Fromm
New Orleans 2004

S0-AQL-021

The Krewe of Rex throws the granddaddy of all Mardi Gras parades on the morning of Fat Tuesday, the final day of Carnival season. See chapter 2. © *Syndey Byrd Photography.*

There's nothing like Mardi Gras in New Orleans (top). It's a 2-week-long party throughout the city, and everybody's invited. See chapter 2. On Bourbon Street (bottom), the action goes on all year. *Top photo: © Jackson Hill/Southern Lights Photography; bottom photo: © David Perry Lawrence/Image Bank.*

Dine alfresco on the pretty balcony of the French Quarter's Royal Café, located in one of the city's most-photographed buildings. See chapter 7. © *Bob Krist.*

Kick up your heels at Jazz Fest (top), held in late April and early May. See chapter 2. All year long you can hear the vintage jazz sound of the Preservation Hall Jazz Band (bottom) at Preservation Hall. See chapter 11. *Top photo: © Syndey Byrd Photography; bottom photo: © Robert Holmes.*

With its magnificent Victorian, Italianate, and Greek Revival houses, the Garden District remains one of the most picturesque (and architecturally distinctive) areas in the city. See chapter 9 for a walking tour of the neighborhood. © Syndey Byrd Photography.

Aaron Neville is a fixture on the New Orleans music scene and often plays in local clubs. See the "Aaron Neville's New Orleans" box in chapter 1 for his favorite things about New Orleans. © George Long Photography.

The James Beard Foundation named Commander's Palace (top) the best restaurant in the entire country. Our vote for the best muffaletta (Frisbee-size hero sandwiches stuffed with Italian cold cuts and cheeses) goes to Central Grocery (bottom). For tips on where to eat in America's fattest city, see chapter 7. *Both photos: © Syndey Byrd Photography.*

Oak Alley is everybody's image of the classic Southern plantation home. See chapter 12.
© Randy Wells/Tony Stone Images.

Frommer's®

New Orleans

2004

by Mary Herczog

Here's what the critics say about Frommer's:

"Amazingly easy to use. Very portable, very complete."
—*Booklist*

"Detailed, accurate, and easy-to-read information for all price ranges."
—*Glamour Magazine*

"Hotel information is close to encyclopedic."
—*Des Moines Sunday Register*

"Frommer's Guides have a way of giving you a real feel for a place."
—*Knight Ridder Newspapers*

WILEY

Wiley Publishing, Inc.

About the Author

Mary Herczog is a freelance writer who also works in the film industry. She is the author of *Frommer's Las Vegas, Las Vegas For Dummies,* and *Los Angeles & Disneyland ® For Dummies* and the coauthor of *California For Dummies.* She would never leave New Orleans if it weren't for July and August.

Published by:

Wiley Publishing, Inc.

111 River St.
Hoboken, NJ 07030

ISBN 0-7645-3869-1
ISSN 0899-2908

Editor: Alexis Lipsitz Flippin
Production Editor: Tammy Ahrens
Cartographer: Roberta Stockwell
Photo Editor: Richard Fox
Production by Wiley Indianapolis Composition Services

Front cover photo: A saxophone player in the Big Easy
Back cover photo: The *Mississippi Queen* riverboat

For information on our other products and services or to obtain technical support, please contact our Customer Care Department within the U.S. at 800-762-2974, outside the U.S. at 317-572-3993 or fax 317-572-4002.

Wiley also publishes its books in a variety of electronic formats. Some content that appears in print may not be available in electronic formats.

Manufactured in the United States of America

5   4   3

Contents

List of Maps

Acknowledgments

As ever, a bayou-full of thank-yous to Alexis Lipsitz Flippin and Frommer's for a job that is a joy. Thank you to Christine deCour and the MCVB of NOLA for helping me eat and sleep. Thanks to Mark Walton for keeping me accurate. Thank you to the Fat Pack (Dave, Nettie, Diana, Robin, Wesly, Chuck) for help with "research." Thank you to Haven Kimmel for answering a certain e-mail. Tim and Leslie got married. Steve Hochman is better than even the best New Orleans meal, better even than the sweetest river wind.

An Invitation to the Reader

In researching this book, we discovered many wonderful places—hotels, restaurants, shops, and more. We're sure you'll find others. Please tell us about them, so we can share the information with your fellow travelers in upcoming editions. If you were disappointed with a recommendation, we'd love to know that, too. Please write to:

Frommer's New Orleans 2004
Wiley Publishing, Inc. • 111 River St. • Hoboken, NJ 07030

An Additional Note

Please be advised that travel information is subject to change at any time—and this is especially true of prices. We therefore suggest that you write or call ahead for confirmation when making your travel plans. The authors, editors, and publisher cannot be held responsible for the experiences of readers while traveling. Your safety is important to us, however, so we encourage you to stay alert and be aware of your surroundings. Keep a close eye on cameras, purses, and wallets, all favorite targets of thieves and pickpockets.

Other Great Guides for Your Trip:

New Orleans For Dummies

Frommer's Portable New Orleans

The Unofficial Guide to New Orleans

Frommer's Irreverent Guide to New Orleans

Frommer's Star Ratings, Icons & Abbreviations

Every hotel, restaurant, and attraction listing in this guide has been ranked for quality, value, service, amenities, and special features using a **star-rating system.** In country, state, and regional guides, we also rate towns and regions to help you narrow down your choices and budget your time accordingly. Hotels and restaurants are rated on a scale of zero (recommended) to three stars (exceptional). Attractions, shopping, nightlife, towns, and regions are rated according to the following scale: zero stars (recommended), one star (highly recommended), two stars (very highly recommended), and three stars (must-see).

In addition to the star-rating system, we also use **seven feature icons** that point you to the great deals, in-the-know advice, and unique experiences that separate travelers from tourists. Throughout the book, look for:

Finds	Special finds—those places only insiders know about
Fun Fact	Fun facts—details that make travelers more informed and their trips more fun
Kids	Best bets for kids and advice for the whole family
Moments	Special moments—those experiences that memories are made of
Overrated	Places or experiences not worth your time or money
Tips	Insider tips—great ways to save time and money
Value	Great values—where to get the best deals

The following **abbreviations** are used for credit cards:

AE	American Express	DISC	Discover	V	Visa
DC	Diners Club	MC	MasterCard		

Frommers.com

Now that you have the guidebook to a great trip, visit our website at **www.frommers.com** for travel information on more than 3,000 destinations. With features updated regularly, we give you instant access to the most current trip-planning information available. At Frommers.com, you'll also find the best prices on airfares, accommodations, and car rentals—and you can even book travel online through our travel booking partners. At Frommers.com, you'll also find the following:

- Online updates to our most popular guidebooks
- Vacation sweepstakes and contest giveaways
- Newsletter highlighting the hottest travel trends
- Online travel message boards with featured travel discussions

What's New in New Orleans

One of the deepest pleasures of New Orleans is that it isn't new; it's old. Really old. It seems like it was old when it was built. Part of that is illusion, of course: a result of the ever-active decay that lends a patina of charm to everything it touches while heavily touching the wallets of hapless building owners trying to stem the tide of water and insect damage. To be honest, the *really* old bits all burned up 200 years ago in two different fires, and the city has been at times as egregious as any other about knocking down historical delights in favor of some more modern structure.

Still, this is the kind of town where, on our first visit, a friend who was herself back for the first time in a decade took us right to her favorite tiny French Quarter bookstore, confident that it would be there because it always had been. And it was. Heck, this is a town where there are restaurants that have been open for 150 years.

That is slowly changing, however. Indeed, that very bookstore, along with some other stores of similar character, is now gone, thanks to greedy French Quarter landlords who upped the rents and lost longtime tenants and gained T-shirt shops. It's a great pity.

Luckily, things move at a snail's pace in New Orleans, compared with, say, Vegas, where 9 establishments have opened and 12 closed since you started reading this paragraph. And while that doesn't ensure that some places listed in this book might not be with us by the time you go to see them, the majority will, and will continue to be.

We took a certain father we are related to for his first trip back to New Orleans in over 30 years, and he said that apart from some of the Bourbon Street music being on tape rather than live and the addition of strobe lights, everything else was exactly the same, which is not to say there haven't been some improvements, with more to come. Thanks to the ever-booming convention business, new hotels continue to pop up, often, happily, utilizing old buildings; the **Ritz-Carlton** (p. 71) took over the Maison Blanche department store, and a **Wyndham** renovated the Whitney bank building into **The Whitney—A Wyndham Historic Hotel** (p. 91).

There are several brand-spanking-new hotels, including the **Cotton Exchange** (p. 87), the **Alexa Hotel** (p. 88), and the **Astor Crown Plaza,** 100 Bourbon St. (© **888/696-4806**), each furthering the trend of putting to good use marvelous old spaces, some very beloved in the annals of New Orleans. Summer 2003 should bring the opening of the **Renaissance Arts Hotel,** 700 Tchoupitoulas St. (© **866/696-4806**), which promises to live up to its Warehouse Art District location with artworks by local artists in each of the 217 rooms.

New Orleans loves nothing more than making a fuss about, well, all sorts of things, running the gamut from the genuinely controversial to matters that other cities might consider, dare we say, trivial?

In the first category, ongoing efforts to help **clean up the French Quarter** have had mixed results but plenty of reaction. The problem is this: The Quarter is a bona fide neighborhood—and we cannot stress this enough—where people have lived for nearly 300 years. But it's also the center of the tourism trade in town, a place full of tour groups, carriage rides, and various unofficial entertainers, from musicians to tap dancers to those folks who spray themselves white and pretend to be statues.

On one hand, greater efforts have been made to crack down on real "quality-of-life" issues like public drunkenness and urination. On the other hand, a recent ordinance was passed that effectively bans tarot-card readers and other street performers from Jackson Square, in an effort to keep those areas available for the artists who hawk their wares there. Musicians are still permitted, however, and the other "performers" can entertain elsewhere, so it's said, though many are skeptical and fear the crackdown will spread citywide. Although shoe-shiners and tap-dancers of questionable quality aren't necessary local components, the fact remains that they are part of a long and vital tradition of **busking** by musicians from Louis Armstrong to Kermit Ruffins. New Orleans without its street performers is just another pretty city. This issue has prompted more than one protest and sit-in.

There have also been concerted efforts on the part of Quarter residents to regulate or otherwise modify the number of **nighttime tours.** It seems that many of the operators not only tell lurid tales of utter falsity, but they also do so using bullhorns, disturbing neighborhood peace and quiet. As you'll see in chapter 8, we recommend only one nighttime ghost tour, which does not engage in such tactics, and we urge you to follow suit.

On the more absurd side, New Orleans was riveted by the drama that ensued when **Galatoire's** fired a venerable waiter, prompting dozens of his longtime customers to write letters of support (which were published in the local newspaper) for both the man and the traditions that this city loves so well. This is the same crowd that complained when Galatoire's went from hand-chipped ice to ice machines and when it began hiring female waitstaff. Did we mention that New Orleans really doesn't take well to change?

A completely unexpected change took place when the **new mayor took office.** Former cable company exec Ray Nagin announced that he was not in favor of an entrenched local tradition, that of **bribing public officials.** (We are not making this up.) It seems that the new mayor had hardly begun his job before people were approaching him with pockets full of cash (one such offer came while he was in the men's room!). Nagin stunned the city when he began cleaning house, dumping all sorts of long-term City Hall employees, rooting out corruption and graft in a way few could recall seeing before.

The physical face of New Orleans will change somewhat when the new **Canal Street streetcar line** is finished, around summer 2004. This development should bring a boom to the deserving Mid-City area.

Work should begin commencing on the ambitious and long-developed **New Orleans Jazz National Historical Park,** within the grounds of Armstrong Park. A collection of five buildings of varying ages (from a classic 1825 Creole cottage to a Masonic hall) will be moved to the site, each providing space for a variety of jazz-related endeavors, including education and research centers, plus a new 6,000-square-foot facility for the fabulous WWOZ radio station.

In the works are **pedestrian-only extensions of St. Claude Avenue and Dumaine Street** (an intersection immortalized as a Carnival gathering space in Professor Longhair's "Go to the Mardi Gras," and one that disappeared when Armstrong Park was carved out of the Treme district) that will lead to a plaza for outdoor concerts.

Speaking of musical heritage and the honoring thereof with parks, the **New Orleans Musical Legends Park** opened at 311 Bourbon St. with statues of Al Hirt and Pete Fountain, and more local legends will be joining them over time.

The **Ogden Museum of Southern Art** (p. 158) should be open by the time you read this (though we'll only believe it when we see it) and will be worth the wait, since it plans to be the largest collection of its kind, properly showcasing the best of Southern visual arts and culture.

Charlotte, North Carolina, lost the Hornets to New Orleans, and although the city has yet to embrace their new basketball team with the fervor they feel for their eternally beleaguered Saints football team, by and large attendance in its first season was good. The team even made it into the 2003 playoffs. Maybe things would improve if they were called something snappy and NOLA-appropriate, like, say, the Jazz? (Joke intended.)

The **New Orleans Jazz & Heritage Festival** continues to be an astonishing amount of fun, even though cranks have complained for 10 years that it's gotten too crowded (oh, like they were there 30 years ago when they were *giving* tickets away, trying to scrap together an audience that topped three figures). So in 2003 the powers that be made a welcome change—Jazz Fest added a new day, Thursday of the first weekend (making both weekends 4 days long). See chapter 2 for more information on Jazz Fest.

The change that comes to all of us sooner or later came in 2003 to **Stan Rice,** the husband and greatest supporter of the city's own great supporter, bestselling author Anne Rice. Stan passed away at 60.

1

The Best of New Orleans

New Orleans should come with a warning label.

See, there's a growing group of residents whom locals call the "never lefts." They are the people who came to New Orleans as tourists: came for Mardi Gras, came for Jazz Fest, or just came. And the city worked its magic on them. They listened to street musicians around Jackson Square. They danced to brass bands in clubs at night. They gazed at lush tropical courtyards hidden behind unassuming building fronts. They strolled down streets time seemed to have forgotten. They kissed beneath flickering gas lamps. They ate incredible meals and topped them off with beignets at 3am at the Café du Monde while watching the passing human parade. They found themselves perusing newspaper ads for houses and apartments, because as their trip's scheduled end date came and went, they were still in New Orleans. They came for Mardi Gras, came for Jazz Fest, just came—and *never left.*

New Orleans does that to people.

This is one of the few cities in America (if not the only one) where you do not feel as if you are in America. It may sound cliché to call New Orleans magical and seductive, but it happens to be the truth. Every one of your senses will be engaged from the moment you arrive here. The city is a visual delight, from the lacy ironwork wrapped around the buildings of the French Quarter to the stately, graceful old homes of the Garden District to the giant oaks that stretch across Esplanade Avenue or drip with ghostly Spanish moss in City Park. But to just call New Orleans picturesque is not doing it justice. Music flows from every doorway or is played right in the street. Jazz, Cajun, blues, whatever—you'll find yourself moving to a rhythm and wondering if the streets really are dancing along with you. There are delicious smells in the moist, honeyed air, which seems to carry a whiff of the Caribbean while caressing your skin, almost as if it were alive.

And then there's the food. Don't get us started on the food.

This is a city that is fully, totally alive. It's sensual and joyous, decadent but not exploitative. Indulgences are many but for the right reason—they are fun. This is a city where every business entirely closes for Mardi Gras; after all, *carnival* roughly means "farewell to flesh." No one's going to say good-bye to such things (as if they ever really do) without a big party.

We tell people that all we do when we go to New Orleans is eat, drink, listen to music, dance, and walk. That's it. In New Orleans, you can do just that for days without getting bored. That's the kind of town it is. In fact, that may be the simplest way to sum up its appeal—which is not an easy task. For years, countless authors have tried to explain its gestalt. You could fill entire bookcases with New Orleans–based or –inspired literature, some written by natives, even more by authors who came for a visit and never left.

We won't kid you, though. There is a downside to all this fun. New Orleans has always been the city of permissive attitudes—it was the first U.S. city where prostitution was sort of legal. Today, loose liquor laws mean not only a party

Greater New Orleans

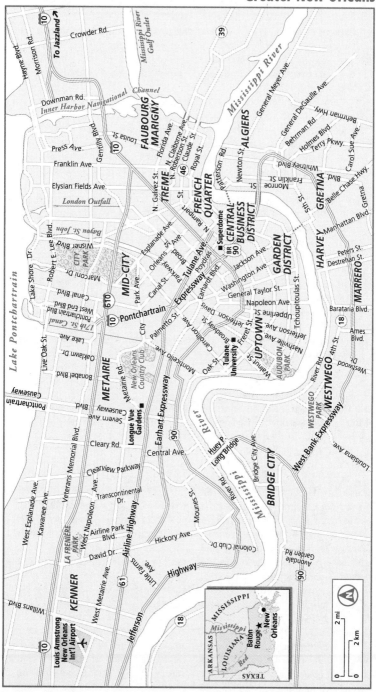

Moments Aaron Neville's New Orleans

Multiple Grammy winner Aaron Neville's unmistakably angelic voice has been a New Orleans landmark for several decades, in his career as a soloist and as one of the Neville Brothers. His latest solo album is entitled *Devotion* (EMD/Cordant). He recently recounted what he loves about his hometown.

"I'm a homebody these days, but I still like riding the St. Charles streetcar and going to the Camellia Grill for breakfast or having blackened redfish or crawfish at K-Paul's, where there's always a line. Is the wait worth it? Oh, yeah! And I like riding the riverboat and checking out Audubon Park now that they have the beautiful natural habitats. I used to go up there a long time ago when they had cages, and I didn't like it. The animals didn't look happy.

"New Orleans has a mystique to it, and it's got a hold on me. This place is like a melting pot, a mixture of so many cultures, with nothing pure. It's got its own attitude. And music for any occasion—people walk here with a musical rhythm. This is one place where you can walk down the street and greet people. Do that in New York or L.A. and people look at you like you are crazy. Here, people say, 'What's up?' and you say, 'Where y'at?' When I play different cities and someone in the audience calls out, 'Where y'at?', I know where they're from. When I was growing up, I thought everyone said that.

"I travel to different countries and cities all over the world, but when I'm coming back from the road, the greatest sight to me is looking out the airplane window and seeing the swamps."

atmosphere but also obnoxious drunks and disgusting displays in the streets. Crime has been high; for a couple of years—1995 and 1996, in particular—this was the most dangerous city in America, although recent concerted efforts to fix that have paid off with lower crime rates.

But those who love New Orleans remain amused by its flaws— they're part of what makes the town real. And it *is* real—it only looks like a movie set because of remarkable historic preservation; the city continues to largely resist efforts to turn itself into an amusement park. For every tacky souvenir store and theme restaurant, there are 10 places that defy commercialization. This town refuses to be turned into something shiny and clean. That wouldn't be the natural order of things, anyway: Thanks to the climate, the city began to decay the moment it was built. Buildings may be worn and shabby, but every brick has a story. You want tidy and sterile? Go elsewhere. You want history and character? Come here.

The best way to get inside New Orleans is to plunge right in. Don't just go for the obvious. Though we've met people who never left Bourbon Street and had a terrific time, the city has so much more to offer. We've also met people who went for recognizable names and quick and easy decisions and then were disappointed that their experiences were no more than adequate.

Look over the advice that follows, and you should be able to sidestep the inevitable tourist traps. We want you to go home having passed a real good time, as the locals say. We won't promise that you won't get your hands dirty—but if the dirt comes from the powdered sugar on a beignet, then you did your trip right.

That is, assuming you do go home. Remember, we warned you, so don't blame us if you come to New Orleans and one day discover that you never left.

1 Frommer's Favorite New Orleans Experiences

- **Beignets & Café au Lait at Café du Monde:** Sit on the crowded patio gazing at the action on Decatur Street and Jackson Square. Gorge on hot French-style doughnuts liberally coated in powdered sugar (everyone will know what you've been doing from the sprinkles on your shirt) and washed down with potent chicory coffee. And do it at any hour of the day—3pm or 3am. It's open 24 hours! See p. 145.

- **Jazz at Preservation Hall:** Drop your four bucks in the hat and squeeze into one of the country's time-honored jazz institutions. Your feet will be moving and your ears will be happy, even if they never knew they liked jazz before. See p. 232.

- **A Crowded Night at the Maple Leaf:** The Maple Leaf is a very "New Orleans" club and a fun place to hang out. On nights when popular bands fill the place to hot, sweaty capacity and the crowd spills over into the street and dances right on the sidewalk, it's sublime. See p. 238.

- **Dinner at Commander's Palace:** This is one of the legendary restaurants that continues to deserve its reputation after many decades. It's romantic, gracious, attentive, and delicious. Though it's perfect for a special occasion, eating there makes *any* meal a special occasion. See p. 137.

- **A Streetcar Ride:** The streetcar named *Desire* may no longer be with us, but the historic St. Charles line still is. Not only is this a convenient way to travel from downtown to uptown (or vice versa), but also the route shows off some of the most beautiful homes in New Orleans. See p. 60.

- **A Cemetery Tour:** New Orleans's above-the-ground tombs are hard to forget once you've seen them, and touring these ghostly cities of the dead provides you with a unique look into the history and culture of the city. See p. 172.

- **A Stroll Through the Garden District:** These elegant (not flashy) old homes, nestled among lush trees, are wonderful to gaze at and envy. At the right time of day, you might have the streets largely to yourself and feel you've slipped back in time—or into an Anne Rice novel. See p. 197.

- **A Stroll Along St. John's Bayou:** Most tourists don't get much beyond the Quarter or else they speed past this low-slung body of water as they head for City Park. Slow down Big Easy style, finally away from the hordes as you meander along the bayou and admire the less high-profile, but no less romantic, neighborhood around it. See p. 162.

- **Bourbon Street After Dark:** Even if you end up hating it, you have to see it at least once. Music spurts and oozes out of windows and doors, drinkers reign supreme, and sex is widely available—on paper, on stage, and on video. It's wild, disgusting, and strangely exhilarating. See chapter 11.

- **Club Hopping in the Frenchmen Section:** This portion of the Faubourg Marigny (the neighborhood that borders the French

Quarter to the north and east) features at least five clubs and several bars, each with its own personality and charm. Stroll from one to the other, dipping in for a bit or just listening to the music pouring out the doors before moving on to sample something farther down the street. See chapter 11.

- **Food, Glorious Food:** With a nearly infinite selection of outstanding restaurants and other food sources, meal planning in New Orleans is very serious indeed. There is never time to do it all: a muffuletta from Central Grocery eaten on the banks of the Mississippi; boiled crawfish or oyster shooting at Acme or Felix's; and amazing, innovative cuisine at the Upperline, Brigtsen's, Emeril's,

Peristyle, or Bayona. Can you eat five meals a day here? We've tried! See chapter 7.

- **Seeing New Orleans Piano Great Eddie Bo:** One of the last in the tradition of New Orleans piano professors is charming and saucy, his playing is marvelous, and his band is hot.
- **Dancing to the ReBirth Brass Band, the Wild Magnolias, and/or Kermit Ruffin:** Dancing to three of the best musical acts New Orleans has to offer (a brass band, the ultimate Mardi Gras Indian combo, and a jazz musician in the tradition of Louis Armstrong, respectively) is the physical manifestation of the word *fun*—and the truest spirit of New Orleans. See chapter 11.

2 Best Hotel Bets

Selecting just one accommodation in New Orleans is a little like picking your favorite flavor of ice cream—there are just so many great options to choose from. You'll find full reviews of all these places in chapter 6, "Where to Stay," plus some other choices that we like almost as much.

- **Best for a Romantic Getaway:** Take an old indigo plantation some blocks away from the Quarter, outfit it with some of the nicest furnishings in town, add in a full lavish breakfast, and you've got **The House on Bayou Road,** 2275 Bayou Rd. (✆ **800/882-2968** or 504/945-0992). Subtract the breakfast and put the operation in a gorgeous old Creole building in the Quarter, add raves from the likes of *Condé Nast Traveler,* and you've got the **Soniat House,** 1133 Chartres St. (✆ **800/544-8808** or 504/522-0570). See p. 82 and 72.
- **Best New Orleans–Specific Hotel Value:** Why stay in an admittedly comfortable, but ultimately generic, luxe hotel room

when for the same price you can have a two- or three-room suite, complete with wide oak floors, tall ceilings, fireplaces, antiques, and balconies overlooking the Quarter (in short, all the elements that make for a truly atmospheric stay)? They start at $195 at the **Hotel Ste. Hélène,** 508 Chartres St. (✆ **800/348-8888** or 504/522-5014), and can be even cheaper in June, July, August, and December. See p. 74.
- **Best Basic Hotel:** You know, just a hotel, albeit a hotel that looks sufficiently NOLA-like. It's friendly, it's sweet, and it's better than *basic* allows it to sound—it's the **Maison Dupuy,** 1001 Toulouse St. (✆ **800/535-9177** or 504/586-8000). See p. 75.
- **Best Breakfast:** Not to say that the fancy meal served over at **The House on Bayou Road** isn't fabulous, but just as good is the multi-course bonanza served up at the **Olde Victorian Inn,** 914 N. Rampart St. (✆ **800/725-2446**

or 504/522-2446), where you get the additional bonus of the adorable owners (who say they have so many menus that it takes 30 days before they repeat a breakfast) cooking for you. See p. 79.

- **Best Reason to Stay in Mid-City:** Soon, this will be the new hot neighborhood to stay in, particularly once the Canal Street streetcar line starts running sometime in 2004. In the meantime, beat the crowds and bunk at the gorgeous **Block-Keller House,** 3620 Canal St. (℗ **800/729-4640** or 504/488-4640), where the skilled owners know their B&B business, or at the friendly, antiques-filled **1896 O'Malley House,** 120 S. Pierce St. (℗ **866/226-1896** or 504/488-5896). See p. 83 and 84.

- **Grandest B&B:** Big rooms filled with big beds and big furniture in a big mansion on St. Charles, a big street, the **Grand Victorian Bed & Breakfast,** 2727 St. Charles Ave. (℗ **800/997-0008** or 504/895-1104), is stately and, well, grand. See p. 92.

- **Best More Modest B&B: Chimes B&B,** 1146 Constantinople St. (℗ **800/729-4640** [for reservations only] or 504/488-4640), is a delightful family-owned guesthouse in the Garden District. The charming owners have been operating the B&B for 15 years, generating loyal return guests. See p. 94.

- **Best Moderately Priced Hotel:** The **Bourbon Orleans Hotel,** 717 Orleans St. (℗ **504/523-2222**), is the best value in its price range. It's centrally located (make sure to ask for a room *not* facing Bourbon Street unless you're sure you want to keep an eye on the nonstop partying), has excellent amenities like coffeemakers and marble bathrooms, and rivals some of the city's more expensive hotels in quality of service. See p. 76.

- **Best for Travelers with Disabilities:** Two of the most accessible and accommodating choices are the **Hotel Monteleone,** 214 Royal St. (℗ **800/535-9595** or 504/523-3341), and the **Windsor Court,** 300 Gravier St. (℗ **800/262-2662** or 504/523-6000). See p. 74 and 86.

- **Best Hotel for Hip Executives:** The innovative minimalist style and myriad of comforts at the recently opened **International House,** 221 Camp St. (℗ **800/633-5770** or 504/553-9550), have justly made this everyone's new favorite hotel. It's the perfect palate cleanser if you can't stand Victorian frills. See p. 88.

- **Best Hotel for Hip Families or Couples:** Well, they could stay at the ultra-hip W, but if you want something a bit more NOLA-specific, try the new **Hotel Monaco,** 333 St. Charles Ave. (℗ **866/561-0010**), where the robes are leopard-colored, foot massages are offered at night, and, on request, you can have an in-room goldfish. See p. 88.

- **Best Health Club:** The hands-down winner is the **Hilton New Orleans Riverside Hotel,** 2 Poydras St. (℗ **800/445-8667** or 504/561-0500). Its Rivercenter Racquet and Health Club features outdoor and indoor tennis courts, squash and racquetball courts, a rooftop jogging track, tanning beds, massage, a hair salon, and a golf studio. See p. 85.

- **Best Little Hotel:** The **Hotel Maison de Ville,** 727 Toulouse St. (℗ **800/634-1600** or 504/561-5858), is a highly regarded member of both the Small Luxury Hotels of the World and the Small Historic Hotels of America. Once you submit to its pampering, you'll understand why. See p. 69.

- **Best Funky Little Hotel: The Frenchmen,** 417 Frenchmen St. (© **800/831-1781** or 504/948-2166), is small but full of pure New Orleans charm. See p. 81.
- **In a Class by Itself:** Of all the hotels in New Orleans, the **Windsor Court,** 300 Gravier St. (© **800/262-2662** or 504/523-6000), stands head and shoulders above the rest. Most guest rooms are suites with Italian marble bathrooms, balconies or bay windows, living rooms, kitchenettes, and dressing rooms. If you choose one of the two-bedroom penthouse suites, you'll have the added luxury of a private library and a terrace that overlooks the mighty Mississippi. See p. 86.

3 Best Dining Bets

It's always hard to quantify such things as restaurant comparisons, particularly in a town that has so many wonderful choices. Below is a list to guide you.

Some of you may wonder why there are no "Best Cajun" and "Best Creole" categories. Our feeling was that New Orleans has no exceptional Cajun restaurants (they're adequate at best), and just about everyone has a different definition of Creole cooking, so narrowing it down was nearly impossible. When we consulted with hard-core New Orleans foodies who like nothing more than debates of this nature, fists were waved in the air. But when the dust settled, a compromise was met—"Best Contemporary Creole." Even that caused some to wail, "But those restaurants aren't Creole!," and the whole thing started up again.

For more complete listings of New Orleans restaurants by cuisine and neighborhood, see chapter 7, "Where to Dine."

- **Best Restaurant in the United States:** Actually, we haven't tried them all, so we can't say for sure, but the James Beard Foundation, which *should* know, recently gave **Commander's Palace,** 1403 Washington Ave. (© **504/899-8221**), its Lifetime Outstanding Restaurant Award. We won't argue. See p. 137.
- **Best Restaurant in the Quarter:** When you finish a meal and every single dish you had was perfect, you know you've eaten somewhere special. That's happened to us at **Peristyle,** 1041 Dumaine St. (© **504/593-9535**), more than once. See p. 114.
- **Best Neighborhood Restaurant:** (and the winner of Best Breakfasts and Best Dish: the praline bacon) **Elizabeth's,** 601 Gallier St. (© **504/944-9272**), serves monster portions of delicious and curious food and is just flat-out wonderful. See p. 125.
- **Best Neighbahood Restaurant:** You know, the old neighbahood where the locals still ask, "Hey, dahwlin', wheah y'at?" This category is a toss-up between the Italian and Creole dishes at **Mandina's,** 3800 Canal St. (© **504/482-9179**), and those found at **Liuzza's,** 3636 Bienville St. (© **504/482-9120**), though the deep-fried dill pickle slices at the latter may tip the scales. See p. 129.
- **Best Spot for a Business Lunch:** Businesspeople across the city favor the casual but classy atmosphere at **Mr. B's Bistro,** 201 Royal St. (© **504/523-2078**), not to mention the fine food. See p. 118.
- **Best Wine List:** The wine cellar at **Brennan's,** 417 Royal St. (© **504/525-9711**), is unsurpassed in New Orleans. (Prices range from $20 to $1,000.) See p. 110.

- **Best for Kids:** Take them to **Café du Monde,** 800 Decatur St. (© **504/581-2914**), where getting powdered sugar all over yourself is half the fun. It's large and open-air, and street performers are always around. See p. 145.
- **Best Really Old Restaurant:** Truth be told, **Antoine's,** 713 St. Louis St. (© **504/581-4422**), isn't all that good, but it's been around and in the same family for 150 years, so find a restaurant older and better—we dare you. Plus, they invented oysters Rockefeller and make the only authentic version (the recipe is a closely guarded secret). See p. 108.
- **Best Gumbo:** More fighting words, but you can't go wrong at **Dooky Chase,** 2301 Orleans Ave. (© **504/821-0060**), or **Galatoire's,** 209 Bourbon St. (© **504/ 525-2021**). See p. 128 and 112.
- **Best Barbecue Shrimp:** That's Cajun style, in a spicy, garlicky butter sauce, and while **Pascal's Manale,** 1838 Napoleon Ave. (© **504/895-4877**), invented it (and has the largest shrimp), the sauce at **Mr. B's Bistro,** 201 Royal St. (© **504/523-2078**), is perfect. If only the two elements could be combined . . . . See p. 141 and 118.
- **Best Oysters:** Or "ersters" as a local would say, and then they would insist that **Felix's Restaurant & Oyster Bar,** 739 Iberville St. (© **504/522-4440**), has the best, unless they insist that **Acme Oyster House,** 724 Iberville St. (© **504/522-5973**), does. We think they are identically good (and let's not even discuss **Casamento's,** 4330 Magazine St., © **504/895-9761**). See p. 122, 121, and 142, respectively.
- **Best Hope for Vegetarians:** You are not forgotten at **Old Dog New Trick Café,** 517 Frenchman Street (© **504/943-6368**), where

an entire menu has been fashioned to taste as good as anything else in this otherwise meat-and-fish-intensive town. See p. 124.
- **Best New Restaurant:** By the time you read this, someplace else new and wonderful may have usurped its place, but regardless, we had such a fine meal at **Muriel's,** 801 Chartres St. (© **504/568-1885**), that we were shocked it could be so good. See p. 113.
- **Best Contemporary Creole:** The food at **Brigtsen's,** 723 Dante St. (© **504/861-7610**), and **Upperline,** 1413 Upperline St. (© **504/ 891-9822**), is consistently interesting, innovative, and delicious. But **Dick & Jenny's,** 4501 Tchoupitoulas St. (© **504/894-9880**), should also make this list. See p. 137 and 139.
- **Best Italian:** We almost hate to tell you, because there are already too many people ahead of us in line (they don't take reservations), but New Orleans's strong Italian presence is best represented at **Irene's Cuisine,** 539 St. Phillip St. (© **504/529-8811**). Get there early or expect a wait. See p. 115.
- **Best Pasta Dish Elsewhere:** The black truffle fettuccine (or whatever) at **Bacco,** 310 Chartres St. (© **504/522-2426**), where the Brennan family (the most prominent name in New Orleans dining and the family that collectively operates over half a dozen restaurants) delivers up yet another marvelous restaurant—eat Italian here, too, and you'll be glad you did. See p. 108.
- **Best Classic New Orleans Restaurant:** Of the three mainstays of New Orleans dining (the others being Galatoire's and Antoine's; see p. 112 and 108), **Arnaud's,** 813 Bienville St. (© **504/523-5433**), is the one

where you can count on getting a consistently good (and maybe even great) meal in the same way, and in the exact same surroundings, that generations of New Orleanians have done before you. See p. 106.

- **Best Desserts:** Desserts in New Orleans tend to run to the familiar; everyone serves bread pudding or flourless chocolate cake. But there are places (most often run by people named Brennan) that stray into more interesting territory with practically Bacchanalian choices. **Commander's Palace** serves a justifiably famous bread pudding soufflé, but don't ignore other possibilities served there, including the chocolate Sheba. Then there is the banana cream pie at **Emeril's**, 800 Tchoupitoulas St. (☏ **504/528-9393**), which reduces grown men to quivering fools. Others are brought to their knees by the white chocolate bread pudding at the **Palace Café** 605 Canal St. (☏ **504/523-1661**). Try 'em all and decide for yourself. See p. 137, 130, and 134.

- **Best Local Dive with Outstanding Food:** Uglesich's Restaurant & Bar, 1238 Baronne St. (☏ **504/523-8571**), is nearly always crowded, looks only slightly better than a dump, and features food so sublime you won't care a bit. (Secretly, we think this is the best restaurant in New Orleans.) See p. 136.

- **Best Burgers:** Locals swear by **Port of Call,** 838 Esplanade Ave. (☏ **504/523-0120**), but its cow-size half-pounder might be too much for some. We throw the vote to the more manageable third-of-a-pound juicy delight at the **Clover Grill,** 900 Bourbon St.

(☏ **504/598-1010**). See p. 118 and 122, respectively.

- **Best Outdoor Dining:** Go to **Bayona,** 430 Dauphine St. (☏ **504/525-4455**), to eat the fabulous food in the beautiful, quiet, and fairly secluded courtyard. It's especially delightful on moonlit nights or balmy spring afternoons. See p. 108.

- **Best View:** The amazing moonlit view of the Mississippi makes **Bella Luna,** 914 N. Peters St. (☏ **504/529-1583**), hard to beat for a special occasion. See p. 109.

- **Best Po' Boys:** The drippy monster creations at **Mother's,** 401 Poydras St. (☏ **504/523-9656**), are the bomb and the buttah. See p. 136.

- **Best Muffulettas:** You really haven't had a sandwich until you've tried a muffuletta, and no one beats **Central Grocery,** 923 Decatur St. (☏ **504/523-1620**). See p. 123.

- **Best Sazerac:** This famous locally invented cocktail can be found all over the city, but connoisseurs agree that its point of origin, the **Sazerac Bar and Grill,** in the Fairmont Hotel, University Place (☏ **504/529-4733**), still has it down perfectly—though as of this writing, the bartender at **Irene's Cuisine,** 539 St. Phillip St., in the French Quarter (☏ **504/529-8811**), who worked at the Sazerac, seems to have learned his lessons well and comes in a close second. See p. 133 and 115.

- **Best Original Dessert:** Lilette, 3637 Magazine St. (☏ **504/895-1636**), serves little rounds of goat-cheese crème fraîche with poached pairs, and it's a combo made for the gods. See p. 141.

2

Mardi Gras, Jazz Fest & Other Festivals

New Orleans is a city that really loves a good party. And what happens when a party gets too big? It becomes a festival. That's what happened over the years to the Jazz & Heritage Festival— it evolved from an event where people were literally begged to take free tickets into a hugely crowded, multiday affair that has, relatively speaking, not that much to do with jazz (but is no less fun for it).

New Orleanians know what makes a great party: really good food and music, and lots of it. That's what you will find at any festival in Louisiana—regardless of what it is ostensibly celebrating. Anything is an excuse for a party here, so you can experience festivals centered around swamps, gumbo, crawfish, frogs, tomatoes, architecture, and more.

This chapter covers some of the largest festivals in New Orleans and the outlying areas; others are listed in the "New Orleans Calendar of Events" in chapter 3, "Planning Your Trip to New Orleans."

You can get information on many of the events mentioned in both chapters by contacting the **New Orleans Metropolitan Convention and Visitors Bureau,** 1520 Sugar Bowl Dr., New Orleans, LA 70112 (*©* **800/672-6124** or 504/566-5055; www.neworleans cvb.com).

1 Mardi Gras

Obviously, the granddaddy of all New Orleans celebrations is Mardi Gras. Thanks to sensational media accounts that zero in on the salacious aspects of this carnival, its rep has gone downhill in the last few years, while the accounts have attracted more and more participants looking for wild action rather than tradition. But despite what you may have heard, Mardi Gras remains one of the most exciting times to visit New Orleans. The truth of the matter is that you can spend several days admiring and reveling in the city's traditions and never even venture into the frat-party atmosphere of Bourbon Street.

Knowledge of some of the long and fascinating history of Mardi Gras may help put matters in perspective. First of all, it's not a festival; it's a *carnival,* which is from a Latin word roughly meaning "farewell to flesh." Mardi Gras is both a day and a time period. It's French for "Fat Tuesday," the day before Ash Wednesday, when Lent begins, and it historically refers to the 5- to 8-week stretch from Twelfth Night (Jan 6) to Mardi Gras day (which can fall as late as Mar 9). With Lent comes fasting and deprivation. The idea was that good Christians would take the opportunity to eat as much as they could in preparation for their impending denial.

The party's origins can be traced to that Roman excuse for an orgy, the **Lupercalia festival.** It will sound strangely familiar to today's Mardi Gras participant:

2 days when all sexual and social order disappeared, cross-dressing was mandatory, and the population ran riot. The early Christian church was naturally appalled by this but was unable to stop it (as someone later said about Storyville and prostitution, you can make it illegal but you can't make it unpopular). Grafting Lupercalia to the beginning of Lent may have been a compromise to bribe everyone into observing Lent, and they may have needed those 40 days to recover!

Carnival, with lavish masked balls and other revels, became popular in Italy and France, and so naturally, the tradition followed the Creoles to New Orleans. The first Carnival balls occurred in 1743, but the first detailed accounts of Mardi Gras–specific festivities showed up in 1824. Informal parades and masked revelers cavorting in the streets characterized the celebrations. By the mid-1800s, Mardi Gras mischief had grown so ugly (the habit of tossing flour on revelers gradually turned into throwing bricks at them) that everyone predicted the end of the tradition. (The more things change, the more they stay the same.)

THE BIRTH OF THE KREWES   Everything changed in 1856. Tired of being left out of the Creoles' Mardi Gras, a group of Americans who belonged to a secret society called Cowbellians formed the Mystick Krewe of Comus (named after the hero of a John Milton poem). On Mardi Gras evening, they presented a torch-lit parade, seemingly out of nowhere, that was breathtaking in its design, effects, and imagination. A new tradition was born. Every Mardi Gras night thereafter (with some exceptions) climaxed with the appearance of Comus, each time grander and more astounding.

And so the new standard was set. Mardi Gras societies became known as **krewes,** and most were made up of prominent society types or businessmen; the event marked the height of the social season. The next krewe to emerge was that of Rex, the king of Carnival. Rex paraded in the morning and later paid public homage to Comus. Their meeting became the high point of Mardi Gras.

Rex was born in part to celebrate the Mardi Gras appearance of the grand duke of Russia, Alexis Alexandrovich Romanov, who had followed the actress Lydia Thompson from New York when she came to star in *Bluebeard*. The city went all out to welcome him, and when it was learned that his favorite song was Lydia's burlesque tune "If Ever I Cease to Love You," every band in the Rex parade was asked to play it. That sprightly melody is now the official song of Mardi Gras, and the **royal colors**—purple for justice, green for faith, and gold for power—were adopted as the festival's official colors. More krewes, such as Momus and Proteus, came into being, each throwing a lavish ball along with its parade and each with an exclusive membership.

The Civil War put a temporary halt to things, but Comus was parading again by 1866. In 1870, the Twelfth Night Revelers krewe was founded and added two new customs that still endure. Members threw trinkets to onlookers (the first thrower was dressed as Santa Claus), and a "queen" reigned over their ball.

As a classic elite Old South institution, Mardi Gras was not exactly at the forefront of promoting racial equality or harmony. Throughout the 19th century, the city's African Americans participated in parades only by carrying torches to illuminate the route (the *flambeaux,* as the torches are known, are still around, a welcome, atmospheric Mardi Gras tradition). In 1909, a black man named William Storey mocked the elaborately garbed Rex by prancing after his float wearing a lard can for a crown. Storey was promptly dubbed "King Zulu." By 1916, his followers had grown so in number that they formed the Krewe of Zulu (officially the Zulu Social Aid and Pleasure Club), developing a parody of Rex and making a mockery of racial stereotypes. The Zulu parade quickly became one of the most popular aspects of Mardi Gras. The most famous King Zulu was Louis Armstrong, who reigned in 1949.

Unfortunately, most krewes remained notable for their lack of blacks, Jews, and women, and as times changed, the public, which was not permitted to join the krewes but was supposed to be happy to pay taxes for postparade cleanup, demanded equality. It was not considered enough that some krewes had begun (grudgingly) inviting blacks to their balls. An ordinance passed in 1992 denies a parade permit to any group that discriminates on the basis of race or religion. (Krewes are still not required to integrate along gender lines, a choice of the all-female krewes as much as the male, though men in drag are a hallmark of Mardi Gras.) Rex acceded to the new regulations, but mighty Comus, in a move that many still feel marked the beginning of the end of classic Mardi Gras, canceled its parade. Proteus and Momus soon followed suit.

Some say the flavor of Mardi Gras had already changed long before the 1992 ordinance.

SPECTACLE & BEAUTY   Parades were always things of spectacle and beauty with literally antique floats: 19th-century caissons with wooden wheels. But the processions had gotten so big over the years that they had to be taken out of the Quarter. The old krewes were gradually replaced by "super krewes" like Bacchus and Endymion, whose membership was nonexclusive. One of their floats was as big as an entire Comus parade. In 1997, the largest parades each had more than 20 floats, celebrity guests, marching bands, dancing groups, motorcycle squads, and a total of many thousands of participants. Celebrities are often the super krewes' kings; the 2001 Bacchus king was Larry King. In 1998, the Krewe of the Americas, completely made up of non–New Orleans residents, paraded for the first time, on Mardi Gras afternoon itself, a sacrilege to natives who long considered this Comus's day.

The trinkets known as **throws** fly thick and fast from the floats of these super krewes, but they lack the tradition of the old krewes. In the 1880s, Rex began throwing trinkets to parade watchers, a forerunner of the Rex doubloon, which was introduced in 1960. Other krewes eventually followed suit, and now throws are mandatory. The ubiquitous beads were originally glass (often from Czechoslovakia) but now are of less expensive plastic. **Doubloons** are another popular souvenir. Usually made of aluminum, these oversize coins show the krewe's coat of arms on one side and the year's parade theme on the other. They are collector's items for natives, many of whom have every krewe's doubloons from many different years. Other throws include **stuffed animals, plastic krewe cups,** and especially the highly prized, hand-painted **Zulu coconuts**.

Alas, the traditional cry of, "Throw me something, Mister," to obtain a trinket has gradually turned into the request/demand, "Show me your tits!" But though it seems Mardi Gras is moving ever further away from its traditions, remember that Comus has in the past disappeared for several years and always rose again. Indeed, Proteus returned for Mardi Gras 2000 to cries of "Welcome back!"

KICKIN' UP YOUR HEELS: MARDI GRAS ACTIVITIES

Mardi Gras can be whatever you want. Don't be suckered by media reports that focus only on the exhibitionism and drunken orgies. Sure, some of Mardi Gras is becoming more and more like spring break as college kids pour into town, eager to have license to do anything. Thankfully, that kind of activity is largely confined to Bourbon Street. If that's what you want, go there. But if you avoid Bourbon Street, you will find an entirely different Mardi Gras experience.

THE SEASON   The date of Fat Tuesday is different each year, but Carnival season always starts on **Twelfth Night,** January 6, as much as 2 months before Mardi Gras. On that night, the Phunny Phorty Phellows kick off the season with a streetcar ride from Carrollton Avenue to Canal Street and back.

Over the following weeks, the city celebrates Mardi Gras in its own inimitable fashion. For most people, this means attending a string of **King Cake parties.** The traditional King Cake is a round, braided confection into which a plastic baby is baked; getting the piece with the baby can be a good omen or can mean you have to throw the next King Cake party. For the high-society crowd, the season brings the year's best parties, some of which hark back to the grand masked balls of the 19th century. Each krewe throws a ball, ostensibly to introduce its royalty for the year. There are dozens of these parties between Twelfth Night and Mardi Gras, but most are not traditional masked balls. (By the way, don't expect to be invited—they are quite exclusive.)

Two or 3 weeks before Mardi Gras itself, parades begin chugging through the streets with increasing frequency. There are also plenty of parodies, like the parade of the **Mystick Krewe of Barkus** and the **Krewe du Vieux**'s yearly expression of decadence (open to the public). Barkus is, as you might guess, a krewe for pets that parades through the Quarter (some of the dogs get quite gussied up) and is a total hoot, while Krewe du Vieux are humans just having a wild time, preening in outrageous costumes.

If you want to experience Mardi Gras but don't want to face the full force of craziness, consider coming for the weekend 10 days before Fat Tuesday (the season officially begins the Fri of this weekend). You can count on 10 to 15 parades during the weekend by lesser-known krewes like Cleopatra, Pontchartrain, Sparta, and Camelot. The crowds are more manageable than the ones you'll find just a week later.

The following weekend there are another 15 parades—the biggies. The parades are bigger, the crowds are bigger(everything's bigger. By this point, the city has succumbed to Carnival fever. After a day of screaming for beads, you'll probably find yourself heading somewhere to get a drink or three. The French Quarter will be the center of late-night revelry; all of the larger bars will be packed. If you travel uptown or to Mid-City to see a parade, however, you might consider staying put and spending your evening at one of the joints nearby. The last parade each day (on both weekends) usually ends around 9:30pm or later; you might be exhausted by the time you get back to the hotel.

LUNDI GRAS   In the 19th century, Rex's **King of Carnival** arrived downtown from the Mississippi River on this night, the Monday before Fat Tuesday. Over the years, the day gradually lost its special significance, becoming just another day of parades. In the 1980s, however, Rex revived Lundi Gras, the old tradition of arriving on the Mississippi.

These days, festivities at the riverfront begin in the afternoon with lots of drink and live music leading up to the King's arrival at around 6pm. Down the levee a few hundred feet at Wolfenberg Park, Zulu has its own Lundi Gras celebration with the king arriving at around 5pm. (In 1999, for the first time, King Zulu met up with Rex in an impressive ceremony.) That night, the **Krewe of Orpheus** holds their parade. It's one of the biggest and most popular parades, thanks to the generosity of the krewe's throws. And although it's a recent addition to the Mardi Gras scene (it began in 1994), it holds fast to old Mardi Gras traditions, including floats designed by master float creator Henri Schindler. For Mardi Gras 2000, venerable Proteus returned to parading, right before Orpheus.

Because Lent begins the following night at midnight, Monday is the final dusk-to-dawn night of Mardi Gras. A good portion of the city forgoes sleep so as not to waste the occasion—which only adds to the craziness.

MARDI GRAS   The day begins early, starting with the two biggest parades, **Zulu** and **Rex,** which run back to back. Zulu starts near the Central Business District at 8:30am; Rex starts Uptown at 10am.

Throughout the early morning, in between the parades, you can also see the elaborately costumed Mardi Gras **"walking clubs,"** like the Jefferson City Buzzards, the Pete Fountain Half Fast, and the Mondo Kayo Social and Marching Club (identifiable by their tropical/banana theme). They walk, they drink, they're usually accompanied by marching bands, and because they probably didn't sleep the night before, they don't move very fast. You can catch these "marchers" anywhere along their St. Charles Avenue route (between Poydras St. and Washington Ave.). Keep your eyes open also for the unofficial marching club, the Julus, which includes members of the New Orleans Klezmer All-Stars and tends to follow the Zulu parade, throwing not coconuts but painted bagels.

It will be early afternoon when Rex spills into the Central Business District. Nearby at about this time, you can find some of the most elusive New Orleans figures, the **Mardi Gras Indians.** The "tribes" of New Orleans are small communities of African Americans and black Creoles (some of whom have Native American ancestors), mostly from the inner city. Their elaborate (and that's an understatement) beaded and feathered costumes, rivaling Bob Mackie Vegas headdresses in outrageousness and size, are entirely made by hand. The men begin working on them on Ash Wednesday, the day after Mardi Gras, to get them ready in time for the next year. Throughout the day, tribes of Indians from all over town converge along the median of Claiborne Avenue, underneath the interstate, where a large crowd of locals is always milling around to see the spectacle. If two tribes meet on the median or back in their neighborhoods, they'll stage a mock confrontation, resettling their territory and common borders. (If you're lucky, you can sometimes catch these confrontations during other times of the year if the Indians are out to celebrate something else, like Jazz Fest or the mayor's inauguration.)

After the parades, the action picks up in the Quarter. En route, you'll see that Mardi Gras is still very much a family tradition, with whole families dressing up in similar costumes. Marvel at how an entire city has shut down so that every citizen can join in the celebrations. Some people don't bother hitting the streets; instead, they hang out on their balconies watching the action below or have barbecues in their courtyards. If you are lucky and seem like the right sort, you might well get invited in.

In the Quarter, the frat-party action is largely confined to Bourbon Street. The more interesting activity is in the lower Quarter and the Frenchmen section of the Faubourg Marigny (just east of the Quarter), where the artists and gay community really know how to celebrate. The costumes are elaborate works of art, some the product of months of work. Although the people may be (okay, probably *will* be) drunk, they are boisterous and enthusiastic, not (for the most part) obnoxious.

As you make your way through the streets, keep your eyes peeled for members of the legendary **Krewe of Comus.** They will be men dressed in tuxes with brooms over their shoulders, holding cowbells. Ask them if they are Comus, and they will deny it, insisting they are Cowbellians. But then they might hand you a vintage Comus doubloon, and the truth will be out.

If you can, try to stay until midnight when the police come through the Quarter, officially shutting down Mardi Gras.

PLANNING A VISIT DURING MARDI GRAS

LODGING   You can't just drop in on Mardi Gras. Accommodations in the city and the nearby suburbs are booked solid, *so make your plans well ahead and book a room as early as possible.* Many people plan a year or more in advance. Prices are usually much higher during Mardi Gras, and most hotels and guesthouses impose minimum-stay requirements.

CLOTHING   As with anything in New Orleans, you must join in if you want to have the best time—simply being a spectator is not enough. And that means a **costume** and **mask** (anything goes). Once you are masked and dressed up, you are automatically part of it all. (Tellingly, the Bourbon St. participants usually do not wear costumes.) A mask tends to bring out the extrovert in everyone. It makes it much easier to talk to strangers or simply to jump up and down begging for beads. It's so simple—a $1.50 piece of plastic will make you part of the spectacle rather than a spectator. As far as costumes go, you need not do anything fancy. You can't possibly compete with those residents who spend all year, and thousands of dollars, on their costumes, but don't feel bad. If anything, feel morally superior to those who don't bother dressing up at all. They aren't in the Carnival spirit, but you are.

If you've come unprepared, several shops in town specialize in Mardi Gras costumes and masks. One of the most reasonable is the **Mardi Gras Center,** 831 Chartres St. (© **504/454-6444**). If you come early enough, they can custom-make a costume to your specifications; if not, they're well stocked with new and used costumes, wigs, masks, hats, and makeup. (See p. 214 for more listings.) You might also try the secondhand stores along Magazine Street that have a large inventory of costumes from the year before—you can usually pick up something quite snazzy for not very much money there.

DINING   If you want to eat at a restaurant during Mardi Gras, make reservations as early as possible. And pay very close attention to **parade routes** (see the map on p. 21), because if there is one between you and your restaurant, you may not be able to cross the street, and you can kiss your dinner goodbye. For those of you who don't plan in advance, this might work to your advantage; restaurants often have a high no-show rate during Mardi Gras for this reason, and so a well-timed drop-in may work.

PARKING   Remember that even though the huge crowds you'll find everywhere add to the general merriment, they also grind traffic to a halt all over town. So our admonition against ever renting a car is even stronger during Mardi Gras. *Don't drive.* Instead, relax and take a cab or walk. Go with the flow. Don't get irritated. Remember, the fun is everywhere, so you don't really have to go anywhere. Parking along any parade route is not allowed 2 hours before and 2 hours after the parade. In addition, although you'll see people leaving their cars on "neutral ground" (the median strip), it's illegal to park there, and chances are good that you'll be towed. Traffic in New Orleans is never worse than *in the*

Tips **Save the Date**

You can always figure out **the date of Mardi Gras** because it falls exactly 47 days before Easter. If you can't find your calendar or just can't be bothered with the math, here are the next 4 years for you: February 24, 2004; February 8, 2005; February 28, 2006, February 20, 2007.

> (Tips **For More Information . . .**
>
> You'll enjoy Mardi Gras more if you've done a little homework before your trip. Contact the **New Orleans Metropolitan Convention and Visitors Bureau,** 1520 Sugar Bowl Dr., New Orleans, LA 70112 (© **800/672-6124;** www.neworleanscvb.com), and ask for current Mardi Gras info.
>
> You'll also want to get your hands on the latest edition of *Arthur Hardy's Mardi Gras Guide.* Your best bet is to contact the magazine directly (© **504/838-6111;** www.mardigrasneworleans.com/arthur). This valuable guide is sold all over town and is full of history, tips, and maps of the parade routes.

hour after a parade. Note: Streetcars and busses do run during Mardi Gras (if they can), but they may have radically altered routes during that time (you won't find anything running on St. Charles Ave.). Contact the Regional Transit Authority (© **504/248-3900;** www.regionaltransit.org) for more information.

SAFETY   Many, many cops are out, making the walk from uptown to downtown safer than at other times of year, but, not surprisingly, the streets of New Orleans are a haven for pickpockets during Mardi Gras. Take precautions.

HOW TO SPEND THE BIG DAY

While the national media focuses only on the Bourbon Street zoo, there are plenty of traditions and family-friendly fun that can be had elsewhere. What you come away with will depend on where you go and who you hang out with. Indeed, you need never see nudity if you plan your day correctly. Basically, there are three ways of doing it: nice, naughty, and nasty. See below for examples of each kind of Mardi Gras experience. Us? We prefer a mix of the first two.

Nice: Hang out exclusively Uptown with the families. Find a spot on St. Charles Avenue, which is entirely closed for the day, and camp out with a blanket, a picnic lunch, and some kids if you can find any, and spend the day there. After **Rex,** there are countless smaller parades (with trucks acting as floats) put on by the Elks and other groups (Zulu, alas, doesn't go through Uptown). Dressed-up families are all around. One side of St. Charles is for the parades and the other is open only to foot traffic, so you can wander about and admire the costumes, with **walking groups** (groups who make their own ad hoc parades) and everyone just milling about on the street. You might well get asked to join in a group barbecue or balcony party. New Orleans kids assure us that Mardi Gras is more fun than Halloween, and we can see why.

Naughty: In the morning, around the start of Zulu, head to Jackson Avenue or Claiborne Avenue and the neighborhoods around those main thoroughfares and look for the **Mardi Gras Indians.** It's a hit-or-miss proposition; the Indians themselves never know when they are going to start and where they are going to be, but running across them on their own turf is one of the great sights and experiences of Mardi Gras. Play it cool, however—this is not your neighborhood. And *do not bring your camera;* this is not an attraction put on for your benefit, and the Indians do not like being treated like a sideshow carnival act. By early to mid-afternoon, they will gather at Indian Ground Zero, on Claiborne under the freeway, where a festival of sorts takes place.

At noon, try to be around the corner of Burgundy and St. Ann streets for the **Bourbon Street** awards. You may not get close enough to actually see the judging, but the participants are all around you so that you can gawk up close and personal at their sometimes R- and X-rated costumes. As you wander the Quarter, keep an eye out (or ask around) for the **Krewe of Kosmic Debris** and the **Society of St. Anne,** marvelously costumed revelers without floats. After the awards (about mid-afternoon), head over to the Frenchmen section, where everyone is in costume, dancing in the street to tribal drums, drinking, and generally celebrating Carnival as it should be, often well into the night.

Nasty: Stay strictly on **Bourbon Street.** Yep, it's every bit as crowded, vulgar, and obscene as you've heard (and you can't even see the floats from here). The street is full of drunks (and the occasional bewildered soul), few (if any) in costume, with balconies full of more drunks, dangling expensive beads (some with X-rated anatomical features on them), which they will hand over in exchange for a glimpse of flesh. Sometimes they show flesh themselves (and they are never the people who ought to be exposing themselves). This is the "anything goes" attitude of Carnival taken to an unimaginative extreme, and while it might be worth getting a quick peep at, it grows boring more quickly than you might think. The city has tried to keep this sort of thing confined just to Bourbon Street, and efforts seem to have paid off. Astonishingly, a mere one street over is like another world. Dauphine Street, just above Bourbon, is largely empty, while Royal Street, below, is full of naughty, not nasty, Mardi Gras participants.

PARADE WATCH

A Mardi Gras parade works a spell on people. There's no other way to explain why thousands of otherwise rational men and women scream, plead, and sometimes expose themselves for no more reward than a plastic bead necklace, a plastic cup, or a little aluminum medallion. Today's parades have become bloated affairs: Natives seem to be unimpressed with a parade of fewer than 20 major floats—and if your parade has 20 floats, it'll need many high school marching bands, the Shriners and their ilk, and a few thousand other participants just to balance it out. Krewe members and guests drop tons of trinkets off their floats in the course of a parade, leaving a trail of trash that is truly astounding. Trees on parade routes have beads hanging in their branches all year long.

In your zeal to catch beads, don't forget to actually look at the parades, where considerable effort goes into the floats. Unfortunately, it's getting more and more common for bead-lust-blinded parade goers to pay little attention to what is actually passing before their eyes (besides the beads), which is really too bad as they are missing some amazing creations. (When the nighttime floats are lit by flambeaux, it is easy for revelers to be suddenly flung back to a time when Mardi Gras meant mystery and magic.) Floats aren't drawn by mules anymore (tractors instead), but the Rex floats come on the same antique wagons the krewe has been using since the 19th century.

There are two environments for viewing each parade. You can choose to stay downtown in the thick of the action, or you can walk out into the neighborhood the parade will traverse (see the map of major parade routes on p. 21). There are still crowds Uptown and in Mid-City, but they're not as large or as rowdy as those farther downtown—and they're much more family oriented. In fact, a good portion of the crowd lined up for a parade on St. Charles Avenue and Canal Street will be local children and families.

Generally, the best place to watch parades on St. Charles Avenue is between Napoleon and Jackson avenues, where the crowds are somewhat smaller and consist mostly of local families and college students. Frankly, we wouldn't attend

Major Mardi Gras Parade Routes

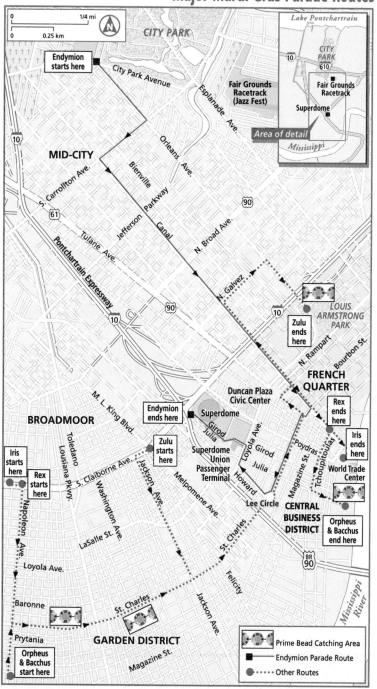

CITY PARK

Endymion starts here

City Park Avenue

Lake Pontchartrain

CITY PARK

Fair Grounds Racetrack

Superdome

Area of detail

Mississippi

Fair Grounds Racetrack (Jazz Fest)

MID-CITY

Orleans Ave.

Bienville

Jefferson Parkway

Canal

N. Broad Ave.

S. Carrollton Ave.

Tulane Ave.

Pontchartrain Expressway

N. Galvez

N. Rampart

Bourbon St.

LOUIS ARMSTRONG PARK

Zulu ends here

FRENCH QUARTER

Duncan Plaza Civic Center

Endymion ends here

Superdome

Rex ends here

Iris ends here

BROADMOOR

M. L. King Blvd.

Zulu starts here

Girod
Julia

Loyola Ave.

Girod

Julia

Howard

Poydras St.

Magazine St.

Tchoupitoulas

World Trade Center

Iris starts here

Rex starts here

Superdome Union Passenger Terminal

Toledano

Lousiana Pkwy.

S. Claiborne Ave.

Jackson Ave.

Washington Ave.

Melpomene Ave.

Lee Circle

CENTRAL BUSINESS DISTRICT

Orpheus & Bacchus end here

Napoleon Ave.

LaSalle St.

Loyola Ave.

Baronne

Prytania

Orpheus & Bacchus start here

St. Charles

St Charles

Felicity

Jackson Ave.

BR 90

GARDEN DISTRICT

St. Charles

Magazine St.

Prime Bead Catching Area

Endymion Parade Route

Other Routes

(Tips Catch Them If You Can: Tips on Getting the Best Throws

So float riders throw beads. "So what?" you think. That's because you've never been in the middle of a Mardi Gras mob before. Trust us, you're going to go crazy for beads, plastic cups, aluminum coins, and other "throws."

First, you stand there passively. All around you, the strands fly thick and fast. You catch a few. "Hmm," you think, "they look kind of good around my neck." Timidly you hold up one hand. You catch a few more. Then you notice the guy next to you/cute college girl in front of you/kid on ladder behind you is getting a lot of beads. A lot more than you. You reach more aggressively for the strands as they fly overhead. Wait, that guy/cute girl/kid got a really good strand! And another! I want one like that! How come I'm not getting any like that!

Now you find yourself shrieking, "Throw me something, Mister!" with everyone. You jump. You wail. You plead. You knock over a kid. You are completely consumed by bead lust. You think, "This is stupid. It's a 5¢ piece of plastic—oh, look, a really glittery strand! I want it I want it I want it! Please, *mistah!!!*"

And that's not even discussing Zulu coconuts.

Now, if there's a trick to bead catching, we're darned if we know it. One surefire way is to be a small child or a cute college girl (or even better, a cute college girl sitting on a tall person's shoulders). If you are none of these, you must plead and beg and whine like everybody else. Local pros stand on ladders, which put them almost at eye level with float riders. Others bring umbrellas or nets, challenging float riders to

a Mardi Gras parade (if we can help it) without children—their delight increases your enjoyment considerably. Don't forget to bring a bag to hold any throws you catch and consider bringing moist towelettes (your hands get dirty), drinks, a blanket or chair to sit on, and a picnic.

These are just a few of the major parades of the last days of Carnival (times and dates are subject to change):

- **Iris** (founded 1917): This women's krewe follows traditional Carnival rules of costume and behavior. It parades on the Saturday afternoon before Mardi Gras along Napoleon Avenue to St. Charles Avenue to Canal Street and then along Convention Center Boulevard.

- **Endymion** (founded 1967): This became one of the early "super krewes" in the 1970s by featuring a glut of floats and celebrity guests like Alice Cooper, Charo, Tom Jones, Dolly Parton, John Goodman, or Chuck Norris (Jason Alexander was the 2002 Grand Marshal). In 2001, the parade had 28 "super floats." It runs Saturday evening down Canal Street to St. Charles Avenue, then on to Howard and Girod streets and into the Superdome for a big party.

- **Bacchus** (founded 1968): The original "super krewe," Bacchus was the first to host international celebrities. It traditionally runs the Sunday before Mardi Gras from Napoleon Avenue to St. Charles Avenue to Canal Street, then along Tchoupitoulas Street and into the Convention Center.

hone their aim. Direct eye contact with a float rider also works. Sob stories invoking real and fictional ailments and family members can't hurt—if you can make yourself heard above the din of everyone else's tale of woe.

Personally, we find the popular pastime of flashing body parts in exchange for beads tacky. So does the city of New Orleans, which, in an effort to reclaim Mardi Gras from the party-hearty types, has sternly asked float riders not to throw to exhibitionists. This tactic hasn't entirely worked, but hopes are that this will largely be confined to Bourbon Street.

But if you really want to score, try positioning yourself at the end of a parade route, particularly for one of the generous super krewes like Orpheus. Throws are of no use to float riders once the parade is over, and toward the end of the ride, they often shovel out their excess inventory in great amounts (even heaving whole packages of beads overboard). By accidentally ending up at the very last block of Zulu, we scored no less than two of the highly prized Zulu coconuts, and a man near us got three.

Note: When beads land on the ground, put your foot over them to claim them; if you reach for them with your hands, you might well get your fingers broken by someone else stepping on them. If you get lucky and are tossed a whole package of beads, don't be greedy—share with your neighbors, who might well trade you a nifty strand in exchange.

- **Orpheus** (founded 1994): One of the youngest krewes, it was founded by a group that includes Harry Connick Jr. and tries to adhere to classic krewe traditions. It is popular for its many amazing floats and for the generosity of its throws. The parade is on the evening of Lundi Gras and follows the same route as Bacchus.
- **Zulu** (founded 1916): Zulu is the liveliest parade, with float riders decked out in woolly wigs and blackface. They carry the most prized of Mardi Gras souvenirs: gold-and-black-painted coconuts. (Each of these coconuts is hand decorated—some more nicely than others—with glitter and paint, so they look phenomenal. But that's not the only reason people want them. These distinctive coconuts are a rarity of sorts—they are made and given out only by Zulu as opposed to the beads that you can get at any parade, so they have become a bit of a status symbol.) The parade runs on Mardi Gras morning from Claiborne Avenue to Jackson Avenue to St. Charles Avenue to Canal Street, and then along Galvez and Orleans streets to Armstrong Park.
- **Rex** (founded 1872): Rex, the original Mardi Gras parade, follows Zulu down St. Charles. It features the King of Carnival and some of the classic floats of Carnival. Various independent walking clubs often precede the parade along its route.

MARDI GRAS MEMORIES: RIDING A FLOAT

Sure, it's fun to watch a Mardi Gras parade, but we all yearn to actually be in one, to ride one of those glorious floats in a fabulous, shiny costume, wearing a mask, tossing beads to an adoring public. Even lifelong New Orleanians almost never get to have that experience, as only a few krewes invite outsiders to ride. So when the Krewe of Orpheus generously offered to let me join their 1999 Mardi Gras parade, I didn't hesitate.

The theme was "Premieres of the French Opera," an homage to the beloved building that burned down in the 1920s. The floats were conceived by master float designer Henri Schindler. I would be riding on *Le Cid* (an opera by Jules Massenet). I had to send in measurements for my costume (float riders must be masked and costumed throughout the parade) and purchase beads to throw. Many, many beads. How many? "Oh, about 50 or 60 gross." "That's more than 7,000 strands!" I said, calculating that this was going to set me back several hundred bucks. "Yeah, you're right—you might want to get a few more."

Orpheus parades on Lundi Gras night, starting at 6pm. I show up at 10am at the Convention Center to load my beads on the float. Several other float riders do the same, and before long, we are surrounded by little fortresses of beads and other throws. My neighbors, noticing my thrifty (read: cheap) beads (the better-quality beads cost a lot more, especially for 7,000 of them), graciously share a few good strands with me so I may bestow them on especially worthy people. I resolve to throw only to people who don't have many beads, who've been overlooked by other float riders, who aren't cute college girls—in short, people like me. (I'd been frustrated all week by float riders who seemed to find me invisible.)

I try on my costume, which is vaguely knightlike (that is, if knights wore shiny metallic fabric and orange polyester). I look like a big pumpkin. The sleeves hang down 4 inches past my fingers. Good thing they had my measurements—imagine if they didn't!

We finally get on the floats at 3:30pm, ready to head to the parade route. My husband, in mandatory tux, will meet me at the finish line near the Convention Center, home of the Orpheus Ball.

4pm: The floats start to move toward the starting point on Tchoupitoulas.

4:30pm: Our float stops. The float in front of us has a flat tire.

4:31pm: Everyone around me starts drinking.

5pm: Float starts to move again.

5:20pm: Float stops moving.

5:45pm: Pizzas (dinner) are delivered to the float. Only in New Orleans.

6pm: Parade starts. It doesn't really affect us. We are float 24, and it's a long, long time until we hit the starting line.

6:05pm to 7:35pm: People still drinking.

7:35pm: Float starts to move again.

7:37pm: Float stops.

8pm: Float starts again. We can see the starting point.

8:05pm: So much for moving.

8:30pm: Everyone is deeply, crushingly bored.

9pm: Even the drinkers have stopped drinking.

9:17pm: I think of my husband at the ball and wonder if I will ever see him again.

9:30pm: Here we go! And it's mayhem. Thousands of people, waving hands, screaming, shrieking, pleading, crying, "Please, Mister, throw me something, throw me something, Mister!" I start to grin and don't stop for hours. I throw beads, feeling, at last, like a queen tossing largesse to the populace. I am sparing in my generosity, however, minding advice not to go overboard too early, lest I run out of beads. I discover my aim isn't bad, and from my upper-level vantage point, I can throw quite far out, to specific people in the back. I also learn that from atop the float, you can see everybody, no matter how small, so if it seems like float riders are ignoring you, it's because they are.

9:35pm: One heavily endowed young woman flashes me and looks expectant, but I say, "Put those away!"

10pm: As we turn onto St. Charles, I hear someone shout my name. It's my cousin's son, a Tulane med student whom I've never actually met before. Of course, since I'm masked and costumed, he still doesn't know what I look like.

10:15pm: Orpheus is known for its generosity, so by now, every parade goer's neck is already thickly covered in beads. There is no bead-challenged person to throw to. Worse, because so many floats have already gone by, everyone only wants the really good beads, not the utilitarian stuff I'm throwing. Oh, dear.

10:45pm: I notice how my friend Ann is really good at taunting the crowd with the good beads. She holds out long, thick strands, shows them off, whips the crowd into a frenzy, then shakes her head sadly and puts them away to await more worthy types.

11pm: The crowd's impatience is high whenever the float comes to a halt—that's when riders supposedly throw the really good stuff. The crowd threatens to turn ugly when I don't. The occasional good strand given by a sympathetic co-rider means I can then appease the angry mob. Lacking a worthy target, I choose to turn my back and throw blindly. Meanwhile, my neat fortress of beads is now in a shambles, and I slip and slide on loose strands, frantically trying to get some to throw before revelers scale the float to rip them from me.

11:04pm: I never want to see another bead as long as I live.

11:05pm: Oh, goody, only about halfway there!

11:06pm to 12:35am: Pleasemisterthrowmesomethingpleasemisterpleasemister c'monmisterheymisterpleasemisterpleasemisterpleasepleaseplease*mistaaaahhh*!

12:40am: I make a horrifying discovery. With less than one-third of the parade to go, I still have several thousand beads left. These are worthless once the parade is over (particularly my crappy cheap beads), so as we hit Canal Street, I start to heave them at a great rate, by the dozen, and sometimes entire packages of several dozen. Suddenly, I am *very* popular. Especially fun is throwing the packages into knots of frat boys and watching them pummel each other for it.

1:30am: We arrive at the Convention Center. Although these people have been watching floats arrive for at least 3 hours, they are still surprisingly fresh and enthusiastic. This howling mob of gowned women and tuxedoed men stands on chairs and tables and shrieks for beads. Among them is my husband, who catches the camera I toss him, so he can take a picture of my dirty, bedraggled self.

1:35am: I descend from the float and proceed to the party. "How was it?" my husband's new friends (he's been sitting there a long time) inquire. "Ask me tomorrow," I say.

2 Cajun Mardi Gras

If Mardi Gras in New Orleans sounds like too much for you, no matter how low-key you keep it, consider driving out to Cajun country, where Mardi Gras traditions are just as strong but considerably more, er, wholesome. **Lafayette,** the capital of French Acadiana, celebrates Carnival in a different manner, one that really reflects the Cajun heritage and spirit. (For the full story, see chapter 12, "Plantation Homes & Cajun Country: Side Trips from New Orleans.") Three full days of activities lead up to Cajun Mardi Gras, making it second in size only to New Orleans's celebration. There's one *big* difference, though: Their final pageant and ball are open to the general public. Don your formal wear and join right in!

Instead of Rex and his queen, the Lafayette festivities are ruled by King Gabriel and Queen Evangeline. They are the fictional hero and heroine of Henry Wadsworth Longfellow's epic poem *Evangeline,* which was based on real-life lovers who were separated during the British expulsion of Acadians from Nova Scotia around the time of the French and Indian War. Their story is still very much alive here among the descendants of those who shared their wanderings.

Things get off to a joyous start with the **Children's Krewe** and **Krewe of Bonaparte** parades and ball, held on the Saturday before Mardi Gras, following a full day of celebration at Acadian Village. On Monday night, Queen Evangeline is honored at the **Queen's Parade.** The **King's Parade,** held the following morning, honors King Gabriel and opens a full day of merriment. Lafayette's African-American community stages the **Parade of King Toussaint L'Ouverture** and **Queen Suzanne Simonne** at about noon, just after the King's Parade. Then the **Krewe of Lafayette** invites everyone to get into the act as its parade winds through the streets. Krewe participants trot along on foot or ride in the vehicle of their choice—some very imaginative modes of transportation turn up every year. The Mardi Gras climax, a formal ball presided over by the king and queen and their royal court, takes place that night. Everything stops promptly at midnight, as Cajuns and visitors alike depart to begin their observance of Lent.

MASKED MEN & A BIG GUMBO   In the Cajun countryside that surrounds Lafayette, there's yet another form of Mardi Gras celebration, one tied to the rural lifestyle. Cajuns firmly believe in sharing, so you're welcome to come along. The celebration goes like this: Bands of masked men dressed in raggedy patchwork costumes (unlike the New Orleans costumes, which are heavy on glitter and shine) and peaked hats known as *capichons* set off on Mardi Gras morning on horseback (but don't count on getting a horse—instead, plan on walking or hitching a ride in a car), led by their *capitaine.* They ride from farm to farm, asking at each, *"Voulez-vous reçevoir le Mardi Gras?"* ("Will you receive the Mardi Gras?") and dismounting as the invariable *"Oui"* comes in reply. Each farmyard then becomes a miniature festival as the revelers *faire le macaque* ("make monkeyshines") with song and dance, much drinking of beer, and other antics loosely labeled "entertainment." As payment for their show, they demand, and get, "a fat little chicken to make a big gumbo" (or sometimes a bag of rice or other ingredients).

When each band has visited its allotted farmyards, they all head back to town where everyone else has already begun the general festivities. There'll be dancing in the streets, rowdy card games, storytelling, and the like until the wee hours, and you can be sure that all those fat little chickens go into the *"gumbo gros"* pot to make a very big gumbo indeed.

You can write or call ahead for particulars on both the urban (Lafayette) and rural (the rest of Cajun Country) Mardi Gras celebrations. For the latter, the towns of **Eunice** and **Mamou** stage some of the most enjoyable celebrations. Contact the **Lafayette Parish Convention and Visitors Commission,** P.O. Box 52066, Lafayette, LA 70505 (© **800/346-1958** in the U.S., 800/543-5340 in Canada, or 337/232-3737; www.lafayettetravel.com) for more information.

3 New Orleans Jazz & Heritage Festival

What began in 1969 as a small gathering in a public park to celebrate the music of New Orleans now ranks as one of the best attended, most respected, and most musically comprehensive festivals in the world. Although people call it Jazz Fest, the full name is New Orleans Jazz & Heritage Festival, and the heritage is about as broad as it can get. Stand in the right place and, depending on which way the wind's blowing, you can catch as many as 10 musical styles from several continents, smell the tantalizing aromas of a dozen or so different food offerings, and meet a U.N.-like spectrum of fellow fest-goers all at once.

While such headliners as Van Morrison, Dave Matthews, Bob Dylan, Sting, and Paul Simon have drawn record-setting crowds in recent years, serious Jazz Fest aficionados savor the lesser-known acts. They range from Mardi Gras Indians to old-time bluesmen who have never played outside the Delta, from Dixieland to avant-garde, from African artists making rare U.S. appearances to the top names in Cajun, zydeco, and, of course, jazz.

Gone are the days when the event was held in Congo Square and only a few hundred people came. Now filling the infield of the Fair Grounds horse-racing track up near City Park, the festival covers the last weekend in April and the first in May (in 2003, a new day was added to the schedule, so it now begins the last Thursday of April). It's set up about as well as such an event can be. When the crowds get big, though—the second Saturday, traditionally, is the busiest—it can be tough to move around, especially if the grounds are muddy from rain. And the lines at the most popular of the several dozen food booths can be frustratingly long. However, the crowds are remarkably well behaved—to make a sweeping generalization, these are not the same types who come for Mardi Gras. Tellingly, there are few, if any, arrests during Jazz Fest.

Attending Jazz Fest means making a few decisions. Hotel and restaurant reservations, not to mention choice plane flights, fill up months (if not a year) in advance, but the schedule is not announced until a couple of months before the event. That may mean scheduling your visit around your own availability, not an appearance by a particular band (unless you go for the whole 11 days). Just about every day at Jazz Fest is a good day, however, so this is not a hardship.

The second Saturday does attract some of the top acts, and each year it sets a record for single-day attendance. But we feel the fun tends to diminish with that many people. Still, the tickets are cheap enough that going early in the day and leaving before the crowds get too big is a viable option. The Thursday before the second weekend is traditionally targeted to locals, with more local bands and generally smaller crowds because fewer tourists are around than on the weekends. (This may also hold true with the new "first" Thursday, in terms of crowds.) It's a great time to hit the best food booths and to check out the crafts areas. Fans of the Neville Brothers, New Orleans's favorite sons, will be pleased to know that they are the traditional closing act on Sunday, with brother Aaron Neville usually making a popular appearance in the gospel tent earlier in the day.

Whenever you decide to go, contact **New Orleans Jazz & Heritage Festival,** 1205 N. Rampart St., New Orleans, LA 70116 (© **504/522-4786;** www.nojazz fest.com), to get the schedule for each weekend and information about other Jazz Fest–related shows around town.

JAZZ FEST POINTERS

Of course, going to Jazz Fest means marathon endurance. With so many stages and musical choices, your mind can almost freeze. The Festival's main feature, the Louisiana Heritage Fair, offers music on 12 stages. You can plot out your day or just wander from stage to stage, catching a few songs by just about everyone. There is something to be said for the latter approach; some of the best Jazz Fest experiences come from discovering a hitherto unknown (at least to you) band or otherwise stumbling across a gem of a musical moment. Or you can camp out at just one stage—from the big ones, which feature famous headliners, to the gospel tent, where magical moments seem to happen several times a day.

Regardless, a typical Jazz Fest day has you arriving sometime after the gates open at 11am and staying until you are pooped or until they close at around 7pm (incredibly the whole thing runs as efficiently as a Swiss train). After you leave the Fair Grounds for the day, get some dinner and then hit the clubs. Every club in the city has Jazz Fest–related bookings. (The increasingly popular LMNOP—Louisiana Music–New Orleans Pride—music industry conference, which runs concurrent with part of Jazz Fest, showcases local acts.) Bouncing from one club to another can keep you out until dawn. Then you get up and start all over again. This is part of the reason we think Jazz Fest is so fun.

There are also many nonmusical aspects of Jazz Fest to distract you, particularly the crafts. Local craftspeople and imported artisans fill a sizable section of the Fair Grounds with displays of their products during the festival. Many of them offer demonstrations. You might get to see Louisiana Native American basket making; Cajun accordion, fiddle, and triangle making; and Mardi Gras Indian beading and costume making. Contemporary arts and crafts—like jewelry, furniture, handblown glass, and painting—are also featured. In addition, you'll find an open marketplace at Congo Square filled with contemporary and traditional African (and African-influenced) crafts and performing artists.

And then, as always in New Orleans, there's the food. The heck with the music—when we dream of Jazz Fest, we are often thinking more about those 50-plus food booths filled with some of the best goodies we've ever tasted. We have friends who, at the end of every Jazz Fest, buy tickets for the very popular soft-shell crab po' boy stand *for next year* so they won't suffer a moment's delay in getting their mouths around one of the best sandwiches they've ever tasted.

The food ranges from local standbys—red beans and rice, jambalaya, étouffée, and gumbo—to more interesting choices such as oyster sacks, the hugely popular sausage bread, *cochon de lait* (a mouthwatering roast pig sandwich), alligator sausage po' boys, and quail and pheasant gumbo. There's crawfish every way including crawfish sushi, crawfish beignets, and the divine crawfish Monica (a white cream sauce over pasta). And that's not even discussing the various Caribbean, African, Spanish, and even vegetarian dishes available. And how about dessert? Lemon crepes, Italian ice cream, Key lime tarts, chocolate snowballs with condensed milk on them—oh, my! There's plenty of cold beer available, too, although you'll have to wait in some mighty long lines to get to it.

But there is even more to the Fest than food, music, and crafts. A number of cultural presentations on a wealth of topics (for starters, local folklore or music) are held daily throughout the fairgrounds. These little jewels are easily over-looked or missed altogether. We encourage you to either buy a program (which lists everything being offered) or drop by one of the information booths scattered around the grounds to look over the listings.

Experienced Fest-goers also know that the Grandstand is the best-kept secret; it's air-conditioned, for one thing, and full of art and photography exhibits, cooking demonstrations by the city's best chefs, a small movie theater that screens New Orleans–related documentaries all day long, and the Heritage Stage, which features interviews and short performances by some of the acts. (This is a chance to perhaps see someone very popular in a more intimate setting, with often unpredictable and wild results—recently, we saw the Five Blind Boys of Alabama with only a couple hundred people, compared with the thousands who struggled to see their full set later in the day.)

Try to purchase tickets as early as February if possible. They're available by mail through **Ticketmaster** (℃ **504/522-5555;** www.ticketmaster.com). To order tickets by phone or to get ticket information, call **New Orleans Jazz & Heritage Festival** (℃ **800/488-5252** outside Louisiana, or 504/522-4786; fax 504/379-3291; www.nojazzfest.com). Admission for adults is $20 in advance and $25 at the gate; $2 for children. Evening events and concerts (order tickets in advance for these events as well) may be attended at an additional cost—usually between $20 and $30, depending on the concert. The good news is that tickets are always available at the gate (there is no sell-out). The bad news is that tickets are always available at the gate, which can lead to severe overcrowding.

Note: No outside beverages are allowed at Jazz Fest. Though there are seats at some of the stages (two jazz tents, the gospel tent, and the blues tent) and some bleachers at another stage, people either sit on the ground, stand, or bring folding chairs or small blankets.

JAZZ FEST PARKING & TRANSPORTATION   Parking at the Fair Grounds is next to impossible. The few available spaces cost $10 a day. We strongly recommend that you take public transportation or one of the available shuttles. The **Regional Transit Authority** operates bus routes from various pickup points to the Fair Grounds. For schedules, contact ℃ **504/248-3900** (www.regionaltransit.org). Taxis, though probably scarce, will also take you to the Fair Grounds at a special-event rate of $3 per person (or the meter reading if it's higher). We recommend **United Cabs** (℃ **504/524-9606**). **New Orleans**

⌜Tips   More Fun on the Bayou

A possible alternative to Jazz Fest, especially for those who feel its size now outweighs the amount of fun it generates, is the **Festival International de Louisiane**. This 6-day celebration of the music and art of southern Louisiana and its French-speaking cousins around the world is held on the blocked-off streets of Lafayette. It usually runs through the last weekend in April. Between the considerably smaller crowds and even smaller price (it's free!), it makes for a nice change of pace from Jazz Fest, with which it overlaps. The festival always manages to come up with a fairly impressive lineup. For information, call or write the Festival International de Louisiane, 735 Jefferson St., Suite 205, Lafayette, LA 70501 (℃ **337/232-8086;** www.festival international.com).

Jazz & Heritage Festival (© **800/488-5252** outside Louisiana, or 504/522-4786; www.nojazzfest.com) has information about shuttle transportation, which is not included in the ticket price.

PACKAGE DEALS   If you want to go to Jazz Fest but would rather have someone else do all the planning, contact **Festival Tours International,** 15237 Sunset Blvd., Suite 17, Pacific Palisades, CA 90272 (© **310/454-4080;** www.gumbo pages.com/festivaltours), which caters to music lovers who don't wish to wear name tags or do other hokey tour activities. Packages include not just accommodations and tickets for Jazz Fest but also a visit to Cajun country for unique personal encounters with local musicians.

If you're flying to New Orleans specifically for the Jazz & Heritage Festival, visit www.nojazzfest.com to get a Jazz Fest promotional code from a list of airlines that offer special fares during the event.

4 Other Top Festivals

THE FRENCH QUARTER FESTIVAL

The 3-day French Quarter Festival in early April is a celebration of the ingredients of French Quarter life. While the diversity of music is nowhere near as great as that found at Jazz Fest, this is rapidly growing as an alternative. There are scores of free outdoor concerts, art shows, and children's activities. Most of the music is of the traditional jazz, brass-band, Cajun/zydeco, or funk variety. Stages are set throughout the Quarter, along Bourbon, Royal, and even down by the river, where the breeze adds to the experience. Jackson Square and Woldenberg Riverfront Park are transformed into the world's largest jazz brunch, with about 60 leading restaurants serving Cajun and Creole specialties; the food is no less abundant than at Jazz Fest, but because it's done by local restaurants, it's no less top-notch. Best of all, it's all located in the Quarter, so you can come and go as you please throughout the day, a boon like no other.

For details, write to **French Quarter Festivals,** 400 N. Peters St., Suite 205, New Orleans, LA 70130 (© **800/673-5725** or 504/522-5730; www.frenchquarter festivals.org).

FESTIVALS ACADIENS

This is a Cajun Country celebration—or rather, several celebrations—held during the third week of September in Lafayette. The festivals, lumped together under the heading Festivals Acadiens, pay tribute to the culture and heritage of Cajun families who have been here since the British expelled them from their Nova Scotia homes nearly 250 years ago. Included among the festivals are the **Bayou Food Festival,** the **Festival de Musique Acadienne,** and the **Louisiana Native Crafts Festival.**

At the **Bayou Food Festival,** you'll be able to taste the cuisine of more than 30 top Cajun restaurants. Specialties such as stuffed crabs, crawfish étouffée, oysters Bienville, shrimp de la Teche, catfish *en brochette,* jambalaya, chicken-and-sausage gumbo, smothered quail, and hot *boudin* (sausage) are everyday eating for Cajuns, and this is a rare opportunity to try them all. The Bayou Food Festival is held in Girard Park, adjacent to the music festival. Admission is free.

The **Festival de Musique Acadienne** began in 1974 when some Cajun musicians were engaged to play briefly for visiting French newspaper editors. It was a rainy night, but some 12,000 Cajun residents showed up to listen. The walls rang for 3 solid hours with old French songs, waltzes, two-steps, Cajun rock rhythms, zydeco, and the special music some have dubbed "Cajun country." It has become an annual affair with more than 50,000 visitors usually on hand. Because of the crowds, the festival is now held outdoors in Girard Park where fans can listen in grassy comfort. Performed almost entirely in French, the music covers both traditional and modern Cajun styles, including zydeco. The music starts early and ends late, and there's no charge to come to the park and listen.

You'll see native Louisiana artisans demonstrating their skills at the **Louisiana Native Crafts Festival.** All crafts presented must have been practiced before or during the early 1900s, and all materials used must be native to Louisiana. Meeting these criteria are such arts as woodcarving, soap making, pirogue making (pronounced *pee*-rogue, it's a Cajun canoe), chair caning, doll making, palmetto weaving, Native American–style basket weaving, quilting, spinning, dyeing, pottery making, jewelry making, and alligator skinning.

For details on Festivals Acadiens, contact the **Lafayette Parish Convention and Visitors Commission,** P.O. Box 52066, Lafayette, LA 70505 (© **800/346-1958** in the U.S., 800/543-5340 in Canada, or 337/232-3737; www.lafayette travel.com).

3

Planning Your Trip to New Orleans

Whatever your idea of the ideal New Orleans trip, this chapter will give you the information to make informed plans and help point you toward some additional resources.

International travelers should also consult chapter 4, "For International Visitors," for information on entry requirements, getting to the United States, and more.

1 Visitor Information

Even a seasoned traveler should consider writing or calling ahead to the **New Orleans Metropolitan Convention and Visitors Bureau,** 1520 Sugar Bowl Dr., New Orleans, LA 70112 (℃ **800/672-6124** or 504/566-5055; www.neworleanscvb.com). The staff is extremely friendly and helpful, and you can easily get any information you can't find in this book from them.

Another source of information is the **New Orleans Multicultural Tourism Network,** Louisiana Superdome, 1520 Sugar Bowl Dr., New Orleans, LA 70112 (℃ **504/523-5652;** www.soulofneworleans.com); you may be particularly interested in their self-directed tours of African-American landmarks.

2 Money

Prices for everything from accommodations to zydeco clubs skyrocket during major events and festivals (see chapter 2, "Mardi Gras, Jazz Fest & Other Festivals"). New Orleans is also quite popular in the fall during what has become the convention season. The heat and humidity of the summer months (July and Aug) keep tourism in the city to its yearly low, so if the weather doesn't bother you, you can find some incredible bargains during those times, especially at hotels.

ATMs Almost all New Orleans ATMs are linked to a national network that most likely includes your bank at home. **Cirrus** (℃ **800/424-7787;** www.mastercard.com) and **PLUS** (℃ **800/843-7587;** www.visa.com) are

the two most popular networks; check the back of your ATM card to see which network your bank belongs to (these days, most banks belong to both).

Some centrally located ATMs in New Orleans are at the **First National Bank of Commerce,** 240 Royal St.; **Hibernia National Bank,** 701 Poydras St.; and **Whitney National Bank,** 228 St. Charles Ave. There are now ATMs all over the French Quarter, a big change from 10 years ago when there was just one.

Expect to pay a $1 to $2 service charge each time you withdraw money from an ATM, in addition to what your home bank charges.

Avoid poorly lit or out-of-the-way ATMs, especially at night. Use an indoor machine or one at a well-trafficked, well-lit location. Put your money away discreetly; don't flash it around or count it in a way that could attract the attention of thieves.

TRAVELER'S CHECKS   Traveler's checks are something of an anachronism from the days before the ATM made cash accessible at any time. But you may want to avoid withdrawal fees and enjoy the security of traveler's checks—provided you don't mind showing identification every time you want to cash one.

You can get traveler's checks at almost any bank. **American Express** offers checks for a service charge ranging from 1% to 4%. You can also get American Express traveler's checks over the phone by calling ✆ **800/221-7282.** Amex gold or platinum cardholders can avoid paying the fee by ordering over the telephone; platinum cardholders can also purchase checks fee-free in person at Amex Travel Service locations (check www.americanexpress.com for the office nearest you). American Automobile Association members can obtain checks without a fee at most AAA offices.

Visa offers traveler's checks at Citibank branches and other financial institutions nationwide; call ✆ **800/ 732-1322** to locate the purchase location near you. **MasterCard** also offers traveler's checks through **Thomas Cook Currency Services;** call ✆ **800/ 223-9920** for a location near you.

If you carry traveler's checks, be sure to keep a record of their serial numbers (separate from the checks, of course) so that you're ensured a refund in case they're lost or stolen.

Most hotels will happily cash traveler's checks for you, and many stores and restaurants are equally pleased to accept them (as are even the food booths at Jazz Fest!).

3 When to Go

With the possible exception of July and August (unless you happen to thrive on heat and humidity), just about any time is the right time to go to New Orleans. Mardi Gras is, of course, the time of year when it's hardest to get a hotel room, but it can also be difficult during the various music festivals throughout the year, especially the Jazz & Heritage Festival (see chapter 2, "Mardi Gras, Jazz Fest & Other Festivals").

It's important to know what's going on when; the city's landscape can change dramatically depending on what festival or convention is happening, and prices can also reflect that. The best time of year, in our opinion, is December, before and during Christmas. The town is gussied up with decorations, there are all kinds of seasonal special events, the weather is nice—but for some reason, tourists become scarce. Hotels, eager to lure any business, lower their rates dramatically, and most restaurants are so empty that you can walk in just about anywhere without a reservation. Take advantage of it.

THE WEATHER

The average mean temperature in New Orleans is an inviting 70°F (20°C), but it can drop or rise considerably in a single day. (We've experienced 40°F [4°C] and rain one day, 80°F [27°C] and humidity the next.) Conditions depend primarily on two things: whether it rains and whether there is direct sunlight or cloud cover. Rain can provide slight and temporary relief on a hot day; for the most part, it hits in sudden (and sometimes dramatically heavy) showers, which disappear as quickly as they arrived. Anytime the sun shines unimpeded, it gets much warmer. The region's high humidity can make even mild warms and colds feel intense. Still, the city's semitropical climate is part of its appeal—a slight bit of moistness makes the air come sensually alive.

New Orleans will be pleasant at almost any time of year except July and August, which can be exceptionally hot and muggy. If you do come during those months, you'll quickly learn to follow the natives' example, staying out of the noonday sun and ducking from one air-conditioned building to another. Winter is very mild by American standards but is punctuated by an occasional cold snap, when the mercury can drop below the freezing point.

In the dead of summer, T-shirts and shorts are absolutely acceptable everywhere except the finest restaurants. In the spring and fall, something a little warmer is in order; in the winter, you should plan to carry a lightweight coat or jacket, though umbrellas and cheap rain jackets are available everywhere for those tourists who inevitably get caught in a sudden, unexpected downpour.

New Orleans Average Temperatures & Rainfall

	Jan	Feb	Mar	Apr	May	June	July	Aug	Sept	Oct	Nov	Dec
High (°F)	61	64	71	78	84	89	90	90	87	80	71	64
Low (°F)	44	47	54	60	67	73	74	74	71	61	54	47
High (°C)	16	18	22	26	29	32	32	32	31	27	22	18
Low (°C)	7	8	12	16	19	23	23	23	22	16	12	8
Days of Rainfall	10	9	9	7	8	10	15	13	10	5	7	10

NEW ORLEANS CALENDAR OF EVENTS

For more information on **Mardi Gras, Jazz Fest, Festivals Acadiens,** and other major area events, see chapter 2, "Mardi Gras, Jazz Fest & Other Festivals." For general information, contact the **New Orleans Metropolitan Convention and Visitors Bureau,** 1520 Sugar Bowl Dr., New Orleans, LA 70112 (© **800/672-6124** or 504/566-5055; www.neworleanscvb.com).

January

Nokia Sugar Bowl Classic. First held in 1934, this is New Orleans's oldest yearly sporting occasion. The football game is the main event, but there are also tennis, swimming, basketball, sailing, running, and flag-football competitions. Fans tend to be really loud, really boisterous, and everywhere during the festivities. For information, contact Nokia Sugar Bowl, 1500 Sugar Bowl Dr., New Orleans, LA 70112 (© **504/525-8573;** www.nokiasugarbowl.com). January 1.

March

Lundi Gras. This is an old tradition that has been revived in the last decade or so. It's free, it's outdoors (celebrations are at Spanish Plaza), and it features music (including a jazz competition) and the arrival of Rex at 6pm, marking the beginning of Mardi Gras. For more information, contact New Orleans Riverwalk Marketplace, 1 Poydras St., New Orleans, LA 70130 (© **504/522-1555**). For more information, see p. 16. Monday before Mardi Gras. February 23, 2004.

Mardi Gras. The culmination of the 2-month-long carnival season, Mardi Gras is the big annual blowout, a citywide party that takes place on Fat Tuesday (the last day before Lent in the Christian calendar). The entire city stops working (sometimes days in advance!) and starts partying in the early morning, and the streets are taken over by some overwhelming parades—which, these days, go through the Central Business District instead of the French Quarter. See chapter 2, "Mardi Gras, Jazz Fest & Other Festivals," for more details. Day before Ash Wednesday. February 24, 2004.

St. Patrick's Day Parades. There are two: One takes place in the French Quarter beginning at Molly's at the Market (1107 Decatur St.), March 14, and the other goes through the Irish Channel neighborhood following a route that begins at Jackson Avenue and Magazine Street, goes over to St. Charles Avenue, turns uptown to Louisiana Avenue, and returns to Jackson Avenue. The parades have the flavor of Mardi Gras, but instead of beads, watchers are pelted with cabbages, carrots, and other veggies. For information on the French Quarter parade, call Molly's at the Market (© **504/525-5169**). The Irish Channel parade takes place in early March. Because there's no organization to contact about this one, you can try the Convention and Visitors Bureau (see p. 32) for more information.

Black Heritage Festival. This festival honors the various African-American cultural contributions to New Orleans. Write or call the Black Heritage Foundation, 4535 S. Prieur St., New Orleans, LA 70125 (© **504/827-0112**) for more info. March 15 and 16.

St. Joseph's Day Parade. In addition to the parade, which takes place the weekend around March 19, you may want to visit the altar devoted to St. Joseph at the American Italian Museum and Library, 537 S. Peters St. For more information, call © **504/522-7294**. March 17 to 19.

Super Sunday. This is the annual Mardi Gras Indians showdown, which takes place on the Sunday nearest St. Joseph's Day. This is an incredible, but sadly under-appreciated event in New Orleans, when the Indians are all in one place; the feathers fly and the chants are ongoing. Unfortunately, there are no contact numbers nor firm times or locations for this event (though it's roughly in the Bayou St. John area and Uptown, around the corner of LaSalle and Washington), and for that matter, recently the two neighborhoods have been doing their respective things on Sundays 2 weeks apart. For more information, you can try checking with www.nola.com or the Metropolitan Tourism board, or just show up in town and drive into that area and ask around. Usually in mid- to late March.

Tennessee Williams New Orleans Literary Festival. A 5-day series celebrating New Orleans's rich literary heritage, this festival includes theatrical performances, readings, discussion panels, master classes, musical events, and literary walking tours dedicated to the playwright. By the way, the focus is not confined to Tennessee Williams. Events take place at venues throughout the city. For info, call © **504/581-1144** or go to www.tennesseewilliams.net. Late March.

Spring Fiesta. The fiesta, which begins with the crowning of the Spring Fiesta queen, is more than half a century old and takes place throughout the city—from the Garden District to the French Quarter to Uptown and beyond. Historical and architectural tours of many of the city's private homes, courtyards, and plantation homes are offered in conjunction with the 5-day event. For the schedule, call the Spring Fiesta Association (© **504/581-1367**). Last 2 weekends in March or early April.

April

The French Quarter Festival. For hard-core jazz fans, this is rapidly becoming an alternative to Jazz Fest, where actual jazz is becoming less and less prominent. It kicks off with a parade down Bourbon Street. Among other things, you can join people dancing in the streets, learn the history of jazz, visit historic homes, and take a ride on a riverboat. Many local restaurants set up booths in Jackson Square, so the eating is exceptionally good. Events are held all over the French Quarter. For information, call or write French Quarter Festivals, 100 Conti St., New Orleans, LA 70130 (© **504/522-5730**; www.french quarterfestivals.org). April 16 to 18, 2004.

New Orleans Jazz & Heritage Festival (Jazz Fest). A 10-day event that draws musicians, music fans, cooks, and craftspeople to celebrate music and life, Jazz Fest rivals Mardi Gras in popularity. Lodgings in the city tend to sell out up to a year ahead, so book early. Events take place at the Fair Grounds Race Track and various venues throughout the city. For information, call or write New Orleans Jazz & Heritage Festival, 1205 N. Rampart St., New Orleans, LA 70116 (© **504/ 522-4786**; www.nojazzfest.com). Look for more information in chapter 2, "Mardi Gras, Jazz Fest & Other Festivals." Usually held the last weekend in April and first weekend in May.

The Crescent City Classic. This 6-mile road race, from Jackson Square to Audubon Park, brings an international field of top runners to the city. For more info, call or write the Classic, P.O. Box 13587, New Orleans, LA 70185 (© **504/861-8686;** www.ccc10k.com). Saturday before Easter.

May

Greek Festival. Located at the Holy Trinity Cathedral's Hellenic Cultural Center, this 3-day festival features Greek folk dancing, specialty foods, crafts, and music. For more information, call or write Holy Trinity Cathedral, 1200 Robert E. Lee Blvd., New Orleans, LA 70122 (© **504/282-0259**). Last weekend of May.

June

The Great French Market Tomato Festival. A celebration of tomato diversity, this daylong event features cooking and tastings in the historic French Market. For more information, call or write the French Market, P.O. Box 51749, New Orleans, LA 70151 (© **504/522-2621;** www. frenchmarket.org). First Sunday in June.

Reggae Riddums Festival. This 3-day gathering of calypso, reggae, and *soca* (a blend of soul and calypso) musicians is held in City Park and includes a heady helping of ethnic foods and arts and crafts. For more information, call or write Ernest Kelly, P.O. Box 6156, New Orleans, LA 70174 (© **888/767-1317** or 504/367-1313). Second week of June.

July

Go Fourth on the River. The annual Fourth of July celebration begins in the morning at the riverfront and continues into the night, culminating into a spectacular fireworks display. For more information, call or write Anna Pepper, 610 S. Peters St., Suite 301, New Orleans, LA 70130 (© **504/587-1791**). July 4th.

New Orleans Wine & Food Experience. During this time, antiques shops and art galleries throughout the French Quarter hold wine and food tastings, winemakers and local chefs conduct seminars, and a variety of vintner dinners and grand tastings are held for your gourmandistic pleasure. More than 150 wines and 40 restaurants are featured every day. For information and this year's schedule, call or write Mary Reynolds, P.O. Box 70514, New Orleans, LA 70172 (© 504/529-9463; www.nowfe.com). Five days in July (though you should call in advance because in 2002, it was held in May).

September

Southern Decadence. All over the French Quarter, thousands of folks—drag queens, mostly—follow a secret parade route, making sure to stop into many bars along the way. People travel from far and wide to be a part of the festivities. There is only an informal organization associated with the festival, and it's hard to get anyone on the phone. For information, try the website www.southern decadence.com or contact *Ambush Magazine* (© 800/876-1484 or 504/522-8047; fax 504/522-0907). Labor Day weekend.

The Rayne Frog Festival. Cajuns can always find an excuse to hold a party, and in this case, they've turned to the lowly frog as an excuse for a *fais do-do* (dance) and a waltz contest. Frog races and frog-jumping contests fill the entertainment bill—and if you arrive without your amphibian, there's a Rent-a-Frog service. A lively frog-eating contest winds things up. For dates and full details, contact Lafayette Parish Convention and Visitors Commission, P.O. Box 52066, Lafayette, LA 70505 (© 800/346-1958 in the U.S., 800/543-5340 in Canada, or 337/232-3808; www.lafayettetravel.com). Labor Day weekend.

Festivals Acadiens. This is a series of happenings that celebrate Cajun music, food, crafts, and culture in and near Lafayette, Louisiana. (Most of the events are in Lafayette.) For more information, contact the **Lafayette Parish Convention and Visitors Commission,** P.O. Box 52066, Lafayette, LA 70505 (© **800/346-1958** in the U.S., 800/543-5340 in Canada, or 337/232-3737; www.lafayettetravel.com). Third week of the month.

Swamp Festival. Sponsored by the Audubon Institute, the Swamp Festival features long days of live swamp music performances (lots of good zydeco here), as well as hands-on contact with Louisiana swamp animals. Admission to the festival is free with zoo admission. For information, call or write the Audubon Institute, 6500 Magazine St., New Orleans, LA 70118 (© **504/861-2537;** www.audoboninstitute.org). Last weekend in September and first weekend in October.

October

Art for Arts' Sake. The arts season begins with gallery openings throughout the city. Julia, Magazine, and Royal streets are where the action is. For more information, contact the Contemporary Arts Center, 900 Camp St., New Orleans, LA 70130 (© **504/523-1216;** www.cacno.org). Throughout the month.

Louisiana Jazz Awareness Month. There are nightly concerts (some of which are free), television and radio specials, and lectures, all sponsored by the Louisiana Jazz Federation. For more information and a schedule, contact the Louisiana Music Commission (© **504/835-5277;** www.louisianamusic.org). All month.

Gumbo Festival. This festival showcases one of the region's signature dishes and celebrates Cajun culture to boot. It's 3 days of gumbo-related events (including the presentation of the royal court of King and Miss Creole Gumbo), plus many hours of Cajun music. The festival is held in Bridge City, on the outskirts of New Orleans. For more information, contact the Gumbo Festival, P.O. Box 9069, Bridge City, LA 70096 (© **504/436-4712**). October 9 to 11.

New Orleans Film Festival. Canal Place Cinemas and other theaters throughout the city screen award-winning local and international films and host writers, actors, and directors over the course of a week. Admission prices range from $4 to $6. For dates, contact the New Orleans Film and Video Society, 843 Carondelet, no. 1, New Orleans, LA 70130 (© **504/523-3818;** www.neworleansfilmfest.com). Mid-month.

Halloween. Rivaling Mardi Gras in terms of costumes, Halloween is certainly celebrated more grandly here than it is in any other American city. After all, New Orleans has a way with ghosts. Events include Boo-at-the-Zoo (Oct 30–31) for children, costume parties (including a Monster Bash at the Ernest N. Morial Convention Center), haunted houses (one of the best is run by the sheriff's department in City Park), the Anne Rice Vampire Lestat Extravaganza, and the Moonlight Witches Run. You can catch the ghoulish action all over the city—many museums get in on the fun with specially designed tours—but the French Quarter, as always, is the center of the Halloween-night universe. October 31.

December

Words & Music: A Literary Fest in New Orleans. This highly ambitious literary and music conference (originated in large part by the folks behind Faulkner House Books) offers 5 days' worth of roundtable discussions with eminent authors (with varying connections to the city), original drama, poetry readings, master classes, plus great music and food. For authors seeking guidance and inspiration and for book lovers in general, call © **504/586-1609** or visit their website www.wordsandmusic.org for dates. December 5 to 9.

Christmas New Orleans Style. New Orleans loves to celebrate, so it should be no surprise that they do Christmas really well. The town is decorated to a fare-thee-well, there is an evening of candlelight caroling in Jackson Square, bonfires line the levees along the River Road on Christmas Eve (to guide Papa Noël, his sled drawn by alligators, on his gift-delivering way), restaurants offer specially created multicourse Réveillon dinners, and hotels throughout the city offer "Papa Noël" rates.

Why? Because despite all the fun and the generally nice (read: not hot and humid) weather, tourism goes *waaay* down at this time of year, and hotels are eager to lure you all in with cheaper rates. This is one of the top times to come to town—you can have the city virtually to yourself. For information, contact French Quarter Festivals, 400 N. Peters St., Suite 205, New Orleans, LA 70130 (© **504/522-5730;** www.french quarterfestivals.org). All month.

Celebration in the Oaks. Lights and lighted figures, designed to illustrate holiday themes, bedeck sections of City Park. This display of winter wonderment is open for driving and walking tours. Driving tours are $12 per family car or van, and walking tours are $5 per person. For information, contact Celebration in the Oaks, 1 Palm Dr., New Orleans,

LA 70124 (© **504/483-9415;** www.neworleanscitypark.com). Late November to early January.

New Year's Eve. The countdown takes place in Jackson Square and is one of the country's biggest and most reliable street parties. In the Southern equivalent of New York's Times Square, revelers watch a lighted ball drop from the top of Jackson Brewery. December 31.

4 Planning Your Trip Online

Researching and booking your trip online can save time and money. Internet users can tap into the same travel-planning databases that were once accessible only to travel agents. The "big three" online travel agencies, **Expedia.com, Travelocity.com,** and **Orbitz.com** sell most of the air tickets bought on the Internet. (Canadian travelers should try expedia.ca and Travelocity.ca; U.K. residents can go for expedia.co.uk and opodo.co.uk.) Each has different business deals with the airlines and may offer different fares on the same flights, so it's wise to shop around. Expedia and Travelocity will also send you **e-mail notification** when a cheap fare becomes available to New Orleans.

Also remember to check **airline websites,** especially those for low-fare carriers such as Southwest or JetBlue, whose fares are often misreported or simply missing from travel agency websites. Even with major airlines, you can often shave a few bucks from a fare by booking directly through the airline and avoiding a travel agency's transaction fee. But you'll get these discounts only by **booking online:** Most airlines now offer online-only fares that even their phone agents know nothing about. For the websites of airlines that fly to and from your destination, go to "Getting There," below.

Shopping online for **hotels** is much easier in the U.S. and Canada than it is in the rest of the world. Of the "big three" sites, **Expedia** may be the best choice, thanks to its long list of special deals. **Travelocity** runs a close second. Hotel specialist sites **hotels.com** and **hoteldiscounts.com** are also reliable. An excellent free program, **TravelAxe** (www.travelaxe.net), can help you search multiple hotel sites at once.

5 Tips for Travelers with Special Needs

TRAVELERS WITH DISABILITIES

Most disabilities shouldn't stop anyone from traveling. There are more options and resources out there than ever before. Be aware, though, that while New Orleans facilities are mostly accessible (especially in the Quarter), with proprietors being most accommodating (opening narrow doors wider to fit wheelchairs and such), you are still dealing with older structures created before thoughts of ease for those with disabilities. Before you book a hotel, **ask questions** based on your needs. If you have mobility issues, you'll probably do best to stay in one of the city's newer hotels, which tend to be more spacious and accommodating. Sidewalks are often bumpy and uneven, and getting on the St. Charles streetcar might be too great a challenge. Streets are better for maneuvering wheelchairs than sidewalks (some French Quarter streets are closed for pedestrian traffic only).

For information about specialized transportation systems, call **LIFT** (© **504/827-7433**).

You can join **The Society for Accessible Travel & Hospitality,** 347 Fifth Ave., Suite 610, New York, NY 10016

(© 212/447-7284; www.sath.org), which offers a wealth of travel resources for all types of disabilities and informed recommendations on destinations, access guides, travel agents, tour operators, vehicle rentals, and companion services. Annual membership costs $45 for adults, $30 for seniors and students. The society's quarterly magazine, *Open World,* is full of good information and resources.

The **Moss Rehab Hospital** (© 215/456-9603; www.mossresource net.org) provides friendly and helpful phone assistance through its **Travel Information Service.**

GAY & LESBIAN TRAVELERS

This is a very gay-friendly town with a high-profile homosexual population that contributes much to the color and flavor of the city. You'll find an abundance of establishments serving gay and lesbian interests, from bars to restaurants to community services to certain businesses.

If you need help finding your way, you can stop by or call the **Lesbian and Gay Community Center,** 2114 Decatur St. (© 504/945-1103; www. lgccno.org); hours vary, so call before stopping in.

Ambush Magazine, 828-A Bourbon St., New Orleans, LA 70116 (© 504/522-8047; www.ambushmag. com), is a weekly entertainment and news publication for the Gulf South's gay, lesbian, bisexual, and transgender communities. The website offers plenty of links to other interesting sites. *Impact Gulf South Gay News* is another popular area publication.

Grace Fellowship, 3151 Dauphine St. (© 504/944-9836), and the **Vieux Carré Metropolitan Community Church,** 1128 St. Roch Ave. (© 504/945-5390), are religious organizations that serve primarily gay and lesbian congregations. Both invite visitors to attend services.

One useful website is **www.gay neworleans.com**, which provides information on lodging, dining, arts, and nightlife as well as links to other information on New Orleans gay life.

SENIOR TRAVEL

Don't be shy about asking for discounts, but always carry some kind of identification, such as a driver's license, that shows your date of birth, especially if you've kept your youthful glow.

Mention the fact that you're a senior citizen when you make your travel reservations. Although all of the major U.S. airlines except America West have cancelled their senior discount and coupon book programs, many hotels still offer discounts for seniors. *Note:* Seniors who show their Medicare card can ride New Orleans streetcars and buses for 40¢.

Members of **AARP** (formerly known as the American Association of Retired Persons), 601 E St. NW, Washington, DC 20049 (© 800/424-3410 or 202/434-2277; www.aarp.org), get discounts on hotels, airfares, and car rentals. AARP offers members a wide range of benefits, including *AARP The Magazine* and a monthly newsletter. Anyone over 50 can join.

6 Getting There

BY PLANE

Among the airlines serving the city's **Louis Armstrong New Orleans International Airport** are **America West** (© 800/235-9292; www.americawest.

com), **American** (© 800/433-7300; www.aa.com), **Continental** (© 800/ 525-0280 or 504/581-2965; www. continental.com), **Delta** (© 800/221- 1212; www.delta.com), **Northwest**

(℃ **800/225-2525;** www.nwa.com), **Southwest** (℃ **800/435-9792;** www. southwest.com), **US Airways** (℃ **800/ 428-4322;** www.usairways.com), and **United** (℃ **800/241-6522;** www.ual. com).

The airport is 15 miles west of the city, in Kenner. You'll find information booths scattered around the airport and in the baggage claim area, as well as a branch of the **Travelers Aid Society** (℃ **504/464-3522**).

See "Planning Your Trip Online," above, for tips on finding airfares. For much more about airfares and savvy air-travel tips and advice, pick up a copy of *Frommer's Fly Safe, Fly Smart* (Wiley Publishing, Inc.).

For information on getting into New Orleans from the airport, see p. 51.

NEW AIR TRAVEL SECURITY MEASURES

In the wake of the continued concerns with the wars on Iraq and terrorism, the airline industry began implementing sweeping security measures in airports. Expect a lengthy check-in process and extensive delays. Although regulations vary from airline to airline, you can expedite the process by arriving at least 2 hours before your scheduled flight; knowing what you can carry on—and what you can't; preparing yourself to be searched (electronic items may require additional screening); knowing that no ticket means no gate access (except for those people with specific medical or parental needs); and carrying an **up-to-date** government-issued (federal, state, or local) photo ID, which is now required to board an airplane.

BY CAR

You can drive to New Orleans via **I-10, I-55, U.S. 90, U.S. 61,** or across the Lake Pontchartrain Causeway on **La. 25.** From any direction, you'll see the city's distinctive and swampy outlying regions; if you can, try to drive in while you can enjoy the scenery in daylight. For the best roadside views, take U.S. 61 or La. 25, but only if you have time to spare. The larger roads are considerably faster.

It's a good idea to call before you leave home to ask for directions to your hotel. Most hotels have parking facilities (for a fee); if they don't, they'll give you the names and addresses of nearby parking lots.

AAA (℃ **504/367-4095;** www.aaa. com) will assist members with trip planning and emergency services.

Driving in New Orleans can be a hassle, and parking is a nightmare. It's a great city for walking, and cabs are plentiful and not too expensive, so you really don't need a car unless you're planning several day trips.

Nevertheless, most major national car-rental companies are represented at the airport. See p. 60 for more information on renting a car and driving in New Orleans.

BY TRAIN

As with the interstates and highways into New Orleans, the passenger rail lines cut through some beautiful scenery. **Amtrak** (℃ **800/USA-RAIL** or 504/528-1610; www.amtrak.com) trains serve the city's **Union Passenger Terminal,** 1001 Loyola Ave.

The New Orleans train station is in the Central Business District. Plenty of taxis wait outside the main entrance to the passenger terminal. Hotels in the French Quarter and the Central Business District are just a short ride away.

4

For International Visitors

Whether it's your first visit or your tenth, a trip to the United States may require an additional degree of planning. This chapter will provide you with essential information, helpful tips, and advice for the more common problems that some visitors encounter.

1 Preparing for Your Trip

ENTRY REQUIREMENTS

Check at any U.S. embassy or consulate for current information and requirements. You can also obtain a visa application and other information online at the **U.S. State Department**'s website, at **www.travel.state.gov**.

VISAS

The U.S. State Department has a **Visa Waiver Program** allowing citizens of certain countries to enter the United States without a visa for stays of up to 90 days. At press time, these included Andorra, Australia, Austria, Belgium, Brunei, Denmark, Finland, France, Germany, Iceland, Ireland, Italy, Japan, Liechtenstein, Luxembourg, Monaco, the Netherlands, New Zealand, Norway, Portugal, San Marino, Singapore, Slovenia, Spain, Sweden, Switzerland, and the United Kingdom. Citizens of these countries need only a valid passport and a round-trip air or cruise ticket in their possession upon arrival. If they first enter the United States, they may also visit Mexico, Canada, Bermuda, and/or the Caribbean islands and return to the United States without a visa. Further information is available from any U.S. embassy or consulate. Canadian citizens may enter the United States without visas; they need only proof of residence.

Citizens of all other countries must have (1) a valid passport that expires at least 6 months later than the scheduled end of their visit to the United States and (2) a tourist visa, which may be obtained without charge from any U.S. consulate.

To obtain a visa, the traveler must submit a completed application form (either in person or by mail) with a 1½-inch-square photo and must demonstrate binding ties to a residence abroad. Usually, you can obtain a visa at once or within 24 hours, but it may take longer during the summer rush June through August. If you cannot go in person, contact the nearest U.S. embassy or consulate for directions on applying by mail. The U.S. consulate or embassy that issues your visa will determine whether you will be issued a multiple- or single-entry visa and any restrictions regarding the length of your stay.

MEDICAL REQUIREMENTS

Unless you're arriving from an area known to be suffering from an **epidemic** (particularly cholera or yellow fever), inoculations or vaccinations are not required for entry into the United States. If you have a medical condition that requires **syringe-administered medications,** carry a valid signed prescription from your physician—the

Federal Aviation Administration (FAA) no longer allows airline passengers to pack syringes in their carry-on baggage without documented proof of medical need. If you have a disease that requires treatment with **narcotics,** you should also carry documented proof with you—smuggling narcotics aboard a plane is a serious offense that carries severe penalties in the U.S.

For HIV-positive visitors, requirements for entering the United States are somewhat vague and change frequently. For up-to-the-minute information, contact the Centers for Disease Control's **National Center for HIV** (℃ **404/332-4559;** www.cdc.gov/hiv/dhap.htm) or the **Gay Men's Health Crisis** (℃ **212/367-1000;** www.gmhc.org).

DRIVER'S LICENSES

Foreign driver's licenses are mostly recognized in the U.S., although you may want to get an international driver's license if your home license is not written in English.

PASSPORT INFORMATION

Safeguard your passport in an inconspicuous, inaccessible place like a money belt. Make a copy of the critical pages, including the passport number, and store it in a safe place, separate from the passport itself. If you lose your passport, visit the nearest consulate of your native country as soon as possible for a replacement. Passport applications are downloadable from the Internet sites listed below.

CUSTOMS

Foreign tourists to Louisiana can receive a refund on taxes paid on tangible goods purchased within the state. You must show your passport (Canadians can show a driver's license) at the time of purchase and *request a tax refund voucher from the vendor.* You will be charged the full amount and given a sales receipt and a refund voucher. If you're leaving New Orleans by plane, go to the Louisiana Tax Free Shopping Refund Center at the airport. Present your sales receipts and vouchers from merchants, your passport, and a round-trip international ticket (the duration of the trip must be less than 90 days). To arrange your refund by mail, you'll need copies of sales receipts, copies of your travel ticket and passport, your original refund vouchers, and a statement explaining why you were not able to claim your refund at the airport. Send these to **Louisiana Tax Free Shopping Refund Center,** P.O. Box 20125, New Orleans, LA 70141 (℃ **504/467-0723**).

WHAT YOU CAN BRING IN

Every visitor more than 21 years of age may bring in, free of duty, the following: (1) 1 liter of wine or hard liquor; (2) 200 cigarettes, 100 cigars (but not from Cuba), or 3 pounds of smoking tobacco; and (3) $100 worth of gifts. These exemptions are offered to travelers who spend at least 72 hours in the United States and who have not claimed them within the preceding 6 months. It is altogether forbidden to bring into the country foodstuffs (particularly fruit, cooked meats, and canned goods) and plants (vegetables, seeds, tropical plants, and the like). Foreign tourists may bring in or take out up to $10,000 in U.S. or foreign currency with no formalities; larger sums must be declared to U.S. Customs on entering or leaving, which includes filing form CM 4790. For more specific information regarding U.S. Customs, contact your nearest U.S. embassy or consulate, or the **U.S. Customs** office at ℃ **202/927-1770** or www.customs.ustreas.gov.

WHAT YOU CAN TAKE HOME

Check with your country's Customs or Foreign Affairs department for the latest guidelines—including information on items that are not allowed to be brought into your home country—before you leave home.

U.K. citizens should contact **HM Customs & Excise, Passenger Enquiries** (ⓒ **0181/910-3744;** www.open.gov.uk).

For a clear summary of **Canadian** rules, write for the booklet *I Declare,* issued by **Revenue Canada,** 2265 St. Laurent Blvd., Ottawa K1G 4KE (ⓒ **506/636-5064**) or see www.ccra-adrc.gc.ca.

Citizens of **Australia** should request the helpful Australian Customs brochure *Know Before You Go.* For more information, contact **Australian Customs Services,** GPO Box 8, Sydney NSW 2001 (ⓒ **02/9213-2000**). Also visit the travel section of www.dfat.gov.au for more info.

For New Zealand Customs information, contact the **New Zealand Customs** Service at ⓒ **09/359-6655** or go online to www.customs.govt.nz.

INSURANCE

Although it's not required of travelers, health insurance is highly recommended. Unlike many European countries, the United States does not usually offer free or low-cost medical care to its citizens or visitors. Doctors and hospitals are expensive and in most cases will require advance payment or proof of coverage before they render their services.

Policies can cover everything from the loss or theft of your baggage and trip cancellation to the guarantee of bail in case you're arrested. Good policies will also cover the costs of an accident, repatriation, or death. Packages such as **Europ Assistance's "Worldwide Healthcare Plan"** are sold by European automobile clubs and travel agencies at attractive rates. **Worldwide Assistance Services, Inc.** (ⓒ **800/821-2828;** www.worldwideassistance.com) is the agent for Europ Assistance in the United States.

Though lack of health insurance may prevent you from being admitted to a hospital in nonemergencies, don't worry about being left on a street corner to die: The American way is to fix you now and bill the living daylights out of you later.

MONEY

CURRENCY The U.S. monetary system is very simple: The most common bills (all ugly, all green) are the $1 (colloquially, a "buck"), $5, $10, and $20 denominations. There are also $50 bills and $100 bills (the last two are usually not welcome as payment for small purchases). All the paper money was recently redesigned, making the famous faces adorning them disproportionately large. The old-style bills are still legal tender.

There are seven denominations of coins: 1¢ (1 cent, or a penny); 5¢ (5 cents, or a nickel); 10¢ (10 cents, or a dime); 25¢ (25 cents, or a quarter); 50¢ (50 cents, or a half dollar); the gold "Sacagawea" coin worth $1; and, prized by collectors, the rare, older, silver dollar.

CURRENCY EXCHANGE The "foreign-exchange bureaus" so common in Europe are rare even at airports in the United States, and nonexistent outside major cities. It's best not to change foreign money (or traveler's checks denominated in a currency other than U.S. dollars) at a small-town bank, or even a branch in a big city; in fact, leave any currency other than U.S. dollars at home—it may prove a greater nuisance to you than it's worth.

In New Orleans, you can find exchange services a block away from the Quarter at the **Whitney National Bank**'s foreign exchange department (228 St. Charles Ave.; ⓒ **504/838-6565**).

TRAVELER'S CHECKS Though traveler's checks are widely accepted, make sure that they're denominated in U.S. dollars, because foreign-currency checks are often difficult to exchange.

The three traveler's checks that are most widely recognized—and least likely to be denied—are **Visa, American Express,** and **Thomas Cook.** Be sure to record the numbers of the checks, and keep that information in a separate place in case they get lost or stolen. Most businesses are pretty good about taking traveler's checks, but you're better off cashing them in at a bank (in small amounts, of course) and paying in cash. *Remember:* You'll need identification, such as a driver's license or passport, to change a traveler's check.

CREDIT CARDS & ATMs Credit cards are the most widely used form of payment in the United States: **Visa** (BarclayCard in Britain); **MasterCard** (Eurocard in Europe, Access in Britain, Chargex in Canada); **American Express; Diners Club;** and **Discover.** There are, however, a handful of stores and restaurants that do not take credit cards, so be sure to ask in advance. Businesses often require a minimum purchase price, usually around $10 or $15, to use a credit card.

It is strongly recommended that you bring at least one major credit card. You must have a credit or charge card to rent a car. Hotels and airlines usually require a credit-card imprint as a deposit against expenses, and in an emergency, a credit card can be priceless.

You'll find **automated teller machines (ATMs)** on just about every block across the country. Most ATMs will allow you to draw U.S. currency against your bank. Check with your bank before leaving home to see if you have a daily withdrawal limit. Expect to be charged up to $3 per transaction, however, if you're not using your own bank's ATM. Most ATMs will also dispense credit-card cash advances from Visa, MasterCard, and American Express—but remember that you will need a personal identification number (PIN) to access your credit card.

SAFETY CONCERNS

GENERAL SAFETY TIPS U.S. urban areas tend to be less safe than those in Europe or Japan. Visitors should always stay alert. In New Orleans, avoid deserted areas (like the outer edges of the French Quarter), especially at night. Don't go into any cemeteries or city parks at night unless there's an event that attracts crowds like a festival or concert. Generally speaking, you can feel safe in areas where there are many people and many open establishments.

Avoid carrying valuables with you on the street, and keep expensive cameras or electronic equipment bagged up or covered when not in use. If you're using a map, try to consult it inconspicuously—or better yet, study it before you leave your room. Hold onto your pocketbook, and place your billfold in an inside pocket. In theaters, restaurants, and other public places, keep your possessions in sight.

Remember also that hotels are open to the public, and in a large hotel, security may not be able to screen everyone entering. Always lock your room door. Don't assume that, once inside your hotel, you no longer need to be aware of your surroundings.

DRIVING SAFETY If you drive off a highway into a doubtful neighborhood, leave the area as quickly as possible. If you have an accident, even on the highway, stay in your car with the doors locked until you assess the situation or until the police arrive. If you're bumped from behind on the street or are involved in a minor accident with no injuries and the situation appears to be suspicious, motion to the other driver to follow you to the nearest well-lit service station or the nearest police precinct if you happen to know where that is. *Never* get out of your car in such situations.

If you see someone on the road who indicates a need for help, do *not* stop.

Take note of the location, drive on to a well-lit area, and telephone the police by dialing ℂ **911.**

Park in well-lit, well-traveled areas, if possible. Always keep your car doors locked whether the car is within your sight or not. Look around before you get out of your car and never leave any packages or valuables in sight. If someone attempts to rob you or steal your car, do *not* try to resist the thief or carjacker. Report the incident to the police department immediately.

Ask your rental agent for directions to your destination and a map with the route clearly marked when you pick up your car.

2 Getting to the United States

THE MAJOR AIRLINES

Operated by the European Travel Network, **www.discount-tickets.com** is a great online source for regular and discounted airfares to destinations around the world. You can also use this site to compare rates and book accommodations, car rentals, and tours. Click on "Special Offers" for the latest package deals.

FROM CANADA Air Canada (ℂ **888/247-2262,** 800/268-7240 in Toronto, or 800/663-3721 in Vancouver; www.aircanada.ca) flies from Toronto and Montreal to Newark, and from Calgary and Vancouver to Houston. From both cities, connecting flights to New Orleans are on Continental Airlines.

Many American carriers also serve similar routes. **American Airlines** (ℂ **800/433-7300;** www.aa.com) connects through Chicago or Dallas; **Continental Airlines** (ℂ **800/231-0856;** www.continental.com) flies from Montreal and Toronto, connecting through Newark (it partners with Air Canada to service other Canadian cities); **Delta** (ℂ **800/241-4141;** www.delta.com) connects through its hubs in Atlanta or Cincinnati; and **United Airlines** (ℂ **800/241-6522;** www.ual.com) flies from Toronto, Calgary, and Vancouver, connecting through Chicago.

FROM THE UNITED KINGDOM & IRELAND There are no direct flights from London to New Orleans, but the following airlines will book you through on a connecting flight.

British Airways (ℂ **0345/222-111** in the U.K. or 800/AIRWAYS in the U.S.; www.britishairways.com) has daily service to New York from London as well as direct flights from Manchester and Glasgow. It can also connect you through Philadelphia or Charlotte, NC. **Virgin Atlantic** (ℂ **01293/747-747** in the U.K. or 800/862-8621 in the U.S.; www.virgin-atlantic.com) flies from London's Heathrow to New York. It can also connect you through Newark, Miami, or Orlando.

American Airlines (ℂ **0181/572-5555** in London, 0345/789-789 elsewhere in the U.K.; www.aa.com) connects through Chicago; **Continental Airlines** (ℂ **01293/776-464** in the U.K. or 800/525-0280 in the U.S.; www.continental.com) connects through Newark or Houston; **Delta Airlines** (ℂ **0800/414-767** in the U.K. or 800/221-1212 in the U.S.; www.delta.com) connects through Atlanta or Cincinnati; and **United Airlines** (ℂ **0181/990-9900** in London or 0800/888-555 elsewhere in the U.K.; www.ual.com) connects through Washington, D.C.'s Dulles or Chicago.

From Ireland, **Aer Lingus** (ℂ **01/886-8888** in Dublin, 800/IRISH-AIR in the U.S.; www.aerlingus.ie) flies to New York, where you can connect to a New Orleans flight.

FROM AUSTRALIA & NEW ZEALAND Qantas (ℂ **13-13-13** in Australia or 800/227-4500 in the U.S.;

www.qantas.com.au) and **Air New Zealand** (✆ **0800/737-000** in New Zealand or 800/262-1234 in the U.S.; www.airnewzealand.co.nz) fly to the West Coast and will book you straight through to New Orleans on a partner airline. You can also take **United** (✆ **2/ 9237-8888** in Sydney, 3/9602-2544 in Melbourne, or 008/230-322 elsewhere in Australia; www.ual.com), which connects through San Francisco or Los Angeles.

IMMIGRATION & CUSTOMS CLEARANCE

Visitors arriving by air, no matter what the port of entry, should cultivate patience and resignation before setting foot on U.S. soil. Getting through immigration control may take as long as 2 hours on some days, especially on summer weekends, so be sure to have this guidebook or something else to read. This is especially true in the aftermath of the September 11, 2001, terrorist attacks, when security clearances have been considerably beefed up at U.S. airports. Add the time it takes to clear Customs, and you'll see that you should make a 2- to 3-hour allowance for delays when you plan your connections between international and domestic flights.

People traveling by air from Canada, Bermuda, and some places in the Caribbean can sometimes clear Customs and Immigration at the point of departure, which is much quicker.

See "Getting There" in chapter 3, "Planning Your Trip to New Orleans," for more information on arriving in New Orleans.

 FAST FACTS: **For the International Traveler**

Automobile Organizations Auto clubs will supply maps, suggested routes, guidebooks, accident and bail-bond insurance, and emergency road service. The **American Automobile Association (AAA)** is the major auto club in the United States. If you belong to an auto club in your home country, inquire about AAA reciprocity before you leave. You may be able to join AAA even if you're not a member of a reciprocal club; to inquire, call AAA (✆ **800/222-4357**). AAA is actually an organization of regional auto clubs; so look under "AAA Automobile Club" in the White Pages of the telephone directory. AAA has a nationwide emergency road service telephone number (✆ **800/AAA-HELP**).

Automobile Rentals See p. 60.

Business Hours Banks are open weekdays from 9am to 3pm, but almost every bank has 24-hour ATMs. Generally, business offices are open weekdays from 9am to 5pm. In New Orleans, many small shops do not open until later in the morning (around 10am), and many stay open until 6pm. Stores are open 6 days a week with many open on Sundays, too; department stores usually stay open until 9pm 1 day a week.

Currency & Exchange See "Money" earlier in this chapter. For the latest market conversion rates, point your Internet browser to www.x-rates.com.

Drinking Laws The legal age for purchase and consumption of alcoholic beverages is 21; proof of age is required and often requested at bars, nightclubs, and restaurants, so it's always a good idea to bring ID when you go out.

Electricity The United States uses 110 to 120 volts AC (60 cycles), compared to 220 to 240 volts AC (50 cycles) in most of Europe, Australia, and New Zealand. If your small appliances use 220 to 240 volts, you'll need a 110-volt transformer and a plug adapter with two flat parallel pins to operate them here. Downward converters that change 220–240 volts to 110–120 volts are hard to find in the United States, so bring one with you.

Embassies & Consulates All embassies are located in Washington, D.C. Some consulates are located in major U.S. cities, and most nations have a mission to the United Nations in New York City. If your country isn't listed below, call directory assistance in Washington, D.C. (© **202/555-1212**), or go online to **www.embassy.org/embassies** for the location and phone number of your national embassy.

The embassy of **Australia** is at 1601 Massachusetts Ave. NW, Washington, DC 20036 (© **202/797-3000;** www.austemb.org). The embassy of **Canada** is at 501 Pennsylvania Ave. NW, Washington, DC 20001 (© **202/682-1740;** www.canadianembassy.org). The embassy of **Ireland** is at 2234 Massachusetts Ave. NW, Washington, DC 20008 (© **202/462-3939;** www.ireland emb.org/contact.html). The embassy of **Japan** is at 2520 Massachusetts Ave. NW, Washington, DC 20008 (© **202/238-6700;** www.us.emb-japan.go.jp). Japanese consulates are located in Atlanta, Kansas City, San Francisco, and Washington D.C. The embassy of **New Zealand** is at 37 Observatory Circle NW, Washington, DC 20008 (© **202/328-4800;** www.nzemb.org). New Zealand consulates are in Los Angeles, Salt Lake City, San Francisco, and Seattle. The embassy of the **United Kingdom** is at 3100 Massachusetts Ave. NW, Washington, DC 20008 (© **202/462-1340;** www.britainusa.com/consular/embassy). Other British consulates are in Atlanta, Boston, Chicago, Cleveland, Houston, Los Angeles, New York, San Francisco, and Seattle.

Emergencies Call © **911** for fire, police, and ambulance. This is a free call from pay phones. If you encounter such traveler's problems as sickness, accident, or lost or stolen baggage, call the **Travelers Aid Society** (© **504/464-3522** at Louis Armstrong New Orleans International Airport), an organization that specializes in helping distressed travelers (they reunite families separated while traveling, provide food and/or shelter to people stranded without cash, and even offer emotional counseling). The local office is at 846 Baronne St. (© **504/525-8726**).

Gasoline (Petrol) Petrol is known as gasoline (or simply "gas") in the United States, and petrol stations are known as both gas stations and service stations. Gasoline is less expensive here than it is in Europe (though prices were going up sharply at press time), and taxes are already included in the printed price. One U.S. gallon equals 3.8 liters or .85 imperial gallons.

Holidays Banks, government offices, post offices, and many stores, restaurants, and museums are closed on the following legal national holidays: January 1 (New Year's Day), the third Monday in January (Martin Luther King Jr. Day), the third Monday in February (Presidents' Day, Washington's Birthday), the last Monday in May (Memorial Day), July 4th (Independence Day), the first Monday in September (Labor Day), the second Monday in October (Columbus Day), November 11 (Veterans' Day/Armistice Day), the fourth Thursday in November (Thanksgiving Day), and December 25 (Christmas). Also, the Tuesday following the first

Monday in November is Election Day and is a federal government holiday in presidential-election years (held every 4 yr., and next in 2004). Most New Orleans businesses are also closed Mardi Gras day.

Legal Aid If you are "pulled over" for a minor infraction (such as speeding), never attempt to pay the fine directly to a police officer; this could be construed as attempted bribery, a much more serious crime. Pay fines by mail, or directly into the hands of the clerk of the court. If accused of a more serious offense, say and do nothing before consulting a lawyer. Here the burden is on the state to prove a person's guilt beyond a reasonable doubt, and everyone has the right to remain silent, whether he or she is suspected of a crime or actually arrested. Once arrested, a person can make one telephone call to a party of his or her choice. Call your embassy or consulate.

Medical Emergencies For an ambulance, dial Ⓒ **911.** For information on hospitals and doctors in New Orleans, see "Fast Facts: New Orleans" in chapter 5.

Restrooms Public toilets are hard to find on the streets of New Orleans. They can be found, though, in bars, restaurants, hotel lobbies, museums, department stores, and service stations—and they will probably be clean (except those in service stations, which can sometimes be frighteningly filthy). Some restaurants and bars display a notice, RESTROOMS ARE FOR CUSTOMERS ONLY, but you can usually ignore this sign—or better yet, avoid arguments by paying for a cup of coffee or soft drink, which will qualify you as a patron. In restrooms with attendants, leaving at least a 25¢ tip is customary.

Taxes In the United States, there is no VAT (value-added tax) or other indirect tax on a national level. Every state, and each city in it, is allowed to levy its own local tax on all purchases, including hotel and restaurant checks, airline tickets, and so on. In New Orleans, the sales tax rate is 9%. See "Customs," earlier in this chapter, for information on receiving a refund on taxes paid on tangible goods purchased in Louisiana.

Telephone The telephone system in the United States is run by private corporations, so rates, especially for long-distance service and operator-assisted calls, can vary widely. Generally, hotel surcharges on long-distance and local calls are astronomical, so you're usually better off using a **public pay telephone.** Many convenience stores and newsstands sell **prepaid calling cards;** these can be the least expensive way to call home. **Local calls** made from public pay phones in most locales cost either 25¢ or 35¢. Pay phones do not accept pennies, and few take anything larger than a quarter.

To call the United States from another country, dial the international access code of that country (00 in the U.K., 0011 in Australia, 0170 in New Zealand); then the country code (1); and then the three-digit area code (504 for New Orleans) and the seven-digit phone number (for example, from the U.K., you'd dial **00-1-504/000-0000**).

For calls between different area codes in the United States and to Canada, dial 1 followed by the area code and the seven-digit number (for example, **1-504/000-0000**).

For calls within New Orleans, just dial the seven-digit number (for example, **000-0000**).

For international calls from the United States, dial the international access code (011) followed by the country code (44 for the U.K., 353 for Ireland, 61 for Australia, 62 for New Zealand, 27 for South Africa; others can be found in the telephone directory's White Pages), then the city code (if applicable) and the telephone number of the person you wish to call (for example, to call Dublin, you'd dial 011+353+1/000-0000).

For local directory assistance ("Information"), dial ℂ 411; for **long-distance information,** dial 1 and then the appropriate area code and 555-1212 (for example, New Orleans directory assistance would be ℂ **1-504/555-1212**).

Telephone Directory There are two kinds of telephone directories in the United States. The so-called **White Pages** list private households and business subscribers in alphabetical order. The inside front cover lists emergency numbers for police, fire, ambulance, the poison-control center, a crime-victims hot line, and so on. The first few pages will tell you how to make long-distance and international calls, complete with country codes and area codes. Government numbers are usually printed on blue paper within the White Pages. Printed on yellow paper, the **Yellow Pages** lists all local services, businesses, industries, and houses of worship according to activity, with an index at the front or back.

Tipping Tipping is so ingrained in the American way of life that the annual income tax of tip-earning service personnel is based on how much they should have received in light of their employers' gross revenues. Accordingly, they may have to pay tax on a tip you didn't actually give them.

Here are some rules of thumb:

In hotels, tip **bellhops** at least $1 per bag ($2–$3 per bag if you have a lot of luggage) and tip the **chamber staff** $2 to $3 per day (more if you've left a disaster area for him or her to clean up). Tip the **doorman** or **concierge** only if he or she has provided you with some specific service (for example, calling a cab for you or obtaining difficult-to-get theater tickets). Tip the **valet-parking attendant** $1 every time you get your car.

In restaurants, bars, and nightclubs, tip **service staff** 15% to 20% of the check, tip **bartenders** 10% to 15%, tip **checkroom attendants** $1 per garment, and tip **valet-parking attendants** $1 per vehicle. Tip the **doorman** only if he has provided you with some specific service (such as calling a cab for you). Tipping is not expected in fast-food restaurants.

As for other service personnel, tip **skycaps** at airports at least $1 per bag ($2–$3 per bag if you have a lot of luggage) and tip **hairdressers** and **barbers** 15% to 20%. Tip **cab drivers** 15% of the fare. Tipping ushers at movies and theaters and gas-station attendants is not expected.

5

Getting to Know New Orleans

New Orleans is a very user-friendly city—that is, if you don't count the unusual directions and the nearly impossible-to-pronounce street names. (More on that later.) It's a manageable size (only about 7 miles long), with most of what the average tourist would want to see concentrated in a few areas.

Some find spending the entire time they're in New Orleans in a haze of delightful decadence a perfectly acceptable way to enjoy a trip. But for those of you who feel that there is a lot to see and do—not to mention eat and drink—in perhaps too short a time, a little planning is in order. This chapter contains some of the ins and outs of New Orleans navigation and gives you some local sources to contact for specialized information.

For an introductory essay about New Orleans and our list of the best of New Orleans, see chapter 1, "The Best of New Orleans."

1 Orientation

ARRIVING

From the airport, you can get to your hotel on the **Airport Shuttle** (© 504/ 522-3500). For $10 per person (one way), the van will take you directly to your hotel. There are Airport Shuttle information desks (staffed 24 hr.) in the airport.

Note: If you plan to take the Airport Shuttle *to* the airport when you depart, you must call a day in advance and let them know what time your flight is leaving. They will then tell you what time they will pick you up.

A **taxi** from the airport to most hotels will cost about $24; if there are three or more passengers, the fare is $8 per person.

If you want to ride in style from the airport to your hotel, try **New Orleans Limousine Service** (© 504/529-5226). Express transfer service for a six-passenger limo is $80.50.

From the airport, you can reach the **Central Business District** by bus for $1.50 (exact change required). Buses run from 6am to 6:30pm. From 6 to 9am and 3 to 6pm, they leave the airport every 12 to 15 minutes and go to the downtown side of Tulane Avenue between Elks Place and South Saratoga Street; at other times, they leave every 23 minutes. For more information, call the **Louisiana Transit Company** (© 504/818-1077).

VISITOR INFORMATION

The **New Orleans Metropolitan Convention and Visitors Bureau,** 1520 Sugar Bowl Dr., New Orleans, LA 70112 (© 800/672-6124 or 504/566-5003; www.neworleanscvb.com), not only has a wide array of well-designed and well-written brochures that cover everything from usual sightseeing questions to cultural history, but also the incredibly friendly and helpful staff can answer almost any random question you may have. If you're having trouble making decisions, they can give you good advice; if you have a special interest, they'll help you plan your visit around it—this is definitely one of the most helpful tourist centers in any major city.

Once you've arrived in the city, you also might want to stop by the **Visitor Information Center,** 529 St. Ann St. (© **504/568-5661**), in the French Quarter. The center is open daily from 9am to 5pm and has walking- and driving-tour maps and booklets on restaurants, accommodations, sightseeing, special tours, and pretty much anything else you might want to know about. The staff is friendly and knowledgeable about both the city and the state.

CITY LAYOUT

"Where y'at?" goes the traditional local greeting. "Where" is easy enough when you are in the French Quarter, the site of the original settlement. A 13-block-long grid between Canal Street and Esplanade Avenue, running from the Mississippi River to North Rampart Street, it's the closest the city comes to a geographic center.

After that, all bets are off. Because of the bend in the river, the streets are laid out at angles and curves that render north, south, east, and west useless. It's time to readjust your thinking: In New Orleans, the compass points are *riverside, lakeside, uptown,* and *downtown.* You'll catch on quickly if you keep in mind that North Rampart Street is the *lakeside* boundary of the Quarter and that St. Charles Avenue extends from the French Quarter, *downtown,* to Tulane University, *uptown.*

Canal Street forms the boundary between new and old New Orleans. Street names change when they cross Canal (Bourbon St., for example, becomes Carondelet St.), and addresses begin at 100 on either side of Canal. In the Quarter, street numbers begin at 400 at the river because 4 blocks of numbered buildings were lost to the river before the levee was built).

MAPS Don't think you can get along without one in New Orleans! There's a free color foldout map in the back of this book that should help you find your way. If you'd like to supplement it with an additional map, call the Convention and Visitors Bureau (see above) or stop by the Visitor Information Center (see above) for a free one or pay for one at any major bookstore. If you rent a car, be sure to ask for maps of the city—the rental agents have good ones.

STREET NAMES As if the streets themselves weren't colorful enough, there are the street names, from Felicity to the jawbreaker Tchoupitoulas (chop-i-*too*-las). How did they get these fanciful monikers? Well, in some cases, from overeducated city fathers who named streets after Greek muses (Calliope and Terpsichore). Some immortalize long-dead and otherwise forgotten women (Julia was a free woman of color, but who was Felicity?).

Many streets in the French Quarter—Burgundy, Dauphine, Toulouse, and Dumaine—honor French royalty or nobility, while St. Peter and St. Ann were favorite baptismal names of the Orleans family. The Faubourg Marigny (Faubourg being the local word for *suburb*) neighborhood was once part of the Marigny (say *Mare*-i-nee) family plantation. After scion Bernard squandered his family's fortune (mostly on gambling), he sold off parcels to the city, naming the streets after his favorite things: Desire, Piety, Poets, Duels, Craps, and so forth.

By the way, if pronunciation seems a mystery, try it with a French accent, and you might actually get it right. Unless it's Chartres (*chart*-ers), that is, or Burgundy (bur-*gun*-dee) Street. And Calliope (cal-lee-*ope*). Oh, never mind. When in doubt, just ask a local. They're used to it.

The City at a Glance

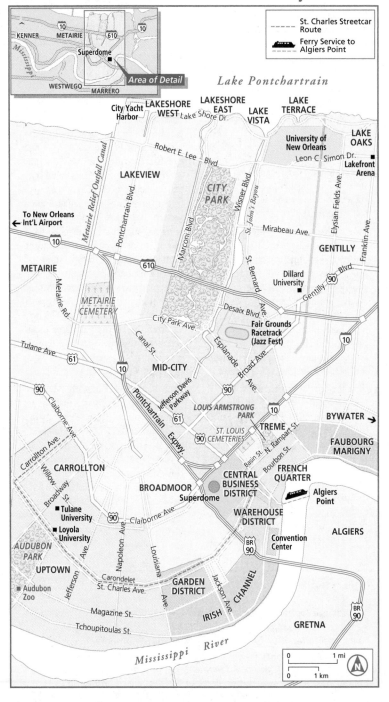

THE NEIGHBORHOODS IN BRIEF

The French Quarter Made up of about 90 square blocks, this section is also known as the *Vieux Carré* ("Old Square") and is enclosed by Canal Street, North Rampart Street, the Mississippi River, and Esplanade Avenue. The Quarter is full of clubs, bars, stores, residences, and museums; its major public area is Jackson Square, bounded by Chartres, Decatur, St. Peter, and St. Ann streets. The most historic and best-preserved area in the city, it's likely to be the focal point of your stay.

Storyville North of the Quarter (just above Rampart St.) is Basin Street, the birthplace of jazz. Or, at least, that's the legend. In fact, jazz probably predates the rise of Storyville (the old red-light district along Basin St.), where it is said to have been born, by a good number of years. To give credit where credit is due, however, Storyville's "sporting houses" did provide a place for the music to grab the ear of a wide segment of the public who came to enjoy the houses', uh, services. King Oliver, Jelly Roll Morton, and Louis Armstrong were among the jazz greats who got their start on Basin Street in the brothels between Canal Street and Beauregard Square.

Apart from a couple of nondescript buildings, no trace of the old Storyville survives (and note this is now a very dangerous neighborhood). A low-income public housing project now sprawls over much of the site, and statues depicting Latin American heroes—Simón Bolívar, Benito Juárez, and Gen. Francisco Morazán—dot the landscape.

Faubourg Marigny This area is east of the French Quarter (on the other side of Esplanade Ave.). Over the past decade, the Marigny has emerged as one of the city's vital centers of activity. Here, you can still find the outlines of a small Creole suburb, and many old-time residents remain. Younger urban dwellers have moved into the area in significant numbers recently. Today, some of the best bars and nightspots in New Orleans are along Frenchmen Street, the Marigny's main drag. Along with the adjacent sections of the French Quarter, the Marigny is also a social center for the city's gay and lesbian communities.

Bywater This riverside neighborhood is past the Faubourg Marigny and is bounded on the east by an industrial canal. It is tempting to misspeak and call it "Backwater," because, at first glance, it seems like a wasteland of light industry and run-down homes. In fact, Bywater has plenty of nice, modest residential sections. Furthermore, it's home to the city's artists-in-hiding, and many local designers have shops among the urban decay. This is in

---

Impressions

'Is it the part of the police department to harass me when this city is the flagrant vice capital of the civilized world?,' Ignatius bellowed. 'This city is famous for its gamblers, prostitutes, exhibitionists, anti-Christs, alcoholics, sodomites, drug addicts, fetishists, onanists, pornographers, frauds, jades, litterbugs, and lesbians, all of whom are only too well protected by graft. If you had a moment, I shall endeavor to discuss the crime problem with you, but don't make the mistake of bothering me.'
　　　　　　　　　　　　　　　　—John Kennedy Toole, *A Confederacy of Dunces*

keeping with the history of the area, which early on was home to artisans as well as communities of immigrants and free people of color.

Mid-City/Esplanade Ridge

Stretching north from the French Quarter to City Park, Esplanade Ridge hugs either side of Esplanade Avenue. This area encompasses a few distinct neighborhoods, all of which have certain things in common. In the 19th century, Esplanade was the grand avenue of New Orleans's Creole society—the St. Charles Avenue of downriver. Many sections of the avenue and houses along it have seen better days, but there is still evidence of those times, especially in the ancient oak trees forming a canopy above the road. If you drive or stroll toward City Park along Esplanade (see Walking Tour 3, "Esplanade Ridge," in chapter 9, "City Strolls"), you can measure the progress of the avenue's development in the styles of its houses.

The oldest section of Esplanade Ridge, **Faubourg Treme,** is located directly across Rampart Street from the French Quarter. Like the Quarter, it was a dense 19th-century Creole community. Unlike the Quarter, Treme (pronounced treh-*may*) has remained almost untouched by preservationists and so has continued to be an organic residential community. Today, it is one of the most vibrant African-American neighborhoods in New Orleans, home to more than a few of the city's best brass bands. Unfortunately, Treme is also plagued by severe crime, so it's not advisable to walk through at night.

Central Business District Historically, **Canal Street** has been New Orleans's main street, and in the 19th century, it also divided the French and American sections of the city. (By the way, there's no

canal—the one that was planned for the spot never came to be.)

The **Central Business District (CBD)** is roughly bounded by Canal Street and the elevated Pontchartrain Expressway (Business Route U.S. 90) between Loyola Avenue and the Mississippi River. Some of the most elegant luxury hotels are in this area. Most of the district was known as Faubourg St. Mary when Americans began settling here after the Louisiana Purchase. Lafayette Square was the center of life here during the 19th century.

Within the CBD is the **Warehouse District.** More than 20 years ago, this area was full of abandoned warehouses and almost nothing else. With the efforts of some dedicated individuals and institutions, however, it's steadily evolving into a residential neighborhood with some commercial activity. Furthermore, this area also serves as the city's art gallery district, with many of the premier galleries concentrated along **Julia Street** (see chapter 10, "Shopping"). Most of these galleries show the works of local and regional contemporary artists. The Contemporary Arts Center and Louisiana Children's Museum (see chapter 8, "Sights to See & Places to Be") are also in this area.

Uptown/The Garden District

Bounded by St. Charles Avenue (lakeside) and Magazine Street (riverside) between Jackson and Louisiana avenues, the Garden District remains one of the most picturesque areas in the city. Originally the site of a plantation, the area was subdivided and developed as a residential neighborhood for wealthy Americans. Throughout the middle of the 19th century, developers built the Victorian, Italianate, and Greek Revival homes that still line the streets. Most of the

How to Make Like the Locals Do

We are so proud of you. Not for you the "I went to New Orleans, but I never got off Bourbon Street." Not for you any tourist trap, or maybe even any other tourist. You want to make like the locals do. Having said that, by and large this book avoids tourist traps, and while it won't help you avoid tourists, it does feature many a spot that has prompted many a local to say, "You've got that place in there?! No one knows about that!" (Not to blow our own horn or anything.) But here are a few more residents-only suggestions, plus a few specific venues, featured elsewhere in this guide, that have their own traditional following. Be aware that making like a local sometimes means heading into areas that will prompt your cab driver (yes, take a cab, if you don't have your own car) to shake their heads about your foolhardy behavior. Ignore them, though do please be cautious. Here, in no particular order:

Po' Boys at Gene's   This is an authentic dive, which, for New Orleans, is about as authentic as it gets. It may be a little *too* local color for you, so just plan to get food to go (it's not really eat-in, anyway). All you get at Gene's are po' boys, but oh, that's all you need. Particularly when the po' boy is the classic Creole hot sausage and cheese (American cheese, please!), fully dressed. Divine. Gene's also offers a roast beef po' boy and a hamburger, but that's it for menu options. No chips, no dessert. One drink comes with your generously sized sandwich. $5 total. Don't you feel local already? Gene's Po-Boys is at 1040 Elysian Fields (*(©* **504/943-3861**).

Fried Chicken at McHardy's   When beloved friends of ours married, they served fried chicken from McHardy's, 1458 N. Broad St. (*(©* **504/949-0000**), at their wedding reception. And you know what? No fancy-pants expensive, catered extravaganza had better food. It's the best fried chicken we've ever eaten (moist, tender, slightly crispy skin, perfectly seasoned, 50¢ a piece), bar none.

After Church at Galatoire's   It's been a tradition since there has been a Galatoire's: residents, all of them in their Sunday finery, standing in line (because that's what you do) at the restaurant many still think is the finest in town, a place where, when the hand-chipped ice was replaced with cubes produced by a (gasp!) machine, demonstrations were held. We exaggerate, but not by much. Purists will tell you that changes like this mean Galatoire's simply isn't what it used to be, but chances are, they are saying that while being waited on by the person who has waited on them for the last 40 years. So you be the judge. See p. 112.

A Real Gospel Brunch   Speaking of church, forget the so-called "Gospel Brunch" at the House of Blues. Go see the real thing in a real place of worship, like the **Guiding Light Missionary Baptist Church,** 2012 Washington Ave. (*(©* **504/891-7654**). It's humble, but it's right and true, and the singing of the choir (not to mention the sometimes fiery preaching) is what it's all about. You may well be the only non-parishioner there, but the congregation is always welcoming. Worship begins at 7am on Sundays, but you don't need to be there before 8:30am. Remember to put some of those dollars you saved by not going to the HOB into the collection plate, but also note that said plate is passed early and often, so pace your giving.

Crescent City Farmers' Markets This is the collective name for the three weekly produce (and other foodstuffs) wonderlands in various city locales. It's *the* place to commune with local gourmands. You may not want to cart home fresh produce, though sampling in season is always a pleasure, but you can bring home some powerful Creole cream cheese, fresh breads and biscuits, and other regional treats. Local chefs do demonstrations (crawfish and shrimp quesadillas!), and gourmet snacks are on sale as well. The markets are held on Thursday from 3pm to 7pm at 3700 Orleans Ave.; Tuesday from 10am to 1pm in the Uptown Square parking lot at 200 Broadway; and Saturday from 8am to noon at 700 Magazine St. For more info, go to www.crescentcityfarmersmarket. org.

Snake & Jake's Xmas Club Lounge Tiny. Cramped. Full of Christmas twinkle lights and locals drinking and some out-of-towners, also drinking, because they consider it their own local lounge when they come to town. See p. 245.

Kermit Ruffins & the Barbecue Swingers Every Thursday night, Kermit Ruffins, he of the smooth trumpet and gravelly, Satchmo-inspired voice, plays at **Vaughan's Lounge.** Because this is his home turf, he feels much freer here, and his sets veer away from tourist-pleasing, conservative performances to looser repertoires. And because his band is called the Barbeque Swingers, and because he loves to cook, he often makes free BBQ before the shows. See p. 234.

Wee Watering Holes The tiny, long, narrow, and claustrophobic **Carrollton Station** and the just plain tiny **Circle Bar** are two music venues popular with locals, who come to see rock acts and singer/songwriters (along with some touring groups). Fans like to drink here as well, regardless of who is on stage. Wait, we can say that about virtually every place on this list! See p. 237 and 243, respectively.

Super Sunday All year long, the Mardi Gras Indians work on their elaborate costumes of hand-sewn beaded mosaics and feathers, creating concoctions that would make even over-the-top designer Bob Mackie burst into tears of helpless envy. And once a year, they meet on their home turfs, to compete, with chants, drums, and costumes, to prove once and for all which tribe is the most glorious, and who is the prettiest. All that work for nothing but honor, pride, and beauty. Watching them parade and square off is one of the great sights of New Orleans, and hardly anyone goes. Perhaps that's because of the location (the Uptown Indians start and end at the corner of Washington Avenue and LaSalle Street; the Mid-City tribes start around Bayou St. John and Orleans Avenue; in both cases, just drive around looking for feathers and listening for drums); perhaps it's because the Indians are supposed to parade on the Sunday closest to St. Joseph's Day (March 19), but that's only if the weather is good (rain and wind are hard on feathers: "Ever seen a wet chicken?" one Indian pointed out) and if the Indians feel like it. Take your chances, though, because it's a sight you won't see anywhere else.

homes had elaborate lawns and gardens, but few of those still exist. The Garden District is located uptown (as opposed to the CBD, which is downtown); the neighborhood west of the Garden District is often called Uptown (not to be confused with the directions people often use here: The Garden District is located uptown from both the Quarter and CBD and is *in* what is collectively referred to as Uptown). (See chapter 9, "City Strolls," for a suggested stroll through this area.)

The Irish Channel The area bounded by Magazine Street and the Mississippi River, Louisiana Avenue, and the Central Business District got its name during the 1800s when more than 100,000 Irish immigrated to New Orleans. As was true elsewhere in the country, the Irish of New Orleans were often considered "expendable" labor, and many were killed while employed at dangerous construction work and other manual labor.

These days, the Channel is significantly less Irish, but it retains its lively spirit and distinctive neighborhood flavor. Much of the area is run-down, but just as much is filled with quiet residential neighborhoods. To get a glimpse of the Irish Channel, go to the antiques shop district on Magazine Street and stroll between Felicity Street and Jackson Avenue.

Algiers Point Directly across the Mississippi River from the Central Business District and the French Quarter and connected by the Canal Street Ferry, Algiers Point is the old town center of Algiers. It is another of the city's original Creole suburbs but probably the one that has changed the least over the decades. Today, you can't see many signs of the area's once-booming railroad and dry-docking industries, but you can see some of the best-preserved small gingerbread and Creole cottages in New Orleans. The neighborhood has recently begun to attract attention as a historic landmark, and it makes for one of the city's most pleasant strolls (see chapter 8, "Sights to See & Places to Be," for tips on how to get here).

SAFETY

The city's high crime rate has made headlines over the past few years. New Orleans has worked hard on the problem, and an increased police force and vigilance have led to a decrease in crime. Problems do still remain, however.

STREET SMARTS The **French Quarter** is fairly safe, thanks to the number of people present at any given time, but some areas are better than others. On the other hand, anything can happen anywhere, so just pay attention and use basic street smarts. On Bourbon Street, be careful when socializing with strangers and be alert to distractions by potential pickpocket teams. Dauphine and Burgundy are in quiet, lovely old parts of the Quarter, but as you near Esplanade, watch out for purse snatchers. At night, stay in well-lighted areas with plenty of both street and pedestrian traffic and take cabs down Esplanade and into the **Faubourg Marigny.**

Impressions

She had understood before she had ever dreamed of a city such as this, where every texture, every color, leapt out at you, where every fragrance was a drug, and the air itself was something alive and breathing.
—Anne Rice, *The Witching Hour*

Conventional wisdom holds that one should not go much above Bourbon toward Rampart alone after dark, though the increased vigilance has meant a decrease in problems. Still, it might be best to stay in a group (or near one) if you can; and if you feel uncomfortable, consider taking a cab, even if it seems silly, for the (very) short ride. In the **Garden District,** as you get past Magazine toward the river, the neighborhoods can be rough, so exercise caution (more cabs, probably). At all times, try to avoid looking distracted or confused. If you appear confident and alert, you will look less like a target.

TRAVEL SMARTS   Don't hang that expensive camera around your neck when it's not in use. Put it out of sight, if you can, in a camera bag or other case. If the bag or case has a shoulder strap, carry it so the bag is on your hip with the strap over the opposite shoulder so that a simple tug won't dislodge it. That goes for purses as well. You might consider using a money belt or other hidden, pick-pocket-proof type of travel wallet. (Women probably won't want to bring purses to clubs where they plan on dancing.) And never leave valuables in the outside pocket of a backpack. Should you stop for a bite to eat, keep everything within easy reach—of you, not a purse snatcher. If you're traveling in a car, place your belongings in the trunk, not under the seat. And it's always a good idea to leave expensive-looking jewelry and other conspicuous valuables at home anyway.

2 Getting Around

You really don't need to rent a car during your stay in New Orleans. Not only is the town just made for walking (thanks to being so flat—and so darn pictur-esque), but also most places you want to go are easily accessible on foot or by some form of the largely excellent public transportation system. Indeed, we find a streetcar ride to be as much entertainment as a practical means of getting around. At night, when you need them most, cabs are easy to come by. Mean-while, driving and parking in the French Quarter bring grief. The streets are nar-row and crowded, and many go one way only (this is easily the most confusing city we have ever driven around). Street parking is minimal (and likely to attract thieves), and parking lots are fiendishly expensive.

Sure, everything takes a bit longer when you are depending on the kindness of strangers to get around, but driving and parking headaches take time, too, and are not conducive to a pleasant vacation. Besides, you need to walk off all those calories you'll be ingesting!

BY PUBLIC TRANSPORTATION

DISCOUNT PASSES   If you won't have a car in New Orleans, we strongly encourage you to invest in a **VisiTour** pass, which entitles you to an unlimited number of rides on all streetcar and bus lines. It costs $5 for 1 day, $12 for 3 days. Many visitors think this was the best tip they got about their New Orleans stay and the finest bargain in town. Passes are available from VisiTour vendors—to find the nearest one, ask at your hotel or guest house or contact the **Regional Transit Authority (RTA)** (© **504/827-2600;** www.regionaltransit.org). You can contact the RTA for information about any part of the city's public trans-portation system.

BUSES   New Orleans has an excellent public bus system, so chances are there's a bus that runs exactly where you want to go. Local fares at press time are $1.25 (you must have exact change in bills or coins), transfers are an extra 25¢, and express buses are $1.25. You can get complete route information by contacting

A Bus Named Desire

"They told me to take a streetcar named Desire and then transfer to one called Cemeteries and ride six blocks and get off at Elysian Fields!"
      Although Blanche's directions wouldn't actually have gotten her to Stella and Stanley's house (Tennessee Williams fiddled with streetcar lines to make his metaphor work), there were indeed once streetcars called Desire and Cemeteries. The signs indicated their ultimate destinations (a street and a district, respectively). However, Blanche's later question, "Is that streetcar named Desire still grinding along the tracks?" must now be answered no. (Unless we are still using that metaphor.)
      The streetcar in question, which used to run through the French Quarter along Bourbon and Royal streets, has, like all but two of its brethren, been replaced by buses. That means you can't take a whirl on the legendary streetcar, but you can still ride buses called Desire and Cemeteries.

the RTA (© 504/827-7802; www.regionaltransit.org) or by picking up one of the excellent city maps available at the Visitor Information Center, 529 St. Ann St., in the French Quarter.

STREETCARS   Besides being a national historic landmark, the **St. Charles Avenue streetcar** is also a convenient and fun way to get from downtown to Uptown and back. The trolleys run 24 hours a day at frequent intervals, and the fare is $1.25 each way (you must have exact change in bills or coins). Streetcars can get crowded at rush hour and when school is out for the day. Board at Canal and Carondelet streets (directly across Canal from Bourbon St. in the French Quarter) or anywhere along St. Charles Avenue, sit back, and look for landmarks or just enjoy the scenery.

The streetcar line extends beyond the point where St. Charles Avenue bends into Carrollton Avenue. The end of the line is at Palmer Park and Playground at Claiborne Avenue, but you'll want to mount a shopping expedition at the Riverbend Shopping Area (see p. 207). It will cost you another $1.25 for the ride back to Canal Street. It costs 10¢ to transfer from the streetcar to a bus.

The **riverfront streetcar** runs for 1.9 miles, from the Old Mint across Canal Street to Riverview, with stops along the way. It's a great step saver as you explore the riverfront. The fare is $1.25, and there's wheelchair ramp access (but not on the St. Charles line).

The exciting news is that sometime in 2003 (oh, don't get your hopes up; figure it's bound to be later), a new streetcar line will run up Canal from the Quarter all the way to City Park Avenue (right to the cemeteries there). This will help ease your travels considerably and open up Mid-City as a viable accommodations option.

BY CAR

If you must have a car, try one of the following car rental agencies: **Avis,** 2024 Canal St. (© 800/331-1212 or 504/523-4317; www.avis.com); **Budget Rent-A-Car,** 1317 Canal St. (© 800/527-0700 or 504/467-2277; www.budget.com); **Dollar Rent-A-Car,** 1910 Airline Hwy., Kenner (© 800/800-4000 or 504/467-2285;

www.dollar.com); **Hertz,** 901 Convention Center Blvd., No. 101 (© **800/ 654-3131** or 504/568-1645; www.hertz.com); **Swifty Car Rental,** 1717 Canal St. (© **504/524-7368**); or **Alamo,** 1806 Airline Hwy., Kenner (© **800/GO-VALUE**; www.goalamo.com).

Rental rates vary according to the time of your visit and from company to company, so call ahead and do some comparison shopping. Ask lots of questions, try different dates and pickup points, and ask about corporate or organizational discounts (such as AAA or frequent-flier-program memberships). And if you're staying for a week or more, be sure to ask about weekly rates, which are cheaper.

To rent a car in the United States, you need a valid driver's license, a passport, and a major credit card. The minimum age is usually 25, but some companies will rent to younger people and add a surcharge. It's a good idea to buy maximum insurance coverage unless you're positive your own auto or credit-card insurance is sufficient. Stick to the major companies because what you might save with smaller companies might not be worth the headache if you have mechanical troubles on the road. Rates vary, so it pays to call around.

New Orleans drivers are often reckless, so drive defensively. The meter maids are an efficient bunch, so take no chances with parking meters. Carry change with you—many meters take only quarters. It's probably best to use your car only for longer jaunts away from congested areas. Most hotels provide guest parking, often for a daily fee; smaller hotels or guesthouses (particularly in the French Quarter) may not have parking facilities but will be able to direct you to a nearby public garage.

The narrow streets and frequent congestion make driving in the French Quarter more difficult than elsewhere in the city. Streets are one-way, and on weekdays during daylight hours, Royal and Bourbon streets between the 300 and 700 blocks are closed to vehicles. The blocks of Chartres Street in front of St. Louis Cathedral are closed at all times. Driving is also trying in the Central Business District, where congestion and limited parking make life difficult for motorists. Do yourself a favor: Park the car and use public transportation in both areas.

Once you get into more residential areas like the Garden District and off main drags like St. Charles Avenue, finding where you are going becomes quite a challenge. Street signs are often no bigger than a postcard and are hard to read at that. At night, they aren't even lit, so deciphering where you are can be next to impossible. If you must drive, we suggest counting the number of streets you have to cross to tell you when to make any turns rather than relying on street signs.

BY TAXI

Taxis are plentiful in New Orleans. They can be hailed easily on the street in the French Quarter and in some parts of the Central Business District, and they are usually lined up at taxi stands at larger hotels. Otherwise, telephone and expect a cab to appear in 3 to 5 minutes. The rate is $2.10 when you enter the taxi and $1.20 per mile thereafter. During special events (like Mardi Gras and Jazz Fest), the rate is $3 per person (or the meter rate if it's greater) no matter where you go in the city.

The city's most reliable company is **United Cabs** (© **504/524-9606**). Their taxis are black and white and are easily confused with Bell Cabs, especially at night; you often can't tell which you've got for sure until the cab has descended upon you. It's embarrassing (and once in a while results in a cranky cab driver) to flag down a cab and then wave them on if they aren't the company you desire, but go ahead. Honestly, it's worth it; while other cab companies may have honest drivers, they nearly always have considerably faster meters (go ahead, test this out; take United one way and someone else for the return trip and compare fares), though that tidbit may be of less significance when it's 2am in a dark neighborhood! (United cabs often have elongated pyramid advertisement signs on top of them, which used to be a sure way of identifying one, but other cab companies have them now, if not as frequently.)

Most taxis can be hired for a special rate for up to five passengers. It's a hassle-free and economical way for a small group to tour far-flung areas of the city (the lakefront, for example). Within the city you pay an hourly rate; out-of-town trips cost double the amount on the meter.

ON FOOT

We can't stress this enough: Walking is by far the best way to see New Orleans. There are too many unique and sometimes glorious sights that you can miss if you whiz past them by using other forms of transportation. Slow down. Have a drink to go. Get a snack. Stroll. Take one of our walking tours (see chapter 9, "City Strolls"). Sure, sometimes it's too hot or humid—or raining too hard—to make walking attractive, but there is always a cab or bus nearby. Do remember to drink lots of water if it's hot and pay close attention to your surroundings. If you enter an area that seems unsafe, retreat.

BY BIKE

One of the best ways to see the city is by bike. The terrain is flat, the breeze feels good, and you can cover a whole lot of ground on two wheels. Two bike stores in and near the French Quarter rent bikes by the hour, day, or longer. **Bicycle Michaels,** 622 Frenchmen St. (© **504/945-9505;** www.bicyclemichaels.com) rents mountain and hybrid bikes; during Jazz Fest it has a fleet of 100 bikes at the ready. Rates are $5 an hour, $16 a day, and $64 for 5 days. **French Quarter Bicycles,** 522 Dumaine St. (© **504/529-3136;** www.fqbikes.com), rents mountain bikes for $5 an hour and $20 a day. Both shops require a credit-card deposit.

BY FERRY

The Canal Street ferry is one of the city's secrets—and it's free for pedestrians. The ride takes you across the Mississippi River from the foot of Canal to Algiers Point (25 min. round-trip), and it affords great views of downtown New Orleans and the commerce on the river. Once in Algiers, you can walk around the old Algiers Point neighborhood and tour Mardi Gras World (see p. 169). At night, with the city's glowing skyline reflecting on the river, a ride on the ferry can be quite romantic. The ferry also does carry car traffic (for free), in case you'd like to do some West Bank driving.

 FAST FACTS: New Orleans

Airport See "Getting There" in chapter 3, "Planning Your Trip to New Orleans," and "Orientation" at the beginning of this chapter.

American Express The local office (© 800/508-0274) is at 201 St. Charles Ave. in the Central Business District. It's open weekdays from 9am to 5pm.

Babysitters It's best to ask at your hotel about babysitting services. If your hotel doesn't offer help finding childcare, try calling **Accent on Children's Arrangements** (© 504/524-1227) or **Dependable Kid Care** (© 504/486-4001).

Convention Center The **Ernest N. Morial Convention Center** (© 504/582-3000) is at 900 Convention Center Blvd. It was built in anticipation of the World's Fair, held in New Orleans in 1984, under "Dutch" Morial's administration. Morial, father of Marc Morial, New Orleans's mayor from 1994 to 2002, was the city's first black mayor.

Emergencies For fire, ambulance, and police, dial © **911.** This is a free call from pay phones.

Hospitals Should you become ill during your visit, most major hotels have in-house doctors on call 24 hours a day. If no one is available at your hotel or guesthouse, call or go to the emergency room at **Ochsner Medical Institutions,** 1516 Jefferson Hwy. (© **504/842-3460**), or the **Tulane University Medical Center,** 1415 Tulane Ave. (© **504/588-5800**).

Information See "Visitor Information," earlier in this chapter.

Liquor Laws The legal drinking age in Louisiana is 21, but don't be surprised if people much younger take a seat next to you at the bar. Alcoholic beverages are available around the clock, 7 days a week. You're allowed to drink on the street but not from a glass or bottle. Bars will often provide a plastic "go cup" so that you can transfer your drink to as you leave (and some have walk-up windows for quick and easy refills).

   One warning: Although the police may look the other way if they see a pedestrian who's had a few too many (as long as he or she is peaceful and is not bothering anyone), they have no tolerance at all for those who are intoxicated behind the wheel.

Maps See "City Layout," earlier in this chapter.

Newspapers & Magazines To find out what's going on around town, you might want to pick up a copy of the daily ***Times-Picayune*** (www.nola.com) or ***Offbeat*** (www.offbeat.com), a monthly guide (probably the most extensive one available) to the city's evening entertainment, art galleries, and special events. It can be found in most hotels, though it's often hard to locate toward the end of the month. The ***Gambit Weekly*** (www.bestof neworleans.com) is the city's free alternative paper and has a good mix of news and entertainment information. It comes out every Thursday. The paper conducts an annual **"Best of New Orleans"** readers' poll; check their website for the results.

Pharmacies The 24-hour pharmacy closest to the French Quarter is **Walgreens,** 3311 Canal St., at Jefferson Davis (© **504/822-8072**). There is also a 24-hour **Rite Aid** at 3401 St. Charles Ave., at Louisiana Ave. (© **504/896-4575**), which is more convenient if you're staying Uptown or in the Garden District.

Photographic Needs A good option for 1-hour film processing is **French Quarter Camera,** 809 Decatur St. (© **504/529-2974**). Disposable and inexpensive cameras, film, and batteries can be found in any of the many corner grocery stores in the Quarter.

Police Dial © **911** for emergencies. This is a free call from pay phones.

Post Office The main post office is at 701 Loyola Ave. There's also a post office in the World Trade Center, at 2 Canal St. If you're in the Quarter, you'll find a post office at 1022 Iberville St., near Burgundy Street. There's another one at 610 S. Maestri Place, near Camp Street. If you have something large or fragile to send home and don't feel like hunting around for packing materials, go to **Royal Mail & Parcel,** 828 Royal St., near St. Ann Street ((*C* 504/522-8523) in the Quarter, or **Mail Box Pack & Ship,** 1201 St. Charles Ave., near Clio Street ((*C* 504/524-5080), uptown. The latter also has pickup service.

Radio   WWOZ (90.7 FM) is *the* New Orleans radio station. They say they are the best in the world, and we aren't inclined to disagree. New Orleans jazz, R&B, brass bands, Mardi Gras Indians, gospel, Cajun, zydeco—it's all here. Don't miss music historian (and former White Panther activist, memorialized in a song by John Lennon) John Sinclair's shows (at press time, Wed from 11am to 2pm and Sun from 3 to 6am), which got him named Best DJ in *OffBeat*'s annual poll. The city's NPR station is WWNO (89.9 FM). Also, Tulane's station, WTUL (91.5 FM), plays very interesting music.

Safety   Be careful while visiting any unfamiliar city. In New Orleans, in particular, don't walk alone at night, and don't go into the cemeteries alone at any time during the day or night. Ask around locally before you go anywhere; people will tell you if you should take a cab instead of walking or using public transportation. Most important, if someone holds you up and demands your wallet, purse, or other personal belongings, don't resist. Also see the "Safety" section earlier in this chapter and the "Safety Concerns" section in chapter 4, "For International Visitors."

Taxes   The sales tax in New Orleans is 9%. An additional 2% tax is added to hotel bills for a total of 11%. Foreign visitors should see "Customs" in section 1 of chapter 4 for details on getting their state sales tax refunded.

Taxis   See "Getting Around," earlier in this chapter.

Time Zone   New Orleans observes central time, the same as Chicago. Between the first Sunday in April and the last Saturday in October, daylight saving time is in effect. During this period, clocks are set 1 hour ahead of standard time. Call (*C* 504/828-4000 for the correct local time.

Transit Information   Local bus routes and schedules can be obtained from the **RTA Ride Line** ((*C* 504/248-3900; www.regionaltransit.org). **Union Passenger Terminal,** 1001 Loyola Ave., provides bus information ((*C* **504/524-7571**) and train information ((*C* **504/528-1610;** www.amtrack.com) and is the place where trains and buses deliver and pick up their passengers who are traveling away from or into New Orleans.

Traveler's Aid Society   This nationwide, nonprofit, social-service organization geared to helping travelers in difficult straits offers services that might include reuniting families separated while traveling, providing food and/or shelter to people stranded without cash, or even emotional counseling. If you're in trouble, seek them out. You can reach the local branch of the society at (*C* **504/525-8726.**

Weather   For an update, call (*C* **504/828-4000.**

6

Where to Stay

If you're doing your New Orleans trip right, you shouldn't be doing much sleeping. But you do have to put your change of clothes somewhere. Fortunately, New Orleans is bursting with hotels of every variety, so you should be able to find something that fits your preferences. During crowded times (Mardi Gras, for example), however, just finding anything might have to be good enough. After all, serious New Orleans visitors often book a year in advance for popular times.

Given a choice, we tend to favor slightly faded, ever-so-faintly-decayed, just-this-side-of-elegant locales; a new, sterile chain or even a luxury hotel doesn't seem right for New Orleans, where atmosphere is everything. Slightly tattered lace curtains, faded antiques, mossy courtyards with banana trees and fountains, a musty, Miss Havisham air—to us, it's all part of the fun. We prefer to stay in a Tennessee Williams play if not an Anne Rice novel (though in summertime, we'll take air-conditioning, thank you very much).

Understandably, this may not appeal to you. (It may, in fact, describe your own home, and who wants their own home on vacation?) Regardless of whether you want the anonymous familiarity of a chain (where every room is identical, but a certain level of quality is assured), serious pampering, major antiques, or a good location, there's a place for you in New Orleans.

Here, however, are a few tips. Don't stay on Bourbon Street unless you absolutely have to or don't mind getting

no sleep. The open-air frat party that is this thoroughfare does mean a free show below your window, but it is hardly conducive to . . . well, just about anything other than participation in the same. (On the other hand, making a night of it on your balcony, people-watching—and people-egging-on—is an activity with its own merits, one enjoyed by a number of happy tourists.) If you must stay on Bourbon Street, try to get a room away from the street.

A first-time visitor might also strongly consider not staying in the Quarter at all. Most of your sightseeing will take place there, but you may want to get away from it all after dinner or simply see a neighborhood whose raison d'être isn't to entertain first-time visitors. Try the beautiful Garden District instead. It's an easy streetcar ride away from the Quarter, and it's close to a number of wonderful clubs and restaurants.

All of the guesthouses in this chapter are first-rate. If you want more information, we highly recommend the **Bed and Breakfast, Inc., Reservation Service** ★★★ (℃ **800/729-4640** or 504/488-4640; www.historiclodging. com), which represents about 50 establishments in every section of the city, among them 19th-century, turn-of-the-20th-century, and modern residences, offering suites, rooms, and cottages. Prices range from $61 to $252 a night. The service can also often find a room for you on relatively short notice.

As a general rule, just to be on the safe side, always book ahead in spring,

New Orleans Accommodations

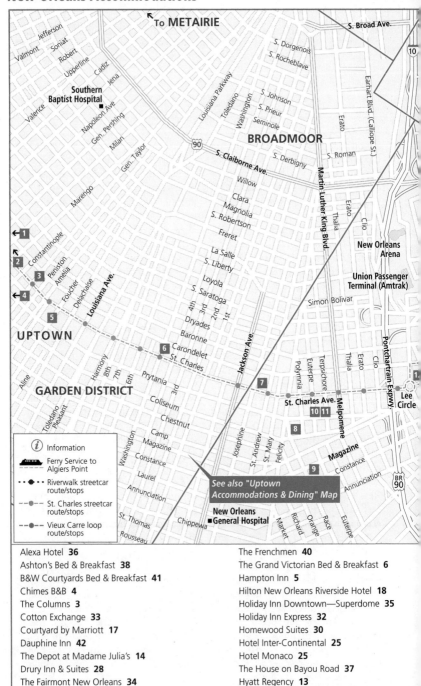

To METAIRIE

S. Broad Ave.

Jefferson
Valmont
Soniat
Robert
Upperline
Cadiz
Jena
Valerice
Southern
Baptist Hospital
Napoleon Ave.
Gen. Pershing
Milan
Gen. Taylor
Marengo
Constantinople
Peniston
Amelia
Foucher
Delachaise
Louisiana Ave.
Harmony
8th 7th 6th
Aline
Toledano
Pleasant

S. Dorgenois
S. Rocheblave
Louisiana Parkway
Toledano
Washington
S. Johnson
S. Prieur
Seminole

BROADMOOR

S. Claiborne Ave.
S. Derbigny
S. Roman
Willow
Clara
Magnolia
S. Robertson
Freret
La Salle
S. Liberty
Loyola
S. Saratoga
4th 3rd 2nd 1st
Dryades
Baronne
Carondelet
St. Charles

UPTOWN

GARDEN DISTRICT

Prytania
3rd
Coliseum
Chestnut
Camp
Magazine
Washington
Constance
Laurel
Annunciation
St. Thomas
Chippewa
Rousseau

Earhart Blvd. (Calliope St.)
Erato
Martin Luther King Blvd.
Erato
Thalia
Clio

New Orleans
Arena

Union Passenger
Terminal (Amtrak)

Simon Bolivar

Jackson Ave.

Terpsichore
Euterpe
Polymnia
St. Charles Ave.
Melpomene

Clio
Thalia
Erato
Clio

Pontchartrain Expwy.

Lee
Circle

10 11
8
Josephine
St. Andrew
St. Mary
Felicity
9

Magazine
Constance
Annunciation

BR
90

New Orleans
General Hospital

Richard
Orange
Race
Euterpe
Market

(i) Information

Ferry Service to
Algiers Point

• ◆ • • Riverwalk streetcar
route/stops

— ● — St. Charles streetcar
route/stops

— ● — Vieux Carre loop
route/stops

See also "Uptown
Accommodations & Dining" Map

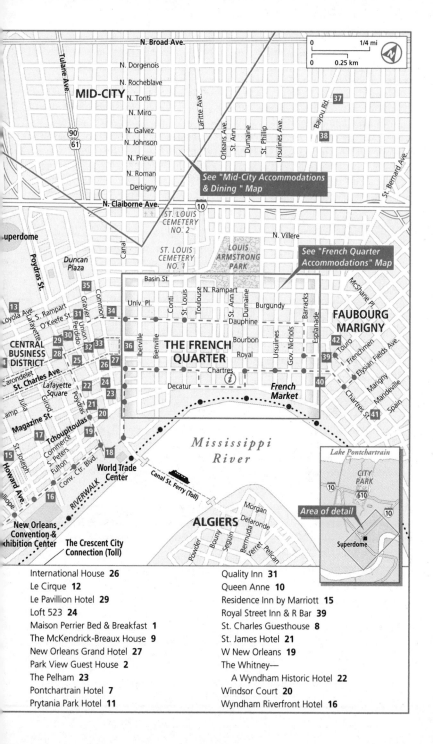

International House **26**
Le Cirque **12**
Le Pavillion Hotel **29**
Loft 523 **24**
Maison Perrier Bed & Breakfast **1**
The McKendrick-Breaux House **9**
New Orleans Grand Hotel **27**
Park View Guest House **2**
The Pelham **23**
Pontchartrain Hotel **7**
Prytania Park Hotel **11**

Quality Inn **31**
Queen Anne **10**
Residence Inn by Marriott **15**
Royal Street Inn & R Bar **39**
St. Charles Guesthouse **8**
St. James Hotel **21**
W New Orleans **19**
The Whitney—
   A Wyndham Historic Hotel **22**
Windsor Court **20**
Wyndham Riverfront Hotel **16**

fall, and winter. And if your trip will coincide with Mardi Gras or Jazz Fest, book *way* ahead (and we can't stress this enough—*please* look at the calendar of events in chapter 3, "Planning Your Trip to New Orleans," to make sure you are not unintentionally coinciding with these events)—up to a year in advance if you want to ensure a room. Sugar Bowl week and other festival times when visitors flood New Orleans also require planning for accommodations, and there's always the chance that a big convention or sports event will be in town, making it difficult to find a room. You might conceivably run across a cancellation and get a last-minute booking, but the chances are remote at best. You should also be aware that rates frequently jump more than a notch or two for Mardi Gras and other festival times (sometimes they even double), and in most cases, there's a 4- or 5-night minimum requirement during those periods.

If you want to miss the crowds and the lodgings squeeze that mark the big festivals, consider coming in the month immediately following Mardi Gras or, if you can stand the heat and humidity, in the summer, when the streets are not nearly as thronged. December, before the Sugar Bowl and New Year's activities, is a good time, too, but perhaps a bit rainy. In both cases, hotel prices fall dramatically and great deals can be had just about everywhere. (And these prices might not be accounted for in the rack rate, so you might have a pleasant surprise!)

There are no recommendable inexpensive *hotels* in the French Quarter. If you're on a budget and must stay there, consider a guesthouse. On the whole, however, you'll have a better selection of inexpensive lodgings outside the Quarter. There are also a handful of hostels in New Orleans; check the Internet site **www.hostels.com** for more information.

You'll find a list of our favorite accommodations in a variety of eclectic categories in chapter 1, "The Best of New Orleans."

The rates we've given in this chapter are for double rooms and do not include the city's 11% hotel tax. You may see some wide ranges of room rates below, which hotels were not eager to break down more specifically for us. Realize that rates often shift according to demand. The high end of the range is for popular times like Mardi Gras and Jazz Fest, and the low end is for quieter periods like the month of December.

1 The French Quarter

For hotels in this section, see the "French Quarter Accommodations" map on p. 69.

VERY EXPENSIVE

Grenoble House   The Grenoble House, an old French Quarter town house built around a courtyard, is small, quiet, and close to everything. Rooms are all apartments (the most private are in the old slave quarters in the back) with full kitchens (including microwaves), sitting/living areas, and bedrooms with expensive mattresses. Furnishings can be disappointingly modern—they clash with the frequently exposed brick walls, if you ask us. Businesspeople like the apartmentlike convenience, while families with teenagers (children under 12 aren't allowed) might look into the two-bedroom accommodations. A special plus here is the personal, attentive service—they will book theater tickets, restaurant reservations, and sightseeing tours and will even arrange a gourmet dinner brought to your suite or a private cocktail party on the patio if you want to entertain.

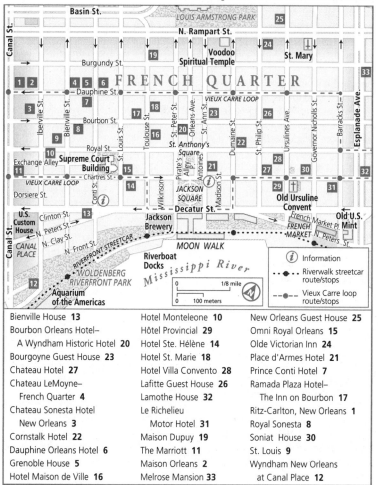

Bienville House **13**
Bourbon Orleans Hotel–
  A Wyndham Historic Hotel **20**
Bourgoyne Guest House **23**
Chateau Hotel **27**
Chateau LeMoyne–
  French Quarter **4**
Chateau Sonesta Hotel
  New Orleans **3**
Cornstalk Hotel **22**
Dauphine Orleans Hotel **6**
Grenoble House **5**
Hotel Maison de Ville **16**

Hotel Monteleone **10**
Hôtel Provincial **29**
Hotel Ste. Hélène **14**
Hotel St. Marie **18**
Hotel Villa Convento **28**
Lafitte Guest House **26**
Lamothe House **32**
Le Richelieu
  Motor Hotel **31**
Maison Dupuy **19**
The Marriott **11**
Maison Orleans **2**
Melrose Mansion **33**

New Orleans Guest House **25**
Omni Royal Orleans **15**
Olde Victorian Inn **24**
Place d'Armes Hotel **21**
Prince Conti Hotel **7**
Ramada Plaza Hotel–
  The Inn on Bourbon **17**
Ritz-Carlton, New Orleans **1**
Royal Sonesta **8**
Soniat House **30**
St. Louis **9**
Wyndham New Orleans
  at Canal Place **12**

Prices reflect that these are suites, but still—you probably can do better in other hotels.

323 Dauphine St., New Orleans, LA 70112. ℂ **800/722-1834** or 504/522-1331. Fax 504/524-4968. www.grenoblehouse.com. 17 suites. $199–$279 1-bedroom suite; $379–$459 2-bedroom suite. Rates include continental breakfast. Weekly rates available. AE, MC, V. No on-site garage. Public garage 1 block away. No children under 12. **Amenities:** Small, unheated pool for dipping plus a Jacuzzi. *In room:* A/C, TV, full kitchen.

Hotel Maison de Ville ★★ A member of *The Small Luxury Hotels of the World,* the Maison de Ville is not quite as sterling as it has been, but it remains so romantic and charming that complaints (that it's not exactly run-down but not quite on the ball with all things as it used to be) only seem intermittently important. At this hotel, where Tennessee Williams was a regular guest in room no. 9, most of the rooms surround an utterly charming courtyard (complete with fountain and banana trees), where it's hard to believe you're in the thick of the Quarter. Rooms (some of which have very tall ceilings and very tall—as in you need steps to reach them—beds) vary dramatically in size; however, some can be downright tiny, so ask when you reserve, as price is no indicator of size. Be careful you don't get a room overlooking the street—Bourbon is less than half a block away and makes its sorry presence known.

The far more spacious Audubon Cottages (larger than many apartments, some with their own private courtyards), located a few blocks away and including a small, inviting pool, can go for less than the cramped queen rooms in the main hotel (and are farther from the hubbub of Bourbon). All rooms are thoroughly lush, with nice touches like feather beds, and the service is helpful and courteous. A wonderful romantic getaway—we just wish the continental breakfast (in both locations) weren't so disappointing.

727 Toulouse St., New Orleans, LA 70130. ℭ **800/634-1600** or 504/561-5858. Fax 504/528-9939. www. maisondeville.com. 16 units, 7 cottages. $195–$245 double; $215–$250 queen; $235–$260 king; $325–$395 suite; $265–$375 1-bedroom cottage; $535–$695 2-bedroom cottage; $770–$960 3-bedroom cottage. AE, DC, DISC, MC, V. Valet parking $23. **Amenities:** Le Bistro restaurant (see p. 113 for a full review); outdoor pool; access to nearby health club; concierge; room service 7am–10pm; massage; laundry; dry cleaning; shoe shine. *In room:* A/C, TV, dataport, minibar, hair dryer.

Maison Orleans ✦✦ This hotel is for those who say, "I'd stay at the Ritz-Carlton if only it were even nicer and had even better service." *Voila!* This place is a boutique hotel, attached to the Ritz, with, get this, 24-hour butler service. Yes, ring a special button, "ask for the sun" (they say themselves), and your own personal Jeeves will fetch it for you. We tested this system and had mixed results (no pony, and a special treat for an anniversary proved a bit staid, but requests for coffee and late-night vanilla ice cream were filled promptly and perfectly), but then again, they had just opened, so glitches should be worked out by now. Another fine touch: A phone call prior to your stay ensures that whatever you want or need (bottled water, chocolates, cheese, a certain kind of bathrobe) will be in your room upon your arrival. You pay extra for most of this, of course, but you deserve it. (Consider Jeeves a mobile honor bar.)

The rooms here are gorgeous little classics of NOLA style: wood floors, paneling, and furniture, superb moldings, fireplace facades, and bathrooms containing about the deepest hotel tub we've seen, a separate shower (though rooms with 05s have smaller bathrooms, with combo tub and shower), quality amenities, and thick bath sheets. You get both local aesthetic *and* modern comforts, though window size can vary. Beds are so ultra-lush, with feather beds, down comforters with soft covers, and a half canopy, that we had to be dragged out of ours in the morning. A continental breakfast is served downstairs, and from 5 to 8pm, an array of snacks is set out. *Note:* If you still have more money to burn, the sole suite, room no. 795, can't be beat for sheer size, beauty, and comfort.

904 Iberville St., New Orleans, LA. 70112. ℭ **504/670-2900**. Fax 504/670-2910. www.maisonorleans.com. 75 rooms. $315–$495. AE, DC, DISC, MC, V. Valet parking $25. **Amenities:** 2 restaurants; continental breakfast plus daily snacks; health club; spa; full access to Ritz-Carlton shops; 24-hr. room service; 24-hr. butler service; special baths drawn by butler. *In room:* AC, TV, minibar (stocked according to personal preference), hair dryer, iron, high-speed Internet access, CD and DVD players (and complimentary selections).

Melrose Mansion ✦ A standout even on a street full of mansions in a town full of pampering guesthouses, the Melrose Mansion has long combined luxury resort living with the best guesthouse offerings. Unfortunately, it seems lately to be resting on its laurels. Service, once impeccable, is less so, and the breakfasts, once handsome feasts, now tend toward the prepackaged and ordinary. It still remains a charming old mansion, beautifully renovated, but it may no longer be justifying its high cost. (For which, please note, it has a very strict cancellation policy; half the reservation is paid up front when you make the reservation and

---

> ### ⎛*Tips* **Staying Safe**
>
> There is, of course, considerable concern about personal safety in New Orleans. Your hotel choice, for the most part, need not be influenced by that. Daytime is mostly safe, and, at night, you will probably be traveling in cabs or, if you're in the French Quarter, in well-populated areas. If you stay above Bourbon Street, closer to Rampart, don't walk back to your hotel alone at night; take a cab or travel in groups.

---

is not refundable. The other half is paid 30 days prior to your stay and, at that point, is also nonrefundable.)

The rooms vary from classic Victorian antiques to lighter country-style decor; we love the bright yellow Miss Kitty's Room (named for a former tenant and burlesque dancer) and the more classic Burgundy Room. Bathrooms can be small, but plush bathrobes and linens help. The Parc Henry suite overlooks the year-round heated pool and, between that and its large dining room and kitchen, seems perfect for entertaining and hanging out.

937 Esplanade Ave., New Orleans, LA 70116. ⓒ **800/650-3323** or 504/944-2255. Fax 504/945-1794. www.melrosegroup.com. 20 units. $225–$250 double; $325–$425 suite. Rates include continental breakfast and cocktail hour. AE, DC, DISC, MC, V. Valet parking $15. **Amenities:** Heated outdoor pool. *In room:* A/C, TV, minibar.

Ramada Plaza Hotel–The Inn on Bourbon
This was formerly a Best Western, but while the change in chain ownership did bring about new (modestly good-looking, vaguely Southern) decor in the rooms, little else is all that different—it's still a pricy chain hotel. The justification is the location: the former site of the 1859 French Opera House—the first opera house built in the United States (it burned down in 1919). Party animals should note that this means the hotel is right in the middle of the liveliest action on Bourbon, and many rooms have balconies overlooking the mayhem below. If you have a serious commitment to sleeping, though, choose another place to stay, or at least request an interior room. On the other hand, there are worse ways to spend a N'Awlins evening than having a pizza on your balcony while enjoying the free show on Bourbon Street below. All rooms have king or double beds. The Bourbon Street Cafeteria serves breakfast.

541 Bourbon St., New Orleans, LA 70130. ⓒ **800/535-7891** or 504/524-7611. Fax 504/568-9427. www.innon bourbon.com. 186 units. $205–$215 double. AE, DC, DISC, MC, V. Valet parking $18. **Amenities:** Bar; outdoor pool; fitness room; concierge; jewelry shop; gift shop; laundry; dry cleaning; express checkout. *In room:* A/C, TV, minibar.

Ritz-Carlton, New Orleans ⭐⭐
Sentimentalists that we are, we were deeply sad to see the venerable Maison Blanche department store go the way of Woolworth's, D. H. Holmes, and other Canal Street shopping landmarks. But for the city's sake, we are pleased to have a Ritz-Carlton take its place, preserving the classic, glazed terra-cotta building and bringing a high-end luxury hotel to the Quarter. Again, being sentimentalists, we would rather find our luxury in a less—how shall we say—*generic* way, but we can't deny that with name-brand recognition comes a reliable standard. And so the staff falls all over themselves to be friendly and helpful, rooms have lovely beds (maybe not as nice as the W in the Central Business District), king rooms are nicer than doubles (well, that may be because we are partial to sage green over blue chintz), and the whole effect is very gracious

and just a bit stuffy, an impression that deepens at night as cocktails are served in the lobby lounge where everything is very civil and jeans and other casual attire are frowned upon. (Indeed, there is supposed to be a dress code after 6pm, but we didn't see it enforced.) Chocolates are served in the clubby library lounge/cigar bar at night, and if you pony up to stay on the concierge floor, gourmet snacks are served nearly round the clock. There are a great many elevators and different levels, so getting around does require some zigzagging to and fro. The spa is by far the nicest in town, and though undeniably expensive, it's gorgeous, and the treatments are utter perfection—it's so far ahead of the pack that it's probably not worth spending money at any other spa facility.

921 Canal St., New Orleans, LA 70112. © **800/241-3333** or 504/524-1331. Fax 504/524-7233. www.ritz carlton.com. 452 units. $415 double; from $560 and way, way up for suites. AE, DC, MC, V. Valet parking $25. Pets accepted. **Amenities:** Top-of-the-line spa and health club (with resistance pool, Jacuzzi, and personal trainers); concierge; shops; massage. *In room:* A/C, TV, dataport, minibar, hair dryer, iron, ironing board, safe, Nintendo.

Royal Sonesta ♠♠ As one of the classiest hotels in the Quarter, the contrast between the boisterous hurly-burly of Bourbon Street and the Sonesta's marbled and chandeliered lobby—recently given a facelift that has made it even more elegant—couldn't be greater. Inside, all is quiet and gracious, and if your room faces the courtyard (complete with a large pool), you are in another world altogether. Big and bustling (a favorite of business travelers, so it always seems busy), this is considered the only acceptable, top-flight Bourbon Street hotel, though noise is still a problem in rooms that face Bourbon (or even the side streets). But because the Sonesta is so large, reaching nearly to Royal Street, unless you do have one of those rooms, you won't believe you are so close to such craziness. Rooms have undergone a major renovation, with posher bedspreads and the like, but the designers miscalculated by including an enormous combo armoire/TV cabinet—leaving scant few inches between it and the end of the king-size beds. New bathrooms gleam with marble and tile, but don't bring a cat inside if you want to swing it. *Note:* This is the best place in the Quarter to catch a cab; they line up at the corner.

300 Bourbon St., New Orleans, LA 70130. © **800/766-3782** or 504/586-0300. Fax 504/586-0335. www.royal sonestano.com. 500 units. $249–$389 double; $479–$1,250 suite. AE, DC, DISC, MC, V. Parking $23 car, $25 oversized. **Amenities:** 2 restaurants; bar; pool; exercise room; concierge; business center; room service 7am–2am; massage. *In room:* A/C, TV, minibar, hair dryer, iron, safe.

Soniat House ♠♠♠ The recipient of endless tributes from various prestigious travel journals, the wonderful and romantic Soniat House lives up to the hype. Keeping a low profile behind a solid wood gate, it is classic Creole—the treasures are hidden off the street. Inside you will find a perfect little hideaway, an oasis of calm that seems impossible in the Quarter. The beyond-efficient staff will spoil you, and the sweet courtyards, candlelit at night, will soothe you.

Rooms do vary, if not in quality then at least in distinction. All have antiques, but if you want, say, high ceilings and really grand furniture (room no. 23 has a 17th-century bed), you are better off in the main house or the suite-filled annex across the street. The rooms in the old kitchen and other buildings are not quite as smashing by comparison. On the main property, bathrooms are small, but across the street, they gain size, not to mention Jacuzzi bathtubs, custom decor, and antique furnishings. Our only real complaint is the extra charge for the admittedly delicious, but small, breakfast (fresh squeezed orange juice and fluffy biscuits made to order)—it seems petty.

1133 Chartres St., New Orleans, LA 70116. ℂ **800/544-8808** or 504/522-0570. Fax 504/522-7208. www.soniathouse.com. 33 units. $195–$325 double; $350–$650 suite; $750 2-bedroom suite. AE, MC, V. Valet parking $19. Children over 12 welcome only in rooms that accommodate 3. **Amenities:** Access to nearby health club and business center (for an additional charge); concierge; same-day laundry/dry cleaning; non-smoking property. In room: A/C, TV, hair dryer, safe.

EXPENSIVE

Chateau LeMoyne–French Quarter ✦
The Chateau LeMoyne is in a good location, just around the corner from Bourbon Street but away from the noise and not far from Canal. It's a nice surprise to find a Holiday Inn housed in century-plus-old buildings, but the ambience stops at your room's threshold. Once inside, matters look pretty much like they do in every Holiday Inn—too bad. Famed architect James Gallier designed one of these 19th-century buildings, and you can still see bits of old brick, old ovens, and exposed cypress beams here and there, along with a graceful curving outdoor staircase. You wish they'd made more of their space, but even the spacious courtyard feels oddly sterile. Maybe it's the new brick, which seems sandblasted free of pesky (but atmospheric) moss.

Suites aren't much different, just with frillier furniture, though the enormous Executive Suite is probably worth budget busting for its four large (if dark) rooms that include a Jacuzzi and sauna.

301 Dauphine St., New Orleans, LA 70112. ℂ **800/447-2830** or 504/581-1303. Fax 504/525-8531. www.chateaulemoyne.com. 171 units. $159–$244 double; $259–$459 suite. Extra person $15. AE, DC, DISC, MC, V. Valet parking $20. **Amenities:** Restaurant (breakfast only); bar; outdoor swimming pool; room service 7am–11pm. In room: A/C, TV, coffeemaker, hair dryer, iron, ironing board.

Chateau Sonesta Hotel New Orleans ✦
On the site of the former D. H. Holmes Canal Street department store (1849), the Chateau Sonesta Hotel maintains the structure's 1913 facade, while inside it's a generic high-end hotel, popular among business groups for its meeting rooms and location. At the Canal Street entrance is a newly erected statue of Ignatius Reilly, hero of *A Confederacy of Dunces,* whom we first met when he was waiting, as all of New Orleans once did, "under the clock"—the old Holmes clock, now located in a bar, was for decades the favored rendezvous point for tout New Orleanians. Guest rooms are large, and many feature balconies overlooking Bourbon or Dauphine streets. In addition to in-house movies, videos are available for rental.

800 Iberville St., New Orleans, LA 70112. ℂ **800/SONESTA** or 504/586-0800. Fax 504/586-1987. www.chateausonesta.com. 251 units. $299–$350 double; $285–$798 suite. Extra person $40, except children under 17. AE, DC, DISC, MC, V. Valet parking $20. **Amenities:** Restaurant; bar; heated outdoor pool; exercise room; concierge; tour desk; gift shop; room service 6:30am–11pm; babysitting; laundry; dry cleaning. In room: A/C, TV, dataport, minibar.

Dauphine Orleans Hotel ✦✦
On a relatively quiet and peaceful block of the Quarter, the Dauphine Orleans Hotel is relaxed, but not unkempt. It's just a block from the action on Bourbon Street, but you wouldn't know it if you were sitting in any of its three secluded courtyards. Guests tend to like the atmosphere a lot. The hotel's buildings have a colorful history: The license a former owner took out to make the place a bordello is proudly displayed in the bar, and its proprietors are happy to admit that ghosts have been sighted on the premises. The hotel's back buildings were once the studio of John James Audubon, and the "patio rooms" across the street from the main building were originally built in 1834 as the home of New Orleans merchant Samuel Herrmann. Rooms are nice enough, with feather pillows and marble bathrooms, and period-style furniture.

415 Dauphine St., New Orleans, LA 70112. (C) **800/508-5554** or 504/586-1800. Fax 504/586-1409. www.dauphineorleans.com. 111 units. $149–$269 double; $149–$289 patio room; $179–$399 suite. Rates include continental breakfast and afternoon tea with welcome drink coupon. Extra person $20. Children under 17 stay free in parents' room. AE, DC, DISC, MC, V. Valet parking $18. **Amenities:** Bar; outdoor pool; small fitness room; Jacuzzi; concierge; complimentary French Quarter and downtown transportation; babysitting; laundry; dry cleaning; guest library. *In room:* A/C, TV, minibar.

Hotel Monteleone 👉👉   Opened in 1886, the Monteleone is the largest hotel in the French Quarter (and was home to Truman Capote's parents when he was born!), and it seems to keep getting bigger without losing a trace of its trademark charm. Because of its size, you can almost always get a reservation here, even when other places are booked. Everyone who stays here loves it, probably because its staff is among the most helpful in town. One recent guest who stayed here with a child with disabilities raved about the facilities.

Until recently, the big problem was the inconsistency among the rooms. But all are being freshly renovated (all but the middle section should be finished by the time you're reading this), but there is still some difference in terms of size and style. Which should you choose? Beats us—some of the new rooms sparkle, others are sort of bland, and the old ones have a faded gentility, in a *Barton Fink* 1940s way. Rooms in the 60s are near the ice machine; rooms from 56 to 59 are slightly bigger (but the bathrooms aren't the new marble) with old high ceilings. Executive suites are just big rooms but have the nicest new furniture, including four-poster beds and Jacuzzis.

One of the city's best-kept secrets is the roof-top pool; on a recent visit, we were among a handful of folks lounging on the flower-filled deck high above the street noise, with unencumbered views of the city and beyond.

214 Royal St., New Orleans, LA 70130. (C) **800/535-9595** or 504/523-3341. Fax 504/561-5803. www.hotel monteleone.com. 573 units. $169–$230 double; $360–$975 suite. Extra person $25. Children under 18 stay free in parents' room. Package rates available. AE, DC, DISC, MC, V. Valet parking $19 car, $21 small SUV. **Amenities:** 3 restaurants; 2 bars (for info on the Carousel Bar, see p. 240); heated rooftop swimming pool (open year-round); fitness center (understocked but with fabulous views of the city and river); Jacuzzi; sauna; concierge; room service 6:30am–11pm; babysitting; laundry. *In room:* A/C, TV, dataport, minibar, coffeemaker, hair dryer, iron, safe.

Hotel Ste. Hélène 👉 *Value*   Being in the shadow of the Omni Royal Orleans, its grand across-the-street neighbor, the Hotel Ste. Hélène could easily be overlooked. But in our opinion, this is what a slightly funky Quarter hotel should be—and you can't beat its close-to-Jackson-Square location. Having said that, the accommodations are a mixed bag. The main hotel has a definite odd New Orleans charm, if you find dark, tiny, and funky charming. The property winds about several buildings (including one down St. Louis Street that has some dynamite suites of such size and classic elegant style you might feel you are in a Merchant-Ivory movie—the best value for high-end money in town, we think). Throughout are interior and exterior courtyards (some with flickering gas lamps) that rooms overlook (interior rooms have windows only on the atrium).

Impressions

There is something left in this people here that makes them like one another, that leads to constant outbursts of the spirit of play, that keeps them from being too confoundedly serious about death and the ballot and reform and other less important things in life.

—Sherwood Anderson, *New Orleans and the Double-Dealer*

Rooms also vary in size and style. Front rooms have balconies overlooking the street; others have beds set in alcoves (we find it romantic, though you might find it claustrophobic) with a sort of low-rent parlor sitting area. Still others are just square rooms. Bathrooms can be tiny but are clean and modern. If some of the "antiques" are actually mock and the hangings and linens aren't all high-end, it still has a good feel to it. Ask for one of the larger street-facing rooms (like those on Chartres, which are also undergoing renovations).

508 Chartres St., New Orleans, LA 70130. ℂ 800/348-3888 or 504/522-5014. Fax 504/523-7140. www. melrosegroup.com. 26 units. $149–$350 double. AE, DC, DISC, MC, V. Parking (about $10) in nearby lot. **Amenities:** Continental breakfast; pool; babysitting; laundry service. In room: A/C, TV.

Lafitte Guest House

Here you'll find the best of both worlds: antique living just blocks from Bourbon Street mayhem (though the Lafitte's cute little parlor seems almost antithetical to rowdy merriment). The three-story brick building, with wrought-iron balconies on the second and third floors, was constructed in 1849 and has been completely restored. Thanks to new owners, there are ongoing upgrades (columns added to the lobby and so forth) plus better beds and new fixtures in the rooms. Each room has its own Victorian flair (though room nos. 5 and 40 have modern furnishings), with memorable touches such as pralines on the pillow, sleeping masks, and sound machines with soothing nature noises.

1003 Bourbon St., New Orleans, LA 70116. ℂ 800/331-7971 or 504/581-2678. Fax 504/581-2677. www.lafitteguesthouse.com. 14 units. $159–$219 double. Extra person $25. AE, DISC, MC, V. Parking $10. **Amenities:** Complimentary breakfast; 24-hr. concierge. In room: A/C, TV.

Maison Dupuy ⦿

We often forget to recommend this place, but that's a mistake. A little out of the main French Quarter action and a tad closer than some might like to dicey Rampart (though the hotel is entirely safe), the Maison Dupuy, with its seven town houses surrounding a good-size courtyard (and a heated pool), is still warm and inviting. While the rooms aren't remarkable, they are comfortable. Though floor space and balconies (with either courtyard or street views—the former is quieter) vary, the staff is most friendly and helpful, the courtyard of sufficiently pleasing ambience, and the location—a quieter end of the Quarter, near a bar with pool tables (a rarity in town)—puts it right in the middle of "oh, they've got rooms available? why not?" category. All that, plus a darn good restaurant (**Dominique's,** reviewed on p. 111) make this a recommendable place.

1001 Toulouse St., New Orleans, LA 70112. ℂ 800/535-9177 or 504/586-8000. Fax 504/525-5334. www.maisondupuy.com. 200 units. $99–$269 superior double; $149–$299 deluxe double with balcony; $329–$838 suite. AE, DC, DISC, MC, V. Valet parking $18 when available. **Amenities:** Restaurant; bar; heated outdoor pool; health club; concierge; room service 6am–midnight; babysitting; same-day laundry/dry cleaning. In room: A/C, TV, minibar.

Omni Royal Orleans ⦿⦿ (Kids)

Despite being part of a chain, this is an elegant hotel that escapes feeling sterile and generic. This is only proper given that it is on the former site of the venerable 1836 St. Louis Exchange Hotel, one of the country's premier hostelries and a center of New Orleans social life until the final years of the Civil War. The original building was finally destroyed by a 1915 hurricane, but the Omni, built in 1960, is a worthy successor, enjoying a prime location smack in the center of the Quarter. Truman Capote and William Styron have stayed here, and there is a Tennessee Williams suite. Furnishings in the guest rooms have grave good taste, full of muted tones and plush furniture, with windows that let you look dreamily out over the Quarter. Suites are vast, making this a good choice for families. Service is swift and conscientious—altogether an especially worthwhile choice.

621 St. Louis St., New Orleans, LA 70140. ✆ **800/THE-OMNI** in the U.S. and Canada, or 504/529-5333. Fax 504/529-7089. www.omniroyalorleans.com. 360 units. $199–$339 double; $339–$800 suite; $1,100 penthouse. Children under 18 stay free in parents' room. AE, DC, DISC, MC, V. Valet parking $21. **Amenities:** Restaurant; 2 bars; heated outdoor pool; health club; concierge; business center; salon; barber shops; 24-hr. room service; massage; babysitting; emergency mending and pressing; florist; sundries shop and newsstand; complimentary shoe shine. *In room:* A/C, TV, dataport, minibar, coffeemaker, iron, ironing board.

St. Louis ⚜ Right in the heart of the Quarter, the St. Louis is a small hotel that surrounds a lush courtyard with a fountain. But it's somewhat disappointingly dull for what ought to be a charming boutique hotel. Some rooms have private balconies overlooking Bienville Street, and all open onto the central courtyard. Rooms are undergoing a remodeling and getting new carpet, drapes, and furniture, which should freshen up a slightly stodgy decor by the time you read this. The otherwise uninteresting bathrooms do have bidets.

730 Bienville St., New Orleans, LA 70130. ✆ **800/535-9111** or 504/581-7300. Fax 504/679-5013. www.stlouishotel.com. 83 units. $145–$335 double; $345–$375 suite. Children under 18 stay free in parents' room. AE, DC, MC, V. Valet parking $19. **Amenities:** Restaurant; access to nearby health club; concierge; room service from restaurant at breakfast; laundry. *In room:* A/C, TV.

Wyndham New Orleans at Canal Place ⚜ At the foot of Canal Street, the Wyndham is technically *in* the French Quarter—but not quite *of* it. It is literally *above* the Quarter: The grand-scale lobby, with its fine paintings and antiques, is on the 11th floor of the Canal Place tower. The guest rooms are on the floors above; each has a marble foyer and bathroom, fine furnishings (including particularly good pillows), and phones with call-waiting and voicemail. Needless to say, this hotel provides some of the city's most expansive views of the river and the French Quarter.

100 Iberville St., New Orleans, LA 70130. ✆ **800/996-3426** or 504/566-7006. Fax 504/553-5120. www.wyndham.com. 437 units. $169–$419 double. Ask about packages and specials. AE, DISC, MC, V. On site parking $25 a day. **Amenities:** Restaurant; bar; heated pool; privileges at a nearby 18-hole golf course; concierge; tour desk; 24-hr. room service; laundry; dry cleaning; direct elevator access to Canal Place shopping center, where guests can use the health center free of charge, or visit the barber shop, salon, and stores. *In room:* A/C, TV, dataports, minibar, coffeemaker, hair dryer, iron.

MODERATE

Bienville House ⚜⚜ A nice little Quarter hotel, better than most (thanks to a combo of location, price, and room quality) though not as good as some (owing to a lack of specific personality). It's generally sedate, except perhaps during Mardi Gras, when the mad gay revelers take over—as they do everywhere, truth be told. The truly friendly and helpful staff adds a lot of welcoming spirit. Rooms mostly have high ceilings; kings have four-poster beds and slightly more interesting furniture than doubles. Some rooms have balconies overlooking the small courtyard that features a good pool for a dip (though the back gate looks out onto a busy street), and all have the standard amenities of a fine hotel. Note that the Iberville Suite is so large it actually made us laugh out loud—and we mean that in a good way.

320 Decatur St., New Orleans, LA 70130. ✆ **800/535-7836** or 504/529-2345. Fax 504/525-6079. www.bienvillehouse.com. 83 units. $89–$650 double. Rates include continental breakfast. AE, DC, DISC, MC, V. Valet parking $15 cars, $19 sport-utility vehicles. **Amenities:** Gamay restaurant (see p. 112 for full review); outdoor pool; room service from Gamay, Tue–Sat 5–10pm. *In room:* A/C, TV, dataport, coffeemaker, hair dryer, iron.

Bourbon Orleans Hotel—A Wyndham Historic Hotel ⚜ A lot of hotels claim to be centrally located in the French Quarter, but the Bourbon Orleans really is. The place takes up an entire block of prime real estate at the intersection of—guess where—Bourbon and Orleans streets. And, while many hotels *claim* to have an interesting history, this one actually does: The oldest part of the hotel is the Orleans Ballroom, constructed in 1815 as a venue for the city's masquerade, carnival, and quadroon balls. In 1881, the building was sold to the Sisters of the Holy Family, members of the South's first order of African-American nuns. The sisters converted the ballroom into a school and remained for 80 years until the building was sold to real estate developers from Baton Rouge, who turned it into an apartment hotel.

Today, the hotel occupies three buildings, and we wish it had more character to go along with its fascinating history. The public spaces are lavishly decorated, but their elegant interest doesn't quite extend to the rather standard guest rooms. Bigger than average, they will give no cause for complaint about either decor or comfort, but you can't help wanting something a little more striking. If you want to escape the excitement of Bourbon Street during your non-waking hours, ask for an interior room.

717 Orleans St., New Orleans, LA 70116. ℂ 504/523-2222. Fax 504/525-8166. www.bourbonorleans.com. 216 units. $125–$198 petite queen or twin; $145–$219 deluxe king or double; $188–$262 junior suite; $241–$398 town house suite; $272–$482 town house suite with balcony. Extra person $20. AE, DC, DISC, MC, V. Valet parking $25. **Amenities:** Restaurant; bar; outdoor pool; concierge; room service 6:30am–10pm; same-day dry cleaning; nightly shoe shine. *In room:* A/C, TV, fax, dataport, coffeemaker, hair dryer, iron, optional voice mail.

Bourgoyne Guest House (Value   This is an eccentric place, with an owner to match. If you dislike stuffy hotels and will happily take things a little worn at the edges in exchange for a relaxed, hangout atmosphere, come here. Accommodations are arranged around a nicely cluttered courtyard, the right spot to visit and regroup before diving back out onto Bourbon Street (whose main action begins just a few feet away). Studios are adequate little rooms with kitchens and bathrooms that appear grimy but are not (we saw the strong potions housekeeping uses; it's just a result of age). The Green Suite is as big and grand as one would like with huge tall rooms, a second smaller bedroom, a bigger bathroom, and a balcony overlooking Bourbon Street. For price and location, it's a heck of a deal, maybe the best in the Quarter. The first floor can suffer from street noise, though that probably depends on the time of year and how far up Bourbon the party travels.

839 Bourbon St., New Orleans, LA 70116. ℂ 504/525-3983 or 504/524-3621. 5 apts. $92 studio double; La Petite Suite $120 double; Green Suite $130 double, $160 triple, $190 quad. MC, V. *In room:* A/C, unstocked fridge, coffeemaker, iron.

Cornstalk Hotel ⭐   Thanks to the famous fence out front, this might be better known as a sightseeing stop than a place to stay, but consider staying here anyway. A gorgeous Victorian home on the National Register of Historic Places, it's nearly as pretty inside as out. Additionally, the location couldn't be better—it's almost at the exact heart of the Quarter on a busy (but not noisy) section of Royal.

The requisite antiques dominate; if you are looking for period charm, look no further. The high-ceilinged rooms have fireplaces or stained-glass windows, and some have plasterwork (ceiling medallions, scrolls, and cherubs) from old plantations. One room (the one with the largest bed) is spectacular, while the rest are charming—you feel as if you have gone back 100 years. Unfortunately, that also applies to things like the plumbing (though apparently they've done some renovating and complaints are down). The large front gallery, set unusually far back from the street, and the upstairs balcony provide perfect spots for sipping coffee in the morning or sherry after a hard day's shopping.

Oh, the fence? Well, it's at least 130 years old (photos indicate it might be even older), is made of cast iron, and looks like cornstalks painted in the appropriate colors. When it was a private home, Harriet Beecher Stowe stayed here—a trip that inspired her to write *Uncle Tom's Cabin.*

915 Royal St., New Orleans, LA. 70116. ✆ **504/523-1515.** Fax 504/522-5558. www.travelguides.com/cornstalk. 14 units. $75–$185 double. AE, MC, V. Limited parking $15. **Amenities:** Continental breakfast. *In room:* A/C, TV.

Hôtel Provincial ✿
Don't mention this to the owners, who are sensitive about it, but word from the ghost tours is that the Provincial is haunted, mostly by soldiers treated here when it was a Civil War hospital. It must not be too much of a problem, though, because guests rave about the hotel and never mention ghostly visitors. With flickering gas lamps, no elevators, no fewer than five patios, and a tranquil setting, this feels less like a hotel than a guesthouse. Both the quiet and the terrific service belie its size, so it seems smaller and more intimate than it is. It's also in a good part of the Quarter on a quiet street off the beaten path. For views of the river (plus higher ceilings), get a room on the third or fourth floor of the back building. Some rooms have half-tester beds (the furniture is a mix of antique and repros). Regular rooms are dark but roomy. Finally, with such a pretty pool area, it's a shame there isn't much in the way of lounging or shade.

1024 Chartres St., New Orleans, LA 70116. ✆ **800/535-7922** or 504/581-4995. Fax 504/581-1018. www.hotelprovincial.com. 94 units. $79–$289 double. Packages available. AE, DC, DISC, MC, V. Valet parking $15. **Amenities:** Restaurant; bar; pool. *In room:* A/C, TV, dataport, iron.

Hotel St. Marie
Location, location, location. Just a little above Bourbon Street on an otherwise quiet street, this hotel—part of the group that also owns the Prince Conti and the Place d'Armes (see below)—should be on your list of "clean and safe backup places to stay if my top choices are full." Surrounding a sterile courtyard with a drab pool (which you will nonetheless bless the heavens for in summer), rooms are generic New Orleans in dark colors, with standard-issue, mock-European hotel furniture. Note that king rooms are more pleasant than doubles, and corner rooms are more spacious, which includes the otherwise dinky bathrooms (a few of which have these odd red lights that could really cause major ocular damage). Some rooms have balconies overlooking the street and courtyard. Hallways are not numbered and can be dim, which could make a tipsy late-night return a challenge.

827 Toulouse St., New Orleans, LA 70112. ✆ **800/366-2743** or 504/561-8951. Fax 504/571-2802. www.hotelstmarie.com. 100 units. $150–$170 double. AE, DC, DISC, MC, V. Valet parking $20. **Amenities:** Restaurant; bar; room service (during dining room hours); laundry; dry cleaning. *In room:* A/C, TV.

Hotel Villa Convento ✿
Local tour guides say this was the original House of the Rising Sun bordello, so if you have a sense of humor (or theater), be sure to pose in your bathrobe on your balcony so that you can be pointed out to passing tour groups. With its rather small public spaces and the personal attention that its owners and operators, the Campo family, give to their guests, the Villa Convento has the feel of a small European inn or guesthouse and does a lot of repeat business. The building is a Creole town house; some rooms open onto the tropical patio, others to the street, and many have balconies. The loft rooms are unique family quarters with a king-size bed on the entry level and twin beds in the loft.

616 Ursulines St., New Orleans, LA 70116. ✆ **800/887-2817** or 504/522-1793. Fax 504/524-1902. www.villaconvento.com. 25 units. $89–$105 double; $155 suite. Extra person $10. Rates include continental breakfast. AE, DC, DISC, MC, V. Parking $6. *In room:* A/C, TV, hair dryer, iron.

Lamothe House ⓖ★   Somehow, a shiny new hotel doesn't seem quite right for New Orleans. More appropriate is slightly faded, somewhat threadbare elegance, and the Lamothe House neatly fits that bill. The Creole-style plain facade of this 1840s town house hides the atmosphere you are looking for—a mossy, brick-lined courtyard with a fish-filled fountain and banana trees and rooms filled with antiques that are worn in the right places but not shabby. A continental breakfast is served in a second-floor dining room that just screams faded gentility. (As the, alas, sometimes cranky staff points out, it's not Victorian style; it *is* Victorian.) It's a short walk to the action in the Quarter and just a couple of blocks to the bustling Frenchmen scene in the Faubourg Marigny. On a steamy night, sitting in the courtyard breathing the fragrant air, you can feel yourself slip out of time.

621 Esplanade Ave., New Orleans, LA 70116. Ⓒ **800/367-5858** or 504/947-1161. Fax 504/943-6536. www.new-orleans.org. 30 units. $64–$275 double. Rates include breakfast. AE, DISC, MC, V. Free parking, except special events. **Amenities:** Pool. *In room:* A/C, TV.

Le Richelieu Hotel ⓖ★ *(Kids)*   First a row mansion, then a macaroni factory, and now a hotel, this building has seen it all. It's at the Esplanade edge of the Quarter—a perfect spot from which to explore the Faubourg Marigny. Le Richelieu is good for families (despite the surcharge for children), being out of the adult action and with a nice pool. The McCartney family thought so; Paul, the late Linda, and their kids stayed here for some months long ago while Wings was recording an album. Management is proudest of the enormous VIP suite—a sort of early-'70s-style apartment with three bedrooms, large bathrooms, a kitchen, a living room, a dining area, and even a steam room. Other rooms are standard high-end motel rooms. Many have balconies, and all overlook either the French Quarter or the courtyard. Le Richelieu is the only hotel in the French Quarter with free self-parking on the premises.

1234 Chartres St., New Orleans, LA 70116. Ⓒ **800/535-9653** or 504/529-2492. Fax 504/524-8179. www.lerichelieuhotel.com. 84 units. $95–$180 double; $200–$550 suite. Extra person or child $15. French Quarter Explorer and honeymoon packages available. AE, DC, DISC, MC, V. Parking $20. **Amenities:** Restaurant; bar; outdoor pool; steam room; concierge; room service 7am–9pm. *In room:* A/C, TV, unstocked fridge, hair dryer, iron.

Olde Victorian Inn ⓖ★★   While long-time clients might have been initially anxious when their beloved P. J. Holbrook retired and sold her business, they soon learned that current owners Keith and Andre West-Harrison took her legacy very seriously. "We changed nothing because the guests loved it, and it works." It certainly works for us. Decor (cutesy, quaint, and cluttered—expect doilies and teddy bears) remains untouched, as do P.J.'s legendary breakfasts, which are made according to P.J.'s own recipes—the inn happily boasts that they can go 30 days without repeating a menu (on a recent visit, they stuffed us with goodies like Creole pancakes topped with peaches poached in homemade vanilla). The yellow Chantilly room (with a balcony overlooking the park) is a favorite (and a bit less fussy). Rooms at the back have bigger bathrooms. The owners brim over with joy for their job, and you quickly feel like a welcome guest in their home. They also have three sweet, well-behaved dogs (not allowed in the rooms) that are equally gracious hosts.

As if visiting here isn't treat enough, the inn now has **Miss Celie's Spa Orleans,** just the cutest little day spa with a touch of Victorian beauty parlor, offering not only mani-pedis but also massage, facials, and even hair stylings (www.spaorleans.com).

914 N. Rampart St., New Orleans, LA 70116. ℂ **800/725-2446** or 504/522-2446. Fax 504/522-8646. www.oldevictorianinn.com. 6 units. $120–$175 double. Rates include full breakfast. Senior discount and weekly rates available. AE, DC, DISC, MC, V. Parking available on street. *In room:* A/C.

Place d'Armes Hotel 𝔊 *Kids*   Parts of this hotel seem a bit grim and old, though its quite large courtyard and amoeba-shaped pool are ideal for hanging out and may make up for it. Plus, it's only half a block from the Café du Monde (p. 145)—very convenient when you need a beignet at 3am. This also makes it a favorite for families traveling with kids. Rooms are homey and furnished in traditional style; however, 32 of them do not have windows and can be cell-like—be sure to ask for a room with a window when you reserve. Breakfast is served in a breakfast room, and the location, just off Jackson Square, makes sightseeing a breeze.

625 St. Ann St., New Orleans, LA 70116. ℂ **800/366-2743** or 504/524-4531. Fax 504/571-3803. www.placedarmes.com. 80 units. $120–$190 double; $190 courtyard room. Rates include continental breakfast. AE, DC, DISC, MC, V. Parking (next door) $16. **Amenities:** Outdoor pool. *In room:* A/C, TV, hair dryer, iron.

Prince Conti Hotel 𝔊   This tiny but friendly hotel with a marvelously help-ful staff (some of whom are decent tour guides in their off hours) is in a great location right off Bourbon and not generally noisy. Second-floor rooms all have fresh striped wallpaper and antiques, but quality varies from big canopy beds to painted iron bedsteads. Bathrooms can be ultra-tiny, with the toilet virtually on top of the sink. Travelers with kids should stay at the hotel's sister location, the Place d'Armes (see above), because it is farther from Bourbon and has a pool.

830 Conti St., New Orleans, LA 70112. ℂ **800/366-2743** or 504/529-4172. Fax 504/581-3802. www.prince contihotel.com. 53 units. $150 double; $215 suite. AE, DC, DISC, MC, V. Valet parking $20. **Amenities:** Restaurant; piano bar; breakfast cafe; room service 7–10am; laundry service. *In room:* A/C, TV, iron.

INEXPENSIVE
New Orleans Guest House   Run for more than 10 years by Ray Cronk and Alvin Payne, this guesthouse is a little off the beaten path (just outside the French Quarter across North Rampart St.), but it's painted a startling hot, Pepto-Bismol pink, so it's hard to miss.

There are rooms in the old Creole main house (1848) and in what used to be the slave quarters. Rooms are simple—call it motel Victorian, with small bath-rooms that are more motel than Victorian. Each has a unique color scheme (not hot pink, in case you were worried). Room no. 7, with its own private balcony, is perhaps the nicest. The courtyard is a veritable tropical garden with a banana tree, more green plants than you can count, some intricately carved old foun-tains, and a couple of fluffy cats. Also in the courtyard are beer and soda vend-ing machines and an icemaker.

1118 Ursulines St., New Orleans, LA 70116. ℂ **800/562-1177** or 504/566-1177. Fax 504/566-1179. www.neworleans.com/nogh. 14 units. $69–$89 double; $79–$109 queen or twin; $99–$119 king or 2 full beds. Rates include continental breakfast. Extra person $25. AE, MC, V. Free parking. *In room:* A/C, TV, hair dryer, iron, safe.

2 The Faubourg Marigny

The Faubourg Marigny is a very distinct neighborhood from the French Quar-ter, though they border each other and are just an easy walk apart. This arty and bohemian neighborhood may be better for a younger crowd who wants to be near the French Quarter without actually being in it.

For hotels in this section, see the "New Orleans Accommodations" map on p. 66.

MODERATE

B&W Courtyards Bed & Breakfast ★★
The deceptively simple facade hides a sweet and very hospitable little B&B, complete with two small courtyards and a fountain. It's located in the Faubourg Marigny next to the bustling nighttime Frenchmen scene, a 10-minute walk or $5 cab ride (at most) to the Quarter. Owners Rob Boyd and Kevin Wu went to ingenious lengths to turn six oddly shaped spaces into comfortable rooms. No two rooms are alike—you enter one through its bathroom. Another room is more like a small, two-story apartment with the bedroom upstairs and a virtually full kitchen downstairs. All are carefully and thoughtfully decorated (check out the remote-control ceiling fans!). Rob and Kevin are adept at giving advice—and strong opinions—not just about the city but about their own local favorites. Breakfast is light (fruit, homemade breads) but beautifully presented. Prepare to be pampered—they take good care of you here.

2425 Chartres St., New Orleans, LA 70117. © **800/585-5731** or 504/945-9418. Fax 504/949-3483. www.bandwcourtyards.com. 8 units. $99–$750 double. Rates include continental breakfast. AE, DISC, MC, V. Free parking available on street. **Amenities:** Jacuzzi; business center. *In room:* A/C, TV, dataport, coffeemaker, hair dryer, iron, safe.

Dauphine Inn ★★
Just about as perfect a B&B as you could want, hidden, as most are in this neighborhood, behind an unassuming facade. But inside is a large, 100-year-old home, including parlors with a perfect combination of period pieces and modern shabby chic, accented by the owner's collection of chirpy pet birds. Rooms—done in sterling taste, with every aesthetic and comfort attended to—are named after local drinks; we are torn between our love for the green Absinthe room (which can be turned into a suite with the adjoining bedroom) and the larger (king-size four-poster bed) yellow Sazerac room. All have pretty, if sometimes small, bathrooms, DVD and CD players (and a library full of options for same), and sweet touches (pillow candy, rubber duckies for the bathtub, and sound machines offering up waves or rain to help you sleep even more soundly) at every turn. The owner went to culinary school to prepare for her breakfast guests, so enjoy those home-baked goodies.

2001 Dauphine St., New Orleans, LA. 70116. © **877/543-7583** or 504/943-0515. Fax 504/948-9926. www.thedauphineinn.com. 3 units. $89–$145 (higher for special events). **Amenities:** Breakfast; DVD and CD library. *In room:* AC, TV, hair dryer, DVD/CD Players, SoundSpa radio, high-speed Internet modem, voicemail.

The Frenchmen ★
This small, sweet, and slightly funky inn is very popular with in-the-know regular visitors. It's not for some, but others become loyal repeat customers. The Frenchmen feels out of the way, but in some respects, the location can't be beat. It's just across from the Quarter and a block away from the main drag of the Frenchmen section of the Faubourg Marigny, where all sorts of clubs and happenings make for a lively night scene.

Housed in two 19th-century buildings that were once grand New Orleans homes, the rooms are each individually decorated and furnished with antiques. They vary in size considerably, however, and some are very small indeed. Standard rooms have one double bed, some rooms have private balconies, and others have a loft bedroom with a sitting area. A small pool and Jacuzzi are in the inn's tropical courtyard, where you can often find guests hanging out at night, talking over the day's activities, planning what they are about to do next, or just making a night of it right there.

417 Frenchmen St. (at Esplanade Ave.), New Orleans, LA 70116. © **800/831-1781** or 504/948-2166. Fax 504/948-2258. www.frenchmenhotel.com. 27 units. $49–$155 double. Rates include breakfast. AE, DISC, MC, V. Free parking, except special events. **Amenities:** Pool; Jacuzzi. *In room:* A/C, TV.

INEXPENSIVE

Royal Street Inn & R Bar ⚲   This is an offbeat, happening little establishment in a residential neighborhood with plenty of street parking and regular police patrols. It's loose but not disorganized, and there couldn't be a better choice for laid-back travelers. Breakfast isn't served, but the inn still bills itself as a B&B. That's because here B&B stands for bed-and-*beverage*—the lobby is the highly enjoyable **R Bar** (p. 243). You check in with the bartender, and as a guest, you get two complimentary cocktails. The right guests—the only kind who will be happy here—will want to hang out in the bar all night. And why not? It's that kind of place.

Regular rooms are small but cute, like a bedroom in a real house but with doors that open directly to the street. Suites are the best value near the Quarter. They're well sized, accommodating up to four (though not without some loss of privacy), and feature kitchenettes as well as their own names and stories. The Ghost in the Attic is a big room (complete with a mural of said ghost) with sloping ceilings, pleasing for those with starving-artist garret fantasies who don't like to give up good furniture. All beds and linens have been recently upgraded, and new murals grace some of the rooms.

1431 Royal St., New Orleans, LA 70116. ✆ **800/449-5535** or 504/948-7499. Fax 504/943-9880. www. royalstreetinn.com. 5 units. $90 double; $130 suite. Price includes tax; rates include bar beverage. AE, DISC, MC, V. Street parking available—purchase special needed permit from the management. **Amenities:** Bar. *In room:* A/C, TV.

3 Mid-City/Esplanade

For hotels in this section, see the "Mid-City Accommodations & Dining" map on p. 83.

EXPENSIVE

The House on Bayou Road ⚲⚲⚲   If you want to stay in a rural and romantic plantation setting but still be near the French Quarter, try the House on Bayou Road, quite probably the most smashing guesthouse in town. Just off Esplanade Avenue, this intimate Creole plantation home, built in the late 1700s for a colonial Spanish diplomat, has been restored by owner Cynthia Reeves, who oversees an operation of virtual perfection.

Each room has its own charm and is individually decorated to a fare-thee-well—slightly cluttered, not quite fussy, but still lovingly done aesthetic. The Bayou St. John Room (the old library) holds a queen-size four-poster bed and has a working fireplace; the Bayou Delacroix has the same kind of bed and a wonderfully large bathtub. The large cottage has three rooms that can be rented separately or together (perfect for a large family). The small Creole cottage is a great romantic getaway spot complete with a porch with a swing and rocking chairs.

The unusually extensive grounds are beautifully manicured, and there's an outdoor pool, Jacuzzi, patio, and screened-in porch. Expect a hearty plantation-style breakfast, and during the day and in the evening there's access to a mini-fridge filled with beverages.

2275 Bayou Rd., New Orleans, LA 70119. ✆ **800/882-2968** or 504/945-0992. Fax 504/945-0993. www.house onbayouroad.com. 8 units, 2 cottages. $155–$320 double. Rates include full breakfast. AE, MC, V. Free off-street parking. **Amenities:** Restaurant; outdoor pool; Jacuzzi. *In room:* A/C, dataport, minibar, hair dryer, iron.

MODERATE

Ashton's Bed & Breakfast ⚲   This charming guesthouse has been undergoing renovations of late and is a fine and worthy alternative to some of its more

Mid-City Accommodations & Dining

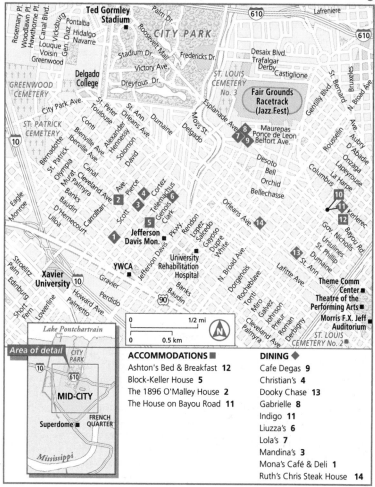

ACCOMMODATIONS ■
Ashton's Bed & Breakfast **12**
Block-Keller House **5**
The 1896 O'Malley House **2**
The House on Bayou Road **11**

DINING ◆
Cafe Degas **9**
Christian's **4**
Dooky Chase **13**
Gabrielle **8**
Indigo **11**
Liuzza's **6**
Lola's **7**
Mandina's **3**
Mona's Café & Deli **1**
Ruth's Chris Steak House **14**

costly compatriots. Decor is a bit grandma-fussy, but we love the nice touch of seasonal decorations in the rooms. One room has a most inviting fluffy white bed, but its bathroom is contained in a curtained-off corner, while another room has merely partitioned off an area for the same. Those with personal-space and privacy issues might want to head to room no. 3, which is most grand, with a four-poster bed and the nicest bathroom in the guesthouse, complete with a claw-foot tub. Virtually all the rooms have wide wooden floorboards. A full breakfast is served, featuring local dishes and flavors such as *pain perdu* and eggs Sardou.

2023 Esplanade Ave., New Orleans, LA 70116. ℂ **800/725-4131** or 504/942-7048. Fax 504/947-9382. www.ashtonsbb.com. 6 units. $125–$155 double. Rates include full breakfast. AE, DISC, MC, V. Free parking. *In room:* A/C, TV, dataport, minibar, hair dryer, iron.

Block-Keller House ⋆⋆ One of two B&Bs in the up-and-coming Mid-City area (sure to become even more popular when the streetcar starts running this way in 2003), this inn is extensively restored with an eye toward both guest comfort and preservation of the full Victorian excess. It's a splendid choice for someone who wants both the classic Victorian B&B experience (look for Victorian excess in the front rooms' gorgeous details) but also guiltily wants a room with modern amenities (Berber carpet, Jacuzzi tubs, and the like). If that's you, stay upstairs or in the newly remodeled bottom level—which was smartly transformed from a grungy basement into a soothing haven with immaculate bathrooms, pale mint walls, and handsome sepia-tone photographs of the rural South. (This would be our base for a lengthy business travel stay.)

However, if you do desire the traditional, ground-floor rooms, with fireplaces and grand old beds, are for you. You'll find comfy communal sitting areas upstairs and in the bottom level. Room nos. 5 and 6 are large (for those with personal space issues), while room no. 4 has a window seat. The hosts are very experienced in B&B running, and it shows in everything they do, including the continental breakfast, which during our stay included feather-light buttermilk biscuits, hard-cooked eggs, fresh cantaloupe and strawberries, and all the trappings. All in all, this place is perfect in looks, style, and service—plus, it's a block away from Mandina's restaurant (p. 129). And say hello for us to Milo, the resident black lab, and his new best friend, Buster the yellow lab pup.

3620 Canal St., New Orleans, LA 70119. ✆ 877/588-3033 or 504/483-3033. Fax 504/483-3032. www.block kellerhouse.com. 9 units. $90–$125. Includes breakfast. AE, MC, V. **Amenities:** Continental breakfast; Internet access. *In room:* A/C, TV.

The 1896 O'Malley House ✦ This is another beautifully restored home turned B&B, in a building dating back to, you guessed it, 1896. Many of the original details, including marvelous tile on the various fireplaces in several of the rooms, are still intact. Second-floor rooms are larger, and most have Jacuzzi tubs. The third floor is a clever use of design and space, with formerly dull wood walls turned most striking by pickling the wood to a lighter color (ask to see the photos of the mysterious science equations found scrawled on one wall). These rooms are smaller and more garretlike, though, frankly, they pale in desirability only if you really *really* want that classic high-ceilinged look. The first floor houses the parlor/sitting area as well as the owners' real estate business (separated from the main B&B by a hallway). Although it's located on a dull stretch of street, the B&B is also mere minutes from a lovely section of Canal.

120 S. Pierce St., New Orleans, LA 70119. ✆ 866/226-1896 or 504/488-5896. www.1896omalleyhouse.com. 8 units. $89–$195. AE, MC, V. Pet friendly. **Amenities:** Continental breakfast. *In room:* A/C, TV, dataport, hair dryer and iron on request.

4 Central Business District

For hotels in this section, please see the "New Orleans Accommodations" map on p. 66.

VERY EXPENSIVE

The Fairmont New Orleans ✦✦ New Orleanians still sometimes think of this as the Roosevelt, and today's Fairmont Hotel upholds its predecessor's tradition of elegance. The marbled and columned lobby runs a full block and is famous for its over-the-top decorations at Christmas time. (Pres. Bill Clinton stayed here for many of his New Orleans overnights.)

Rooms are done with pleasant if dull good taste—just fine for business or if you don't demand much personality. Big TVs, good mattresses, even better cotton sheets and down pillows, plus high ceilings make this place much more comfortable and less stuffy than similar rooms at peer hotels. Note that some of the suites are positively enormous (and the hotel has so many suites that they'll often offer upgrades for a nominal fee). For the business traveler, the Fairmont offers in-room computer hookups and fax machines in the suites.

123 Baronne St., New Orleans, LA 70112. (C) 800/441-1414 or 504/529-7111. Fax 504/529-4764. www. fairmont.com. 700 units. $109–$330 double. Extra person $30. AE, DC, DISC, MC, V. Valet parking $19. **Amenities:** Restaurant; 2 bars (including the Sazerac Bar and Grill; see p. 133); brand-new rooftop outdoor pool; tennis courts; rooftop health club (small but sporting enough machines); concierge; tour desk; activities desk; business center; gift shop; salon; 24-hr. room service; massage; babysitting; laundry service; newsstand; currency exchange. *In room:* A/C, TV, dataport, hair dryer, iron.

Hilton New Orleans Riverside Hotel ⭐ (Kids)   The Hilton is in the neighborhood of the Windsor Court (see below) but in a more central location—right at the riverfront near the World Trade Center of New Orleans, the New Orleans Convention Center, and the Aquarium. It's a self-contained complex of nearly a dozen restaurants, bistros, and bars; two gift shops; a full and exceptional racquet and health club; a huge exhibition space; and no fewer than 38 conference rooms. In addition, Harrah's Casino and the Riverwalk Marketplace are accessible from the hotel's lobby, which contains a nine-story atrium. Given all that, this is a top choice for families—there is much in the way of child-friendly entertainment right in the hotel or within a block or two. Guest rooms are spacious, and many have fabulous views of the river or the city.

2 Poydras St., New Orleans, LA 70140. (C) 800/445-8667 or 504/561-0500. Fax 504/568-1721. www.new orleans.hilton.com. 1,600 units. $225–$475 double; $650–$2,000 suite. Special packages available. AE, DC, DISC, MC, V. Valet parking $25; self-parking $20. **Amenities:** 2 restaurants; 2 bars (for a listing of one of them, Pete Fountain's, see p. 234); concierge; airport transportation; 24-hr. room service; laundry, dry cleaning, and pressing service; eligible for membership ($27 for 3 days) in the hotel's Rivercenter Racquet and Health Club. *In room:* A/C, TV, dataport, minibar, coffeemaker, hair dryer, iron.

Hotel Inter-Continental ⭐   The red granite Hotel Inter-Continental rises from the heart of the Central Business District within walking distance of the French Quarter and the Mississippi River attractions. It's a favorite of groups (including rock groups; the Stones stayed here two tours ago) and conventions. You should consider it, too. Room renovations are ongoing. A strong, fresh decor features custom furniture; deep, rich colors (not precisely gaudy but strong); dark woods; lots of marble; better bathrooms; and many nice touches including "the best beds in town" (the mattresses are quite comfortable indeed) and some classy-looking amenities. These handsome rooms feel quite luxurious and are the best in the immediate area, though they're probably too stuffy for families. Some rooms have balconies that overlook the courtyard, although said courtyard is modern and industrial in appearance.

444 St. Charles Ave., New Orleans, LA 70130. (C) 800/327-0200 or 504/525-5566. Fax 504/523-7310. http://new-orleans.interconti.com. 482 units. $305–$325 double; $500–$2,000 suite. AE, DC, DISC, MC, V. Valet parking $25. **Amenities:** The Veranda Restaurant (p. 135), Pete's Pub serving lunch daily; bar; outdoor rooftop pool; health club (focusing on cardiovascular machines); concierge; business center; gift shop; barbershop and salon; 24-hr. room service; massage; laundry/dry cleaning service. *In room:* A/C, TV, dataport, minibar, coffeemaker, hair dryer, iron, safe.

Hyatt Regency ⭐   If your trip to New Orleans revolves around an event at the Superdome, you should consider the Hyatt. The hotel occupies a 32-story building with guest rooms surrounding a seemingly bottomless central atrium. The public spaces are in grand corporate style, and so, as you'd expect, the lobby cafes generally attract a lunchtime crowd from the Central Business District. (If

there's a Saints home game, however, expect to find a football crowd—the hotel's **Hyttops Sports Bar & Grill** is a popular hangout.) Guest rooms were clearly designed with the business traveler and the conventioneer in mind.

500 Poydras Plaza, New Orleans, LA 70113. © **800/233-1234** or 504/561-1234. Fax 504/587-4141. www.neworleans.hyatt.com. 1,184 units. $219–$244 double; $525–$1,000 suite. AE, DC, DISC, MC, V. Valet parking $18. **Amenities:** 2 restaurants; bar and grill; heated rooftop pool; exercise room; Jacuzzi; concierge; free shuttle service to the French Quarter; business center; gift shop; salon; room service during limited hours; babysitting; florist. *In room:* A/C, TV, dataport, hair dryer, iron.

Loft 523 ⭐

We bet you've never seen anything like this, not even in New York, from which these spacious loft-style units drew their inspiration. Loft 523, in an old carriage and dry-goods warehouse in the Central Business District, is the latest innovation from local developer Sean Cummings, whose International House, a block away (see below), continues to wow with edge and elegance. Each of the 18 lofts is a marvel of modern design, sort of a Jetson's-futuristic-meets-NYC-minimalist-fantasy. They are sleek and handsome, but those wanting plushy and overstuffed will be miserable as soon as they see the concrete floors. Beds are platforms, surprisingly comfortable with Frette linens (but just a chenille throw blanket over that; ask for the down comforters if the night brings a chill). A Sony CD/DVD Surround Sound system adds sonic warmth, and the bathrooms are so big you could fit the entire ReBirth Brass Band inside. (Check out that Agape "spoon" tub.) But here's where Cummings and company break from N.Y./L.A. detached cool: Throughout are reminders of the building's provenance—old wood planks form the floor downstairs, turn-of-the-20th-century tin ceiling tiles outfit the elevators, and columns from the old warehouse decorate the lounge. Note that room service is spotty— all the food comes from the International House's restaurant, down the street.

523 Gravier St., New Orleans, LA 70130. © **800/633-5770** or 504/200-6523. Fax 504/483-6522. www.loft523.com. 18 units, 3 of them penthouses. $259–$359 double; $859–$1100 suite. AE, MC, V. Valet parking $22. **Amenities:** Lounge; health club. *In room:* A/C, TV, hair dryer, iron, safe, wireless Internet access, remote-control stereo system.

JW Marriott Hotel New Orleans ⭐

The hotel formerly known as Le Meridian and ever so briefly as the New Orleans Grand is so committed to appearing classy that it covers the electrical cords of its lamps with shirred designer fabric. You can't fault the location on Canal right across from the Quarter (excellent for viewing Mardi Gras parades), but ultimately, it's elegant but boring—yes, we're spoiled—more for business travelers who don't plan on spending much time in their rooms (the public areas are far more grand than the actual rooms). Double rooms have extra wide twin beds (a sure sign they aren't catering to families), with a chaise lounge in the king room and sofas in doubles. Corner "deluxe" king rooms have extra windows for an additional view. Bathrooms are divided into two parts, with a large dressing area and a dinky toilet/tub space.

614 Canal St., New Orleans, LA 70130. © **888/364-1200** or 504/525-6500. Fax 504/586-1543. www. marriott.com. 494 units. $184–355 double; $1,000–$3,500 suite. AE, DC, DISC, MC, V. Valet parking $26. **Amenities:** Restaurant; 2 bars; heated outdoor pool; health club (offering free aerobics and spinning classes); sauna; 24-hr. concierge; business center; gift shop; salon; 24-hr. room service; massage; babysitting; laundry; dry cleaning; jewelry store; art gallery. *In room:* A/C, TV, dataport, minibar, coffeemaker, hair dryer, iron, safe.

Windsor Court ⭐⭐⭐

Condé Nast Traveler not long ago voted the Windsor Court the Best Hotel in North America (and probably did it a disservice— who, after all, could ever live up to such hype?). In any case, there may be a finer hotel on the continent, but it can't be found in New Orleans. The unassuming,

Spending the Night in Chains

For those of you who prefer the predictability of a chain hotel, there's a **Marriott** ✦ at 555 Canal St. at the edge of the Quarter (✆ **800/654-3990** or 504/581-1000).

In the Central Business District (CBD), check out the new **Holiday Inn Express,** 221 Carondelet St. (✆ **504-962-5572**), or consider the slightly spiffier **Cotton Exchange** next door at 231 Carondelet St. (which shares facilities with the Holiday Inn), in the historic building of the same name (✆ **504-962-5572**). **Residence Inn by Marriott** ✦, 345 St. Joseph St. (✆ **800/ 331-3131** or 504/522-1300), and a **Courtyard by Marriott** ✦, 300 Julia St. (✆ **504-598-9898**), are both a couple of blocks from the Convention Center. The brand-new **Homewood Suites,** at 409 Baronne St., is pretty dazzling, in a generic way (✆ **504/581-5599**), while the new **Quality Inn,** at 210 O'Keefe Ave., seems clean and fine (✆ **504/525-6800**).

The **Holiday Inn Downtown–Superdome** ✦ is, natch, right by the Superdome at 330 Loyola Ave. (✆ **800/HOLIDAY** or 504/581-1600).

And if all the rooms in town are booked, you might try to see if one of the chains down by the airport has something for you.

---

somewhat office-building exterior is camouflage for the quiet but posh delights found within. Two corridors downstairs are mini-galleries that display original 17th-, 18th-, and 19th-century art, and a plush reading area with an international newspaper rack is on the second floor. Everything is very, very chic and consequently just a little chilly. It's not too stiff for restless children, but it still feels more like a grownup hotel. The level of service is extraordinarily high; we doubt it could be much better were this Windsor Castle rather than Windsor Court.

The accommodations are exceptionally spacious, with classy, not flashy, decor. Almost all are suites (either really big, or downright huge) featuring large bay windows or a private balcony overlooking the river (get a river view if at all possible) or the city, a private foyer, a large living room, a bedroom with French doors, a large marble bathroom with particularly luxe amenities (plush robes, high-quality personal-care items, thick towels, a hamper, extra hair dryers), two dressing rooms, and a "petite kitchen."

300 Gravier St., New Orleans, LA 70130. ✆ **800/262-2662** or 504/523-6000. Fax 504/596-4749. www. windsorcourthotel.com. 324 units. $290–$400 standard double; $370–$505 junior suite; $400–$700 full suite; $700–$1,150 2-bedroom suite. Children under 12 stay free in parents' room. AE, DC, DISC, MC, V. Valet parking $22. **Amenities:** The Grill Room restaurant (p. 131); Polo Club Lounge; health club with resort-size pool, sauna, and steam room; concierge; 24-hr. suite service (much more than your average room service); in-room massage; laundry; dry cleaning. *In room:* A/C, TV, minibar, hair dryer, safe.

W New Orleans ✦✦   While we have strong feelings indeed about staying in more New Orleans–appropriate, site-specific accommodations, we cheerfully admit that this is one fun hotel, and what is New Orleans about if not fun? There are certainly no more playful rooms in town, done up as they are in reds, blacks, and golds—frosty chic, to be sure, but oh, so comfortable, thanks to feather everything (pillows, comforters, beds—and yes, allergy sufferers, they have foam alternatives). There are nifty amenities and gewgaws galore; suites offer little different from the rooms except more space and, indeed, more of everything (two TVs, two VCRs, two bathrooms, one Oujia board). Not all rooms have views, but the ones that do, especially those of the river, are outstanding. The ultra-chic bar was designed by hip bar/club owner Rande "Mr. Cindy Crawford" Gerber. We do wish this whole experience wasn't so, well, New York, but then again, we find ourselves having so much fun it's kinda hard to get all that worked up about it.

333 Poydras St., New Orleans, LA 70130. © **800/522-6963** or 504/525-9444. Fax 504/581-7179. www. whotels.com. 423 units. $469–$900 double. AE, DC, DISC, MC, V. Valet parking $28. **Amenities:** Restaurant; bar; swimming pool; fitness center; concierge; business services; 24-hr. room service; massage. *In room:* A/C, TV/VCR, minibar, coffeemaker, hair dryer, iron, safe, CD player.

EXPENSIVE

Alexa Hotel　This boutique hotel–wannabe is connected to the larger and more traditionally elegant Astor Crown Plaza by a series of corridors and elevators, which makes for confusion if no one at the front desk warns you about this or lets you know that all the major facilities—like the business center, health club, and pool—are over at the sister property. Then why, you may ask, should you stay here rather than there? It's cheaper. Rooms are narrow and small—as in you-can-kick-the-wall-at-the-end-of-the-bed-if-you-are-tall size, though the exposed brick wall and period-style furniture helps, as does the pretty dark marble in the petite, shower-only bathrooms. Rooms also contain a desk with a comfortable executive's chair and a dataport, and guests have access to two good restaurants, making this hotel a smart bet for the solo business traveler (rooms with two double beds are much too cramped) with no claustrophobia issues.

119 Royal St., New Orleans, Louisiana 70130. © **888/884-3366** or 504/962-0600. Fax 504/962-0601. www.alexahotelneworleans.com. 192 units. $99–$269 double; $450 suite. **Amenities:** Bourbon House Seafood restaurant (p. 109); bar; swimming pool; fitness room; concierge. *In room:* AC, TV, hair dryer, iron, safety deposit box.

Hotel Monaco ★★ *Kids*　There is much to like about this surprisingly whimsical boutique hotel, which recently took over (and beautifully preserved) the 1925 Masonic Temple. It's self-consciously quirky (check out the seashell fireplace in the lobby sitting area), but who cares when that translates to faux-fur throws on the beds (which also have down comforters and mosquito-net half-canopies), leopard-patterned bathrobes, and, upon request, an in-room goldfish? It's a riot of silliness influenced by the kinda now, kinda wow style of the W chain, but much wilder. Bathrooms are small but appointed richly enough so that you don't mind. Public areas are most inviting (go ahead, canoodle in that jungle-frivolous lounge at the end of the hall), even more so thanks to complimentary evening wine and foot massages. The health club is housed in what appears to be the old ballroom. All in all, it's adult playful, but still good for families—especially during Papa Nöel season, when rooms go for something like $85 a night. Plus, the hotel is pet-friendly, so bring Fido along!

333 St. Charles Ave., New Orleans, LA 70130. © **866/561-0010** or 504/561-0010. Fax 504/561-0036. www.monaco-neworleans.com. 250 units. $135–$295 double. AE, DC, DISC, MC, V. Valet parking $29 (cheaper garages within walking distance of hotel). Special dog packages for canine guests. **Amenities:** Cobalt restaurant (p. 132); fitness room; concierge; salon; 24-hr. room service; babysitting; laundry; dry cleaning; wine reception; free foot massage. *In room:* AC, TV, dataport, hair dryer, iron, CD player, duel line phones.

International House ★★★　A standout from the start, the International House has set a new standard with its creative design and meticulous attention to detail, and other hotels in the area should be paying careful attention: The bar has been raised. Record company and film execs should love it, but so should anyone who's had enough of Victorian sweetness and needs a palate cleanser. Here, a wonderful old beaux-arts bank building has been transformed into a modern space that still pays tribute to its locale. Consequently, in the graceful lobby, classical pilasters stand next to modern wrought-iron chandeliers.

Interiors are the embodiment of minimalist chic. Rooms are simple with muted, monochromatic (okay, beige) tones, tall ceilings and ceiling fans, up-to-the-minute bathroom fixtures, but also black-and-white photos of local musicians and characters, books about the city, and other clever decorating touches that anchor the room in its New Orleans setting. (This is significant; without them, you could easily plant this hotel in L.A. and not notice a difference.) The commitment to hip, neat, cool, and groovy means dark corridors and hard-to-read room numbers, and although the big bathrooms boast large tubs or space-age glassed-in showers, they do come off as a bit industrial. But compensations include cushy touches like feather pillows, large TVs with movie channels, your own private phone number in your room, and CD players with CDs.

221 Camp St., New Orleans, LA 70130. ℭ **800/633-5770** or 504/553-9550. Fax 504/553-9560. www.ihhotel.com. 119 units. $149–$379 double; $369–$1,799 suite. AE, DC, DISC, MC, V. Valet parking $22. **Amenities:** Lemon Grass restaurant (p. 133); bar; health club; 24-hr. concierge; gift shop; room service 8am–10pm; dry cleaning. *In room:* A/C, TV, dataport, minibar, hair dryer, iron, CD player.

Le Cirque   A smart, sharp, and chic version of the generic business hotel—sort of like a Crowne Plaza, if it was done up in chartreuse and that new misty gray-blue that's all the rage. Oddly, it's not set up as a business hotel, lacking amenities such as separate dataports, but it does offer 4,000 square feet of meeting space. Rooms are average size; the ones with king beds are a bit cramped thanks to all the furniture crammed in along with it (chair, desk, TV). Queen rooms are even smaller. The bar, however, is one of the hippest in town. *A tip:* The hotel offers rides in a complimentary town car (first come, first served) anywhere within a 2-mile radius.

936 St Charles Ave., New Orleans, LA 7013. ℭ **888/487-8782** or 504/962-0900. Fax 504/962-0901. www.hotellecirque.com. 136 units. $69–$299. AE, DC, DISC, MC, V. **Amenities:** Restaurant; bar; concierge; limited car service; limited-hours room service; babysitting; laundry; dry cleaning. *In room:* A/C, TV, hair dryer, iron, safes, newspaper.

The Pelham   This small hotel, in a renovated building that dates from the late 1800s, is one of the new wave of boutique hotels. From the outside and in its public areas, the Pelham feels like an upscale apartment building. Centrally located rooms are generally less bright than those on the exterior of the building; all have in-room safes. If you're not interested in staying right in the French Quarter or if you're looking for something with less public atmosphere than a hotel and more anonymity than a B&B, the Pelham is a good option.

444 Common St., New Orleans, LA 70130. ℭ **888/211-3447** or 504/522-4444. Fax 504/539-9010. www.neworleanscollection.com/pelham. 60 units. $79–$399 double. AE, DC, DISC, MC, V. Parking $19 cars, $22 trucks plus tax. **Amenities:** Concierge; laundry service. *In room:* A/C, TV, dataport, hair dryer, iron, safe.

Wyndham Riverfront Hotel ⊛   There couldn't be a better location if you're attending an event at the Convention Center: It's right across the street. But the rooms feel less like they're in a business hotel and more like "use-convention-as-excuse-for-New Orleans-junket." Not that there's a party-hearty vibe, but the rooms just aren't set up for real business travelers like those in your average Marriott. Instead, rooms are prefab elegant with stately wallpaper and armchairs, far more aesthetically pleasing than most big hotels. Some can be small, but the second floor has quite tall ceilings, which offset that effect. Bathrooms are nothing special but contain many fruity/flowery amenities from Bath & Bodyworks. Towels are thick but pillows rubbery. We did get a sense that the staff can be somewhat overwhelmed when a convention is staying there, but they were never less than gracious.

701 Convention Center Blvd., New Orleans, LA 70130. ☎ **800/WYNDHAM** or 504/524-8200. Fax 504/524-0600. www.wyndham.com. 202 units. $189–$220 double. AE, DC, DISC, MC, V. Valet parking $25. **Amenities:** Restaurant; bar; pool; exercise room; concierge; gift shop; room service 7am–11pm; laundry; dry cleaning. *In room:* A/C, TV, minibar, coffeemaker, hair dryer, iron, safe.

MODERATE

Drury Inn & Suites *Value*   This family-owned chain looks all too generic outside, but inside is a pleasant surprise, with grander-than-expected public spaces and rooms that are fancier than those in the average chain, not to mention clean and new. All have high ceilings (except for those on the 5th floor) and a decent amount of square footage, though bathrooms are small (with sinks in the dressing area). The beds are hard, but otherwise the furniture is good-quality generic-hotel average. There is a nice little heated rooftop pool plus a small exercise room. All that plus a generous comp breakfast makes this not a bad little bargain for the area.

820 Poydras St., New Orleans, LA 70112-1016. ☎ **504/529-7800.** Fax 504/581-3320. www.drury hotels.com/properties/neworleans.cfm. 156 units. $114 regular room; $149 suite. AE, DC, DISC, MC, V. $15 parking. **Amenities:** Daily full breakfast buffet; Mon–Thurs evening complimentary cocktails; heated pool; exercise room; laundry/dry cleaning services. *In room:* A/C, TV, coffeemaker, hair dryer, iron, free local calls, some suites have whirlpool tubs.

Le Pavillion Hotel ⭐   Established in 1907 in a prime Central Business District location, Le Pavillion was the first hotel in New Orleans to have elevators. It's now a member of Historic Hotels of America. The building is a long, slender rectangle with a prominent columned motor entrance. The lobby is stunning, just what you want in a big, grand hotel, with giant columns and chandeliers. The standard guest rooms are all rather pretty and have similar furnishings, but they differ in size. "Bay Rooms" are standard with two double beds and bay windows. Suites are actually hit or miss in terms of decor, with the nadir being the mind-bogglingly ugly Art Deco Suite. Much better is the Plantation Suite, decorated in—you guessed it—antiques including pieces by Mallard, C. Lee (who, as a slave, studied under Mallard), Mitchell Rammelsberg, Belter, Badouine, and Marcotte. Late-night peanut butter and jelly sandwiches plus chocolates and milk are offered in the lobby.

833 Poydras St., New Orleans, LA 70112. ☎ **800/535-9095** or 504/581-3111. Fax 504/522-5543. www.le pavillon.com. 226 units. $139–$159 double; $275–$1,695 suite. AE, DC, DISC, MC, V. Valet parking $25. **Amenities:** Restaurant; bar; heated outdoor pool; fitness center and whirlpool spa; concierge; 24-hr. room service; babysitting; laundry; dry cleaning. *In room:* A/C, TV, dataport, minibar, hair dryer, iron.

St. James Hotel ⭐   A fine preservation job has given what could have been an eyesore derelict (if historic) building a new useful function. Actually, this is two different buildings, one of which used to be—get this!—the St. James Infirmary, sung about so memorably by many a mournful jazz musician. But because the restorers had to make do with a non-uniform space, rooms vary in size and style, and a few lack windows. You want high ceilings? Ask for a room in the back building. Rooms on the top floor have exposed brick and wood. All rooms have marble bathrooms, and two suites and a room share a small, private brick courtyard with a fountain—a nice setup for a small group. There is a teeny-weeny pool—you might be forgiven for considering it really just a large puddle with nice tile. Overall, this is a good and friendly find, located just a block or two within the Central Business District and thus just a few blocks from the Quarter.

330 Magazine St., New Orleans, LA 70130. ☎ **888/211-3447** or 504/304-4000. www.saintjameshotel.com. 86 units. $99–$299 double. AE, DC, DISC, MC, V. Valet parking $18.95. **Amenities:** Pool; health club;

concierge; room service Mon–Sat 6:30am–10am; babysitting; laundry; dry cleaning. *In room:* Coffeemaker, hair dryer, iron, safe.

The Whitney—A Wyndham Historic Hotel ★ A clever and welcome use of space as a grand old bank building has been converted into a fine modern hotel. The unique results include gawk-worthy public spaces; be sure to look up at all the fanciful, wedding-cake-decoration old plasterwork (they don't make 'em like that any more—pity) and help us wonder how the heck safecrackers got past those thick slab of doors. Best of all is the imposing lobby, full of stately pillars (doubtless the grandeur intimidated many a loan applicant of yesteryear), now part restaurant but also still part working bank—it puts other swellegant establishments in town to shame.

Rooms are a little too stately to classify as true business efficient but also a little too generic to make this a proper romantic getaway. Having said that, we found the beds most comfortable and were pleased with the spacious bathrooms. Overall, the Whitney has more character than your average upscale chain, so it ultimately gets a positive vote. If you are a hoity-toity businessman (and one who probably doesn't use expressions like *hoity-toity*), you will probably like it a lot. And if you are a preservationist, you will probably like it even more.

610 Poydras St., New Orleans, LA. 70130 ✆ **504/581-4222.** 93 units. $159–$339. AE, DC, DISC, MC, V. Valet parking $20.16 cars, $22.40 oversized. **Amenities:** Restaurant; lobby bar; private dining room; fitness center; business services; room service 6am–11pm. *In room:* A/C, TV, dataport, minibar, coffee- and tea-making facilities, hair dryer, iron, CD player.

INEXPENSIVE

The Depot at Madame Julia's ★ *Finds* A second establishment from the couple who run the St. Charles Guesthouse in the Garden District (p. 96), the Depot takes up part of a whole complex of buildings dating from the 1800s and is an alternative to more commercial hotels in the Central Business District.

Low prices and a guesthouse environment mean a number of good things—including rooms with character and a proprietor who loves to help guests with all the details of their stay—but it also means shared bathrooms, rooms on the small and cozy side, and a location that, although quiet on the weekends, can get noisy in the mornings as the working neighborhood gets going. (Still being gentrified, the neighborhood is hit or miss, but more of the former than the latter thanks to artsy Julia Street.) A mere 7 blocks (safe in the daytime) from the Quarter, it's a quick walk or a short streetcar ride, which makes it an affordable alternative to the Quarter's much more expensive accommodations. The budget-conscious and those who prefer their hotels with personality will consider this a find.

748 O'Keefe St., New Orleans, LA 70113. ✆ **504/529-2952.** Fax 504/529-1908. 25 units, all with shared bathrooms. $65–$85 double. Breakfast included. AE, personal checks (if paid in advance). Off-street parking available. *In room:* A/C.

5 Uptown/The Garden District

For hotels in this section, see the "Uptown Accommodations & Dining" map on p. 93 or the "New Orleans Accommodations" map on p. 66.

VERY EXPENSIVE

Pontchartrain Hotel ★ If you have a weakness for faded grandeur and evocative atmosphere (and we do), here's your spot. If, on the other hand, you prefer antiseptic clean, you're in the wrong place. This dignified hotel has long been a local landmark. Back in the day, it was the place for the likes of Rita

Hayworth and Aly Kahn to tryst, courtesy of adjoining suites—Ms. Hayworth's still has the fanciful floral murals on walls and woodwork. Tom and Nicole spent an anniversary here. All rooms have been recently redone—each getting at least new paint and carpet and some totally gutted to the walls. New rooms have mock French Provincial furniture and newer bathrooms (they are working on boosting the water pressure)—but regardless, it still looks like an old, formerly grand hotel, even with the newer fixtures. Beds are comfortable and rooms more spacious than many typical hotel rooms. Room 409, however, is a dinky exception (indeed, any room ending in 01 or 09 is going to be on the smaller side). Service is friendly but a bit more lackadaisical than one might desire. Anne Rice fans take note: Rowan and Michael lived here while renovating their house in *The Witching Hour.* Just to reiterate: While there are some out there who write us cranky letters complaining that the Pontchartrain doesn't live up to their high standards, we and like-minded others pretty much think it's the cat's meow.

2031 St. Charles Ave., New Orleans, LA 70140. ℭ **800/777-6193** or 504/524-0581. Fax 504/529-1165. www.pontchartrainhotel.com. 118 units. $95–$380 double. Extra person $10; during special events $25. Seasonal packages and special promotional rates available. AE, DC, DISC, MC, V. Parking $18. **Amenities:** Restaurant; bar; access to nearby spa with health club and outdoor pool; 24-hr. room service. *In room:* A/C, TV, coffeemaker, hair dryer, iron, safe.

EXPENSIVE

The Grand Victorian Bed & Breakfast ★★   Owner Bonnie Rabe confounded and delighted her new St. Charles neighbors when she took a crumbling Queen Anne–style Victorian mansion right on the corner of Washington (2 blocks from Lafayette cemetery and Commander's Palace with a streetcar stop right in front) and, over the course of many arduous months, resurrected it into a showcase B&B. The location makes its porches and balconies a perfect place to spend Mardi Gras; parade viewing doesn't come any more comfortable or convenient.

The stunning rooms are full of antiques (each has an impressive four-poster or wood canopy bed—though a couple are small thanks to their vintage) with the slightly fussy details demanded by big Victorian rooms. Linens, pillows, and towels are ultra plush, and some bathrooms have big Jacuzzi tubs. The largest room—our favorite—overlooks the street corner (and has its own St. Charles view balcony) and so is potentially noisy. You can always request one toward the back. A generous continental breakfast is served, and friendly Bonnie is ready with suggestions on how to spend your time. Though Bonnie does live on the third floor, she is not always there, so as in any B&B, do not expect 24-hour service.

2727 St. Charles Ave., New Orleans, LA 70130. ℭ **800/977-0008** or 504/895-1104. Fax 504/896-8688. www.gvbb.com. 8 units. $150–$350 double. Rates include breakfast. AE, DISC, MC, V. *In room:* A/C, TV, dataport, hair dryer, iron.

Queen Anne ★   A somewhat different take on lodging from the same folks who bring you the Prytania Park Hotel (see below), this was a one-family home for 130 years. The owners had to pass muster with the mayor, the governor, and the park service when they renovated it, and the result is perhaps the grandest building for a B&B in town. Furnishings are a bit sterile, however—hotel-room furniture masquerading as antique (though mattresses are top of the line). The Queen Anne is not our first choice for decor, but the stately rooms (each of which has some exquisite detail like beautifully tiled nonworking fireplaces or 10- to 14-foot ceilings) pull it off. The tiniest room has quite a large bathroom,

Uptown Accommodations & Dining

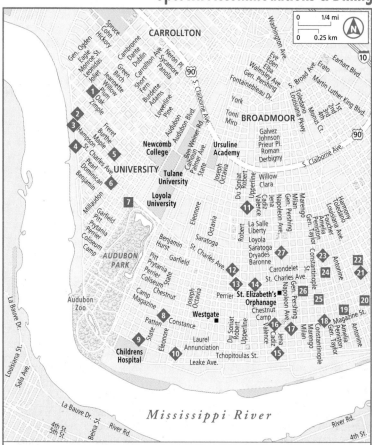

Map labels:

CARROLLTON

BROADMOOR

UNIVERSITY

Newcomb College
Ursuline Academy
Tulane University
Loyola University

AUDUBON PARK

Audubon Zoo

St. Elizabeth's Orphanage
Westgate

Childrens Hospital

Mississippi River

KENNER   METAIRIE
BRIDGE CITY
WESTWEGO   MARRERO
FRENCH QUARTER
Superdome
Area of detail

ACCOMMODATIONS ■

Chimes B&B **25**
The Columns **24**
Hampton Inn **22**
Maison Perrier Bed & Breakfast **26**
Park View Guest House **7**

DINING ◆

Bluebird Cafe **21**
La Boulangerie **16**
Brigtsen's **2**
Camellia Grill **4**
Casamento's **17**
Clancy's **9**
Dante's Kitchen **3**
Dick & Jenny's **15**
Dunbar's Creole Cooking **11**
Foodie's Kitchen **6**
Franky & Johnny's **10**
Gautreau's **12**
Jacques-Imo's **1**
Kelsey's **18**
La Crêpe Nanou **13**

Lilette **19**
Martin Wine Cellar and Delicatessen **23**
Martinique Bistro **8**
Mystic Cafe **20**
Pascal's Manale **27**
PJ's Coffee & Tea Company **5**
Reginelli's **8**
Upperline **14**

while the three attic rooms are too conventional to be worth your while. The inn is nicely located near the Mardi Gras parade route.

1625 Prytania St., New Orleans, LA 70130. Registration is at the Prytania Park Hotel on Terpsichore St. between Prytania St. and St. Charles Ave. © **800/862-1984** or 504/524-0427. Fax 504/522-2977. www.the queenanne.com. 12 units. $159–$179 double. Rates include continental breakfast. AE, DC, DISC, MC, V. Self-parking $10. **Amenities:** Free shuttle to Convention Center, Harrah's Casino, and French Quarter; laundry services. *In room:* A/C, TV, unstocked fridge, hair dryer, safe, microwave.

MODERATE

Chimes B&B ★★★ *(Finds)*   This is a real hidden gem, one that truly allows you to experience the city away from the typical tourist experience. The Chimes is in a less fashionable but more neighborhoodlike portion of the Garden District, just 2 blocks off St. Charles Avenue. Your hosts, Jill and Charles Abbyad, have run this B&B (located in the old servants' quarters behind their house, surrounding a small, sweet courtyard) for over 15 years, and their experience shows.

Rooms vary in size from a generous L-shape to a two-story loft type (with a very small bathroom) to some that are downright cozy. All have antiques (including romantic old beds) but are so tastefully underdecorated, particularly in contrast to other B&Bs, that they are positively Zen. An ambitious continental breakfast is served in the hosts' house, and chatting with them can be so enjoyable you might get off to a late start. The Abbyads know and love their city, and their friendliness and charm are among the reasons they have so many loyal, repeat customers. One recent guest, veteran of many New Orleans hotels, spent one night here and proclaimed that on subsequent trips, she would stay nowhere else but here. (The Chimes is unfortunately not set up to accommodate guests with disabilities.)

1146 Constantinople St., New Orleans, LA 70115. © **800/729-4640** (for reservations only) or 504/488-4640. Fax 504/899-9858. www.historiclodging.com/chimes.html. 5 units. $115–$155 double; off-season rates lower. Rates include breakfast. Look for rates, availability, and featured specials online. AE, MC, V. Limited off-street free parking. Well-behaved pets accepted. *In room:* A/C, TV, dataport, coffeemaker, hair dryer, iron.

The Columns ★   New Orleans made a mistake when it tore down its famous bordellos. If somebody had turned one of the grander ones into a hotel, imagine how many people would stay there! The next best thing is the Columns, whose interior was used by Louis Malle for his film about Storyville, *Pretty Baby*. Please don't lounge around the lobby in your underwear, however, even if it is Victorian (the underwear, not the lobby). Built in 1883, the building is one of the city's greatest examples of a late-19th-century Louisiana residence. The grand, columned porch is a highly popular evening scene thanks to the bar inside. The immediate interior is utterly smashing; we challenge any other hotel to match the grand staircase and stained-glass-window combination.

Unfortunately, the magnificence of the setting is hurt by the relentlessly casual attitude toward the public areas. Cheesy furniture downstairs, an empty, neglected ballroom, and stale cigarette smoke in that gorgeous stairway (courtesy of the bar) detract mightily from the experience, making it perilously close to seedy in some spots—too bad. This could be a deeply romantic hotel, ponderously Victorian, and we mean that in a good way. But bar revenue reigns supreme, so the smoke is probably there to stay. Consequently, the prices may not be justified, fabulous hangout or not. Low-end rooms are cozy with quilts and old bedsteads. High-end rooms are indeed that—it's the difference between the master's room and the servants' quarters. We particularly like room 16, with its grand furniture and floor-to-ceiling shutters that lead out to a private, second-story porch.

3811 St. Charles Ave., New Orleans, LA 70115. ℂ 800/445-9308 or 504/899-9308. Fax 504/899-8170. www.thecolumns.com. 20 units. $110–$180 double. Rates include full breakfast. AE, MC, V. Parking available on street. **Amenities:** Bar. *In room:* A/C.

Hampton Inn   This is a top choice for a chain hotel, if you don't mind being a bit out of the way (we don't—it's quite nice up here on St. Charles in a grand section of town that is generally not overly touristed but is right on the Mardi Gras parade route). The public areas are slightly more stylish than that found in other chains, and there are welcome touches like free coffee in the lobby and complimentary cheese and tea served daily from 6 to 7pm. The style does not extend to the rooms, however, which are pretty mundane. But they're not *that* bad (the bedspreads and mustard-colored walls excepted). There are all kinds of personality-enhancing details (decent photos for artwork, ever-so-slight arts-and-crafts detailing on furniture, and big TVs) hidden in that bland color scheme.

3626 St. Charles Ave., New Orleans, LA 70115. ℂ 800/426-7866 or 504/899-9990. Fax 504/899-9908. www.neworleanshamptoninns.com. 100 units. $129–$159 double. Rates include continental breakfast, free local calls, and free incoming faxes. AE, DC, DISC, MC, V. Free parking. **Amenities:** Small outdoor lap pool; laundry; dry cleaning. *In room:* AC, TV, dataport, coffeemaker, hair dryer, iron.

Maison Perrier Bed & Breakfast ⚜   This 1894 painted-lady Victorian (it may or may not have been a turn-of-the-century "gentlemen's club") has been restored to a gleaming fare-thee-well. Rooms are teasingly named after the ladies who may have worked here and each has its own colorful charm, plus at least one special detail: a high four-poster bed, say, or fabulous old tile around a (non-working) fireplace. Downstairs is a warm parlor and a rec room that is more modern than not, but the hosts ply you with beverages and afternoon baked goods (plus weekend wine and cheese gatherings), and the vibe is convivial. Breakfast is large, prepared by a resident cook who knows the way to a guest's heart is through Southern specialties like puff pancakes and Creole grits. The owners offer full concierge services.

4117 Perrier St. (2 blocks riverside from St. Charles Ave., 3 blocks downtown from Napoleon Ave.), New Orleans, LA 70115. ℂ 888/610-1807 or 504/897-1807. Fax 504/897-1399. www.maisonperrier.com. $120–$250 double. Rates include breakfast. AE, DISC, MC, V. Parking available on street. **Amenities:** Concierge; business center; laundry service. *In room:* A/C, TV, dataport, minibar, hair dryer, iron.

The McKendrick-Breaux House ⚜⚜   Owner Eddie Breaux saved this 1865 building just as it was about to fall down and turned it into one of the city's best B&Bs. The antiques-filled rooms are spacious (some of the bathrooms are downright huge), quaint, and meticulously decorated but not fussy. The public areas are simple, elegant, and comfortable. Really, the whole place couldn't be in better taste, and yet it's not intimidating, thanks to the warmth that comes from Breaux and his staff. They are utterly hospitable and, like the best guesthouse hosts, quite knowledgeable about the city they love, and ready to help you make plans.

1474 Magazine St., New Orleans, LA 70130. ℂ 888/570-1700 or 504/586-1700. Fax 504/522-7134. www.mckendrick-breaux.com. 9 units. $125–$195 double. Rates include tax and breakfast. AE, MC, V. Limited free off-street parking. **Amenities:** Jacuzzi in courtyard. *In room:* A/C, TV, dataport, hair dryer, iron.

Prytania Park Hotel   This 1840s building (which once housed Huey Long's girlfriend) is now equal parts motel and funky simulated Quarter digs. Rooms vary: Some have been redone to the owner's pride (adding darker wood tones and four-poster beds plus bathrooms that still have a Holiday Inn feel), but we kind of prefer the older section with its pine furniture, tall ceilings, and non-working fireplaces. All rooms have lots of good reading lights. Some units have balconies or loft bedrooms (accessible by spiral staircases). Those without the loft can be small, and the new dark wood furniture makes it a bit ponderous.

1525 Prytania St. (enter off Terpsichore St.), New Orleans, LA 70130. © **800/862-1984** or 504/524-0427. Fax 504/522-2977. www.prytaniaparkhotel.com. 62 units. $109 double; $119 suite. Extra person $10. Rates include continental breakfast. Children under 12 stay free in parents' room. Seasonal rates and special packages available. AE, DC, DISC, MC, V. Off-street parking available. **Amenities:** Free shuttle to Convention Center and French Quarter. *In room:* A/C, TV, minibar.

INEXPENSIVE

Park View Guest House ⭐   If you can't live without Bourbon Street and bars mere steps away from your hotel entrance, then this is not the place for you. But if a true getaway to you means a step back in time, come to this way-uptown guesthouse that feels at once like a truly old-fashioned hotel (as well it should; it was built in 1881) and a glamorous Belle Epoque mansion with all the trimmings. Antiques-filled rooms (including some imposing beds and armoires) are becoming plusher every minute, benefiting from the addition of down comforters, better amenities, and hair dryers. All rooms have high ceilings, and some have balconies overlooking Audubon Park, which is right across the street—go for an old-fashioned late-afternoon promenade. The St. Charles streetcar stops right outside, so it's easy to get to and from the Quarter, still in a period mood. The front desk is staffed 24 hours a day, there's a tour desk, and guests have the use of a refrigerator and ice machine.

7004 St. Charles Ave., New Orleans, LA 70118. © **888/533-0746** or 504/861-7564. Fax 504/861-1225. www.parkviewguesthouse.com. 22 units, 17 with private bathroom. $85–$150. Rates include continental breakfast. Extra person $10. AE, DISC, MC, V. Parking available on street. *In room:* A/C.

St. Charles Guesthouse   Very much worth checking out for those on a budget, the St. Charles Guesthouse—the first such accommodation in the Garden District and much copied over the last 20 years—is not fancy, but it's one of the friendliest hotels in town. Rooms are plain and run from low-end backpacker lodgings, which have no air-conditioning (even the management describes them as "small and spartan"), to larger chambers with air-conditioning and private bathrooms—nice enough but nothing special. That's okay. The place does have the required New Orleans–atmosphere elements: high ceilings, a long staircase, and antiques (there is such a fine line between "antique" and "old furniture"), not to mention the banana tree–ringed courtyard. It's only a short walk through the quiet and very pretty neighborhood to the St. Charles Avenue streetcar line.

1748 Prytania St., New Orleans, LA 70130. © **504/523-6556.** Fax 504/522-6340. www.stcharlesguest house.com. 35 units, 23 with private bathroom. $45–$95 double. Rates include continental breakfast. AE, MC, V. Parking available on street. **Amenities:** Outdoor pool. *In room:* No phone.

7

Where to Dine

After being in New Orleans for just a short amount of time, you will find yourself talking less about the sights and more about the food—if not constantly about the food: what you ate already, what you are going to be eating later, what you wish you had time to eat. We are going to take a stand and say to heck with New York and San Francisco: New Orleans has the best food in the United States. (There are natives who will gladly fight you if you say otherwise.)

This is the city where the great chefs of the world come to eat—if they don't work here already. Many people love to do nothing more than wax nostalgic about great meals they have had here, describing entrees in practically pornographic detail. It is nearly impossible to have a bad meal in this town; at worst, it will be mediocre, and with proper guidance, you should even be able to avoid that.

There is, however, a reason why a 1997 study of U.S. eating habits proclaimed New Orleans the fattest city in the country—a fact the locals will cheerfully volunteer to you—they are terribly proud of it (alas, they've lost the title to Houston). At times, it might seem that everything is fried or served with a sauce, and sometimes both. This, of course, defeats the potentially healthful quality of seafood, the predominant offering. "It ain't the fish, it's the battah that makes you fat," explains a local. Vegetables seem rare—or an afterthought at best.

Some of you may fret about this. Some of you may be watching your waistlines, to which we say, with all due understanding and respect, "So what?" You're on vacation. Vow to make it up when you get home. Even if it were possible to maintain your diet here, you'd just be miserable from the deprivation, and you wouldn't be getting the full New Orleans experience anyway. It's part of that all-important decadence. Give in.

Sure, you might consider ordering salads whenever you can or opting for blackened rather than fried fish in an effort to trim those calories and fat grams. But don't go into contortions about it. If you are doing your trip properly, you will be walking and dancing so much that your scale might not be as unfriendly as you fear when you return home.

Our favorite restaurants in various categories, all of them sure to incite an argument, are listed in chapter 1, "The Best of New Orleans."

1 A Taste of New Orleans

Boy, does this city love to eat. And boy, does it offer visitors a range of choices. Thanks to influences from French provincial, Spanish, Italian, West Indian, African, and Native American cuisines, it covers the whole span from down-home Southern cooking to the most creative and artistic gourmet dishes. New Orleans is one of the few cities in America that can justify a visit solely for cooking and cuisine.

New Orleans Dining

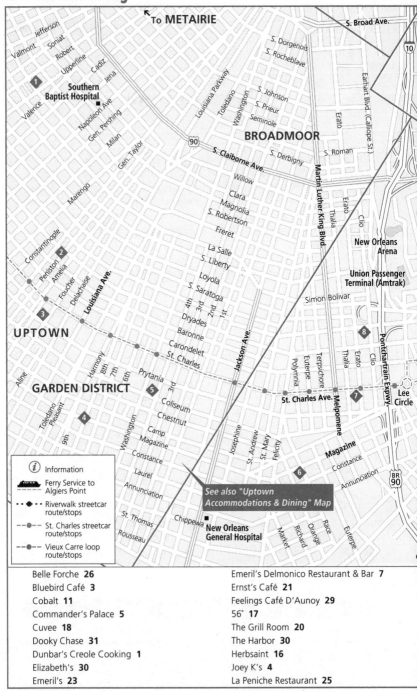

Belle Forche **26**
Bluebird Café **3**
Cobalt **11**
Commander's Palace **5**
Cuvee **18**
Dooky Chase **31**
Dunbar's Creole Cooking **1**
Elizabeth's **30**
Emeril's **23**

Emeril's Delmonico Restaurant & Bar **7**
Ernst's Café **21**
Feelings Café D'Aunoy **29**
56° **17**
The Grill Room **20**
The Harbor **30**
Herbsaint **16**
Joey K's **4**
La Peniche Restaurant **25**

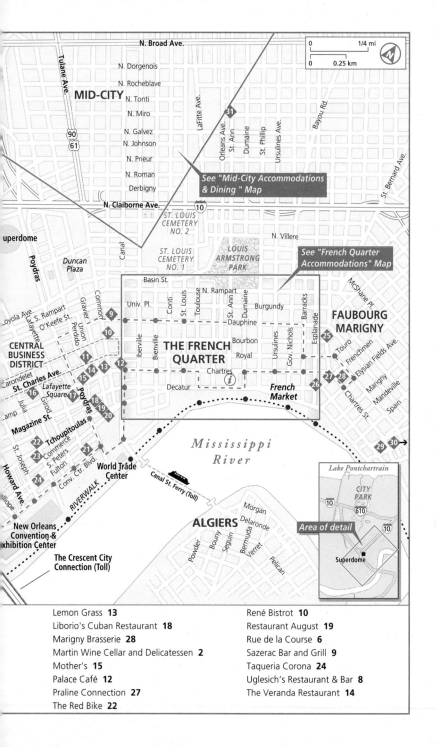

N. Broad Ave.

MID-CITY

N. Dorgenois
N. Rocheblave
N. Tonti
N. Miro
N. Galvez
N. Johnson
N. Prieur
N. Roman
Derbigny

Tulane Ave.

90
61

LaFitte Ave.

Orleans Ave.
St. Ann
Dumaine
St. Phillip
Ursulines Ave.

Bayou Rd.

St. Bernard Ave.

31

See "Mid-City Accommodations & Dining" Map

N. Claiborne Ave.

10

ST. LOUIS CEMETERY NO. 2

N. Villere

ST. LOUIS CEMETERY NO. 1

LOUIS ARMSTRONG PARK

uperdome

Duncan Plaza

Canal

Basin St.

See "French Quarter Accommodations" Map

Poydras

Univ. Pl.

N. Rampart
Conti
St. Louis
Toulouse
St. Ann
Dumaine
Burgundy

Barracks

Esplanade

McShane Pl.

FAUBOURG MARIGNY

oyola Ave.
S. Rampart
O'Keefe St.
Lafayette

Common

Gravier
Union
Perdido

9

Dauphine

Iberville
Bienville

THE FRENCH QUARTER

Bourbon

Royal

Ursulines
Gov. Nichols

25

Touro

Frenchmen

Elysian Fields Ave.

CENTRAL BUSINESS DISTRICT

St. Charles Ave.

Carondelet

Lafayette Square

10

11

15 14 13

16   17

12

Chartres

Decatur

i

French Market

26

27 28

Chartres St.

Marigny

Mandeville

Spain

amp
Julia

Magazine St.

Tchoupitoulas

18
19
20

St. Joseph

22
23

Commerce
S. Peters
Fulton

21

Conv. Ctr. Blvd.

World Trade Center

Mississippi River

29 30

Howard Ave.

lliope

RIVERWALK

New Orleans Convention & xhibition Center

Canal St. Ferry (Toll)

Morgan

ALGIERS

Delaronde

Powder
Bouny
Seguin
Bermuda
Verret

Pelican

Lake Pontchartrain

CITY PARK

10
610

Area of detail

10

Superdome

The Crescent City Connection (Toll)

0   1/4 mi
0   0.25 km

Lemon Grass **13**
Liborio's Cuban Restaurant **18**
Marigny Brasserie **28**
Martin Wine Cellar and Delicatessen **2**
Mother's **15**
Palace Café **12**
Praline Connection **27**
The Red Bike **22**

René Bistrot **10**
Restaurant August **19**
Rue de la Course **6**
Sazerac Bar and Grill **9**
Taqueria Corona **24**
Uglesich's Restaurant & Bar **8**
The Veranda Restaurant **14**

Impressions

Living in New Orleans is like drinking blubber through a straw. Even the air is caloric.

—Andrei Codrescu, "Fantastic Fast"

Many of the famous dishes here started out as provincial French recipes brought to the New World by early settlers. Native Americans introduced the settlers to native herbs and *filé* (ground sassafras leaves); the Spanish added saffron and peppers to the mix somewhat later. From the West Indies came new vegetables, spices, and sugar cane, and when slave boats arrived, landing many black women in the kitchens of white slave owners, an African influence was added. Out of all this came the distinctive Creole culinary style unique to New Orleans. Later, Italian immigrants added yet another dimension to the city's tables. In addition, many traditional Old South dishes remain on menus.

From this international past, residents of New Orleans have inherited a love of exciting culinary combinations, and from the city's old-world traditions, they've retained an appreciation for fine service in elegant surroundings. There are lots of ironies here, too; you can get gourmet dishes served in the plainest of settings and plain meals (such as boiled crawfish or red beans and rice) in the fanciest of eateries. New Orleanians are voracious restaurant goers and are notoriously strict in the qualities they expect from an eating establishment. If a place is below par, it probably won't last very long.

YOU GOT YOUR CAJUN IN MY CREOLE!

Cajun and Creole are the two classic New Orleans cuisines. What's the difference? It lies chiefly in distance between city and countryside.

Cajun cooking came from country folk—the Acadians who left France for Nova Scotia in the 1600s and, after being expelled from Canada by the British in the 1700s, made their way to the swamps and bayous of rural Louisiana. French dishes traveled with them, but along the way recipes were adapted to locally available ingredients. Their cuisine tends to be a lot like their music: spicy and robust. Etouffée, a classic dish, features sausage, duck, poultry, pork, and seafood prepared in a rich roux and served over rice. It's usually accompanied by something deep-fried. Creole dishes, on the other hand, were developed by French and Spanish city dwellers and feature delicate sauces and ingredients of the highest quality.

In practice, however, the two cuisines have discovered such a happy marriage in New Orleans that it's often difficult to distinguish between them. Because Creole is already such a hodgepodge—there are so many different ways of defining it that two entirely different restaurants might correctly call themselves Creole—it may soon swallow up Cajun food as just another influence. Paul Prudhomme of K-Paul's Louisiana Kitchen calls the result of Cajun and Creole cross-fertilization "Louisiana food." He goes on to say, "Nowhere else have all the ethnic groups merged to combine all these different tastes, and the only way you'll know the difference, honey, is to live 'em!" No matter how a New Orleans restaurant classifies its culinary offerings, you're bound to find one or two examples of Cajun and Creole cooking on the menu.

OF BEIGNETS, BOUDIN & DIRTY RICE

Many of the foods in New Orleans are unique to the region and consequently may be unfamiliar to first-time visitors. Here's a list that will help you navigate any New Orleans menu:

andouille (ahn-doo-*we*): A spicy Cajun sausage made with pork.

bananas Foster: Bananas sautéed in liqueur, brown sugar, cinnamon, and butter; then drenched in rum, set ablaze, and served over vanilla ice cream.

beignet (bin-*yay*): A big, puffy, deep-fried doughnut (don't look for the hole), liberally sprinkled with powdered sugar—the more sugar, the better.

boudin (boo-*dan*): A type of sausage containing onion, spices, pork, and rice.

café brûlot (cah-*fay* brew-*low*): Coffee mixed with spices and liqueurs and served flaming.

chaurice (cho-*reece*): A hard sausage used chiefly for flavoring beans or soups.

crawfish: A tiny, lobsterlike creature plentiful in the waters around New Orleans and eaten in every conceivable way. When it's served whole and boiled, separate the head from the tail and then remove the first two sections of the tail shell. Squeeze the tail at its base, and the meat should pop right out—you'll get the hang of it.

daube: Beef or sometimes veal.

dirty rice: A popular menu item, it looks dirty because of the spices and other ingredients in which it's cooked—usually chicken livers and gizzards, onions, chopped celery, green bell pepper, cayenne, black and white peppers, and chicken stock.

dressed: Served with the works—used when ordering a sandwich.

eggs hussarde: Poached eggs with hollandaise, *marchand de vin* sauce, tomatoes, and ham. *Marchand de vin* is a wine sauce flavored with onions, shallots, celery, carrots, garlic, red wine, beef broth, and herbs.

eggs Sardou: Legend has it that Antoine Alciatore created this dish especially for French playwright Victorien Sardou (author *of La Tosca*). It includes poached eggs, artichoke bottoms, anchovy filets, hollandaise, and truffles or ham as a garnish.

étouffée (ay-too-*fay*): A Cajun stew (usually containing crawfish) served with rice.

filé (*fee*-lay): A thickener made of ground sassafras leaves. Filé is frequently used to thicken gumbo.

grillades (gree-*yads*): Thin slices of beef or veal smothered in a tomato-and-beef-flavored gravy, often served with grits.

grits: Grains of dried corn that have been ground and hulled. A staple of the Southern breakfast table, grits are most frequently served with butter and salt (not maple syrup or brown sugar) or red-eye gravy.

gumbo: A thick, spicy soup always served with rice and usually containing crab, shrimp, sometimes oysters, and okra in a roux base.

hurricane: A local drink of rum and passion-fruit punch.

hush puppies: Fried balls of cornmeal, often served as a side dish with seafood.

jambalaya (jum-ba-*lie*-ya): A jumble of yellow rice, sausage, seafood, vegetables, and spices.

lagniappe (lan-*yap*): A little something extra you neither paid for nor deserve—like the 13th doughnut when you order a dozen.

muffuletta: A mountainous sandwich made with Italian sausage, deli meats, one or two kinds of cheese, olive salad (pickled olives, celery, carrots, cauliflower, and capers), and oil and vinegar, piled onto a round loaf (about 8 inches in diameter) of Italian bread made specially for these incredible sandwiches.

oysters Rockefeller: Oysters on the half shell in a creamy sauce with spinach, so called because Rockefeller was the only name rich enough to match the taste.

pain perdu (pan *pair*-du): Literally "lost bread," this is New Orleans's version of French toast, made with French bread. You'll find a large variety of toppings on pain perdu as you make your way around New Orleans.

po' boy: A sandwich on French bread with different fillings (similar to submarine sandwiches and grinders). Most po' boys are filled with fried seafood, but they can be anything you want, from roast beef to fried eggs to french fries. Yes, french fries.

pralines (*praw*-leens): A very sweet confection made of brown sugar and pecans; they come in "original" and creamy styles.

rémoulade: A spicy sauce, usually over shrimp. The one at Commander's Palace is a concoction of homemade mayonnaise, boiled egg yolks, horseradish, Creole mustard, and lemon juice. But several New Orleans restaurants claim to have invented it, and who can say who is right at this point?

roux: A mixture of flour and fat that's slowly cooked over low heat, used to thicken stews, soups, and sauces.

Sazerac: A cocktail of bourbon or rye (Canadian whiskey) with bitters.

shrimp Creole: Shrimp in a tomato sauce seasoned with what's known around town as "the trinity": onions, garlic, and green bell pepper.

tasso: A local variety of ham. No weak little honey-baked version, this one's smoked and seasoned with red pepper.

2 Restaurants by Cuisine

AMERICAN & NEW AMERICAN

Bluebird Cafe ★★ (Uptown/Garden District, $, p. 141)

Cobalt ★★ (Central Business District, $$$, p. 132)

Emeril's ★★ (Central Business District, $$$, p. 130)

Ernst's Café (Central Business District, $, p. 135)

Feelings Cafe D'Aunoy ★ (Faubourg Marigny, $$, p. 125)

The Grill Room ★ (Central Business District, $$$$, p. 131)

Indigo ★ (Mid-City/Esplanade, $$, p. 128)

Nola ★★ (French Quarter, $$$, p. 114)

The Pelican Club ★ (French Quarter, $$$, p. 114)

Peristyle ★★★ (French Quarter, $$$, p. 114)

The Red Bike ★ (Central Business District, $$, p. 134)

Rémoulade (French Quarter, $$, p. 119)

ASIAN FUSION

56° ★ (Central Business District, $$$, p. 132)

Key to abbreviations: $$$$ = Very Expensive; $$$ = Expensive; $$ = Moderate; $ = Inexpensive

BAKERY

Café au Lait ✿ (French Quarter, $, p. 145)

La Boulangerie ✿✿✿ (Uptown and Mid-City, $, p. 145)

La Madeleine ✿ (French Quarter, $, p. 145)

La Marquise ✿ (French Quarter, $, p. 146)

BISTRO

Cafe Degas ✿✿ (Mid-City/Esplanade, $$ p. 127)

Herbsaint ✿✿ (Central Business District, $$, p. 133)

Lilette ✿ (Uptown/Garden District, $$, p. 141)

Peristyle ✿✿✿ (French Quarter, $$$, p. 114)

CAFES/COFFEE

Café au Lait ✿ (French Quarter, $, p. 145)

Café Beignet ✿ (French Quarter, $, p. 122)

Café du Monde ✿✿✿ (French Quarter, $, p. 145)

Clover Grill ✿ (p. 122, $)

La Madeleine ✿ (French Quarter, $, p. 145)

La Marquise ✿ (French Quarter, $, p. 146)

P.J.'s Coffee & Tea Company ✿ (17 locations in New Orleans, $, p. 146)

Royal Blend Coffee & Tea House ✿ (French Quarter and Central Business District, $, p. 146)

Rue de la Course ✿ (Central Business District and various other neighborhoods, $, p. 146)

CAJUN

Brigtsen's ✿✿ (Uptown/Garden District, $$$, p. 137)

K-Paul's Louisiana Kitchen ✿ (French Quarter, $$$, p. 112)

Olde N'Awlins Cookery ✿ (French Quarter, $$, p. 118)

Petunia's ✿ (French Quarter, $ p. 124)

Rémoulade (French Quarter, $$, p. 119)

CARIBBEAN CRIOLLE

Belle Forché ✿ (Faubourg Marigny, $$, p. 124)

CONTEMPORARY LOUISIANA

Dante's Kitchen ✿ (Uptown/Garden District, $$, p. 139)

201 Restaurant & Bar ✿ (French Quarter, $$, p. 121)

CONTINENTAL

Bella Luna ✿ (French Quarter, $$$, p. 109)

Sazerac Bar and Grill ✿ (Central Business District, $$$, p.133)

The Veranda Restaurant ✿ (Central Business District, $$, p. 135)

CREOLE

Antoine's ✿ (French Quarter, $$$, p. 108)

Arnaud's ✿ (French Quarter, $$$$, p. 106)

Bacco ✿✿ (French Quarter, $$$, p. 108)

Brennan's ✿ (French Quarter, $$$, p. 110)

Brigtsen's ✿✿ (Uptown/Garden District, $$$, p. 137)

Broussard's ✿ (French Quarter, $$$, p. 110)

Cafe Sbisa (French Quarter, $$, p. 115)

Christian's ✿✿ (Mid-City/Esplanade, $$, p. 127)

Clancy's ✿✿ (Uptown/Garden District, $$$, p. 137)

Commander's Palace ✿✿✿ (Uptown/Garden District, $$$, p. 137)

Court of Two Sisters (French Quarter, $$$, p. 111)

Cuvee ✿✿ (Central Business District, $$$, p. 132)

Dick & Jenny's ✿✿ (Uptown/Garden District, $$, p. 139)

Dooky Chase ✿ (Mid-City/Esplanade, $$, p. 128)

Elizabeth's ✿✿✿ (Faubourg Marigny, $, p. 125)

Emeril's ★★ (Central Business District, $$$$, p. 130)

Emeril's Delmonico Restaurant and Bar ★ (Central Business District, $$$$, p. 131)

Feelings Cafe D'Aunoy ★ (Faubourg Marigny, $$, p. 125)

Felix's Restaurant & Oyster Bar ★★ (French Quarter, $, p. 122)

Gabrielle ★★ (Mid-City/ Esplanade, $$, p. 128)

Gamay ★★ (French Quarter, $$$, p. 112)

Gautreau's ★ (Uptown/Garden District, $$, p. 140)

Jacques-Imo's ★★ (Uptown/ Garden District, $$$, p. 140)

Joey K's ★ (Uptown/Garden District, $, p. 143)

Kelsey's ★ (Uptown/Garden District, $$, p. 140)

K-Paul's Louisiana Kitchen ★ (French Quarter, $$$, p. 112)

La Peniche Restaurant ★ (Faubourg Marigny, $, p. 126)

Liuzza's ★★ (Mid-City/Esplanade, $$, p. 129)

Mandina's ★★ (Mid-City/ Esplanade, $$, p. 129)

Mother's ★★ (Central Business District, $, p. 136)

Mr. B's Bistro ★★ (French Quarter, $$, p. 118)

Muriel's ★★ (French Quarter, $$$, p. 113)

Napoleon House ★ (French Quarter, $, p. 124)

Nola ★★ (French Quarter, $$$, p. 114)

Olde N'Awlins Cookery ★ (French Quarter, $$, p. 118)

Palace Café ★★ (Central Business District, $$, p. 134)

Petunia's ★ (French Quarter, $, p. 124)

Praline Connection (Faubourg Marigny, $, p. 127)

Ralph & Kacoo's (French Quarter, $$, p. 119)

Rémoulade (French Quarter, $$, p. 119)

Royal Café ★ (French Quarter, $$, p. 119)

Sazerac Bar and Grill ★ (Central Business District, $$$, p. 133)

Tujague's ★ (French Quarter, $$, p. 120)

Upperline ★★★ (Uptown/Garden District, $$$, p. 139)

The Veranda Restaurant ★ (Central Business District, $$, p. 135)

Wolfe's of New Orleans ★★ (Metairie, $$$, p. 143)

CUBAN

Liborio's Cuban Restaurant ★ (Central Business District, $$, p. 134)

DELI

Foodie's Kitchen ★★★ (Metairie, $, p. 144)

ECLECTIC

Bella Luna ★ (French Quarter, $$$, p. 109)

Dick & Jenny's ★★ (Uptown/ Garden District, $$, p. 139)

Jacques-Imo's ★★ (Uptown/ Garden District, $$$, p. 140)

Marigny Brasserie ★★ (Faubourg Marigny, $$, p. 125)

Muriel's ★★ (French Quarter, $$$, p. 113)

The Red Bike ★ (Central Business District, $$, p. 134)

Upperline ★★★ (Uptown/Garden District, $$$, p. 139)

FRENCH

Brennan's ★ (French Quarter, $$$, p. 110)

Cafe Degas ★★ (Mid-City/ Esplanade, $$, p. 127)

Galatoire's ★ (French Quarter, $$$, p. 112)

Irene's Cuisine ★★ (French Quarter, $$, p. 115)

La Crêpe Nanou ★ (Uptown/ Garden District, $$, p. 140)

Martinique Bistro ★★ (Uptown/Garden District, $$$, p. 138)

Peristyle ✿✿✿ (French Quarter, $$$, p. 114)

René Bistrot ✿ (Central Business District, $$, p. 135)

Restaurant August ✿ (Central Business District, $$, p. 135)

HAMBURGERS

Camellia Grill ✿✿ (Uptown/ Garden District, $, p. 142)

Port of Call ✿✿ (French Quarter, $$, p. 118)

INTERNATIONAL

Bayona ✿✿ (French Quarter, $$$, p. 108)

Dominique's ✿ (French Quarter, $$$, p. 111)

Le Bistro ✿✿ (French Quarter, $$$, p. 113)

Lola's ✿✿✿ (Mid-City/Esplanade, $$, p. 129)

Marisol ✿ (French Quarter, $$$, p. 113)

ITALIAN

Angeli on Decatur ✿✿ (French Quarter, $, p. 121)

Bacco ✿✿ (French Quarter, $$$, p. 108)

Café Giovanni ✿ (French Quarter, $$$, p. 110)

Irene's Cuisine ✿✿ (French Quarter, $$, p. 115)

Liuzza's ✿✿ (Mid-City/Esplanade, $$, p. 129)

Mama Rosa's ✿ (French Quarter, $, p. 123)

Mandina's ✿✿ (Mid-City/ Esplanade, $$, p. 129)

Maximo's Italian Grill ✿ (French Quarter, $$, p. 117)

Napoleon House ✿ (French Quarter, $, p. 124)

Pascal's Manale ✿ (Uptown/ Garden District, $$, p. 141)

Peristyle ✿✿✿ (French Quarter, $$$, p. 114)

JAPANESE

Samurai Sushi ✿ (French Quarter, $$, p. 120)

MEDITERRANEAN

Angeli on Decatur ✿✿ (French Quarter, $, p. 121)

Mystic Cafe ✿✿ (Uptown/Garden District, $, p. 143)

MEXICAN

Taqueria Corona ✿✿ (Central Business District, $, p. 136)

MIDDLE EASTERN

Mona's Café & Deli ✿✿ (Faubourg Marigny, $, p. 126)

PIZZA

Louisiana Pizza Kitchen (French Quarter, $, p. 123)

Mama Rosa's ✿ (French Quarter, $, p. 123)

SANDWICHES

Acme Oyster House ✿✿ (French Quarter, $, p. 121)

Café au Lait ✿ (French Quarter, $, p. 145)

Café Maspero ✿ (French Quarter, $, p. 122)

Camellia Grill ✿✿ (Uptown/ Garden District, $, p. 142)

Johnny's Po-Boys ✿✿ (French Quarter, $, p. 122)

Martin Wine Cellar and Delicatessen ✿✿ (Uptown/ Garden District, $, p. 143)

Mother's ✿✿ (Central Business District, $, p. 136)

Royal Blend Coffee & Tea House ✿ (French Quarter and Central Business District, $, p. 146)

Uglesich's Restaurant & Bar ✿✿ (Central Business District, $, p. 136)

SEAFOOD

Acme Oyster House ✿✿ (French Quarter, $, p. 121)

Bourbon House Seafood ✿ (French Quarter, $$$, p. 109)

Bruning's Seafood on the Lake ✿ (Lake Pontchartrain, $$, p. 144)

Café Maspero ✿ (French Quarter, $, p. 122)

Casamento's ✹✹ (Uptown/Garden District, $, p. 142)

Deanie's Seafood Bucktown USA ✹ (Metairie, $$, p. 144)

Felix's Restaurant & Oyster Bar ✹✹ (French Quarter, $, p. 122)

Franky & Johnny's ✹ (Uptown/Garden District, $, p. 142)

Joey K's ✹ (Uptown/Garden District, $, p. 143)

Olde N'Awlins Cookery ✹ (French Quarter, $$, p. 118)

Pascal's Manale ✹ (Uptown/ Garden District, $$, p. 141)

Ralph & Kacoo's (French Quarter, $$, p. 119)

Red Fish Grill ✹ (French Quarter, $$, p. 119)

Rib Room ✹ (French Quarter, $$$, p. 115)

Uglesich's Restaurant & Bar ✹✹ (Central Business District, $, p. 136)

SOUL FOOD

Dooky Chase ✹ (Mid-City/ Esplanade, $$, p. 128)

Dunbar's Creole Cooking ✹✹ (Uptown/Garden District, $, p. 142)

The Harbor ✹ (Faubourg Marigny, $, p. 126)

Jacques-Imo's ✹✹ (Uptown/ Garden District, $$$, p. 140)

Praline Connection (Faubourg Marigny, $, p. 127)

SPANISH

Lola's ✹✹✹ (Mid-City/Esplanade, $$, p. 129)

STEAK

Dickie Brennan's Steakhouse ✹✹ (French Quarter, $$$, p. 111)

Pascal's Manale ✹ (Uptown/ Garden District, $$, p. 141)

Rib Room ✹ (French Quarter, $$$, p. 115)

Ruth's Chris Steak House ✹ (Mid-City/Esplanade, $$$, p. 127)

VEGETARIAN

Old Dog New Trick Café ✹ (French Quarter, $, p. 124)

VIETNAMESE

Lemon Grass ✹✹ (Central Business District, $$, p. 133)

3 The French Quarter

VERY EXPENSIVE

Arnaud's ✹ CREOLE   Arnaud's may have the lowest profile of all the classic old New Orleans restaurants, but it's probably the most reliable in terms of quality. In addition to the formal (and seriously New Orleans) dining room, it now has a more casual jazz bistro featuring lovely lunches that put the other grande dame establishments to shame, with entertainment (and an extra cover charge) at night. Apart from the signature appetizer, shrimp Arnaud (boiled shrimp topped with a spicy rémoulade sauce), we like the crabmeat Ravigotte (crab tossed with a Creole mustard–based sauce, hearts of palm, and other veggies). Rave-producing fish dishes include snapper or trout Pontchartrain (topped with crabmeat), the spicy pompano Duarte, and pompano David and tuna Napoleon, lighter fish dishes and good choices for those watching waistlines. Any filet mignon entree is superb (the meat is often better than what's served in most steakhouses in town). Desserts aren't quite as magnificent, but the Chocolate Devastation is worth trying, and one crème brûlée fan said Arnaud's was the best she'd ever had.

Arnaud's also operates a less formal, less expensive brasserie, **Rémoulade** (p. 119), right next door.

French Quarter Dining

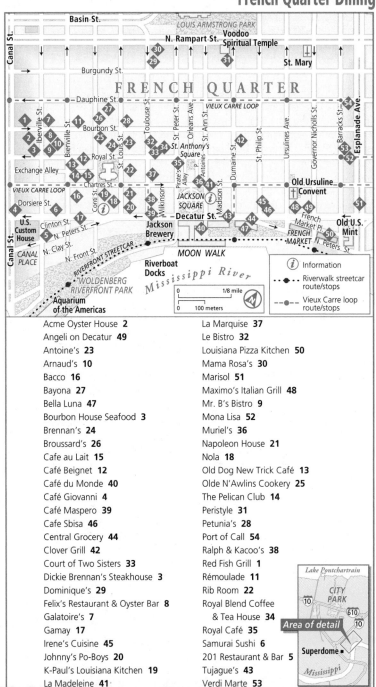

Acme Oyster House **2**
Angeli on Decatur **49**
Antoine's **23**
Arnaud's **10**
Bacco **16**
Bayona **27**
Bella Luna **47**
Bourbon House Seafood **3**
Brennan's **24**
Broussard's **26**
Cafe au Lait **15**
Café Beignet **12**
Café du Monde **40**
Café Giovanni **4**
Café Maspero **39**
Cafe Sbisa **46**
Central Grocery **44**
Clover Grill **42**
Court of Two Sisters **33**
Dickie Brennan's Steakhouse **3**
Dominique's **29**
Felix's Restaurant & Oyster Bar **8**
Galatoire's **7**
Gamay **17**
Irene's Cuisine **45**
Johnny's Po-Boys **20**
K-Paul's Louisiana Kitchen **19**
La Madeleine **41**

La Marquise **37**
Le Bistro **32**
Louisiana Pizza Kitchen **50**
Mama Rosa's **30**
Marisol **51**
Maximo's Italian Grill **48**
Mr. B's Bistro **9**
Mona Lisa **52**
Muriel's **36**
Napoleon House **21**
Nola **18**
Old Dog New Trick Café **13**
Olde N'Awlins Cookery **25**
The Pelican Club **14**
Peristyle **31**
Petunia's **28**
Port of Call **54**
Ralph & Kacoo's **38**
Red Fish Grill **1**
Rémoulade **11**
Rib Room **22**
Royal Blend Coffee
   & Tea House **34**
Royal Café **35**
Samurai Sushi **6**
201 Restaurant & Bar **5**
Tujague's **43**
Verdi Marte **53**

813 Bienville St. ℂ **504/523-5433.** www.arnauds.com. Reservations recommended. Jackets required in main dining room at dinner. Main courses $19–$38. AE, DC, DISC, MC, V. Mon–Fri 11:30am–2:30pm; Sun Jazz brunch 10am–2:30pm; Sun–Thurs 6–10pm; Fri–Sat 6–10:30pm.

EXPENSIVE

Antoine's ⚜ CREOLE   Owned and operated by the same family for an astonishing 150 years, Antoine's is, unfortunately, beginning to show its age. With its 15 dining rooms and massive menu (more than 150 items), it was once the ultimate in fine dining in New Orleans. Thomas Wolfe said he ate the best meal of his life here, and author Frances Parkinson Keyes immortalized it in her mystery *Dinner at Antoine's.* But subtle murmurs about a decline in quality have become outright complaints. It has been the subject of many discussions, in print and among locals, on how the food quality has gone sharply downhill and how knowing your waiter has become a necessity. It is the waiter, after all, who determines which of those 15 dining rooms you sit in, and some locals have found themselves in the front room, where only (gasp!) *tourists* get seated.

Still, it's hard to ignore a legend, and so with some caution you may wish to investigate for yourself. Locals—loyal customers all, mind you—will advise you to focus on starters and dessert and skip the entrees. They're right; at best, the latter are bland but acceptable. You might order a side of creamed spinach, which is classic comfort food. Oysters Rockefeller (served hot in the shell, and covered with a mysterious green sauce—Antoine's invented it and still won't give out the recipe) will live up to its rep, and the infamous football-size (and football-shaped) baked Alaska is surely the most frivolous dessert ever. After he won the Nobel Prize for literature, William Faulkner got one inscribed "the Ignoble Prize."

713 St. Louis St. ℂ **504/581-4422.** www.antoines.com. Reservations required. Jacket required and tie recommended at dinner. Main courses $22–$38. AE, DC, MC, V. Mon–Sat 11:30am–2pm and 5:30–9:30pm.

Bacco ⚜⚜ ITALIAN/CREOLE   Bacco is romantic and candlelit at night, more affordable and casual at lunchtime. Don't expect spaghetti and marinara sauce here. Instead, think rich, arresting creations such as *ravioli ripieni di formaggio,* featuring four creamy cheeses all melting into a sauce of olive oil, tomatoes, and browned garlic. Or try the *cannelloni con fungi,* stuffed with wild mushrooms and fresh herbs, and covered in a goat cheese and chive sauce. The menu changes regularly, but our latest trip featured an appetizer of truffled egg rolled in herbed bread crumbs with Gorgonzola cream sauce—it goes without saying that it was rich, but it's a combo you need to experience. Truffle pasta made us so happy we asked for the recipe, and the pumpkin *panna cotta* for dessert was something we told people about for months. Alas, the latter was a seasonal special, but because this is a Brennan (the most prominent name in New Orleans dining, as the family collectively operates over half a dozen restaurants in the area) restaurant, desserts are generally above average—including possibly the best version of tiramisu we've ever had.

310 Chartres St. ℂ **504/522-2426.** www.bacco.com. Reservations recommended. Main courses $18–$31. AE, DC, MC, V. Daily 11:30am–2pm and 6–10pm.

Bayona ⚜⚜ INTERNATIONAL   Bayona's reputation as one of the top newer (lately, that means less than 15 years old!) restaurants is so well deserved that patrons have been known to burst into applause driving by. Chef-owner Susan Spicer is a local treasure—she also is behind Herbsaint and Cobalt, both reviewed in this chapter—and Bayona's lovely courtyard only adds to the pleasures of the experience.

Impressions

The Louisiana diet will kill a man as surely as the sword.

—King of the Hill

Be sure to begin with the outstanding cream of garlic soup, a perennial favorite. Appetizers include grilled shrimp with cilantro sauce and black bean cakes, and delicate, flavorful veal sweetbreads sautéed with scallions and diced potatoes in sherry vinaigrette. Knockout entrees have included medallions of lamb loin with a lavender honey aioli (a mayonnaise-based sauce) and a zinfandel demi-glace; a perfectly grilled pork chop with a stuffing of fontina cheese, fresh sage, and prosciutto; and yet another lamb dish, this one topped with goat cheese, that may have been the best lamb we've ever tasted. Heaven. Entrees come with a well-balanced selection of sides such as gnocchi, puréed butternut squash, or fresh sweet corn. And lunch brings a smoked duck (with apple butter and jelly) sandwich that has been boxed to go on many a plane flight!

430 Dauphine St. ✆ **504/525-4455.** www.bayona.com. Reservations required at dinner, recommended at lunch. Main courses at lunch $9–$14, at dinner $16–$28. AE, DC, DISC, MC, V. Mon–Fri 11:30am–2pm; Mon–Thurs 6–9:30pm; Fri–Sat 6–10:30pm.

Bella Luna ✦ ECLECTIC/CONTINENTAL   With its sweeping view of the Mississippi, Bella Luna is considered the most romantic restaurant in town, but no one can quite agree on the food, which has both its fans and its detractors. We are coming down on the side of the former—and not just because entrees are garnished with curious herbs from the chef/owner's garden (which he maintains over at the Ursuline Convent).

The menu changes periodically, but we'll list some things to look for: Definitely try the fettuccine appetizer, prepared tableside. It's a wonderfully fresh pasta, happily light for a dish that can sometimes be gluey and heavy. A salmon tower with white truffle oil, cucumber, and red onion with Louisiana *choupique* (fish) caviar and capers—well, gee, doesn't that sound good? It is. Skip the meat entrees, like an ultimately uninteresting veal chop, in favor of fish dishes such as sautéed redfish in a sweet basil pesto crust. Even ordinary dishes like mashed potatoes are done well, light as air, fluffy as a cloud, and maybe containing garlic, truffles, or something else that's equally delightful. Desserts include a bananas Foster bread pudding, a milk-chocolate-and-cappuccino cheesecake, and a slightly less successful chocolate-and-Jack Daniel's ice cream. Do ask if your table has a good view (the closer to the windows, the better). Note that service can be uneven, so don't go unless you can linger—which you may well want to, hypnotized by Old Man River rolling along.

914 N. Peters St. ✆ **504/529-1583.** Reservations recommended. Dress is business casual. Main courses $16–$28. AE, DC, DISC, MC, V. Mon–Sat 6–10:30pm; Sun 6–9:30pm.

Bourbon House Seafood ✦ SEAFOOD   The latest entry from Dickie Brennan, this is a modern take on the classic New Orleans fish house, both aesthetically and gastronomically. It's a big, cheerful room with balcony seating perfect for spying or canoodling. The menu features all kinds of fish, from platters of fresh boiled or raw seafood to entrees like baked fish Grieg (soft, tender fish in a meunière sauce that is neither overpowering nor overly buttery) and grilled Gulf fish on a ragout of local legumes. There's fried stuff as well, like crab claws with a mustardy rémoulade sauce. If either the sweetbreads with crabmeat or the bouillabaisse (stewed in a tomato tarragon broth) are offered on the specials, get them. For dessert, we favor the lemon Creole cream cheese cheesecake, but others prefer the house specialty, a crunchy chocolate blondie (a type of brownie pie). Breakfast/brunch brings other Creole traditional breakfast favorites, like *pain perdu.*

144 Bourbon St. ℂ 504/522-0111. Reservations recommended. Main courses breakfast $5.25–$20, lunch $8.50–$20, dinner $19–$27. AE, DISC, MC, V. Daily 6:30am–10am; 11:30am–2:30pm; 5:30pm–11pm.

Brennan's ⊛ FRENCH/CREOLE   For more than 40 years, breakfast at Brennan's has been a New Orleans tradition, a feast that has surely kept many a heart surgeon busy. Don't expect any California health-conscious fruit-and-granola options here; this multicourse extravaganza is unabashedly sauce- and egg-intensive. It's also costly—it's not hard to drop $50 on breakfast—so you might be better off sticking with the fixed-price meal (though it often limits your choices). Breakfast at Brennan's has changed very little over the years, and that is part of the restaurant's charm, as is the building, constructed by Edgar Degas's great-grandfather and childhood home of tragic chess master Paul Morphy. Dine here and you will find yourself rubbing elbows with loyal locals (including transplant Trent Reznor, leader of the band Nine Inch Nails, who is a regular and a favorite of the staff) and tourists in search of a classic. Enjoy dishes such as eggs Portuguese (poached on top of a tomato concoction, served in a puff pastry with hollandaise ladled over the whole), the fine turtle soup, and the superb onion soup made with a roux. You can justify it all by making this your main meal of the day. Breakfast and lunch are quite crowded; dinner is less so (head straight to the gas lamp–lined balcony for dinner), probably due to a less-solid reputation for that meal. Even with a reservation, expect a wait.

417 Royal St. ℂ 504/525-9711. www.brennansneworleans.com. Reservations recommended. Main courses $20–$39; fixed-price lunch $35; fixed-price 4-course dinner $39. AE, DC, DISC, MC, V. Daily 8am–2:30pm and 6–10pm. Closed Christmas.

Broussard's ⊛ CREOLE   Unfairly dismissed as a tourist trap (which, in truth, it was for some years), Broussard's is a perfectly fine alternative if your top choices are booked up. You can really have a very fine meal here. Chef Gunther Preuss and his wife, Evelyn, own the place, which includes an elegant, formal dining room and a lovely courtyard. "Gunther has a way with crab," claims his press material, and once we stopped giggling over that turn of phrase, we had to admit it was true. Try the appetizer of crabmeat Florentine, which includes spinach and is covered in a brie sauce. Be sure to order the baked filet of redfish Herbsaint (a local anise-flavored liqueur), clever and delicious in its components, which include impossibly sweet crabmeat and lemon risotto. Pompano Napoleon (grilled, with pepper-crushed scallops and shrimp, puff pastry, and a mustard-caper sauce) is a signature dish, but with phrases like "pepper-crushed" and "mustard-caper sauce," one would expect a bit more punch. Many of the desserts are happily heavy and creamy. The double chocolate Marquise Nelly Melba is as fun to eat as it is to say (it's a bittersweet chocolate parfait), while the chocolate profiteroles comes with Godiva fudge sauce.

819 Conti St. ℂ 504/581-3866. www.broussards.com. Reservations recommended. No jeans, shorts, sneakers, or T-shirts. Main courses $22–$36. AE, MC, V. Daily 5:30–10pm.

Café Giovanni ⊛ ITALIAN   Though Chef Duke LoCicero has been winning culinary awards right and left, Café Giovanni is kind of a mixed bag, thanks to a combo of fine food, lackadaisical service, and—of course—the dreaded (or highly enjoyable, depending on your conversational needs during dinner and your love of schmaltz) singing waiters (to be found Wednesday, Friday, and Saturday nights, singing opera with all their might). Still, any place that serves the gastronomic wonder that is fresh, buttery crescenza cheese on panettone *pain perdu* (Italian Christmas cake merged with local French toast . . . kinda), smeared over foie gras and topped off with a reduction sauce that ought to be illegal, well, we can overlook a little operatic noise. Though Chef Duke is renowned for his pastas, including a duck-and-rabbit ragout over pappardelle (the duck overpowered the rabbit in this rich dish) and pasta Gambino, which tosses shrimp, garlic, cream, and other tidbits together, these may not be all that much better than the pastas found over at Irene's Cuisine (p. 115).

117 Decatur St. © **504/529-2154.** www.cafegiovanni.com. Main courses $16–$26. AE, DC, DISC, MC, V. Daily 5:30–10pm.

Court of Two Sisters *Overrated* CREOLE   This is probably the prettiest restaurant in town (thanks to a huge, foliage-filled courtyard located in a 2-centuries-old building), but even major ambience can't obscure the problems with the food. You'll find the only daily jazz brunch in town here, but it suffers from the typical buffet problem—too many dishes, none of which succeed except maybe the made-to-order items like eggs Benedict. Avoid the vinegary ceviche, but try the seafood slaw (we give it a thumbs up). Dinner may be even worse; apart from a Caesar salad (made in the traditional style, at tableside), there is little, if anything, to recommend. It's a pity, because you can't ask for a better setting.

613 Royal St. © **504/522-7261.** www.courtoftwosisters.com. Reservations recommended for dinner and brunch. Main courses $18–$30; fixed-price menu $39; brunch $23. AE, DC, DISC, MC, V. Daily 9am–3pm and 5:30–10pm.

Dickie Brennan's Steakhouse ★★ STEAK   Carnivores should be pleased with this particular Brennan family establishment, which has the feel of a contemporary clubhouse. All the meat is USDA Prime, and great care is taken to cook it just as the customer dictates. The house filet comes surrounded by quite good creamed spinach and Pontalba potatoes (diced roasted potatoes sautéed with garlic, onions, wild mushrooms, ham, and scallions). We rather prefer the tender, flavorful rib-eye, but do get creamed spinach on the side. Start with the napoleon (layered puff pastry) of tomato and Gorgonzola cheese, topped with rémoulade sauce—it's a little busy, but you'll enjoy it. Steak Diane is butter-soft with a slightly sweet flavor. Prime beef salad is heavy on the dressing, but luckily the dressing is not cloying. Surprisingly, the tuna (with mango and maque choux—a side dish made with corn) is quite good. Don't miss the bananas Foster bread pudding, which proves that there can still be new twists on this old faithful dish.

716 Iberville St. © **504/522-2467.** www.dbrennanssteakhouse.com. Reservations recommended. Main courses $15–$35. AE, DC, DISC, MC, V. Mon–Fri 11:30am–2:30pm and 5:30–10pm; Sat–Sun 5:30–10pm.

Dominique's ★ INTERNATIONAL   Here's yet another reason for the New Orleans restaurant scene to be grateful to Le Bistro at the Maison de Ville. Like Bayona's Susan Spicer and others before him, Chef Dominique Macquet (originally from the Indian Ocean island of Mauritius) worked at Le Bistro before opening up his eponymous restaurant. Named one of the seven best new restaurants in America by *Bon Appétit* in 1998, this medium-size bistro is well worth a little trot up the Rue Toulouse—worth it, that is, as long as you want to try cutting-edge dishes like duck pastrami and duck prosciutto, and trust us, you do. The menu changes regularly, but if offered, both the foie gras seared with Bing cherries, and the Three-Way Duck Salad (duck confit with baby spinach, duck crackling, and duck prosciutto with a nectarine and Gewürztraminer vinaigrette) are very good. Entrees vary—the grilled filet of beef *farci,* with Boursin cheese rösti potatoes, carrot and molasses flan, and shallot jus, is most enjoyable, but you can probably skip the "signature" Maine lobster. For dessert, try the chocolate soufflé or the "cappamisu" (cappuccino-flavored tiramisu).

In the Maison Dupuy Hotel, 1001 Toulouse St. ✆ **504/522-8800.** www.dominiquesrestaurant.com. Reservations recommended. Main courses $22–$30. AE, DC, DISC, MC, V. Daily 7–10:30am and 6–10pm.

Galatoire's ✿ FRENCH

The venerable Galatoire's causes heated discussions these days among local foodies: Is it still the best restaurant in New Orleans or is it past its prime? Locals love it because they've gone for regular Sunday-evening dinners for years, and all the old waiters know their names. We love it because in *A Streetcar Named Desire* Stella took Blanche there to escape Stanley's poker game. It was Tennessee Williams' favorite restaurant (his table is the one right behind the word RESTAURANT on the window). Galatoire's has been run by the same family since 1905, and its traditions remain intact. A spectacular renovation of the upstairs dining room, which had been closed since World War II, provided much-needed additional seating.

Galatoire's is worth the trip, though you may not have the same experience as a knowledgeable local unless you get a waiter who can really guide you (ask for John). We love the lump crabmeat appetizer (think coleslaw, only with crab instead of cabbage), the shrimp rémoulade, and the oysters Rockefeller. For an entree, get the red snapper or redfish topped with sautéed crabmeat meunière (a delightful butter sauce)—it will probably be one of the finest fish dishes you'll have during your stay. Don't miss out on the terrific creamed spinach and the puffy potatoes with béarnaise sauce, which will make you swear off regular french fries forever.

209 Bourbon St. ✆ **504/525-2021.** www.galatoires.com. Reservations accepted for upstairs. Jackets required after 5pm and all day Sun. Main courses $14–$27. AE, DC, DISC, MC, V. Sun noon–10pm; Tues–Sat 11:30am–10pm. Closed Memorial Day, July 4th, Thanksgiving, and Christmas.

Gamay ✿✿ CREOLE

This is another offering from the chef/owners of Gabrielle (see p. 128). Gamay is a little bit more starched and formal than its predecessor, but the contemporary Creole food is so darn good that we don't really care all that much. The menu changes often, but if you can, try appetizers like barbecue shrimp pie or grilled Mayhorn cheese with Beluga caviar and oysters. Among the entrees, the almond-crusted soft-shell crab with garlic shrimp and saffron pasta was too huge and rich to finish, though we did give it a gallant try. A Gulf fish of the day came with balsamic vinegar sauce and flash-fried spinach that was at once both sweet and savory. Dessert options include the heavenly strawberry shortcake and a large wedge of chocolate layer cake.

In the Bienville House hotel, 320 Decatur St. ✆ **504/299-8800.** Reservations recommended. Main courses $18–$28. AE, DC, DISC, MC, V. Mon–Fri 11:30am–2pm and 5:30–10:30pm; Sat 5:30–10:30pm.

K-Paul's Louisiana Kitchen ✿ CAJUN/CREOLE

Paul Prudhomme was at the center of the Cajun revolution of the early '80s, when Cajun food became known throughout the world. His reputation and his line of spices continue today, which is probably why there is constantly a line outside his restaurant. Unfortunately, although the American regional food is still good, it's not spectacular and certainly is not worth the wait (upwards of 1½ hr.). The portions are

Paul-size (that is, large) and as spicy as you might imagine, but nothing that special. Indeed, it feels as if the menu hasn't changed all that dramatically in quite some time. More interesting and innovative food is available all over town, and at some places you can get Prudhomme-influenced food (any restaurant in town that serves Creole food or has blackened fish is a Prudhomme-influenced restaurant) without the long wait (other places take reservations).

Different menu items are offered daily, but you can't go wrong with jambalaya (spicy!) or bronzed or blackened anything (really spicy!). One vegetarian friend claims the fried eggplant dish he had there was one of his lifetime outstanding meals (you have to ask for it; it's not regularly featured on the menu).

416 Chartres St. © **504/524-7394**. www.kpauls.com. Reservations accepted for upstairs dining room only. Main courses at lunch $17–$23, at dinner $26–$36. AE, DC, DISC, MC, V. Mon–Sat 5:30–10pm.

Le Bistro ★★ INTERNATIONAL   This tiny jewel of a bistro, part of the superb Hotel Maison de Ville, is easy to overlook among the higher-profile choices in the French Quarter. But it's a favorite among in-the-know locals, who think of it as a training ground for new chefs who then go on to make a splash at their own restaurants (as Susan Spicer has at Bayona). Patrons also bask in the warm Gallic glow of hospitality emitted by long-time maitre d' Patrick, who will remember your name and your favorite dish and who will insist that you try the crème brûlée (he's right, Le Bistro's version is as good as it gets).

The menu changes regularly, but a recent dinner visit produced uniformly marvelous dishes such as a Beggar's Purse (a little concoction made of phyllo dough), an oyster appetizer, and generous entrees of wild boar and swordfish. It's also an excellent choice for lunch, with selections like the rich country pâté, lovely salads, and especially the signature dish of mussels with thick french fries and homemade mayonnaise. Don't forget to finish with the crème brûlée, and tell Patrick we said, "Hi."

In the Hotel Maison de Ville, 727 Toulouse St. © **504/528-9206**. www.maisondeville.com. Reservations recommended. Main courses $21–$28. AE, DC, DISC, MC, V. Mon–Sat 11:30am–2pm; daily 6–10pm.

Marisol ★ INTERNATIONAL   Located in a charming and inexplicably cursed space—that is, one that has seen many restaurants come and go in a short number of years—Marisol itself seems to be struggling. While the menu is considerably less complicated than it was originally (all to the better; the dishes then were ambitious but by and large unsuccessful), it still isn't anything to get worked up over (apart from an excellent Thai crab and coconut soup). There is, however, a nice soft-shell crab on jasmine rice, a very good roast chicken on Tuscan bread salad, and adequate fish dishes like pan-seared Spanish mackerel in a slightly salty sherry vinegar sauce. Service can be heedless and slow—too bad— this is one of the nicest courtyards in town, and dining here on a sultry night can be bliss. So we have a suggestion: At this writing, they have an extensive cheese course, two or three dozen choices at least, so coming here for cheese and wine should be a marvelous option.

437 Esplanade Ave. © **504/943-1912**. www.marisolrestaurant.com. Reservations recommended. Main courses $18–$28. AE, DC, MC, V. Tues–Fri 11am–2pm and 6–10pm; Fri–Sat 6–11pm; Sun brunch 11am–2pm.

Muriel's ★★ CREOLE/ECLECTIC   Conventional wisdom would have it that any restaurant this close to tourist-hub Jackson Square—as in, across the street from it—would have to serve overpriced, mediocre food. But then conventional wisdom notes the Gothic-parlor look to the dining rooms in the newish Muriel's (among the pretty touches: a wall covered in antique photos, a dressing table fit for Miss DuBois, a floating doorway leading nowhere) and decides to sit down just to be polite. Then conventional wisdom eats excellent seared scallops with balsamic vinegar, smoked oysters with bacon, and house salad with vanilla-bean vinaigrette, poached pears, and Stilton—and skips the seared foie gras because it's a bit too dry—following it up with perfect grilled barbecue shrimp, equally good lamb, and Dijon mustard–crusted salmon. Sated and fully satisfied, conventional wisdom then floats upstairs, past the table set for the in-house ghosts, and into the Séance Room, which looks like a gypsy den crossed with a bordello, and has a drink. Conventional wisdom is reminded that rules are made to be broken and vows to tell everyone to come here.

801 Chartres (at St. Ann). ✆ **504/568-1885.** Reservations suggested. Main courses $9.50–$13 lunch, $15.50–$26 dinner. AE, DISC, MC, V. Wed–Sun 11:30am–3:30pm; Sun–Thurs 5:30pm–10pm; Fri–Sat 5:30pm–11pm.

Nola ⋆⋆ CREOLE/NEW AMERICAN   This modern two-story building with a glass-enclosed elevator is the most casual and the least expensive of chef Emeril Lagasse's three restaurants, and the most conveniently located for the average tourist. As with Lagasse's other restaurants, the dining experience can be a bit hit-and-miss (perhaps this will change now that Chef Lagasse's sitcom foray has ended). We've had frequent problems with attitude here (at least when making reservations and when showing up for them; the service thereafter is fine, if slow at times), but when the food is on, it's spectacular—especially since Neal Swidler, from Emeril's Delmonico, became chef de cuisine—we think he's one to watch. Try smoked duck pizza with Brie and white truffle aioli as a starter, or any filet (we especially liked the one with red potatoes, walnuts, and bacon in a port wine reduction, with bleu cheese and shallot crisps), but proceed with caution when the "Vietnamese" influences show up, as they aren't reliable. Vegetarians will be thrilled with the portobello mushroom en croûte (with ratatouille, truffled mascarpone, and brie cream sauce). And no one will complain about the desserts; don't miss the fried apple pie, and try a taste of the pineapple–lemon grass ice cream if it's served that night.

534 St. Louis St. ✆ **504/522-6652.** www.emerils.com. Reservations recommended. Main courses $20–$32. AE, DC, DISC, MC, V. Mon–Sat 11:30am–2pm; Sun–Thurs 6–10:30pm; Fri–Sat 6pm–11pm.

The Pelican Club ⋆ NEW AMERICAN   Just a short stroll from the House of Blues, the Pelican Club is worth investigating, particularly for its reasonably priced three-course fixed-price meal. The appetizers are a bit more inventive than the entrees (you could easily make a meal of them), but everything is quite tasty. Escargots come in a tequila garlic butter sauce (which you will probably find yourself sopping up with bread), topped with tiny puff pastries. Oysters are garnished with apple-smoked bacon—even oysterphobes won't have a problem with these babies. Special salads are served each evening; a recent visit found arugula, Gorgonzola, and apple in balsamic dressing. Tender lamb comes coated in rosemary-flavored bread crumbs with a spicy pepper jelly, and fish is cooked to perfection. Interesting sides like wild-mushroom bread pudding accompany the entrees. The desserts are certainly standouts. Try the flat (rather than puffy) white chocolate bread pudding, creamy chocolate pecan pie, or amazing profiteroles filled with coffee ice cream and topped with three sauces.

615 Bienville St., entrance in Exchange Alley. ✆ **504/523-1504.** Reservations recommended. Main courses $18–$42; fixed-price early dinner $25. AE, DC, DISC, MC, V. Daily 5–10pm.

Peristyle ⋆⋆⋆ FRENCH/AMERICAN/ITALIAN/BISTRO   It's had its share of ups and downs over the years (the death of the original chef-owner, a devastating fire in 1999), but Peristyle rises back up each time better than ever and is right now perhaps the best restaurant in town. Fighting words, but come try chef-owner Anne Kearney's food and see what you think. The space is brighter and perhaps noisier than in its past incarnation (it still occupies the site of Marti's, where Tennessee Williams used to sit daily on the balcony and play poker), but we are here to say we've eaten several meals here in the last couple years, and there hasn't been a clunker dish yet. From lovely salads and fun appetizers like the caramelized onion tart or the country pâté of the day to the always generous-size (and isn't that a relief?) entree portions (recently, we fought over which was more outstanding—farm-raised quail with roasted shallot–applewood bacon–pecan relish; sage-marinated pork chop with butternut squash gnocchi; or lemon-fennel tuna with crispy potato cake), it's all just a delight, innovative without being threatening, and a near-perfect melding of flavors. And yes, the desserts are wonderful, though we do tend to burn out by then, having stuffed ourselves silly.

1041 Dumaine St. ℂ **504/593-9535.** Reservations recommended. Main courses $24–$27. AE, DC, MC, V. Fri 11:30am–1:30pm; Tues–Sat 6–10pm.

Rib Room ⭐ SEAFOOD/STEAK   This is where New Orleanians come to eat beef. And who can fault their choice of surroundings? The solid and cozy Old English feel of this room is complete with natural-brick and open ovens at the back. But while the meat is good, it is not outstanding, and the acclaimed prime rib is just a bit tough and more than lacking in flavor. There are also filets, sirloins, brochettes, tournedos, and steak *au poivre,* plus some seafood dishes. Carnivores, landlubbers, and ichthyophobes will be happier here than at one of the city's Creole restaurants, but it is not the must-do that its reputation would have you believe.

In the Omni Royal Orleans hotel, 621 St. Louis St. ℂ **504/529-7045.** www.omniroyalorleans.com. Reservations recommended. Main courses $24–$34. AE, DC, DISC, MC, V. Daily 6:30–10:30am, 11:30am–2:30pm (serving lunch Mon–Sat, brunch Sun), and 6–10pm.

MODERATE

Cafe Sbisa CREOLE   Right across from the French Market, Cafe Sbisa opened in 1899 and in the 1970s was one of the first restaurants to experiment with Creole cooking. After a brief closure, it has once again become a local favorite. But here's one instance where you may not want to go where the locals go. We found the food decidedly mediocre. Barbecued shrimp came in a sauce something like heavy Worcestershire. It was adequate but disappointing. A special of wild boar was tough and chewy and its preparation bland. A salad special, with Bibb lettuce, unusual zebra tomatoes, and lemon vinaigrette, was memorable, however. You can't fault the atmosphere, which is classy and unpretentious, with live piano music some nights. The waitstaff is almost smothering in their friendly, effusive care. Sbisa offers a Sunday jazz brunch.

1011 Decatur St. ℂ **504/522-5565.** www.cafesbisa.com. Reservations recommended. Main courses $15–$25. AE, DC, DISC, MC, V. Sun–Thurs 5:30–10:30pm; Fri–Sat 5:30–11pm; Sun brunch 10:30am–3pm.

Irene's Cuisine ⭐⭐ FRENCH/ITALIAN   Irene's is somewhat off the regular tourist dining path, and locals would probably prefer to keep it that way—it's hard enough getting into one of their favorite neighborhood bistros. In fact, in a constantly uncertain and changing world, waiting upwards of 90 minutes for a table at Irene's is something you can count on. But those same locals feel the French provincial and Italian food is worth it, and you may as well. Once you do enter, after being lured in from a block away by the potent smell of garlic,

Finds Chuck Taggart's Red Beans & Rice

Chuck Taggart is a native New Orleanian currently residing in Los Angeles. For more than 10 years he has been a music programmer and DJ, producing and hosting "Down Home" on KCSN, 88.5 FM, a program featuring Louisiana music and roots and traditional music from around the world. He is the creator, author, editor, and webmaster of the Gumbo Pages (www.gumbopages.com), a site devoted to Louisiana music, culture, and cuisine. He is also a culinary arts student at UCLA Extension and aspires to become a chef—if he can ever tear himself away from his cushy day job.

Red beans and rice is the quintessential New Orleans dish, traditionally served on Mondays. It's going to take a little practice before you get it right. You'll probably want to fiddle with it each time you make it and arrive at the exact combinations of seasonings you like. Feel free to alter this recipe to your taste, but don't stray too far.

1 pound dried red kidney beans
1 large onion, chopped
1 bell pepper, chopped
5 ribs celery, chopped
As much minced garlic as you like (I like lots, 5 or 6 cloves)
1 large smoked ham hock, 1 big chunk of Creole-style pickle meat (pickled pork), or ¾ pound smoked ham, diced
1 to 1½ pounds mild or hot smoked sausage or andouille, sliced
½ to 1 teaspoon dried thyme leaves, crushed
1 or 2 bay leaves
Crystal hot sauce or Tabasco, to taste
A few dashes Worcestershire sauce
Creole seasoning blend or red pepper, to taste
Salt and freshly ground black pepper, to taste
Fresh Creole hot sausage or chaurice, grilled or pan-fried, 1 link or patty per person, for serving (optional)
Pickled onions (optional)
White long-grain rice, for serving

you will find a dark, cluttered tavern, not unromantic (provided you don't mind a noise level that's a decibel or so above hushed), with ultra-friendly waiters who seem delighted you came and who keep the crowds happy with prompt service.

The menu is heavier on meats and fish than pasta; salads come with a tangy balsamic dressing; and soups can be intriguing combinations, such as the sweet potato andouille sausage concoction. On a recent visit, we were thrilled by soft-shell-crab pasta, an entirely successful Italian/New Orleans hybrid consisting of a whole fried crustacean atop a bed of pasta with a cream sauce of garlic, crawfish, tomatoes, and wads of whole basil leaves. The panned oysters and grilled shrimp appetizer can be magnificent and don't forget the *pollo rosemarino*—five pieces of chicken marinated, partly cooked, marinated again, and then cooked a final time. Desserts, alas, are the usual dull New Orleans suspects (repeat after me: crème brûlée, bread pudding, chocolate torte . . .).

Soak the beans overnight if possible. The next day, drain and put fresh water in the pot. Bring the beans to a rolling boil. Make sure the beans are always covered by water, or they will discolor and harden. Boil the beans for 45 to 60 minutes until they are tender but not falling apart. Drain.

While the beans are boiling, sauté the trinity (onions, celery, and bell pepper) until the onions turn translucent. Add the garlic and sauté for 2 more minutes, stirring occasionally. After the beans are boiled and drained, add the sautéed vegetables to the beans and then add the meat, the seasonings, and just enough water to cover.

Bring to a boil and then reduce heat to a low simmer. Cook at least 2 to 3 hours until the whole thing gets nice and creamy. Adjust seasonings as you go along. Keep tasting it. Stir occasionally, making sure it doesn't burn or stick to the bottom of the pot. (If the beans are old—say, more than 6 to 12 months—they won't get creamy. Make sure the beans are reasonably fresh. If they're still not getting creamy, take 1 or 2 cups of beans out and mash them, then return them to the pot and stir.)

If you can, stick the beans in the fridge overnight. Reheat with a little water to get the right consistency and serve for dinner the next day. They'll taste a lot better.

Serve generous ladles of beans over hot white long-grain rice with good French bread and good beer. I also love to serve grilled or pan-fried fresh Creole hot sausage or chaurice on the side. (And pickled onions.) Serves 8 regular people or 6 hungry ones.

Vegetarian Red Beans & Rice

Sacrilege, you say? Maybe. But a lot of folks who don't eat pork, or meat of any kind, can still enjoy this dish. It's not the same, of course, but it's still pretty damned good. Follow the same above, except:

- Omit the meat
- Add 2 tablespoons vegetable oil along with the seasonings
- Add 1 teaspoon (or to taste) liquid-smoke seasoning

539 St. Phillip St. ② **504/529-8811.** Reservations accepted only for Christmas Eve, New Year's Eve, and Valentine's Day. Main courses $14–$18. AE, MC, V. Sun–Thurs 5:30–10:30pm; Fri–Sat 5:30–11pm. Closed New Year's Day, July 4th, Labor Day, and Thanksgiving.

Maximo's Italian Grill ✷ ITALIAN With its brick walls blanketed by Herman Leonard jazz photos (one of the largest collections in the world), friendly atmosphere, and cool and hot jazz on the sound system, we are glad indeed that Maximo's is open late. It's a good choice for reliable Italian food and casual comfort dining after an early show (or a lengthy afternoon nap!). On the antipasto platter, you're likely to find lovely portobello mushrooms, prosciutto-wrapped fruit, and a selection of olives. Try the prosciutto-wrapped grilled asparagus, and order anything that comes "fire roasted" (it has something complicated to do with peppers). Note that this is a very veggie-compatible place, with some delectable, entirely meat-free entrees. Go for the zabaglione (a fluffy Italian dessert made with eggs and sugar and not much else) or the Black Max (flourless chocolate cake) for dessert. The wine list is excellent.

1117 Decatur St. ℂ **504/586-8883.** www.maximositaliangrill.com. Reservations recommended. Main courses $9.95–$30. AE, DC, DISC, MC, V. Daily 6pm–until the last person leaves.

Mr. B's Bistro ★★ CONTEMPORARY CREOLE   This deceptively simple place only helps solidify the Brennan family's reputation as excellent restaurant owners. It draws a steady group of regulars for lunch several days a week, always at their regular tables—some local businesspeople just don't consider it a week without lunch here. For visitors, it's a fine place to recover from intense Royal Street shopping.

The food, mostly modern interpretations of Creole classics, is simple but peppered with spices that elevate the flavors into something your mouth really thanks you for. The crab cakes are about as good as this dish gets. Superb, too, is the not-too-spicy andouille sausage—get it in everything you can. Gumbo Ya Ya is a hearty, country-style rendition with chicken and sausage, perfect for a rainy day. The unusual pasta jambalaya is a variation on a classic dish—Gulf shrimp, andouille, duck, and chicken, tossed with spinach fettuccine. The Cajun barbecued shrimp are huge and plump, with a rich, thick, buttery sauce. It's so tasty it makes you greedy for every drop of sauce, completely oblivious to the silly bib they make you wear. Seemingly simple desserts feature just the right amount of sweet. Recent standouts were chocolate molten "up" cake with raspberry coulis and a particularly good version of the humble bread pudding.

201 Royal St. ℂ **504/523-2078.** www.mrbsbistro.com. Reservations recommended, but not required. Main courses $17–$28. AE, DC, DISC, MC, V. Mon–Sat 11:30am–3pm; Sun brunch 10:30am–3pm; Sun–Fri 5:30–10pm; Sat 5–10pm.

Olde N'Awlins Cookery ★ CREOLE/CAJUN/SEAFOOD   A good standby if your first choices are full, this family-operated restaurant serves up reliably good traditional Cajun and Creole favorites such as jambalaya, blackened redfish, and shrimp Creole. Try the Cajun barbecued shrimp and don't forget to ask for plenty of extra bread to sop up the rich, buttery, spicy sauce. Oooh, fattening. Housed in an 1849 building that's been a private house, a brothel, a bistro bar, and a disco, it makes use of the original old brick and a charming courtyard to create a very pleasant and—dare we say it?—decidedly New Orleans atmosphere.

The restaurant also offers an extensive breakfast menu with many specialty egg dishes including Atchafalaya (poached, with alligator sausage) and *des Allemandes* (poached, on fried catfish). Breakfast is served until 4pm daily and includes hash browns, grits, toast, coffee, choice of meat, and a variety of side dishes (red beans, grilled veggies, and so forth). You will probably have to wait to be seated at peak hours.

729 Conti St. ℂ **504/529-3663.** www.oldenawlinscookery.com. Reservations accepted only for parties of 5 or more. Breakfast items $7–$12; complete breakfast $7; main courses $5.75–$15 at lunch, $15–$25 at dinner. AE, MC, V. Daily 8am–11pm.

Port of Call ★★ HAMBURGERS   Sometimes you just need a burger—particularly when you've been eating many things with sauce. Locals feel strongly that the half-pound monsters served at the cozy (and we mean it) Port of Call are the best in town. We are going to take a stand and say that, while they are certainly terrific, all that meat may be too much of a good thing. The Port of Call is just a half-step above a dive, but it's a convivial place with a staff that's attentive (if somewhat harried during busy hours). The hamburgers come with a baked potato (because you might not have gotten enough food), and there also are pizzas, excellent filet mignon, rib-eye steaks, and New York strip steaks. Because businesspeople come here from all over the city, it's often jammed at regular eating hours, so try it before 7pm, when people who work in the Quarter begin to gather here. Take-out service is available.

838 Esplanade Ave. © 504/523-0120. www.portofcallneworleans.com. Main courses $6–$21. AE, MC, V. Sun–Thurs 11am–1am; Fri–Sat 11am–2am.

Ralph & Kacoo's CREOLE/SEAFOOD   This is a satisfying, reliable place for seafood, nothing we would consider writing home about, but a decent backup place. The Creole dishes are quite good, portions are more than ample, prices are reasonable, and the high volume of business means everything is fresh. Start with fried crawfish tails or the killer onion rings, and if you're adventurous, give the blackened alligator with hollandaise a try. For those on restricted diets, there's a special "heart-healthy" menu. Be sure to try the satin pie for dessert— it's a creamy, mousselike concoction of peanut butter and a thin layer of chocolate that will please even non–peanut butter fans.

519 Toulouse St. © **504/522-5226.** www.ralphandkacoos.com. Reservations necessary. Main courses $14–$40. AE, DC, DISC, MC, V. Mon–Thurs 11:30am–9pm; Fri–Sat 11am–11pm; Sun 11am–10pm.

Red Fish Grill ☆ SEAFOOD   Red Fish is far better than anything else in its price range on Bourbon Street, and—surprise!—it's another Brennan restaurant. Ralph Brennan's place serves many New Orleans specialties with an emphasis on—surprise again—fish. Skip the dull salads in favor of appetizers like shrimp rémoulade napoleon (layered between fried green tomatoes) or grilled shrimp and shiitake mushroom quesadillas. For your entree, go right to the fish they do so well. Whatever you have will be light and flaky with flavors that complement one another, rich (it *is* New Orleans) but not overly so. The signature dish is a pan-seared catfish topped with sweet potato crust and an andouille cream drizzle. It's so outstanding, we asked for the recipe so we could try to re-create it at home. (We couldn't really, but it was fun trying.) Also splendid is the grilled Gulf fish with a pecan butter sauce.

115 Bourbon St. © 504/598-1200. www.redfishgrill.com. Reservations limited. Main courses $8.75–$16 at lunch, $14–$29 at dinner. AE, DC, MC, V. Daily 11am–3pm and 5–11pm.

Rémoulade CREOLE/CAJUN/AMERICAN   An informal cafe offshoot of the venerable Arnaud's, Rémoulade is certainly better than the otherwise exceedingly tourist-trap restaurants on Bourbon Street (Red Fish Grill being the exception), offering average but adequate local food at reasonable prices. You are best off ignoring the undistinguished jambalayas, gumbos, and so forth in favor of trying some of the Arnaud's specialties featured here—particularly the fine turtle soup and shrimp rémoulade. Burgers and pizza fill out the menu. *Note:* This is one of the few places in town that serves Brocatto's Italian ice cream. A visit for a serving of this fabulous local product (it's impossibly thick and creamy) is a mandatory pit stop for us on a hot day.

309 Bourbon St. © 504/523-0377. Main courses $5–$17. AE, DISC, MC, V. Daily 11:30am–midnight.

Royal Café ☆ CREOLE   The Royal Café is felicitously located in perhaps the most photographed building in the Quarter—a corner edifice with multilevels of intricate wrought-iron lacework on the balconies. Being suckers for setting, we wouldn't blame you if you chose to eat here strictly for the chance to sit on that same balcony, ferns overhead, Quarter life going on below. Just don't blame us if the food is only average. Skip the disappointing shrimp rémoulade and merely okay salads and go for the hearty and just-right gumbo or the Louisiana french dip, which is more accurately described as a roast beef po' boy—it drips with gravy and will stick to your ribs. Desserts such as the Dark Chocolate Desire Cake and the Godiva Meltdown Ice Cream Extravaganza are not refined but are bursts of sugar that should make you even happier as you enjoy your view.

700 Royal St. ℂ 504/528-9086. www.royalcafe.com. Reservations required for parties of 6 or more. Main courses $12–$24. AE, MC, V. Mon–Fri 11am–3pm; Sat–Sun 10am–3pm; daily 6–10pm.

Samurai Sushi ★ JAPANESE   Lord knows we love a cream sauce as much as, and probably more than, the next person, to say nothing of our deep commitment to deep-fried anything, but sometimes something's gotta give (like our waistbands), and that's why, if we can't get our hands on a plain green salad, we end up eating sushi. If you find yourself needing a similar break, you could do worse than trying out this French Quarter sushi place, which also delivers both in the Quarter and the Central Business District. While the crawfish tail sushi is hit or miss, the Crunchy Roll (a California roll topped with tempura—see, we always come back to deep-fried) and the spicy tuna roll are worth checking out, as is the enjoyably named Flying Fish Roll. They also have teriyaki and so forth. And it is interesting to see how a town known for fish does it raw.

239 Decatur St. ℂ 504/525-9595. Sushi $3.50–$7.50 for pieces/rolls; lunch specials $6.25–$11; dinner $15–$26. AE, DC, DISC, MC, V. Mon–Thurs 11:30am–10pm; Fri 11:30am–10:30pm; Sat 5–10:30pm; Sun 5–10pm.

Tujague's ★ CREOLE   Dating back to 1856, Tujague's (pronounced *two*-jacks) is every bit as venerable and aged as the big-name New Orleans restaurants (heck, in the bar they've got a mirror that has been in place for 150 yr.!), and yet no one ever mentions it—which is a shame. It may not be a knockout, but it's authentic and solid.

Finds Food on the Fly

Time has a way of disappearing, never again to be accounted for, in New Orleans. This is really not a problem, but still, you gotta eat, if only to keep your strength up for all that, well, whatever it was that you did or will do. So if you find yourself strapped for time, lacking a reservation, or just too exhausted to leave your hotel room, here are some options that deliver. (You might also take note of listings below for the exceptional Foodie's Kitchen and Martin Wine Cellar, both of whom offer superb take-out choices, the best in the city. Alas, neither delivers at this time.)

The **Verdi Marte**, 1201 Royal St. (ℂ 504/525-4767), is a favorite with Quarter dwellers (they also deliver to the Faubourg Marigny). It's open 24 hours with bargain-basement prices for local dishes, plus decent salads and fine barbecue. **Mona Lisa** ★, 1212 Royal St. (ℂ 504/522-6746), will deliver better-than-fine pizza and Italian dishes to you in the Quarter seven days a week.

For those staying uptown or near City Park, there's even better pizza (try the Mediterranean, which is roasted garlic cloves and bell peppers, or the Sun Pie, with goat cheese and pesto) from **Reginelli's** ★, 741 State St. (ℂ 504/899-1414) or 874 Harrison St. (ℂ 504/488-0133). They'll also deliver in the Quarter. We love Reginelli's 'cause they were open during Mardi Gras and actually delivered our pizza in the promised 45 minutes!

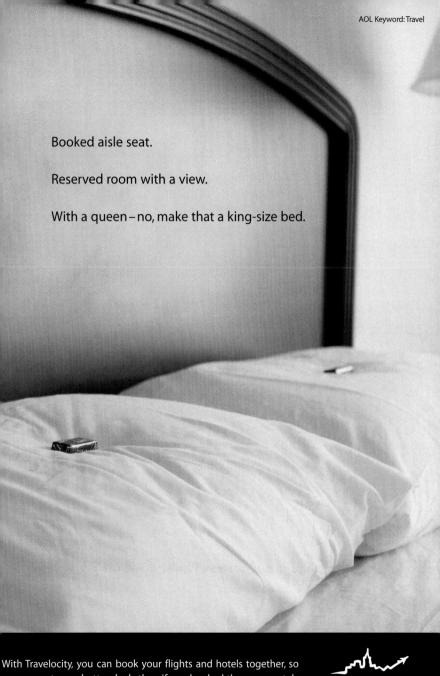

Booked aisle seat.

Reserved room with a view.

With a queen – no, make that a king-size bed.

With Travelocity, you can book your flights and hotels together, so you can get even better deals than if you booked them separately. You'll save time and money without compromising the quality of your trip. Choose your airline seat, search for alternate airports, pick your hotel room type, even choose the neighborhood you'd like to stay in

Travelocity

Visit www.travelocity.com or call 1-888-TRAVELOCITY

Tujague's does not have a menu; instead, each night, it offers a set six-course (it seems one course is coffee) meal. You will eat what they cook that night. Don't expect fancy or nouvelle: This is real local food. Meals start with a sinus-clearing shrimp rémoulade (with red or white sauce, or both if you can't make up your mind), heads to a fine gumbo (not as thick as some, but that's not a liability), then to a sample of a so-tender-you-cut-it-with-a-fork brisket, and then on to whatever is happening for an entree. There's likely to be filet mignon for sure, but skip it (it's ordinary) in favor of items like stuffed shrimp or perfect fettuccine or Bonne Femme chicken, a baked garlic number from the original owner's recipe (the restaurant has it every night, but you have to ask for it). Finish with a classic, the right-on-the-money bread pudding.

823 Decatur St. ⓒ 504/525-8676. www.tujaguesrestaurant.com. Reservations recommended. 3-course lunch $15–$17, 6-course dinner $30–$36. AE, DC, DISC, MC, V. Daily 11am–3pm and 5–10pm.

201 Restaurant & Bar ⭐ CONTEMPORARY LOUISIANA   They do fish very nicely, with a decidedly Asian influence, at this casual but spiffy place. It's a simple space, a typical New Orleans high-ceilinged room, mercifully largely intact except for the addition of some modern and Depression-era lamps. The menu changes occasionally, but at a recent meal, we were most pleased by shrimp-and-scallop pot stickers with a spicy but sweet red-pepper dipping sauce, and a macadamia-crusted fish with ginger soy butter. There are some fine red-meat dishes, but the lighter offerings show off the Asian flair to better advantage, while making both your waistline and taste buds equally happy.

201 Decatur St. (at Iberville St.). ⓒ 504/561-0007. www.201restaurant.com. Reservations recommended. Main courses $18–$28. AE, DC, DISC, MC, V. Sun–Thurs 6–11pm; Fri–Sat 6pm–midnight.

INEXPENSIVE

Acme Oyster House ⭐⭐ SEAFOOD/SANDWICHES   This joint is always loud, often crowded, and the kind of place where you're likely to run into obnoxious fellow travelers. But if you need an oyster fix or you've never tried oyster shooting (taking a raw oyster, possibly doused in sauce, and letting it slide right down your throat), come here. There's nothing quite like standing at the oyster bar, eating a dozen or so freshly shucked oysters on the half-shell. (You can have them at a table, but somehow they taste better at the bar.) If you can't quite stomach them raw, try the oyster po' boy, with beer, of course. Acme offers fresh-baked bread pudding and cheesecake on the dessert menu, but of course, dessert is not why you come here.

724 Iberville St. ⓒ 504/522-5973. www.acmeoyster.com. Oysters $4–$6.50 per half–whole dozen, respectively; po' boys $5.50–$7.50; New Orleans specialties $6–$8; seafood $11–$14. AE, DC, DISC, MC, V. Sun–Thurs 11am–10pm; Fri–Sat 11am–11pm.

Angeli on Decatur ⭐⭐ ITALIAN/MEDITERRANEAN   This is a highly welcome addition to the Quarter, featuring terrific (if not particularly New Orleans–specific) food with further praise for its nearly round-the-clock hours and local delivery service—all things hungry locals and tourists crave. Brought to you by the team behind the Garden District's popular Mystic Cafe, Angeli is a nice (and at night, dimly lit) space that doesn't overdo the angel theme. It's conveniently accessible after a day's busy sightseeing or a night's busy club-hopping. It's perfect for a light, actually rather healthy meal, a much-needed alternative to some of the extravaganzas offered by more formal restaurants in town. Portions are substantial—splitting a Greek salad produced two full plates of fresh, lovely veggies and a couple of pieces of garlic bread. Add to that a small pizza (they do them all well, but the Mystical—roasted garlic, goat cheese, onions, sun-dried tomatoes—is a top choice), and you've got a tasty, affordable meal for two, at any hour and even in your hotel room.

1141 Decatur St. (at Gov. Nicholls St.). ✆ **504/566-0077.** Main courses $6.95–$18. AE, MC, V. Mon–Thurs 10am–4am; Fri–Sat 24 hr.

Café Beignet ⭐ CAFE   This is a full-service, bistro-style cafe. At breakfast you can get Belgian waffles, an omelet soufflé, bagels and lox, or brioche French toast. Items on the lunch menu include gumbo, crawfish pie, vegetable sandwiches, and salads. And, of course, beignets.

334B Royal St. ✆ **504/524-5530.** All items under $7. No credit cards. Daily 7am–5pm.

Café Maspero ⭐ SEAFOOD/SANDWICHES   Upon hearing complaints about the increasing presence in the Quarter of "foreign" restaurants, such as Subway and the Hard Rock Cafe, one local commented, "Good. That must mean the line will be shorter at Café Maspero." Locals do indeed line up for burgers, deli sandwiches (including a veggie muffuletta!), seafood, grilled marinated chicken, and so on, in some of the largest portions you'll ever run into. And there's an impressive list of wines, beers, and cocktails. Everything is delicious and is sold at low, low prices.

601 Decatur St. ✆ **504/523-6250.** Main courses $4.25–$9. No credit cards. Sun–Thurs 11am–11pm; Fri–Sat 11am–midnight.

Clover Grill ⭐ COFFEEHOUSE   We are cross lately with the Clover Grill. Once a place where the irreverent menu ("We're here to serve people and make them feel prettier than they are") competed with the even more outrageous staff for smart-aleck behavior, it has lost its luster. The menu has fewer jokes, and the once charmingly sassy staff is straying lately toward surly. But the burgers are still juicy and perfect and apparently are still cooked under a hubcap (they say it seals in the juices). It seems to work well enough that we'll go out on a limb and declare them the best burgers in New Orleans, over the usual favorites at the Port of Call. Breakfast is still served around the clock, and there are still drag queens sitting at the tables or counters. But too many times lately we've come in at night requesting a shake, only to be told "no shakes." Unacceptable for a 24-hour diner. Go—but tell them they are on probation until they reclaim their original joie de vivre.

900 Bourbon St. ✆ **504/598-1010.** www.clovergrill.com. All items under $7. AE, MC, V. Daily 24 hr.

Felix's Restaurant & Oyster Bar ⭐⭐ SEAFOOD/CREOLE   Like its neighbor the Acme Oyster House, Felix's is a crowded and noisy place, full of locals and tourists taking advantage of the late hours. It's more or less the same as the Acme. Each has its die-hard fans, convinced their particular choice is the superior one. Have your oysters raw, in a stew, in a soup, Rockefeller or Bienville style, in spaghetti, or even in an omelet. If oysters aren't your bag, the fried or grilled fish, chicken, steaks, spaghetti, omelets, and Creole cooking are mighty good, too. If you want something blackened, they'll fry it up to order. They usually also have boiled crawfish in season.

739 Iberville St./210 Bourbon (2 entrances). ✆ **504/522-4440.** www.felixs.com. Main courses $10–$20. AE, MC, V. Mon–Thurs 10am–midnight; Fri 10am–1am; Sat 10am–1:30am; Sun 10am–10pm.

Johnny's Po-Boys ⭐⭐ SANDWICHES   For location (right near a busy part of the Quarter) and menu simplicity (po' boys and more po' boys), you can't ask for much more than Johnny's. They put anything you could possibly imagine (and some things you couldn't) on huge hunks of French bread, including the archetypal fried seafood (add some Tabasco, we strongly advise), deli meats, cheese omelets, ham and eggs, and the starch-o-rama that is a French Fry Po' Boy. You need to try it. *Really.* Johnny boasts that "even my failures are edible," and that says it all. And they deliver!

511 St. Louis St. ℭ **504/524-8129.** Everything under $11. No credit cards. Mon–Fri 8am–4:30pm; Sat–Sun 9am–4pm.

Louisiana Pizza Kitchen PIZZA The Louisiana Pizza Kitchen is a local favorite for its creative pies and atmosphere. Pastas have a significant place on the menu, but diners come for the pizzas and Caesar salad. Individual-size pizzas, baked in a wood-fired oven, feature a wide variety of toppings (shrimp and roasted garlic are two of the most popular). The best thing about their pizza is that your toppings won't get lost in an overabundance of cheese and tomato sauce.

95 French Market Place. ℭ **504/522-9500.** Pizzas $5.75–$9.50; pastas $6–$14. AE, DC, DISC, MC, V. Sun–Thurs 11am–10pm; Fri–Sat 11am–11pm. There is another branch at 615 S. Carrollton Ave. (ℭ **504/ 866-5900**).

Mama Rosa's ★ ITALIAN/PIZZA Done in by sauces and hankering for something plain? Get a big slice of pizza here. Although the decor (typical red-and-white-checked tablecloths, a jukebox, and a bar) is nothing to brag about, the pizzas are. You can get a 10- or 14-inch pie with a variety of toppings for a very

---

 Whole Lotta Muffuletta Goin' On

Muffulettas are sandwiches of (pardon the expression) heroic proportions, enormous concoctions of round Italian bread, Italian cold cuts and cheeses, and olive salad. One person cannot eat a whole one—at least not in one sitting. (And if you can, don't complain to us about your stomachache.) Instead, share; a half makes a good meal, and a quarter is a filling snack. They may not sound like much on paper, but once you try one, you'll be hooked.

Several places in town claim to have invented the muffuletta and also claim to make the best one. (Some fancy restaurants have their own upscale version—they are often delicious but bear no resemblance to the real McCoy.) Popular opinion, shared by the author, awards the crown to Central Grocery. But why take our word for it? Muffuletta comparison-shopping can be a very rewarding pastime.

Judging from the line that forms at lunchtime, many others agree with us that **Central Grocery** ★★★, 923 Decatur St. (ℭ **504/523-1620**), makes the best muffuletta. There are a few seats at the back of this crowded, heavenly smelling Italian grocery, or you can order to go. Best of all, they ship, so once you're hooked—and you will be—you need not wait until your next trip for a muffuletta fix. Take your sandwich across the street and eat it on the banks of the Mississippi for an inexpensive romantic meal (about $7 for a whole sandwich).

Then there are those who swear by the heated muffulettas served at the **Napoleon House** ★, 500 Chartres St. (ℭ **504/524-9752**). Others find them blasphemous. We recommend that you start with cold and work up to heated—it's a different taste sensation.

reasonable price. The crusts are thick—almost as thick as a pan pizza—and the more you put on them, the better they are. You can also get mini-muffulettas as appetizers. The staff can be a bit surly, but you're not here for the ambience. Delivery is available.

616 N. Rampart St. ✆ **504/523-5546**. Main courses $5.50–$15. AE, DC, DISC, MC, V. Sun–Thurs 11am–10pm; Fri–Sat 10am–11pm.

Napoleon House ✪ CREOLE/ITALIAN   Folklore has it that the name of this place derives from a bit of wishful thinking: Around the time of Napoleon's death, a plot was hatched here to snatch the Little Corporal from his island exile and bring him to live in New Orleans. The third floor was added expressly for the purpose of providing him with a home. Alas, it probably isn't true: The building dates from a couple of years after Napoleon's death. But let's not let the truth get in the way of a good story, or a good hangout, which this is at any time of day, but particularly late at night, when it's dark enough to hatch your own secret plans. Somewhere between tourist-geared and local-friendly, it serves large portions of adequate versions of traditional New Orleans food (po' boys, jambalaya), plus the only heated muffuletta in town.

500 Chartres St. ✆ **504/524-9752**. Main courses $3.25–$25. AE, DISC, MC, V. Mon–Thurs 11am–midnight; Fri–Sat 11am–1am; Sun 11am–7pm.

Old Dog New Trick Café ✪ VEGETARIAN   This cafe has moved from its original location in the heart of the Quarter, but vegetarians must seek it out, because it's one of the rare local places that caters just to them. Large portions and small prices make this a pleasing, healthy stop. The cafe calls itself "vegan friendly." It does have dishes with cheese but can make them without, and some tuna sneaks onto the menu. The desserts are absolutely vegan. Regardless of their specific denomination, the sandwiches, salads, and stuffed pitas, not to mention the polenta and a variety of tofu dishes, have been voted Best Vegetarian by *Gambit* readers. Delivery is available. (The name is in honor of Ben the Boston Terrier; the veggie burgers are "Ben burgers" for further homage.) Brunch is served on weekends.

517 Frenchmen St. ✆ **504/943-6368**. www.olddognewtrick.com. Main courses $6.95–$11. AE, MC, V. Sun–Thurs 11:30am–9pm; Fri–Sat 11:30am–10pm; Sun brunch 11:30am–3pm.

Petunia's ✪ CAJUN/CREOLE   Petunia's, located in an 1830s town house, dishes up enormous portions of New Orleans specialties like shrimp Creole, Cajun pasta with shrimp and andouille, and a variety of fresh seafood. Breakfast and Sunday brunch are popular, with a broad selection of crepes that, at 14 inches, are billed as the world's largest. Options include the St. Marie, a blend of spinach, cheddar, chicken, and hollandaise and the St. Francis, filled with shrimp, crab ratatouille, and Swiss cheese. If you have room for dessert, try the dessert crepes or the peanut butter pie.

817 St. Louis St. (between Bourbon and Dauphine sts.). ✆ **504/522-6440**. www.petuniasrestaurant.com. Reservations recommended at dinner. Main courses at breakfast and lunch $6.95–$15, at dinner $14–$27. AE, DC, DISC, MC, V. Daily 8am–11pm.

4 The Faubourg Marigny

For the restaurants in this section, see the "New Orleans Dining" map on p. 98.

EXPENSIVE

Belle Forché ✪ CARIBBEAN CRIOLLE   Just when you think you've got Cajun and Creole figured out, they throw *Criolle* into the mix. What it means is that Caribbean cuisine influences the menu at this mermaid-emblazoned Marigny-based bistro as much as actual Creole and Cajun food do. Swoon, as we do, over the flash-fried oysters "in tuxedo" (with shaved black and white truffles over the top) and the divinely unusual gumbo soup that combines cilantro and coconut milk (plus dollops of tasso and eggplant) to a happy effect. Filet of beef is topped with crabmeat and perches on a whole artichoke bottom, while mahimahi finds itself crusted in plantains. Finally, save room for the sweet banana beignets, which might even make Café du Monde jealous.

1407 Decatur St. ⓒ 504/940-0722. www.belleforche.com. Reservations recommended. Main courses $17–$28. AE, DC, MC, V. Tues–Sun 5:30–10:30pm. Cafe menu till 2:30am Thurs, Fri, and Sat.

MODERATE

Feelings Cafe D'Aunoy ⓖ AMERICAN/CREOLE   This modest neighborhood joint is a short cab ride away from the French Quarter. Friendly and funky, it serves tasty, solid (if not spectacular) food. It feels like a true local find—because it is—and can be a welcome break from the scene in the Quarter or from more intense dining. Try to get a table in the pretty courtyard or on the balcony overlooking it (particularly delightful on a balmy night), though the dining rooms are perfectly pleasant. The piano player is a neighborhood character; be sure to have a drink at the lively bar and chat with him. A recent visit produced oysters en brochette, pâté de maison, seafood-stuffed eggplant (shrimp, crabmeat, and crawfish tails in a casserole with spicy sausage and crisp fried eggplant), and a chocolate mousse/peanut butter pie for dessert.

2600 Chartres St. ⓒ 504/945-2222. www.feelingscafe.com. Reservations not required. Main courses $13–$24. AE, DC, DISC, MC, V. Sun and Fri 11am–2pm; Sun–Thurs 6–10pm; Fri–Sat 6–11pm.

Marigny Brasserie ⓖⓖ ECLECTIC   Originally a neighborhood cafe (and still operating in its original location as such), this is perhaps our first choice for a nice meal in the Frenchman/Marigny section of town—not because the food is so outstandingly innovative, but it's interesting enough, and everything we tried was pleasing to various degrees. Strongly recommended is the Serrano fig salad—aged goat cheese wrapped in Serrano ham and tossed with mixed greens in a fig vinaigrette—and the seasonal tomato and Spanish tarragon salad, one of those lovely green creations that have finally started showing up on New Orleans menus. The mushroom-crusted salmon, on a bed of fragrant sesame sticky rice and topped with lump crabmeat, was so juicy and nonfishy that it turned a former salmon avoider into a salmon believer. Rack of lamb has a sweet cherry demi-glace topping, but the seared tuna, while a fine cut of fish, needs a sauce of its own. The original Marigny Cafe is still a good choice for breakfast or lunch and is one block away, up Frenchman at the corner of Royal and Touros.

640 Frenchman St. ⓒ 504/945-4472. www.marignybrasserie.com. Reservations suggested. Main courses $16–$24. AE, MC, V. Mon–Thurs 5:30pm–10pm; Fri–Sat 5:30pm–midnight.

INEXPENSIVE

Elizabeth's ⓖⓖⓖ CREOLE   The average tourist may not head over to the Bywater because, well, because it's not the Quarter. That's too bad—not only will they miss a true N'Awlins neighbahood, but they will also miss experiences like Elizabeth's. Forget paying huge sums for average and goopy breakfast food. Here you eat, as they say, "Real Food, Done Real Good"—and, we add, real cheap. Food like Creole Rice Calas (sweet rice fritters), a classic breakfast dish that is nearly extinct from menus around town. Food calling for health advisories, like the praline bacon (topped with sugar and pecans—"pork candy" the shameless chef calls it; you must not miss this, but they only have it at breakfast time), or stuffed French toast (*pain perdu* piled high with cream cheese flavored with strawberries), or the breakfast po' boy, a monster sandwich the size of the Sunday *Picayune* rolled up. Daily specials are also worth getting regardless of what they are (one day, we had an Asian pupu platter—spring rolls, stuffed chicken wings with a piquant sauce, plus half a catfish stuffed with oyster cornbread dressing). All this great food, plus splendid, smart, and friendly service (the advantage of an informal cafe). We strongly suggest that you not be an average tourist and get yourself down to the Bywater. Out of the way or not, this is one of the city's best restaurants. We'll meet you there—and let's walk back together (it's a hike, but doable) to justify an extra order of praline bacon.

601 Gallier St. ⒸＣ **504/944-9272.** www.elizabeths-restaurant.com. Everything under $10. MC, V. Tues–Sat 7am–2:30pm.

The Harbor ⒶＳＯＵＬ FOOD Definitely out of the way (as with Elizabeth's, just take a cab), the Harbor has been a favorite of knowledgeable locals since 1949. This is the place to go for huge portions of authentic soul food, all for ridiculously low prices. (A combination plate will set you back $4.40.) You order at the counter, where all the women call you "Baby," set yourself down at a beat-up table, admire the zero decor, note that you are the only nonlocal, and dig in. Smothered pork chops, fried chicken, barbecued ribs, turkey wings, greens, red beans and rice—this is not gourmet, and we mean that as a compliment. It is hearty and filling, and you will probably be sorry you can't try everything, though at these prices, it won't be for lack of funds. Get there early, as they tend to run out of food. Oh, and if you want their famous banana pudding—and you do, you really do—you must order it early in the day (call ahead), with orders ready at 3pm.

2529 Dauphine St. Ⓒ **504/947-1819.** All items under $9. No credit cards. Daily 6am–5pm.

La Peniche Restaurant ⒶＣＲＥＯＬＥ A short walk into the Marigny brings you to this homey (as opposed to "homely") dive; take the walk, because rents in the Quarter are too high for any place that looks like this to be a true bargain. It's open 24 hours, except for Wednesday, which means you are just moments away from fried fish, po' boys, burgers, and even quiche. Good brunch options exist as well, which is why it's packed during that time. Come for specials like bronzed (with Cajun spices) pork, and be sure to have some chocolate layer cake (like homemade!) and peanut butter chocolate chip pie.

1940 Dauphine St. Ⓒ **504/943-1460.** Everything under $15. Cash only. Open Thurs 9am–Tues 2am.

Mona's Café & Deli ⒶⒶ MIDDLE EASTERN This local favorite finally expanded from its original Mid-City location into other parts of the city, with varying results. Unfortunately, the original location, which was by far the most reliable, was virtually destroyed in an arson fire. For the time being, we recommend coming here (and ordering the marinated chicken and the basmati rice with saffron) and avoiding, at least for the time being, the latest addition on Magazine Street, which still seems to be finding its way. There, the food is not bad (except for perhaps the rather nasty, and unauthentic, chicken swarma), but the strictly ordinary Middle Eastern fare (hummus, kebobs, and so forth) won't make a believer out of anyone with no prior exposure to this kind of cuisine. Once the Mid-City location is back up and running, it should be better than either of the other two mentioned here.

504 Frenchman St. Ⓒ **504/949-4115.** Sandwiches $2.75–$3.75; main courses $6–$11. AE, DISC, MC, V. Mon–Thurs 11am–9pm; Fri–Sat 11am–10pm; Sun noon–6pm. They also have locations Uptown, 3151 Calhoun St., and at 4126 Magazine St.

Praline Connection *Overrated* CREOLE/SOUL FOOD   To some NOLA residents, this might be heresy (but we know just as many others who will back us up), but we think the Praline Connection is completely overrated and eminently missable. It's probably riding on sentiment and tradition, so if this review helps shake things up and gets it back into shape, well, then, good. This used to be the place to come for solid, reliable, and even—once upon a time—marvelous Creole and soul food. The crowds still come, not noting that what they are getting is often dry and dull. For now, we suggest you instead head to Dunbar's or, better still, the Harbor (not far from here in the Marigny), where you can get the same type of food with somewhat less crowding, more atmosphere, and cheaper prices.

542 Frenchmen St. ⓒ **504/943-3934.** www.pralineconnection.com. Main courses $6.95–$19. AE, DC, DISC, MC, V. Sun–Thurs 11am–10:30pm; Fri–Sat 11am–midnight. **Praline Connection II**, 907 S. Peters St. (ⓒ **504/523-3973**), offers the same menu and a larger dining room. Closed Sat–Sun.

5 Mid-City/Esplanade

For a map of the restaurants in this section, see the "Mid-City Accommodations & Dining" map on p. 83.

EXPENSIVE

Ruth's Chris Steak House ⚐ STEAK   Even though branches of Ruth's Chris have popped up all over the country in the past few years, you won't get an argument locally if you pronounce this the best steak in town. This Mid-City location is the original Ruth's Chris, and if you're looking for prime beef—corn fed, custom aged, cut by hand, and beautifully prepared—this is your place. Pork chops and one or two other meats appear on the menu, but these are vastly outnumbered by beef dishes: This is a steakhouse through and through. Private dining rooms are available.

711 N. Broad St. ⓒ **504/486-0810.** www.ruthschris.com. Reservations recommended. Main courses $24–$58. AE, DC, DISC, MC, V. Mon–Wed 11:30am–10pm; Thurs 11:30am–10:30pm; Fri 11:30am–11pm; Sat 5–11pm; Sun noon–9:30pm.

MODERATE

Cafe Degas ⚐⚐ BISTRO/FRENCH   Just an adorable, friendly, charming French bistro—a delightful neighborhood restaurant, and one that doesn't emphasize fried food (trust us, that's a combo that's hard to find in this town!). If you want to have a nice meal, without the fuss and feathers, Degas should do the trick in terms of both the food and the atmosphere. There are daily dinner and lunch specials—think quiches and real, live salads (always a happy find in this town) and simple but fun fish and meat dishes, all featuring big but straightforward flavors, presented in generous portions. You can go light (a salad, a plate of pâtés and cheeses) or heavy (filet of beef tenderloin with a green peppercorn brandy sauce)—either way, you'll feel like you ate something worthwhile. Though it's French, this is not France, and this bistro is informal enough that you can go wearing blue jeans.

3127 Esplanade Ave. ⓒ **504/945-5635.** www.cafedegas.com. Reservations recommended. Main courses $9.50–$20. AE, DC, DISC, MC, V. Mon 5:30–10pm; Tues–Fri 11:30am–2:30pm and 5:30–10pm; Sun brunch 10:30am–3pm; Sat–Sun 6–10pm.

Christian's ⚐⚐ CREOLE   Ever had a three-course meal in a church? Here's your chance. Christian's is doubly well named. It's owned by Christian Ansel (whose culinary pedigree is strong; he's the grandson of a nephew of Jean Galatoire) and occupies a former church. Renovations preserved the architecture, including the high-beamed ceiling and (secular) stained-glass windows. The old altar is the waiters' station, and the sermon board out front lists the menu. Locals account for about 80% of the clientele. They come for appetizers like smoked soft-shell crabs, perfect plump crab cakes, oysters Roland (baked in a garlic-butter sauce with mushrooms, parsley, bread crumbs, and Creole seasoning), crawfish Carolyn (in a spicy cream-brandy-Parmesan cheese sauce, rather like the "dynamite" served at some sushi restaurants), and a strong rendition of oysters *en brochette*. The roasted duck is heavenly, as is the gumbo. Daily fish specials include delights such as sheepshead (yes, that's a fish) stuffed with shrimp and crabmeat, lightly breaded, and fried with aioli; broiled filet of grouper with red onion *beurre blanc* and sautéed scallops; or catfish stuffed and fried ("Cajun corndog" said the waiter). For dessert, try the intriguing "Slip," if it's offered. How can you go wrong with ice cream on a praline cookie?

3835 Iberville St. ✆ **504/482-4924.** Reservations recommended. Main courses $18–$30. AE, DC, MC, V. Tues–Fri 11:30am–2pm and 5:30–9:30pm; Sat 5:30–9:30pm.

Dooky Chase ⭐ SOUL FOOD/CREOLE   African and African-American influences are key components in the city's multicultural cuisine. In the traditional rooms of Dooky Chase, classic soul food interacts gloriously with the city's French, Sicilian, and Italian traditions. Chef Leah Chase dishes up one of the city's best bowls of gumbo—no small achievement—along with more esoteric dishes such as shrimp Clemenceau, an unlikely but successful casserole of sautéed shellfish, mushrooms, peas, and potatoes. The fried chicken is exquisite, as are the sautéed veal, the grits, the grillades, and the court bouillon—a first cousin of gumbo in which okra is replaced by tomatoes, onions, and garlic, along with generous chunks of catfish. Keep an eye out for touring jazz artists or prominent black politicians who may well occupy the adjoining tables. Prices are a bit high and service is brisk (though always friendly), but Dooky Chase does offer a vintage New Orleans experience.

2301 Orleans Ave. ✆ **504/821-2294.** Reservations recommended at dinner. Main courses $10–$25; fixed-price 4-course meal $25; Creole feast $38. AE, DC, DISC, MC, V. Sun–Thurs 11:30am–10pm; Fri–Sat 11:30am–11pm.

Gabrielle ⭐⭐ CREOLE   This rather small, but casually elegant contemporary Creole restaurant just outside the French Quarter is gaining a big reputation around town, thanks to some superb food from a chef who studied under Paul Prudhomme and Frank Brigtsen. The menu can change, but foie gras is likely to be generously portioned and even more likely to melt in your mouth. For a main course, try Creole cream cheese–crusted lamb chops, stuffed flounder with lobster dressing or roast chicken with shrimp and lavender honey mustard sauce. The Peppermint Patti dessert is the most popular, a concoction made of chocolate cake, peppermint ice cream, and chocolate sauce. There's a small bar here, and the wine list is quite nice.

Gabrielle offers an early-evening special Tuesday through Thursday from 5:30 to 6:15pm. You get a choice of three appetizers, two entrees, and two desserts for only $16.

3201 Esplanade Ave. ✆ **504/948-6233.** Reservations recommended. Main courses $16–$30; early-evening special (Tues–Thurs 5:30–6:15pm) $16. AE, DC, DISC, MC, V. Oct–May Fri 11:30am–2pm; year-round Tues–Sat 5:30–10pm.

Indigo ⭐ NEW AMERICAN   Apparently it wasn't enough for Cynthia Reeves to own and operate arguably the best guesthouse in the city; having accomplished that, she had to turn her sights to something else ambitious, and this lovely new restaurant is the result. Named for the product of the former plantation on which a part of the restaurant lies (as does her B&B, the House on Bayou Road, see

p. 82), Indigo is a romantic space already chock-full of savvy locals looking for a new dining experience. It's a tad expensive, but the food is generating nearly universal raves, thanks to clever and talented chef Randy Lewis. We ourselves swoon over the creamy crawfish vichyssoise (accompanied by a sweet little crawfish grilled-cheese sandwich) and various appetizers and *amuse-bouches* that use lobster or truffle flour or both. Fish—like the Romesco powder-dusted sea bass—is beyond just right and probably your best choice for an entree. We were a bit sad that the molten chocolate cake dessert was not at all molten in the center, but the caramel ice cream on the side consoled us.

2285 Bayou Rd. (C) **504/947-0123**. www.indigonola.com. Reservations recommended. Main courses $18–$29. AE, DC, DISC, MC, V. Tues–Sat 6–10pm; Sun brunch 11am–2pm; Sun 6pm–9:30pm.

Liuzza's ✿✿ CREOLE/ITALIAN Actual moment from a Liuzza's visit: The crusty waitress hands a menu to a customer ("Here you go, Bay-bee") and then abruptly closes it. "Bay-bee," she instructs, gesticulating with a finger, "Numba One, or Numba Two—but *definitely* Numba One." Naturally, the Number One special was ordered (it proved to be a seafood lasagna, dripping with a white cream sauce) and devoured (despite its enormous size).

Yep, this is a neighborhood institution (since 1947; it's humble, small, and often crowded with regulars) and when the waitress talks, you betcha you listen. Presumably, she will also tell you to get the heavenly fried onion rings or the deep-fried dill pickle slices ("You people will batter and deep-fry anything that isn't nailed down!," said yet another astonished visitor); if she doesn't, we just did. Still more recommended menu items are the Galboroni Pasta (spaghettini with spicy marinara sauce, pepperoni strips, and stuffed artichoke hearts), shrimp-artichoke fettuccine, and mega-rich fettuccine Alfredo. Po' boy lovers can't go wrong with the excellent fried seafood po' boys. If it's carbo overload you seek, you can get a french-fry po' boy with mayo (the sandwich for which the name "po' boy" was coined). Or try the excellent and sweet barbecue (Jack Daniels is concealed in the sauce) over pulled pork. Great inexpensive food in an establishment dripping with New Orleans atmosphere—don't miss it, Bay-bee.

3636 Bienville St. (C) **504/482-9120**. www.liuzzas.com. Main courses at lunch $3.95–$20, at dinner $7.50–$20. AE, DC, DISC, MC, V. Mon–Sat 10:30am–10:30pm.

Lola's ✿✿✿ SPANISH/INTERNATIONAL "Please, oh please, don't mention Lola's in the book!" beg our local foodie friends. Why? Because this small, special place doesn't take reservations, and the nightly wait is already long as it is. But we are going to spill the beans anyway while assuring you that this is worth waiting for, thanks to incredible Spanish dishes, from various paellas to starters such as garlic shrimp tapas and a heck of a garlic soup. Try to arrive 15 to 30 minutes before opening time and wait in line. If you come later and there's a mob, don't be discouraged: Service is attentive and food comes quickly, so your wait shouldn't be too long. Don't forget to bring cash—and try not to get ahead of our friends in line!

3312 Esplanade Ave. (C) **504/488-6946**. Main courses $8.75–$14. No credit cards or out-of-town checks. Sun–Thurs 6–10pm; Fri–Sat 6–10:30pm.

Mandina's ✿✿ CREOLE/ITALIAN In a city renowned for its small, funky, local joints as well as its fine-dining establishments, dis is da ultimate neighbahood N'Awlins restaurant. Tommy Mandina's family has owned and operated this restaurant and bar since the late 1800s, and the menu hasn't changed much in the last 50 years or so. This is a good thing. Mandina's gets crowded at lunch, so try to go a little early or late to beat the crowd. And don't be afraid of your waiter— surly or gruff as he may be, his advice is always good.

(Finds **Nicholas Payton's Gumbo Recipe**

Trumpeter Nicholas Payton is following in the tradition of New Orleans greats from Louis Armstrong to Wynton Marsalis. His Verve recordings include Nick@Night, Gumbo Nouveau, the 1997 Grammy-winning Doc Cheatham & Nicholas Payton, and his newest release, Dear Louis.

   1 pound smoked sausage
   1 pound hot sausage
   1 pound seasoned ham
   1 pound chicken necks or gizzards
   1 large onion
   1 bell pepper
   ½ cup parsley
   2 pounds shrimp
   1 pound crabmeat or fresh crab
   salt and pepper
   1 cup flour
   filé

Put all the meats and vegetables in a large pot and sauté them. Do not add the seafood yet. In another pot, boil the shrimp heads in water for stock. After the meats and vegetables are sautéed, add the shrimp stock (without the heads) and the rest of the seafood to the pot. Brown the flour in a dry frying pan to make the roux. When the flour is browned, add a little at a time to the pot. The roux and the filé are used to thicken the gumbo, so add it according to how thick you wish to have your gumbo. Add salt and pepper to taste. Cook for about another hour, skimming the gumbo occasionally.

Standouts among the appetizers are the greasy but yummy fried onion rings, the excellent tangy shrimp rémoulade, and the crawfish cakes. Soups are always fine as well, especially seafood gumbo and turtle soup au sherry. Then go for the wonderful red beans and rice with Italian sausage, the trout meunière, the grilled trout, or our favorite comfort food, the sweet Italian sausage and spaghetti combo—hardly innovative gourmet, but exactly the way we remember it from childhood. Finish up with rum-soaked Creole bread pudding, and you'll have such a taste of New Orleans you'll feel like a native from da old neighbahood.

3800 Canal St. ℂ **504/482-9179.** Main courses $7.50–$23. No credit cards. Mon–Thurs 11am–10:30pm; Fri–Sat 11am–11pm; Sun noon–9pm.

6 Central Business District

For restaurants in this section, see the "New Orleans Dining" map on p. 98.

VERY EXPENSIVE

Emeril's ⨁⨁ CREOLE/NEW AMERICAN   We are giving Emeril's first (and still best) restaurant two stars mostly on the firm belief that matters are still being properly overseen here, but given how thin the Chef is spreading himself these days (all those other restaurants, in several different cities, plus the Food Network show—at least, thank heavens, his sitcom is no more), we increasingly wish he would get himself off TV and back into the kitchen. And we are still cranky about how attitudinal the staff and service can be. Having said that, when this restaurant is on its game, doggonit, there isn't much better eating to be had.

Emeril first came into prominence in the kitchen of Commander's Palace, and his specialty is what he calls *New* New Orleans Cuisine, based on and using key ingredients of Creole classics but taking them in exciting directions. Everything in his bustling, noisy Warehouse District restaurant is homemade, from the bacon to the Worcestershire sauce to the andouille sausage and home-cured tasso. Each plate dances with color and texture, and side dishes are perfectly paired with entrees (such as grilled Creole-seasoned chicken with savory corn-and-andouille bread pudding). The menu often changes, although some favorites remain, and the daily specials are always exciting and wildly varied (such as crawfish-and-morel-mushroom-stuffed artichoke bottoms with foie gras, roasted onion ragout, and a drizzle of celery purée). The signature dessert, astonishingly rich banana cream pie with banana crust and caramel drizzle sauce, will leave you moaning and pounding on the table (we've seen it happen).

800 Tchoupitoulas St. (©) **504/528-9393.** www.emerils.com. Reservations required at dinner. Main courses $22–$36; menu degustation (tasting menu) $75. AE, DC, DISC, MC, V. Mon–Fri 11:30am–2pm; Mon–Sat 6–11pm.

Emeril's Delmonico Restaurant and Bar ✦ CREOLE   Delmonico's was intended less as a venue for Emeril to show off the innovative cooking that has made him a star and more as a chance for him to experiment with classic Creole dishes. Locals remain underwhelmed, however; though it does a brisk business (and boasts one of the loveliest interiors in New Orleans), it seems there are many who have yet to be blown away by the food. This may be because it's so rich and sauce-intensive and, also, so costly. But it can be fun to see what Emeril is up to in this context. Certainly, any complaints of ours are muffled by mouthfuls of the cream-and-truffle angel hair pasta topped with crispy crab cakes. You can easily blow your budget on the tasting menu, and perhaps you should, particularly when it features such decadent delights as smoked salmon and wild-mushroom truffle stew topped with over-easy eggs, shaved black truffle, black truffle emulsion, crispy parsley, and a drizzle of white truffle oil. (We get dizzy just thinking about it.) If you want to treat your waistline, try the Caesar salad for two; it's very traditional (which means none of that gloppy, creamy dressing), and is most peppery and tangy. The desserts are all splendid variations on local favorites, but you can skip the crème brûlée.

1300 St. Charles Ave. (©) **504/525-4937.** www.emerils.com. Reservations required. Main courses $18–$30. AE, DC, DISC, MC, V. Mon–Fri 11:30am–2pm; Sun 10:30am–2pm; Sun–Thurs 6–10pm; Fri–Sat 6–11pm.

The Grill Room ✦ NEW AMERICAN   This is a special-event place where the silverware is heavy, the linens are thick, and all the diners are dressed to the nines. The Grill Room is an elegant and stately place whose chefs constantly win culinary awards (it's the training ground for chefs, like Kevin Graham, who go on to start their own, innovative restaurants) and whose cuisine (New American with a New Orleans influence), service, and wine list are all flawless. Like the

---

Impressions

New Orleans is one place you can eat and drink the most, and suffer the least.

—William Makepeace Thackeray

Windsor Court in general, the restaurant has an upper-crust-English-meets-upper-crust-Southern character, evident in everything from its 19th-century British paintings to the gracious, attentive service.

We've had outstanding meals at the Grill Room, and we've had good meals at the Grill Room, and which you get probably depends on who is cooking when you go. The appetizers seem to withstand the vagaries of restaurant life the best, so do try their "catfish & caviar," which is catfish rémoulade topped with sevruga—believe us when we say it works. They used to have the best pastry chef in town, but desserts seem to have lost some of their flash lately, though as long as they keep Valrhona chocolate pâté on the menu, we will be happy.

In the Windsor Court Hotel, 300 Gravier St. ✆ 504/522-1992. www.orient-express.com. Reservations recommended. Jacket required at dinner. Main courses $16–$25 at lunch, $28–$39 at dinner. AE, DC, DISC, MC, V. Daily 7am–10:30am; Sun 7–9am; Mon–Sat 11:30am–2pm; Sun brunch 10:30am–2pm; Sun–Thurs 6–10pm; Fri–Sat 6–10:30pm.

EXPENSIVE

Cobalt ⭐⭐ REGIONAL AMERICAN   The latest restaurant from local wonder girl Susan Spicer is another winner (compared with her others: It's a bit better than Bayona at this time, but a bit more expensive than Herbsaint). The space, located in the fab Hotel Monaco, is a little too self-consciously hip for New Orleans (and noisy on the nights when a jazz band plays)—you would be forgiven for thinking you were in NYC. But that's nitpicking. Who cares when you can eat dishes such as these: a stunning, duck confit "debris" (not too too rich, just a touch of tarragon) on a perfect biscuit; a nicely dressed Bibb lettuce salad with bleu cheese and roasted pears; a solid combo of goat cheese and white-bean ravioli and sweet butternut squash purée; and tender venison with ancho-berry sauce. If the appetizer special of Indonesian beef with crisp rice and sweet onions is on the menu, get it. Finish up with a cunning "Cobalt PB&J," a thick peanut butter mousse with grape ice cream.

333 St. Charles Ave. ✆ 504/565-5595. www.cobaltrestaurant.com. Dinner reservations suggested. Main courses at lunch $9–$16, at dinner $16–$28. AE, DC, DISC, MC, V. Mon–Fri 7:30–9:30am and 11:30am–2pm; daily 5:30–10pm; Sat and Sun 8:30am–10:30am and 5:30–10pm.

Cuvee ⭐⭐ CONTEMPORARY CREOLE   Cuvee is one of a group of newer restaurants that have been earning almost unanimous raves from local tourist foodies, and we strongly suggest you discover why for yourself. Should you indeed end up in this cozy, brick-lined room (suggesting a wine cellar, natch), try to order—assuming the seasonally changing menu allows—the lovely spicy mirliton (a fruit that's kind of like a cross between a pear and a yucca plant) napoleon (with shrimp rémoulade) appetizer, though the pan-seared scallops with citrus *beurre blanc* isn't a bad second choice. We loved the pan-seared duck breast with duck confit and foie gras, combined with a Roquefort risotto—a medley that ranks among the city's best duck dishes. Don't miss the crunchy wonder that is the chocolate macadamia nut torte—it's like the ultimate candy bar. An exquisite wine list helps you impress dates by providing phonetic pronunciations for all the wines.

322 Magazine St. ✆ 504/587-9001. www.restaurantcuvee.com. Reservations highly suggested. Main courses at lunch $7–$15, at dinner $18–$28. AE, DC, MC, V. Mon–Fri 11:30am–2:30pm and 6–10pm; Fri–Sat 6–11pm.

56° ⭐ ASIAN FUSION   It's the prime temperature at which wine should be stored. Well, we figured you might ask. Anyway, this is a new restaurant by Chef Minh, the figure behind Lemon Grass over at the International House. While the menu is more heavily Vietnamese-influenced at Lemon Grass, here (a lovely former bank space in the Whitney Hotel) matters go a little more continental. We recently tried, and liked, the tempura shrimp with a sweet corn cake and the fried coconut shrimp with the Oriental slaw appetizer, but we also tried, and loved, a mussel noodle and broth dish, and a firm and earthy wild mushroom pasta. Truth be told, it is expensive, absolutely, and not as immediately memorable as Lemon Grass, but Chef Minh's cooking is something special no matter where it happens, so we suggest that if you are curious, come at lunch, where you will miss nothing except the bigger bill to be had at dinner.

In the Whitney Windham Hotel, 610 Poydras St. ℂ 504/212-5656. Reservations suggested. Main courses at lunch $11.50–$17.50, at dinner $16.50–$29. AE, DC, MC, V. Daily 6–10am and 11am–2pm; Sun–Thurs 6–10pm; Fri–Sat 6–11pm.

Sazerac Bar and Grill ⌖ CONTINENTAL/CREOLE   A top-to-bottom renovation has so completely redesigned the venerable Sazerac (yep, the cocktail was invented in the adjoining bar, which remains unchanged from its Art Deco days) that it is unrecognizable to bewildered locals. Once they get over the confusion, they are pleased to note that a once rather claustrophobic experience has been turned into a more airy one, with the room now open to the Fairmont's famous block-long lobby. It's a good choice for dining in the area; a recent meal found diners eating every bit of turtle soup, barbecue shrimp pasta, blackened red snapper with pecan-butter sauce, and sugar cane–glazed duck with a sweet potato andouille *timbale* (fried or baked pastry dough, filled with cooked food).

In the Fairmont Hotel, 123 Baronne St. ℂ 504/529-4733. Reservations recommended. Jackets recommended at dinner. Main courses $20–$30. AE, DC, DISC, MC, V. Mon–Sat 6am–2pm; Sun brunch 7am–2pm; daily 5:30–9pm.

MODERATE

Herbsaint ⌖⌖ BISTRO   We know, we just go on and on about chef Susan Spicer and her restaurants. We'd say we are sorry, but we really aren't. French-American, as opposed to Bayona's more Mediterranean slant, Herbsaint (that would be the locally made pastis found in, among other places, the popular local cocktail, the Sazerac) is the more affordable venue to try Spicer's recipes (even the entrees are comfortably under $20). Be sure to try the Herbsaint, tomato, and shrimp bisque—it sent us into rhapsodies, and we aren't even soup fans—and the "small plate" of shrimp with green-chile grits ("Not as good as Uglisech's," says one NOLA foodie, "but a close second."). Salads can come delectably decorated with figs, bleu cheese, and a sherry vinaigrette. For once, vegetarians will not feel left out; the herbed gnocchi with eggplant tomato sauce is a marvelous dish, while the carnivores will be equally as pleased with the cane-braised short ribs. The desserts are stand outs; we could eat the coconut macadamia nut pie every day of our life, though we would save room for the chocolate beignets with their molten boozy interior. Okay, we aren't going to go on and on, but only because that takes up valuable time, when we all could be eating here instead.

701 St. Charles Ave. ℂ 504/524-4114. www.herbsaint.com. Reservations suggested for lunch, and for 2 or more for dinner. $14–$24. AE, DC, DISC, MC, V. Mon–Fri 11:30am–2:30pm; Mon–Sat 5:30–10:30pm.

Lemon Grass ⌖⌖ VIETNAMESE   Don't feel you are missing out on local cuisine by trying the modern Vietnamese creations found in this hip Asian cafe—for one thing, New Orleans has some of the best Vietnamese restaurants in the world, outside of Vietnam. Chef Minh is as influenced by his adopted town as his homeland. Crawfish can pop up in dishes, and Minh's take on shrimp mirliton (a fruit that's kind of like a cross between a pear and a yucca plant) is well worth trying. Appetizers are terrific, one and all, but a highlight is the flash-fried oysters crusted with nuts and served with wasabi leek confit. We adore the spicy chicken roti, among the entrees, as well as the felicitously named Happy Pancake. Save room for the decidedly European desserts, including our favorite, a fluffy dark and white chocolate mousse.

In the International House, 217 Camp St. ℂ **504/523-1200.** Reservations recommended. Main courses $13–$27. AE, MC, V. Daily 7:30–10am and 11:30am–2:30pm; Sun–Thurs 6–10pm; Fri–Sat 6–11pm.

Liborio's Cuban Restaurant ⭐ CUBAN   Nicely located in the Central Business District, this Cuban cafe attracts many local business folk at lunchtime, but despite the crowds, that might be the best time to go, when prices are very affordable (they do seem to be needlessly high at dinnertime). Plus, it's a fun space—the chartreuse sponged walls and pillowy parachute-fabric upholstering the ceiling make for a festive and more aesthetically pleasing look than you might think from reading the description. Lazy ceiling fans and photos from the homeland put you in mind of Hemingway's Havana. Order the day's special or be like us, partial to Cuban specialties like tender, garlicky roast pork, the flat-bread Cuban sandwich, and sweet fried plantains.

321 Magazine St. ℂ **504/581-9680.** Reservations suggested. Main courses at lunch $6.50–$14, at dinner $11–$20. AE, DC, DISC, MC, V. Mon–Sat 11am–3pm; Tues–Sat 5:30–9:30pm.

Palace Café ⭐⭐ CONTEMPORARY CREOLE   This is where to go for low-key and nonintimidating romantic dining. Housed attractively in the historic Werlein's for Music building, this popular Brennan family restaurant admittedly went through a bit of a slump but happily has resurged. But don't take our word for it; newcomers and longtime NOLA visitors should make this discovery for themselves. But when you do go, be sure to order the crabmeat cheesecake appetizer (a table-poundingly good dish if ever there was one), and possibly the escargots as well. As for main courses, they do fish especially well (note these dishes from a recent menu: andouille-crusted fish with a cayenne *beurre blanc* and chive *aioli,* and Gulf shrimp Tchefuncte—that's toasted garlic and green onions in a Creole *meunière* sauce). For dessert, they invented the by-now ubiquitous white chocolate bread pudding, and no matter what others may claim, they have the best. But do pester them about the Mississippi Mud Pie, seven layers of chocolate mousse from lightest to darkest, our personal favorite dessert ever and missing for some time from the menu. Its continued absence is really the only thing we have to complain about here.

605 Canal St. ℂ **504/523-1661.** www.palacecafe.com. Reservations recommended. Main courses $11–$25. AE, DC, DISC, MC, V. Mon–Fri 11:30am–2:30pm; Sat–Sun brunch 10:30am–2:30pm; daily 5:30–10pm.

The Red Bike ⭐ NEW AMERICAN/ECLECTIC   A fine choice if you're looking for a healthy alternative to the endless array of sauces offered elsewhere in the city. It's conveniently located in the Warehouse District, making it a handy place for a pit stop during gallery hopping. Inside the attractive cafe setting, you will find all sorts of yummy sandwiches on the house bread (for sale, along with other bakery delights, at the counter) including a recommended curried turkey salad. Salads are hearty, and most menu selections use interesting cheeses, herbs, and veggies. Brunch can be particularly nice, with a variety of egg dishes. The prices here are so reasonable that the place teeters just on the edge of the "inexpensive" category.

746 Tchoupitoulas St. ℂ **504/529-BIKE.** Main courses at lunch $7–$11, at dinner $9–$16. AE, DC, MC, V. Mon–Fri 11am–2:30pm; Sat–Sun 10am–2:30pm; Thurs–Sat 6–9:30pm.

René Bistrot ⌘ FRENCH   This relatively new restaurant is a chic, sophisticated, slightly snooty modern hotel bistro. Everything is fresh and pretty—
indeed, the "purse" made of phyllo stuffed with mushrooms and cream is almost
too pretty to eat. The menu isn't overwhelmingly interesting (mushroom and
arugula salad with sweet beets is a nice starter in addition to the purse) but on
the other hand, they serve a perfect steak frites: The steak is pounded thin and
peppered, topped with a dollop of herb butter, and the pommes frites on the
side are brilliant. It's an archetype of that dish and reason enough to come here.
Oh, and it's gotten lots of national accolades, including being named one of
Esquire magazine's Best New Restaurants of 2002 and one of America's 50 Best
Hotel Restaurants in *Food & Wine* magazine in May 2003.

817 Common St. (in the Renaissance Pere Marquette Hotel). ⌀ **504/412-2580**. www.renebistrot.com.
Reservations recommended. $17–$20. AE, MC, V. Sun–Thurs 6:30–10:30am, 11:30am–2:30pm, and 6–10pm;
Fri–Sat 6–11am, 11:30am–2:30pm, and 6–10pm.

Restaurant August ⌘ FRENCH   Harkening back to elegant New Orleans
dining (Frette linens and chandeliers; classy, but the effect is more dated than
nostalgic formal), but with a nouvelle twist on what would have been classic
New Orleans cuisine, August's chef John Besh has received a great deal of attention, but for our tastes, his contemporary French food is, overall, a bit too
dainty, fussy, and expensive. Having said that, an appetizer of baked goat cheese,
sour cherry tapenade, and Serrano ham mixes sweet and sour most successfully.
The house salad is combined with "roasted pumpkin seeds" (a concoction just
like peanut brittle in form and texture), pheasant comes both roasted and crispy,
and desserts are unusual (especially the lavender almond milk soup with lavender mousse and lavender white chocolate parfait). Vegetarians should be warned
that ham is used liberally and not wisely—it pops up even in fine dishes—but
the waitstaff seems willing to make adjustments if need be.

301 Tchoupitoulas St. ⌀ **504/299-9777**. www.rest-august.com. Reservations recommended. Main courses
$17–$37. AE, DC, MC, V. Mon–Fri 11am–2pm; daily 5:30–10pm.

The Veranda Restaurant ⌘ CONTINENTAL/CREOLE   This is one of
the more unusual dining spaces in town, thanks to a glass-enclosed courtyard
(one heck of a show during a thunderstorm). Buffet buffs will think themselves
in heaven with a buffet lunch option; you will find no gloppy macaroni and
cheese here but rather all sorts of culinary wonders. Regular dining is less
impressive but still tasty; consider Louisiana crab cakes in a light Creole mustard
sauce for a starter. The Creole herb–encrusted chicken breast, and the duo of
black bean and spinach ravioli in a chipotle pepper cream are other stars.
Healthy-choice entrees are marked (and for that matter, they're offered!) on the
menu. Leave room for one (or two) of several marvelous chocolate cakes.

In the Hotel Inter-Continental, 444 St. Charles Ave. ⌀ **504/585-4383**. Reservations recommended. Main
courses $16–$26. AE, DC, DISC, MC, V. Mon–Sun 6:30am–2pm and 5:30–10pm; Sun brunch 11am–2:30pm.

INEXPENSIVE

Ernst's Café AMERICAN   The same family has run the restaurant and bar in
this old brick building since 1902. Located right next to Harrah's casino and featuring live blues music on Friday and Saturday nights, it's a big local scene.
Sandwiches, hamburgers, fried shrimp, salads, red beans and rice, and po' boys
are on offer here.

600 S. Peters St. ⌀ **504/525-8544**. www.ernstcafe.net. Main courses $6.50–$9.95. AE, DC, MC, V. Mon–Sat
11am–2am; Sun 3pm–midnight.

Mother's ★★ SANDWICHES/CREOLE   Perhaps the proudest of all restaurants when New Orleans was named Fattest City in the U.S. was Mother's, whose overstuffed, mountain-size po' boys absolutely helped contribute to the results. It has long lines and zero atmosphere, but who cares when faced with a Famous Ferdi Special—a giant roll filled with baked ham (the homemade house specialty), roast beef, gravy, and debris (the bits of beef that fall off when the roast is carved)? There's other food, including one of the best breakfasts in the city, but the po' boys are what New Orleans goes for, and you should, too. (We can never decide between the Ferdi, the fried shrimp, or the soft-shell crab, when in season, and end up getting all three.) Mother's is within walking distance of the Louisiana Superdome and a number of major hotels. Be sure to allow time to stand in line, as there nearly always is one, though it can move quickly. (If you are lucky, decades-long customer Charlie will be volunteering to help oversee the crowds. He used to look like James Dean and has the photo to prove it—and he still sings like Elvis, and might charm you with a tune.) Mother's recently expanded, but it seems the new facilities are mostly for private functions.

401 Poydras St. ⓒ **504/523-9656.** www.mothersrestaurant.com. Menu items $1.75–$20. AE, DISC, MC, V. Mon–Sat 5am–10pm; Sun 7am–9pm.

Taqueria Corona ★★ MEXICAN   It's hard to get good Mexican food outside of, well, Mexico and Southern California, and so when fans find a place like Taqueria Corona, they almost weep with gratitude and delight. Here you'll find football-size burritos tasting just the right way (and that means not the generic fast-food way, thanks), grilled tacos, combo platters, even gazpacho—and all of it for minimal prices. Be sure to order a side of *cebollitas,* grilled and seasoned green onions.

857 Fulton St. ⓒ **504/524-9805.** Most items under $10. AE, DISC, MC, V. Mon–Sat 11:30am–2pm; Sun–Thurs 5–9:30pm; Fri–Sat 5–10pm. There's also an Uptown location: 5900 Magazine St., near Nashville (ⓒ **504/897-3974**).

Uglesich's Restaurant & Bar ★★ SANDWICHES/SEAFOOD   It's dangerous to call any one place "the best in New Orleans," but it's mighty tempting to make an exception for "Ugly's," a tiny, crowded, greasy neighborhood place that serves some of the most divine seafood in town. At lunchtime, especially during busy tourist seasons, you might have a very long wait before you order at the counter, another wait for a table, and a third wait for your food. But we swear it will be worth it. Obviously, others who should know think so; you might well end up sitting next to some of the best chefs in town because this is where *they* go for lunch. (You might just want to skip Uglesich's altogether during Jazz Fest and Mardi Gras. If you do go, at least bring a book or a bunch of chatty friends. During a recent Jazz Fest visit, the wait took from 2½ to—get this—*4* hours. Even dedicated fans find it hard to justify that sort of time commitment.)

It's hard to narrow down the dishes, and it's also hard to try new ones when you can't stay away from the splendid old favorites. Among the musts are fried green tomatoes with shrimp rémoulade, shrimp in creamy sauce on a fried cake of grits, voodoo shrimp (in a peppery butter sauce), and trout all kinds of ways. Order extra bread to sop up the sauce, but be sure to ask for it unbuttered. You'll be full, you might smell of grease, and you might well come back for more the next day.

Note: At press time, the owner was mulling retirement, so please call and make sure the restaurant is still open when you plan to go.

1238 Baronne St. ⓒ **504/523-8571** or 504/525-4925. Menu items $7–$14. No credit cards. Mon–Fri 9:30am–4pm; open 1 Sat a month. Closed July–Aug.

7 Uptown/The Garden District

For a map of restaurants in this section, see either the "New Orleans Dining" map on p. 98 or the "Uptown Accommodations & Dining" map on p. 93.

EXPENSIVE

Brigtsen's ★★ CAJUN/CREOLE   In a setting both elegant and homey, chef Frank Brigsten serves some of the city's best contemporary Creole cuisine. Nestled in a converted 19th-century house at the Riverbend, Brigtsen's is warm, intimate, and romantic. The individual dining rooms are small and cozy, and the menu changes daily.

Brigsten has a special touch with rabbit; one of his most mouthwatering dishes is an appetizer of rabbit tenderloin on a tasso-Parmesan grits cake with sautéed spinach and a Creole mustard sauce. The rabbit and andouille gumbo is delicious, intensely flavored, and well balanced. You can't miss with any of the soups, especially the lovely butternut squash shrimp bisque, and there's an entree to please everyone. One of the most popular dishes is roast duck with cornbread dressing and pecan gravy, with the duck skin roasted to a delightful crackle. We enjoyed the broiled fish of the day (sheepshead on a recent visit) with crabmeat, Parmesan crust, and a delicate, tangy lemon mousseline sauce, and pan-roasted drum fish topped with lots of lump crabmeat and chanterelle mushrooms, surrounded by a wonderful crab broth. Save room for dessert, perhaps the signature banana bread pudding with banana rum sauce. Brigsten's offers one of the loveliest evenings you'll spend in a Crescent City restaurant. And the "Early Evening" dinner special is as good a bargain as you'll find.

723 Dante St. ✆ **504/861-7610.** www.brigtsens.com. Reservations required. Main courses $18–$26; 3-course "Early Evening" dinner (Tues–Thurs 5:30–6:30pm) $17. AE, DC, MC, V. Tues–Sat 5:30–10pm.

Clancy's ★★ CREOLE   Your friendly cab driver may insist that Clancy's is "out of town," because this local favorite is so far uptown, but it's really not that much farther than a trip to the zoo or to Brigtsen's (see above). The food and neighborhood vibe alone should be worth the trip; it's a relief to get off the tourist path. The locals who cram into the smallish, oh-so-New Orleans room nightly will advise you to order the night's specials rather than sticking to the menu (though the duck dish on the menu is as good as duck gets). Do try the renowned fried oysters with brie appetizer. Recently, we tried smoked fried soft-shell crab topped with crabmeat (smoke flavor not overpowering, crab perfectly fried without a drop of grease to taint the dish), and veal topped with crabmeat and béarnaise sauce. Food too heavy? What the heck—make it even more so with desserts like lemon icebox pie. One local said it was even better than his grandma's!

6100 Annunciation St. ✆ **504/895-1111.** Reservations recommended. Main courses $17–$27. AE, DC, DISC, MC, V. Tues–Fri 11:30am–2pm; Mon–Thurs 5:30–10:30pm; Fri–Sat 5:30–11pm.

Commander's Palace ★★★ CREOLE   Recently awarded the Lifetime Outstanding Restaurant Award by the James Beard Foundation, Commander's is one of those places that lives up to its reputation. It's not just the food—which is never less than good—it's the whole package. In a beautiful 1880s Victorian

---

Impressions

In some places they eat to live. In our town, we live to eat.

—Ella Brennan

house, it consists of a nearly endless series of dining rooms, from large to inti-mate, each more appealing and romantic than the last. On balmy nights, you can eat in the lovely courtyard. (Although the back garden room was recently remodeled, the original building remains our favorite place to dine.) The wait-staff is incredibly attentive; several people pamper you throughout your meal (someone we know ordered the chocolate soufflé, and it fell before it was brought out to them, so to "make it up"—not that they needed to—they brought her and two fellow travelers five lagniappe special desserts; needless to say, they had to roll out of the restaurant). Each night features a multicourse fixed-price menu for around $35, which features the evening's specialties but also allows you to mix and match off the regular menu—a good bargain and a great splurge. And lunch is even more affordable: from $14 to $15 for appetizer and entree (and 25¢ martinis if you buy at least an entree!).

The famous turtle soup with sherry is outstanding, so thick it's nearly a stew. Don't miss it. Other marvelous appetizer choices include the shrimp and tasso with five-pepper jelly; carpaccio salad with roasted eggplant and garlic; and the hearty crawfish bisque with homemade biscuits. Main-course selections change seasonally, but you are best off sticking with Creole-type offerings—such as the frequently available and dreamy boned and roasted Mississippi quail, stuffed with Creole crawfish sausage, or the mixed grill (including lamb and rabbit sausage!) or even the dauntingly thick pork chop—rather than, say, more nou-velle-cuisine choices such as ultimately bland pan-fried fish. There's an excellent wine list, and the menu offers suggestions for wine with each entree.

Your serving team will tell you to try the famous bread pudding soufflé. Trust them. But all the desserts are exceptional; chocolate lovers should not overlook the chocolate Sheba, a sort of solid chocolate mousse, ever so slightly chilled and covered in nuts. And everyone should consider the Creole cream cheesecake, which will make you rethink your position on cheesecakes if you were on the fence. Then there is the gorgeous rendition of pecan pie a la mode and the not-on-the-menu-so-ask-for-it chocolate molten soufflé.

This is one must-do New Orleans restaurant, particularly appropriate for spe-cial occasions—but you can simply call your trip to New Orleans a special occa-sion, and we won't tell.

1403 Washington Ave. ⓒ **504/899-8221.** www.commanderspalace.com. Reservations required. Jackets required at night; no shorts, T-shirts, or tennis shoes. Main courses $29–$32; full brunch $20–$32; fixed-price $29–$36. AE, DC, DISC, MC, V. Mon–Fri 11:30am–1:30pm; Sat 11:30am–12:30pm; Sun brunch 10:30am–1:30pm; daily 6–9:30pm.

Martinique Bistro 🎯🎯 FRENCH   This place is just far enough uptown to be off the regular tourist radar. Because it has only 44 seats when the courtyard is not open (100 with), you might have trouble getting a table. Nonetheless, this sweet little bistro, a local favorite, is well worth the cab ride and potential wait. The yellow-squash soup is out of this world, and main courses such as the shrimp with sun-dried mango and curry are quite dazzling as well. If available, don't miss the lamb confit (tender shredded lamb mixed with preserved lemon and orange rind) on top of *pain perdu* (the Creole version of French toast). Do try the sorbet sampler (flavors such as mango, bitter lemon, and even imported French currents). If the weather permits, be sure to sit in the jasmine-scented courtyard.

5908 Magazine St. ⓒ **504/891-8495.** Reservations recommended. Main courses $15–$23. MC, V. Nov–May Sun–Thurs 5:30–10pm, Fri–Sat 5:30–10:30pm; June–Oct Sun–Thurs 6–10pm, Fri–Sat 6–10:30pm.

Upperline ★★★ ECLECTIC/CREOLE   In a small, charming house in a largely residential area, the Upperline is more low-key than high-profile places such as Emeril's. In its own way, though, it's every bit as inventive. It's a great place to try imaginative food at reasonable (by fancy restaurant standards) prices. Owner JoAnn Clevenger and her staff are quite friendly, and their attitude is reflected in the part of the menu where they actually—gasp!—recommend dishes at *other* restaurants. Perhaps you can afford to be so generous when your own offerings are so strong. Standout appetizers include fried green tomatoes with shrimp rémoulade sauce (they invented this dish, which is now featured just about everywhere in town), spicy shrimp on jalapeño cornbread, duck confit, and fried sweetbreads. For entrees, there's moist, herb-crusted pork loin, roast duck with a tingly sauce (either plum or port wine), and a fall-off-the-bone lamb shank. If you're lucky, there will be a special menu like the all-garlic meal, in which even dessert contains garlic. For dessert, try warm honey-pecan bread pudding or chocolate-hazelnut mousse. The award-winning wine list focuses primarily on California selections.

1413 Upperline St. © 504/891-9822. www.upperline.com. Reservations required. Main courses $18–$24. AE, DC, MC, V. Sun, Wed, and Thurs 5:30–9:30pm; Fri–Sat 5:30–10pm.

MODERATE

Dante's Kitchen ★ CONTEMPORARY LOUISIANA   It's daring for a restaurant to open near an established favorite, even more so if it's directly across the street with no other eating establishments nearby. But Dante's Kitchen has held its own against the justly fabled Brigtsen's, offering its own takes on local cuisine, for more moderate prices. Sitting inside is like sitting in any nice restaurant; outside, the serenity of the patio can be disturbed by street traffic and the occasional passing train (which frankly, we think is quite cool). A recent meal found us swooning over plump grilled shrimp in creamy grits, and the bizarre and eminently successful combo salad of warm, pecan-crusted goat cheese, pulled pork, arugula, and pears in a mimosa-balsamic vinaigrette. Really. Roast duck was perfect, though the cornbread dressing was dry, and an herb-crusted salmon on a pasta putanesca is deceptively healthy, so go for it. Desserts can be boring.

736 Dante St. © **504/861-3121.** www.danteskitchen.com. Reservations for parties of 6 or more only. Entrees $14–$21. AE, DISC, MC, V. Mon–Fri 11:30am–2:30pm; Sun–Thurs 6pm–9pm; Fri–Sat 6pm–10pm.

Dick & Jenny's ★★ ECLECTIC/CREOLE   Don't let out-of-the-way-on-a-depressing-industrial-street (or, for that matter, their refusal to take reservations) keep you away from this marvelous restaurant (one of the best in town, but easy to overlook thanks to the setting). It was good from its opening a couple years ago, and it's only gotten better. However, the room is still small, and the wait may still be long, so you might want to time your visit for an off-hour or day. When you do get there, you might eat as we recently did: steamed artichoke with warm brie crab dip, smoked salmon and dill cream cheese terrine with blue crab beignet and lemon aioli, a hearty white-bean-and-roast-lamb soup—and that's just the appetizers! Duck Quattro is, naturally, duck four ways (confit, foie gras, duck liver cognac flan, and seared breast with white beans; enough to share tastes, but you won't, because you will be greedy about this excellent food, we predict), falling-apart 5-hour-braised brisket with cheddar mashed potatoes, and desserts such as a crispy chocolate fritter or lemon mascarpone crepes.

4501 Tchoupitoulas St. © **504/894-9880.** Main courses $12–$19. AE, DISC, MC, V. Tues–Thurs 5:30–10pm; Fri–Sat 5:30–10:30pm.

Gautreau's ⊛ CREOLE A long time NOLA tradition that has seen its share of ups and downs, Gautreau's (and its haute Creole food) is currently experiencing one of its "ups." Having said that, there are other restaurants in town that more swiftly spur us to repeat visits. But it's hard to fault Gautreau's, a classy "old timey" restaurant (dress up just a touch; you'll fit in better with the formal locals) with a menu that changes frequently. Here's what we had recently: the sweet mixed greens with pears, goat cheese and a port vinaigrette—a marvelous salad in a town not known for salads (we wish it were larger), and the arugula salad with Gorgonzola vinaigrette and a subtle but distinctive use of herbs as an accent. Pork chops are novel-thick, set on sweet potato hash with braised red cabbage and apple-sage butter. Sautéed drum fish comes on caramelized-onion and spinach risotto with roasted red pepper aioli. Flourless chocolate cake is ubiquitous in this town, but here is the place to have it, where it's soft and fudgey.

1728 Soniat St. ⓒ 504/899-7397. http://ebiz.hibernia.com/gautreaus. Reservations recommended. Main courses $17–$32. DC, DISC, MC, V. Mon–Sat 6–10pm.

Jacques-Imo's ⊛⊛ ECLECTIC/CREOLE/SOUL FOOD It never failed: Every time a local found out we were heading uptown to Jacques-Imo's for dinner, he'd let out a whoop of joy. Or get all moonie-eyed. Even our cab driver sat up straight when we said we were going to Oak Street for dinner. "You going to Jacques-Imo's?" That's because Jacques-Imo's is the type of funky, colorful neighborhood joint that the natives love. But all the eclectic decor and good-time vibe would be for naught if the food was less than stellar. It's great, in fact—a serendipitous amalgam of traditional Creole, Southern soul, and New Wave innovative. The fried chicken is already a classic, we often order the catfish stuffed with crabmeat, and the shrimp Creole was the best version we've ever had—big fat shrimp swimming in a perfectly balanced Creole tomato sauce. A shrimp and alligator-sausage "cheesecake" (more like a quiche) was a tasty starter, while lovers of chicken livers will want the version here, on toast in a dark brown sauce. Try the three-layer chocolate (white, milk, and dark) mousse pie for dessert. The chef is the chef/owner from the much-loved and much-lamented Chez Helene, the model for the restaurant in the 1980s sitcom *Frank's Place*. Get there early, or you'll have to wait for a table; but is that so bad when you're sharing a cold one under a banana tree on a warm Louisiana evening with a bunch of laid-back, like-minded souls?

8324 Oak St. ⓒ 504/861-0886. www.jacquesimoscafe.com. Main courses $17–$25. AE, DC, DISC, MC, V. Mon–Thurs 6–10pm; Fri–Sat 5:30–10:30pm.

Kelsey's ⊛ CONTEMPORARY CREOLE For 8 years, chef Randy Barlow worked at K-Paul's with Paul Prudhomme, and the influence is apparent. The house specialty is eggplant Kelsey, a batter-fried eggplant pirogue (in the shape of a boat) stuffed with seafood seasoned with Parmesan and Romano cheeses, tomatoes, garlic, olive oil, parsley, and lemon juice. Fried green tomatoes sit atop spinach Florentine, while the Eggplant Delight (topped with barbecued shrimp) is another appetizer standout. Skip the disappointing garlic soup, and if you order salad, ask them to go light on the dressing.

3923 Magazine St. ⓒ 504/897-6722. www.kelseysrest.com. Reservations recommended. Main courses at lunch $9–$14, at dinner $18–$26. AE, DC, DISC, MC, V. Tues–Sat 11:30am–2:30pm and 6–10pm; Fri–Sat 5:30–10pm; Sunday brunch 10:30am–2pm; Sun 5:30–9:30pm.

La Crêpe Nanou ⊛ FRENCH Voted the top French bistro in New Orleans in the Zagat survey, La Crêpe Nanou is another not-so-secret local secret. It's always crowded. It's a romantic spot (windows angled into the ceiling let you gaze at the stars) that is simultaneously 19th century and quite modern. You can order crepes wrapped around a variety of stuffings, including crawfish. But you might want to save your crepe consumption for dessert (big and messy, full of chocolate and whipped cream) and concentrate instead on the big healthy salads and moist, flaky fish, particularly the whole grilled fish with herbs. It's big enough for two and is done to perfection. You can usually find knowledgeable locals ordering the mussels and extra bread to sop up the garlic white-wine sauce. Meat dishes come with your choice of sauce (garlic or cognac, for example).

1410 Robert St,. ✆ **504/899-2670.** Main courses $8.95–$16.95. AE, DC, MC, V. Sun–Thurs 6–10pm; Fri–Sat 6–11pm.

Lilette ✦ BISTRO   Recently expanded, Lilette seems to have (we sincerely hope) broken the curse of a space where other endeavors have dropped like flies. It did so with a chic rendition of a classic New Orleans bistro. Go at lunch, when choices are more interesting but less expensive. You will get fancy (sometimes oddly hearty) and nicely composed dishes such as boudin noir (dark sausage) with homemade mustard, arugula with white balsamic vinaigrette, and grilled beets with goat cheese, but also surprises like a pulled pork sandwich with aioli. Don't miss the curious dessert, little rounds of goat cheese crème fraîche, delicately paired with pears poached in liquid flavored with vanilla beans and raisins, topped with lavender honey, a marriage made on Mt. Olympus.

3637 Magazine St,. ✆ **504-895-1636.** Reservations suggested. Main courses at lunch $8–$17, at dinner $18–$29. AE, DISC, MC, V. Tues–Sat 11:30am–2pm; Tues–Thurs 6–10pm; Fri–Sat 6–11pm.

Pascal's Manale ✦ ITALIAN/STEAK/SEAFOOD   Barbecued shrimp. This restaurant has built its reputation on that one dish, and you should come here, if only for that. The place is crowded and noisy and verges on expensive, but it grows on you. Don't expect fancy decor—the emphasis is on food and conviviality. (Sunday nights especially feel like social gatherings.) Here you are going to get hearty, traditional N'Awlins fare, in a hearty, traditional N'Awlins setting. And there's nothing wrong with that, as long as you don't expect anything more. It's still a top-notch place for raw oysters. The barbecue shrimp sauce may no longer be the best in the city (we are more partial these days to the buttery wonder served over at Mr. B's), but the shrimp within it—plump, sweet, kitten-size—are. Be sure to add sherry to the turtle soup, and be extra sure to skip the dull and even possibly icky desserts. Instead, get another order of shrimp. Just try not to think about your arteries too much; lick your fingers, enjoy, and vow to walk your socks off tomorrow.

1838 Napoleon Ave. ✆ **504/895-4877.** Reservations recommended. Main courses $11–$24. AE, DC, DISC, MC, V. Mon–Fri 11:30am–10pm; Sat 4–10pm; Sun 4–9pm. Closed Sun from Memorial Day to Labor Day.

INEXPENSIVE

Note: **Foodie's** (reviewed below) now has a new, smaller location in Uptown at 7457 St. Charles Ave. (✆ **504/865-8646**).

Bluebird Cafe ✦✦ AMERICAN   Employees here tell the story of a man who awoke from an extended coma with these two words: *Huevos rancheros.* As soon as possible, he returned to the Bluebird for his favorite dish. A similar scene repeats each weekend morning when locals wake up with Bluebird on the brain. Why? Because this place consistently offers breakfast and lunch food that can restore and sustain your vital functions. Try the buckwheat pecan waffle, cheese grits, or homemade sausage and corned beef hash. You can also build your own omelet or see why the *huevos rancheros* enjoys its reputation (if you don't like runny eggs, ask for scrambled *huevos*). At midmorning on weekends, there is always a wait (up to 30 min.) out front. It's worth it.

3625 Prytania St. ✆ **504/895-7166.** All items under $7.95. No credit cards. Mon–Fri 7am–3pm; Sat–Sun 8am–3pm.

Camellia Grill 🐾🐾 HAMBURGERS/SANDWICHES   Even though it's *only* been a part of the city's food culture since 1946, the Camellia Grill seems to have always been there. Right off the St. Charles Avenue streetcar, it's a fixture in many people's lives. As you sit on a stool at the double-U-shaped counter, white-jacketed waiters pamper you while shouting cryptic orders to the chefs. There's often a wait because the Camellia serves some of the best breakfasts and burgers anywhere, but the wait is always worth it. The Camellia is famous for its omelets—heavy and fluffy at the same time and almost as big as a rolled-up newspaper. Notable omelet choices are the chili and cheese, and the potato, onion, and cheese (a personal favorite). Don't forget the pecan waffle, a work of art. If you're feeling really decadent, go with a friend, order omelets, and split a waffle on the side. The burgers are big and sloppy and among the best in town. Wash it all down with one of the famous chocolate freezes and then contemplate a slice of the celebrated pie for dessert (the chocolate pecan is to die for).

626 S. Carrollton Ave. ✆ **504/866-9573.** All items under $10. No credit cards. Mon–Thurs 9am–1am; Fri 9am–3am; Sat 8am–3am; Sun 8am–1am.

Casamento's 🐾🐾 SEAFOOD   This restaurant takes oysters so seriously that it simply closes down when they're not in season. It pays off—this is *the* oyster place. You pay a bit more for a dozen, but your reward is a presentation that shows the care that the staff puts in; the oysters are cleanly scrubbed and well selected. You might also take the plunge and order an oyster loaf: a big, fat loaf of bread fried in butter, filled with oysters (or shrimp), and fried again to seal it. Casamento's also has terrific gumbo—perhaps the best in town. The joint is small (you have to walk through the kitchen to get to the restrooms), but the atmosphere is light, with the waitresses serving up jokes and poking good-natured fun at you, at each other, or at the guys behind the oyster bar.

4330 Magazine St. ✆ **504/895-9761.** Main courses $4.95–$11. No credit cards. Tues–Sun 11:30am–1:30pm and 5:30–9pm. Closed June to mid-Sept.

Dunbar's Creole Cooking 🐾🐾 SOUL FOOD   For a genuine soul food experience, come to this small, super-friendly establishment run by the very charming Tina Dunbar. A no-decor, big-kitchen place, Dunbar's caters to blue-collar locals in search of breakfast (which can run as little as $1) or lunch. You'll feast on huge, soul-warming, and generally amazing Southern dishes, including gumbo, cornbread, and bread pudding, with daily specials listed on a board. Even the health-conscious will be happy here, with dishes such as the excellent red beans and rice. Service is down-home, and attire is definitely come-as-you-are.

4927 Freret St. ✆ **504/899-0734.** Main courses $5–$15. AE, DISC, MC, V. Mon–Sat 7am–9pm.

Franky & Johnny's 🐾 SEAFOOD   This is a favorite local hole-in-the-wall neighborhood joint with either zero atmosphere or enough for three restaurants, depending on how you view these things. And by "things" we mean plastic checked tablecloths, a ratty but friendly bar, and locals eating enormous soft-shell-crab po' boys with the crab legs hanging out of the bread and their mouths. You got your po' boys, your boiled or fried seafood platters with two kinds of salad, and goodness knows, you got your beer. Try that soft-shell-crab po' boy or the red beans and rice and other down-home dishes and know you are some-where that isn't for tourists—and enjoy it all the more.

321 Arabella St. (and Tchoupitoulas St.). ℭ **504/899-9146.** Main courses $5.95–$15. AE, DISC, MC, V. Daily 11am–10pm.

Joey K's ✯ CREOLE/SEAFOOD   This is just a little local corner hangout, though one that savvy tourists have long been hip to. Indeed, it was a tourist who told us to order the Trout Tchoupitoulas, and boy, were we happy—lovely pan-fried trout topped with grilled veggies and shrimp. Daily blackboard specials like brisket, lamb shank, white beans with pork chops, or Creole jambalaya won't fail to please. Order it all to go, and you'll be dining like a real Uptown local.

3001 Magazine St. ℭ **504/891-0997.** Main courses $5.95–$13. DC, MC, V. Mon–Fri 11am–10pm; Sat 8am–10pm.

Martin Wine Cellar and Delicatessen ✯✯ SANDWICHES   Martin's saved us during one busy pre–Mardi Gras weekend when parades and crowds prevented us from hitting a sit-down restaurant for lunch. A gourmet liquor and food store, Martin's also has a full-service deli counter. In addition to the usual deli suspects, they offer about two dozen specialty sandwiches, elaborate concoctions like the Dave's Special: rare roast beef, coleslaw, pâté de Campagne, and special mustard on rye. We ordered it on onion bread instead, and it made our list of the Ten Best Sandwiches of All Time. Weekdays feature daily specials (lamb shanks, barbecue shrimp, garlic soup), and then there is the cheese counter, the packaged salads, and the fresh breads to explore. It's all inexpensive and delicious. It's just 2 blocks lakeside of St. Charles, making this is the perfect Garden District spot for take-out or picnic fixings.

3827 Baronne St. ℭ **504/896-7380.** www.martinwine.com. Everything under $10. AE, DC, DISC, MC, V. Mon–Sat 9am–6:30pm; Sun 10am–4pm. They also have a location in Metairie at 714 Elmeer, in the 1200 block of Veterans Memorial Blvd. (ℭ **504/896-7300**).

Mystic Cafe ✯✯ MEDITERRANEAN   Local vegetarians flock here, though the cafe is technically Mediterranean (which means anything from Italy to Turkey), and some dishes include meat. The food is mostly butter-free and can be made without sugar upon request. Vegans and the heart-conscious will find plenty of whole-grain, high-quality olive oil–cooked options. We've had some wonderful salads and sandwiches here. Some might find it a welcome relief from the usual full-throttle New Orleans fare (we plead guilty to this ourselves), but others might feel they are dining in California.

3244 Magazine St. ℭ **504/891-1992.** Main courses $5.75–$11. AE, DC, DISC, MC, V. Sun–Thurs 11am–11pm; Fri–Sat 11am–midnight.

8 Metairie

Note: **Martin Wine Cellar,** reviewed above, has an additional, larger location in Metairie, almost across the street from Foodie's Kitchen (reviewed below), which makes for a very nice dilemma, indeed. The location is 714 Elmeer (ℭ **504/ 896-7300**).

EXPENSIVE

Wolfe's of New Orleans ✯✯ CONTEMPORARY CREOLE   You might be feeling awfully cheated, trapped out there in a good-quality, well-priced, and dull chain hotel in Metairie. Here you are, miles, it seems, from all the fun. Ha! You've got something other tourists don't: easy access to Wolfe's. The chef-owner spent 8 years at Emeril's, so you know delights are coming: appetizers like gnocchi with lump crabmeat and lobster, topped with flash-fried parsley, house-cured bacon, and smoked tomato fondue. A tomato chive cream cioppino with shellfish, plus shrimp toast if you ask nicely. Shiitake and goat-cheese cheesecake. A beautiful dark-roux gumbo. Dry-rub smoked brisket with bleu cheese, homemade andouille sausage, and candied pecan risotto with a caramelized shallot reduction. Can you tell we love writing lists like this? Do not under any circumstances leave without tasting Miss Ellie's (that's the chef's mom) white chocolate butter bars. The menu changes seasonally (we suggest the $45 tasting option), but you can see what treats will be there regardless. It's all set in a pretty room more reminiscent of a restaurant set in Uptown, and we thought that even before we had the Lemon Drop Martinis.

7224 Ponchartrain Blvd. ⓒ **504/284-6004.** www.wolfesofneworleans.com. Reservations suggested. Main courses $18–$24. AE, DC, MC, V. Mon–Fri 11:30am–2pm; Mon–Thurs 5:30pm–9:30pm; Fri–Sat 5:30pm–11pm.

MODERATE

Deanie's Seafood Bucktown USA ✸ SEAFOOD   The very model of a neighborhood restaurant, Deanie's, with its monster portions and generally high-quality food, is worth making the drive to Metairie. From the new potatoes (boiled in crab juice) that are plunked on the table when you arrive, to the almost ridiculously high piles of fried seafood that follow, it's one silly and savory experience. Even the salads are large; try the unusual sweet fig and balsamic dressing (made in-house). Opinions differ on whether their barbecue shrimp is the best in town (we think not, but we like it just fine), but note that the portion for two is so large that it's more reasonable (and more affordable) to just split the portion for one—and you may *still* have leftovers!

1713 Lake Ave. ⓒ **504/831-4141.** www.deanies.com. Main courses $11–$35. AE, MC, V. Sun–Thurs 11am–10pm; Fri–Sat 11am–11pm. **Note:** Deanie's has a new location in the French Quarter at 841 Iberville (ⓒ **504/581-1316**).

INEXPENSIVE

Foodie's Kitchen ✸✸✸ DELI   It's kind of a disservice to sum up Foodie's with a simple "Deli" categorization, but how else can you readily describe the latest Brennan family gourmet extravaganza? Foodie's features fantastic sandwiches (and smart prep chefs who will make suggestions like ordering the Rock N' Remi shrimp—shrimp rémoulade—on slipper bread rather than the pita it normally comes on; doing so instantly landed the resulting creation on our Best Sandwiches of All Time list), complex fresh salads, and lovely and daily changing hot menu items. A bakery section offers hearty breads like the five-cheese loaf and desserts to thrill (including a chocolate truffle cupcake that had a certain Frommer's author's mother actually licking and gnawing its paper casing), and prepared-food sections include packaged Commander's Palace turtle soup, all to either eat in or (more likely) take out. Foodie's calls it "great food for busy people." Ourselves, we call it a blessing from heaven, as we swing by on the way to the airport to pick up the aforementioned turtle soup.

720 Veteran's Blvd. ⓒ **504/837-9695.** www.foodieskitchen.com. Most items under $10. AE, DISC, MC, V. Mon–Fri 10am–9pm; Sat–Sun 8am–9pm. **Note:** Foodie's now has a new, smaller location in Uptown at 7457 St. Charles Ave. (ⓒ **504/865-TOGO** [8646]).

9 Lake Pontchartrain

MODERATE

Bruning's Seafood on the Lake ✸ SEAFOOD   Bruning's has served a classic New Orleans seafood menu since 1859, and it is now run by fifth- and sixth-generation Brunings who use traditional family recipes. (They had to do some rebuilding after the restaurant sustained heavy damage from Hurricane George in 1998.) The broiled seafood is especially good, as is the seafood gumbo. The fried dishes are grease free. A good buy, if you can't make up your mind, is the generous seafood platter. There's a children's menu, and all entrees come with salad, toast, and a potato.

1922 West End Pkwy. ① **504/282-9395.** Main courses $8.95–$18. AE, DISC, MC, V. Sun–Thurs 11am–9:30pm; Fri–Sat 11am–10:30pm.

10 Coffee, Tea & Sweets

Café au Lait ⭐ COFFEE/BAKERY/SANDWICHES   This is a good little coffeehouse space (that also serves, as of right now, an impressive menu of mostly sandwiches and salads) in an area of the Quarter sadly lacking much of this type of food. We like their freeze drinks (icy blends of coffee and chocolate) on any hot day.

307 Chartres St. ① **504/528-9933.** Coffee $1.70–$3.50; main courses $4.50–$13. AE, DC, DISC, MC, V. Mon–Sat 8am–6pm; Sun 8am–5pm.

Café du Monde ⭐⭐⭐ COFFEE   Excuse us while we wax rhapsodic. Since 1862, Café du Monde has been selling café au lait and beignets (and nothing but) on the edge of Jackson Square. A New Orleans landmark, it's *the* place for people-watching. Not only is it a must-stop on any trip to New Orleans, you may find yourself wandering back several times a day: for your morning beignet and coffee, your afternoon snack, and best of all, your 3am pick-me-up. What's a beignet? (Say ben-*yay,* by the way.) A square French doughnut–type object, hot and covered in powdered sugar. You might be tempted to shake off some of the sugar. Don't. Trust us. Pour more on, even. You'll be glad you did. Just don't wear black, or everyone will know what you've been eating. At three for about $1, they're a hell of a deal. Wash them down with chicory coffee, listen to the nearby buskers, ignore people trying to get your table, and try to figure out how many more stops you can squeeze in during your visit.

In the French Market, 800 Decatur St. ① **504/581-2914.** www.cafedumonde.com. Coffee, milk, hot chocolate, and beignets (3 for $1.35). No credit cards. Daily 24 hr. Closed Christmas. Additional locations at Riverwalk Mall, New Orleans Centre at the Superdome, original location in the New Orleans French Market.

La Boulangerie ⭐⭐⭐ BAKERY   Honestly, one food-related area that New Orleans actually fails in is bread; many a local restaurant serves a sorry, flaky bit of staleness. But this bakery would be a jewel even if it were in a major bread city. Perhaps the only authentic baguettes in the city (the owners are from France, so they are particular about their bread, as you might guess), the loaves are crusty on the outside, soft and flavorful on the inside. But we forget about the baguettes, perfect though they may be, because of the olive bread, an oval loaf studded with olives, and just slightly greasy (in a good way) with olive oil. Heaven. And, oh, the bleu cheese bread they make only on weekends. They also do marvelous croissants, chocolate-filled croissants, and other pastries. Olive bread—and for that matter, many products—sell out early, so here is one (perhaps the only) reason to be an early bird in New Orleans. No coffee, though.

4526 Magazine St (uptown). ① **504/269-3777.** Loaf of bread $2–$6. No credit cards. Tues–Sat 6am–7pm; Sun 7am–1pm. Also at 3143 Ponce de Leon (Mid-City) (① **504/940-0577;** Tues–Sat 7am–6pm, Sun 8am–2pm) and 625 St. Charles Ave. (① **504/569-1925;** daily 6am–6pm).

La Madeleine ⭐ BAKERY/COFFEE   La Madeleine is one of the French Quarter's most charming casual eateries, though its location means it's nearly always crowded with tourists. One of a chain of French bakeries, it has a wood-burning brick oven that turns out a wide variety of breads, croissants, and brioches—and claims that the skills for making these treats come right from France, so it's all authentic. We like their thick-chunk chocolate chip cookie, even if they don't serve milk to wash it down with. Don't order their main dishes—stick with their wonderful baked goods.

547 St. Ann St. (at Chartres St.). (©) 504/568-0073. www.lamadeleine.com. Pastries $1.35–$2.60; main courses $3.90–$9.25. AE, DISC, MC, V. Daily 7am–9pm.

La Marquise ★ PASTRIES/COFFEE, TEA, AND SWEETS   Tiny La Marquise serves French pastries in the crowded front room, which also holds the display counter, and outside on a small but delightful patio. Maurice Delechelle is the master baker and guiding hand here, and you'd be hard-pressed to find more delectable goodies. There are *galettes bretonnes* (butter cookies), *pain au chocolat* (a rectangle of croissant dough wrapped around a chocolate bar and then baked), *cygne* swans (cream-filled éclairs in the shape of swans), *choux à la crème* (cream puffs), and *mille-feuilles* (napoleons) as well as croissants, brioches, and a wide assortment of strudels and Danish pastries. La Marquise is almost always crowded; if there are no seats on the patio, Jackson Square is just a few steps away. **Croissant D'Or** ★, a larger version of La Marquise operated by the same folks, is at 617 Ursulines St. (© **504/524-4663**). It's a quiet and calm place with the same great snacks, and you can almost always find an open table.

625 Chartres St. (©) 504/524-0420. Pastries $2.75–$5. No credit cards. Daily 7am–7pm.

P.J.'s Coffee & Tea Company ★ COFFEE   P.J.'s is a local institution, with 17 locations around town at last count. It offers a great variety of teas and coffees, and it roasts its own coffee beans. The iced coffee is made by a cold-water process that requires 12 hours of brewing. P.J.'s also serves mochas, cappuccinos, and lattes. The granita is prepared with P.J.'s Espresso Dolce iced coffee concentrate, frozen with milk and sugar, and served as a coffee "slushee"—great on hot, muggy days.

5432 Magazine St. (©) 504/895-0273. www.pjscoffee.com. 95¢–$4. AE, MC, V. Mon–Fri 6:30am–11pm; Sat–Sun 7am–11pm. P.J.'s has branches at Tulane University ((©) 504/865-5705), 644 Camp St. ((©) 504/529-3658), 634 Frenchmen St. ((©) 504/949-2295), and 7624 Maple St. ((©) 504/866-7031), among other locations.

Royal Blend Coffee & Tea House ★ COFFEE/SANDWICHES   This place is set back off the street; to reach it you walk through a courtyard. Order a sandwich, quiche, or salad at the counter and take it out into the courtyard. On Saturday afternoons, weather permitting, a guitarist serenades diners. (You can also eat inside, but it's not as much fun.) If you're just in the mood for coffee and pastry, they have plenty of that, too, and the pastry menu changes daily.

621 Royal St. (©) 504/523-2716. www.royalblendcoffee.com. Pastries 85¢–$2.95; lunch items $3.25–$6.45. AE, MC, V. Sun–Thurs 7am–8pm; Fri–Sat 7am–11pm. Royal Blend has branches at 222 Carondelet St. ((©) 504/529-2005) and at 204 Metairie Rd. in Metairie ((©) 504/835-7779).

Rue de la Course ★ COFFEE   This is your basic comfy boho coffeehouse: cavernous in appearance, thanks to a very tall ceiling; manned by cool, friendly college kids; and full of locals seeking a quick pick-me-up, lingering over the paper, or poring over their journals. In addition to prepared coffee and tea, Rue de la Course sells loose tea and coffee by the pound as well as a few newspapers and local magazines.

1500 Magazine St. (©) 504/529-1455. No credit cards. Mon–Fri 7:30am–11pm; Sat–Sun 8am–11pm. Other locations: 3128 Magazine St. ((©) 504/899-0242), 219 N. Peters St. ((©) 504/523-0206), 401 Carondelet St. ((©) 504/586-0401), and 6501 Willow St.((©) 504/862-8063). Hours vary.

Sights to See & Places to Be

We admit that our favorite New Orleans activities involve walking, eating, listening to music, and dancing. If that's all you do while you're visiting, we won't complain. Still, some people feel guilty if they don't take in some culture or history while they're on vacation.

And besides, there will be occasions when you'll need to escape the rain or heat. New Orleans offers several fine museums and a world-class aquarium and zoo, all of which, in addition to being interesting in and of themselves, make marvelous refuges from the weather (except perhaps for the zoo).

Frankly, New Orleans itself is one big sight—it's one of the most unusual-looking cities in America, and being nice and flat, it's just made for exploring on foot. So get out there and do it (see the walking tours in chapter 9, "City Strolls," if you'd like some structure).

Don't confine yourself to the French Quarter. Yes, it certainly is a seductive place, but to go to New Orleans and never leave the Quarter is like going to New York, remaining in Greenwich Village, and believing you've seen Manhattan. Make sure you also take time to do things like stroll the lush Garden District, marvel at the oaks in City Park, ride the streetcar down St. Charles Avenue and gape with jealousy at the gorgeous homes, or go visit some gators on a swamp tour.

But if you leave the Quarter only to visit clubs and restaurants, we won't blame you a bit.

SUGGESTED ITINERARIES

If You Have 1 Day

If you have only a day in New Orleans, you might as well spend it all in the **French Quarter**—after all, you could easily spend a much longer trip entirely within its confines. (We just won't let you do so if you have the additional time.) But this is a day that will include all the important factors of a New Orleans visit: eating, walking, drinking, eating some more, listening to music, and dancing.

Start your day with beignets and coffee at **Café du Monde.** Then take the **walking tour** of the Quarter in the next chapter; it gives you a bit of history in addition to pointing out individual buildings, and it

also helps you slow down and admire the grand architecture of this unique neighborhood. For lunch, have a muffuletta at **Central Grocery** (split it with somebody; they're gigantic) and thread your way through the buildings across the street to eat it by the banks of the **Mississippi River.** If you want something more elaborate, sample the modern Creole offerings of **Mr. B's Bistro & Bar.**

After lunch, go to the historic **Cabildo,** with its fine exhibits illustrating New Orleans and Louisiana history and culture, and/or the **Presbytère,** which has just been turned into a wonderful new Mardi Gras museum. Afterward, pop in to nearby **Faulkner House Books** (see chapter 10)—not only did the author live there for a time, you can also choose a literary souvenir from the comprehensive selection of New Orleans–related books.

Then start **walking.** Walk down Royal Street and admire the antiques. Round the corner and drop in at the new Chartres Street address of **A Gallery for Fine Photography;** it's like a museum of photos, many of which relate to local culture and history. (One of these would make a high-quality, albeit pricey, souvenir.) Swing by the shops toward the Esplanade Avenue end of Decatur Street. Be sure to check out the **Voodoo Museum;** it's more tourist voodoo than not, but there is some real information. As you wander, don't forget to admire the varying colors of buildings, the intricate iron lacework on the balconies, and so forth. This is quite a place they've got here.

As evening approaches, take a walk on Bourbon Street. Sure, it's gaudy, loud, and kind of disgusting and comes off as a combination giant T-shirt shop and bar. At the right time of day, when things are starting to heat up but the real obnoxious types aren't too drunk, when different kinds of music pour from every door, when captivating smells waft from restaurants, it's also seductive and exhilarating. Have a pre-dinner drink at the darkly mysterious Lafitte's Blacksmith Shop (the oldest building in town) or the darkly romantic Napoleon House or sample a Hurricane at the not-so-dark-but-always-rowdy Pat O'Brien's.

And then get out of the Quarter. If you have one dinner to eat in New Orleans, you must eat at Commander's Palace. You might not totally agree with the James Beard folks who voted it best restaurant in the United States, but we doubt you will be disappointed.

Afterward, you can check out who's playing at Tipitina's or the Maple Leaf, or you may just want to head back to the Quarter. If you opt for a romantic buggy ride, we won't make fun of you. Do not miss hearing some jazz at Preservation Hall—it's cheap, and it's the real McCoy. You might also want to navigate Bourbon Street; now that night has fallen, the scene will have truly kicked in. You have to see it once, even if you never want to see it again. For equal fun, less like that found at a frat party, head to the Frenchmen section of the Faubourg Marigny, where there are at least five clubs and a couple of bars within a few blocks. Wander from one to another, sometimes never even going inside (the music can be heard outside just as easily), simply mingling with the friendly crowds. You can also drop by Donna's for some fine local music.

Suddenly feeling hungry again? Grab a dozen oysters at **Acme** or **Felix's.** (Or make another trip to Café du Monde. It's been known to happen.) Have you exercised restraint and missed one of the three bars mentioned above? Go now. If you don't collapse exhausted—and full—in your bed, you haven't done your day properly.

If You Have 2 Days

Get out of the Quarter, get out of the Quarter, get out of the Quarter. Are we getting through to you? You can come back; you probably still have serious shopping (if not serious drinking) to do. But today, you must begin to see what else New Orleans has to offer.

Hop on the **St. Charles Avenue streetcar** first thing. Admire the gorgeous homes along the way (if you are awake enough) and get off at the end for breakfast at the **Camellia Grill.** The pecan waffle should get you going. It will also convince you of the need for more walking. Good. Get back on the streetcar, get off in the **Garden District,** and take the walking tour in the next chapter. Aside from its historical significance and interest, this neighborhood, full of fabulous houses and lush greenery, is just plain beautiful. Then get back on the streetcar—this time pay attention to those beautiful houses—and get off at Lee Circle. Walk or cab to lunch at either **Uglesich's** (if you have the time to wait in line and the appetite for some of the finest, and most fattening, seafood in town) or **Mother's** (if po' boys are more your speed).

Now catch the bus to **City Park,** where you can admire the oaks and go to the **art museum.** On the way back, be sure to head down **Esplanade Avenue** (in a vehicle, please—it's too far to walk, and parts are too unsavory), perhaps even getting out to stroll along St. John's Bayou. Again, admire the beautiful homes and majestic oaks, different from what you've seen in the Garden District but no less memorable. If you return to the Quarter for additional shopping and drinking, you can also go by the **Aquarium of the Americas**—it's a particularly good one (and open until 8pm on Fri and Sat).

At night, sample what's new and happening in New Orleans cooking. We recommend the more-or-less-contemporary Creole food at the **Upperline** or **Brigtsen's,** but

the omnipresent sounds of "Bam!" and "Turn it up a notch" may understandably draw you to **Emeril's.** The first two make some clubs convenient; head to Tip's or the Maple Leaf if you didn't get there the previous night, **Mid City** for some zydeco and bowling, or the **Howlin' Wolf** for serious headliners. Or all of them if you are up for it. Try to be.

If You Have 3 Days

Yes, we are dragging you out of the Quarter again, but we will let you come back later.

Get back on the St. Charles Avenue streetcar and head to **Audubon Park** and the **zoo,** which is one of the best in the country but is small enough to see in a short time. Although we love that streetcar ride and take it whenever we can, you might want a change of scenery, in which case you can take a **riverboat** to the park. Afterward, head over to **Joey K's** or **Mystic Cafe** on Magazine Street and have some lunch (or try **Pascal's Manale, Camellia Grill,** or **Martin Wine Cellar,** which are nearby) and then meander down Magazine Street for some shopping (more affordable than much you'll find in the Quarter), hopping on and off the bus as you spot stores that interest you. Finish up at the **art galleries** on Julia Street.

Sometime today, take a **walking tour.** There is one for practically every interest (from those offered by the Park Service to African-American heritage tours), and we particularly like cemetery tours, which allow you to see one of New Orleans's most iconic sights in a safe

---

Impressions

Yet to all men whose desire only is to live a short life, but a merry one, I have no hesitation in recommending New Orleans.

—Henry Fearon, "Sketches of America," 1817

New Orleans Attractions

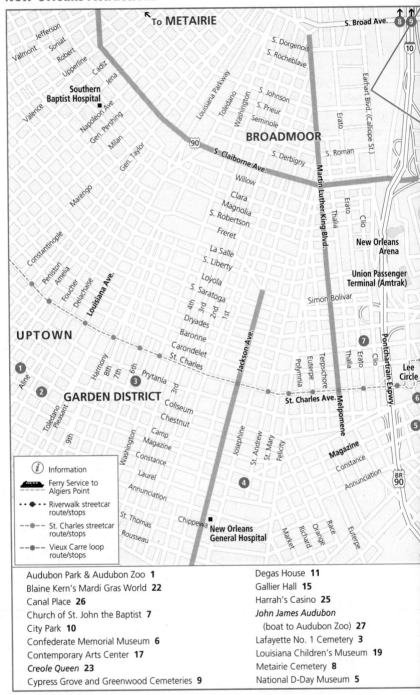

Audubon Park & Audubon Zoo **1**

Blaine Kern's Mardi Gras World **22**

Canal Place **26**

Church of St. John the Baptist **7**

City Park **10**

Confederate Memorial Museum **6**

Contemporary Arts Center **17**

Creole Queen **23**

Cypress Grove and Greenwood Cemeteries **9**

Degas House **11**

Gallier Hall **15**

Harrah's Casino **25**

John James Audubon
(boat to Audubon Zoo) **27**

Lafayette No. 1 Cemetery **3**

Louisiana Children's Museum **19**

Metairie Cemetery **8**

National D-Day Museum **5**

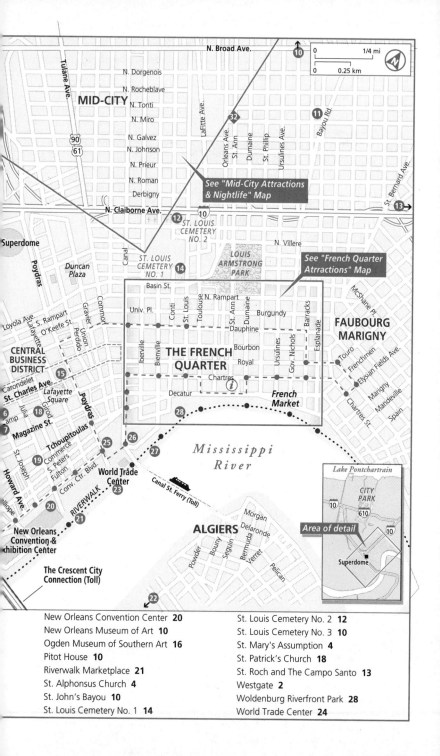

New Orleans Convention Center **20**
New Orleans Museum of Art **10**
Ogden Museum of Southern Art **16**
Pitot House **10**
Riverwalk Marketplace **21**
St. Alphonsus Church **4**
St. John's Bayou **10**
St. Louis Cemetery No. 1 **14**

St. Louis Cemetery No. 2 **12**
St. Louis Cemetery No. 3 **10**
St. Mary's Assumption **4**
St. Patrick's Church **18**
St. Roch and The Campo Santo **13**
Westgate **2**
Woldenburg Riverfront Park **28**
World Trade Center **24**

and informative manner. You can fit in a tour of **Lafayette Cemetery** on your way to Magazine Street, or you can go back to the Quarter for a tour of St. Louis No. 1. (Or do these before you head over to the park.) Other possibilities include a literary heritage tour, voodoo tours, and nighttime ghost and vampire tours—though these are of dubious veracity and should be taken strictly for entertainment purposes.

1 The French Quarter

Those who have been to Disneyland might be forgiven if they experience some déjà vu upon first seeing the French Quarter. It's somewhat more worn, of course, and, in spots, a whole lot smellier. But it's also real. However, thanks perhaps in part to Disney, many tourists treat the Quarter like a theme park, going from bar to bar instead of ride to ride, broadcasting their every move with rowdy shrieks of merriment.

Fine—except, it isn't an amusement park constructed just for the delight of out-of-towners. It's an actual neighborhood, one of the most visually interesting in America, and one that has existed for more than 200 years. (Some of the people living in the Quarter are the fifth generation of their family to do so.)

There's a great deal to the French Quarter—history, architecture, cultural oddities—and to overlook all that in favor of T-shirt shops and the ubiquitous bars is a darn shame, which is not to say we don't understand, and rather enjoy, the lure of the more playful angle of the area. And as much as we find **Bourbon Street** tacky and often disgusting, we walk down it at least once every time we are in town. We just don't want you to end up like some tourists who never even get *off* Bourbon. (And regardless of where you go in the Quarter, please remember that you are walking by people's homes. You wouldn't like it if someone did something biologically disgusting on your doorstep, so please afford French Quarter dwellers the same courtesy.)

A French engineer named Adrien de Pauger laid out the Quarter in 1718, and today it's a great anomaly in America. Almost all other American cities have torn down or gutted their historic centers, but thanks to a strict preservation policy, the area looks exactly as it always has and is still the center of town.

Aside from Bourbon Street, you will find the most bustling activity at **Jackson Square,** where musicians, artists, fortunetellers, jugglers, and those peculiar "living statue" performance artists (a step below mime, and that's pretty pathetic) gather to sell their wares or entertain for change. **Royal Street** is home to numerous pricey antiques shops, with other interesting stores on **Chartres and Decatur streets** and the cross streets between.

The closer you get to **Esplanade Avenue** and toward **Rampart Street,** the more residential the Quarter becomes, and buildings are entirely homes (in the business sections, the ground floors are commercial and the stories above apartments). Walk through these areas, and peep in through any open gate; surprises await in the form of graceful brick and flagstone-lined courtyards filled with foliage and bubbling fountains. Follow the French Quarter stroll in chapter 9, "City Strolls," and you'll see a few of the nicest courtyards in the Quarter.

The Vieux Carré Commission is ever vigilant about balancing contemporary economic interests in the Quarter with concerns for historic preservation. Not only has the commission encouraged restoration, but it has also joined in the battle to hold back certain would-be intruders of the modern world. There's not a traffic light in the whole of the French Quarter—they're relegated to fringe streets—and streetlights are of the old gaslight style. In 1996, large city buses

French Quarter Attractions

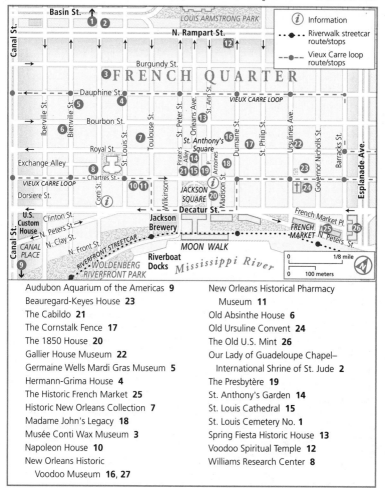

Audubon Aquarium of the Americas **9**

Beauregard-Keyes House **23**

The Cabildo **21**

The Cornstalk Fence **17**

The 1850 House **20**

Gallier House Museum **22**

Germaine Wells Mardi Gras Museum **5**

Hermann-Grima House **4**

The Historic French Market **25**

Historic New Orleans Collection **7**

Madame John's Legacy **18**

Musée Conti Wax Museum **3**

Napoleon House **10**

New Orleans Historic
   Voodoo Museum **16**, **27**

New Orleans Historical Pharmacy
   Museum **11**

Old Absinthe House **6**

Old Ursuline Convent **24**

The Old U.S. Mint **26**

Our Lady of Guadeloupe Chapel–
   International Shrine of St. Jude **2**

The Presbytère **19**

St. Anthony's Garden **14**

St. Louis Cathedral **15**

St. Louis Cemetery No. 1 **1**

Spring Fiesta Historic House **13**

Voodoo Spiritual Temple **12**

Williams Research Center **8**

were banned from the neighborhood. During a good part of each day, Royal and Bourbon streets are pedestrian malls, and no vehicles are *ever* allowed in the area around Jackson Square. We also applaud the hard-drawn lines that have mostly kept out the generic chain stores that populate most city centers these days, threatening to turn all of America into one big mall, one city indistinguishable from any other.

   Though much of New Orleans is made for walking, the Quarter is particularly pedestrian-friendly. The streets are laid out in an almost perfect rectangle, so it's nearly impossible to get lost. It's also so well traveled that it is nearly always safe, particularly in the central parts. Again, as you get toward the fringes (especially near Rampart) and as night falls, you should exercise caution; stay in the more bustling parts and try not to walk alone.

   The French Quarter walking tour in chapter 9 will give you the best overview of the historic buildings in the area and of the city's history. Many other attractions that aren't in the walking tour are listed in this chapter, so make sure to cross-reference as you go along. For attractions in this section, see the "French Quarter Attractions" map on p. 153.

MAJOR ATTRACTIONS

Audubon Aquarium of the Americas ★★★ *Kids* With all the other delights New Orleans offers, it's easy to overlook the Audubon Institute's Aquarium of the Americas—despite its million-gallon size. Who wants to look at fish when you could be eating them? But this is a world-class aquarium, highly entertaining and painlessly educational, with beautifully constructed exhibits. Kids love it, even those too impatient to read the graphics, but adults shouldn't overlook it, if for no other reason than it's a handy refuge from the rain.

The aquarium is on the banks of the Mississippi River, a very easy walk from the main Quarter action. Five major exhibit areas and dozens of smaller aquariums hold a veritable ocean of aquatic life native to the region (especially the Mississippi River and Gulf of Mexico) and to North, Central, and South America. You can walk through the underwater tunnel in the Caribbean Reef exhibit and wave to finny friends swimming all around you, view a shark-filled re-creation of the Gulf of Mexico, or drop in to see the penguin exhibit. We particularly like the walk-through Waters of the Americas, where you wander in rain forests (complete with birds and piranhas) and see what goes on below the surface of swamps; one look will quash any thoughts of a dip in a bayou. Not to be missed are a riveting exhibit on jellyfish, the impossibly cute giant sea otters, and the sea-horse exhibit. By the time you read this, the new **Insectarium** (yep, an insect museum) should be open to entertain you and/or give you the willies.

The **IMAX theater** ★★ shows two or three films at regular intervals. The Audubon Institute also runs the city's zoo at Audubon Park uptown (p. 171). **Combination tickets** for the aquarium, the IMAX theater, the zoo, and a riverboat ride to the zoo are $37 for adults, $19 for children. You can also buy tickets for different combinations of the attractions.

1 Canal St., at the River ⓒ **800/774-7394** or 504/581-4629. www.auduboninstitute.org. Aquarium $14 adults, $10 seniors, $6.50 children 2–12. IMAX $7.75 adults, $6.75 seniors, $5 children. Combination aquarium/IMAX tickets $18 adults, $15 seniors, $11 children. Aquarium opens daily at 9:30; closing hours vary by season. IMAX daily 10am–6pm. Shows every hour on the hour; advanced tickets recommended. Closed Mardi Gras and Christmas.

The Historic French Market ★★ *Kids* Legend has it that the site of the French Market was originally used by Native Americans as a bartering market. It began to grow into an official market in 1812. From around 1840 to 1870, it was part of Gallatin Street, an impossibly rough area so full of bars, drunken sailors, and criminals of every shape and size that it made Bourbon Street look like Disneyland. Today, it's a mixed bag (and not nearly as colorful as its past). The 24-hour Farmer's Market makes a fun amble as you admire everything from fresh produce and fish to more tourist-oriented items like hot sauces and Cajun and Creole mixes. Snacks like gator on a stick (when was the last time you had that?) will amuse the kids. The Flea Market, a bit farther down from the Farmer's Market, is considered a must-shop place, but the reality is that the goods are kind of junky: T-shirts, jewelry, hats, purses, toys, sunglasses, and so on. Still, some good deals can be had (even better if you are up for bargaining), so the savvy might find it the right place for souvenir shopping. The flea market is open daily.

On Decatur St., toward Esplanade Ave. from Jackson Sq. Open daily roughly 9am–6pm.

St. Louis Cathedral ★ The St. Louis Cathedral prides itself on being the oldest continuously active cathedral in the United States. What usually doesn't get mentioned is that it is also one of the ugliest. The outside is all right, but the rather grim interior wouldn't give even a minor European church a run for its money.

Still, its history is impressive and somewhat dramatic. The cathedral formed the center of the original settlement, and it is still the major landmark of the French Quarter. This is the third building to stand on this spot. A hurricane destroyed the first in 1722. On Good Friday 1788, the bells of its replacement were kept silent for religious reasons rather than ringing out the alarm for a fire—which eventually went out of control and burned down more than 850 buildings, including the cathedral itself.

Rebuilt in 1794, the structure was remodeled and enlarged between 1845 and 1851 by J. N. B. de Pouilly. The brick used in its construction was taken from the original town cemetery and was covered with stucco to protect the mortar from dampness. It's worth going in to catch one of the free docent tours; the knowledgeable guides are full of fun facts about the windows and murals and how the building nearly collapsed once from water table sinkage. Be sure to look at the slope of the floor; clever architectural design somehow keeps the building upright even as it continues to sink.

615 Pere Antoine Alley. ⓒ **504/525-9585.** Fax 504/525-9583. www.saintlouiscathedral.org. Free admission. Mon–Sat 9am–5pm; Sun 2–5pm. Free tours run continuously.

HISTORIC BUILDINGS

Beauregard-Keyes House ⓖ   This "raised cottage," with its Doric columns and handsome twin staircases, was built as a residence by a wealthy New Orleans auctioneer, Joseph Le Carpentier, in 1826. Confederate Gen. P. G. T. Beauregard lived in the house with several members of his family for 18 months between 1865 and 1867, and from 1944 until 1970, it was the residence of Frances Parkinson Keyes (pronounced *Cause*), who wrote many novels about the region. One of them, *Madame Castel's Lodger,* concerns the general's stay in this house. *Dinner at Antoine's,* perhaps her most famous novel, was also written here. Mrs. Keyes left her home to a foundation, and the house, rear buildings, and garden are open to the public. The gift shop has a wide selection of her novels.

1113 Chartres St., at Ursulines St. ⓒ **504/523-7257.** Fax 504/523-7257. Admission $5 adults, $4 seniors, students, and AAA members, $2 children ages 6–13, free for children under 6. Mon–Sat 10am–3pm. Closed Sun and holidays. Tours on the hour.

The 1850 House ⓖ   James Gallier Sr. and his son designed the historic Pontalba Buildings for the Baroness Micaela Almonester de Pontalba (see box below), who had them built in 1849 (see stop no. 32 of "Walking Tour 1: The French Quarter" in chapter 9, "City Strolls") in an effort to combat the deterioration of the older part of the city. The rows of town houses on either side of Jackson Square were the largest private buildings in the country at the time. Legend has it that the Baroness, miffed that her friend Andrew Jackson wouldn't tip his hat to her, had his statue erected in the square, where to this day he continues to doff his chapeau toward her apartment on the top floor of the Upper Pontalba. It's probably not true, but we never stand in the way of a good story.

In this house, the Louisiana State Museum presents a demonstration of life in 1850, when the buildings opened for residential use. The self-guided tour uses a fact-filled sheet that explains in detail the history of the interior and the uses of the rooms, which are filled with period furnishings arranged to show how the rooms were typically used. It vividly illustrates the difference between the "upstairs" portion of the house, where the upper-middle-class family lived in comfort (and the children were largely confined to a nursery and raised by servants), and the "downstairs," where the staff toiled in considerable drudgery to make their bosses comfortable. It's a surprisingly enjoyable look at life in the "good old days"; it might have you reconsidering just how good they were.

Lower Pontalba Building. 523 St. Ann St., Jackson Sq. ℂ **800/568-6968** or 504/568-6968. Fax 504/568-4995. http://lsm.crt.state.la.us/site/1850ex.htm. Admission $5 adults, $4 seniors and students, free for children under 13. Tues–Sun 9am–5pm. Closed state holidays.

Old Absinthe House The Old Absinthe House was built in 1806 and now houses the Old Absinthe House bar and two restaurants. The drink for which the building and bar were named is now outlawed in this country (it caused blindness and madness), but you can sip a legal libation in the bar and feel at one with the famous types who came before you, listed on a plaque outside: William Thackeray, Oscar Wilde, Sarah Bernhardt, and Walt Whitman. Andrew Jackson and the Lafitte brothers plotted their desperate defense of New Orleans here in 1815.

The house was a speakeasy during Prohibition, and when federal officers closed it in 1924, the interior was mysteriously stripped of its antique fixtures—including the long marble-topped bar and the old water dripper that was used to infuse water into the absinthe. Just as mysteriously, they all reappeared down the street at a corner establishment called, oddly enough, the Old Absinthe House Bar (400 Bourbon St.). The latter recently closed, and a neon-bedecked daiquiri shack opened in its stead. Needless to say, the fixtures are nowhere in sight.

240 Bourbon St., between Iberville and Bienville sts. ℂ **504/523-3181.** www.oldabsinthehouse.com. Free admission. Daily 9am–2am.

Old Ursuline Convent ⭐⭐ Forget tales of America being founded by brawny, brave, tough guys in buckskin and beards. The real pioneers—at least, in Louisiana—were well-educated French women clad in 40 pounds of black wool robes. That's right; you don't know tough until you know the Ursuline nuns, and this city would have been a very different place without them.

The Sisters of Ursula came to the mudhole that was New Orleans in 1727 after a journey that several times nearly saw them lost at sea or to pirates or disease. Once in town, they provided the first decent medical care (saving countless lives) and later founded the local first school and orphanage for girls. They also helped raise girls shipped over from France as marriage material for local men, teaching the girls everything from languages to homemaking of the most exacting sort (laying the foundation for who knows how many local families).

The convent dates from 1752 (the Sisters themselves moved uptown in 1824, where they remain to this day), and it is the oldest building in the Mississippi River Valley and the only surviving building from the French Colonial period in the United States. It also houses Catholic archives dating back to 1718. Unfortunately, tours here can be disappointing affairs; docents' histories ramble all over the place, rarely painting the full, thrilling picture of these extraordinary ladies to whom New Orleans owes so much.

1110 Chartres St., at Ursulines St. ℂ **504/529-3040.** Admission $5 adults, $4 seniors, $2 students, free for children under 8. Tours Tues–Fri 10am–3pm on the hour (closed for lunch at noon); Sat–Sun 11:15am, 1pm, and 2pm.

The Old U.S. Mint ⭐⭐ *Kids* The Old U.S. Mint, a Louisiana State Museum complex, houses exhibits on New Orleans jazz and on the city's Carnival celebrations. The first exhibit contains a comprehensive collection of pictures, musical

Lady Bountiful: Baroness de Pontalba

New Orleans owes a great debt to Baroness Micaela Almonester de Pontalba and her family—without them, Jackson Square would be a mudhole. Her father, Don Almonester, used his money and influence to have the St. Louis Cathedral, Cabildo, and Presbytère built. The Baroness was responsible for the two long brick apartment buildings that flank Jackson Square and for the renovation that turned the center of the square into what it is today.

Born in 1795 into the most influential family in New Orleans, she married her cousin, who stole her inheritance. When she wanted a separation at a time when such things were unheard of, her father-in-law shot her several times and then shot himself. She survived, though some of her fingers did not. In subsequent portraits, she would hide the wounded hand in her dress. In the end, she got her money back—she used it for those French Quarter improvements—and also ended up taking care of her (eventually) slightly nutty husband for the rest of his life. She died in Paris in 1874, and her home there is now the residence of the American ambassador. The book *Intimate Enemies* by Christina Vella (Louisiana State University Press, 1997) has all the details about this remarkable woman.

instruments, and other artifacts connected with jazz greats—Louis Armstrong's first trumpet is here. It tells of the development of the jazz tradition and New Orleans's place in that history. Across the hall is a stunning array of Carnival mementos from New Orleans and other communities across Louisiana—from ornate Mardi Gras costumes to a street scene complete with maskers and a parade float.

400 Esplanade Ave., at N. Peters St. (enter on Esplanade Ave. or Barracks St.). © 800/568-6968 or 504/568-6968. Fax 504/568-4995. Admission $5 adults, $4 seniors and students, free for children under 13. Tues–Sun 9am–5pm.

Our Lady of Guadeloupe Chapel—International Shrine of St. Jude ⊛
This is known as the "funeral chapel." It was erected (in 1826) conveniently near St. Louis Cemetery No. 1, specifically for funeral services, so as not to spread disease through the Quarter. We like it for three reasons: the catacomblike devotional chapel with plaques thanking the Virgin Mary for favors granted, the gift shop full of religious medals including a number of obscure saints, and the statue of St. Expedite. He got his name, according to legend, when his crate arrived with no identification other than the word *expedite* stamped on the outside. Now he's the saint you pray to when you want things in a hurry. (We are not making this up.) Expedite has his cults in France and Spain and is also popular among the voodoo folks. He's just inside the door on the right.

411 N. Rampart St., at Conti St. Parish office. © 504/525-1551. www.saintjudeshrine.com.

MUSEUMS

In addition to the destinations listed here, you might be interested in the **Germaine Wells Mardi Gras Museum** at 813 Bienville St., on the second floor of Arnaud's restaurant (© **504/523-5433;** fax 504/581-7908), where you'll find a private collection of Mardi Gras costumes and ball gowns dating from around 1910 to 1960. Admission is free, and the museum is open during restaurant hours.

The **Ogden Museum of Southern Art** (which will feature five floors of the finest collection of Southern art anywhere, everything from acrylics to sculpture to mixed media) should be open by the time you read this (I'll believe it when I see it). It's at 925 Camp St. (© **504/539-9600**; www.ogdenmuseum.org) and is open Monday to Saturday from 10am to 5pm.

The Cabildo 🐊🐊🐊 Constructed from 1795 to 1799 as the Spanish government seat in New Orleans, the Cabildo was the site of the signing of the Louisiana Purchase transfer. It was severely damaged by fire in 1988 and closed for 5 years for reconstruction, which included total restoration of the roof by French artisans using 600-year-old timber-framing techniques. It is now the center of the Louisiana State Museum's facilities in the French Quarter. It's conveniently located right on Jackson Square and is quite worth your time.

A multiroom exhibition informatively, entertainingly, and exhaustively traces the history of Louisiana from exploration through Reconstruction from a multicultural perspective. It covers all aspects of life, not just the obvious discussions of slavery and the battle for statehood. Topics include antebellum music, mourning and burial customs (a big deal when much of your population is succumbing to yellow fever), immigrants and how they fared here, and the changing roles of women in the South (which occupies a large space). As you wander through, each room seems more interesting than the last. Throughout are portraits of nearly all the prominent figures from Louisiana history plus other fabulous artifacts, including Napoléon's death mask.

701 Chartres St. © **800/568-6968** or 504/568-6968. Fax 504/568-4995. Admission $5 adults, $4 students and seniors, free for children under 13. Tues–Sun 9am–5pm.

Gallier House Museum 🐊 James Gallier Jr. designed and built the Gallier House Museum as his residence in 1857. Anne Rice fans will want to at least walk by—this is the house she was thinking of when she described Louis and Lestat's New Orleans residence in *Interview with the Vampire.* Gallier and his father were leading New Orleans architects—they also designed the old French Opera House, the original St. Charles Exchange Hotel, Municipality Hall (now Gallier Hall), and the Pontalba Buildings. This carefully restored town house contains an early working bathroom, a passive ventilation system, and furnishings of the period. Leaders of local ghost tours swear that Gallier haunts the place. Inquire about seasonal special programs.

1118 and 1132 Royal St., between Governor Nicholls and Ursuline sts. © **504/525-5661.** www.gnofn. org/~hggh. Admission $6 adults, $5 seniors, students, AAA members, and children ages 8–18, free for children under 8. Mon–Fri 10am–4pm. Tours offered Mon–Fri at 10am, 11am, noon, 1:30pm, 2:30pm, 3:30pm, and selected Sun.

Hermann-Grima House 🐊 Brought to you by the same folks who run the Gallier House (see above), the 1831 Hermann-Grima House is a symmetrical Federal-style building (perhaps the first in the Quarter) that's very different from its French surroundings. The knowledgeable docents who give the regular tours make this a satisfactory stop at any time, but keep an eye out for the frequent special tours. At Halloween, for example, the house is draped in typical 1800s mourning, and the docents explain mourning customs. The house, which stretches from St. Louis Street to Conti Street, passed through two different families before becoming a boardinghouse in the 1920s. It has been meticulously restored and researched, and the tour is one of the city's more historically accurate offerings. On Thursdays, from October through May, cooking demonstrations take place in the authentic 1830s kitchen, using methods of the era. (Alas, health rules prevent those on the tour from sampling the results.) The house also contains one of the Quarter's last surviving stables, complete with stalls.

820 St. Louis St. © 504/525-5661. www.gnofn.org/~hggh. Admission $6 adults, $5 seniors, students, AAA members, and children ages 8–18, free for children under 8. Mon–Fri 10am–4pm. Tours offered Mon–Fri at 10am, 11am, noon, 1:30pm, 2:30pm, and 3:30pm.

Historic New Orleans Collection–Museum/Research Center ★★   The Historic New Orleans Collection's museum of local and regional history is almost hidden away within a complex of historic French Quarter buildings. The oldest, constructed in the late 18th century, was one of the few structures to escape the disastrous fire of 1794. These buildings were owned by the collection's founders, Gen. and Mrs. L. Kemper Williams. Their former residence, behind the courtyard, is open to the public for tours. There are also excellent tours of the Louisiana history galleries, which feature choice items from the collection—expertly preserved and displayed art, maps, and original documents like the transfer papers for the Louisiana Purchase of 1803. The collection is owned and managed by a private foundation, not a governmental organization, and therefore offers more historical perspective and artifacts than boosterism. The Williams Gallery, also on the site, is free to the public and presents changing exhibitions that focus on Louisiana's history and culture.

If you want to see another grandly restored French Quarter building (and a researcher's dream), visit the **Williams Research Center,** 410 Chartres St., near Conti Street (© **504/598-7171**), which houses and displays the bulk of the collection's many thousands of items. Admission is free.

533 Royal St., between St. Louis and Toulouse sts. © **504/523-4662**. Fax 504/598-7108. www.hnoc.org. Free admission; tours $4. Tues–Sat 10am–4:30pm; tours Tues–Sat 10am, 11am, 2pm, 3pm. Closed major holidays, Mardi Gras.

Madame John's Legacy ★   The second-oldest building in the Mississippi Valley (after the Ursuline Convent) and a rare example of Creole architecture that miraculously survived the 1794 fire, Madame John's Legacy has finally been opened to the public.

Built around 1788 on the foundations of an earlier home destroyed in the fire of that year, the house has had a number of owners and renters (including the son of Governor Claiborne), but none of them were named John (or even Madame!). It acquired its moniker courtesy of author George Washington Cable, who used the house as a setting for his short story "Tite Poulette." The protagonist was a quadroon named Madame John after her lover, who willed this house to her.

There are no tours, but you can enjoy two exhibits: one on the history and legends of the house (including glimpses into the style and manner of Creole life) and another of art by self-taught/primitive artists.

632 Dumaine St. © 504/568-6968. Admission $3 adults, $2 students and seniors, free for children under 13. Tues–Sun 9am–5pm.

Musée Conti Wax Museum ★ *Kids*   You might wonder about the advisability of a wax museum in a place as hot as New Orleans, but the Musée Conti holds up fine. This place is pretty neat—and downright spooky in spots. (And, of course, when it is hot, this is a good place to cool off!) A large section is devoted to a sketch of Louisiana legends (Andrew Jackson, Napoléon, Jean Lafitte, Marie Laveau, Huey Long, a Mardi Gras Indian, Louis Armstrong, and Pete Fountain) and historical episodes. Whether or not these figures are the exact reproductions touted and prized by so many other wax museums is highly dubious, but the descriptions, especially of the historical scenes, are surprisingly informative and witty.

917 Conti St. ⓒ **504/525-2605.** www.get-waxed.com. Admission $6.75 adults, $6.25 seniors (over 62), $5.75 children ages 4–17, free for children under 4. Mon–Sat 10am–5pm; Sun noon–5pm. Closed Mardi Gras and Christmas.

New Orleans Historic Voodoo Museum ⭐ Some of the hard-core voodoo practitioners in town might scoff at the Voodoo Museum, and perhaps rightly so. It is largely designed for tourists, but it is also probably the best opportunity for tourists to get acquainted with the history and culture of voodoo. Don't expect high-quality, comprehensive exhibits—the place is dark, dusty, and musty. There are occult objects from all over the globe plus some articles that allegedly belonged to the legendary Marie Laveau. Unless someone on staff talks you through it (which they will, if you ask), you might come away with more confusion than facts. Still, it's an adequate introduction. Who wouldn't want to bring home a voodoo doll from here? The people who run the museum are involved in voodoo, and there is generally a voodoo priestess on site, giving readings and making personal gris-gris bags. Again, it's voodoo for tourists, but for most tourists, it's probably the right amount. (Don't confuse this place with the Marie Laveau House of Voodoo on Bourbon Street.) The museum recently split into two parts, with exhibits on classic voodoo found at the old Dumaine Street location and a focus on contemporary voodoo at the new Peters Street space.

The museum can arrange psychic readings and visits to voodoo rituals if you want to delve deeper into the subject.

217 N. Peters St. (contemporary voodoo exhibits). ⓒ **504/522-5223.** And 724 Dumaine St., at Bourbon St. (historic voodoo). ⓒ **504/523-7685.** Admission $7 adults, $5.50 students, seniors, and military, $4.50 high school students, $3.50 grade school students. Cemetery tour $22; tour of the Undead $22. Daily 10am–8pm.

New Orleans Historical Pharmacy Museum ⭐ Founded in 1950, the New Orleans Pharmacy Museum is just what the name implies. In 1823, the first licensed pharmacist in the United States, Louis J. Dufilho Jr., opened an apothecary shop here. The Creole-style town house doubled as his home, and he cultivated the herbs he needed for his medicines in the interior courtyard. Inside you'll find old apothecary bottles, voodoo potions, pill tile, and suppository molds as well as the old glass cosmetics counter (pharmacists of the 1800s also manufactured makeup and perfumes). Unfortunately, the old-timey atmosphere is assisted by itty-bitty information cards attached to the exhibits with minimal facts listed in ancient typefaces or spidery handwriting—too bad. As alternative medicine gains acceptance, it's fascinating to look back at a time when medicine was barely more than snake-oil potions.

514 Chartres St., at St. Louis St. ⓒ **504/565-8027.** www.pharmacymuseum.org. Admission $2 adults, $1 seniors and students, free for children under 12. Tues–Sun 10am–5pm.

The Presbytère ⭐⭐⭐ The Presbytère was planned as housing for the clergy but was never used for that purpose. Currently, it's part of the Louisiana State

Museum, which has just turned the entire building into a smashing Mardi Gras museum, one that puts all other efforts in town to shame. (Blaine Kern's Mardi Gras World in Algiers Point is also a cool experience, and it wouldn't be overkill to do both if you're interested. At Mardi Gras World, you'll see floats being made, but the tour experience could be a bit better, and it's out of the way.)

Five major themes (History, Masking, Parades, Balls, and the Courir du Mardi Gras) trace the history of this high-profile but frankly little-understood (outside of New Orleans) annual event. The exhibits are stunning and the attention to detail is startling, with everything from elaborate Mardi Gras Indian costumes to Rex Queen jewelry from the turn of the 20th century. A re-creation of a float allows you to pretend you are throwing beads to a crowd on a screen in front of you. Heck, even some of the restrooms masquerade (appropriately) as the ubiquitous Fat Tuesday port-a-potties! There is almost too much to see, so allow a couple of hours, and don't forget to check out the gift shop, the only place in town where you can buy those coveted Zulu beads.

751 Chartres St., Jackson Sq. ⓒ **800/568-6968** or 504/568-6968. Fax 504/568-4995. Admission $5 adults, $4 seniors and students, free for children under 13. Tues–Sun 9am–5pm.

Woldenberg Riverfront Park ⭐   Made up of just under 20 acres of newly repaired green space, Woldenberg Riverfront Park has historically been the city's promenade; now it's an oasis of greenery in the heart of the city with numerous works by popular local artists scattered throughout. The park includes a large lawn with a brick promenade leading to the Mississippi, and it is home to hundreds of trees—oaks, magnolias, willows, and crape myrtles—and thousands of shrubs.

The **Moonwalk** has steps that allow you to get right down to Old Muddy—on foggy nights, you feel as if you are floating above the water. There are many benches from which to view the city's main industry—its busy port (second in the world only to Amsterdam in annual tonnage). To your right you'll see the Greater New Orleans Bridge and the World Trade Center of New Orleans (formerly the International Trade Mart) skyscraper as well as the Toulouse Street wharf, the departure point for excursion steamboats.

Along the Mississippi from the Moonwalk at the old Governor Nicholls Street wharf to the Aquarium of the Americas at Canal St. ⓒ **504/861-2537.** Daily dawn–dusk.

2 Outside the French Quarter
UPTOWN & THE GARDEN DISTRICT

If you can see just one thing outside the French Quarter, make it the Garden District. It has no significant historic buildings or important museums—it's simply beautiful. In some ways, even more so than the Quarter, this is New Orleans. Authors as diverse as Truman Capote and Anne Rice have been enchanted by its spell. Gorgeous homes stand quietly amidst lush foliage, elegant but ever so slightly (or more) decayed. You can see why this is the setting for so many novels; it's hard to imagine that anything real actually happens here.

But it does. Like the Quarter, this is a neighborhood, so please be courteous as you wander around. Seeing the sights consists mostly of looking at the exteriors of nice houses, so we suggest that you turn to "Walking Tour 2: The Garden District" (see chapter 9, "City Strolls"), which will help guide you to the Garden District's treasures and explain a little of its history. Use the listings in chapter 10, "Shopping," to find the best shops, galleries, and bookstores on **Magazine Street,** the main shopping strip that bounds the Garden District.

Meanwhile, a little background: Across Canal Street from the Quarter, "American" New Orleans begins. After the Louisiana Purchase of 1803, an essentially French-Creole city came under the auspices of a government determined to develop it as an American city. As American citizens moved in, tensions between Creole society and the newcomers began to increase. Some historians lay this at the feet of Creole snobbery; others blame the naive and uncultured Americans. In any case, Creole society succeeded in maintaining a relatively distinct social world, deflecting American settlement upriver of Canal Street (uptown); the Americans in turn came to dominate the city with sheer numbers of immigrants. Newcomers bought up land in what had been the old Gravier Plantation (now the uptown area) and began to build a parallel city. Very soon, Americans came to dominate the local business scene, centered along Canal Street. In 1833, the American enclave that we now know as the Garden District was incorporated as Lafayette City, and—thanks in large part to the New Orleans–Carrollton Railroad, which covered the route of today's St. Charles Avenue streetcar—the Americans kept right on expanding until they reached the tiny resort town of Carrollton. It wasn't until 1852 that the various sections came together officially as a united New Orleans.

TROLLING ST. JOHN'S BAYOU & LAKE PONTCHARTRAIN ✦✦✦

St. John's Bayou is a body of water that originally extended from the outskirts of New Orleans to Lake Pontchartrain, and it's one of the most important reasons New Orleans is where it is today. Jean Baptiste Le Moyne, Sieur de Bienville, was commissioned to establish a settlement in Louisiana that would both make money and protect French holdings in the New World from British expansion. Bienville chose the spot where New Orleans now sits because he recognized the strategic importance of "back-door" access to the Gulf of Mexico provided by the bayou's linkage to the lake. Boats could enter the lake from the Gulf and then follow the bayou until they were within easy portage distance of the mouth of the Mississippi River. Area Native American tribes had used this route for years.

The early path from the city to the bayou is today's Bayou Road, an extension of Governor Nicholls Street in the French Quarter. Modern-day Gentilly Boulevard, which crosses the bayou, was another Native American trail—it led around the lake and on to settlements in Florida.

As New Orleans grew and prospered, the bayou became a suburb as planters moved out along its shores. In the early 1800s, a canal was dug to connect the waterway with the city, reaching a basin at the edge of Congo Square. The basin became a popular recreation area with fine restaurants and dance halls (as well as meeting places for voodoo practitioners, who held secret ceremonies along its shores). Gradually, New Orleans reached beyond the French Quarter and enveloped the whole area—overtaking farmland, plantation homes, and resorts.

The canal is gone, filled in long ago, and the bayou is a meek re-creation of itself. It is no longer navigable (even if it were, bridges were built too low to permit the passage of boats of any size), but residents still prize their waterfront sites, and rowboats and sailboats make use of the bayou's surface. This is one of the prettiest areas of New Orleans—full of the old houses tourists love to marvel at without the hustle, bustle, and confusion of more high-profile locations. A walk along the banks and through the nearby neighborhoods is one of our favorite things to do on a nice afternoon.

GETTING THERE   The simplest way to reach St. John's Bayou from the French Quarter is to drive straight up Esplanade Avenue about 20 blocks (you

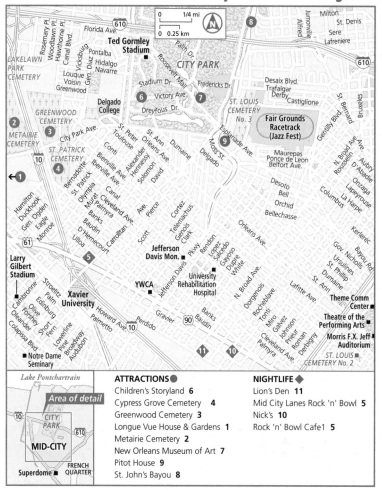

ATTRACTIONS ●

Children's Storyland **6**
Cypress Grove Cemetery **4**
Greenwood Cemetery **3**
Longue Vue House & Gardens **1**
Metairie Cemetery **2**
New Orleans Museum of Art **7**
Pitot House **9**
St. John's Bayou **8**

NIGHTLIFE ◆

Lion's Den **11**
Mid City Lanes Rock 'n' Bowl **5**
Nick's **10**
Rock 'n' Bowl Cafe1 **5**

can also grab the bus that says "Esplanade" at any of the bus stops along the avenue). Or take the Esplanade Ridge walking tour in chapter 9, "City Strolls." Right before you reach the bayou, you'll pass **St. Louis Cemetery No. 3** (just past Leda St.). It's the final resting place of many prominent New Orleanians, among them Father Adrien Rouquette, who lived and worked among the Choctaw; Storyville photographer E. J. Bellocq; and Thomy Lafon, the black philanthropist who bought the old Orleans Ballroom as an orphanage for African-American children and put an end to its infamous "quadroon balls." Just past the cemetery, turn left onto Moss Street, which runs along the banks of St. John's Bayou. If you want to see an example of an 18th-century West Indies–style plantation house, stop at the **Pitot House,** 1440 Moss St. (see later in this chapter).

To continue, drive along Wisner Boulevard, on the opposite bank of St. John's Bayou from Moss Street, and you'll pass some of New Orleans's grandest modern homes—a sharp contrast to those on Moss Street. If you want to go all the way to Lake Pontchartrain, here's a good route: Stay on Wisner to Robert E. Lee Boulevard, turn right, drive to Elysian Fields Avenue, and then turn left. That's the University of New Orleans campus on your left.

Turn left onto the broad concrete highway, Lake Shore Drive. It runs for 5½ miles along the lake, and in the summer, the parkway alongside its seawall is usually swarming with swimmers and picnickers. On the other side are more luxurious, modern residences.

Lake Pontchartrain is some 40 miles long and 25 miles wide. Native Americans once lived along both sides, and it was a major waterway long before white people were seen in this hemisphere. You can drive across it over the 23¾-mile Greater New Orleans Causeway, the longest bridge in the world.

When you cross the mouth of St. John's Bayou, you'll be where **the old Spanish Fort** was built in 1770. Its remains are now nestled amid modern homes. In the early 1800s, there was a lighthouse here, and in the 1820s, a railroad brought New Orleanians out to a hotel, a casino, a bandstand, bathing houses, and restaurants that made this a popular resort area.

Look for the **Mardi Gras fountain** on your left. Bronze plaques around its base are inscribed with the names of Mardi Gras krewes, and if you time your visit to coincide with sundown, you'll see the fountain beautifully lit in the Mardi Gras colors of purple (for justice), green (for faith), and gold (for power).

At the end of Lake Shore Drive, when you come to the old white Coast Guard lighthouse, you'll know you've reached **West End.** This interesting little park is home to several yacht clubs, a marina, and a number of restaurants, many of which have been here for years and look just the way you'd expect—not too fancy but with a good view out over the water. This old fishing community has, over the years, become the main pleasure-boating center of New Orleans; the Southern Yacht Club here was established in 1840, making it the second oldest in the country. After the railroad began bringing pleasure-seekers here from the city in the 1870s, showboats and floating circuses often pulled up and docked for waterside performances.

MUSEUMS & GALLERIES

Confederate Memorial Museum ★★   Not far from the French Quarter, the Confederate Museum was established in 1891 (giving it a claim to being the oldest surviving museum in Louisiana) and currently houses the second-largest collection of Confederate memorabilia in the country. It opened so soon after the end of the war that many of the donated items are in excellent condition. Among these are 125 battle flags, 50 Confederate uniforms, guns, swords, photographs, and oil paintings. You'll see personal effects of Confederate Gen. P. G. T. Beauregard and Confederate Pres. Jefferson Davis (including his evening clothes), part of Robert E. Lee's silver camp service, and many portraits of Confederate military and civilian personalities. It's somewhat cluttered and not that well laid out—for the most part, only buffs will find much of interest here, though they can have remarkable temporary exhibitions like a most moving one on Jefferson Davis's youngest daughter, Winnie.

929 Camp St., at St. Joseph's. ℂ **504/523-4522.** www.confederatemuseum.com. Admission $5 adults, $4 students and seniors, $2 children under 12. Mon–Sat 10am–4pm.

Contemporary Arts Center ★★   Redesigned in the early '90s to much critical applause, the Contemporary Arts Center (CAC) is a main anchor of the city's young arts district (once the city's old Warehouse District, it's now home to a handful of leading local galleries). Over the past 2 decades, the center has consistently exhibited influential and groundbreaking work by regional, national, and international artists in various mediums. The CAC staggers its shows, so there should always be something worth seeing hanging on the walls; it also presents theater, performance art, dance, and music concerts. Individual exhibitions hang for 6 to 8 weeks, and performances are weekly.

900 Camp St. ☎ **504/528-3805.** Fax 504/528-3828. www.cacno.org. Gallery admission $5 adults, $3 seniors and students, free for members and kids 15 and under, free to all on Thurs. Performance and event tickets $3–$25. Tues–Sun 11am–5pm.

National D-Day Museum ⭐⭐⭐ Opened on D-day, June 6, 2000, this is the creation of the late best-selling author (and *Saving Private Ryan* consultant) Stephen Ambrose, and it is the only museum of its kind in the country. It tells the story of all 19 U.S. amphibious operations worldwide on that fateful day of June 6, 1944 (Normandy may have been the subject of a Spielberg movie, but many other battles were waged and won). A rich collection of artifacts (including some British Spitfire airplanes) coupled with top-of-the-line educational materials (including an oral history station) makes this new museum one of the highlights of New Orleans.

Many of the exhibits emphasize personal stories, including audio exhibits featuring civilians and soldiers alike relating their own experiences. A panorama allows visitors to see just what it was like on those notorious beaches. There is also a copy of Eisenhower's contingency speech, in which he planned to apologize to the country for the failure of D-day—thankfully, it was a speech that was never needed nor delivered.

945 Magazine St., in the Historic Warehouse District. ☎ **504/527-6012.** www.ddaymuseum.org. Admission $10 adults, $6 seniors, $5 children ages 5–17, free for children under 5. Daily 9am–5pm. Closed holidays.

New Orleans Museum of Art ⭐⭐ Often called NOMA, this museum is located in an idyllic section of City Park. The front portion of the museum is the original large, imposing neoclassical building ("sufficiently modified to give a subtropical appearance," said the architect Samuel Marx); the rear portion is a striking contrast of curves and contemporary styles.

The museum opened in 1911 after a gift to the City Park Commission from Isaac Delgado, a sugar broker and Jamaican immigrant. Today, it houses a 40,000-piece collection including pre-Columbian and Native American ethnographic art; 16th- through 20th-century European paintings, drawings, sculptures, and prints; early American art; Asian art; and one of the six largest decorative glass collections in the United States. A 5-acre sculpture garden is currently under construction and should be open sometime in 2003. Be sure to pick up a guide pamphlet from the information desk at the entrance.

The changing exhibits frequently have regional resonance, such as the extensive retrospective on Degas, which focused on the time he spent in the city, or the one devoted to religious art and objects collected from local churches. Another exhibit focused on—how's this for a complete change of pace—"dirty pictures" throughout the modern era!

1 Collins Diboll Circle, at City Park and Esplanade. ☎ **504/488-2631.** Fax 504/488-6662. www.noma.org. Admission $6 adults, $5 seniors (over 64), $3 children 3–17, free to Louisiana residents. Thurs 10am–noon; Tues–Sun 10am–5pm. Closed most major holidays.

Westgate ⭐ Death buffs and other morbid types will be thrilled to visit Westgate (also known as the "House of Death"), while others will come down with a serious case of the creeps. The hard-to-miss purple-and-black building is a gallery of "necromantic art" run by Leilah Wendell and Daniel Kemp, who inaugurated this project in 1979. Both are authors of metaphysical books about the personification of death, and the gallery is dedicated to Azrael, the embodiment of "what Western cultures refer to as the Angel of Death," says Wendell. The art, much of it by Wendell, uses plenty of death imagery with a heavy emphasis on its romance. The results are graphic and powerful. Some will find this deeply disturbing, but it certainly is one of the most unusual galleries in town and is worth a trip for the open-minded and curious. The owners are actually far more friendly and helpful than you might think. Their on-site shop—the **Original Necrotorium**—sells "necromantic" art and jewelry.

5219 Magazine St., at the corner of Bellecastle St., Uptown. ✆ 504/899-3077. www.westgatenecromantic. com. Free admission; donations accepted. Tues–Sat noon–5pm.

HISTORIC NEW ORLEANS CHURCHES

Church and religion are not likely to be the first things that jump to mind in a city known for its debauchery. But New Orleans remains a very Catholic city—don't forget that Mardi Gras is a pre-Lenten celebration. In fact, religion of one form or another directed much of the city's early history and molded its culture in countless ways.

Church of St. John the Baptist ✪ You may have noticed a large gilded dome prominently set in the New Orleans skyline (especially as you drive on the elevated expressway). That's the Church of St. John the Baptist, built by the Irish in 1871. Its most noteworthy features (besides the exceptional exterior brickwork) are the beautiful stained-glass windows crafted by artists in Munich and the Stations of the Cross and sacristy murals painted during and after World War II by Belgian artist Dom Gregory Dewit.

1139 Oretha Castle Haley Blvd., at U.S. 90. ✆ 504/525-1726.

St. Alphonsus Church ✪ The Irish built St. Alphonsus Church in 1855 because they refused to worship at St. Mary's (see below) with their German-speaking neighbors. The gallery and columns may vaguely remind you of the St. Louis Cathedral in the French Quarter, though we find it more spooky and atmospheric. That's probably why portions of Anne Rice's *The Witching Hour* take place here. The church no longer holds Mass. Ironically, when St. Mary's was restored, St. Alphonsus was closed, and the congregation moved across the street. Hopes for similar restoration here are high. Currently, the church operates an Arts and Cultural Center, which includes an Irish Art museum. You can tour the interior and the museum 2 days a week, Thursday and Saturday, from 10am to 2pm, with a self-guided audiotape (live tour guides must be arranged in advance).

2030 Constance St., at St. Andrew St. ✆ 504/522-6748. For information, call the Friends of St. Alphonsus at ✆ 504/482-0008.

St. Mary's Assumption ✪ Built in 1860 by the German Catholics, this is a more baroque and grand church than its Irish neighbor across the street (see above), complete with dozens of life-size saint's statues, and it's the beneficiary of a major restoration project. The two churches make an interesting contrast to each other. The hero of the yellow fever epidemic of 1867, Fr. Francis Xavier Seelos, is buried in the church. Credited with the working of many miracles, he was beatified in 2000—and to say this was a big deal is to make an understatement. If you visit the church, you're likely to see letters of petition on his tomb. Still more *Witching Hour* action takes place here, including Rowan and Michael's wedding.

2030 Assumption St., at Josephine St. ℭ **504/522-6748**. Tours of the Fr. Seelos shrine are offered Mon–Sat; call ℭ **504/525-2495** to arrange a tour.

St. Patrick's Church   The original St. Patrick's was a tiny wooden building founded to serve the spiritual needs of Irish Catholics. The present building, begun in 1838, was constructed around the old one, which was then dismantled. The distinguished architect James Gallier Sr. designed much of the interior, including the altar. It opened in 1840, proudly proclaiming itself as the "American" Catholics' answer to the St. Louis Cathedral in the French Quarter (where, according to the Americans, God spoke only in French).

724 Camp St., at Girod St. ℭ **504/525-4413**.

St. Roch and the Campo Santo ⍟ *Finds*   St. Roch is the patron saint of plague victims; a local priest prayed to him to keep his flock safe during an epidemic in 1867. When everyone came through all right, the priest made good on his promise to build St. Roch a chapel. The Gothic result is fine enough, but what is best is the small room just off the altar, where successful supplicants to St. Roch leave gifts, usually in the form of plaster anatomical parts or medical supplies, to represent what the saint healed for them. The resulting collection of bizarre artifacts (everything from eyeballs and crutches to organs and false limbs) is either deeply moving or the greatest creepy spontaneous folk-art installation you've ever seen. The chapel is not always open, so call first.

1725 St. Roch Ave., at N. Derbigny St. ℭ **504/945-5961**.

MORE INTERESTING NEW ORLEANS BUILDINGS

Degas House ⍟   Legendary French Impressionist Edgar Degas felt very tender toward New Orleans; his mother and grandmother were born here, and he spent several months in 1872 and 1873 visiting his brother at this house. It was a trip that resulted in a number of paintings, and this is the only residence or studio associated with Degas anywhere in the world that is open to the public. One of his paintings showed the garden of the house behind his brother's. His brother liked that view, too; he later ran off with the wife of the judge who lived there. His wife and children later took back her maiden name, Musson. The Musson home, as it is formally known, was erected in 1854 and has since been sliced in two and redone in an Italianate manner. Both buildings have been restored and are open to the public via a tour. Both also house a very nice (though fairly humble) B&B setup.

2306 Esplanade Ave., north of the Quarter, before you reach N. Broad Ave. ℭ **504/821-5009**. www.degas house.com. $10 donation requested. Daily 10am–3pm by advance appointment only.

Gallier Hall   This impressive Greek Revival building was the inspiration of James Gallier Sr. Erected between 1845 and 1853, it served as City Hall for just over a century and has been the site of many important events in the city's history—especially during the Reconstruction and Huey Long eras. Several important figures in Louisiana history lay in state in Gallier Hall, including Jefferson Davis and General Beauregard. Of late, it was local legend Ernie K-Doe who was so honored. More than 5,000 mourners came to Gallier Hall on July 14, 2001, to pay their respects to the flamboyant R&B musician, who was laid out in a white costume and a silver crown and scepter and delivered to his final resting place in the company of a big, brassy jazz procession.

545 St. Charles Ave. Not usually open to the public.

Jackson Barracks and Military Museum ☆ This series of fine old brick buildings with white columns is on an extension of Rampart Street downriver from the French Quarter. The buildings were built in 1834 and 1835 for troops who were stationed at the river forts. Some say Andrew Jackson, who never quite trusted New Orleans Creoles, planned the barracks to be as secure against attack from the city as from outside forces. The barracks now serve as headquarters for the Louisiana National Guard, and there's an extensive military museum in the old powder magazine and in a new annex, which has a large collection of military items from every American war. Call before you go to confirm that the barracks and museum are open.

6400 St. Claude Ave. ℂ **504/278-8242.** Fax 504/278-8614. Free admission. Museum hours Mon–Fri 8am–4pm. Closed weekends except by appointment.

Pitot House ☆ The Pitot House is a typical West Indies–style plantation home, restored and furnished with early-19th-century Louisiana and American antiques. Dating from 1799, it originally stood where the nearby modern Catholic school is. In 1810, it became the home of James Pitot, the first mayor of incorporated New Orleans (he served 1804–05). Tours here are usually given by a most knowledgeable docent and are surprisingly interesting and informative.

1440 Moss St., near Esplanade Ave. ℂ **504/482-0312.** Fax 504/482-0363. Admission $5 adults, $4 seniors and students, $2 children under 12, parties of 10 or more $3 each. Wed–Sat 10am–3pm. Last tour begins at 2pm.

The Superdome ☆ Completed in 1975 (at a cost of around $180 million), the Superdome is a landmark civic structure. It's a 27-story windowless building with a seating capacity of 76,000 and a computerized climate-control system

---

Finds **The Healing Powers of Beer**

The little town of Abita Springs, on the opposite side of Lake Pontchartrain from New Orleans, was a big destination for elite New Orleanians in the 19th century, who were drawn to its artesian springs of ozone water, for years considered to have restorative or healing powers. Today, the town attracts visitors who want to hike through the Piney Woods along the Tammany Trace, those who are on their way to the Honey Island Swamp, and those who are looking to take a deep draught of its famous liquid—and we don't mean the water. The **Abita Brewing Company** ☆☆, at 21084 Hwy. 36, Covington (ℂ **800/737-2311** or 985/893-3143; www.abita.com), brews up one of the most successful regional microbrew brands in the country, served in bars and sold in convenience stores throughout Louisiana and across the South. In 1994, the brewery moved down the road, and its original building was converted into the Abita Brewpub, a restaurant and Abita product central store. Despite the much larger scale of the overall brewing operation, the beer is still made in small batches. Free tours of the brewery are held on Saturday at 1pm and 2:30pm and Sunday at 1pm. Take I-10 west from New Orleans to the Causeway, go east on I-12 toward Slidell (3 miles), take the Abita Springs exit (65), and drive north along Hwy. 59 (4 miles).

that uses more than 9,000 tons of equipment. It's one of the largest buildings in the world in diameter (680 ft.), and its grounds cover some 13 acres. Inside, no posts obstruct the spectator's view of whatever's going on (the Superdome is the home of several sporting events as well as conventions, trade shows, balls, and large theatrical and musical productions), while movable partitions and seats allow the building to be configured for almost any event. *Note:* At press time, tours of the facility had been canceled, with no immediate plans to reinstate them.

1500 block of Poydras St., near Rampart St. ✆ **504/587-3808**. www.superdome.com.

FLOATING ACROSS THE RIVER TO ALGIERS POINT

Algiers, annexed by New Orleans in 1870, stretches across the Mississippi River from New Orleans and is easily accessible via the free ferry that runs from the base of Canal Street. *Take note:* This ferry is one of New Orleans's best-kept secrets—it's a great way to get out onto the river and see the skyline. With such easy access (a ferry leaves every 15–20 min.), who knows why the Point hasn't been better assimilated into the larger city, but it hasn't. Though it's only about a ¼ mile across the river from downtown and the French Quarter, it still has the feel of an undisturbed turn-of-the-20th-century suburb. Strolling around here is a delightfully low-key way to spend an hour or two.

The last ferry returns at around 11:15pm, but be sure to check the schedule before you set out, just in case. While you're over there, you might want to stop in at . . .

Blaine Kern's Mardi Gras World ★★ *(Kids)* Few cities can boast a thriving float-making industry. New Orleans can, and no float maker thrives more than Blaine Kern, who makes more than three-quarters of the floats used by the various krewes every Carnival season. Blaine Kern's Mardi Gras World offers tours of its collection of float sculptures and its studios, where you can see floats being made year-round. Visitors see sculptors at work, doing everything from making small "sketches" of the figures to creating and painting the enormous sculptures that adorn Mardi Gras floats each year. You can even try on some heavily bejeweled and dazzling costumes (definitely bring your camera!). Although they could do more with this tour, the entire package does add up to a most enjoyable experience, and it is rather nifty to see the floats up close.

223 Newton St., Algiers Point. ✆ **800/362-8213** or 504/361-7821. www.mardigrasworld.com. Admission $13.50 adults, $10 seniors (over 62), $5.50 children 3–12, free for children under 3. Daily 9:30am–4:30pm. Closed Mardi Gras, Easter, Thanksgiving, Christmas. Cross the river on the Canal St. Ferry and take the free shuttle from the dock (it meets every ferry).

3 Parks & Gardens

PARKS

Audubon Park ★★ *(Kids)* Across from Loyola and Tulane universities, Audubon Park and the adjacent Audubon Zoo (see "A Day at the Zoo," below) sprawl over 340 acres, extending from St. Charles Avenue all the way to the Mississippi River. This tract once belonged to city founder Jean-Baptiste Le Moyne and later was part of the Etienne de Boré plantation, where sugar was granulated for the first time in 1794. Although John James Audubon, the country's best-known ornithologist, lived only briefly in New Orleans (in a cottage on Dauphine St. in the French Quarter), the city has honored him by naming both the park and the zoo after him. There is no historical evidence to suggest that Audubon was much of a golfer; nevertheless, a golf course now fills the middle of the park that bears his name.

The huge trees with black bark are live oaks; some go back to plantation days, and more than 200 additional ones were recently planted here. They're evergreens and shed only once a year, in early spring. With the exception of the trees, it's not the most visually interesting park in the world—it's just pretty and a nice place to be. Visitors can enjoy a picnic in the shade of the trees, feed ducks in a lagoon, and pretend they're Thoreau. Or they can look with envy at the lovely old houses whose backyards literally bump up against the park. The park includes the Odgen Entrance Pavilion and Garden (at St. Charles Ave.) and a smattering of gazebos, shelters, fountains, and statuary.

Without question, the most utilized feature of the park is the 1¾-mile paved traffic-free road that loops around the lagoon and golf course. It was estimated a few years ago that between 2,000 and 3,000 joggers use the track each day, joined by cyclists, walkers, and in-line skaters. Along the track are 18 exercise stations; tennis courts and horseback riding facilities can be found elsewhere in the park. Check out the pavilion on the riverbank for one of the most pleasant views of the Mississippi you'll find. The Audubon Zoo is toward the back of the park, across Magazine Street.

Horseback rides through the park strike us as an appropriate way to see the grounds. Rides are available (organized, with a guide) from **Cascade Stables,** 700 East Dr., directly next to the zoo (© **504/891-2246**). Open Tuesday through Sunday (except major holidays) from 9am to 4pm, rides cost $20 for 45 minutes. Call in advance.

6500 Magazine St., between Broadway and Exposition Blvd. © **504/581-4629**. www.auduboninstitute.org. **Note:** The park opens daily at 6am. Officially closes at 10pm.

Chalmette Battlefield/Jean Lafitte National Historical Park & Preserve ✦✦

On the grounds of what is now Chalmette National Historical Park, the bloody **Battle of New Orleans** was waged on January 14, 1815. Ironically, the battle should never have been fought because a treaty signed 2 weeks before in Ghent, Belgium, had ended the War of 1812. But word had not yet reached Congress, the commander of the British forces, or Andrew Jackson, who stood with American forces to defend New Orleans and the mouth of the Mississippi River. The battle did, however, succeed in uniting Americans and Creoles in New Orleans and in making Jackson a hero in this city.

You can visit the battleground and see markers that allow you to follow the course of the battle. The Beauregard plantation house on the grounds contains exhibits on the battle, and the Visitor Center presents a film and other exhibits. There's a National Cemetery in the park, established in 1864. It holds only two American veterans from the Battle of New Orleans, but some 14,000 Union soldiers who fell in the Civil War are buried here. For a terrific view of the Mississippi River, climb the levee in back of the Beauregard House. To reach the park, take St. Claude Avenue southeast from the French Quarter until it becomes St. Bernard Highway, approximately 7 miles.

8606 W. St. Bernard Hwy. © **504/281-0510**. www.nps.gov/jela. Free admission. Daily 9am–5pm.

City Park ✦✦✦

Once part of the Louis Allard plantation, City Park has been here a long time and has seen it all—including that favorite pastime among 18th-century New Orleans gentry: dueling. At the entrance, you'll see a statue of Gen. P. G. T. Beauregard, whose order to fire on Fort Sumter opened the Civil War and who New Orleanians fondly refer to as "the Great Creole." The extensive, beautifully landscaped grounds hold botanical gardens and a conservatory, four golf courses, picnic areas, a restaurant, lagoons for boating and fishing, tennis courts, horses for hire and lovely trails to ride them on, a bandstand, two miniature trains, and **Children's Storyland,** an amusement area with a carousel ride for children (see "Especially for Kids," later in this chapter). At Christmastime, the mighty oaks, already dripping with Spanish moss, are strung with lights—quite a magical sight—and during Halloween, there is a fabulous haunted house. You'll also find the **New Orleans Museum of Art** at Collins Diboll Circle, on Lelong Avenue, in a building that is itself a work of art (see "Museums & Galleries," earlier in this chapter).

1 Palm Dr. ✆ **504/482-4888**. www.neworleanscitypark.com. Daily 6am–7pm.

GARDENS

Audubon Louisiana Nature Center ⭐   Part of the Audubon Institute, Joe Brown Park is an 86-acre tract of Louisiana forest in the far eastern part of the city where guided walks are given daily (except Mon). A nature film is shown on weekdays, and weekends offer additional activities (canoeing, bird-watching, arts and crafts workshops, and others). Three miles of trails and a wheelchair-accessible raised wooden walkway are available for public use. The Nature Center offers exhibits and hands-on activities and has a **planetarium** offering shows on Saturday and Sunday (laser rock shows on Friday and Saturday nights). Call ✆ **504/246-STAR** for the current planetarium schedule.

In Joe Brown Memorial Park, Nature Center Drive, New Orleans East. ✆ **800/774-7394** or 504/246-9381. www.auduboninstitute.org. Admission $5 adults, $4 seniors, $3 children. Tues–Fri 9am–5pm; Sat 10am–5pm; Sun noon–5pm. Take I-10 to Exit 244, pass Plaza Shopping Center, and turn left onto Nature Center Drive.

Longue Vue House & Gardens ⭐⭐   The Longue Vue mansion is a unique expression of Greek Revival architecture set on an 8-acre estate. It was constructed from 1939 to 1942. Longue Vue House and Gardens is listed on the National Register of Historic Places and is accredited by the American Association of Museums.

Styled in the manner of an English country house, the mansion was designed to foster a close rapport between indoors and outdoors, with vistas of formal terraces and pastoral woods. Some parts of the enchanting gardens were inspired by those of Generalife, the former summerhouse of the sultans in Granada, Spain. Besides the colorful flowering plants, there are formal boxwood parterres, fountains, and a colonnaded loggia. Highlights are the Canal Garden, the Walled Garden, the Wild Garden (which features native irises), and the Spanish Court with its pebbled walkways, fountains, and changing horticultural displays.

7 Bamboo Rd., New Orleans, near Metairie. ✆ **504/488-5488**. www.longuevue.com. Admission $10 adults, $9 seniors, $5 children and students. Mon–Sat 10am–4:30pm; Sun 1–5pm. Hourly tours start at 10am. Closed Jan 1, Mardi Gras, July 4th, Labor Day, Thanksgiving, Dec 24–25, and Easter Sun.

A DAY AT THE ZOO

Audubon Zoo ⭐⭐⭐ *Kids*   It's been more than 20 years since the Audubon Zoo underwent a total renovation that turned it from one of the worst zoos in the country into one of the best. The achievement is still worth noting, and the result is a place of justifiable civic pride that delights even non-zoo fans. While a terrific destination for visitors with children, this small and sweet attraction offers a good change of pace for anyone. Note that on hot and humid days, you should plan your visit for early or late in the day; otherwise, the animals will be sleeping off the heat.

Here, in a setting of subtropical plants, waterfalls, and lagoons, some 1,800 animals (including rare and endangered species) live in natural habitats rather than cages. Don't miss the replica of a Louisiana swamp (complete with a rare white gator) or the "Butterflies in Flight" exhibit, where more than 1,000 butterflies live among lush, colorful vegetation.

A memorable way to visit the zoo is to arrive on the sternwheeler *John James Audubon* (see "Organized Tours," later in this chapter) and depart on the St. Charles Avenue streetcar. You can reach the streetcar by walking through Audubon Park or by taking the free shuttle bus.

During your visit to the zoo, look for the bronze statue of naturalist John James Audubon standing in a grove of trees with a notebook and pencil in hand. Also, look for a funny-looking mound near the river—it was constructed so that the children of this flatland city could see what a hill looked like.

6500 Magazine St. Ⓒ 504/581-4629. www.auduboninstitute.org. Admission $10 adults, $6 seniors (over 64), $5 children 2–12. Daily 9:30am–5pm; 9:30am–6pm weekends in the summer. Last ticket sold 1 hour before closing. Closed holidays.

4 New Orleans Cemeteries ★★★

Along with Spanish moss and lacy iron balconies, the cities of the dead are part of the indelible landscape of New Orleans. Their ghostly and inscrutable presence enthralls visitors, who are used to traditional methods of burial—in the ground or in mausoleums.

Why are bodies here buried above ground? Well, it rains in New Orleans—a lot—and then it floods. Soon after New Orleans was settled, it became apparent that Uncle Etienne had an unpleasant habit of bobbing back to the surface (doubtless no longer looking his best). Add to that cholera and yellow fever epidemics, which helped increase not only the number of bodies but also the infection possibility, and given that the cemetery of the time was inside the Vieux Carré, it's all pretty disgusting to think about.

So in 1789, the city opened St. Louis No. 1, right outside the city walls (which no longer exist) on what is now Rampart Street. The "condo crypt" look—the dead are placed in vaults that look like miniature buildings—was inspired to a certain extent by the famous Père Lachaise cemetery in Paris. Crypts were laid out haphazardly in St. Louis No. 1, which quickly filled up even as the city outgrew the Vieux Carré and expanded around the cemetery. Other cemeteries soon followed and eventually were incorporated into the city proper. They have designated lanes, making for a more orderly appearance. The rows of tombs look like nothing so much as a city—a city where the dead inhabitants peer over the shoulders of the living.

These little houses of the dead, in addition to solving the problem of below-ground burial, are even more functional. There are two types of crypts: the aforementioned "family vaults" and the "oven crypts"—so called because of their resemblance to bread ovens in a wall. A coffin is slid inside, and the combination of heat and humidity acts like a slow form of cremation. In a year or so, the occupant is reduced to bone. As the space is needed, the bones are pushed to the back, coffin pieces are removed, and another coffin is inserted. In the larger family vaults (made of whitewashed brick), there are a couple of shelves and the same thing happens. As family members die, the bones are swept off the shelves into a pit below, and everyone eventually lies jumbled together. The result is sometimes dozens of names, going back generations, on a single spot. It's a very efficient use of cemetery space, far more so than conventional sweeping expanses of graveyard landscaping.

> ### *Tips* Safety First
>
> You will be warned against going to the cemeteries alone and urged to go with a scheduled tour group (see "Organized Tours," later in this chapter). Thanks to their location and layout—some are in dicey neighborhoods, and the crypts obscure threats to your safety—some cemeteries can be quite risky, making visitors prime pickings for muggers and so forth. Other cemeteries, those with better security and in better neighborhoods, not to mention with layouts that permit driving, are probably safe. Ironically, two of the most hazardous, St. Louis No. 1 and Lafayette No. 1, are often so full of tour groups that you could actually go there without one and be fairly safe. On the other hand, a good tour is fun and informative, so why not take the precaution?
>
> If you're going to make a day of the cemeteries, you should also think about renting a car. You won't be driving through horrendous downtown traffic, you can visit tombs at your own pace, and you'll feel safer.

For many years, New Orleans cemeteries were in shambles. Crypts lay open, exposing their pitiful contents—if they weren't robbed of them—bricks lay everywhere, marble tablets were shattered, and visitors might even trip over stray bones. Thanks to local civic efforts, several of the worst eyesores have been cleaned up, though some remain in deplorable shape. A faux voodoo practice continues in some of the St. Louis cemeteries, where visitors are encouraged to scrawl Xs on the tombs. Please don't do this; not only is it a made-up voodoo ritual, it destroys the fragile tombs.

For more information, we highly recommend Robert Florence's *New Orleans Cemeteries: Life in the Cities of the Dead* (Batture Press, 1997). It's full of photos, facts, and human-interest stories and is available at bookstores throughout the city.

THREE CEMETERIES YOU SHOULD SEE WITH A TOUR

St. Louis No. 1   This is the oldest extant cemetery (1789) and the most iconic. Here lie Marie Laveau, Bernard Marigny, and assorted other New Orleans characters. Louis the vampire from Anne Rice's *Vampire Chronicles* even has his (empty) tomb here. Also, the acid-dropping scene from *Easy Rider* was shot here.
Basin St. between Conti and St. Louis sts.

St. Louis No. 2   Established in 1823, the city's next-oldest cemetery, unfortunately, is in such a terrible neighborhood (next to the so-called Storyville Projects) that regular cemetery tours don't usually bother with it. If there is a tour running when you are in town, go—it's worth it. The Emperor of the Universe, R&B legend Ernie K-Doe, was laid to rest here in 2001, joining Marie Laveau II, some Storyville characters, and others who lie within its 3 blocks.

Note: As of this writing, there is no regular tour of St. Louis No. 2, which is absolutely unsafe. Do not go there, even in a large group, without an official tour.
N. Claiborne Ave. between Iberville and St. Louis sts.

Lafayette No. 1   Right across the street from Commander's Palace restaurant, this is the lush uptown cemetery. Once in horrible condition, it's been beautifully restored. Anne Rice's Mayfair witches have their family tomb here.
1427 Sixth St.

SOME CEMETERIES YOU COULD SEE ON YOUR OWN

If you decide to visit the below on your own, please exercise caution. Take a cab to and from or consider renting a car for the day. Most of these cemeteries (such as St. Louis No. 3 and Metairie) have offices that can sometimes provide maps; if they run out, they will give you directions to any grave location you like. All have sort-of-regular hours—figure from 9am to 4pm as a safe bet.

Cypress Grove and Greenwood Cemeteries   Located across the street from each other, both were founded in the mid-1800s by the Firemen's Charitable and Benevolent Association. Each has some highly original tombs; keep your eyes open for the ones made entirely of iron. These two cemeteries are an easy bus ride up Canal Street from the Quarter.

120 City Park Ave. and 5242 Canal Blvd. By car, take Esplanade north to City Park Ave., turn left until it becomes Metairie Ave.

Metairie Cemetery   Don't be fooled by the slightly more modern look—some of the most amazing tombs in New Orleans are here. Not to be missed is the pyramid-and-Sphinx Brunswig mausoleum and the "ruined castle" Egan family tomb, not to mention the former resting place of Storyville madam Josie Arlington. (Her mortified family had her body moved when her crypt became a tourist attraction, but the tomb remains exactly the same, including the statue of a young woman knocking on the door. Legend had it that it was Josie herself, being turned away from her father's house or a virgin being denied entrance to Josie's brothel—she claimed never to despoil anyone. The reality is that it's just a copy of a statute Josie liked.) Ruth of Ruth's Chris Steakhouse was entombed here in 2002 in a marble edifice that looks remarkably like one of her famous pieces of beef.

5100 Pontchartrain Blvd. (©) 504/486-6331. By car, take Esplanade north to City Park Ave., turn left until it becomes Metairie Ave.

St. Louis No. 3   Conveniently located next to the Fair Grounds racetrack (home of the Jazz Fest), St. Louis No. 3 was built on top of a former graveyard for lepers. Storyville photographer E. J. Bellocq lies here. The Esplanade Avenue bus will take you there.

3421 Esplanade Ave.

5 Voodoo

Voodoo's mystical presence is one of the most common motifs in New Orleans. The problem is that the presence is mostly reduced to a tourist gimmick. Every gift shop seems to have voodoo dolls for sale, there is a **Voodoo Museum** (p. 160), and Marie Laveau, the famous voodoo queen, comes off as the town's patron saint. But lost among the kitsch is a very real religion with a serious past and considerable cultural importance.

Voodoo's roots can be traced in part back to the African **Yoruba** religion, which incorporates the worship of several different spiritual forces that include a supreme being, deities, and the spirits of ancestors. When Africans were kidnapped, enslaved, and brought to Brazil—and, ultimately, Haiti—beginning in the 1500s, they brought their religion with them.

By the 1700s, 30,000 slaves a year were brought to Haiti. Voodoo began to emerge at this time as different African religions met and melded. (The word *voodoo* comes from an African word meaning "god" or "spirit.") Slaves were forced to convert to Catholicism, but they found it easy to practice both religions. Voodoo gods were given saints' names, and voodoo worship more or less continued, appropriating certain Catholic rituals and beliefs. Rituals involved participants dancing in a frenzy to increasingly wild drumbeats and eventually falling into a trancelike state, during which a *loa* (a spirit and/or lower-level deity intermediary between humans and gods) would take possession of them.

Voodoo didn't immediately take root in New Orleans, thanks to repressive slaveholders and an edict banning its practice. But the edict was repealed after the Louisiana Purchase in 1803, and in 1804, when slaves in Haiti revolted and overthrew the government, free blacks came to New Orleans in great numbers, as did fleeing plantation owners with their own slaves, all bringing a fresh infusion of voodoo.

Napoleonic law forced slave owners to give their slaves Sundays off and to provide them with a gathering place. **Congo Square** on Rampart Street, part of what is now Louis Armstrong Park, became the place for slaves to gather for voodoo or drumming rituals. Voodoo then was a way for slaves to have their own community and a certain amount of freedom. The religion emphasized knowledge of family and gave power to ancestors. Further, women were usually the powerful forces in voodoo—priestesses ran matters more often than priests—and this appealed to women in a time when women simply didn't have that kind of authority and power.

These gatherings naturally attracted white onlookers, as did the rituals held (often by free people of color) along St. John's Bayou. The local papers of the 1800s are full of lurid accounts of voodoo "orgies" and of whites being possessed by spirits, otherwise losing control, or being arrested after being caught in a naked pose. Thanks to the white scrutiny, the Congo Square gatherings became more like performance pieces, emphasizing drumming and music rather than religious rituals. Because of the square's proximity to what became Storyville, legend has it that madams from the houses would come down to the Sunday gatherings and hire some of the performers to entertain at their houses.

It was during the 1800s that the famous voodoo priestesses came to some prominence. Mostly free women of color, they were devout religious practitioners and very good businesswomen who had a steady clientele of whites secretly coming to them for help in love or money matters. During the 1900s, voodoo largely went back underground.

It is estimated that today as much as 15% of the population of New Orleans practices voodoo. The most common public perception of voodoo involves casting spells or sticking pins in voodoo dolls. Most of that is Hollywood nonsense. Voodoo dolls do exist, as do gris-gris bags—little packets of herbs, stones, and other bits and pieces designed to bring luck, love, health, or what have you (*gris* means "gray," to symbolize a magic somewhere between white and black). Other rituals more or less incorporate magic, but most of it is done for good, not for evil. Ask a real practitioner about helping you with the latter, and you will probably get some nasty looks.

Most of the stores and places in New Orleans that advertise voodoo are set up strictly for tourism. This is not to say that some facts can't be found there or that you shouldn't buy a mass-produced gris-gris bag or voodoo doll as a souvenir. For an introduction to voodoo, check out the New Orleans Historic Voodoo Museum (see the "Museums & Galleries" section earlier in this chapter). If you want to know about true voodoo, however, you need to seek out real voodoo temples or practitioners, of which there are several in New Orleans (you can find them at the temples listed below or by calling Ava Kay, who works on her own—see

That Voodoo That You Do

Voodoo is a nature-based traditional African religion. It is the religion that the slaves brought here when they were taken from Africa. The word literally means "spirit deity and God, the creator of the universe." The word itself means God, but it was taken out of context.

African people were not brought to the New World to have themselves or their culture glorified. Anything that was not white and Protestant or Catholic was looked upon as demonic. And it was not. We are all worshipping God in our own ways. And it is every culture's prerogative to do so.

People confuse negative magic with voodoo. It is not. That is not dealing with the religion of voodoo but the intent to harm. That is hoodoo. And it is not voodoo.

I was drawn to it by my family. My mother used to do candles, and she was very psychic, and she would tell me about spirits and ghosts and how to protect myself from spirits. And I grew up in a neighborhood where people would hoodoo each other. Being born on Halloween, I've always been drawn to spiritual things. I started becoming actively involved in traditional African religions over 25 years ago, but it was always part of my culture.

I had to go through levels of study and initiation with elders here and in Haiti. My Yoruba/Santeria initiation was in Atlanta. Additionally, I am a priestess of Oya, the goddess of hurricanes, the queen of the spirit world, and the queen of the marketplace. I did her initiation about 12 years ago.

Voodoo is a viable religion because people feel that by using the rituals and the prayers and all of the implements they can do things and have power and control over their own lives. People lack something in their lives, and there is a void that traditional religions do not seem to fill, at least, the way they practice it. Voodoo a lot of times fills that void, helps a person get more in touch with their spiritual self.

The voodoo dolls are greatly overrated. They are used to help you focus, and you can use them in healing. I do not sell pins with my dolls. In Haiti, I've seen the dolls, and they are never with pins. It's Hollywood to think that. People will use them that way, but it's black magic. The focal point can be positive or negative, but negative work will come back to you.

You can definitely be another religion along with voodoo, any religion. I have a lot of Jewish people who work with me and also go to synagogue. I am Catholic, I go to church, I take Communion, I sing in the choir for midnight Mass. Everyone in my church knows I'm very Catholic, but also I'm a voodoo and Yoruba priestess.

—Ava Kay Jones

Ava Kay Jones has a law degree from Loyola University and is a practicing Voodoo and Yoruba priestess. She also heads the Voodoo Macumba dance troupe, and her booth at Jazz Fest is annually one of the most popular. She is available for readings, gris-gris bags, and other items of voodoo interest at ℂ 504/484-6499 by appointment only.

"That Voodoo That You Do" box above). If you want to know still more, check out Robert Tallant's book *Voodoo in New Orleans* (Pelican Pocket, 1983).

VOODOO TEMPLES ⭐⭐

Here are two authentic voodoo temples, attached to two botanicas selling everything you might need for potions and spells. The public is welcome, and the employees are happy to educate the honestly curious, but don't go if you just want to giggle and gawk.

The Island of Salvation Botanica and the **Temple Simbi-sen Jak,** 835 Piety St. (📞 **504/948-9961**), are run by Sallie Glassman, voodoo priestess and author of a deck of voodoo tarot cards. The staff at the well-stocked botanica is very interested in educating the public. If you demonstrate the right enthusiasm, they might show you the temple, or you might get invited to their Saturday-night ceremony—but be aware that you will be required to participate: It is not something to observe as a performance. The botanica is open Wednesday through Sunday from 10am to 5:30pm, but due to morning readings, browsers are usually not allowed in until noon.

Located right in the French Quarter, the **Voodoo Spiritual Temple,** 828 N. Rampart St. (📞 **504/522-9627**), is the real McCoy—interested tourists are welcome, but please be respectful. Priestess Miriam belonged to the Spiritual Church in Chicago before setting up this spiritual house, which has a store attached. The main room is a temple, full of fascinating altars. There are both personal and open rituals; the curious might try the Thursday-night drumming workshops, which sometimes turn into rituals. The staff wants to increase others' knowledge of voodoo and sweep away myths and ignorance, so the honestly inquisitive are quite welcome. It's open daily from 10:30am to 5:30pm.

VISITING MARIE LAVEAU

Marie Laveau is the most famous New Orleans voodoo queen. Though she was a real woman, her life has been so mythologized that it is nearly impossible to separate fact from fiction. But who really wants to? Certainly we know that she was born a free woman of color in 1794 and married Jacques Paris in 1819. Paris disappeared about 4 years later, and Marie later took up with Christophe Glapion.

Along the way, Marie, a hairdresser by trade, became known for her psychic abilities and powerful gris-gris. It didn't hurt that her day job allowed her into the best houses, where she heard all the good gossip and could apply it to her other clientele. In one famous story, a young woman about to be forced into a marriage with a much older, wealthy man approached Marie. She wanted to marry her young lover instead. Marie counseled patience. The marriage went forward, and the happy groom died from a heart attack while dancing with his bride at the reception. After a respectable time, the wealthy widow was free to marry her lover.

Marie wholeheartedly believed in voodoo and turned it into a good business, too. Her home at what is now 1020 St. Ann St. (you can now see only the building itself) was purportedly a gift from a grateful client. A devout Catholic, Marie continued to attend daily Mass and was publicly noted for her charity work that included regular visits to inmates awaiting execution.

Her death in 1881 was noted by the *Times-Picayune,* though voodoo was not mentioned. Her lookalike daughter, Marie II, took over her work, leading some to believe (mistakenly) that Marie I lived a very long time, looking quite well indeed—which only added to her legend. But Marie II allegedly worked more for the darker side than her mother. Her eventual reward, the story goes, was death by poison (delivered by whom is unknown). Today, visitors can bring Marie tokens (candles, Mardi Gras beads, change) and ask her for favors—she's buried in **St. Louis Cemetery No. 1.**

6 Anne Rice's New Orleans (★

Love her or loathe her, Anne Rice is a one-woman cottage industry in New Orleans and one of the town's biggest boosters. Many tourists come here just because they have read her books; she writes seductive descriptions of her hometown that are actually quite accurate—minus the vampires, witches, and ghosts, of course. Rice uses many real locales; the Gallier House, for example, was the inspiration for the home of vampires Lestat and Louis in *Interview with the Vampire*. Her own childhood homes and present dwelling turn up in *Violin* and *The Witching Hour*. Even her nonhorror novel *Exit to Eden* sent its protagonists on a romantic trip to New Orleans, exulting in the sensual tropical air and gorging on barbecued shrimp at **Pascal's Manale** (p. 141).

Anne Rice (née O'Brien) was born on October 4, 1941, in New Orleans to Irish parents. When she was 16, her family moved to Texas, where she met her husband, the late Stan Rice. They married in 1961 and moved to California a few years later, living for years in the San Francisco area. *Interview with the Vampire* was published in 1976, and in the 1980s, the Rices and their son packed up and moved back to New Orleans.

Rice continues to put out about one novel a year, often set at least in part in the city she loves. She always does her first book signing at the **Garden District Book Shop,** 2727 Prytania St. (p. 213), and, as her fortunes have grown, she has bought a number of significant buildings from her youth. This has earned praise from some, who see the salvation of decaying landmarks, and the ire of others, who see it as the consumption of pieces of local history for someone's private enjoyment.

Of late, Rice has been cutting back on her public activities—several years ago, she closed her tour company, she no longer allows a weekly tour through her Garden District home, and last year, she decided to dismantle her doll museum and sell off the contents, and put its location, St. Elizabeth's Orphanage, also up for sale.

Between her personal life and her novels (and the overlap therein), there are any number of Anne Rice landmarks around town. The faithful could make a day of it; vampire spotting is strictly up to you.

ANNE RICE IN THE FRENCH QUARTER

The romance of the French Quarter seems to attract vampires, who found easy pickins in its dark corners in the days before electricity.

St. Louis Cemetery No. 1, 400 Basin St. A tomb (empty, of course) with Louis the vampire's name is located here in the "Vampire Chronicle" books, and Louis occasionally goes to sit on it and brood. Rumor has it that Rice has purchased a tomb here for her eventual use. *Note:* Keep your wits about you here, not because of vampires but because this isn't the safest neighborhood. See p. 173 for more on cemetery tours.

Gallier House, 1132 Royal St. This famously preserved museum is said by Rice scholars to be the model for the house on Rue Royal that was home to vampires Lestat and Louis in *Interview with the Vampire*. Also see p. 158.

Anne Rice's New Orleans

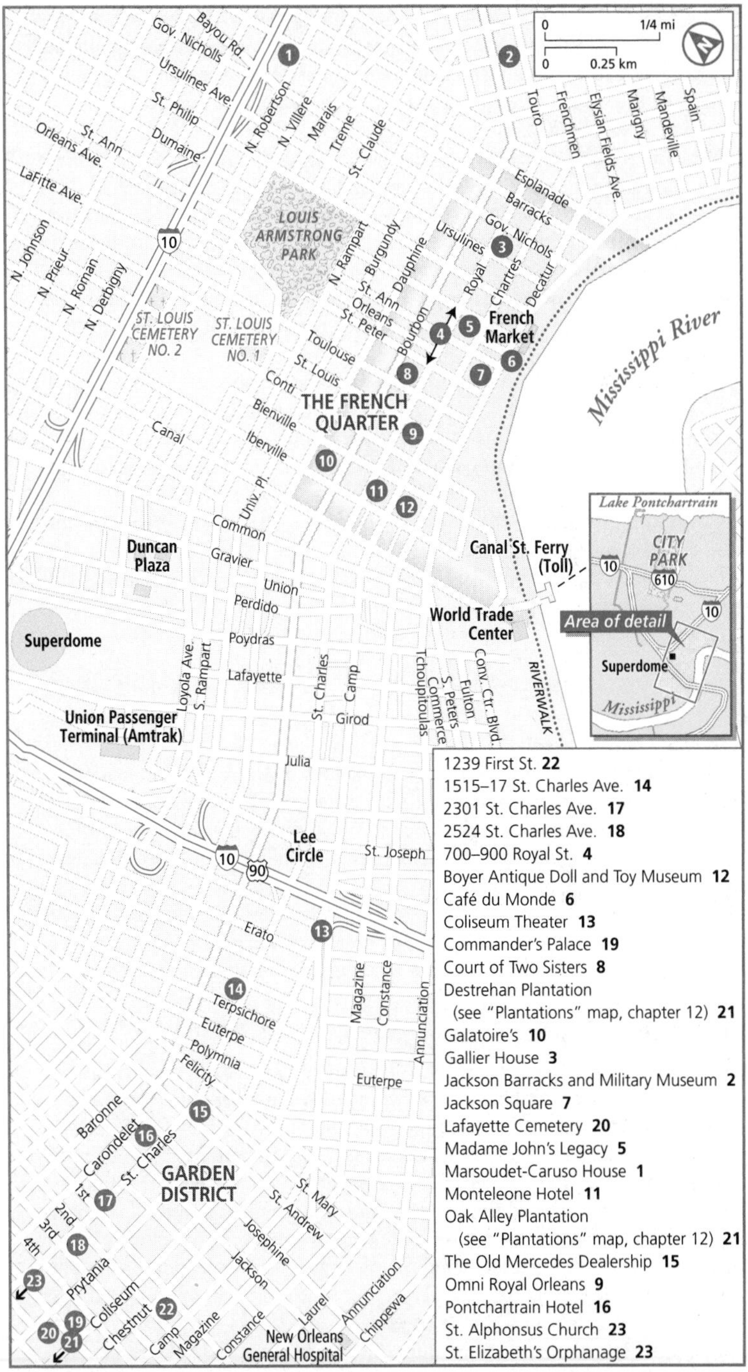
0 1/4 mi
0 0.25 km
Bayou Rd.
Gov. Nicholls
Ursulines Ave.
St. Philip
Dumaine
St. Ann
Orleans Ave.
LaFitte Ave.
N. Robertson
N. Villere
Marais
Treme
St. Claude
Touro
Frenchmen
Elysian Fields Ave.
Marigny
Mandeville
Spain
Esplanade
Barracks
Gov. Nichols
Ursulines
LOUIS ARMSTRONG PARK
N. Rampart
Burgundy
Dauphine
Royal
Chartres
Decatur
St. Ann
Orleans
St. Peter
Bourbon
French Market
N. Johnson
N. Prieur
N. Roman
N. Derbigny
ST. LOUIS CEMETERY NO. 2
ST. LOUIS CEMETERY NO. 1
Toulouse
St. Louis
Conti
Bienville
Iberville
THE FRENCH QUARTER
Mississippi River
Canal
Univ. Pl.
Common
Gravier
Union
Perdido
Poydras
Lafayette
Duncan Plaza
Canal St. Ferry (Toll)
World Trade Center
Superdome
Loyola Ave.
S. Rampart
St. Charles
Camp
Tchoupitoulas
Commerce
S. Peters
Fulton
Conv. Ctr. Blvd.
RIVERWALK
Girod
Union Passenger Terminal (Amtrak)
Julia
Lake Pontchartrain
CITY PARK
Area of detail
Superdome
Mississippi
Lee Circle
St. Joseph
Erato
Terpsichore
Euterpe
Polymnia
Felicity
Magazine
Constance
Annunciation
Euterpe
Baronne
Carondelet
St. Charles
GARDEN DISTRICT
1st
2nd
3rd
4th
Prytania
Coliseum
Chestnut
Camp
Magazine
Constance
Laurel
Annunciation
Chippewa
St. Mary
St. Andrew
Josephine
Jackson
New Orleans General Hospital
1239 First St. 22
1515–17 St. Charles Ave. 14
2301 St. Charles Ave. 17
2524 St. Charles Ave. 18
700–900 Royal St. 4
Boyer Antique Doll and Toy Museum 12
Café du Monde 6
Coliseum Theater 13
Commander's Palace 19
Court of Two Sisters 8
Destrehan Plantation (see "Plantations" map, chapter 12) 21
Galatoire's 10
Gallier House 3
Jackson Barracks and Military Museum 2
Jackson Square 7
Lafayette Cemetery 20
Madame John's Legacy 5
Marsoudet-Caruso House 1
Monteleone Hotel 11
Oak Alley Plantation (see "Plantations" map, chapter 12) 21
The Old Mercedes Dealership 15
Omni Royal Orleans 9
Pontchartrain Hotel 16
St. Alphonsus Church 23
St. Elizabeth's Orphanage 23

The stretch of 700 to 900 Royal St. Quite a few of the exteriors for the *Interview with the Vampire* movie were filmed along this stretch—though the set decorators had to labor long and hard to erase all traces of the 20th century. Try to imagine the streets covered in mud. Then try to imagine how folks who live around here felt about it.

Madame John's Legacy, 632 Dumaine St. In the *Interview with the Vampire* movie, this is the house from which the caskets are being carried as Brad Pitt's voice-over describes Lestat and the little vampire Claudia going out on the town: "An infant prodigy with a lust for killing that matched his own. Together, they finished off whole families." Also see p. 159.

Café du Monde, 800 Decatur St. Lestat visits this restaurant in *The Tale of the Body Thief,* and Michael and Rowan snack here in *The Witching Hour.* Also see p. 145.

Jackson Square. It's here that Claudia makes an important decision regarding Lestat's fate in *Interview with the Vampire* and that Raglan James meets Lestat in *The Tale of the Body Thief.*

Omni Royal Orleans hotel, at 621 St. Louis St. Katherine and Julien Mayfair stay here—it's still the St. Louis Hotel—in *The Witching Hour.* Also see p. 75.

Court of Two Sisters, 613 Royal St. Characters in *The Witching Hour* dine here. Also see p. 111.

Galatoire's, 209 Bourbon St. Characters from several books, including *The Witching Hour,* dine here as well. Also see p. 112.

Hotel Monteleone, 214 Royal St. This was Aaron Lightner's house in *The Witching Hour.*

Boyer Antiques Doll & Toy Museum, 241 Chartres St. In the *Interview with the Vampire* movie, this is the shop where Claudia admires a doll and then deals with the patronizing shopkeeper in typical vampire fashion.

Marsoudet-Caruso House, 1519 Esplanade Ave. A few blocks north of the French Quarter at the intersection of Esplanade and Claiborne avenues, this is the house where Louis scents the smell of old death in the *Interview with the Vampire* movie and finds the moldering Lestat shrinking from helicopters in a musty chair.

Jackson Barracks, south of the French Quarter along the Mississippi. This area was used for numerous exteriors in the *Interview with the Vampire* movie, including the scene where Louis and Claudia run for their ship after setting Lestat on fire.

ANNE RICE IN THE GARDEN DISTRICT

Rice's books increasingly have featured the Garden District and the area around it, perhaps because she and her family live and own a number of properties there.

Coliseum Theater, 1233 Coliseum St. In the film version of *Interview with the Vampire,* this is the theater where Louis sees *Tequila Sunrise.*

The property at 1515–17 St. Charles Ave. Rice told the New Orleans City Council that she purchased this property and that she plans to use it for a commercial venture. She had previously said she was considering opening a theme restaurant called **Cafe Lestat** sometime in the future. Draw your own conclusions.

Pontchartrain Hotel, 2031 St. Charles St. This upscale hotel (p. 91) and its restaurant, the Caribbean Room (now closed), appear in *The Witching Hour.*

The old Mercedes dealership (now Al Copeland's Cheesecake restaurant), 2001 St. Charles Ave. This building was at the center of a dispute that amused the city for months. The vampire Lestat disappeared from this world through an image of himself in the window of this building. When Straya (as it was then) opened, Rice (who rumor had it wanted to open her own cafe on the site) criticized owner Al Copeland with a full-page ad in the daily newspaper. Lestat (wink, wink—word on the street was that it was Copeland himself) then mysteriously returned to this realm and bought an ad of his own, congratulating Copeland for his "stroke of genius."

St. Alphonsus Church, 2030 Constance St. This is a small church with a stunning interior (p. 166). It was the O'Brien family church—Anne's parents married here, and she was baptized and received communion here. She also took Alphonsus as her confirmation name. Readers will recognize this as a setting in *The Witching Hour.*

1239 First St. This historic property (see "Walking Tour 2: The Garden District" in chapter 9, "City Strolls") is Anne Rice's primary residence. The Mayfair house in *The Witching Hour* matches her home in almost every detail, including address.

2301 St. Charles Ave. This spacious, two-story white house was Rice's childhood home.

2524 St. Charles Ave. Rice's family moved into this traditional-style raised villa when Anne was 14. It's prominently featured in her novel *Violin.*

Commander's Palace, 1403 Washington Ave. Rice readers will recognize this restaurant as a favorite of the Mayfair family (also see p. 137).

Lafayette No. 1. This centerpiece of the Garden District is also a frequent setting in Rice's work, especially as a roaming ground for Lestat and Claudia in *Interview with the Vampire* and as the graveyard for the Mayfairs in *The Witching Hour.*

7 Organized Tours

There are some advantages to taking tours. Though many are touristy (by definition), someone else does the planning, it's an easy way to get to outlying areas, and if the tour guide is good, you should learn a lot in a fairly entertaining way. *But be warned:* Though we can't vouch for the accuracy of this information, we have heard reports that some hotel concierges take kickbacks from the tour companies they recommend—a widespread practice around the world. Obviously, not every concierge is on the take, and some may have honest opinions about the merits of one company over another. The way to avoid this problem is to cut out the middleman; no matter how you learned about it, pay the fee directly to the company, not to your concierge. No reputable firm will insist you pay someone else first. In addition, except for the outstanding Historic New Orleans Walking Tours, most tour companies seem to be hit or miss, depending on the guide you get.

For information on organized and self-guided tours of the plantation houses outside New Orleans, see chapter 12, "Plantation Homes & Cajun Country: Side Trips from New Orleans."

IN THE FRENCH QUARTER

Note: Chapter 9, "City Strolls," includes a French Quarter walking tour you can do on your own.

Historic New Orleans Walking Tours ★★★ (© 504/947-2120; www.tour neworleans.com) is the place to go for authenticity, rather than sensationalism. Here, the tour guides are carefully chosen for their combination of knowledge and entertaining manner, and we cannot recommend the guides or the tours highly enough. The daily French Quarter tours are the best straightforward, nonspecialized walking tours of this neighborhood; $12 adults. They also offer a Voodoo tour and a Haunted tour, $15 adults; and a Garden District tour, $14 adults; students and seniors $2 dollars off on all tours.

The nonprofit volunteer group **Friends of the Cabildo** (© 504/523-3939) also offers an excellent 2-hour walking tour of the Quarter. It leaves from in front of the 1850 House Museum Store, at 523 St. Ann St. on Jackson Square. The requested donation is $10 per adult, $8 for seniors (over 65) and children 13 to 20; it's free for children under 13. Tours leave Tuesday through Sunday at 10am and 1:30pm and Monday at 1:30pm, except holidays. No reservations—just show up, donation in hand. The Friends also offers great seasonal tours—like the terrific one offered at Halloween of local courtyards otherwise not open to the public, where guides dressed as the ghosts of local historical figures tell their tales.

Stop by the **Jean Lafitte National Park and Preserve's Folklife and Visitor Center,** 419 Decatur St., near Conti Street (© **504/589-2636**), for details on its excellent free walking tour conducted by National Park Service rangers. The History of New Orleans tour covers about a mile in the French Quarter and brings to life the city's history and the ethnic roots of its unique cultural mix. No reservations are required for this tour, but only 25 people are taken in a group. The tour starts at 9:30am daily (except for Mardi Gras); the office opens at 9am, and it's strongly suggested you get there then to ensure that you get a ticket.

The Bienville Foundation ✦✦, run by Roberts Batson (© **504/945-6789;** nolabienville@aol.com), offers a live on stage Scandal Tour and a highly popular and recommended Gay Heritage Tour. The tours last roughly 2½ hours and generally cost $20 per person. Times and departure locations also change seasonally, so call or e-mail to find out what's happening when.

Kenneth Holdrich, a professor of American literature at the University of New Orleans, runs **Heritage Literary Tours** ✦✦✦, 732 Frenchmen St. (© **504/ 949-9805**). Aside from his considerable academic credentials, he knew both Tennessee Williams and the mother of John Kennedy Toole. In addition to a general tour about the considerable literary legacy of the French Quarter, some tours, arranged in advance, can be designed around a specific author, like the Tennessee Williams tour. The narratives are full of facts both literary and historical, are loaded with anecdotes, and are often downright humorous. Group tour rates available ($20 for adults) are "scheduled for your convenience."

Le Monde Creole ✦✦ (© **504/568-1801**) offers a unique tour that uses the dramatic lives of one classic Creole family as a microcosm of the Creole world of the 19th century. This is the sister operation of **Laura Plantation** (p. 257). At the city location, you can learn about Creole city life and the extraordinary story of Laura's family, off the plantation and in the Vieux Carré, while viewing French Quarter courtyards associated with the family. Guides are some of the best in the city, and this is probably the only operation that also offers tours in French. Tours are 2½ hours, twice daily at 10:30am and 1:30pm, Sun 10am and 1:30pm. Prices for adults are $20, $15 for children; kids under 12 are free. Reservations are required.

BEYOND THE FRENCH QUARTER

Author Robert Florence (who has written two excellent books about New Orleans cemeteries as well as our Garden District walking tour in chapter 9, "City Strolls") loves his work, and his **Historic New Orleans Walking Tours** ✦✦✦ (© **504/947-2120**) are full of meticulously researched facts and more than a few good stories. A very thorough (more thorough even than the one in chapter 9) tour of the Garden District and Lafayette Cemetery (a section of town not many of the other companies go into) leaves daily at 11am and 1:45pm from the Garden District Book Shop (in the Rink, corner of Washington Ave. and Prytania St.). Rates are $14 for adults, students and seniors $12, free for children under 12.

Tours by Isabelle ✸ (✆ **504/391-3544;** www.toursbyisabelle.com) offers 8 different tours for small groups in 13 air-conditioned passenger vans. Prices and departure times vary. Make reservations as far in advance as possible. For $47, you can join Isabelle's afternoon Combo Tour, which begins at 1pm and adds Longue Vue House and Gardens to a tour of the French Quarter, St. Louis cemetery no. 3, Bayou St. John, the shores of Lake Pontchartrain, and the Uptown and downtown neighborhoods. Many more tours are available; contact them for more information.

Gray Line, 2 Canal St., Suite 1300 (✆ **800/535-7786** or 504/569-1401; www.graylineneworleans.com), offers tours of the entire city, including the French Quarter, in comfortable motor coaches. But take our word for it: The Quarter demands a more in-depth examination than a view from a bus window will provide. Take one of these generally informative tours only as a prelude to exploring the Quarter in detail. Gray Line also offers a tour that includes a 2-hour cruise on the **steamboat *Natchez*** (www.steamboatnatchez.com), plus plantation tours and walking tours.

Good Old Days (✆ **504/523-0804**) offers 3-hour daily van tours of the city for $45; children 11 and under go half price. The company also offers a plantation tour $60, and carriage tours for $105 an hour.

SWAMP TOURS

Everyone should take a swamp tour at least once in their lives—first of all, they're fun, and gator spotting and other typical swamp tour activities can be instructional. As far as the swamps go, the swamp itself is less important than the tour operator, and everyone seems to have their own favorite tour operators.

In addition to the tour providers listed below, Jean Lafitte and Gray Line (see above) both offer **swamp tours,** which can be a hoot, particularly if you get a guide who calls alligators to your boat for a little snack of chicken (please keep your hands inside the boat—they tend to look a lot like chicken to a gator). On all of the following tours, you're likely to see alligators, bald eagles, waterfowl, egrets, owls, herons, ospreys, feral hogs, otters, beavers, frogs, turtles, raccoons, deer, and nutria (maybe even a black bear or a mink)—and a morning spent floating on the bayou can be mighty pleasant.

Half Pint's Swamp Adventures ✸ (✆ **318/280-5976**) offers private guided tours of the "beauty, serenity, and exotic wildlife" of the Atchafalaya Basin, the nation's largest swamp. Half Pint is more folk hero than man, and his tours come highly recommended. Prices change often; call for the most updated information.

Lil' Cajun Swamp Tours ✸ (✆ **800/725-3213** or 504/689-3213; www.lilcajunswamptours.com) offers a good tour of Lafitte's bayous. Capt. Cyrus Blanchard, "a Cajun French-speaking gentleman," knows the bayous like the back of his hand. The tour lasts 2 hours and costs about $17 for adults, $15 for seniors, and $13 for children 3 to 12 if you drive yourself to the boat launch. With transportation from New Orleans, the cost is $31 for adults, $21 for children. (Note that the boat used on the Lil' Cajun Swamp Tours is much larger than the boat used on many of the other tours—it seats up to 67 people and can be noisier and more crowded than you might like.)

Dr. Wagner's Honey Island Swamp Tours ✮✮ (© 985/641-1769 or 504/242-5877; www.honeyislandswamp.com) takes you by boat into the interior of Honey Island Swamp to view wildlife with native professional naturalist guides. Dr. Wagner, the primary tour guide, is a trained wetland ecologist and provides a solid educational experience to go with the purer swamp excitement. Tours last approximately 2 hours. Prices are $20 for adults, $10 for children under 12 if you drive to the launch site yourself; the rate is $45, $25 for children if you want a narrated hotel pickup in New Orleans.

Cypress Swamp Tours ✮✮ (© 800/633-0503; www.cypressswamp.com), a small company located on Bayou Segnette in the town of Westwego (a town that is also a sentence, and good for them), offers an "authentic Cajun Heritage" tour (no fake Cajuns, but we bet some heavy put-on accents!). It includes free transportation from most downtown hotels. Prices for the 2-hour swamp tour are $22 for adults and $12 for children. Your best bet may be the combo swamp and Destrehan Plantation tour ($48 adults and $35 children; lunch included).

Blue Dog Seafood Tours ✮ (© 800/875-4287 or 985/649-1255; www.blue dogtours.com) takes visitors on—you guessed it—seafood tours. You can harvest fish or go shrimping, and at the end of the experience the boat crew will cook for you! The Louisiana Seafood Experience tour is approximately 2 hours on the boat, with 10am or 2pm departures; luncheon is served from noon until 2pm ($75 per person; transportation from and return to your New Orleans hotel, add $15 per person). The Shrimping Tour costs $300 per person and includes a Louisiana feast at the end of the day.

MYSTICAL & MYSTERIOUS TOURS

An increased interest in the supernatural, ghostly side of New Orleans—let's go right ahead and blame Anne Rice—has meant an increased number of tours catering to the vampire set. It has also resulted in some rather humorous infighting as rival tour operators have accused each other of stealing their shtick—and customers. We enjoy a good nighttime ghost tour of the Quarter as much as anyone, but we also have to admit that what's available is really hit or miss in presentation (it depends on who conducts your particular tour) and more miss than hit with regard to facts. Go for the entertainment value, not for the education (with some exceptions—see below).

While most of the ghost tours are a bunch of hooey hokum (many using bullhorns during nighttime tours and disturbing neighborhood peace and quiet), we are pleased that there is one we can send you to with a clear conscience: **Historic New Orleans Walking Tours** ✮✮✮ (© 504/947-2120). They offer a Cemetery and Voodoo Tour, the only one that is fact- and not sensation-based, though it is no less entertaining for it. The trip goes through St. Louis Cemetery No. 1, Congo Square, and an active voodoo temple. It leaves Monday through Saturday at 10am and 1pm, Sunday at 10am only, from the courtyard at 334-B Royal St. Rates are $15 for adults, students and seniors $13, free for children under 12. They are also offering a nighttime haunted tour, perhaps the only one in town where well-researched guides will offer genuine thrills and chills. Leaves 7:30pm from 508 Toulouse St.

Magic Walking Tours ✮, 714 N. Rampart. (© 504/588-9693; www.tour neworleans.com), created by Richard Rochester, was apparently the first to up the ante on the evening tours, offering a bit of theatrical spectacle along with ghost stories. When others copied the concept, Rochester toned down the gimmicks (though with his long hair, top hat, and special-effect contact lenses, he makes up for it). The guides are generally good, but Richard's the best—he knows how to spin a yarn, and his history of the town is marvelous to listen to. Several guided walking tours are offered daily: St. Louis Cemetery No. 1 (which is probably the only voodoo-free cemetery tour out there), the French Quarter, the Garden District, the Voodoo Tour, and the Vampire and Ghost-Hunt Walking Tour. Reservations are not necessary, but call ahead for tour schedules. Meeting places vary according to the tour. Tours cost $15 for adults, $13 for students and seniors, and are free for children under 6.

Haunted History Tours ✪, 97 Fontainebleau Dr. (© **888/6-GHOSTS** or 504/861-2727; www.hauntedhistorytours.com), is the Magic Walking Tours' big rival and the place to go if you want theatrics along with facts (and we use the term *facts* very loosely). Expect fake snakes and blood, costumes, and gizmos. They offer everything from a voodoo/cemetery tour to a nocturnal vampire tour of the Quarter. Prices are $18 for adults, $12 seniors and students, $9 for children; meeting places and departure times vary with the offerings.

BOAT TOURS

For those interested in doing the Mark Twain thing, a number of operators offer riverboat cruises; some cruises have specific destinations like the zoo or Chalmette, while others just cruise the river and harbor without stopping. They're touristy, but they can be fun if you're in the right mood, and they are good for families. Docks are at the foot of Toulouse and Canal streets, and there's ample parking. Call for reservations, which are required for all these tours, and to confirm prices and schedules.

The steamboat *Natchez,* 2 Canal St., Suite 1300 (© **800/233-BOAT** or 504/569-1415), a marvelous three-deck sternwheeler docked at the wharf behind the Jackson Brewery, offers two 2-hour daytime cruises daily at 11:30am and 2:30pm. The narration is by professional guides, and there is a cocktail bar, live jazz, an optional lunch, and a gift shop. Daytime fares are $18 for adults and $9 for children; evening cruises (not including dinner) are $28 for adults, $14 for children. Children under 3 ride free. There's also a jazz dinner cruise with an optional buffet every evening.

Aboard the sternwheeler *John James Audubon,* 2 Canal St., Suite 1300 (© **800/233-BOAT** or 504/586-8777), passengers travel the Mississippi, tour the busy port, and dock to visit the Audubon Zoo and the Aquarium of the Americas. There are four trips daily, departing from the Riverwalk in front of the Aquarium at 10am, noon, 2pm, and 4pm. Return trips from the zoo leave at 11am, 1pm, 3pm, and 5pm. One-way or round-trip tickets can be purchased with or without aquarium, zoo, and IMAX admission. Combination tickets that save you several dollars are available.

The paddle-wheeler *Creole Queen,* Riverwalk Dock (© **800/445-4109** or 504/524-0814), departs from the Poydras Street Wharf adjacent to the Riverwalk at 10:30am and 2pm for 2½-hour narrated excursions to the port and to the historic site of the Battle of New Orleans. There is also a 7pm jazz dinner cruise. The boat has a covered promenade deck, and its inner lounges are air-conditioned and heated. Food and cocktail service are available on all cruises. Daytime fares are $17 for adults ($23 with lunch), $9 for children ($15 with lunch); the nighttime jazz cruise is $48 for adults, $25 for children. Children under 3 ride free. They also offer swamp tours and harbor cruises; prices vary.

CARRIAGE TOURS

Corny it may be, but there is a sheepish romantic lure to the old horse-drawn carriages that pick up passengers at Jackson Square and take them for day and nighttime tours of the Quarter. (They are actually mule-drawn because mules can take heat and humidity while horses can't.) The mules are decked out with ribbons, flowers, or even hats, and the drivers seem to be in a fierce competition to win the "most unusual city story" award. Once again, the "facts" presented are probably dubious but should be most entertaining. Carriages wait at the Decatur Street end of Jackson Square from 9am to midnight in good weather; the charge is $8 per adult and $5 for kids under 12 for a ride that lasts roughly half an hour.

Private horse-and-carriage tours offered by **Good Old Days Buggies** (© 504/ 523-0804) include hotel or restaurant pickup and cost $105 an hour.

ANTIQUING TOURS

Antiquing in New Orleans can be an overwhelming experience, especially if you have your heart set on something in particular. For that, you might need a little expert help, and that's why Macon Riddle founded **Let's Go Antiquing!,** 1412 Fourth St. (© 504/899-3027). She'll organize and customize antiques-shopping tours to fit your needs. Hotel pickup is included, and she will even make lunch reservations for you. If you find something and need to ship it home, she'll take care of that, too.

8 Especially for Kids

New Orleans is one of those destinations that may be more fun *sans enfants.* Don't get us wrong—there are plenty of unusual things to do during daylight hours that will wear out everyone under 12 or over 40, but any adult confined to his or her hotel room past 9pm has entirely missed the point of vacationing here. Still, we suppose it's in everyone's best interest to introduce the little tykes to the land of big food and big music so that they'll beg to return when they're old enough to go clubbing with Mom and Dad. In the meantime, you can entertain them with a combination of conventional and unconventional, only–in–New Orleans activities.

The **French Quarter** in and of itself is fascinating to children over 7. A walkabout with a rest stop for beignets at **Café du Monde** (p. 145) will while away a pleasant morning and give you an opportunity to see the architecture and peek into the shops. Continue (or begin) their roots-music education with a visit to the **Jazz Museum** at the Old U.S. Mint (p. 156) and later to **Preservation Hall** (p. 232) for a show. For those progeny who aren't terrifically self-conscious, a **horse-and-buggy ride** (see "Carriage Tours," above) around the Quarter is very appealing—but save it for later when they start getting tired and you need a tiny bribe to keep them going. (If you happen to be in New Orleans in December, be sure to take a **carriage ride** through City Park, when thousands of lights turn the landscape and trees into fairy-tale scenery.)

The **Musée Conti Wax Museum** (p. 159), which features effigies of local historical figures and holds guided tours at 11am and 2pm, is an acceptable pick if the weather turns on you. **Riverwalk Marketplace** (p. 207), the glass-enclosed shopping center on the edge of the Quarter on Canal Street, also appeals to kids with its relaxed atmosphere and food vendors. The **Canal Street ferry** (p. 62), which crosses the Mississippi River to Algiers, is free to pedestrians and offers views of the harbor and skyline. Shuttle service is then available from the Algiers ferry landing to **Blaine Kern's Mardi Gras World** (p. 169), where the floats and costumes alone should intrigue even adolescents—whether they'll admit it or not.

Returning to Canal Street, you'll find the **Audubon Aquarium of the Americas** (p. 154) with lots of jellyfish, sea horses, and other creatures from the deep and the not-so-deep. The *John James Audubon* riverboat (p. 185) chugs from the aquarium to lovely **Audubon Park** (p. 169) and the highly regarded **Audubon Zoo** (see "A Day at the Zoo," earlier in this chapter). The park is fronted by magnificent old oak trees.

The following destinations are also particularly well suited for younger children.

Children's Storyland 🅡🅡 *(Kids)* The under-8 set will be delighted with this playground (rated one of the 10 best in the country by *Child* magazine), where well-known children's stories and rhymes have inspired the decor.

Kids and adults will enjoy the carousel, Ferris wheel, bumper cars, and other rides at the **Carousel Gardens,** also in City Park. It's open weekends only from 11am to 4:30pm. Admission is $1 for anyone over 2; $6 buys unlimited rides.

City Park at Victory Ave. 🔾 **504/483-9381.** Admission $2 adults and children ages 2 and up, free for children under 2. Wed–Fri 10am–12:30pm; Sat–Sun 10am–4:30pm. Closed weekdays Dec–Feb.

Louisiana Children's Museum 🅡🅡🅡 *(Kids)* This popular two-story interactive museum is really a playground in disguise that will keep kids occupied for a good couple of hours. Along with changing exhibits, the museum offers an art shop with regularly scheduled projects, a mini–grocery store, a chance to be a "star anchor" at a simulated television studio, and lots of activities exploring music, fitness, water, and life itself. If you belong to your local science museum, check your membership card for reciprocal entry privileges.

420 Julia St., at Tchoupitoulas St. 🔾 **504/523-1357.** Fax 504/529-3666. www.lcm.org. Admission $6. Tues–Sat 9:30am–4:30pm; Sun noon–4:30pm; summer Mon–Sat 9:30am–4:30pm.

9 Gambling

After years of political and legal wrangling—much of which is still an ongoing source of fun in the daily paper—**Harrah's Casino** finally opened. "Oh, goody," we said, along with other even more sarcastic things, as we experienced severe disorientation stepping inside for the first time. It's exactly like a Vegas casino (100,000 sq. ft. of nearly 3,000 slot machines and 120 tables plus buffet and twice-nightly live "Mardi Gras parade" shows), which is mighty shocking to the system and also a bit peculiar because like many a Vegas casino it is Mardi Gras/New Orleans–themed—but exactly like a Vegas casino interpretation of same, which means it's almost exactly *not* like the real thing. We can't understand anyone coming here (and listen, we're fond of Vegas, so we're not anti-casino in general). But if you must go, it can be found on Canal Street at the river (🔾 **504/533-6000**).

There's also 24-hour riverboat gambling in the area. Outside the city, you can find the **Boomtown Belle Casino** (🔾 **504/366-7711** for information and directions) on the West Bank; the **Treasure Chest Casino** (🔾 **504/443-8000**) docked on Lake Pontchartrain in Kenner; and **Bally's Casino** (🔾 **504/248-3200**) docked on the south shore of Lake Pontchartrain.

10 Weddings in New Orleans

While it is true that Vegas remains the top place for weddings—as well it should, with no waiting period and a ceremony perhaps as short as 10 minutes from start (obtaining license) to finish (kiss the bride!)—New Orleans is becoming nearly as popular a nuptial destination. Potential happy couples should be aware, however, that Louisiana requires a 72-hour waiting period (unless you know the right judge to waive it—don't laugh; we did) once you have the marriage license. In addition to the nearly endless number of romantic spots from which to choose, you can get hitched at the **French Quarter Chapel,** 333 Burgundy St. (© **504/598-6808;** www.frenchquarterwedding.com). This 24-hour chapel will officiate for traditional and civil ceremonies as well as "alternative lifestyle" unions. A voodoo priestess is on call to oversee commitment ceremonies.

A quick ferry ride to Algiers Point to see Judge Mary "KK" Norman (© **504/368-4099**) is for the no-frills justice-of-the-peace approach. Some folks are more creative and, yes, romantic and want a ceremony in a French Quarter courtyard, city park, or anywhere else; the **Wedding Ministry** (© **877/878-2933** or 504/831-3007; www.theweddingministry.com) offers a personalized ceremony for all religions as well as nonreligious ceremonies (they even do same-sex unions). If you prefer a standard service in a big St. Charles Avenue mansion, the **House of Broel** (© **800/827-4325** or 504/525-1000; www.houseof broel.com) offers packages for 2 to 200 people.

11 Sporting Events

In addition to the pro teams listed below, don't forget that this is a college town, with plenty of sports action available. And the city continues to draw big-time sporting events—most recently hosting the NCAA Men's Final Four Basketball Championship in March 2003.

New Orleans Hornets The arrival of the former Charlotte Hornets to occupy the New Orleans Arena starting with the 2002–2003 season had more to do with the owner's ongoing dispute with Charlotte officials than with any great Crescent City demand for basketball. Remember, this is a town that couldn't even hold on to a team named the Jazz and its floppy-socked star player "Pistol" Pete Maravich, a tenure that lasted just 4 years before moving to anything-but-jazzy Utah in 1979. The Hornets were actually pretty good in their first season here—making the playoffs, even—though they had trouble filling the arena regularly. If they keep winning, though, maybe the NBA will catch on this time.

1501 Girod St. © **504/301-4000.** Ticket info: © **504/525-HOOP.** Fax 504/301-4121. www.nba.com/ hornets. Tickets $7–$210.

New Orleans Saints Since entering the NFL in 1967, the team has been known to frustrated (but intensely loyal) fans as the Ain'ts. In those 30-odd years, several much newer teams have made it to the Super Bowl while it's rare for this one to even get into the playoffs. And frankly, its home, the Superdome, ain't so super any more. But its history is littered with colorful characters (former coach Mike Ditka, former quarterback Archie Manning, former running back Ricky Williams), and the city long ago embraced the team as lovable losers. And when they actually *do* win, well, let's just say it doesn't take much to give New Orleans an excuse to party.

Superdome, 1500 block of Poydras. Saints home office: 5800 Airline Dr., Metairie. © **504/733-0255.** Ticket info: © **504/731-1700.** www.superdome.com. Tickets $53–$80.

9

City Strolls

We've said it before, and we will keep saying it: This town was made for walking. Except maybe at the height of the summer months when heat and humidity—especially humidity—make you not want to do much of anything except sit gasping in the nearest shade, sipping cool drinks.

This unique-looking city is one of the most beautiful in the country, and to not stroll through it and marvel at it is a huge loss. Everywhere, you will find gorgeous buildings, each more interesting than the last. The French Quarter and the Garden District have their own distinct appearances, and both are easily manageable on foot.

Put on some good walking shoes, breathe in that river wind and tropical breeze, and take a walk. Go slow—there's a reason New Orleans is called the Big Easy. Admire the iron lacework on one building and see how it differs from another. Peek through gateways, particularly in the French Quarter, where simple facades hide exquisite secrets in the form of surprising courtyards with fountains, brickwork, and thick foliage. Gawk at the mighty oaks, some with swaying Spanish moss dripping from their branches, lining the streets. Don't just look at the stops on each tour below; if you're doing things right, there should be plenty to see in between the stops we detailed.

Take a stroll along St. John's Bayou, turning at any corner that strikes your fancy. If you're lucky or if you walk at the right time of day (especially early in the morning), you might have a street or two to yourself. Imagine taking this walk 100 years ago; it would have looked almost exactly the way it does now. At certain times, ghosts seem to flit just out of sight around every corner. But don't get so carried away with daydreams and fantasies that you forget to be aware of your surroundings; these areas should be safe, but be careful just in case.

The following walking tours will give you a nice overview and are perfect for answering the "That looks interesting—what the heck *is* it?" kind of questions that arise during a casual stroll. Formal professional walking tours (like the ones offered by **Historic New Orleans Walking Tours; © 504/ 947-2120;** www.tourneworleans.com) cover more ground and go into considerably more detail, though they tend to deal only with the French Quarter and the Garden District. Below you will find our personalized walking tours of the French Quarter and the Garden District, as well as a stroll along a less traveled route (Esplanade Ridge) that should prove no less rewarding.

WALKING TOUR 1   THE FRENCH QUARTER

Start:	The intersection of Royal and Bienville streets.
Finish:	Jackson Square.
Time:	Allow approximately 1½ hours, not including time spent in shops or historic homes.

Best Times: Any day before 8am (when it's still quiet and deserted), up to 10am (when the day begins in the French Quarter).

Worst Times: At night. Some attractions won't be open, and you won't be able to get a good look at the architecture.

Even if it's the only recreational time you spend in New Orleans, you owe it to yourself to experience the French Quarter, also known by the French name Vieux Carré, or "old square." Made up of just over 80 city blocks, this is perhaps the densest urban area in the country, and it's a living monument to history. Here, the colonial empires of France, Spain, and, to a lesser extent, Britain intersected with the emerging American nation. Still, somehow the place seems timeless, at once recognizably old and vibrantly alive. Today's residents and merchants are stewards of a rich tradition of individuality, creativity, and disregard for many of the concerns of the world beyond. This tour is designed to acquaint you with a bit of the style and history of this place and its important landmarks and to lead you through some of its more picturesque regions.

From the corner of Royal and Bienville streets, head into the Quarter (away from Canal St.). As you walk along Royal, imagine that streetcar named *Desire* rattling along its tracks. It traveled along Royal and Bourbon streets until 1948. (It was replaced by the bus named *Desire*. Really.) You can also imagine how noisy these narrow streets were when the streetcars were in place. Your first stop is:

① 339–343 Royal St.

Also known as the Rillieux-Waldhorn House, this is now the home of Waldhorn Antiques (est. 1881). The building was built between 1795 and 1800 for Vincent Rillieux, the great-grandfather of the French Impressionist artist Edgar Degas. Offices of the (second) Bank of the United States occupied the building from 1820 until 1836 when, thanks to President Jackson's famous veto, its charter expired. Note the wrought-iron balconies—an example of excellent Spanish colonial workmanship.

② The Bank of Louisiana

Across the street, this old bank was erected in 1826 at 334 Royal St. by Philip Hamblet and Tobias Bickle, after the designs of Benjamin Fox. Its Greek Revival edifice was erected in the early 1860s, and the bank was liquidated in 1867. The building has suffered a number of fires (in 1840, 1861, and 1931) and has served as the Louisiana State Capitol, an auction exchange, a criminal court, a juvenile court, and a social hall for the American Legion. It now houses the police station for the Vieux Carré.

Cross Conti Street to:

③ 403 Royal St.

Benjamin H. B. Latrobe died of yellow fever shortly after completing designs for the Louisiana State Bank, which opened in this building in 1821. At the time of his death, Latrobe was one of the nation's most eminent architects, having designed the Bank of Pennsylvania in Philadelphia (1796) and contributed to the design of the U.S. Capitol. You can see the monogram "LSB" on the Creole-style iron balcony railing.

④ Brennan's Restaurant

Brennan's opened in this building at 417 Royal St., also built by Vincent Rillieux, in 1955 (see p. 110 for a full listing). The structure was erected after the fire of 1794 destroyed more than 200 of the original buildings along this street. From 1805 to 1841, it was home to the Banque de la Louisiane. The world-famous chess champion Paul Charles Morphy moved here as a child in 1841. The parents of Edgar Degas also lived here.

1 339–343 Royal St.
2 The Bank of Louisiana
3 403 Royal Street
4 Brennan's Restaurant
5 437 Royal St.
6 New Orleans
   Court Building
7 The Brulatour Court
8 The Merieult House
9 The Court of Two Sisters
10 Old Town Praline Shop
11 Le Monnier Mansion
12 The LaBranche House
13 714 St. Peter St.

14 Pat O'Brien's
15 Preservation Hall
16 Plique-LaBranche
   House
17 623 Bourbon St.
18 Bourbon Orleans Hotel
19 Le Pretre Mansion
20 707 Dumaine St.
21 Madame John's Legacy
22 Lafitte's Blacksmith
   Shop
23 The Thierry House
24 618–630 Governor
   Nicholls St.
25 The Lalaurie Home

26 The Gallier House
   Museum
27 The Beauregard-Keyes
   House
28 The Archbishop Antoine
   Blanc Memorial
29 The Old U.S. Mint
30 The Old French Market
31 Decatur Street
32 The Pontalba Buildings
33 The Presbytère
34 St. Louis Cathedral
35 Faulkner House Books
36 The Cabildo

❺ 437 Royal St.

Masonic lodge meetings were held regularly in a drugstore here in the early 1800s, but that's not what made the place famous. What did? Proprietor and druggist Antoine A. Peychaud served after-meeting drinks of bitters and cognac to lodge members in small egg cups, whose French name (*coquetier*) was Americanized to "cocktail."

❻ New Orleans Court Building

Built in 1909, this courthouse at 400 Royal St. covers the length of the block across from Brennan's. The baroque edifice, made of Georgia marble, certainly seems out of place in the French Quarter—especially considering that many Spanish-era structures were demolished to make way for it. Originally home to parish and state courts, the building is being renovated for use by the Louisiana Supreme Court and the Fourth Circuit Court of Appeals.

Cross St. Louis Street to:

❼ The Brulatour Court

This structure at 520 Royal St. was built in 1816 as a home for François

Seignouret, a furniture-maker and wine importer from Bordeaux—his furniture, with a signature "S" carved into each piece, still commands the respect of collectors. From 1870 to 1887, wine importer Pierre Brulatour occupied the building. WDSU-TV now maintains offices here, but during business hours you're welcome to walk into the courtyard—it's one of the few four-walled courtyards in the French Quarter and among the more exotic. Also, from the street, notice the elaborate, fan-shaped guard screen (*garde de frise*) on the right end of the third-floor balcony—look closely for Seignouret's "S" carved into the screen.

❽ The Merieult House

Built for the merchant Jean François Merieult in 1792, this house at 533 Royal St. was the only building in the area left standing after the fire of 1794. Legend has it that Napoléon repeatedly offered Madame Merieult great riches in exchange for her hair (he wanted it for a wig to present to a Turkish sultan). She refused. Nowadays, it's home to the Historic New Orleans Collection—Museum/Research Center. (See p. 159 for tour times and more information.)

Cross Toulouse Street to:

❾ The Court of Two Sisters

This structure at 613 Royal St. was built in 1832 for a local bank president on the site of the 18th-century home of a French governor. The two sisters were Emma and Bertha Camors (whose father owned the building); from 1886 to 1906, they ran a curio store here.

❿ Old Town Praline Shop

Walk through this shop's entrance to the back of the store to see another of the French Quarter's magnificent courtyards. This 1777 building, at 627 Royal St., is where opera singer Adelina Patti first came for a visit and then lived after becoming something of a local heroine in 1860. The 17-year-old girl's popularity as a last-minute stand-in lead soprano in *Lucia di Lammermoor* saved the local opera company from financial ruin.

⓫ Le Monnier Mansion

This 640 Royal St. structure once towered above every other French Quarter building as the city's first "skyscraper"—all of three stories high when it was built in 1811. A fourth story was added in 1876. George W. Cable, the celebrated author of *Old Creole Days,* chose this building as the residence of his fictional hero, Sieur George.

Cross St. Peter Street to:

⓬ The LaBranche House

Now the Royal Café, at 700 Royal St., this is probably the most photographed building in the Quarter—and no wonder. Take a look at the lacy cast-iron grillwork, with its delicate oak leaf and acorn design, that fairly drips from all three floors. There are actually 11 LaBranche buildings (three-story brick row houses built between 1835 and 1840 for the widow of wealthy sugar planter Jean Baptiste LaBranche). Eight face St. Peter Street, one faces Royal, and two face Pirates Alley.

Turn right at St. Peter Street and continue to:

⓭ 714 St. Peter St.

Built in 1829 by a prominent physician, this was a boardinghouse run by Antoine Alciatore for several years during the 1860s. His cooking became so popular with the locals that he eventually gave up catering to open the famous Antoine's restaurant, still operated by his descendants.

⓮ Pat O'Brien's

You've probably heard of this famous New Orleans nightspot at 718 St. Peter St. (see p. 241 for more information). The building was completed in 1790 for a wealthy planter and was known as the Maison de Flechier.

Later, Louis Tabary put on popular plays here. It's said that the first grand opera in America was performed within these walls. The courtyard is open to visitors and is well worth a look—if you can see it past the crowds consuming the Hurricane drinks for which the place is famous.

⑮ Preservation Hall
Scores of people descend on this spot, at 726 St. Peter St., nightly to hear traditional New Orleans jazz. A daytime stop affords a glimpse, through the big, ornate iron gate, of a lush tropical courtyard in back. Erle Stanley Gardner, the author who brought us Perry Mason, lived in an apartment above the Hall.

⑯ Plique-LaBranche House
This house, at 730 St. Peter St., was built in 1825, sold to Giraud M. Plique in 1827, and sold to Jean Baptiste LaBranche in 1829. The wrought-iron balcony dates from the 1820s. This is believed to be the site of New Orleans's first theater, which burned in the fire of 1816, but that is the subject of some debate.

Continue up St. Peter Street until you reach Bourbon Street. Turn left onto Bourbon Street.

⑰ 623 Bourbon St.
Tennessee Williams and Truman Capote lived in this house, though not together (get your mind out of the gutter!). It's owned by Lindy Boggs, a much-beloved local politician (and mother of NPR and ABC commentator Cokie Roberts), who took over her husband's Congressional seat after his death. She is now the U.S. special envoy to the Vatican.

Turn around and head the other way down Bourbon Street. At the corner of Bourbon and Orleans streets, look down Orleans Street, toward the river, at:

⑱ Bourbon Orleans Hotel
This building at 717 Orleans St. was the site of the famous quadroon balls,

where wealthy white men would come to form alliances (read: acquire a mistress) with free women of color, who were one-eighth to one-fourth black. Look at the balcony and imagine the assignations that went on there while the balls were in session. The building later became a convent.

Turn left onto Orleans and follow it a block to Dauphine (pronounced daw-*feen*) Street. On the corner is:

⑲ Le Pretre Mansion
In 1839, Jean Baptiste Le Pretre bought this 1836 Greek Revival house at 716 Dauphine St. and added the romantic cast-iron galleries. The house is the subject of a real-life horror story: Sometime in the 19th century, a Turk, supposedly the brother of a sultan, arrived in New Orleans and rented the Le Pretre house. He was conspicuously wealthy, and his entourage included many servants and more than a few beautiful young girls—all thought to have been stolen from the sultan.

Rumors quickly spread about the situation, even as the home became the scene of lavish entertainment with guest lists that included the cream of society. One night, shrieks came from inside the house; the next morning, neighbors entered and found the tenant's body lying in a pool of blood surrounded by the bodies of the young beauties. The mystery remains unsolved. Local ghost experts say you can hear exotic music and shrieks on the right night.

Follow Dauphine Street 2 blocks to Dumaine Street and turn right. You'll find an interesting little cottage at:

⑳ 707 Dumaine St.
After the 1794 fire, all houses in the French Quarter were required by law to have flat tile roofs. Most have since been covered with conventional roofs, but this Spanish colonial cottage is still in compliance with the flat-roof rule.

㉑ Madame John's Legacy

This structure, at 632 Dumaine St., was once thought to be the oldest building on the Mississippi River. Recent research suggests, however, that only a few parts of the original building survived the 1788 fire and were used in its reconstruction. The house was originally erected in 1726, 8 years after the founding of New Orleans. Its first owner was a ship captain who died in the 1729 Natchez Massacre; upon his death, the house passed to the captain of a Lafitte-era smuggling ship.

It has had no fewer than 21 owners since. The present structure is a fine example of a French "raised cottage." The aboveground basement is of brick-between-posts construction (locally made bricks were too soft to be the primary building material), covered with boards laid horizontally. The hipped, dormered roof extends out over the veranda. Its name, incidentally, comes from George W. Cable's fictional character that was bequeathed the house in the short story "Tite Poulette." Now a part of the Louisiana State Museum complex (p. 159), it's open for tours.

Take a left at the corner of Dumaine and Chartres streets and follow Chartres to the next corner; make a left onto St. Philip Street and continue to the corner of St. Philip and Bourbon streets to:

㉒ Lafitte's Blacksmith Shop

For many years, this structure, at 941 Bourbon St., has been a bar (for the full story, see chapter 11, "New Orleans After Dark"), but the legend is that Jean Lafitte and his pirates posed as blacksmiths here while using it as headquarters for selling goods they'd plundered on the high seas. It has survived in its original condition, reflecting the architectural influence of French colonials who escaped St. Domingue in the late 1700s.

It may be the oldest building in the Mississippi Valley, but that has not been documented. You can still see the brick-between-posts construction, which is usually covered with plaster. The modern-day owners of the building have resisted invasions of chrome and plastic, which makes the interior an excellent place to imagine life in the Quarter in the 19th century.

Turn left onto Bourbon Street and follow it 2 blocks to Governor Nicholls Street. Turn right.

㉓ The Thierry House

The structure at 721 Governor Nicholls St. was built in 1814 and announced the arrival of the Greek Revival style of architecture in New Orleans. It was designed in part by architect Henry S. Boneval Latrobe, son of Benjamin H. B. Latrobe, when he was 19 years old.

Cross Royal Street to:

㉔ 618–630 Governor Nicholls St.

Henry Clay's brother, John, built a house for his wife here in 1828, and in 1871, a two-story building was added at the rear of its garden. In the rear building, Frances Xavier Cabrini (now a Catholic saint) conducted a school.

Backtrack to the corner of Royal and Governor Nicholls streets. Take a left onto Royal and look for:

㉕ The Lalaurie Home

Many people simply refer to this place, at 1140 Royal St., as "the haunted house." Here's why: When Madame Delphine Macarty de Lopez Blanque wed Dr. Louis Lalaurie, it was her third marriage—she'd already been widowed twice. The Lalauries moved into this residence in 1832, and they soon were impressing the city with extravagant parties. One night in 1834, however, fire broke out and neighbors crashed through a locked door to find seven starving slaves chained in painful positions, unable to move. The sight, combined with Delphine's stories of past slaves having "committed suicide," enraged her neighbors. Madame Lalaurie and her family escaped a mob's wrath and fled to Paris. Several years later she died in Europe, and her body was returned to New Orleans—and even then she had to be buried in secrecy.

The building was a Union headquarters during the Civil War and later was a gambling house. Through the years, stories have circulated of ghosts inhabiting the building, especially that of one young slave child who fell from the roof trying to escape Delphine's cruelties.

㉖ The Gallier House Museum

This house, at 1132 Royal St., was built by James Gallier Jr. as his residence in 1857. Gallier and his father were two of the city's leading architects (see p. 158 for more details). Anne Rice was thinking of this house when she described where Lestat and Louis lived in *Interview with the Vampire.*

Turn left onto Ursulines Street, toward the river.

TAKE A BREAK
If you need a little rest or sustenance at this point, you can stop in the popular **Croissant D'Or**, 617 Ursulines St. They probably aren't actually made of gold (if so, they aren't priced accordingly), but the croissants and pastries here are very good, and the ambience—inside or out on the patio—is equal to the eats.

At the corner of Ursulines and Chartres streets is:

㉗ The Beauregard-Keyes House

This "raised cottage" at 1113 Chartres St. was built as a residence in 1826 by Joseph Le Carpentier, though it has several other claims to fame (see p. 155 for details). Notice the Doric columns and handsome twin staircases.

㉘ The Archbishop Antoine Blanc Memorial

Across the street, the complex at 1112–1114 Chartres St., which was completed in 1752, includes the Old Ursuline Convent (see p. 156 for more information) and the Archiepiscopal Residence.

Continue walking along Chartres Street until you get to Esplanade (pronounced es-pla-*nade*) Avenue, which served as the parade ground for troops quartered on Barracks Street. Along with St. Charles Avenue, it is one of the city's most picturesque historic thoroughfares. Some of the grandest town houses built in the late 1800s grace this wide, tree-lined avenue. (If you're interested in viewing some of these houses, Walking Tour 3, later in this chapter, concentrates on the architecture of Esplanade Ridge.)

The entire 400 block of Esplanade is occupied by:

㉙ The Old U.S. Mint

This was once the site of Fort St. Charles, one of the defenses built to protect New Orleans in 1792. It was here that Andrew Jackson reviewed the "troops"—pirates, volunteers, and a nucleus of trained soldiers—he later led in the Battle of New Orleans. (For more information, see p. 156.)

Follow Esplanade toward the river and turn right at the corner of North Peters Street. Follow North Peters until it intersects with Decatur Street. This is the back end of:

㉚ The Old French Market

This European-style market has been here for well over 150 years, and today it has a farmer's market and stalls featuring everything from gator on a stick to somewhat tacky souvenir items. On most weekends, the Esplanade end of the market houses a flea market.

When you leave the French Market, exit on the side away from the river onto:

㉛ Decatur Street

Not long ago, this section of Decatur—from Jackson Square all the way over to Esplanade—was a seedy, run-down area of wild bars and cheap rooming houses. Fortunately, few of either remain. Instead, this portion of the strip has fallen into step with the rest of the Quarter, sporting a number of restaurants and trendy bars. (The stretch of Decatur between Ursulines and Esplanade streets has retained more of the rundown aesthetic, with secondhand shops that are worth taking a browse through and smaller, darker bars.)

As you walk toward St. Ann Street along Decatur, you'll pass 923 and 919 Decatur St., where the Café de Refugies and Hôtel de la Marine were located in the 1700s and early 1800s. These were reputed to be gathering places for pirates, smugglers, and European refugees (some of them outlaws)—a far cry from today's scene.

TAKE A BREAK
If you're walking in the area of 923 Decatur St. around lunchtime, pop into the **Central Grocery** and pick up a muffuletta sandwich (p. 123). There are little tables at which to eat inside, or you can take your food and sit outside, maybe right on the riverbank.

Decatur Street will take you to Jackson Square. Turn right onto St. Ann Street; the twin four-story, redbrick buildings here and on the St. Peter Street side of the square are:

32 The Pontalba Buildings

These buildings sport some of the most impressive cast-iron balcony railings in the French Quarter. They also represent one of the first eras of revitalization in the Quarter. In the mid-1800s, Baroness Micaela Almonester Pontalba inherited rows of buildings along both sides of the Place d'Armes from her father, Don Almonester (who had been responsible for rebuilding the St. Louis Cathedral; see p. 155). In an effort to counteract the emerging preeminence of the American sector across Canal Street, she decided to raze the structures and, in their place, build high-end apartments and commercial space.

The Pontalba buildings were begun in 1849 under her very direct supervision; you can see her mark today in the entwined initials "A.P." in the ironwork. The buildings were designed in a traditional Creole-European style, with commercial space on the street level, housing above, and a courtyard in the rear. The row houses on St. Ann Street, now owned by the State of Louisiana, were completed in 1851.

Baroness Pontalba is also responsible for the current design of Jackson Square, including the cast-iron fence and the equestrian statue of Andrew Jackson (see p. 155 and 157 for more on the statue and Baroness Pontalba, respectively).

At the corner of St. Ann and Chartres streets, turn left and continue around Jackson Square; you will see:

33 The Presbytère

This, the Cabildo, and the St. Louis Cathedral (see later stops on this walk for both of the above)—all designed by Gilberto Guillemard—were the first major public buildings in the Louisiana Territory. The Presbytère, at 751 Chartres St., was originally designed to be the rectory of the cathedral. Baroness Pontalba's father financed the building's beginnings, but he died in 1798, leaving only the first floor done. The building was finally completed in 1813. It was never used as a rectory, however, but was rented and then purchased (in 1853) by the city to be used as a courthouse. It now houses wonderful exhibits on the history of Mardi Gras (p. 160).

Next you'll come to:

34 St. Louis Cathedral

The building standing here today is the third erected on this spot—the first was destroyed by a hurricane in 1722, the second by fire in 1788. The cathedral was rebuilt in 1794; the central tower was later designed by Henry S. Boneval Latrobe, and the building was remodeled and enlarged between 1845 and 1851. (See p. 154 for more information.)

On the other side of the cathedral, you'll come to Pirates Alley. Go right down Pirates Alley to:

㉟ Faulkner House Books

In 1925, William Faulkner lived at 624 Pirates Alley and worked on his first novels, *Mosquitoes* and *Soldiers' Pay*. While here, he contributed to the *Times-Picayune* and to a literary magazine, the *Double Dealer*. This is a great stop for Faulkner lovers and collectors of literature. (See p. 213 for more information.)

Return to Jackson Square. On the right side of the cathedral on the corner of Chartres and St. Peter streets (as you face the Mississippi River), and also facing Jackson Square, is:

㊱ The Cabildo

In the 1750s, this was the site of a French police station and guardhouse. Part of that building was incorporated into the original Cabildo, statehouse of the Spanish governing body (the "Very Illustrious Cabildo"). The Cabildo was still under reconstruction when the transfer papers for the Louisiana Purchase were signed in a room on the second floor in 1803. Since then, it

has served as New Orleans's City Hall, the Louisiana State Supreme Court, and since 1911, a facility of the Louisiana State Museum. (See p. 158 for details.)

One further note: If you think those old Civil War cannons out front look pitifully small and ineffective by modern standards, think again. In 1921, in a near-deadly prank, one was loaded with powder, an iron ball was rammed down its muzzle, and it was fired in the dead of night. That missile traveled from the Cabildo's portico across the wide expanse of the Mississippi and some 6 blocks inland before landing in a house in Algiers, narrowly missing its occupants.

WINDING DOWN
You've finished! Now go back across Decatur Street to **Café du Monde**, 813 Decatur St., in the French Market—no trip to New Orleans is complete without a leisurely stop here for beignets (p. 145) and coffee. If you still have energy left, hike up the levee and relax on a bench.

WALKING TOUR 2   THE GARDEN DISTRICT

Start:	Prytania Street and Washington Avenue.
Finish:	Lafayette Cemetery.
Time:	45 minutes to 1½ hours.
Best Times:	Daylight.
Worst Times:	Night, when you won't be able to get a good look at the architecture.

Walking through the architecturally phenomenal Garden District, you could get the impression that you've entered an entirely separate city from New Orleans as defined by the French Quarter—or, perhaps more specifically, entered a different time period. Although the Garden District was indeed once a separate city (Lafayette) from the Vieux Carré and was established during a later period, the fact that this neighborhood was created by a different group of people most profoundly distinguishes it from the old section, the French Quarter.

The French Quarter was initially established by Creoles during the French and Spanish colonial periods, and the Garden District was created by Americans after the 1803 Louisiana Purchase. Antebellum New Orleans's lucrative combination of Mississippi River commerce, regional abundance of cash crops, slave trade, and national banks fueled the local economy, resulting in a remarkable building boom that extended for several square miles through Uptown.

Although very few people from the United States lived in New Orleans during its colonial era, after the Louisiana Purchase, thousands of Americans flooded the city and clashed with the Creoles. Friction arose between the two groups due to mutual snobbery, a language barrier, religious division, and, most significantly, competition over burgeoning commerce. Americans were arriving at the brink of a boom time to make fortunes. With inferior business experience, education, and organizational skills, the Creoles worried that "les Americains" would work them out of business. Americans were, therefore, kept out of the already overcrowded French Quarter. Feeling snubbed, the Americans moved upriver to create a residential district of astounding opulence. The Garden District is, therefore, a study of a cultural clash reflected through architecture, with Americans creating an identity by boldly introducing styles and forms familiar to them and previously unknown in colonial Louisiana.

Note: The houses described on this tour are not open to the public. This is a residential area—please do not disturb the occupants and respect everyone in the neighborhood.

To reach the Garden District, take the St. Charles streetcar to Washington Avenue (stop 16) and walk 1 block toward the river to:

❶ The Garden District Book Shop

Inside the historic property known as the Rink, you will find this store at 2727 Prytania St., an excellent starting point for a Garden District tour. Built in 1884 as the Crescent City Skating Rink, the building subsequently acted as a livery stable, mortuary facility, grocery store, and gas station. You probably will not view the interiors of any private homes, but the book shop's stellar collection of regional titles allows you a revealing glimpse into the neighborhood's majestic homes.

This is Anne Rice's favorite bookstore, and she always holds her first book signing here when a new book is released. (The shop stocks a supply of her signed first editions.) Owner Britton Trice schedules signings by many regionally and nationally acclaimed authors. The Rink also offers P.J.'s Coffee Shop, restrooms, and air-conditioning (crucial in the summer).

Across Prytania Street, you'll find:

❷ Colonel Short's Villa

This house, at 1448 Fourth St., was built by architect Henry Howard for Kentucky Colonel Robert Short. The story goes that Short's wife complained of missing the cornfields in her native Iowa, so he bought her the cornstalk fence. A revisionist explanation supplied by a recent owner is that the wife saw that it was the most expensive fence in the building catalog and requested it. Second Civil War occupational governor Nathaniel Banks was quartered here.

Continuing down Prytania, you'll find:

❸ Briggs-Staub House

Located at 2605 Prytania St., this is the Garden District's only example of Gothic Revival architecture. Because this style reminded the Protestant Americans of the Roman Catholicism of their Creole antagonists, it did not become popular. Original owner Charles Briggs did not hold African slaves but did employ Irish servants, for whom he built the relatively large adjacent servant quarters. Irish immigration was then starting to create the Irish Channel neighborhood across Magazine Street from the Garden District.

❹ Our Mother of Perpetual Help Chapel

Once an active Catholic chapel, this site, at 2523 Prytania St., is currently

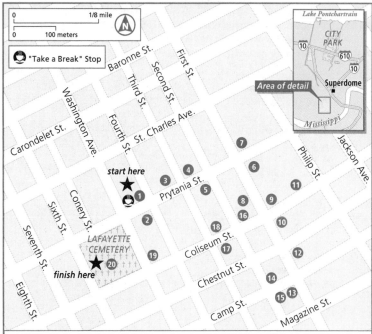

0 | 1/8 mile
0 | 100 meters

N

"Take a Break" Stop

Baronne St.
Third St.
Second St.
First St.
Washington Ave.
Carondelet St.
Fourth St.
St. Charles Ave.
Conery St.
Sixth St.
Seventh St.
Eighth St.
Prytania St.
Coliseum St.
Chestnut St.
Camp St.
Magazine St.
Philip St.
Jackson Ave.

start here

finish here

LAFAYETTE CEMETERY

Lake Pontchartrain
CITY PARK
10
610
10
Area of detail
Superdome
Mississippi

1 The Garden District Book Shop
2 Colonel Short's Villa
3 Briggs-Staub House
4 Our Mother of Perpetual Help Chapel
5 Women's Opera Guild House
6 Toby's Corner
7 Bradish Johnson House and
     Louise S. McGehee Schools
8 Archie Manning House
9 Pritchard-Pigott House
10 Morris-Israel House

11 The Seven Sisters
12 Brevard-Mahat-Rice House
13 Payne-Strachan House
14 Warwick Manor
15 1137 Second St.
16 Joseph Merrick Jones House
17 Musson-Bell House
18 Robinson House
19 Commander's Palace
     Restaurant
20 Lafayette Cemetery

owned by Anne Rice. Rice also owns the Marigny-Claiborne House (built for the daughter-in-law of Bernard Marigny) on the other side of the block at 2524 St. Charles Ave. It's the setting for her novel *Violin*. The author's childhood home is down the street at 2301 St. Charles Ave.

⑤ Women's Opera Guild House

Some of the Garden District's most memorable homes incorporate more than one style. Designed by William Freret in 1858, this building, at 2504 Prytania St., combines Greek Revival

and Queen Anne styles. Now owned by the Women's Opera Guild, the home can be toured by special arrangement (ℂ **504/899-1945**).

⑥ Toby's Corner

Located at 2340 Prytania St., the Garden District's oldest known home dates to at least 1838. Built for Philadelphia wheelwright Thomas Toby, it is in Greek Revival style, which was then very popular throughout the United States. Although the home represents an American attempt at creating a non-Creole architectural identity, this Anglicized style required Creole building techniques such as raising the house up on brick piers to combat flooding and encourage air circulation.

❼ Bradish Johnson House and Louise S. McGehee School

Paris-trained architect James Freret designed this French Second Empire–style mansion at 2343 Prytania St., which was built for sugar factor Bradish Johnson in 1872 at a cost of $100,000 (that's almost $1.5 million today). Contrast this house's awesome detail with the stark classical simplicity of Toby's Corner (see above) across the street—a visual indication of the effect that one generation of outrageous fortune had on Garden District architecture. Since 1929, the building has been the private Louise S. McGehee School for girls.

Turn down First Street (away from St. Charles) and it's less than a block to:

❽ Archie Manning House

This house, at 1420 First St., is the home of former New Orleans Saints superstar quarterback Archie Manning and the childhood home of his son, Peyton Manning, himself an NFL quarterback for the Indianapolis Colts.

❾ Pritchard-Pigott House

This Greek Revival double-galleried town house is located at 1407 First St. As fortunes compounded, the typical Garden District house size grew. Americans introduced two house forms: the cottage (as in Toby's Corner; see above) and the grander town house (seen here).

❿ Morris-Israel House

As time passed, Garden District homes moved away from the simplicity of Greek Revival and became more playful with design. By the 1860s, the Italianate style was popular, as seen in this double-galleried town house at 1331 First St. Architect Samuel Jamison designed this house and the

Carroll-Crawford House on the next corner (1315 First St.); note the identical ornate cast-iron galleries. The Morris-Israel House is reputedly haunted.

Follow Coliseum Street to the left less than half a block to:

⓫ The Seven Sisters

This row of "shotgun" houses at 2329–2305 Coliseum St. gets its nickname from a story that a 19th-century Garden District resident had seven daughters whom he wanted to keep close to home, so he built these homes as wedding gifts. That story is not true. If you count the "Seven Sisters," you will find eight. (They were actually built on speculation.)

An explanation for the name "shotgun" is that, if you fire a gun through the front door, the bullet will go right out the back. Also, a West African word for this native African house form sounds something like "shotgun." The shotgun house effectively circulates air and is commonly found in hot climates. Its relatively small size makes the shotgun house a rarity along the imposing streets of the Garden District, but it is extremely popular throughout the rest of New Orleans.

Now turn around and go back to First Street and turn left. At the corner of First and Chestnut, you'll see:

⓬ Brevard-Mahat-Rice House

Designed in 1857 as a Greek Revival town house and later augmented with an Italianate bay, this house, at 1239 First St., is a fine example of "transitional" architecture. It was historically called Rosegate for the rosette pattern on the fence. (The fence's woven diamond pattern is believed to be the precursor to the chain-link fence.) This is the home of novelist Anne Rice and the setting for her *Witching Hour* novels.

⓭ Payne-Strachan House

Jefferson Davis, president of the Confederate States of America, died at this house at 1134 First St. Davis fell ill while traveling and was taken here, the home of his friend Judge Charles Fenner (son-in-law of owner Jacob Payne). A stone marker in front of the house bears the date of Davis's death, December 6, 1889. (Davis was buried in magnificent Metairie Cemetery for 2 years and then was disinterred and moved to Virginia.) This house is a classic antebellum Greek Revival home. Note the sky-blue ceiling of the gallery—the color is believed to keep winged insects from nesting there and to ward off evil spirits. Many Garden District homes adhere to this tradition.

Turn left on Camp and go less than a block to:

⓮ Warwick Manor

An example of Georgian architecture, this house, at 2427 Camp St., is one of the few homes in the vicinity that's not a single-family residence. Note the buzzers, which indicate rented apartments.

⓯ 1137 Second St.

This house is an example of the type of Victorian architecture popularized in Uptown New Orleans toward the end of the 19th century. Many who built such homes were from the Northeast and left New Orleans in the summer; otherwise, it would be odd to see this kind of claustrophobic house, normally intended for cool climates, in New Orleans. Note the exquisite stained glass and rounded railing on the gallery.

Turn right onto Second Street and go 2 blocks to the corner of Coliseum, where you'll see the:

⓰ Joseph Merrick Jones House

This house, at 2425 Coliseum St., is the home of Nine Inch Nails singer Trent Reznor. When he moved in, more anti-noise ordinances began being introduced into city council proceedings. Could it be a coincidence that his next-door neighbor is City Councilwoman Peggy Wilson?

Turn left onto Coliseum Street and go 1 block to Third Street. Turn left to get to the:

⓱ Musson-Bell House

This house, at 1331 Third St., is the 1853 home of Michel Musson, one of the few French Creoles then living in the Garden District. Musson was the uncle of French Impressionist artist Edgar Degas, who once lived with Musson on Esplanade Avenue during a visit to New Orleans. On the Coliseum Street side of the house is the foundation of a cistern. These water tanks were so common in the Garden District that Mark Twain once commented that it looked as if everybody in the neighborhood had a private brewery. Cisterns were destroyed at the turn of the 20th century when mosquitoes, which breed in standing water, were found to be carriers of yellow fever and malaria.

Turn around and cross Coliseum to see:

⓲ Robinson House

Built between 1859 and 1865 by architect Henry Howard for tobacco grower and merchant Walter Robinson, this house, at 1415 Third St., is one of the Garden District's most striking and unusual homes. Walk past the house to appreciate its scale—the outbuildings, visible from the front, are actually connected to the side of the main house. The entire roof is a large vat that once collected water and acted as a cistern. Gravity provided water pressure and the Garden District's earliest indoor plumbing.

Walk down Coliseum Street 2 blocks to the corner of Washington Avenue. There you'll find:

⓳ Commander's Palace Restaurant

Established in 1883 by Emile Commander, this turreted Victorian structure (a bordello back in the 1920s), at 1403 Washington Ave., is now the pride of the Brennan family, the most visible and successful restaurateurs in New Orleans. Commander's is perennially rated one of the nation's top restaurants, and the jazz brunch—a tradition that originated here—is extremely popular.

⑳ Lafayette Cemetery

Established in 1833, this "city of the dead," on Washington Avenue between Prytania and Coliseum streets, is one of New Orleans's oldest cemeteries. It has examples of all the classic aboveground, multiple-burial techniques and features a number of interesting Anne Rice–related sites (the Mayfair witches' family tomb is here, for example). Although the cemetery gates display New Orleans Police Department signs that say "patrolled," that is not true. Be careful in this and all cemeteries, as predatory crime is a possibility. A guided tour is recommended.

Walk to St. Charles Avenue to pick up the streetcar (there is a stop right there) or flag down a cab to return to the French Quarter.

WINDING DOWN
Now go back to your first stop, the Rink, where you can enjoy a cup of coffee and some light refreshments at P.J.'s Coffee Shop.

WALKING TOUR 3 **ESPLANADE RIDGE**

Start:	Esplanade Avenue and Johnson Street.
Finish:	City Park.
Time:	Allow approximately 1½ hours, not including museum, cemetery, and shopping stops.
Best Times:	Monday through Saturday, early or late morning.
Worst Times:	Sunday, when attractions are closed. Also, you certainly don't want to walk in this area after dark; if you decide to stay in City Park or in the upper Esplanade area until early evening, plan to return on the bus or by taxi.

This is another region of New Orleans that many visitors overlook—even when they drive through it on the way to City Park, the New Orleans Museum of Art, or the Jazz and Heritage Festival. If you're heading to those attractions, consider taking this stroll or leaving enough time for sightseeing from your car. We particularly enjoy the stretch along St. John's Bayou—mostly as slow and quiet as the sluggish water itself. Historically, the Esplanade Ridge area is Creole society's answer to St. Charles Avenue—it's an equally lush boulevard with stately homes and seemingly ancient trees stretching overhead. Originally, it was the site of homes of the descendants of the earliest settlers. The avenue had its finest days toward the end of the 19th century, and some of the neighborhoods along its path, especially the Faubourg Treme, are visibly suffering. If it is a little worn compared with St. Charles Avenue, Esplanade Avenue is still closer to the soul of the city (read: Regular people live here, whereas St. Charles always was for the well heeled and is that way now more than ever).

You can catch a bus on Esplanade Avenue at the French Quarter, headed toward the park to your starting point. Otherwise, stroll (about 15 min.) up Esplanade Avenue to:

❶ 2023 Esplanade Ave.

Originally a plantation home, this was designed in 1860 for A. B. Charpentier.

The building is now operating as Ashton's Bed & Breakfast (see p. 82 for a full listing).

❷ Widow Castanedo's House

Juan Rodriguez purchased this land in the 1780s, and his granddaughter,

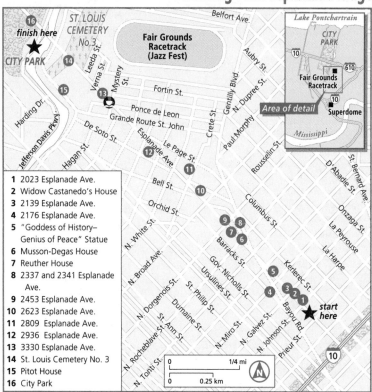

ST. LOUIS CEMETERY No. 3

16 finish here

CITY PARK

Belfort Ave.

Fair Grounds Racetrack (Jazz Fest)

14

15

Harding Dr.

Jefferson Davis Pkwy.

Leeda St.

Verna St.

Mystery St.

13

De Soto St.

Hagan St.

Fortin St.

Ponce de Leon

Grande Route St. John

Esplanade Ave.

Le Page St.

12

11

Bell St.

Orchid St.

N. White St.

N. Broad Ave.

N. Dorgenois St.

N. Rocheblave St.

N. Tonti St.

St. Philip St.

St. Ann St.

Dumaine St.

N. Miro St.

Gentilly Blvd.

N. Dupree St.

Crete St.

Paul Morphy

Rousselin St.

Columbus St.

Barracks St.

Gov. Nicholls St.

Ursulines St.

N. Galvez St.

N. Johnson St.

Prieur St.

Bayou Rd.

Aubry St.

D'Abadie Ave.

St. Bernard Ave.

Onzaga St.

La Peyrouse

La Harpe

Kerlerec St.

10

9 **8**

7 **6**

5

4 **3** **2** **1**

start here

10

Lake Pontchartrain

CITY PARK

10

610

Fair Grounds Racetrack

10

Area of detail

Superdome

Mississippi

0   1/4 mi
0   0.25 km

N

1 2023 Esplanade Ave.
2 Widow Castanedo's House
3 2139 Esplanade Ave.
4 2176 Esplanade Ave.
5 "Goddess of History–Genius of Peace" Statue
6 Musson-Degas House
7 Reuther House
8 2337 and 2341 Esplanade Ave.
9 2453 Esplanade Ave.
10 2623 Esplanade Ave.
11 2809 Esplanade Ave.
12 2936 Esplanade Ave.
13 3330 Esplanade Ave.
14 St. Louis Cemetery No. 3
15 Pitot House
16 City Park

Widow Castanedo, lived in this home at 2033–2035 Esplanade Ave. until her death in 1861. At that time, the house was a smaller, Spanish colonial–style plantation home. Before Esplanade Avenue extended this far from the river, the house was located in what is now the middle of the street. The widow tried and failed to block the extension of the street. The house was moved to its present site and was enlarged sometime around the 1890s. It has a late-Italianate appearance, and is split down the middle and inhabited today by two sisters.

❸ 2139 Esplanade Ave.

This building is a great example of the typical "Esplanade Ridge Style." Note the Ionic columns on the upper level.

On the opposite side of the street is:

❹ 2176 Esplanade Ave.

A simple, classic-style town house, this was the second Bayou Road home built by Hubert Gerard, who also built the Mechling guesthouse at no. 2023 (see above).

After you cross North Miro Street, Esplanade Avenue crosses the diagonal Bayou Road, which was the route to the French-Canadian settlements at St. John's Bayou in the late 17th century. Veer left at the fork to stay on Esplanade Avenue and look for:

❺ Goddess of History—Genius of Peace Statue

This victory monument stands on the triangular piece of land at the intersection of Bayou Road, Esplanade Avenue, and Miro Street. In 1886, the land, known to earlier generations as Gayarre Place, was given to the city by Charles Gayarre. George H. Dunbar donated the statue to be placed there. The original terra-cotta statue was destroyed in 1938, and the present one, made of cement and marble, is a replacement.

⑥ Musson-Degas House

The Musson family rented this house, at 2306 Esplanade Ave., for many years. Estelle Musson married René Degas, brother of Edgar Degas, the French Impressionist artist. (She and her descendants dropped his last name after he ran off with a neighbor's wife.) Degas is said to have painted the portrait of Estelle that is now in the New Orleans Museum of Art, as well as many other works, during the time he spent living at no. 2306.

The house was built in 1854, and the Italianate decorations were added later when it was split into two buildings. The right-hand one is currently open as an homage to Degas, and the left-hand one is being restored with the grand hopes of someday reuniting the two halves. This is the only studio or residence of Degas' open to the public in the world, so do come poke around, but know that you'll need an advance appointment first to get in (see p. 167 for more information).

⑦ Reuther House

The current resident of this house, at 2326 Esplanade Ave., has a collection of small metal houses, cinder-block sculptures, and a beautiful metal-crafted marlin on display on the front porch, which is readily visible from the street. The house is known as the Reuther House because it was owned by Joseph Reuther, a baker, in 1913.

In passing, take a look at nos. 2325, 2329, and 2331—all are interesting examples of Creole cottages. Then, continue to:

⑧ 2337 and 2341 Esplanade Ave.

These houses were identical structures when they were built in 1862 for John Budd Slawson, owner of a horse-drawn streetcar company that

operated along Bayou Road in the 19th century. Back then, they were both single-story shotgun-style houses. Notice the unusual ironwork underneath the front roof overhang.

Cross North Dorgenois Street to:

⑨ 2453 Esplanade Ave.

Until the other was demolished, this house was one of a pair at the corner of Dorgenois Street. Though its architecture has been changed extensively, it's one of the few remaining mansard-roofed homes on Esplanade Ridge.

Cross North Broad Avenue to:

⑩ 2623 Esplanade Ave.

Here is a classical revival Victorian home built in 1896 by Louis A. Jung. Note the Corinthian columns. The Jungs donated the triangular piece of land at Esplanade Avenue, Broad Street, and Crete Street to the city on the condition that it remain public property. It is officially known as DeSoto Park and is graced by a fence in the Art Nouveau style.

⑪ 2809 Esplanade Ave.

This is one of the more decorative Victorian Queen Anne center-hall houses on Esplanade Ridge.

⑫ 2936 Esplanade Ave.

A nice example of what's known as a Gothic villa.

TAKE A BREAK
At the intersection of Mystery Street and Esplanade Avenue, you'll find a little grouping of shops and restaurants. If you're in the area at lunchtime, you might want to stop at **Café Degas** for a leisurely meal—if the weather is nice, the semi-outdoor setting is exceedingly pleasant. If you just want a snack or some picnic food for City Park, we highly recommend a quick sandwich or salad from **Wholefoods**. You can also opt for a break at the **Brew Time** coffeehouse behind Café Degas. Additionally, the bread at **La Boulangerie** is the best in the city. Enjoy!

Continue to:

⓭ 3330 Esplanade Ave.

A galleried frame home built in the Creole-cottage style.

On your right is:

⓮ St. Louis Cemetery No. 3

This was the site of the public Bayou Cemetery, established in 1835. It was purchased by the St. Louis diocese in 1856 and contains the burial monuments of many of the diocese's priests. If you've been putting off going into the cemeteries because of concerns over safety, this is one you can explore on your own—though you should still keep your wits about you and be aware of your surroundings. You can pick up brochures in the office, which is right inside the gate.

From the cemetery, head back out to Esplanade Avenue and continue walking toward City Park. When you get to the bridge, go left, following the signs, along St. John's Bayou (one of the nicest and least touristy areas of the city), to:

⓯ Pitot House

This house, at 1440 Moss St., is open for public viewing (see p. 168 for a full description).

Head back to Esplanade Avenue, cross the bridge, and walk straight into:

⓰ City Park

Where you can explore the amphitheater, museum, and gardens (see p. 170 for more details).

Shopping

Shopping in New Orleans is a highly evolved leisure activity with a shop for every strategy and a fix for every shopaholic—and every budget. Don't assume those endless T-shirt shops on Bourbon Street or even the costly antiques stores on Royal Street are all that New Orleans has to offer. The range of shopping here is as good as it gets—many a clever person has come to New Orleans just to open up a quaint boutique filled with strange items gathered from all parts of the globe or produced by local, somewhat twisted, folk artists.

Want to totally redecorate your house? You can do that here whether you want a complete Victorian look or top-to-bottom folk art. Want to double your record or CD collection? This town is made of music. Want to bring home the perfect souvenir? From an antique sofa that costs about as much as a semester at college to 50¢ Mardi Gras beads, you'll have plenty of options.

Searching for these treasures will be part of what contributes to your calorie-burning walks. Many a well-spent day, or even days, can be had strolling the Quarter window-shopping. But don't forget the many options on Magazine Street. Antiques aficionados eschew exorbitant Royal Street for Magazine because they know the best buys are found there.

New Orleans has always been a place for fine homes and fine furnishings, and as people trade up, they leave some great antiques for the rest of us. Many came from Europe in the early days, while others were crafted right in the city by cabinetmakers internationally known for their exquisite pieces. Antiquing has become so popular in New Orleans that there are even people who will take you on a personalized guided tour of city shops (p. 186). In addition, the **Royal Street Guild** (② **504/524-1260;** www.royalstreet guild.com), an association of some of the city's antiques dealers, has put together brochures that are available at most hotels.

You'll also notice below that the city's art galleries are clustered around the antiques shops and on Julia Street as well. Over the past 20 years (notice that's about as long as the Contemporary Arts Center has been open), New Orleans has grown to be an important regional and national market for contemporary fine arts.

Of course, if you're just looking for some souvenirs, whole colonies of shops in the French Quarter sell postcards, posters, sunglasses, and T-shirts. Most of them are cheap and ghastly, if not in flamingly bad taste. You might also consider bringing home Cajun spices, pralines, a Cajun or zydeco CD or two, or a box of beignet mix; these are the things that truly say you've been to New Orleans.

General hours for the stores in New Orleans are from 10am to 5pm, but call ahead to make sure.

1 Major Hunting Grounds

CANAL PLACE　At the foot of Canal Street (365 Canal St.), where the street reaches the Mississippi River, this shopping center holds more than 50 shops, many of them branches of some of this country's most elegant retailers. Stores in this sophisticated setting include Brooks Brothers, Bally of Switzerland, Saks Fifth Avenue, Gucci, Williams-Sonoma, and Jaeger. Open Monday through Wednesday from 10am to 6pm, Thursday from 10am to 8pm, Friday and Saturday from 10am to 7pm, and Sunday from noon to 6pm.

THE FRENCH MARKET　Shops within the Market begin on Decatur Street across from Jackson Square; offerings include candy, cookware, fashion, crafts, toys, New Orleans memorabilia, and jewelry. It's open from 10am to 6pm (and the Café du Monde, next to the Farmer's Market, is open 24 hours). Quite honestly, you'll find a lot of junk here, but there are some good buys mixed in, and it's always fun to stroll through—and grab a nibble.

JACKSON BREWERY　Just across from Jackson Square at 600–620 Decatur St., the old brewery building has been transformed into a jumble of shops, cafes, delicatessens, restaurants, and entertainment. Keep in mind that many shops in the Brewery close at 5:30 or 6pm, before the Brewery itself. (Open Sun–Thurs from 10am–9pm, Fri–Sat from 10am–10pm.)

JULIA STREET　From Camp Street down to the river on Julia Street, you'll find some of the city's best contemporary art galleries (many are listed below, under "Art Galleries"). Some of the works are a bit pricey, but there are good deals to be had if you're collecting and fine art to be seen if you're not.

MAGAZINE STREET　This is the Garden District's premier shopping street. More than 140 shops (some of which are listed below) line the street in 19th-century brick storefronts and quaint cottagelike buildings. Among the offerings are antiques, art galleries, boutiques, crafts, and dolls. If you're so inclined, you could shop all the way from Washington Street to Audubon Park. The most likely section goes, roughly, from the 3500 to 4200 blocks (from about Aline St. to Milan St., with the odd block or so of nothing). Be sure to pick up a copy of *Shopper's Dream,* a free guide and map to most (if not all) of the stores on the 6 miles of Magazine Street, which is available all along the street.

NEW ORLEANS CENTRE　New Orleans's newest shopping center, at 1400 Poydras St., features a glass atrium and includes stores like Lord & Taylor and Macy's. There are three levels of specialty shops and restaurants. Open Monday through Saturday from 10am to 8pm and Sunday from noon to 6pm.

RIVERBEND　To reach this district (in the Carrollton area), ride the St. Charles Avenue streetcar to stop 44 and then walk down Maple Street 1 block to Dublin Park, the site of an old public market that was once lined with open stalls. Nowadays, a variety of renovated shops inhabit the old general store, a produce warehouse made of barge board, and the town surveyor's raised-cottage home.

RIVERWALK MARKETPLACE　A mall is a mall is a mall, unless it has picture windows offering a Mississippi River panorama. Even though you almost certainly have a mall at home, this one, at 1 Poydras St., is worth visiting. Besides, if you packed wrong and need T-shirts instead of sweaters or vice versa, this is the closest Gap to the Quarter. Note that the best river views are in the section of the mall closest to the Convention Center. Stop by the Fudgery, a candy store that offers regular and highly entertaining musical fudge-making demos. There is also a branch of Café du Monde for beignet fixes. Otherwise, it's the usual mall suspects. Open Monday through Thursday from 10am to 9pm, Friday and Saturday from 10am to 10pm, and Sunday from 12:30 to 5:30pm.

2 Shopping A to Z

ANTIQUES

Audubon Antiques   Audubon has everything from collectible curios to authentic antique treasures at reasonable prices. There are two floors of goods, so be prepared to lose yourself. 2025 Magazine St. ⓒ **504/581-5704.** Mon–Sat 10:30am–5pm, Sun call first.

Bush Antiques and Beds Au Beau Reve   This wonderful treasure trove features impressive European religious art and objects and a beautiful array of beds—sadly, the latter are out of most of our price ranges, but they are really fantastic to look at. An extra treat is the collection of folk art on the rear patio. 2109–2111 Magazine St. ⓒ **504/581-3518.** Fax 504/581-6889. www.bushantiques.com. Mon–Sat 10am–5pm.

Dixon & Harris of Royal   Dixon & Harris features 18th- and 19th-century European fine art and antiques, jewelry, grandfather clocks, and Oriental rugs. The collection of tall-case clocks is one of the largest in the country; the individual clocks are awe-inspiring. The company is a long-standing family-run business; it has helped many younger collectors make some of their initial purchases. 237 Royal St. ⓒ **800/848-5148** or 504/524-0282. www.dixon-antiques.net. Mon–Sat 9am–5:30pm, Sun 10am–5pm.

Jack Sutton Antiques   In some ways, the Suttons are to jewelry and antiques what the Brennans are to food: one family, different businesses. There are a number of Suttons around New Orleans, mostly on Royal. This one, our favorite, specializes in jewelry and objects. The selection of estate jewelry (*estate* meaning "older than yesterday but less than 100 years") is often better than that at other antiques stores—the author's engagement ring came from here—but due to the ebb and flow of the estate business, you can never be sure what may be offered. The store encourages special requests and has a room devoted to "men's gift items" such as antique gambling, cigar, and drinking paraphernalia. 315 Royal St. ⓒ **504/522-0555.** Mon–Sat 10am–5:30pm, Sun 11am–5pm.

Keil's Antiques   Keil's was established in 1899 and is currently run by the fourth generation of the founding family. The shop has a considerable collection of 18th- and 19th-century French and English furniture, chandeliers, jewelry, and decorative items. 325 Royal St. ⓒ **504/522-4552.** www.keilsantiques.com. Mon–Sat 9am–5pm.

Lucullus   An unusual shop, Lucullus has a wonderful collection of culinary antiques as well as 17th-, 18th-, and 19th-century furnishings to "complement the grand pursuits of cooking, dining, and imbibing." They recently opened a second shop at 3932 Magazine St., ⓒ **504/894-0500.** 610 Chartres St. ⓒ **504/528-9620.** Mon–Sat 9:30am–5pm. Closed on Mon during the summer.

Magazine Arcade Antiques   This large, fascinating shop holds an exceptional collection of 18th- and 19th-century European, Asian, and American furnishings as well as music boxes, dollhouse miniatures, European and Oriental porcelain, cloisonné, lacquer, cameos, opera glasses, old medical equipment, wind-up phonographs, antique toys, and scores of other items. Allow yourself plenty of time to browse through it all. 3017 Magazine St. © **504/895-5451.** Mon and Wed–Sat 10am–5pm.

Manheim Galleries At Manheim Galleries, you'll find an enormous collection of continental, English, and Oriental furnishings along with porcelains, jade, silver, and fine paintings. Manheim Galleries is also the agent for Boehm Birds. 409 Royal St. © **504/568-1901.** www.idamanheimantiques.com. Mon–Sat 9am–5pm.

Miss Edna's Antiques Miss Edna's carries eclectic antiques—furniture, specialty items, curios—and paintings, with a focus on 19th-century works. Miss Edna recently moved a few feet up Magazine, doubling her inventory and expanding her art collection. 2035 Magazine St. © **504/524-1897.** Mon–Sat 10am–5pm.

Rothschild's Antiques Rothschild's is a fourth-generation furniture merchandiser. Some of the most interesting things you'll find here are antique and custom-made jewelry (the store is also a full-service jeweler). There's a fine selection of antique silver, marble mantels, porcelains, and English and French furnishings. Rothschild's devotes tens of thousands of square feet to displaying and warehousing antiques. 241 and 321 Royal St. © **504/523-5816** or 504/523-2281. www.rothschildsantiques.com. Mon–Sat 9:30am–5:30pm, Sun by appointment.

Sigle's Antiques & Metalcraft If you've fallen in love with the lacy ironwork that drips from French Quarter balconies, this is the place to pick out some pieces to take home. In addition, Sigle's has converted some of the ironwork into useful household items such as plant holders. 935 Royal St. © **504/522-7647.** Mon–Sat 10am–noon and 1–4:30pm.

Whisnant Galleries The quantity and variety of merchandise in this shop is mind-boggling. You'll find all sorts of unusual and unique antique collectibles including items from Ethiopia, Russia, Greece, South America, Morocco, and other parts of North Africa and the Middle East. 222 Chartres St. © **504/524-9766.** www.whisnantantiques.com. Mon–Sat 9:30am–5:30pm, Sun 10am–5pm.

ART GALLERIES
With one major exception, galleries in New Orleans follow the landscape of antiques shops: **Royal and Magazine streets.**

Since the opening of the Contemporary Arts Center (p. 164), however, galleries also keep popping up around **Julia Street** and the **Warehouse District.** Some are listed below, but there are many others. All are strong contemporary fine-art galleries, but it can be hard to tell them apart. If you're contemplating a gallery-hopping jaunt, start at Julia Street.

Ariodante A contemporary craft gallery, Ariodante features handcrafted furniture, glass, ceramics, jewelry, and decorative accessories by nationally acclaimed artists. Rotating shows offer a detailed look at works by various artists. 535 Julia St. © **504/524-3233.** www.ariodante.com. Tues–Sat 11am–5pm.

Arthur Roger Gallery Arthur Roger sets the pace for the city's fine-art galleries. Since opening in New Orleans 20 years ago, Roger has played a major role in developing the art community and in tying it to the art world in New York. Time and again, he has taken chances—moving early into the Warehouse District and briefly opening a second gallery in New York—and he continues to do so, scheduling shows that range from strongly regional work to the far-flung. The gallery represents many artists including Francis Pavy (who did the 1997 Jazz Fest poster), Ida Kohlmeyer, Douglas Bourgeois, Paul Lucas, Clyde Connell,

Willie Birch, Gene Koss, and George Dureau. 432 Julia St. ✆ **504/522-1999.** www.artroger.com. Mon–Sat 10am–5pm.

Bergen Putman Gallery   Bergen Putman Gallery has the city's largest selection of posters and limited-edition graphics on such subjects as Mardi Gras, jazz, and the city itself and by such artists as Erté, Icart, Nagel, Maimon, and Tarkay. Bergen also features a large collection of works by sought-after African-American artists. The service by Margarita and her staff is friendly and extremely personable. 730 Royal St. ✆ **800/621-6179** or 504/523-7882. www.bergengalleries.com. Daily 9am–9pm.

Berta's and Mina's Antiquities   In years past, this was just another place that bought and sold antiques and secondhand furniture and art. That all ended on the day in 1993 that Nilo Lanzas (Berta's husband and Mina's dad) began painting. Now you can barely see the furniture in the shop for all the new art. Dubbed "folk art" or "outsider art," Lanzas's works (which he paints right near the counter—for about 10–12 hours a day!) are colorful scenes from life in New Orleans or his native Latin America, stories out of the Bible, or images sprung from his imagination. His paintings are on wood with titles or commentaries painted on the frames; he also makes some tin sculptures and woodcarvings. 4138 Magazine St. ✆ **504/895-6201.** Mon–Sat 10am–6pm, Sun 11am–6pm.

Bryant Galleries   This gallery represents renowned artists Ed Dwight, Fritzner Lamour, and Leonardo Nierman as well as other American, European, and Haitian artists. The varied work on display here may include jazz bronzes, glasswork, and graphics. The staff is very friendly and helpful. 316 Royal St. ✆ **800/844-1994** or 504/525-5584. Sun–Wed 10am–6pm, Thurs–Sat 10am–9pm.

Carabaux Galleries   This gallery's collection is built around the works of William Tolliver, an African-American artist from Mississippi whose untimely death at the age of 48 in 2000 received national coverage. Tolliver came to painting relatively late in his life and without formal training. Despite this, he quickly became an internationally recognized contemporary Impressionist painter. (He was chosen to create the official poster for the 1996 Summer Olympics.) At Carabaux Galleries, formally Galerie Royale, you can find a selection of Tolliver's museum-quality pieces as well as work by other artists including Salvador Dalí, Bonny Stanglmaier, and Verna Hart. 3646 Magazine St. ✆ **504/894-1588.** www. groyale.com. Mon–Sat 11am–6pm, or by appointment.

Cole Pratt Gallery, Ltd.   This gallery showcases the work of Southern artists whose creations include abstract and realist paintings, sculptures, and ceramics. The art is of the highest quality and the prices are surprisingly reasonable. 3800 Magazine St. ✆ **504/891-6789.** Fax 504/891-6611. www.coleprattgallery.com. Tues–Sat 10am–5pm.

The Davis Galleries   One of two world-class galleries in New Orleans (the other being A Gallery for Fine Photography; see below), this may be the best place in the world for Central and West African traditional art. The owner makes regular trips to Africa for collecting. Works on display might include sculpture, costuming, basketry, textiles, weapons, and jewelry. 904 Louisiana Ave. ✆ **504/895-5206.** By appointment only.

Diane Genre Oriental Art and Antiques   If all of the 18th- and 19th-century European antiques in the stores along Royal are starting to look the same, it's time to step into Diane Genre's shop. By comparison, the atmosphere in here seems as delicate as one of the ancient East Asian porcelains on display.

Hold your breath and get an eyeful of furniture, 18th-century Japanese wood-block prints, and a world-class collection of Chinese and Japanese textiles. There are also scrolls, screens, engravings, and lacquers. 431 Royal St. ℰ **504/595-8945.** Fax 504-899-8651. www.dianegenreorientalart.com. By appointment only.

Galerie Simonne Stern   Galerie Simonne Stern features paintings, drawings, and sculptures by contemporary artists. Recent shows have included the works of John Alexander, George Dunbar, and Simon Gunning. 518 Julia St. ℰ **504/529-1118.** www.sterngallery.com. Tues–Sat 10am–5pm, Mon by appointment.

A Gallery for Fine Photography   It would be a mistake to skip this incredibly well-stocked photography gallery (one of two world-class galleries in New Orleans—the other is The Davis Galleries; see above). Even if you aren't in the market, it's worth looking around. Owner Joshua Mann Pailet calls this "the only museum in the world that's for sale." It really is like a museum of photography, with just about every period and style represented and frequent shows of contemporary artists. When they aren't swamped, the staff is more than happy to show you some of the many photos in the files. The gallery emphasizes New Orleans and Southern history and contemporary culture (you can buy Ernest Bellocq's legendary Storyville photos) as well as black culture and music. There is something in just about every price range as well as a terrific collection of photography books if that better fits your budget. ***Note:*** The gallery recently relocated around the corner to a new space at 241 Chartres St. ℰ **504/568-1313.** www.agallery.com. Mon–Sat 10am–6pm, Sun 11am–6pm.

Hanson Gallery   Hanson Gallery shows paintings, sculptures, and limited-edition prints by contemporary artists such as Peter Max, Frederick Hart, Pradzynski, Anoro, Thysell, Deckbar, Zjawinska, Erickson, LeRoy Neiman, Richard MacDonald, and Behrens. 229 Royal St. ℰ **504/524-8211.** www.hansongallery-nola.com. Mon–Sat 10am–6pm, Sun 11am–5pm.

Kurt E. Schon, Ltd.   Here you'll find the country's largest inventory of 19th-century European paintings. Works include French and British Impressionist and post-Impressionist paintings as well as art from the Royal Academy and the French Salon. Only a fraction of the paintings in the gallery's inventory are housed at this location, but if you're a serious collector, you can make an appointment to visit the St. Louis Street gallery at 510 St. Louis St. 523 Royal St. ℰ **504/524-5462.** www.kurteschonltd.com. Mon–Fri 9am–5pm, Sat 9am–3pm.

LeMieux Galleries   LeMieux represents contemporary artists and fine crafts-people from Louisiana and the Gulf Coast. They include our personal favorite local artist, Leslie Staub (and her Church of the Soul and Church of Nature series), Dr. Bob, Charles Barbier, Pat Bernard, Mary Lee Eggart, Leslie Elliott-smith, JoAnn Greenberg, David Lambert, Shirley Rabe Masinter, Evelyn Menge, Dennis Perrin, Kathleen Sidwell, and Kate Trepagnier. 332 Julia St. ℰ **504/522-5988.** Fax 504/522-5682. www.lemieuxgalleries.com. Mon–Sat 10am–6pm.

Marguerite Oestreicher Fine Arts   Like the other Julia Street galleries, this one concentrates on contemporary painting, sculpture, and photography. It also consistently shows work by emerging artists. The gallery's recent shows have included works by Drew Galloway and Raine Bedsole. 720 Julia St. ℰ **504/581-9253.** Tues–Sat 10am–5pm and by appointment.

Mario Villa   Mario Villa is New Orleans's undisputed king of design—or at least the city's most ubiquitous designer. To get the full experience, drop into Villa's uptown showroom. Within 5 minutes, you can get a good idea of his aesthetic. There are canvas rugs; plush sofas; wrought-iron chairs, lamps, and tables with organic twists and turns; and a liberal spray of photographs and paintings. It may not be to your taste, but Villa's work is certainly provocative and visually stimulating. Take a moment to look at one of the beds in the front rooms—if they won't enhance your dreams, for good or ill, nothing will. 3908 Magazine St. ✆ **504/895-8731.** Fax 504/895-8167. www.mariovillagallery.com. Tues–Sat 10am–5pm.

New Orleans School of Glassworks and Printmaking Studio This institution serves multiple purposes. Here, within 20,000 square feet of studio space, are a 550-pound tank of hot molten glass and a pre–Civil War press. Established glasswork artists and master printmakers display their work in the on-site gallery and teach classes in glassblowing, kiln-fired glass, hand-engraved printmaking, papermaking, and bookbinding. Absolutely unique to the area, the place is worth a visit during gallery hours. Daily glassblowing and fusing demonstrations are open for viewing. 727 Magazine St. ✆ **504/529-7277.** www.new orleansglassworks.com. Mon–Sat 11am–5pm. Closed Sat June–Aug.

Peligro A bit out of the way but worth checking out, Peligro is one of the best folk-art galleries in the city, with an emphasis on primitive and outsider art (but also work from Latin American countries). The owners have a terrific eye for up-and-coming artists. At times they have smaller items that make for marvelous, original gifts. 305 Decatur St. ✆ **504/581-1706.** Mon–Thurs 10am–6pm, Fri–Sat 10am–8pm, Sun noon–6pm.

The Rodrigue Gallery of New Orleans Blue Dog is the Freddie Krueger of New Orleans; once you've seen Cajun artist George Rodrigue's creation, it invades your consciousness and torments your life. Oh, the staring, otherworldly, bordering-on-kitsch canine has its fans, but it scares us. This gallery is the source for all your Blue Dog needs. 721 Royal St. ✆ **504/581-4244.** www.george rodrique.com. Daily 10am–6pm.

Shadyside Potsalot Pottery If you want to see a master potter at work, Shadyside Pottery is an excellent place to stop. Charles Bohn, who apprenticed in Japan, can be seen at his wheel all day Tuesday through Friday and until midafternoon on Saturday. He specializes in the Japanese tradition of *Raku,* a type of pottery that has a "cracked" look. In addition to his own work, Bohn carries some glass pieces and a selection of Japanese kites by Mitsuyoshi Kawamoto. 3823 Magazine St. ✆ **504/897-1710.** Mon–Sat 10am–5pm.

Wyndy Morehead Fine Arts This gallery shows contemporary fine art in many media. It represents more than 75 local and national artists including Nofa Dixon, Robert Rector, William Lewis, Ron Richmond, and Joan Steiman. 3926 Magazine St. ✆ **504/269-8333.** www.wyndymoreheadfinearts.com. Mon–Sat 10am–5:30pm.

BATH & BEAUTY PRODUCTS & DAY SPAS

Earthsavers Need some serious detoxing after days of debauching, New Orleans style? This is the place to go. It features an impressive variety of holistic and otherwise healthy body-care products (including the very popular but sometimes hard-to-find Kiehl's line)—everything for every part of the body. The massive selection of aromatherapy products even includes a line for your dog. Earthsavers also offers facials, massages, and other salon-type pampering services. A pick-me-up here just might help you get through the rest of that wearying round of eating, drinking, and dancing you have planned. 434 Chartres St.

© **877/581-4999** or 504/581-4999. Fax 504/586-0550. www.earthsaversonline.com. Mon–Wed and Fri–Sat 10am–6pm, Thurs 10am–8pm, Sun noon–5pm.

Hove   Founded in 1931, Hove is the oldest perfumery in the city. It features all-natural scents (except the musk, which is synthetic), and the selection is almost overwhelming. Strips with various options, for both men and women, are laid out to help you. This is the place to establish your signature scent. 824 Royal St. *©* **504/525-7827.** www.hoveparfumeur.com. Mon–Sat 10am–5pm.

BOOKS
Literary enthusiasts will find many destinations in New Orleans. **Maple Street Book Shop,** 7523 Maple St. (*©* **504/866-4916**), is an uptown mecca for bookworms; the **Maple Street Children's Book Shop** is next door at 7529 Maple St. (*©* **504/861-2105**); and **Beaucoup Books** is at 5414 Magazine St. (*©* **504/895-2663**).

Beckham's Bookshop   Beckham's has two entire floors of old editions, rare secondhand books, and thousands of classical LPs that will tie up your whole afternoon or morning if you don't tear yourself away. The owners also operate **Librairie Bookshop,** 823 Chartres St. (*©* **504/525-4837**), which has a sizable collection of secondhand books. 228 Decatur St. *©* **504/522-9875.** Daily 10am–6pm.

Crescent City Books   Two floors of dusty treasures (the emphasis is on history, social history, literary criticism, philosophy, and art) and a staff that ranges from nonchalant to quite sweet and helpful. 204 Chartres St. *©* **800/546-4013** or 504/524-4997. www.crescentcitybooks.com. Daily 10am–6pm.

Faubourg Marigny Bookstore   This well-stocked gay and lesbian bookstore also carries some local titles. It has a used section, CDs, posters, cards, and gifts (all with a more or less gay or lesbian slant) and holds regular readings and signings. The staff makes this a fine resource center—you can call them for local gay and lesbian info. 600 Frenchmen St. *©* **504/943-9875.** Mon–Fri 10am–8pm, Sat–Sun 10am–6pm.

Faulkner House Books   This shop is on a lot of walking tours of the French Quarter because it's where Nobel Prize–winner William Faulkner lived while he was writing his early works *Mosquitoes* and *Soldiers' Pay.* Those who step inside instead of just snapping a photo and walking on will find something remarkable: possibly the best selection per square foot of any bookstore in the whole wide world, with every bit of shelf space occupied by a book that's both highly collectible and of literary value. The shop holds a large collection of Faulkner first editions and rare and first-edition classics by many other authors, and it has a particularly comprehensive collection of New Orleans–related work. Taking up one room and a hallway, Faulkner House feels like a portion of somebody's private home—which it is—but the selection of books here is almost magical. 624 Pirates Alley. *©* **504/524-2940.** Daily 10am–6pm.

Garden District Book Shop   Owner Britton Trice has stocked his medium-size shop with just about every regional book you can think of; if you want a New Orleans or Louisiana-specific book, no matter what the exact focus (interiors, exteriors, food, Creoles, you name it), you should be able to find it here. This is also where Anne Rice does book signings whenever she has a new release. They usually have autographed copies of her books plus fancy special editions of Rice titles that they publish themselves and a large selection of signed books by local and nonlocal authors (from Clive Barker to James Lee Burke). 2727 Prytania St. (in the Rink). *©* **504/895-2266.** Fax 504/895-0111. Mon–Sat 10am–6pm, Sun 11am–5pm.

Kaboom   On the edge of the Quarter, Kaboom is a bit off the beaten path, but bibliophiles should make the trek. This is a reader's bookstore, thanks to an owner whose knowledge of literature is almost scary. The stock (used books only) tends to lean heavily on fiction, but there is little you won't find here. 915 Barracks St. © **504/529-5780**. kaboombooks@bellsouth.net. Daily 11am–6pm.

Octavia Books   We do love our independent bookstores, and although this may be a bit far uptown, a lovely patio, complete with waterfall, is the customer's reward—what better way to linger over a purchase from stock that is chosen with obvious literary care? Book signings and other literary events are common. 513 Octavia St. (at Laurel St.). © **504/899-7323**. www.octaviabooks.com. Mon–Sat 10am–6pm.

CANDIES & PRALINES

Aunt Sally's Praline Shop   At Aunt Sally's, you can watch skilled workers perform the 150-year-old process of cooking the original Creole pecan pralines right before your eyes. You'll know they're fresh. The large store also has a broad selection of regional cookbooks, books on the history of New Orleans and its environs, Creole and Cajun foods, folk and souvenir dolls, and local memorabilia. In addition, Aunt Sally's has a collection of zydeco, Cajun, R&B, and jazz CDs and cassettes. They'll ship any purchase. In the French Market, 810 Decatur St. © **800/642-7257** or 504/944-6090. www.auntsallys.com. Daily 8am–8pm.

Blue Frog Chocolates   If you've noticed our chocolate bias, you know how happy we are at this store, which has the finest chocolate and candy collection in the city. Just for starters is Belgium liquor-filled chocolate; Michel Cluizel fresh butter creams from France; Joseph Schmidt's (often referred to as the "Nipples of Venus"), which are plump and dense; Jordan Almonds (good ones are difficult to find); Dulce De Leche (Argentina) served over ice cream—or as Ann Streiffer, owner with husband Rick, suggested, "Eat it with a spoon from the jar." If you are looking for the quintessential New Orleans favor, see the doubloons, alligators, and Mardi Gras golden-wrapped delights. We could go on about the 21 different colors of M&Ms or the chocolate film for your camera, but we'll stop and let you experience it when you arrive. 5707 Magazine St. © **504/269-5707**. www.bluefrogchocolates.com. Mon–Fri 10am–5:30pm, Sat 10am–4pm.

Laura's Candies   Laura's is said to be the city's oldest candy store, established in 1913. It has fabulous pralines, but it also has rich, delectable golf ball–size truffles—our personal favorite indulgence, although they've gotten a bit pricey as of late. 938 Royal St. © **504/524-9259**. www.laurascandies.com. Daily 9:30am–5:30pm.

Leah's Candy Kitchen   After you've tried all of the city's Creole candy shops, you might very well come to the conclusion that Leah's tops the list. Everything here, from the candy fillings to the chocolate-covered pecan brittle, is made from scratch by second- and third-generation members of Leah Johnson's praline-cookin' family. 714 St. Louis St. © **888/523-5324** or 504/523-5662. www.leahspralines.com. Daily 10am–6pm.

Southern Candy Makers   Here is yet another place to taste test pralines. Our group of experts found these a bit nontraditional but quite good. 334 Decatur St. © **504/523-5544**. Fax 504/523-5540. www.southerncandymakers.com. Daily 10am–7pm.

COSTUMES & MASKS

Costumery is big business in New Orleans, and not just in the days before Lent. In this city, you never know *when* you're going to want or need a costume. A number of shops in New Orleans specialize in props for Mardi Gras, Halloween, and other occasions. Here's a tip: New Orleanians often sell their costumes back to these shops after Ash Wednesday, and you can sometimes pick up a one-time-worn outfit at a small fraction of its original cost.

Little Shop of Fantasy   In the Little Shop of Fantasy, owners Laura and Anne Guccione sell the work of a number of local artists and more than 20 mask makers. Mike creates the feathered masks, Jill does the velvet hats and costumes, and Laura and Anne produce homemade toiletries. Some of the masks and hats are just fun and fanciful, but there are many fashionable ones as well. There are lots of clever voodoo items here, too, plus unusual toys and novelties. 517 St. Louis. ℂ **504/ 529-4243**. www.littleshopoffantasy.com. Mon–Tues and Thurs–Sat 11am–6pm, Sun 1–6pm.

Mardi Gras Center   Mardi Gras Center carries sizes 2 to 50 and has a wide selection of new, ready-made costumes as well as used outfits. It also carries accessories such as beads, doubloons, wigs, masks, hats, makeup, jewelry, and Mardi Gras decorations. The Mardi Gras Center is also a good place to stop for Halloween supplies. 831 Chartres St. ℂ **504/454-6444**. www.mardigrascenter.com. Mon–Sat 10am–5pm, Sun 10am–3pm.

Uptown Costume & Dance Company   The walls of this small store are covered with spooky monster masks, goofy arrow-through-the-head-type tricks, hats, wigs, makeup, and all other manner of playfulness. It draws a steady, year-long stream of loyal customers: kids going to parties, dancers, clowns, actors, and so forth. Conventioneers come here for rental disguises. At Mardi Gras, though, things really get cooking. The shop designs party uniforms for a number of Mardi Gras krewe members. Owner Cheryll Berlier also creates a limited number of wacky Mardi Gras tuxedo jackets, which get gobbled up quickly. 4326 Magazine St. ℂ **504/895-7969**. Mon–Fri 10am–6pm, Sat 10am–5pm.

FASHION & VINTAGE CLOTHING

Body Hangings   Cloaks have seen more favorable eras. Ever hopeful, though, this place is keeping the flame alive until the Sherlock Holmes look comes back in style. It has a good collection of capes, scarves, and cloaks. Men's and women's cloaks are available in wool, cotton, corduroy, and velveteen. 835 Decatur St. ℂ **800/574-1823** or 504/524-9856. www.bodyhangings.com. Daily 10am–6pm.

The Grace Note   Primarily a clothing store, Grace Note also features some gifts. It's a bit pricey, but the clothes are stunning. The designers here work with vintage and new materials, and what they come up with is usually lush, memorable, and very touchable. If you want to swan around town, feeling as though you've stepped out of an 1800s novel, this is the place for you. The gift items come from "architectural or religious fragments"—think distressed wood and peeling paint—producing one-of-a-kind objects that evoke turn-of-the-20th-century through '40s styles. 900 Royal St. ℂ **504/522-1513**. Mon–Sat 10am–6pm, Sun 11am–5pm.

House of Lounge   If you want to be a couch potato, you might as well be a well-dressed one. Or do you want to treat your humble bedroom more like a boudoir? House of Lounge offers all sorts of silky robes and impressive "hostess gowns," plus sexy lingerie (and admittedly, there isn't much difference between the categories). 2044 Magazine St. ℂ **504/671-8300**. www.houseoflounge.com. Mon–Sat 10am–6pm, Sun noon–5pm.

Ms. Spratt's   If you aren't a plus size, this plus-size boutique might well make you wish you were. The clothes—career wear, after 5, funky, and glam— are colorful, wildly fun, and expressive. The whimsical items are many; we especially liked the tin cutouts of "plus-size" angels and the assortment of fan pulls. 4537 Magazine St. ℂ **504/891-0063**. Mon–Sat 10:30am–5:30pm.

Trashy Diva   Despite the name, there is nothing trashy about the vintage clothes found here. They are absolute treasures, not the usual haphazard bulk found at other vintage shops, unique and in terrific shape, dating from the turn of the 20th century to the 1960s. The drawback is that you will pay through the nose for them. Many items are at least three figures—indeed, there was one showpiece 1920s flapper dress on display behind the counter recently, made of pure gold cloth, all yours for a mere $700. You can also admire garments from divas like Bette Davis and Joan Crawford that are on display. 2048 Magazine St. ✆ 888/818-DIVA or 504/299-8777. www.trashydiva.com. Daily noon–6pm.

Violet's   This is our greatest temptation among French Quarter shops, given how we feel about romantic, Edwardian, and '20s-inspired clothes in lush fabrics like velvet and satin. There are some dazzling creations here with appropriate accessories (jewelry, hats, scarves) as well. They also have a Violet's Two at 507 St. Ann St. (✆ **504/588-9894**). 808 Chartres St. ✆ **504/569-0088**. Fax 504/569-0089. Daily 10am–8pm.

Yvonne LaFleur—New Orleans   Yvonne LaFleur, a confessed incurable romantic, is the creator of beautifully feminine original designs. Her custom millinery, silk dresses, evening gowns, lingerie, and sportswear are surprisingly affordable, and all are enhanced by her signature perfume. Her store is in the Riverbend district. 8131 Hampson St. ✆ **504/866-9666**. www.yvonnelafleur.com. Mon–Wed and Fri–Sat 10am–6pm, Thurs 10am–8pm.

FOOD & DRINK

Martin Wine Cellar   If you're a wine lover or connoisseur—or if you want to become one—Martin Wine Cellar may be your most significant find in New Orleans. It carries an eye-popping selection of wines, spirits, and champagnes at surprisingly reasonable prices. It's not rare to find a $10 wine recommended and described in baffling detail. The store has an extensive selection of preserves, coffees, teas, crackers, biscotti, cookies, cheeses, and even cigars that are a perfect accompaniment to drinks (and that are often imported and hard to find elsewhere). There's also a deli in the store. A bigger location is at 714 Elmeer Ave. (in the 1200 block of Veterans Memorial Blvd.) in Metairie (✆ **504/896-7300**). 3827 Baronne St. ✆ 504/899-7411. www.martinwine.com. Mon–Sat 9am–7pm, Sun 10am–4pm.

FURNITURE

Prince & Pauper   Yes, we know furniture is hardly something you can easily fit into your carry-on luggage, but if you long to have an interior like some of the newer New Orleans homes, come to this fabulous store, which is stuffed full of items like dining room tables made from wood from old homes and plantations or romantic teak beds made in Indonesia and so much more. Though of late, their emphasis is leaning more towards French Regency—not our taste, but maybe yours. They ship, so don't worry. 2801 Magazine St. ✆ **504/899-2378**. Mon–Sat 10am–6pm, Sun 11–5pm.

GIFTS

Accent Annex Mardi Gras Headquarters   Need some Mardi Gras beads, masks, and other accouterments? This is one of the biggest suppliers of such things, and it has just about everything you need to properly celebrate Mardi Gras or stock up for that party you want to throw back home. String some green, gold, and purple beads around your neck, and everyone will know where you've been. Note the reasonably priced bags of used beads. Riverwalk. ✆ **504/568-9000**. www.accentannex.com. Mon–Sat 10am–9pm, Sun 11am–7pm.

Aux Belles Choses   This shop feels as though it could be located at a lonely crossroads in rural France. Maybe it's all the pretty dried plants and flowers (you can get arrangements made here). Or perhaps it's the endless variety of country French home, kitchen, and garden items. If you like creamy French soaps, especially with exotic scents, you'll probably leave with a handful—this place has many that are hard to find on this side of the Atlantic. 3912 Magazine St. ✆ 504/ 891-1009. www.abcneworleans.com. Mon–Sat 10am–5pm.

Bellanoche   One more ultra-fine shop, dripping with comfort and luxury, from the proprietor of the Belladonna day spa (2900 Magazine St., Kim Dudek. Bellanoche carries the best in bed linens, with lines like Bella Notte (washable embroidered satin) and Matteo & Co., as well as accessories such as dreamy pouf slipper/shoes by both Olivia Rose Tal and Amy Jo Gladstone. Touching these bed fabrics and marveling at the colors is enough to make "bedridden" something in which to look forward. 3708 Magazine St. ✆ 504/891-6483. www.belladonna dayspa.com. Tues–Sat 10am–6pm.

The Black Butterfly   The Black Butterfly is a place for any collector or admirer of miniatures. This fourth-generation shop (in business since 1894) is filled with porcelain, brass, wood, and pewter figures as well as dollhouse furniture and accessories. The store also has a collection of miniature soldiers and a selection of trains and cars. 727 Royal St. ✆ 504/524-6464. www.blackbutterfly.com. Mon–Sat 11am–6pm.

Casa del Corazón   Gifts, sundries, and folk arts "from the warm latitudes" with an emphasis on Latin America are here, with some Spanish, Italian, and African items. Among recent choices were Day of the Dead figures, pottery, crosses with milagro figures on them, some small furniture pieces (including antique Mexican wedding chests), ceremonial masks, religious amulets, and good-luck soaps. 901 Chartres St. ✆ 504/569-9555. Fax 504/525-9944. www.casacorazon. com. Daily 10am–5pm.

Gallery Inferno   This is the retail space for the artists who work at Studio Inferno in the Bywater, creating all kinds of clever glassworks, from a local perspective. While the vases and so forth are all quite lovely, we are especially fond of glass variations on milagros, images of hearts, eyes, hands, and other body parts topped with a flame, each with its own symbolic meeting. Very affordable, they make distinctive gifts. 3336 Magazine St. ✆ 504/891-1006. Tues–Thurs noon–5pm, Fri noon–6pm.

Importicos   You might think there is plenty of exotica for sale in New Orleans, but this store goes well beyond the bounds—literally, as the owners regularly travel to Indonesia, among other countries, for high-quality ethnic imports. If you've been to Bali, you will recognize some of the carved wooden doodads for sale here. Selections include handcrafted silver jewelry, pottery, textiles, antique and museum reproduction earrings, and leather, wood, stone, and metal items, often made especially for the shop. You'll also find teak, mahogany, and wrought-iron furniture and reproductions of 17th- and 18th-century mirrors. 5523 Magazine St. (✆ 504/891-6141; www.importicos.com); daily 10am–6pm. 736 Royal St. ✆ 504/523-3100. Mon–Thurs 10am–6pm, Fri–Sat 10am–7pm, Sun 11am–7pm.

Janet Molero   The owner of this store is an interior designer, but we like her shop for its assortment of fragrant candles and other gifts. 3935 Magazine St. ✆ 504/269-8305. www.janetmolero.com. Mon–Sat 10am–5pm.

Living Room   The friendly owner here has done a fine job assembling the wares at her original folk-craft store, almost making up for the loss of the site's former occupant, the beloved Olive Book Store. The Living Room holds an eclectic assortment of old and new furnishings, knickknacks (think frames made of wood from old plantations, old spoons, and other recycled materials), fine art, and antiques. Be sure to say hi to the store dogs, Louise and Oil ("Earl" with an accent), who are neighborhood characters (Earl is featured as Mr. Louisiana in a recent book called *Dog Bless America*). The Uptown Living Room, 3324 Magazine St. (✆ **504/891-8251**) offers a similar, but just different enough to make it worth its own trip, selection of gifts and folk art as well as fun fashions. 927 Royal St. ✆ 504/595-8860. Mon–Sat 10am–6pm, Sun noon–6pm.

Lost Nation Casting   Ed and Sarah Huber have re-created an old-world art for modern-day uses. Their store showcases items hand-cast in their own molds from reconstituted stone. Based mainly on classical, Renaissance, baroque, and Victorian designs, pieces are available for the home, courtyard, or garden. If you're looking for a highly artistic New Orleans water meter cover, it's here and ready to hang. 4332 Magazine St. ✆ 504/894-9660. Tues–Sat 11am–6pm.

Orient Expressed Imports   This shop features a fascinating collection of antiques, santos, and objets d'art from around the world—too much stuff for the shop to hold, so be sure to ask for the key to the warehouse next door. The shop also offers its own line of hand-smocked children's clothing plus toys and gifts. 3905 Magazine St. ✆ 888/856-3948 or 504/899-3060. www.orientexpressed.com. Mon–Sat 10am–5pm.

The Private Connection and Pieces   This shop specializes in the arts of Indonesia, including handcrafted gifts and jewelry, unique furniture, and architectural pieces. It also carries both antique and contemporary furnishings. 1116 Decatur St. ✆ 888/263-9693 or 504/593-9526 in the French Quarter. 3927 Magazine St. ✆ 504/899-4944. 538 Madison. ✆ 877/410-2254. www.theprivateconnection.com. All locations Mon–Sat 9am–6pm.

Scriptura   If you can't bear to scratch down notes with a pencil on a steno pad from the drugstore, you're a prime candidate for a romp through Scriptura. This store has everything related to the elegant art of scribbling. You can get designer stationery, glass fountain pens, sealing wax, and all types of generic or specific (travel, cigar, wine, restaurant) journals. This is the kind of place where you can find a gift for that impossible-to-shop-for person in your life. They have also opened a new location at 328 Chartres St. (✆ **504/229-1234**). 5423 Magazine St. ✆ 504/897-1555. www.scriptura.com. Mon–Fri 10am–6pm, Sat 10am–5pm.

Shop of the Two Sisters   This shop has upscale "girly" items such as throw pillows, lamps, sconces, accessories, unique accent pieces (with an emphasis on florals and fruits), and upholstery. Here you'll find consumerism at its most beautiful, but be prepared to pay for it. 1800 Magazine St. ✆ 504/525-2747. www.shopoftwosisters.com. Mon–Sat 10am–6pm.

Simon of New Orleans   Folk artist Simon, whose brightly painted signs are seen throughout New Orleans in homes and businesses, will paint to order your own personal sign and ship it to you. This gallery and shop is shared with Simon's wife, Maria, who has particularly good taste in primitive furniture, antiques, and hodgepodgery. 2126 Magazine St. ✆ 504/561-0088. Mon–Sat 10am–5pm.

Three Dog Bakery   An increasingly high-profile chain of dog treats that mimic the sugary-chocolately delights humans love, but dogs can't eat. Here they are made dog-friendly and are a big hit with guilt-ridden travelers who left Fido and Rover at home. 827 Royal St. ℂ 504/525-2253. Fax 504/525-2252. www.threedog.com. Daily 10am–6pm.

Utopia   Utopia seems to be popular with a specific demographic combination: mothers with their college-age daughters. Most of the products here are natural or organically derived, and many are meant to calm your spirits. There's a variety of women's casual clothing (much of it made of flax and flaxseed) in neutral colors. Many small, earth-colored furniture items—mirrors, chests, lamps, and hanging shelves—are strewn about. 5408 Magazine St. ℂ 504/899-8488. www. utopianola.com. Mon–Sat 10am–6pm, Sun noon–5pm.

Vintage 429   "Fun. Funky. Fabulous" is how they bill themselves, and it is a pretty jocular place, full of autographed memorabilia and some quite pretty antique jewelry and good old watches. It's all eye-catching, though a little too pricey for impulse buys. 429 Royal St. ℂ 866-VINT429 or 504/529-2288. www. vintage429.com. Mon–Sat 10am–6pm, Sun 10am–5pm.

HATS

Little Shop of Fantasy   This store (see "Costumes & Masks," earlier in this chapter) also sells fun costume hats.

Meyer the Hatter   Meyer's opened more than 100 years ago and has been in the same family ever since. Today, the haberdashery has one of the largest selections of fine hats and caps in the South. Men will find distinguished international labels like Stetson, Kangol, Akubra, Dobbs, and Borsalino (and there are some hats for women as well). 120 St. Charles Ave. ℂ 800/882-4287 or 504/525-1048. www.meyerthehatter.com. Mon–Sat 10am–5:45pm.

JEWELRY

Bedazzle   If you like contemporary jewelry, head for Bedazzle, where jewelry is art. It has everything you'd expect to find in a traditional jewelry store, only the merchandise is a lot more interesting. The staff is extremely helpful and friendly—and is patient with rubberneckers. 635 St. Peter St. ℂ 504/529-3248. Fax 504/524-27627. www.bedazzlejewelry.com. Daily 10:30am–6pm.

Brass Lion   This store is stuffed full of new, rather frilly jewelry from different designers. All the selections are romantic and often have a vintage feel to them. Appropriately enough, the store recently added vintage and estate jewelry at some of the most affordable prices in town—often only three figures. 516 Royal St. ℂ 504/525-9815. Daily 10am–6pm.

Hoover Watches & Jewels   A clever, and not unreasonably priced, collection of antique and contemporary jewelry and watches, chosen with considerable care. As lagniappe, owner Stacy Hoover loves to give tourists all kinds of insider tips to New Orleans. 301 Royal St. ℂ 504/522-7289. Fax 504/522-7093. www.hoover watchesandjewels.com. Mon–Thurs 10:30am–5:30pm, Fri–Sat 10:30am–6:30pm, Sun noon–5pm.

Katy Beh Contemporary Jewelry   The modern design of the store's structure sets the stage for what is housed within. Katy Beh, herself a jewelry artist, personally selected pieces made by celebrated designers and fresh new talent from across the U.S. Bring in your own stones to be remade into a distinctive piece or choose a new luxurious gold, silver, or gemstone item. 3701 Magazine St. ℂ 504/896-9600. www.katybeh.com. Mon–Sat 10am–5pm.

Mignon Faget, Ltd.   Mignon Faget is one of the biggest personalities in New Orleans's jewelry universe. The designer is a New Orleans native; in fact, some of her ancestors moved here to escape the French Revolution, while others were long-time plantation owners. Today, in her main studio display room, you can see some of her signature styles—gold, silver, and bronze d'oré fashioned into pendants, bracelets, rings, earrings, shirt studs, and cufflinks. There are other stores at 710 Dublin St. (© **504/865-7361**), uptown in the Riverbend area, and an Uptown location at 3801 Magazine St. (© **504/891-2005**). Canal Place, Level 1. © **800/ 375-7557** or 504/524-2973. www.mignonfaget.com. Mon–Sat 10am–7pm, Sun noon–6pm.

Sabai Jewelry Gallery This store offers a unique array of Asian and hand-crafted jewelry. The stones (all natural) and settings are displayed on antique wooden block prints (some on flat stones embedded in rice). But the best part is when one discovers the lack of designer prices that usually tag along with incredible designs. The Asian photographs, silk pillows, and beaded bags are interesting gift items. Unlike most shops on Magazine, this is open 7 days a week. 3115 Magazine St. © **504/899-9555**. 924 Royal St. © **504/525-6211**. Daily 10am–6pm.

MUSIC

In addition to the giant **Tower Records** at 408 N. Peters St. (© **504/529-4411**), there are a few other places you should check out for music, especially if you still have a turntable.

Beckham's Bookshop It's better known for its fine collection of used books (see "Books" earlier in this chapter), but Beckham's also has a large selection of secondhand classical LPs. 228 Decatur St. © **504/522-9875**. Daily 10am–6pm.

Louisiana Music Factory This popular store carries a large selection of regional music—including Cajun, zydeco, R&B, jazz, blues, and gospel—plus books, posters, and T-shirts. It also has frequent live music and beer bashes—shop while you bop! 210 Decatur St. © **504/586-1094**. www.louisianamusicfactory.com. Daily 10am–7pm.

Rock & Roll Records & Collectibles The name says it all—kind of. The owners say (and who are we to dispute?) that this is the largest and best collection of vinyl anywhere—including 45s and 78s—which means the shop carries many more genres than just rock 'n' roll. This place is record nerd heaven—the walls are lined with classics and floor space is at a minimum thanks to boxes and crates full of records. Prices are negotiable. 1214 Decatur St. © **504/561-5683**. www. rockcollectibles.org. Daily 10am–8pm.

THE OCCULT

The Bottom of the Cup Tearoom It's been open since 1929 and bills itself as the "oldest tearoom in the United States." In addition to having a psychic consultation, you can also purchase books, jewelry, crystal balls, tarot cards, crystals, and healing wands. 732 Royal St. © **504/523-1204**. Mon–Fri 10am–6pm, Sat–Sun 11am–7pm.

Esoterica This is the hip witch store for all your occult needs. Well, maybe not all, but they cover both pagan witch and voodoo rituals with their potions, herbs, gris-gris bags, and selection of related books plus similar magical and death-oriented jewelry. 541 Dumaine St. © **504/581-7711**. www.onewitch.com. Daily noon–10pm.

Marie Laveau's House of Voodoo This is the place for voodoo dolls and gris-gris bags. It's tourist voodoo, to be sure, but such items make great souvenirs for the right friends, and it's a fun store to poke around in. 739 Bourbon St. © **504/ 581-3751**. Daily 10am–midnight.

11

New Orleans After Dark

New Orleans is one of the most beautiful cities in the United States, possibly the world, but we won't mind if you never see the sights—provided, however, that the omission is because you are spending the daylight hours recovering from the equally extraordinary nightlife.

This is a city of music and rhythm. It is impossible to imagine New Orleans without a soundtrack of jazz, Cajun, and zydeco. Music streams from every doorway, and sometimes it seems people are dancing down the street. Sometimes they really are. (After all, this is the town that sends you to your grave with music and then dances back from the cemetery.) You walk along Bourbon Street, for example, and with every step you hear music of all varieties. Maybe none of it is world class, but that doesn't matter too much. It's just that it's there and in such variety. Plus, it's darn infectious.

This is also the city of decadence and good times rolling. Not to mention really loose liquor laws and drinks in "go" cups (plastic containers you can take with you—many bars and clubs even have walk-up windows for easy refills). And all this increases at night. We aren't just talking about the open-air frat party that is Bourbon Street some (okay, most) evenings. In fact, we prefer not to talk about that at all.

Most important is that virtually every night dozens of clubs all over town offer music that can range from average to extraordinary but is never less than danceable. In most places, cover prices vary from night to night

and performer to performer, but rarely will you have to pay more than $10—and then only for more highfalutin places like the House of Blues.

When the clubs get too full, no matter; the crowd spills into the street, talking, drinking, and still dancing right there on the sidewalk (the music is often plenty audible out there). Sometimes the action outside is even more fun than inside, not to mention less hot and sweaty.

Club hopping is easy, though with some exceptions some of the better choices will require leaving the Quarter by cab or some other vehicle. Don't worry—most are a cheap cab ride away, and many are within an additional, even cheaper cab ride, if not walking distance, of each other. We strongly urge you to leave the Quarter at night to visit some of the town's better joints.

However, if you aren't up to that, don't fret. Several of the best jazz and brass band clubs are right in the Quarter. And only steps away is the scene in the Frenchmen section of the Faubourg Marigny, where at least five clubs are going at once within 3 blocks of each other. People wander from one to the other, sometimes never bothering to pay the cover price and go inside. If you do your evening right, those calories you consumed all day long will be gone by morning.

Or, yes, you could spend your night running from bar to bar. There is no lack. With such great music available, that seems a waste of time, however; if all you wanted to do was drink, you could have stayed home and enjoyed yourself just as much. Still, it is New Orleans, and some of these places are as convivial and atmospheric as you will ever find; ducking into a few isn't a bad idea at all. And of course, everything only gets livelier and wilder as the evening goes on.

Speaking of which, don't be fooled by the times given in local listings for band performances. If it says 10pm, the band will probably go on closer to midnight and keep playing until late. Really late. This isn't always true—once in a blue moon, an act will go on when billed and finish up rather early—but chances are good that if you come late, even really late, you will still catch quite a bit of the act you came to see.

However you decide to do it, don't miss it. New Orleans at night is not New Orleans during the day, and not to take advantage of it is to miss out. You could stay in your hotel room with the covers pulled over your head,

but if that's what you want, you came to the wrong city: Just tell yourself you'll sleep when you get home.

For up-to-date information on what's happening around town, look for current editions of *Gambit, Offbeat,* and *Where,* all distributed free in most hotels and all record stores. You can also check out *Offbeat* on the Internet (www.nola.com; once you get to the NOLA home page, go to the music and entertainment section). Other sources include the *Times-Picayune*'s daily entertainment calendar and Friday's **"Lagniappe"** section of the newspaper. Additionally, **WWOZ** (90.7 FM) broadcasts the local music schedule several times throughout the day.

For the nightlife listings in this chapter, see either the "New Orleans Nightlife," "French Quarter Nightlife," or "Uptown Nightlife" maps in this chapter or the "Mid-City Attractions & Nightlife" map on p. 163 of chapter 8, "Sights to See & Places to Be."

1 The Rhythms of New Orleans

The late New Orleans R&B legend Ernie K-Doe was once quoted as saying, "I'm not sure, but I think all music came from New Orleans." What might be a more accurate account—and relatively hyperbole-free—is that all music came *to* New Orleans. Any style you can name, from African field hollers to industrial techno-rock, has found its way to the Crescent City, where it's been blended, shaken, and stirred into a new, distinctive, and usually frothy concoction that, it seems, could have come from nowhere else.

"Yeah," you scoff, "but what about classical music?" Well, maybe you've never heard how pianist James Booker, an eye-patched eccentric even by New Orleans standards, could make a Bach chorale strut like a second-line umbrella twirler. Or maybe you're forgetting that Wynton Marsalis has Grammy Awards for both jazz and classical recordings, not to mention a 1997 Pulitzer Prize for his slavery-themed jazz oratorio *Blood on the Fields.*

On the other side of the spectrum, don't forget that Trent Reznor, the man behind the brutal sounds and imagery of the industrial act Nine Inch Nails, has chosen to live and record in New Orleans—not because of the good property values but because the aesthetics and atmosphere suit him. (His studio is in a former funeral home, natch.)

Even more unusual is the New Orleans Klezmer All Stars ensemble, a group of musicians that plays the lively music of Eastern European Jewish troubadours with a few New Orleans embellishments. You're not required to dance at their performances, but you'll probably find it impossible not to.

Of course, what you're most likely to experience is somewhere in the middle, music more truly rooted in the Crescent City—the Storyville jazz descended from Louis Armstrong and Jelly Roll Morton, the bubbly R&B transmitted via Fats Domino and Professor Longhair, the Mardi Gras Indians and the brass bands of the second lines that recently have gotten exuberant, youthful infusions of funk and hip-hop.

Finding music in New Orleans is no trick. Walk anywhere in the vicinity of Bourbon Street and your ears will be assaulted by a variety of sounds. If you're really interested, it's worth a little effort to seek out the good stuff and avoid the tourist-oriented caricatures that will be thrust at you. Consult the free monthly *Offbeat*, available at many businesses in the French Quarter and elsewhere around town, for what's playing at such clubs as the Howlin' Wolf, Donna's, the Maple Leaf, Tipitina's, or the gotta-see-it-to-believe-it Mid City Lanes bowling alley, home of the famed Rock 'n' Bowl. Listen to public radio station WWOZ-FM (90.7 FM), which plays the best of New Orleans music and gives concert info. For planning in advance, both *Offbeat* (www.nola.com; once you get to the NOLA home page, go to the music and entertainment section) and the radio station (www.wwoz.org) have easily accessible websites.

THE JAZZ LIFE OF NEW ORLEANS

by George Hocutt

Jazz historian and executive producer of the Grammy Award–winning
album Doc Cheatham & Nicholas Payton

New Orleans did not invent jazz, but the crescents in the Mississippi River became the crucible in which jazz evolved. The city's French Catholic background has always inspired a more tolerant attitude toward the simple pleasures of the world than did the Puritan fathers from Plymouth Rock. Melodic sounds of all kinds were one of those pleasures.

Music was of great importance to the Louisiana settlers and their Creole offspring, and the city early on had a fascination with marching bands and parades. As early as 1787, Governor Miro entertained a gathering of Indian leaders with a parade. Eventually, bands were required for nearly every occasion—Mardi Gras, dedications, religious holidays, cornerstone layings, weddings, funerals, ad infinitum. With this plethora of musical activities, one major ingredient was in great need: musicians.

The musicians of early New Orleans were expected to do just what the word implied—provide music. They were not categorized or labeled by any brand or style of music. They were considered tradesmen just like other skilled craftsmen such as carpenters, shoemakers, what have you. From an afternoon parade, they might be required to play at the opera and then possibly a late dance. At the dance, the program would call for waltzes, gallops, gavottes, and quadrilles, among others. (The jazz song "Tiger Rag" derived from a quadrille.) Obviously, these 19th-century instrumentalists were quite accomplished and versatile.

In the early 19th century, slaves were allowed to congregate in the area known as **Congo Square** for dancing to the rhythms of their homelands' drums and other percussive instruments. With the passing of time, many slaves, former slaves, and free men of color became accomplished instrumentalists. There were Negro marching bands in New Orleans before the Civil War, and many continued playing during the city's occupation by simply changing their gray uniforms for the Union blue.

Some of these musicians, possibly graduates of the Congo Square gatherings, brought to their playing a native rhythm that was likely a primitive syncopation. In an evolutionary way, many of New Orleans's musicians began absorbing this amalgam of European and African influences. Then came the addition of the very personal statements of the blues, work songs, hollers, and spirituals. The music was changing and was taking on a certain American and distinctly New Orleanian aura.

In the 1870s, two men were born who were to have a profound effect on the music. **"Papa" Jack Laine** was born in 1873 and **Charles "Buddy" Bolden** in 1878, both in New Orleans.

Bolden, a cornetist who would later be known as the First Man of Jazz, began playing dances and parties around 1895. By 1897, he had put together the band that most old-timers remember. They also remember that, when Bolden put his cornet up and blew loud from Johnson Park in uptown New Orleans, he could be heard for miles around. Fans said, "Buddy's callin' his chickens home." Unfortunately, Bolden was committed to an institution for the insane in 1907, where he died in 1931, never having recorded.

At approximately the same time, Papa Jack, primarily a drummer, formed several groups simultaneously, all called the Reliance Band. They played all over the Gulf Coast and in New Orleans and were extremely popular. Almost all the early white New Orleans jazzmen played in one of Laine's groups. He withdrew from the music business around the time of World War I, but his legacy lived on through the many greats he fostered; later known as Papa Jack's children.

Much of what we know of these two pioneers we have learned from taped interviews with men who were already old at the time they were interviewed—but not old enough to remember the music scene before Bolden and Laine. Names that have emerged, though dimly, include the legendary Mass Quamba, William Martin, Picayune Butler, and a performer known as Old Corn Meal. All of them likely added their own touches to the evolution of New Orleans music.

Concurrent with Bolden and Laine's contributions to the musical life of the city, another event that would affect the spread of jazz everywhere was unfolding. **Storyville,** the only prescribed district for legalized prostitution ever attempted in this country, operated from 1897 to 1917. The most elegant houses were along the lake side of Rampart Street between Iberville and Conti streets. Among them were the Arlington and Lulu White's Mahogany Hall.

No documentation or mention in the taped oral histories of early New Orleans jazzmen (contained in the jazz archives at Tulane University) tells us of an orchestra ever playing in any of the houses, but most of them did have a piano player in the parlor. Among those entertainers were Spencer Williams, later a very successful songwriter; Tony Jackson, who wrote *Pretty Baby;* and the immortal **Jelly Roll Morton.**

Born Ferdinand Joseph Lamothe (his actual name, established by jazz researcher Lawrence Gushee from Jelly's baptismal certificate) in 1890, Morton was the first true jazz composer and, next to Louis Armstrong, the most important figure in early jazz. His compositions were recorded well into the swing era and are still performed today. He was inducted into the Rock and Roll Hall of Fame in the Early Influence category.

Although the houses did not use bands for entertainment, there were many playing opportunities in the bars and clubs that dotted Storyville and the adjacent areas. These clubs—the Arlington Annex, the Cadillac, Frank Early's, 101 Ranch, the Frenchmen's, Pete Lala's, among others—all featured bands. The great musicians of New Orleans all played in the clubs and doubled during the day in the multitude of brass bands that were always in demand. All the prominent names of early New Orleans jazz served this apprenticeship, including Freddy

Keppard, King Oliver, Kid Ory, Sidney Bechet, Papa Celestin, "Big Eye" Louis Nelson, Buddy Petit, Bunk Johnson, Johnny and Baby Dodds, Alphonse Picou, Achille Baquet, Lorenzo Tio, and Tommy Ladnier. The list could go on and on.

As early as 1916, some New Orleans bands that included many of Papa Jack's children decided to try the musical climate in Chicago. Freddy Keppard and the Original Creole Band had been spreading music from New Orleans throughout the country in concerts and on vaudeville stages, but the groups going to Chicago made extended stays at specified clubs. The most successful group was the **Original Dixieland Jazz Band,** led by Nick LaRocca. The ODJB moved on from Chicago to open at Reisenweber's Cafe in New York City in 1917. They were a smash. Everybody loved the new music from New Orleans. After an abortive attempt by Columbia Records, they cut the first jazz record ever, released by Victor Records on February 16, 1917. The record, coupling "Livery Stable Blues" and "Dixie Jazz Band One Step," was an instant hit and was soon topping whatever hit parade existed at that time. The jazz flood had started.

In October 1917, the houses of Storyville were completely shut down by order of the U.S. Navy, and a great many jobs for entertainers and musicians started drying up. The performers began to look elsewhere for work. Apparently, word was filtering back to the city of the success the former New Orleanians were enjoying up north. Many decided to follow that example.

Kid Ory headed to California, where he made the first black jazz record. King Oliver traveled to Chicago in 1919, taking Johnny Dodds and other New Orleans musicians with him. After a brief sojourn in California, he returned to Chicago, and in 1922, he sent for **Louis Armstrong** to come up and join King Oliver's Creole Jazz Band—arguably the greatest collection of jazz musicians ever assembled (and all but one were natives of New Orleans). A young Emmett Hardy, the legendary white cornetist, went on tour with Bea Palmer and, while playing in Davenport, Iowa, was reportedly an influence on the great Bix Beiderbecke. Bix got his earliest musical experience by playing along with Nick LaRocca records. The New Orleans Rhythm Kings, all New Orleans musicians, opened at the Friars Inn in Chicago in 1922; cornetist Paul Mares certainly influenced Beiderbecke, who was attending school nearby and often sat in with the band. Jazz was spreading rapidly, and New Orleans musicians were in great demand by other groups around the country. Every other leader wanted to bring that something special to his music.

After leaving Oliver, Louis Armstrong, already the greatest soloist in jazz, went on to become one of the greatest entertainers and stars we have ever known. At one time, his were probably the most identifiable face and voice in the world. Nearly 30 years after his death, his records are still bestsellers. He transcended New Orleans and became a national treasure.

Sidney Bechet settled in France after World War II and became a huge star performer and prolific composer. On his wedding day, a total holiday was declared in Antibes, and the entire city participated in a massive wedding party, dancing to music he had written.

New Orleans is still producing jazz greats. There is Harry Connick Jr., who is making his mark in Hollywood as well as in music. **Ellis Marsalis** has fathered a group of jazz-playing sons, including trumpeter Wynton, who won a 1997 Pulitzer Prize for his composition *Blood on the Fields,* the first such award for a jazz composer. **Nicholas Payton** is another rising trumpet player from New Orleans. In 1998, Payton and Doc Cheatham shared the Grammy Award for best instrumental recording for their performance of "Stardust" on the album *Doc Cheatham & Nicholas Payton.* Obviously, the city still abounds with creativity.

Much remains in New Orleans for the adventurous jazz fan and explorer. Morton's home still stands on Frenchmen Street. Buddy Bolden's house is on First Street in Uptown, and a monument to him stands in Holt Cemetery, where he was buried in an unmarked grave. A plaque marks the house on Chartres Street where Danny Barker was born. At Rampart and Conti streets, one of Lulu White's buildings remains standing. Down the street is Frank Early's saloon (now a neighborhood convenience store). There is more, but that should give you an idea. Search them out. You can get six free pamphlets detailing different jazz history walking tours, sponsored by the New Orleans Jazz Commission by contacting the New Orleans Jazz National Historic Park, 916 N. Peters (© 504/589-4841; www.nps.gov/neor), or by visiting the Louisiana Music Factory store (p. 220). Alternatively, look at some of the books about music we've recommended on p. 297.

Music still resounds around the town. Although many of the originals are gone, **Preservation Hall** continues to showcase younger players. The **Palm Court Jazz Cafe** offers good jazz 5 nights a week. **Donna's** books great local music, including brass bands that currently also perform in the streets of the city. **Snug Harbor** on Frenchmen Street presents a broad spectrum of jazz from traditional to modern. **Fritzel's** on Bourbon Street hosts weekend jam sessions. The Hilton has a sensational Sunday morning jazz brunch and is home to **Pete Fountain's club.** The Dukes of Dixieland appear nightly on the *Natchez,* a riverboat excursion. Other bands play for daytime sailings.

So certainly there is life in the old gal yet. Whether it's in the water, the air, or that good Creole cooking, jazz continues to grow in the fertile soil that settles on the banks of the curves of the Mississippi River.

BRASS BANDS

If your idea of New Orleans brass bands is merely the postfuneral "second line" parade of "When the Saints Go Marching In," you're in for some joyous surprises. In recent years, young African-American kids have picked up the tradition and given it new life while also stimulating renewed interest in some of the veteran practitioners. At its roots, it's primal jazz nonpareil, with group improvisations, unexpected turns, and spirit to burn.

The key act of the current revival was the **ReBirth Brass Band,** a gaggle of teens and preteens who in the late 1980s and early 1990s tossed pop-funk tunes like "Grazin' in the Grass" and the Doobie Brothers' "Takin' It to the Streets" into their mix of New Orleans standards. They even had a local hit with "Do Whatcha Wanna." The group's still around, though trumpeter Kermit Ruffins, who as a preteen Louis Armstrong look- and sound-alike was the centerpiece, left several years ago to form his own versatile jazz band, the Barbecue Swingers. Others working today in the same vein include **New Birth** and **Olympia,** while such newer arrivals as the **Soul Rebels** and **Coolbone** have added hip-hop and reggae styles to the blend, often with terrific results. At the same time, older ensembles like the **Olympia Brass Band** have gained from the interest. One highlight of Jazz Fest week is the free brass band showdown held at the Louisiana Music Factory record store in the Quarter. And once a week or so, you can catch the best brass bands at **Donna's.**

CAJUN & ZYDECO

Two of the music styles often associated with New Orleans are technically not from there at all. Both Cajun and zydeco really originated in the bayou of southwest Louisiana, a good 3 hours away. And while it's customary for the two to be named in the same breath, they are not the same thing—though they are arguably two sides of the same coin.

The foundations of the two styles lie in the arrival of two different French-speaking peoples in the swamp country: the Acadians, French migrants who were booted out of Nova Scotia by the English in 1755, and the Creole people who were jettisoned by or escaped from the Caribbean slave trade of the same era. Entwined by the pervasive poverty and hardship of the region and by their common status as underclass peoples—the white Acadians, or Cajuns as the name was eventually corrupted, were beaten by schoolteachers for speaking French well into the 20th century, while the Creoles suffered the same oppression as blacks elsewhere—the cultures blended in many ways, nowhere more evidently than in their music.

Introduction of the button accordion and its folksy, diatonic scale was a key development. It added a richness and power to what had largely been fiddle and guitar music. Early recordings of such seminal figures as Joe Falcon (a white man) and Amede Ardoin (a Creole) reveal a rough-hewn music tied to ancient tunes rooted in France and elsewhere, with hints of influence from the sounds starting to arrive through the radio and recordings of popular tunes. Such acts as the **Hackberry Ramblers,** who still perform today with a couple of more or less original members, played the dance-hall circuits from New Orleans into Texas through the 1930s. Many added drums and amplifiers and steel guitars as they became available to fill out the sound.

In the postwar era, the styles began to separate more, with the Cajuns gravitating toward country and western swing and Creole musicians heavily influenced by the urban blues. The purer music of the region was suppressed and nearly lost in the 1950s, though such figures as **D. L. Menard** (the Cajun Hank Williams) and **Clifton Chenier** (the King of Zydeco) pioneered exciting new strains in their respective directions. Chenier, at first performing with just his brother Cleveland on washboard percussion, was among those who took up the chromatic "piano"-style accordion, which suited the blues in ways the button accordion could not. Menard, as his nickname indicates, melded Cajun with the style of the country balladeer he idolized (and met once, providing a tale he's joyously told countless times). In 1959, Menard wrote "La Porte Den Arriere" (The Back Door), which along with the traditional "Jolie Blon" is certainly the most-performed song in the Cajun repertoire.

The great folk music boom of the early 1960s spilled over to Cajun music, and such figures as the **Balfa Brothers** and fiddler **Dennis McGee** suddenly had the opportunity to perform at such folk festivals as the famed Newport gathering. A turning point came when a Cajun group received a standing ovation at the 1964 Newport Festival. It was a real boost for the form and for Cajun pride, both of which seemed on the verge of extinction. With such younger musicians as **Marc Savoy,** who had begun producing homemade accordions of fine quality, providing new energy and commitment, and such entrepreneurs as Floyd Soileau recording the styles of the region, Cajun music gained new life.

This spawned a new generation, proud of their Cajun musical legacy but also fueled by rock-and-roll. Leading the way are fiddler **Michael Doucet** and his band, **Beausoleil,** now Cajun music's best-known band. Even if he hasn't always delighted the purists, Doucet has been a tireless ambassador for his heritage.

In zydeco, Clifton Chenier led the way from the '50s on, with a handful of others (the late Boozoo Chavis, John Delafose, Rockin' Sydney) adding their own embellishments. Chenier, recorded by Ville Platte's Floyd Soileau and Berkeley-based Chris Strackwitz's Arhoolie Records, became internationally famous, even playing the esteemed Montreaux Jazz Festival in Switzerland. His name loomed so large over the field that, at his death in the mid-'80s, there seemed to be no one ready to step into his royal shoes.

But after a little drifting, zydeco has, arguably, grown stronger than ever. A new generation, including Chenier's son C.J. and Delafose's son Geno, is updating the old traditions, while such figures as **Keith Frank, Nathan Williams,** and the late **Beau Jocque,** who died in 1999, have added their own variations of funk, hip-hop, and blues.

RHYTHM & BLUES

Technically, the blues is not a New Orleans form, belonging more to the rural delta and, in its urban forms, Texas and Chicago. But rhythm and blues, with its gospel and African-Caribbean bloodlines, carries a Crescent City heartbeat. In the '50s, **Fats Domino,** along with his great producer-collaborator Dave Bartholemew, fused those elements into such seminal songs as "Blueberry Hill" and "Walkin' to New Orleans"—music that still fuels much of the New Orleans R&B sound today. At the same time, such then-unheralded figures as **Professor Longhair** and **"Champion" Jack Dupree** developed earthier variations of the piano-based sound, contrasting mournful woe with party-time spirit.

The keepers of the flame today are the **Neville Brothers,** who in their various combinations and incarnations (the Meters, Aaron Neville's solo projects, and so on) have explored and expanded just about every direction of this music.

And if the Nevilles are the royal family of New Orleans music, **Irma Thomas** is its duchess of soul. Though she only had one national hit ("Wish Somebody Would Care"), her feel for a song and her magnanimous spirit have led devotees to make regular pilgrimages to her club, the Lion's Den, to hear her perform. It's well worth joining them, but take a cab—it's not in a neighborhood in which you'd want to walk around.

2 Jazz & Blues Clubs

This being New Orleans, jazz and blues are everywhere—though not all of it is worth hearing. Not that any of it is bad, per se. It's just that there is world-class stuff out there competing with tourist traps for your ears, so don't just settle for the first sight (or sound) of brass instruments you find. Seek out the really good stuff, and you'll be rewarded. It's hard to predict opening/closing hours of New Orleans's nightlife. Many bars are open all the time, and because many clubs are in many bars (bars that have stages on which live bands play), there are no set opening and closing hours. In general, know that most clubs hours both start and end late, if they ever end at all.

THE FRENCH QUARTER & THE FAUBOURG MARIGNY

Donna's   A corner bar at the very northern edge of the Quarter, Donna's has become one of the top spots for great local music, including the revival of the brass band experience and a variety of jazz and blues traditions. A recent makeover, with a better-placed stage and table and chairs, has made it even more appealing. But the main asset may be Donna herself, monitoring the door to make sure you don't bring in drinks from outside and making sure you do order something inside. She's been one of the true boosters of new generations of New Orleans music (she's managed both the hip-hop-edged brass band Soul Rebels and the new-funk ensemble

Galactic) and has helped promote awareness of veteran brass bands like Treme and Olympia. As with most real New Orleans hangouts, atmosphere is minimal, but spirits (liquid and otherwise) are high. The cover charge for performances is usually no more than the cost of a good mixed drink. Well worth a stop on an evening of club hopping. ***Note:*** Donna's is in a transitional neighborhood, so be careful entering and leaving. 800 N. Rampart St. ℭ **504/596-6914.** Cover varies.

Fritzel's European Jazz Pub   You might walk right past this small establishment, but that would be a big mistake because the 1831 building brings some of the city's best musicians to play on its tiny stage. In addition to the regular weekend program of late-night jazz (Fri and Sat from 10:30pm, Sun from 10pm), there are frequent jam sessions in the wee hours during the week when performers end their stints elsewhere and gather to play "Musicians' Music." The full bar also stocks a variety of schnapps (served ice-cold) and German beers. 733 Bourbon St. ℭ **504/561-0432.** No cover; 1-drink minimum per set.

Funky Butt   Fret not—this is not a strip bar. Jazz aficionados will connect the name with a tune associated with New Orleans's own Buddy Bolden. There was another Funky Butt club in the early days of jazz; this more recent arrival is operated by the owner of the Magic Walking Tours. Downstairs is a typical funky bar; upstairs is a slightly more pleasing and mature performance space than that at other clubs in town (though not all of the sightlines are so great). It's leaning toward, if not totally achieving, smoky jazz nightclub ambience. Bookings emphasize jazz but can also include anything from the Wild Magnolias (the most famous of the Mardi Gras Indians; it's something special to see them here) to an amazing Billie Holiday tribute band. Creole and vegetarian food is available, and the club is only a block from Donna's (see above). ***Note:*** Although the club itself is safe, the neighborhood around it isn't always. Take a cab (yes, it seems silly, but even from Bourbon Street) to and from this area unless you're in a large group or in the city during a crowded time (Mardi Gras, Jazz Fest). 714 N. Rampart St. ℭ **504/558-0872.** www.funkybutt.com. Cover varies.

Funky Pirate   Decorated to resemble a pirates' lair, the Funky Pirate lives up to its name—especially the "funky" part. The Pirate is as far from urbane modern jazz as you can get, so there's no chance you'll confuse it with the Funky Butt (see above). The place seems to be perpetually full of loud beer drinkers, and at night it can get jam-packed. "Big" Al Carson and the Blues Masters hold court here playing live blues, and Big Al lives up to his name—especially the "big" part. 727 Bourbon St. ℭ **504/523-1960.** No cover, but 1-drink minimum.

Howl at the Moon   Look for piano bar music in a somewhat sophisticated atmosphere, thanks to a red-walled parlorlike room. 125 Bourbon St. ℭ **504/410-9000.** Sun–Thurs 4pm–2am, Fri–Sat 4pm–till . . . .

John Wehner's Famous Door   John Wehner no longer owns the club, so it's up to you to see how Famous it still is. Open since 1934, the Famous Door is the oldest music club on Bourbon Street. Many local jazz, pop, and rock musicians have passed through here. One of them, Harry Connick Jr., played his first gigs here at the age of 13. So far, it seems the club is similar to its old identity, but that may have changed by the time you read this. 339 Bourbon St. ℭ **504/522-7626.** Occasional cover. 1-drink minimum per set.

Maison Bourbon   Despite its location and the sign saying the building is "dedicated to the preservation of jazz" (which seems a clear attempt to confuse tourists into thinking this is the legendary Preservation Hall), Maison Bourbon

New Orleans Nightlife

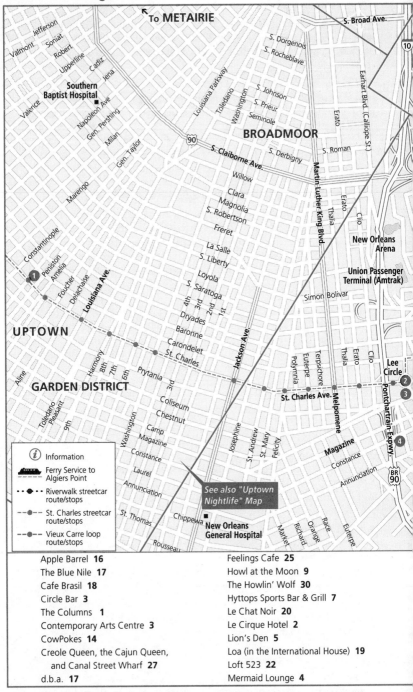

To METAIRIE

Southern Baptist Hospital

BROADMOOR

S. Claiborne Ave.

New Orleans Arena

Union Passenger Terminal (Amtrak)

UPTOWN

Lee Circle

GARDEN DISTRICT

St. Charles Ave.

Magazine

See also "Uptown Nightlife" Map

New Orleans General Hospital

(i) Information

Ferry Service to Algiers Point

Riverwalk streetcar route/stops

St. Charles streetcar route/stops

Vieux Carre loop route/stops

Apple Barrel **16**	Feelings Cafe **25**
The Blue Nile **17**	Howl at the Moon **9**
Cafe Brasil **18**	The Howlin' Wolf **30**
Circle Bar **3**	Hyttops Sports Bar & Grill **7**
The Columns **1**	Le Chat Noir **20**
Contemporary Arts Centre **3**	Le Cirque Hotel **2**
CowPokes **14**	Lion's Den **5**
Creole Queen, the Cajun Queen,	Loa (in the International House) **19**
and Canal Street Wharf **27**	Loft 523 **22**
d.b.a. **17**	Mermaid Lounge **4**

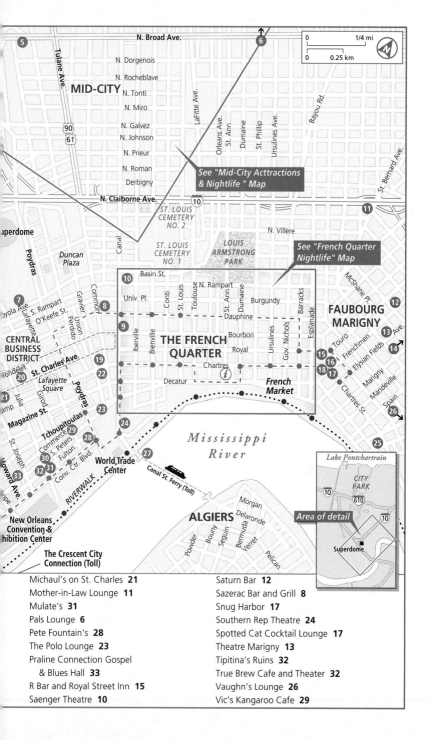

is not a tourist trap. The music is very authentic, and often superb, jazz. Stepping into the brick-lined room, or even just peering in from the street, takes you away from the mayhem outside. From about midafternoon until the wee hours, Dixieland and traditional jazz hold forth, often at loud and lively volume. Players include Wallace Davenport, Steve Slocum, and Tommy Yetta. Patrons must be at least 21 years old. 641 Bourbon St. ☎ **504/522-8818.** 1-drink minimum.

Palm Court Jazz Café   This is one of the most stylish jazz haunts in the Quarter. It's an elegant setting in which to catch top-notch jazz groups Wednesday through Sunday. The music varies nightly but is generally traditional or classic jazz. If you collect jazz records, peek at the records for sale in a back alcove. *Tip:* You might want to make reservations—it's that kind of place. 1204 Decatur St. ☎ **504/525-0200.** Cover $5 per person at tables; no cover at bar.

Preservation Hall   The gray, bombed-out building that looks as if it was erected just shortly after the dawn of time (or at least the dawn of New Orleans) doesn't seem like much, but it's a mecca for traditional jazz fans. This is an essential spot for anyone coming to New Orleans. No amplification, no air-conditioning—it doesn't get any more authentic than this. And it is one of your must-do stops on your trip.

With no seats, terrible sightlines, and constant crowds, you won't be able to see much, but you won't care because you will be having too fun and cheerfully sweaty a time. Even if you don't consider yourself interested in jazz, there is a seriously good time to be had here, and you very probably will come away with a new appreciation for the music. Patrons start lining up at 6:15pm—the doors open at 8pm, so the trick to avoid the line is to get there either just as the doors open or later in the evening. The band plays until midnight, and the first audience usually empties out around 10pm.

A 30-year-old sign on the wall gives prices for requests, but it's out-of-date. As the doorwoman said, "If we still took $5 for 'Saints Go Marchin' In,' they'd be playing it all night." (One night, some big spenders tossed seven $100 bills for seven rounds of "Saints.") Try about $10, and for other requests, "Just offer something." Thanks to the casual atmosphere, not to mention cheap cover, Preservation Hall is one of the few nightspots where it's appropriate to take kids. Early in the evening, you'll notice a number of local families doing just that. 726 St. Peter St. ☎ **800/785-5772** or 504/523-8939 after 8pm. www.preservationhall.com. Cover $5.

Snug Harbor   If your idea of jazz extends beyond Dixieland and if you prefer a concert-type setting over a messy nightclub, get your hands on Snug Harbor's monthly schedule. On the fringes of the French Quarter (1 block beyond Esplanade Ave.), Snug Harbor is the city's premier showcase for contemporary jazz, with a few blues and R&B combos thrown in for good measure. Here, jazz is presented as it should be: part entertainment, part art, and often, part intellectual stimulation. This is the surest place to find Ellis Marsalis (patriarch of the Marsalis dynasty) and Charmaine Neville (of the Neville family).

Not only does Snug offer good music, but the two-level seating provides universally good viewing of the bandstand. You should buy tickets in advance, but be warned: Waiting for a show usually means hanging in the crowded, low-ceilinged bar, where personal space is at a minimum—not recommended for claustrophobes. 626 Frenchmen St. ☎ **504/949-0696.** www.snugjazz.com. Cover $12–$20, depending on performer.

French Quarter Nightlife

ELSEWHERE AROUND THE CITY

Pete Fountain's   Pete Fountain has managed to make his name synonymous with New Orleans music. He grew up playing around town, moved to Chicago with the Dukes of Dixieland, joined Lawrence Welk's orchestra, and then, for more than 20 years, held forth in his own Bourbon Street club. These days, you'll find him here in a re-creation of his former Quarter premises, with seating for more than twice as many as the old club. Pete is featured in one show a night, a couple times a week. You'll need reservations. In the New Orleans Hilton, 2 Poydras St. ℭ **504/561-0500.** Cover $19 (includes 1 drink).

Praline Connection Gospel & Blues Hall   There are two Praline Connections in New Orleans, both operated by the same company. One is a restaurant on Frenchmen Street (p. 127) that serves regional soul food. The 9,000-square-foot Praline Connection Gospel & Blues Hall is a restaurant as well (with the same cuisine), but here you get live music with dinner on Thursday, Friday, and Saturday nights. Sunday brings a great gospel buffet brunch. Reservations are strongly recommended. 907 S. Peters St. ℭ **504/523-3973** for reservations and information. www.pralineconnection.com. Prices change often; call for updated price information.

Vaughan's Lounge   Tucked deep in the Bywater section of New Orleans, Vaughan's Lounge is way down home and right now one of the most happening spots for jazz in town. It's in a residential neighborhood and feels almost as though you're in someone's house. The long bar takes up so much room that people almost fall over the band at the end of the room. In the back room, you might find people playing Ping-Pong. Thursday—Kermit Ruffin's night—is the night to go to Vaughan's. Go early and get some of the barbecue Kermit is often cooking up before a show—he likes to barbecue as much as he likes to play, and he tends to bring his grill along with him wherever he is playing. When he isn't playing and helping out with the eats, you might catch a Mardi Gras Indian practice. Be sure to call ahead to see if there will be live music on, and be sure to take a taxi. 4229 Dauphine St. ℭ **504/947-5562.** Cover varies.

3 Cajun & Zydeco Joints

Most of the so-called Cajun joints in New Orleans are really Cajun for tourists, in both sound and setting. If you want the real thing, you are better off going out to bayou country. Which is not to say some of the finest Cajun bands don't play in New Orleans—it's just that you are likely to find, say, the world-renowned Beausoleil at the Maple Leaf or the Grammy-nominated Hackberry Ramblers at the Mermaid Lounge, neither of which is a Cajun club. None of this should be taken to mean that terrific and authentic Cajun bands don't play at the places listed below—it's just that it's hit-or-miss in terms of true quality. What these spots do offer, however, is a place to learn to Cajun dance, which is not only a skill that comes in handy in New Orleans (trust us, when crowds start to two-step, you'll want to join in) and a dandy way to burn off calories—but it's also just darn fun.

Michaul's on St. Charles   Michaul's attempts to re-create the Cajun dance hall experience, and for a prefab kind of place, it does it well enough. If you've experienced the real thing, you'll turn up your nose, but if you haven't, it'll do. Come for the free dance lessons; call for specific times (they change frequently). 840 St. Charles Ave. ℭ **504/522-5517.** www.michauls.com. No cover.

Mid City Lanes Rock 'n' Bowl   Anything we just said about tourist traps and inauthentic experiences does not apply here. It does not get any more authentic than a club set in the middle of a bowling alley, which is itself set in the middle

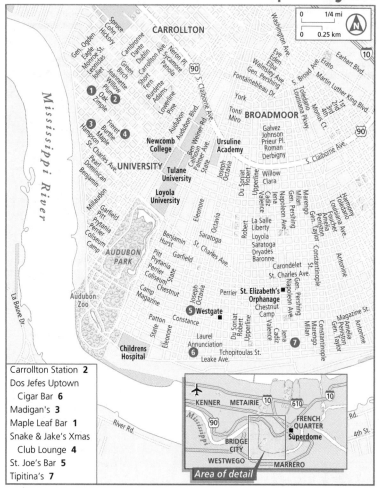

Uptown Nightlife

of a strip mall. Actually, as a bowling alley, Mid City bowling is nothing to write home about unless you like lanes that slope. But as a club, it's one of the finest and best experiences in New Orleans. Certainly it's the best place for zydeco, particularly on the nights devoted to Zydeco Wars, when the audience votes on whether, say, Geno Delafose or C. J. Chenier is the King of Zydeco. Mid City is not limited to just zydeco; it also features top New Orleans rock and R&B groups and some touring acts. On good nights (though we do wonder if Mid City has any that aren't), the dance floor is crowded beyond belief, the noise level is ridiculous, the humidity level is 300%, and you won't want to leave. You might even bowl a few frames. (Expect to wait for a lane.) For this listing, see map on p. 163. 4133 S. Carrollton Ave. ✆ **504/482-3133.** www.rockandbowl.com. Bowling: daytime and evening $12 per hour; show admission $5–$10.

Mulate's A branch of the original (out in Cajun country) and a not-unlikely place to find authentic, and decent, Cajun bands. The stage and dance area are relatively spacious, and the food isn't bad. It's in the same neighborhood as Michaul's (see above), so if you get the Cajun bug, you can easily do both places in a night. 201 Julia St., at Convention Center Blvd. ℂ 800/854-9149 or 504/522-1492. www.mulates.com. No cover.

4 Rhythm, Rock & the Rest of the Music Scene

Most clubs in New Orleans feature an eclectic lineup that reflects the town's music scene; the ReBirth Brass Band, for example, attracts as many rock fans as it does brass band fans. Consequently, the bulk of the club scene escapes categorization (and, of course, booking policies are often subject to change)—even the local papers refer to club lineups as "mixed bags." If you want a specific sound, you have to look at listings (in *Offbeat* and *Gambit* magazines, for example) night by night. Some places are generally good fun on their own regardless of who is playing; any night at the **Maple Leaf** (see below) is going to be a good one, while wandering from spot to spot in the Frenchmen section is a well-spent evening. Really, in New Orleans, you can't go too wrong going just about anywhere simply to hang out. And in the process, you might get exposed to a new, wonderful genre of music or an incredible band.

THE FRENCH QUARTER & THE FAUBOURG MARIGNY

Blue Nile　Taking over the old Dream Palace/Tin Roof space on Frenchman Street (a building that still needs some work) and giving the interior a facelift (the title color naturally features, but so do tangerine and red), this club should be a part of your Frenchman Street hopping, as they book a variety of acts, everything from rock to jazz to world, both local and out of town. The sound could be better, though. 534 Frenchman St. ℂ 504/948-2583 or 504/948-BLUE. Cover varies.

Cafe Brasil　Day (when it is a great place to get a cup of coffee and to hear gossip) or night (when it delivers danceable music), Cafe Brasil is the center of the increasingly lively and popular Frenchmen section of the Faubourg Marigny. It features Latin or Caribbean music, R&B, or jazz almost every night, and chances are whatever is playing will be infectious. Anticipate a hip and trendy, though still casual, crowd and be prepared to act cool. The decent-size dance floor fills up quickly, and the crowd spills into the street to see and be seen, and even to check out the vendors who are often there hawking wares. 2100 Chartres St. ℂ 504/949-0851. Cover varies according to performer.

Checkpoint Charlie's　Somewhere between a biker bar and a college hangout, the dark Checkpoint Charlie's only *seems* intimidating—an effect that's helped by the hard rock sounds usually blaring from the stage. It's easy to overlook straight rock with all the other New Orleans sounds around, but this would be the place to start trying to find it. R&B and blues also sneak into the mix as well as the occasional acoustic open-mike night. A full bar, food, and pool tables help soften the ambience for the easily intimidated, and it's open 24 hours, making it a less touristy place for a quick drink during the day. Plus, there's a coin laundry, so a dusty traveler can clean up while enjoying the music. And right across the street is a fire station known for its hunky firemen, who, on sultry nights, sit outside and admire the views. Admire them right back. 501 Esplanade Ave. ℂ 504/947-0979. No cover.

House of Blues　New Orleans was a natural place for this franchise to set up shop, but its presence in the French Quarter seems rather unnatural. With all the great, funky, authentic music clubs in town, why build one with ersatz "authenticity" that wouldn't be out of place in Disneyland's Pirates of the Caribbean? And while it's noble that they've patronized many deserving Southern "primitive" artists to line the walls with colorful works, there's a certain Hearst Castle grab-bag element to that, too, which diminishes the value and cultural context of the individual works. That isn't to say the facility is without its good points. The music room has adequate sightlines and good sound, and the chain's financial muscle assures first-rate bookings, from local legends like the Neville Brothers to such ace out-of-towners as Los Lobos and Nanci Griffith. The nouvelle Orleans menu in the bustling restaurant, too, is high quality, from a piquant jambalaya to fancy-schmancy pizzas. But patronizing this club rather than the real thing, like Tipitina's (which lost considerable business after the HOB opened), is akin to eating at McDonald's rather than Mother's. 225 Decatur St. ℭ 504/529-2583. www.hob.com. Cover varies.

Jimmy Buffett's Margaritaville Cafe & Storyville Tavern   Yeah, Jimmy Buffett occasionally plays here, and yeah, they serve margaritas. Don't mind us if we sound grumpy; Buffett means well (isn't that practically his whole shtick as an artist?), but he took over a perfectly nice little jazz club (the Storyville Tavern, and by the way, it is not in or even all that near Storyville) and made it part of the brand-name takeover of the Quarter. Lineups are solid if unimaginative. There's no cover—they'll try to sell you food and merchandise instead. It's not as bad as, say, the Hard Rock Cafe, but still . . . . 1104 Decatur St. ℭ 504/592-2565. www.margaritavillecafe.com. No cover.

Shim-Sham Club   After taking over a longtime jazz club space, the Shim-Sham club has evolved into an interesting scene—"a little decadent, a little bohemian," says one local who frequents the place. The club books perhaps the most eclectic lineup in town: In addition to a current burlesque review, you can expect regular '80s and S&M nights, gigs by local or touring punk or metal outfits, maybe even shows by Louis Prima protégé and torch-carrier Sam Butara, proto-grunge legends the Melvins, or a surprise late-night show by Counting Crows lead singer, Adam Duritz, and friends. Seating can be either cabaret style (tables and chairs) or standing room. There is also a secret scene that revolves around the upstairs bar, which you only get to enter by invitation. Act nice and look like fun and maybe you'll get lucky. 615 Toulouse St. ℭ 504/565-5400. www.shimshamclub.com. Cover varies.

The Spotted Cat Cocktail Lounge   It may be small, but this is one of the nicest clubs in town and *the* place on Frenchman to go for late-night canoodling or an otherwise intimate evening, with chocolate martinis and local acts playing nightly. Traditional jazz is regularly featured, and on Mondays and Fridays the New Orleans Jazz Vipers offer a fresh take on classic jazz. 623 Frenchman St. ℭ 504/943-3887. www.thespottedcat.com. No cover.

ELSEWHERE AROUND THE CITY

Throughout this book, we keep nagging you to leave the Quarter. This advice is most important at night. It's not that there aren't some worthwhile, memorable clubs in the Quarter or at the fringes. It's just that there are so many terrific (and, in some cases, outright better) ones elsewhere. They aren't hard to find—any cab driver knows where they are. And not only do they feature some of the best music in town (if not, on some nights, in the country), they aren't designed as tourist destinations, so your experience will be that much more legitimate.

Carrollton Station   A long, narrow space means that folks at the back won't get to see much of what's up on stage, but hey, that puts them closer to the bar, so everyone wins. Way uptown in the Riverbend area, Carrollton Station is a gourmet beer house that schedules local and touring blues, classic New Orleans, and R&B musicians (plus some singer-songwriter types) Wednesday through Sunday, generally beginning at 10pm. (The bar opens at 3pm.) The crowd is a good mix of college students, music aficionados, and fans of whatever act is appearing on a given night. 8140 Willow St. © 504/865-9190. www.carrolltonstation.com. Cover varies.

The Howlin' Wolf This is arguably the premier club in town in terms of the quality and fame of its bookings, especially since a remodeling job increased capacity nearly fourfold—and made it a competitor with the House of Blues. Good. Better a local nonchain gets the business. (Unfortunately for Tipitina's, the renovations coincided with Tip's losing a large chunk of its capacity, which limited the kinds of bands willing to play Tip's; Howlin' Wolf took up the slack.) The new look includes upstairs seating (or standing), which can be closed off for smaller shows. Howlin' Wolf draws some top touring rock acts, though it is not at all limited to rock—El Vez, the Mexican Elvis, is as likely to play as a country band or the latest in indie and alternative rock (recent performers included Frank Black, the Jon Spencer Blues Explosion, and Iris DeMent). The renovations did not extend to the decor, so don't look for House of Blues–like pirate booty or even the posters and other memorabilia Tip's uses to commemorate its history. 828 S. Peters St., in the Warehouse District. © 504/522-WOLF. www.howlin-wolf.com. Cover none–$15.

Lion's Den A true neighborhood dive, but it's well worth stopping by should Miss Irma Thomas be in residence. Lately, she seems to be around only when she's not touring, but you might get lucky—luckier still if she's even cooking up some red beans and rice. Thomas has only one hit to her credit ("Wish Somebody Would Care"), but she's still a great, sassy live R&B and soul act with a devoted following, who can never get enough of "You Can Have My Husband, But Please Don't Mess with My Man" and other delights. She puts on one hell of a show, and it's well worth treading into this otherwise unsavory neighborhood to see it. Heck, some folks come all the way from England every year during Jazz Fest just to watch her play. For this listing, see map on p. 230. 2655 Gravier St., at N. Broad Ave. in Mid-City. © 504/821-3745. Cover varies.

Maple Leaf Bar This is what a New Orleans club is all about. It's medium-size but feels smaller when a crowd is packed in, and by 11pm on most nights, it is, with personal space at times becoming something you can only wistfully remember. But that's no problem. The stage is against the window facing the street, so more often than not, the crowd spills onto the sidewalk and into the street to dance and drink (and escape the heat and sweat, which are prodigious despite a high ceiling). You can hear the music just as well, watch the musicians' rear ends, and then dance some more. With a party atmosphere like this, outside is almost more fun than in. But inside is mighty fine. A good bar and a rather pretty patio (the other place to escape the crush) make the Maple Leaf worth hanging out at even if you don't care about the music on a particular night. But if Beausoleil or the ReBirth Brass Band is playing, do not miss it; go and dance till you drop. 8316 Oak St. © 504/866-9359. Cover varies, depending on day of week and performer.

Mermaid Lounge Although it's very hard to find, thanks to a series of one-way streets (that all seem to lead away from the club) and its location in a cul-de-sac on the edge of the Warehouse District, the Mermaid Lounge is worth the effort. (You might call the club and ask plaintively how to get there. They might tell you.) An eclectic booking policy attracts everything from the Hackberry

Ramblers (the Grammy-nominated Cajun band that has been playing together for nearly 70 years!) to hard-core grunge—and yet, the blue-haired pierced kids still come to dance to the Cajun bands in the tiny, cramped, dark, L-shaped space (yes, there is a mermaid motif throughout). It all adds up to one of the coolest vibes in town. As always, regulars avoid paying the cover charge by standing out on the sidewalk, where the music sounds just fine. Because it's not well marked even if you figure out how to get there, they might be your signpost. 1100 Constance St. © **504/524-4747.** Cover $0–$10.

Rock 'n' Bowl Cafe   Located right under Mid City Lanes (hence the name), this is a huge room (bowling-alley size) that helps take care of the constant overflow from upstairs. Dark and bleak, thanks to the black paint job (with one large mural) and lack of windows, the Rock 'n' Bowl Cafe offers essentially the same acts as Mid City, though perhaps not as much zydeco. On some nights, the clubs split the bill—pay one price, see two bands, one upstairs and one downstairs—which can lead to strange, or not so, combinations of acts such as the Latino and Southwestern-flavored Iguanas and the exuberant roots rock of Dash Rip Rock. For this listing, see the "Mid City Attractions & Nightlife" map on p. 163. 4133 S. Carrollton Ave. © **504/482-3133.** www.rockandbowl.com. Cover usually $5–$7.

Tipitina's   Dedicated to the late piano master Professor Longhair and featured in the movie *The Big Easy,* Tip's was long *the* New Orleans club. But due to circumstances both external (increased competition from House of Blues and others as well as the club's capacity being cut in half by city authorities) and internal (locals say the bookings have not been up to snuff for some time), its star has faded considerably. It remains a reliable place for top local bands, though.

The place is nothing fancy—just four walls, a wraparound balcony, and a stage. Oh, and a couple of bars, of course, including one that serves the people milling outside the club, which as at other top locales is as much a part of the atmosphere as what's inside. Bookings range from top indigenous acts (a brass bands blowout is a perennial highlight of Jazz Fest week) to touring alt-rock and roots acts, both U.S.-based and international. It's uptown and a bit out of the way, but it's definitely worth the cab ride on the right night. A stop here after dinner at the relatively nearby Upperline (p. 139) or as one destination in a night of club hopping can make for a memorable experience, depending on what you're drinking. They also have two other rooms; Tips French Quarter and the Ruins at this point are being used only for special events. 501 Napoleon Ave., Uptown. © **504/895-8477** or 504/897-3943 for concert line. www.tipitinas.com. Cover varies.

5 The Bar Scene

You won't have any trouble finding a place to drink in New Orleans. Heck, thanks to "go" (or *geaux*) cups, you won't have to spend a minute without a drink in your hand. (It's legal to have liquor outside as long as it's in a plastic cup. Actually, given the number of people who take advantage of this law, it almost seems illegal *not* to have such a cup in your hand.)

Bourbon Street comes off like a blocks-long bar—and smells like it, too. It's sort of pointless to single out any one drinking establishment there; not only are they ultimately all more or less similar, but their clientele hardly varies. The crowd is simply moving down the street from one locale to the next. If we sound a bit scornful about drinking in New Orleans, it's because so many seem to treat a visit as nothing more than a license to get blotto, and the streets as one big place to regurgitate. Not only is this obnoxious, but there's a lot more to this town.

Which is not to entirely dismiss drinking as a recreational activity (or, better still, as a sociological study). Certainly, New Orleans provides some of the most convivial, quaint, or downright eccentric spots to do so; in many cases, the places are worth going to even if you plan to imbibe nothing stronger than a soda.

Note that many of the clubs listed above are terrific spots to hoist a few (or a dozen), while some of the bars below also provide music—but that is strictly background for their real design. Piano bars, in particular, have begun to pop up in New Orleans like mushrooms after a good rain. They're everywhere; in addition to the ones listed below, you can find a piano bar in almost every large hotel, and plenty of others off by themselves.

Many bars stay open all the time or have varying hours depending upon the night or the season. If you have your heart set on a particular place, it's always best to call and make sure what their hours will be for that day. Unless noted, none of the places listed below has a cover charge.

THE FRENCH QUARTER & THE FAUBOURG MARIGNY

In addition to the places below, you might consider the clubby bar at **Dickie Brennan's Steakhouse,** 716 Iberville St. (p. 111; ✆ **504/522-2467**), a place where manly men go to drink strong drinks, smoke smelly cigars (they have a vast selection for sale), and chat up girlie girls. Or you could enjoy the low-key sophistication found at **Beque's at the Royal Sonesta,** 300 Bourbon St. (✆ **504/586-0300**), where a jazz trio is usually playing.

The Abbey Despite the name, this place is more basement rumpus room (walls covered with stickers and old album covers) than Gothic church (well, there are some motley stained-glass windows). But the jukebox plays the Cramps and "I Wanna Be Your Dog," and the clientele is very David Lynchian (and maybe still left over from the place's heyday 15 years ago!), so it's okay by us. 1123 Decatur St. ✆ 504/523-7150.

Apple Barrel A small, dusty, wooden-floored watering hole complete with jukebox and darts (of course). You can find refuge here from the hectic Frenchmen scene—or gear up to join in. 609 Frenchmen St. ✆ 504/949-9399.

The Bombay Club This posh piano bar features jazz Wednesday through Saturday evenings. It's also a restaurant (the food is not great) and a martini bar—the drink has been a specialty here for years, so don't accuse the club of trying to ride the current martini trend. In fact, the Bombay's martinis are hailed as the best in town. The bar bills itself as casually elegant—a polite way of saying don't wear jeans and shorts. 830 Conti St. ✆ 504/586-0972.

Carousel Bar & Lounge Piano music is featured here Tuesdays through Saturdays, but the real attraction is the bar itself—it really is a carousel, and it really does revolve. The music goes on until 2am, and who knows if the carousel ever stops revolving. A top choice for those not interested in Bourbon frat party fun or even the young and the frenzied on Frenchman St. And if the bartender isn't busy or indifferent, they make a fine Sazarac. In the Monteleone Hotel, 214 Royal St. ✆ 504/523-3341.

Coyote Ugly The bar made famous by the movie (or at the least the soundtrack to the movie), where comely female bartenders dance on the bar and hose down the rowdy patrons with water and liquid, has set up shop in the French Quarter. Like it needed another rowdy bar . . . like this kind of scene hasn't been happening (with boys) over at the Corner Pocket (see later in this chapter), where they are at least honest that they are parading around for the dough. 225 N. Peters St. ✆ 504/561-0003.

Pat O'Brien's & the Mighty Hurricane

Pat O'Brien's, 718 St. Peter St. (© **504/525-4823;** www.patobriens.com), is world famous for the gigantic, rum-based drink with the big-wind name. The formula (according to legend) was stumbled upon by bar owners Charlie Cantrell and George Oechsner while they were experimenting with Caribbean rum during World War II. The drink is served in signature 29-ounce hurricane lamp–style glasses. The bar now offers a 3-gallon Magnum Hurricane that stands taller than many small children. It's served with a handful of straws and takes a group to finish (we profoundly hope)—all of whom must drink standing up. Naturally, the offerings and reputation attract the tourists and college yahoos in droves. Some nights, the line can stretch out the door and down the street, which seems quite silly given how many other drinking options there are mere feet away.

Which is not to say that Pat's isn't worth a stop—it's a reliable, rowdy, friendly introduction to New Orleans. Just don't expect to be the only person who thinks so. Fortunately, it's large enough to accommodate nearly everyone—in three different bars, including a large lounge that usually offers entertainment (an emcee and alternating piano players)—with the highlight, on nonrainy days at least, being the attractive tropical patio. Don't look there for quiet, though. The party-hearty atmosphere thrives in that section, and on pretty days, tables can be hard to come by.

Even if it is a gimmick, what trip to New Orleans is complete without sampling the famous Hurricane? There's no minimum and no cover, but if you buy a drink and it comes in a glass, you'll be paying for the glass until you turn it in at the register for a $3 refund.

Crescent City Brewhouse   When this place opened in 1991, it was the first new brewery in New Orleans in more than 70 years, and now it's the place to go for microbrewery desires. 527 Decatur St. © **504/522-0571.**

d.b.a.   A little too prefab yuppie safe for us, in a city full of great bars that just happened organically, but their live bookings are increasing in profile, with regular jazz groups and even acts like Walter "Wolfman" Washington, and the list of 160 beers (best selection in the city), wines, and other drinks is most impressive. 618 Frenchman St. © **504/942-3731.** www.drinkgoodstuff.com/no.

El Matador   Your first stop on a Frenchman district crawl (even though it's on the edge of, not precisely in, same), this deep, dark, moody corner bar and club is just enough essential steps above seedy top make it a worthwhile stop. Music happens later at night (so it could be your last stop, as well), with an emphasis on danceable (or at least bounceable) rhythms. 504 Esplanade Ave., at Decatur St. © **504/586-0790.**

Fahy's Irish Pub   One night, we went looking for a bar with pool tables and you know what? New Orleans (or at least, the Quarter) doesn't have a lot of 'em. So it was with a relief we found Fahy's, a corner neighborhood pub (which attracts a pool-playin' crowd) that keeps its two tables in good condition. 540 Burgundy St. © **504/586-9806.**

Feelings Cafe   Here's a funky, low-key neighborhood restaurant and hangout set around a classic New Orleans courtyard, which is where most folks drink—unless they are hanging out with the fabulous piano player, singing the night away. (See p. 125 for the restaurant listing.) It's authentic in the right ways but is also more cheerful than some of the darker, hole-in-the-wall spots that deserve that adjective. Though it's a bit out of the way in the Faubourg Marigny, everyone who goes there comes back raving about it. 2600 Chartres St. ✆ **504/945-2222.** www.feelingscafe.com.

Gennifer Flowers Kelsto Club   Yeah, you read that right. The tabloid darling ('cause she was President Clinton's mistress before he was president) sings torch songs and standards at her own New Orleans club (across the street from Antoine's [p. 68]—and what must the Old Guard there be thinking about this?) on Thursday, Friday and Saturday nights (there is a piano player the other nights). No, we don't know what to make of it, either. 720 St. Louis Street. ✆ **504/524-1111.** http://204.27.90.194/kelsto.htm. No cover.

Hard Rock Cafe *(Overrated*   Gag. This prefab commercial horror is particularly offensive in New Orleans, where there is real music to be had at every turn. It bemuses us to see tourists lined up outside this place when original experiences—as opposed to assembly-line experiences—are just feet away. Better burgers and better beer are to be found elsewhere as well. 418 N. Peters St. ✆ **504/529-5617.** www.hardrock.com.

Kerry Irish Pub   This traditional Irish pub has a variety of beers and other spirits but is most proud of its properly poured pints of Guinness and hard cider. The pub is a good bet for live Irish and "alternative" folk music; it's also a place to throw darts and shoot pool. In case you want one last nightcap on your way back through the Quarter, you should know that Kerry specializes in very-late-night drinking. 331 Decatur St. ✆ **504/527-5954.**

Lafitte's Blacksmith Shop   It's some steps away from the main action on Bourbon, but you'll know Lafitte's when you see it. Dating from the 1770s, it's the oldest building in the Quarter—possibly in the Mississippi Valley (though that's not documented)—and it looks it. Legend has it that the privateer brothers Pierre and Jean Lafitte used the smithy as a "blind" for their lucrative trade in contraband (and, some say, slaves they'd captured on the high seas). Like all legends, that's probably not true.

   The owner managed to maintain the exposed-brick interior when he rescued the building from deterioration in the '40s. At night, when you step inside and it's entirely lit by candles (*Offbeat* magazine claims Lafitte's patented the word *dank*), the past of the Lafitte brothers doesn't seem so distant. (Unfortunately, the owner's penchant for treating good friends such as Tennessee Williams and Lucius Beebe to refreshments was stronger than his business acumen, and he eventually lost the building.) In other towns, this would be a tourist trap. Here, it feels authentic. Definitely worth swinging by even if you don't drink. 941 Bourbon St. ✆ **504/522-9377.**

Napoleon House Bar & Cafe   Set in a landmark building, the Napoleon House is just the place to go to have a quiet drink (as opposed to the very loud drinks found elsewhere in the Quarter) and maybe hatch some schemes. (See p. 124 for the restaurant listing.) Like Lafitte's (see above), it's dark, dark, dark, with walls you really wish could talk. Also like Lafitte's, it seems too perfect to be real—surely this must be constructed just for the tourists. It's not. Even locals like it here. 500 Chartres St. ✆ **504/524-9752.** www.napoleonhouse.com.

O'Flaherty's Irish Channel Pub   Over the years, the city's Irish Channel (uptown along Magazine St.) has become visibly less Irish in character. O'Flaherty's is taking up some of the slack. This is the place to go hear the best in local Celtic music, and on Saturdays, there's also Irish dancing. The supposedly haunted courtyard in the 18th-century building is almost as big a draw as the Irish atmosphere. 514 Toulouse St. ℂ **504/529-1317.**

R Bar and Royal Street Inn   The R (short for Royal Street) Bar is a little taste of New York's East Village in the Faubourg Marigny. It is a quintessential neighborhood bar in a neighborhood full of artists, wannabe artists, punk rock intellectuals, urban gentrifiers, and well-rounded hipsters. It's a talkers' bar (crowds tend to gather in layers along the bar) and a haven for strutting, overconfident pool players. On certain nights, you can get a haircut and a drink for $10. Sometimes the cuts aren't bad, depending on how much the gal wielding the scissors has had to drink. The R Bar has a large selection of imported beers and one of the best alternative and art-rock jukeboxes in the city. Thanks to all this (or perhaps in spite of some of it), it's just a cool little local bar. You'll see a sign behind the bar for the Royal Street Inn, otherwise known as the R Bar Inn, a B&B (bed-and-beverage, that is). If you like the bar, you'll probably love the accommodations, too (p. 82). 1431 Royal St. ℂ **504/948-7499.** www.royalstreetinn.com.

Saturn Bar   Genuine barflies or just slumming celebs? It's so hard to tell when they are passed out in the crumbling (and we mean it) booths or blending in with the pack-rat collection that passes as decor. The Saturn Bar is among the hipster set's most beloved dives, but it's hard to decide if the love is genuine or comes from a postmodern, ironic appreciation of the grubby, art-project (we can only hope) interior. Must be seen to be believed. 3067 St. Claude Ave., in the Faubourg Marigny. ℂ **504/949-7532.**

ELSEWHERE AROUND THE CITY

In addition to those listed below, hang with the local beautiful people at any of the following: **Loa,** the bar at the International House hotel, 221 Camp St., in the Central Business District (for more information on this hotel, see p. 88) is a hip and happening hangout. Hot on its heels for hipness and with a slightly higher energy level is the bar at **Loft 523,** a gorgeous space that beautifully shows off the old timbers that hold up this former warehouse; for information on the hotel, see p. 86. And the bar at **Hotel Le Cirque,** 936 St. Charles Ave. (ℂ **504/962-0900**), is another cool locale for grown-ups with minimal body fat.

Circle Bar   This tiny bar is among the most bohemian-hip in town, courtesy of the slightly twisted folks behind Snake & Jake's. Ambience is the key; it's got the ever-popular "elegant decay" look, from peeling wallpaper to a neon glow from an old K&B drugstore sign on the ceiling. The jukebox keeps the quirky romantic mood going, thanks to bewitching, mood-enhancing selections from the Velvet Underground, Dusty Springfield, and Curtis Mayfield. The clientele is real and real laid-back. Live music includes mostly local acts such as the sarcastically depressed Glyn Styler. Bet you'll see us there. 1032 St. Charles Ave., in the CBD at Lee Circle. ℂ **504/588-2616.**

The Columns   Here's a local favorite for drinks on the white-columned porch under spreading oak trees. Why? Well, aside from the Old South setting, beers at happy hour are a measly $2, and mixed drinks are not much more. But stay on the patio, or be engulfed in cigarette smoke in the dark interior bar. 3811 St. Charles Ave., Uptown. ℂ **504/899-9308.** www.thecolumns.com.

Dos Jefes Uptown Cigar Bar   Dos Jefes has a post-college, young, yuppie-ish clientele (mostly men, it seems). The patio outside has banana trees and iron chairs, and it's nicer than inside—carpet and cigars are a bad combination. The bar has a good selection of beer on tap and piano music until midnight Tuesdays through Saturdays. 5535 Tchoupitoulas St., Uptown. ℂ **504/891-8500.**

Hyttops Sports Bar & Grill   So you think you're a sports fan; well, here's your chance to prove it. Hyttops is in the lobby of the Hyatt, which is connected to the Superdome, the arena of the Sugar Bowl and New Orleans Saints home games. Everywhere you turn in the bar there's a television (many of them big-screen) featuring some athletic event. Because of its location, Hyttops is swamped with fans after Superdome events. If the arena is sold out, many fans like to go here to get as close to the action as they can. In the Hyatt Regency, 500 Poydras Plaza. ℂ **504/561-1234.**

Madigan's   Madigan's is a casual watering hole that has live music on Sundays. 800 S. Carrollton Ave., Uptown. ℂ **504/866-9455.** No cover most nights.

Mother-in-Law Lounge   Ernie K-Doe may be gone, but this shrine to his glorious self and funky lounges everywhere lives on, thanks to wife, Antoinette, the keeper of the K-Doe legend and the bar's owner. Named after his biggest hit, a rousing 1961 number-one pop/R&B novelty, this is a true neighborhood dive bar, weird and wonderful, distinguished by the K-Doe memorabilia that lines the walls. Antoinette (a total kick) makes perhaps the best gumbo we have ever had, and if you are lucky, she will be serving it when you come by. K-Doe himself, in the form of a startlingly lifelike mannequin, which has become a celebrity of sorts around town, still holds court. You may want to be careful in the neighborhood, but once you're there, be sure to play one of K-Doe's songs on the jukebox and drink a toast to the man who billed himself as "Emperor the Universe." Call first—hours are erratic (and often early). 1500 N. Claiborne Ave., northeast of the Quarter. ℂ **504/947-1078.** www.kdoe.com. Call for hours.

Nick's   The slogan here is "Looks like the oldest bar in town!"—and it does. Behind the barroom, you'll find billiards and occasional performances by live musicians. Nick's is famous for shots of drinks with vulgar names, and special drink prices are offered on weekdays. For this listing, see map on p. 163. 2400 Tulane Ave., Mid-City. ℂ **504/821-9128.**

Pals Lounge   This used to be a nondescript corner neighborhood bar called Yvonne's that was only open for a couple of hours in the afternoon. Now, well-heeled backers have turned it into a hipster bar, upping the age and economic demographic considerably, and offering an alternative watering hole for the increasingly gentrified St. John's Bayou neighborhood. Between the fresh and clean renovation, the liquor selection, and the occasional live music, it's a good place to drink and one not yet on the tourist radar. 949 N. Rendon St., St. John's Bayou. ℂ **504/488-PALS.**

The Polo Lounge   The Windsor Court is, without a doubt, the city's finest hotel (p. 86), and the Polo Lounge is the place to go if you're feeling particularly stylish. Sazeracs and cigars are popular here. Don't expect to find any kids; if you like to seal your deals with a drink, this is likely to be your first choice. In the Windsor Court hotel, 300 Gravier St., in the CBD. ℂ **504/523-6000.**

Sazerac Bar and Grill   In the posh Fairmont Hotel (p. 84), the renovated Sazerac Bar is frequented by the city's young professionals and was featured in the movie *The Pelican Brief.* The African walnut bar and murals by Paul Ninas complete the upscale atmosphere. Here is where you should try the famous Sazerac cocktail (a multi-layered combination of rye whiskey, bitters, sugar, herbsaint, and a hint of lemon oil), not because they make it the best (that award probably goes to Bayona; see p. 108) but because you are here. But do tell the bartender to make it from scratch, not from a pre-mix. In the Fairmont Hotel, University Place, in the CBD. *©* 504/529-4733. www.fairmont.com.

Snake & Jake's Xmas Club Lounge   Though admittedly off the beaten path, this tiny, friendly dive is the perfect place for those looking for an authentic neighborhood bar. Co-owned by local musician Dave Clements, decorated (sort of) with Christmas lights, and featuring a great jukebox heavy on soul and R&B, this is the kind of place where everybody not only knows your name, they know your dog's name 'cause you can bring the dog, too. There is almost no light at all, so make friends and prepare to be surprised. Naturally, Snake & Jake's can get really hot, crowded, and sweaty—if you're lucky. *Gambit* readers voted Jose, the bartender, the best in the city. 7612 Oak St., Uptown. *©* 504/861-2802.

St. Joe's Bar   An agreeably dark (but not pretentious), nonseedy corner bar, this is a very typical New Orleans friendly-but-not-overbearing place. Its Upper Magazine location means it's more neighborhood- than business-oriented. Folkart crosses hang from the (apparently) hammered tin ceiling, and the place is often seasonally decorated. At Halloween, the cobwebs look as if they should be permanent. It has a pleasant patio, a pool table, and a well-stocked jukebox with the likes of Ray Charles and the Grateful Dead. 5535 Magazine St., Uptown. *©* 504/899-3744.

Vic's Kangaroo Cafe   Really missing the brief Australia craze of the mid-'80s? Actually remember *Crocodile Dundee*? Drop by Vic's for a fix (or call; the last four digits of the phone number spell "g'day"). Despite the perplexing gimmick (how did Australian Vic land in New Orleans?), this is a friendly bar that caters to the local after-work crowd. Enjoy some shepherd's pie, wash it down with a sample of the nice selection of beers on tap, play a round of pool or darts, and generally have a—oh dear, we are going to say it—g'day. 636 Tchoupitoulas St., in the CBD. *©* 504/524-4329.

6 Burlesque & Strip Clubs

As if there weren't enough to Bourbon Street, what with the booze and the music and the booze, there is the sex industry—kind of. In addition to numerous stores offering what we will euphemistically call marital aids, there are quite a few strip joints—some topless, some bottomless, some offering "live sex acts." If you make a habit of such places, you'll be in heaven. If you are merely curious or are simply in the mood for a naughty evening, this might be the time and place to try one. ***But beware:*** The lack of cover charges means they'll insist you buy a few overpriced, watered-down drinks. Plus, if you are looking for true risqué thrills, you'll likely be disappointed. Those "live love acts" are at best simulated and at worst utterly tame (imagine nude aerobics done by not-half-bad dancers). A promising trend are the "burlesque shows" offered at several of the more upscale "Gentlemen's" clubs, where true strip and tease is making a classy comeback. These shows are costly ($40 and up) but much more in line with the kind of erotic naughty fun you might want.

7 Gay Nightlife

The gay community is quite strong and visible in New Orleans, and the gay bars are some of the most bustling places in town—full of action nearly 24 hours a day. Thanks to "go" cups and the generally transient nature of bar activity, most New Orleans gay bars don't have a strict identity or a specific demographic to their crowds. Though some may attract a slightly younger or more leather crowd (as examples), that doesn't preclude a healthy mix of older patrons and suit-wearers. Below you'll find listings of New Orleans's most popular gay nightspots.

For more information, you can check **Ambush,** 828-A Bourbon St. (*©* **504/ 522-8049;** www.ambushmag.com), a great source for the gay community in New Orleans and for visitors. The magazine's website has a lot of handy-dandy links to other sites of gay interest, including info on local gay bars (www.gaybars. com/states/louisian.htm). Once you're in New Orleans, you can call the office or pick up a copy at Tower Records, 408 N. Peters St., near Conti Street in the French Quarter or at Lenny's News, 5420 Magazine St., near Leontine Street, Uptown.

BARS
In addition to those listed below, you might also try the **Golden Lantern,** 1239 Royal St. (*©* **504/529-2860**), a nice neighborhood spot where the bartender knows the patrons by name. It's the second-oldest gay bar in town, and one longtime patron said that "it used to look like one half of Noah's Ark—with one of everything, one drag queen, one leather boy, one guy in a suit." If Levi's and leather is your scene, then **Rawhide,** 740 Burgundy St. (*©* **504/525-8106;** www.rawhide2010.com), is your best bet; during Mardi Gras, it hosts a great gay costume contest that's not to be missed. The rest of the year, it's a hustler bar. Both of these places are in the French Quarter, as are the establishments listed below. There is no cover unless noted.

The Bourbon Pub-Parade Disco This is more or less the most centrally located of the gay bars, with many of the other popular gay bars nearby. The downstairs pub offers a video bar (often featuring surprisingly cutting edge, innovative stuff) and is the calmer of the two; it's open 24 hours daily and usually gets most crowded in the hour just before the Parade Disco opens. (*Note:* From 5 to 9pm, a $5 cover charge gets you all the draft beer you can drink.) The Parade Disco is upstairs and features a high-tech dance floor complete with lasers and smoke. Consistently voted by several sources as a top dance club (in all of America), it usually opens around 9pm except on Sunday, when it gets going in the afternoon. 801 Bourbon St. *©* 504/529-2107. www.bourbonpub.com.

Café Lafitte in Exile When Tom Caplinger left Lafitte's Blacksmith Shop behind, friends say it broke his heart. But he rallied and opened a place down the block, bringing pals and patrons like Tennessee Williams with him. It's one of the oldest gay bars in the United States, having been around since 1953. There's a bar downstairs, and upstairs you'll find a pool table and a balcony that overlooks Bourbon Street. The whole shebang is open 24 hours daily. This is a cruise bar, but it doesn't attract a teenybopper or twinkie crowd. One of the most popular weekly events is the Sunday evening "Trash Disco," when, you guessed it, they play trashy disco music from the '70s and everyone has a lot of fun. 901 Bourbon St. *©* 504/522-8397. www.lafittes.com.

The Corner Pocket While the boast that they have the hottest male strippers in town may be perhaps too generous, you can decide for yourself by checking out this bar Thursday through Sunday nights after 10pm. Locals who aren't a bit ashamed of themselves claim the cutest boys can be found on Friday nights, and sigh that the management has the strippers wear the sort of garments that prevent peeking (not that that prevents anyone from trying). The bar itself is none too special (and despite the name, the only draw for the pool table is that players might not be especially clothed), with the average age of the clientele around 70. 940 St. Louis St. © 504/568-9829. www.cornerpocket.net.

CowPokes Looking for a gay country bar? Never let it be said that Frommer's lets you down. This is a particularly nice gay country bar, though it resides in a transitional neighborhood, so do let a cab bring you out for some of the weekly activities, including free line-dance lessons on Tuesdays and Thursdays and karaoke on Wednesdays. 2240 St. Claude. © 504/947-0505. www.cowpokesno.com.

Good Friends Bar & Queens Head Pub This bar and pub is very friendly to visitors and often wins the Gay Achievement Award for Best Neighborhood Gay Bar. They describe themselves as "always snappy casual!" The local clientele is happy to offer suggestions about where you might find the type of entertainment you're looking for. Downstairs is a mahogany bar and a pool table. Upstairs is the quiet Queens Head Pub, which was recently decorated in the style of a Victorian English pub. The bar is open 24 hours. 740 Dauphine St. © 504/566-7191. www.goodfriendsbar.com.

LeRoundup LeRoundup attracts the most diverse crowd around. You'll find transsexuals lining up at the bar with drag queens and well-groomed men in khakis and Levi's. Expect encounters with working boys. It's open 24 hours. 819 St. Louis St. © 504/561-8340. www.leroundup.com.

DANCE CLUBS

Oz Oz is the place to see and be seen, with a primarily young crowd (like its across-the-street neighbor, the Bourbon Pub-Parade Disco; see above). It was ranked the city's best dance club by *Gambit* magazine, and *Details* magazine named it one of the top 50 clubs in the country. The music is great, there's an incredible laser light show, and from time to time there are go-go boys atop the bar. Oz hosts frequent theme nights, so call ahead if you're going and want to dress accordingly. 800 Bourbon St. © 877/599-8200 or 504/592-8200. www.ozneworleans.com. Cover varies; straights pay extra.

735 Night Club & Bar Oz continues, for the moment, to rule as top NOLA dance club, but this newish venue might be making them work harder. For one thing, 18-year-olds can join in the fun, and for now at least, straight guests don't have to pay extra. (Yes, we all wonder how anyone can tell.) The result is a mixed crowd that works a good-size dance floor and is happy to catch their collective breath admiring a decor of velvet and animal prints (timeless, both of them). 735 Bourbon St. © 504/581-6740. www.club735.com.

8 The Performing Arts

New Orleans has historically been a center for all sorts of culture, especially the performing arts. In its cultural heyday, it had a thriving classical music community, many theaters, and what may have been the first opera house on the continent. Today, after a period in which the high arts were at a pretty low ebb, things are on the mend. There are a number of local theaters and repertory groups; you'll find opera, symphony orchestras, chamber groups, ballet, and modern dance in the city; and some very good traveling musical theater companies also make their way to town. Note that ticket prices vary widely according to performance, and events are sometimes sold out; if you're interested in attending something specific, plan ahead.

PERFORMING ARTS COMPANIES
OPERA
It wasn't until 1943 that the **New Orleans Opera Association** (© 504/529-2278; www.neworleansopera.org) was formed, which presents several operas a season. Stars from New York's Metropolitan Opera Company frequently appear in leading roles, supported by talented local voices. The Met's touring company occasionally performs here, too. For most performances, seats start at $30.

DANCE
The **New Orleans Ballet Association** (© 504/522-0996; www.nobadance.com), which merged recently with the Cincinnati Ballet, is the city's professional ballet company. Check the newspapers for current performances. The ballet's season generally runs September through April.

CLASSICAL MUSIC
The **Louisiana Philharmonic Orchestra** (© 504/523-6530; www.lpomusic.com) plays a subscription series of concerts during the fall-to-spring season and offers pops concerts on weekends in June and July; tickets start at $11.

MAJOR CONCERT HALLS & AUDITORIUMS
The Mahalia Jackson Theater of the Performing Arts   The Mahalia Jackson Theater has become the favored venue for lavish touring musical shows as well as concerts. You can catch opera and ballet in season as well as circuses, prizefights, ice shows, and the popular summer pops symphony concerts. 801 N. Rampart St. © 504/565-7470.

New Orleans Municipal Auditorium   Just across a flowered walkway from the Mahalia Jackson Theater of the Performing Arts, this auditorium has been used for just about every kind of entertainment—from the circus to touring theatrical companies to ballets and concerts. 1201 St. Peter St. © 504/522-0996 or 504/565-7490 for ticket information.

THEATERS
In addition to the listings below, possibilities for theatrical performances and concerts include **True Brew Cafe and Theater** and the **Louisiana Superdome** (© 800/756-7074 or 504/587-3663; fax 504/587-3848; www.superdome.com), which frequently hosts entertainment that's not even remotely connected with sports.

Contemporary Arts Center   Located in the Warehouse District, the Contemporary Arts Center is best known for its changing exhibitions of contemporary art. Also on the premises are two theaters that frequently feature dance performances and concerts as well as experimental works by local playwrights. Call for the current schedule. 900 Camp St. © 504/523-1216. www.cacno.org.

Le Chat Noir   This cool-cat, swanky, cabaret-style theater in the Warehouse District (with tables and candles) features rotating performances of a variety of entertainment: jazz, cabaret shows (think Broadway tunes), musical revues, and plays. They usually, but not exclusively, feature local talent (Thurs–Sun). They also have live piano music in their Bar Noir every day except Monday from 6pm.

Prices run $5 to $20 depending, and reservations are suggested. 715 St. Charles Ave. (C) **504/581-5812**. www.cabaretlechatnoir.com.

Le Petit Théâtre du Vieux Carré *(Kids)*   You may hear this place referred to as "The Little Theater in the French Quarter." It's home to one of the oldest non-professional theater troupes in the country. Throughout its season (early fall to late spring), the theater puts on a series of well-chosen and familiar musicals and plays. It's community theater, but it might provide an appropriate family nighttime activity. 616 St. Peter St. (C) **504/522-2081**. www.lepetittheatre.com.

Saenger Theatre   The restoration of the Saenger Theatre has been big news in New Orleans. It was regarded as a world-class venue when it first opened in 1927, and its finery has been completely restored. The decor is Renaissance Florentine with Greek and Roman sculpture, fine marble statues, and cut-glass chandeliers. The ceiling is alive with twinkling stars and clouds so real you expect them to drift. Settings like this one are fast disappearing from the American theater scene, and New Orleans is to be congratulated for preserving such opulence. Touring Broadway productions play regularly, and popular music concerts are also held here. 143 N. Rampart St. (C) **504/525-1052**. www.saengertheatre.com.

Southern Rep Theatre   The Southern Rep Theatre, the city's newest theater, focuses on the work of Southern playwrights and actors. Located near the Canal Place movie theater, the Southern Rep is comfortable, intimate, and easily accessible from all downtown and French Quarter hotels. During the summer, novices get a chance to show their stuff as part of the theater's New Playwrights series. At other times, expect to find productions by or (occasionally) about famous Southern playwrights. Ample parking is available in the shopping center garage. Canal Place Shopping Centre, Level 3. (C) **504/835-6002**. www.southernrep.com. Tickets $20.

9 An Evening Cruise

The *Creole Queen* and the *Cajun Queen* ((C) **800/445-4109** or 504/524-0814), riverboat cruisers built in the tradition of their forebears, host lovely (if a bit touristy) Creole dinners and jazz cruises nightly. Both boats are operated by the same company; sometimes only one runs at a time. Departures are at 8pm (boarding at 7pm) from the Canal Street Wharf. The fare of $45 per person includes a sumptuous Creole buffet (it's $22 without the meal), and there's bar service as well as live jazz and dancing against a backdrop of the city's sparkling skyline. Schedules are subject to change, so call ahead to confirm days and times.

12

Plantation Homes &
Cajun Country:
Side Trips from New Orleans

If you have time (to us, that means an overall trip lasting more than 3 days), you should strongly consider a sojourn into the countryside around the city. This chapter starts off by following the River Road and the plantation homes that line the banks of the Mississippi, heading upriver from New Orleans; the second part will take you a little more than 100 miles west of New Orleans to the heart of Acadiana, or Cajun Country.

How much time you devote to these trips depends on your schedule. On the River Road trip, you can see many of the highlights in a day trip, but it's quite possible to keep rambling north to visit the plantation homes in the St. Francisville area, an exploration that will call for an overnight stay. The Cajun Country trip pretty much requires an overnight, and you'll have no trouble filling the time if you can spend a few more days in the region.

1 The Plantations Along the Great River Road

If your image of plantations comes strictly from repeated viewings of *Gone with the Wind,* you may well be disappointed when you go plantation hopping. That particular Tara was a Hollywood creation—indeed, in Margaret Mitchell's novel, Tara was quite different, a rambling structure of no particular style.

Plantation houses, at least the ones that are extant and open to public tours, are often more humble in scale (it wasn't until after 1850 that the houses got bigger, and most of these predate that). They also come in two models: the Creole style, which tends to be a low-slung, simple affair (Creoles preferring to keep the goodies on the inside where they can actually be enjoyed), and the American style, which are closer to classic antebellum grandeur. Nevertheless, these houses run smaller than you might think; even the "big" ones feel a bit cramped compared with certain lavish mansions built by turn-of-the-20th-century oil barons and today's nouveau riche. If your fantasies would be dashed without pillars and porticos, consider sticking to Destrehan, San Francisco, Oak Alley, and Madewood (see their listings later in this chapter).

In the beginning, the Creole planters of Louisiana were rugged frontier people. As they spread out along the Mississippi from New Orleans, they cleared swamplands with a mighty energy. Indigo, the area's first cash crop, had to be transported downriver to New Orleans. Even as you drive on the modern highways that course through some of the bayous, you can easily imagine the challenges those early settlers faced.

Plantations Along the Great River Road

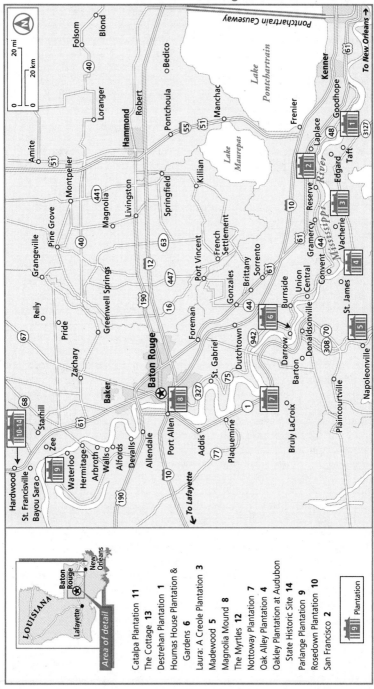

Catalpa Plantation **11**
The Cottage **13**
Destrehan Plantation **1**
Houmas House Plantation & Gardens **6**
Laura: A Creole Plantation **3**
Madewood **5**
Magnolia Mound **8**
The Myrtles **12**
Nottoway Plantation **7**
Oak Alley Plantation **4**
Oakley Plantation at Audubon State Historic Site **14**
Parlange Plantation **9**
Rosedown Plantation **10**
San Francisco **2**

In spite of all the obstacles, however, fields were cleared, swamps were drained, and crops were planted. Rough flatboats and keelboats were able to get the produce to market in New Orleans—if they weren't capsized by rapids, snags, sandbars, and floating debris, and if their cargoes weren't captured by bands of river pirates. These farming men (and a few extraordinary women) poled their boats to New Orleans, collected their pay for the journey, and then went on wild sprees of drinking, gambling, and brawling—behavior that gave the Creoles of the French Quarter their first (and lasting) impression of Americans as barbarians.

By the 1800s, Louisiana planters had introduced farming on a large scale, based primarily on their use of (and dependence on) slave labor. With cheap labor available, more and more acres went under cultivation. King Cotton, which proved to be a most profitable crop, arrived on the scene around this time. So did sugar cane, which brought huge monetary returns, especially after Etienne de Boré discovered the secret of successful granulation. Rice also became a secondary crop. But, natural dangers risked disaster for planters: A hurricane could wipe out a whole year's work, and a swift change in the capricious Mississippi's course could inundate entire plantations. So, there were always small fortunes to be made in the area—and then lost.

THE RIVERBOATS   After 1812, the planters turned to a newly invented water vessel for speedier and safer transportation of their crops to the market. When the first of the steamboats (the *New Orleans,* built in Pittsburgh) chugged downriver belching sooty smoke, it was so dirty, dangerous, and potentially explosive that it was dubbed a "floating volcano."

Over a 30-year period, however, as vast improvements were made, the steamboats came to be viewed as veritable floating pleasure palaces. The need to move goods to market may have floated the boat, so to speak, but the lavish staterooms and ornate "grand salons" put a whole new face on river travel and made a profound change in plantation life. A planter and his wife, children, and slaves could now travel the river with ease and comfort; many set up dual residences and spent the winters in elegant town houses in New Orleans. After months of isolation in the country, where visitors were few, the sociability of the city—with its grand balls, theatrical performances, elaborate banquets, and other entertainment—was a welcome relief. Also, it became possible to ship fine furnishings upriver to plantation homes, allowing the planters to enjoy a more comfortable and elegant lifestyle in the fields.

The riverboats did have a darker side, however. Along with families, merchants, peddlers, and European visitors, the boats were the realm of some cunning and colorful characters: the riverboat gambler and "confidence" (or "con") man. Plantation owners were drawn like magnets to the sharp-witted, silver-tongued professional gamers, crooks, and cranks. Huge fortunes were won and lost on the river, and more than a few deeds to plantations changed hands at the table on a river steamboat.

BUILDING THE PLANTATION HOUSES   During this period of prosperity, from the 1820s until the beginning of the Civil War, most of the impressive plantation homes were built. It was also during this time that many of the grand town houses in cities like New Orleans and Natchez were erected.

The plantation home was the focal point of a self-sustaining community and generally was located near the riverfront; it may have been graced with a wide, oak-lined avenue leading from its entrance to a wharf (though some were much more modest). On either side of the avenue would frequently be *garçonnières* (much smaller houses, sometimes used to give adolescent sons and their friends privacy or as guesthouses for travelers who stopped for a night's lodging). Behind the main house, the kitchen was often separate from the house because of the danger of fire, and the overseer's office was almost always close enough for convenience. Some plantations had, behind these two structures, pigeon houses or dovecotes—and all had the inevitable slave quarters, usually in twin lines bordering a lane leading to cotton or sugar cane fields. When cotton gins and sugar mills came along, they were generally built across the fields, out of sight of the main house.

When the main houses were first raised, they were much like the simple "raised cottage" known as Madame John's Legacy on Dumaine Street in New Orleans (p. 159)—with long, sloping roofs, cement-covered brick walls on the ground floor, and wood and brick (brick between posts) construction in the living quarters on the second floor. These structures suited the sultry Louisiana climate and swampy building sites and made use of native materials. Houses of the colonial period in this region were distinctly influenced by styles from the West Indies, very different from the grander revival styles that followed in the 1800s.

In the 1820s, homes that combined traces of the West Indian style with some Greek Revival and Georgian influences—a style that has been dubbed Louisiana Classic—began to appear. Large, rounded columns usually surrounded the main body of the house, wide galleries reaching from the columns to the walls encircled upper floors, and the roof was dormered. The upper and lower floors consisted of four large rooms (two on either side) flanking a wide central hall. They were constructed of native materials, with a few imported interior details such as fireplace mantels. There were no stone quarries in Louisiana; if stone was used (which wasn't very often), it had to be shipped by sea from New England and transported up the Mississippi from New Orleans. Because the river flowed through banks of clay, however, bricks could be made on the spot. Cypress, too, was plentiful, and it did well in the hot, humid climate, which could quickly rot other woods. To protect the homemade bricks from dampness, they were plastered or covered with cement. Sometimes the outer coating was tinted, although more often it was left to mellow to a soft off-white. The columns were almost always of plastered brick and very occasionally of cypress wood; the capitals were of these materials or, rarely, of iron.

GRAND & GRANDER   By the 1850s, many planters were quite prosperous, and their homes became more grandiose. Many embraced extravagant Victorian architecture and gave it a unique Louisiana flavor; others tended to borrow from the features of northern Italian villas, and some plantation homes followed Gothic lines (notably the fantastic San Francisco plantation, sometimes called "steamboat Gothic"; see p. 256). Planters and their families traveled to Europe more frequently during this period, and they brought back ornate furnishings. European masters were imported for fine woodworking until Louisiana artisans such as Mallard and Seignouret developed skills that rivaled or surpassed the Europeans. Ceilings were adorned with elaborate medallions from which glittering crystal chandeliers hung, and on wooden mantels and wainscoting, the art of *faux marbre* (false marble) began to appear. The wealthiest plantation owners were determined to make their country homes every bit as elegant as their New Orleans town houses.

Plantation houses also expanded in size over time, with some coming to have as many as 30 or 40 rooms. Families were quite large, and social life in the country consisted of visits from neighbors or friends who might stay several days or weeks. After all, travel was difficult; there was very little dropping by or popping in during those times. And certainly a Louisiana version of keeping up with the Joneses had its place as well: The Madewood house on Bayou Lafourche was built for no other reason than to outshine Woodlawn, the beautiful home of the builder's brother (unfortunately, this one's not open to the public).

The planters' enormous wealth stemmed from an economy based on human servitude. The injustice and frequent cruelty of slavery, however, were the seeds of its own demise. Whether or not the issue of slavery caused the Civil War, it soon became a central target of the Union effort. When emancipation came, it had an inestimable effect on plantations all across the South. Farming as it had been practiced on the plantations was impossible without that large, cheap labor base. During Reconstruction, lands were often confiscated and turned over intact to people who later proved unable to run the large-scale operations; many were broken up into smaller, more manageable farms. Increasing international competition began to erode the cotton and sugar markets that had built the planters' large fortunes. The culture represented by the few houses that remain today emerged and died away in a span of less than 100 years.

THE PLANTATION HOUSES TODAY Where dozens of grand homes once dotted the landscape along and around the river, relatively few now remain. Several houses that survived the Civil War have since fallen victim to fires or floods, and some have been torn down to make way for other things such as industrial plants. Others, too costly to be maintained, have been left to the ravages of dampness and decay. A few, however, have been saved, preserved, and treated to the installation of modern conveniences such as plumbing and electricity. Most of the old houses are private residences, but you can visit others for a small admission fee (which, in some instances, supplements the owner's own resources to keep up the old house).

Tours of plantations are a hit-or-miss affair—much depends on your guide—and if you do several, you'll begin to hear many of the same facts about plantation life after a while. The problem is that often the history of the house in question is lost in time, or it never had a particularly good story to begin with; consequently, other details, like the practicalities of plantation living, have to be thrown in to fill out a tour. The exceptions are mostly noted below.

PLANNING YOUR TRIP

All the plantation homes shown on the map on p. 251 are within easy driving distance of New Orleans. How many you can tour in a day will depend on your endurance behind the wheel, your walking stamina (you'll cover a lot of ground touring the houses), how early you set out, how many of the same details you can stand to hear repeated, and how late you want to return (the small highways get a little intimidating after dark). You'll be driving through some ravaged countryside—this is oil and chemical company country now—though you will probably see more sugar cane than you've seen in your entire life. Also, don't expect to enjoy broad river views as you drive along the Great River Road (the name of the roadway on *both* sides of the Mississippi); you'll have to drive up on the levee for that. You will, however, pass through little towns that date from plantation days, and you'll have the luxury of turning off to inspect interesting old churches or aboveground cemeteries.

If you have minimal time, we suggest viewing just the Laura and Oak Alley plantations (see below); they are just a mile apart, and each offers a different perspective on plantation life (Laura being classic understated Creole, while Tara-esque Oak

Alley represents the showy Americans) and the tourism industry (Oak Alley is slick and glitzy, while Laura is more low-key but a superb presentation). Both are approximately an hour's drive from New Orleans.

If you're in New Orleans on **Christmas Eve,** consider driving along the River Road to see the huge bonfires residents build on the levees to light the way for the Christ Child and Papa Noël (who rides in a sleigh drawn by—what else?—eight alligators!). They spend weeks collecting wood, trash, and anything else flammable to make the fires blaze brightly—and often explode with fireworks.

Not all Louisiana plantations actually bordered the Mississippi River (many were on bayous that also provided water transportation), and some of the grand old homes are too far away from New Orleans to be visited in a single day. These are listed separately with the recommendation that you try to stay overnight at one that offers the option. There are also listings for lodgings in St. Francisville, later in this chapter, which can serve as a convenient plantation tour base.

ORGANIZED TOURS

A plantation house bus tour is a stress-free way to visit the River Road region from New Orleans (someone else does the planning and deals with directions and tricky turns), though most of the tours visit only one or two of the houses described below. In general, tour guides are well informed, and the buses are an easy, comfortable way to get around in unfamiliar territory. Almost every New Orleans tour company operates a River Road plantation tour.

The 7-hour tour offered by **Gray Line** (℗ 800/535-7786 or 504/569-1401; www.graylineneworleans.com) is a reliable choice. The tour (usually between 20 and 40 people) visits two plantations, Nottoway and Oak Alley, and drives by six others. The $47 price ($24 for children) includes admission fees. Tours depart at 9am on Monday, Wednesday, Friday, and Saturday. The cost of lunch at a not particularly good country restaurant is not included and generally runs $8 to $10, sometimes more.

If you prefer a smaller tour group, **Tours by Isabelle** (℗ **504/391-3544;** www.toursbyisabelle.com) takes up to 13 people in a comfortable van on an 8-hour expedition to visit Oak Alley, Madewood, and Nottoway plantations. The cost ($95) includes lunch in the formal dining room of the Madewood plantation mansion. The tour runs only when six or more people request it, so you might have to wait a day or two for a large enough group. Other tours by Isabelle include a 4½-hour Cajun Bayou Tour for $55 (the boat tour is 1½ hr.), the 5½-hour Westbank Plantation Tour for $63 (which includes guided tours of Oak Ally and Laura plantations and stops in front of Whitney, Josephine, and Evergreen plantations), and the Grand Tour for $105 (which includes a visit to Oak Alley Plantation, lunch, Laura, and a Cajun Bayou Tour).

PLANTATIONS BETWEEN NEW ORLEANS & BATON ROUGE

The plantations below are listed in the order in which they appear on the map, running along the Mississippi, north, out of New Orleans. Many people choose one or two homes—Oak Alley, Nottoway, Laura, Madewood, and Tezcuco are popular ones—and find the quickest route (get a good map). If you choose to follow the route along the riverbanks, know that you will have to cross the Mississippi a few times to see every plantation; there is a bridge just downriver from Destrehan, one between San Francisco and Laura plantations. The river does wind, so distances along it are deceiving; give yourself more time than you think you'll need to arrive at your destination. All of the plantations discussed in this section are roughly 1 hour from New Orleans and approximately 15 minutes from each other.

Note: Unfortunately, **Tezcuco Plantation** was completely destroyed by fire in May 2002. The 147-year-old plantation home was built by Benjamin Tureaud in 1855 and was called Tezcuco, which was taken from the name of a lake not far from Mexico City. The word *tezcuco* means "resting place." For more information, go to www.cr.nps.gov/nr/travel/louisiana/tez.htm.

Destrehan Plantation ★★

An appearance in *Interview with the Vampire*, not to mention its proximity to New Orleans (perhaps 30 min. away), has made Destrehan Manor a popular plantation jaunt. It's also the oldest intact plantation home in the lower Mississippi Valley open to the public. It was built in 1787 by a free person of color for a wealthy Frenchman and was modified between 1830 and 1840 from its already dated French Colonial style to Greek Revival. Its warmly colored, graceful lines should please nearly everyone's aesthetic sensibilities. In addition to playing the role of Louis's ancestral home in *Interview*, it also supplied some later interiors.

The tour, led by costumed guides who stay in character (it's better than it sounds), is worth taking. The house stayed in the original family's possession until 1910 (some female descendants are still on the board that oversees the place), so a fair amount is documented, and some of the furnishings (including a table used by Lafayette) are original. One of the rooms has been left deliberately unrenovated, and its messy deconstructed state shows you the humble rawness under the usual public grandeur.

Also of important note, this is perhaps the only plantation that is truly accessible for those with disabilities; there is an elevator to take wheelchairs up to the second floor (where the true living spaces are located).

La. 48 (P.O. Box 5), Destrehan, LA 70047. ℂ **985/764-9315.** www.destrehanplantation.org. Admission $10 adults, $5 teenagers, $3 children 6–12, free for children under 6. Daily 9am–4pm. Closed New Year's Day, Mardi Gras, Easter, Thanksgiving, Dec 24–25.

San Francisco ★

This fanciful mansion, a brightly colored creation known as steamboat Gothic, is a farther schlepp from Destrehan (its closest neighbor) than it seems on the map. But it's worth the trip if you want to see something other than a cookie-cutter plantation home. Located 2 miles north of Reserve, the house was built between 1853 and 1856 by Edmond B. Marmillion. Unfortunately, Marmillion died shortly after its completion and never occupied the home, which was willed to his sons, Valsin and Charles. In 1855, while on a grand tour of Europe, Valsin met and married Louise Seybold. Valsin and Louise undertook to decorate the home in high style, and when they were finished, Valsin jokingly declared to his friends that he was *sans fruscin,* or "without a cent" to his name. This is how the plantation home gained its first name, St. Frusquin. When Achille Bougère bought the estate, the name was changed to San Francisco.

The three-story Gothic house has broad galleries that look for all the world like a ship's double decks, and twin stairs lead to a broad main portal much like one that leads to a steamboat's grand salon. (Novelist Frances Parkinson Keyes visited the house and used it as the setting for her novel *Steamboat Gothic.*) Inside, the owner created beauty in every room through the use of carved woodwork and paintings alive with flowers, birds, nymphs, and cherubs on walls and ceilings of cypress tongue-and-groove boards.

2646 Hwy 44, Garyville, LA 70051. ℂ **985/535-2341.** www.sanfranciscoplantation.org. Admission $10 adults, $5 students ages 12–17, $3 children 6–11, free for children under 6. Daily 9:30am–5pm (last tours between 4–4:40pm, depending on season). Closed New Year's Day, Mardi Gras, Easter, Thanksgiving Day, Dec 24–25.

Laura: A Creole Plantation ★★★ *Tips*   If you see only one plantation, make it this one. Laura is the very model of a modern plantation—that is, when you figure that today's crop is tourism, not sugar cane or indigo. And it's all thanks to the vision of developer and general manager Norman Marmillion, who was determined to make this property rise above the average antebellum mansion. The hoopskirted tours found elsewhere are banished in favor of a comprehensive view of daily life on an 18th- and 19th-century plantation, a cultural history of Louisiana's Creole population, and a dramatic, entertaining, in-depth look at one extended Creole family.

This is a classic Creole house, simple on the outside but with real magic within. Unlike many other plantation homes, much is known about this house and the family that lived here, thanks to extensive records (more than 5,000 documents researched in France), particularly the detailed memoirs of Laura Locoul (for whom the plantation is named). On display are more than 375 original artifacts, making this the largest collection in the region of items belonging to one plantation family. They cover a 200-year period and include household items like clothes and jewelry. The property itself is a labor of love, as all the buildings are slowly being renovated (next up, the slave quarters).

Basic tours of the main building and the property last about 55 minutes and are organized around true (albeit spiced-up) stories from the history of the home and its residents. (*Of special note:* The stories that eventually became the beloved Br'er Rabbit were first collected here by a folklorist in the 1870s.) Special tours are available on subjects including Creole architecture, Creole women, children, slaves, and the "Americanization of Louisiana." The special tours last about 1½ hours and must be scheduled in advance. Every day they offer tours in both English and French and have handouts in several additional languages. *Note:* To learn about Laura's family's life in the big city of New Orleans, go on the **Le Monde Creole** tours (p. 182).

2247 La. 18, Vacherie, LA 70090. ✆ **888/799-7690** or 225/265-7690. www.lauraplantation.com. Admission $10 adults, $5 students and children, free for children under 6. Closed major holidays.

Oak Alley Plantation ★★★   This is precisely what comes to mind when most people think "plantation." A splendid white house, its porch lined with giant columns, approached by a magnificent drive lined with stately oak trees— yep, it's all here. Consequently, this is the most famous (and probably most photographed) plantation house in Louisiana. (Parts of *Interview with the Vampire* and *Primary Colors* were shot here.) It's also the slickest operation, with a large parking lot, an expensive lunch buffet (bring your own picnic), hoopskirted guides, and golf carts traversing the blacktopped lanes around the property. It's an interesting contrast with Laura (see above), and they are just a mile apart, so we highly recommend that you visit both.

The house was built in 1839 by Jacques Telesphore Roman III and was named Bon Séjour—but if you walk out to the levee and look back at the quarter-mile avenue of 300-year-old live oaks, you'll see why steamboat passengers quickly dubbed it "Oak Alley." Roman was so enamored of the trees that he planned his house to have exactly as many columns—28 in all. The fluted Doric columns completely surround the Greek Revival house and support a broad second-story gallery. Oak Alley lay disintegrating until 1914, when Mr. and Mrs. Jefferson Hardin of New Orleans bought it. Then, in 1925, it passed to Mr. and Mrs. Andrew Stewart, whose loving restoration is responsible for its National Historic Landmark designation.

Little is known about the families who lived here; consequently, tours focus on more general plantation facts. Over the last few years, renovations have given the rooms and furnishings a facelift, returning the house to its 1830s roots, and though the furnishings are not original, they are strict to the time period and mostly correspond to the Romans' actual inventory.

Overnight accommodations are available in five really nice century-old Creole cottages (complete with sitting rooms, porches, and air-conditioning). Rates are $105 to $135 and include breakfast but not a tour. The overpriced restaurant is open for breakfast and lunch daily from 9am to 3pm.

3645 La. 18 (60 miles from New Orleans), Vacherie, LA 70090. ℂ **800/44-ALLEY** or 225/265-2151. www.oakalleyplantation.com. Admission $10 adults, $5 students, $3 children 6–12, free for children under 6. Daily 9am–5pm except March–Oct. 9am–5:30pm. Closed part of New Year's Day, Thanksgiving, Christmas.

Madewood ★★
This imposing house, a two-story Greek Revival on Bayou Lafourche, just below Napoleonville, is one of the best-preserved plantation mansions and is the place to fulfill your own plantation dreams—literally. The overnight accommodations, unlike those offered by other plantation homes, are in the main house, allowing you and the other guests a chance to run around the 20 rooms at night, pretending it's yours, all yours. Once you hear the recent history, however, you might be rather glad it's not.

A youngest brother originally built Madewood for the sole purpose of outdoing his older brother's elegant mansion, Woodlawn. Four years were spent cutting lumber and making bricks, and another four were spent in actual construction. It was finally completed in 1848, but the owner never got to gloat over his brother—he died of yellow fever just before it was finished. As with many of the grand plantation homes, Madewood fell into disrepair and stood empty for a while until it was bought in 1964 by the parents of the present owner, Keith Marshall. When you hear the stories and see the photos of the laborious renovation (done in large part by the Marshalls and their friends), you realize how much work it is to save, and then continue to keep up, these glorious houses.

If you do **stay overnight,** you'll get the run of the place in the evening as well as grand canopied or half-tester (curtains at the head end) beds, wine and cheese in the library, a multicourse dinner of Southern specialties (served by a charming woman whose family has worked at Madewood for seven generations; be sure to chat with her), brandy in the parlor, and coffee in bed the next morning followed by a full plantation breakfast. Now that's gracious Southern living. If you're lucky, Marshall and his wife, Millie Ball, will join you and share their stories. Rates are $259 for two per night, which includes wine and cheese, dinner, after-dinner brandy and coffee, and a full breakfast. Rooms in the elegant 1820s raised cottage are more secluded with fewer formal furnishings. A bronze plaque in one tells you that Brad Pitt slept there while filming *Interview with the Vampire.*

4250 La. 308, Napoleonville, LA 70390. ℂ **800/375-7151** or 504/369-7151. Fax 504/369-9848. www.madewood.com. Admission $8 adults, $4 children under 12 and students. Daily 10am–4pm. Closed New Year's Eve, New Year's Day, Thanksgiving, and Christmas.

Houmas House Plantation & Gardens ★
This is a different sort of plantation house in that it is actually two houses joined together. The original structure was a mere four rooms built in 1790. In 1840, a larger, Greek Revival–style house was built next to it, and some time over the subsequent years a roof was put over both, joining them together. The property, a former sugar plantation, has had multiple owners and little is known about them. The late Dr. George Crozat of New Orleans purchased the house some years ago and restored it as

a comfortable home for himself and his mother, bringing in authentic period furnishings. Two of his nieces still live on the third floor.

Live oaks, magnolias, and formal gardens frame Houmas House in a way that is precisely what comes to mind when most of us think "plantation house." It so closely fits this image that its exterior was used in the film *Hush, Hush, Sweet Charlotte*. The inside is a bit disappointing, but scenes from *All My Children* were shot here, so be sure to ask for those Susan Lucci stories (they've got 'em).

40136 La. 942, Burnside (58 miles from New Orleans; mailing address: 40136 Hwy. 942, Darrow, LA 70725). (C) 888/323-8314. Fax 225/474-0480. www.houmashouse.com. Admission (including guided tour) $10 adults, $6 children ages 13–17, $3 children ages 6–12, free for children under 6. Daily 10am–5pm; Nov–Jan closes at 4pm. Closed New Year's Day, Thanksgiving, and Christmas. Take I-10 from New Orleans or Baton Rouge. Exit on La. 44 to Burnside and turn right on La. 942.

Nottoway Plantation ★★ There are two reasons to come to this particular plantation. The first is the house itself, dating from 1858, the largest existing plantation house in the South, a mammoth structure with 64 rooms (covering 53,000 sq. ft.), an opening (window or door) for every day in the year, and pillars that could challenge those holding up the White House. It was saved from Civil War destruction by a northern gunboat officer who had once been a guest here, and kindness still blesses it. With handsome interiors featuring marvelous curlicue plasterwork, hand-carved Corinthian columns of cypress wood in the ballroom, beautiful archways, original crystal chandeliers, and other details, it's been lovingly restored over the years by a series of owners (one of whom, in her 90s, still lives on site and runs her doll shop there in the afternoons). This is everything you want in a dazzling Old South mansion.

The second reason to visit is that, by coming here, you have the opportunity to have Judy Davis as your guide. An educated, eloquent, witty raconteur with the timing of a stand-up comic monologist, Davis may well be the best tour guide we have ever had. And if you are really lucky, she might sing for you. You can stay in the plantation in rooms running from $135 to $250, but though this includes a "wake up" call of coffee and a sweet potato muffin, plus a full breakfast, and a tour, it may not be worth the money, as the least-costly rooms are sweet but showing their age (not in the good way), and the costly rooms, while dazzling, often permit only late check-ins and early check-outs because they are on the daily tours. Randolph Hall restaurant serves a not very good lunch from 11am to 3pm and dinner from 6 to 9pm.

Mississippi River Road (P.O. Box 160), White Castle, LA 70788. (C) 866/LASOUTH or 225/545-2730. Fax 225/545-8632. www.nottoway.com. Admission $10 adults, $4 children ages 4–12, free for children under 4. Daily 9am–5pm. Closed Christmas. From New Orleans, follow I-10 west to La. 22 exit, then turn left on La. 70 across Sunshine Bridge. Exit onto La. 1 and drive 14 miles north through Donaldsonville. From Baton Rouge, take I-10 west to Plaquemine exit and then La. 1 south for 18 miles.

DINING

Note that many of the plantations operate their own restaurants, but none of them are very good.

IN VACHERIE

B&C Seafood Market & Cajun Deli ★ CAJUN/SEAFOOD We believe in "when in Rome," so if you are out scouting plantations, join the locals and stop off at this decidedly low-atmosphere family operation for some fresh seafood (the house specialty—boiled or fried), gumbo, jambalaya, po' boys, and our favorite, fried boudin (sausage) balls (they make a great car snack).

2155 Hwy 18. (C) 225/265-8356. All items $6–$20. AE, DISC, MC, V. Mon–Sat 9am–6pm.

IN DONALDSONVILLE

Lafitte's Landing Restaurant ★★ FRENCH/CAJUN   Sadly, this long-time landmark restaurant burned to the ground in late 1998, but the owners refused to let bad luck keep them down for long. They opened up their former home as the Bittersweet Plantation and operate a bed-and-breakfast along with this restaurant. Chef John Folse has cooked for Reagan, Gorbachev, and the Pope—why not let him cook for you?

404 Claiborne Ave. ℂ **225/473-1232.** Fax 225/473-1161. www.jfolse.com. Reservations recommended. Main courses $17–$28. AE, DISC, MC, V. Wed–Sat 6–10pm; Fri and Sun brunch 11am–3pm.

ST. FRANCISVILLE & SURROUNDING PLANTATIONS

St. Francisville, 30 miles northwest of Baton Rouge, doesn't look like much on approach, but by the time you get to the center of town, you are utterly charmed. Many of the plantations described below are clustered around St. Francisville, which is a roughly 2-hour drive from New Orleans and pretty much requires an overnight stay. You can get into the spirit of things and plan to stay at one of the plantations described below, or you may choose to stay in St. Francisville (they have several B&Bs there; see below for listings of St. Francisville). We strongly suggest staying here (if not *at* one of said plantations) overnight rather than going back and forth from Baton Rouge, where there is very little of interest aside from one plantation home. Contact the **St. Francisville tourism information office** for more information (ℂ **225/635-6330;** 9am–5pm daily).

If you do decide to stay in Baton Rouge, which is 77 miles northwest of New Orleans, however, contact the **Baton Rouge Area Convention and Visitors Bureau,** 730 North Blvd., Baton Rouge, LA 70802 (ℂ **800/LA-ROUGE;** www.bracvb.com), and ask for its useful "Baton Rouge Visitors Guide," which contains maps of attractions in the city and surrounding area.

Magnolia Mound ★   This home was built in the late 1700s as a small settler's house. As prosperity came to the lower Mississippi Valley, the house was enlarged and renovated, eventually becoming the center of a 900-acre plantation. Its single story is nearly 5 feet off the ground and has a front porch 80 feet across. The hand-carved woodwork and the ceiling in the parlor are authentically restored. Magnolia Mound takes its name from its setting within a grove of trees on a bluff overlooking the Mississippi. One of the oldest wooden structures in the state, it is typical French Creole in architecture and is furnished in Louisiana and early Federal style. Costumed guides take you through. Magnolia Mound recently completed renovations of slave cabins on the site.

2161 Nicholson Dr., Baton Rouge, LA 70802. ℂ **225/343-4955.** Fax 225/343-6739. http://asterix.ednet. lsu.edu/~anderson/magnolia/mmp.html#mag. Admission $8 adults, $6 seniors, $6 students 13–22, $3 children 5–12, free for children under 5. Tues–Sat 10am–4pm; Sun 1–4pm. Last tour begins at 3:15pm.

Parlange Plantation ★   This plantation is one of the few that still functions as a working farm. Built in 1750 by Marquis Vincent de Ternant, the house is one of the oldest in the state, and its two stories rise above a raised brick basement. Galleries encircle the house, which is flanked by two brick *pigeonniers* (large houses for pigeons). Indigo was planted here at first; in the 1800s, sugar cane became the plantation's main crop. Today, the plantation grows sugar cane, corn, and soybeans, and also supports its own cattle. During the Civil War, this house was host to generals from both sides (Gen. Nathaniel Banks of the Union and Gen. Dick Taylor of the Confederacy)—not, of course, at the same time. Parlange is a National Historic Landmark and is owned by relatives of the original builders.

8211 False River Rd., New Roads, LA 70760. ✆ **225/638-8410.** Admission $10 adults, $5 children 6–12. By appointment only. From Baton Rouge, take U.S. 190 19 miles west and then La. Hwy 1 another 8 miles north.

Oakley Plantation at Audubon State Historic Site 🏛

Oakley Plantation, 3 miles east of U.S. 61, features the old house where John James Audubon came to study and paint the wildlife of this part of Louisiana. Built in 1799, it is a three-story frame house with the raised basement typical of that era. A curved stairway joins the two galleries, and the whole house has a simplicity that bespeaks its age. When Audubon was here, he tutored a daughter of the family and painted some 32 of his *Birds of America* series. When you visit the house today, you will see some original prints from Audubon's elephant folio and many fine antiques. A walk through the gardens and nature trails will explain why this location had such appeal for Audubon. Oakley is part of the 100-acre Audubon State Commemorative Area, a wildlife sanctuary that would have gladdened the naturalist's heart. There's a gift shop in the kitchen building, but you can still see the huge old fireplace where the family's meals were cooked.

La. 965 (P.O. Box 546), St. Francisville, LA 70775. ✆ **888/677-2838** or 225/635-3739. Fax 225/784-0578. Admission $2 adults, free for seniors (over 62) and children under 12. Daily 9am–5pm. Closed New Year's Day, Thanksgiving, Christmas.

Rosedown Plantation 🏛🏛

By far the most impressive and historic of the more far-flung plantations, Rosedown is notable for its dramatic gardens and a tour stuffed with intriguing bits of facts and trivia, courtesy of more than 8,000 documents in their archives. Just east of St. Francisville, Rosedown was completed in 1834 for Daniel Turnbull (whose son, William, married Martha Washington's great-great-granddaughter) on land granted by the Spanish in 1789 to a founder of the Port of Bayou Sara on the Mississippi River. The two-story house, flanked by one-story wings, combines classic and indigenous Louisiana styles. It has the typical columns and wide galleries across the front, and it's made of cement-covered brick. A wide avenue of ancient oaks, their branches meeting overhead, leads up to the house. The 28 acres of historic gardens were begun in 1835 and came to be one of the great horticultural collections of the 19th century as well as one of the nation's most significant historical gardens in the 20th century. Fittingly, marble statues of gods and goddesses (brought back from trips to Europe by the family) dot the winding pathways. Unfortunately, ownership of Rosedown has changed a couple of times, finally landing in the hands of the State of Louisiana. In the process, many of its wonderful family treasures have been lost (well, sold, but don't get anyone started on *that* scandal) and other bits suffered as well, so what you see will depend on an ongoing process. Still, you can easily spend 2 hours wandering through house and gardens. Overnight accommodations are available as well, through a private company.

12501 Hwy. 10 (at I-10 and U.S. 61), St. Francisville, LA 70775. ✆ **888/376-1867** or 225/635-3332. Fax 225/784-1382. Admission (house tour and historic gardens) $10 adults, $8 seniors, $4 students 6–17, free for children under 5. Daily 9am–5pm. Closed New Year's Day, Thanksgiving, and Christmas.

Catalpa Plantation

Unless you are just a die-hard plantation buff, this relatively humble Victorian home is probably not worth going out of your way for. It's not all that historic or notable architecturally. On the other hand, it is still owned by the original family, which is practically unheard of among plantations these days. The oaks that line the drive up to the house grew from acorns planted by the present owner's great-great-great-grandfather, and tours do feature all sorts of curious stories about the family heirlooms that still lie within its walls. The slightly dented silver tea service, for example, lay buried in a pond during the Civil War; the lovely hand-painted china was done by none other than John James Audubon. This sense of family history and direct connection with the past is rare, so that alone may make your visit worthwhile.

Off U.S. 61 (P.O. Box 131), St. Francisville, LA 70775. ℂ **225/635-3372.** Admission $6 adults, $3 children 6–12, free for children under 6. Tours available by appointment.

The Myrtles ℱ A little over 1 mile north of the intersection with Louisiana Highway 10, along U.S. Highway 61, is this beautiful, if a tad dull, house built in 1795. Its gallery is 110 feet long, and the elaborate iron grillwork is reminiscent of the French Quarter. The Myrtles is in an astonishingly good state of preservation, especially inside, where the intricate plaster moldings in each room are intact. The house is set in a grove of great old live oaks; the grounds are not as big as at Rosedown (well, nothing else really is) but are still worth a ramble through. Too bad it's all set right on the noisy highway, which helps dispel any fantasy about drifting back to another era.

Overnight accommodations are available, and although we were merely underwhelmed, we have since gotten many complaints from other guests; the place needs an overhaul, and until it's done, we can't really recommend staying here. They do offer "mystery" tours Friday and Saturday nights, wherein guides tell tales of various ghosts haunting the place; these tend to be kitschy fun, which is just fine if that's what you're looking for (we say that because we once heard, in an occult shop, a woman sincerely complaining that no real ghosts turned up when she stayed there). **Kearn's Carriage House** (on the property) serves fancy dinners and simple lunches and is a worthwhile place to eat.

7747 U.S. 61 (P.O. Box 1100), St. Francisville, LA 70775. ℂ **225/635-6277.** Fax 225/635-5837. www.myrtles plantation.com. Admission $8 adults, $4 children. Daily 9am–5pm. Closed major holidays.

The Cottage ℱ This rambling country home, 5 miles north of St. Francisville, is really a series of buildings constructed between 1795 and 1859. It's not that much to see, inside or out, and the accommodations pale when compared to what's offered at Madewood. Still, the low, two-story house has a long gallery out front, a nice place to sit and relax for an evening, perhaps joined by the owners' sociable dogs.

The first house was built entirely of virgin cypress taken from the grounds. Many of the outbuildings date from 1811, when Judge Thomas Butler (of the "Fighting Butlers," prominent in American history) acquired the property. After his victory in the Battle of New Orleans, Gen. Andrew Jackson, along with a troop of officers that included no fewer than *eight* Butlers, stopped off here for a 3-week stay on his way from New Orleans to Natchez. The Cottage's interior looks very much as it did when the Butlers lived here, with hand-screened wallpaper, a 19th-century loveseat (with space for a chaperone), and needlepoint fire screens made by the ladies of the family. This is a working family farm of some 360 acres.

The four **guest rooms** ($95 double, including breakfast) are a mix of elegant (huge four-poster canopy beds) and funky (icky motel-room carpeting) and are not available January, February, or major holidays. But there is a small pool, and you do have breakfast in the elegant dining room of the main house.

10528 Cottage Lane (at U.S. 61), St. Francisville, LA 70775. ℂ **225/635-3674.** www.cottageplantation.com. Admission $6. Daily for tours 9:30am–4:30pm. Closed major holidays.

ACCOMMODATIONS IN ST. FRANCISVILLE

In addition to the establishments listed below, you might consider spending the night at Madewood, Nottoway Plantation, or Rosedown Plantation, described in the previous section. All should be booked well in advance.

If the accommodations listed below are booked up, call the St. Francisville **tourism information office** for a list of (and suggestions regarding) local B&Bs (© 225/635-6330).

Barrow House Inn ★★   The Barrow House Inn is actually two guesthouses, the Barrow House and the Printer's House. Both are listed on the National Register of Historic Places and are located in the heart of St. Francisville's charming historic district. The Printer's House, dating from the 1780s, is the oldest in town and was built by the monks for whom St. Francisville is named. Across the street is the New England saltbox–style Barrow House (ca. 1809). Owned and operated by Shirley Dittloff and her son Christopher, the houses have been restored and furnished with 1840s to 1880s antiques. The Dittloffs offer a choice of continental or full breakfast, and their acclaimed gourmet dinner (guests only) is served by candlelight in the historic dining room. In addition to numerous pampering touches, guests also have access to a mini–space exploration museum dedicated to Shirley's father, Jim Chamberlin, a pioneer in American space history.

9779 Royal St. (P.O. Box 2550), St. Francisville, LA 70775. © **225/635-4791.** Fax 225/635-1863. www.topten inn.com. 8 units, all with private bathroom. $95–$125 double; $140–$160 suite. Extra person $30. DISC, MC, V. **Amenities:** Gourmet dinner, complimentary wine, continental or full breakfast; gift shop; horseshoes; designated smoking areas; cassette walking tour. *In room:* A/C, TV, canopy beds.

Butler Greenwood Plantation B&B ★★   This is a dynamite place to stay (as a plantation tour, it's nothing you won't see elsewhere—though it is one of few that is still owned and occupied by the original family, and still a full-time family home), starting with the setting, extensive grounds full of tangled oak trees, plus a pond with resident ducks. The front main house (a tour can be arranged for $5) is full of original family furnishings. The guest quarters are seven cottages, each with its own personality, from the **Old Kitchen** (with a working fireplace and the original 150-foot well, covered by glass so guests can peer down it) to the **Gazebo,** with old church windows, to the storybook-cunning three-story **Dovecot.** Each unit has been set in such a way that it has its own bit of privacy and is decorated with a mix of old and new furnishings. Some have ugly kitchen units, and some have decks overlooking a mini-gorge. Continental breakfasts are brought to the cottages in the morning. It all adds up to a

---

(Finds Grandmother's Buttons

Once in St. Francisville, do stop by **Grandmother's Buttons** ★, at 9814 Royal St. (© **800/580-6941** or 225/635-4107; www.grandmothersbuttons.com). The owner makes jewelry from antique and vintage buttons (from Victorian brass picture buttons to 1940s Bakelite)—one-of-a-kind, amazing creations. We've bought more earrings, brooches, and other gewgaws from here than we could ever possibly wear. Don't overlook their much-more-interesting-than-you-might-think Button Museum. Hours are Monday through Saturday from 10am to 5:30pm, Sunday from noon to 5:30pm.

splendid romantic private retreat. Be sure to ask the owner about her true-crime book, which just happens to detail a true crime she herself survived.

8345 U.S. Hwy. 61, St. Francisville, LA 70775. ✆ 225/635-6312. Fax 225/635-6370. www.butlergreenwood. com. 7 units, all with private bathrooms. $125–$175. Rates include continental breakfast and tour of the main plantation house. AE, MC, V. **Amenities:** Pool; nature walks. *In room:* All cottages contain A/C, cable TV, kitchens, Jacuzzi, and porches or decks; some cottages have working fireplaces or four-poster beds.

The St. Francisville Inn ✦   Formerly the Wolf-Schlesinger House, this is a budget alternative to local B&Bs. Rooms are motel-comfortable (the top end choice is the queen with the Jacuzzi tub) and plain, but the owners inject plenty of family-friendly hospitality, and that makes anything pretty. They certainly go all out for the breakfast buffet; it's small but top-heavy with choices (bacon, grits, filled crepes, plus a bunch of desserts). There is a real-size pool, plus an antiques shop. If you are traveling with a large party, the inn can accommodate more than a small B&B (and is potentially more interesting than just a chain hotel), and the owners can also do rather tasty group dinners in the various dining rooms.

5720 Commerce St., St. Francisville, LA 70775. ✆ 800/488-6502 or 225/635-6502. Fax 225/635-6421. www.stfrancisvilleinn.com. 10 units. $60–$95. Full buffet breakfast included in rates. AE, DC, DISC, MC, V. **Amenities:** Pool; shop. *In room:* A/C, TV.

DINING IN ST. FRANCISVILLE

Magnolia Cafe ✦✦ *(Finds* CAFE   This lively, friendly place certainly caters to plantation-hopping tourists with their decidedly nonlocal menu (though locals still come here, drawn by the good food, fine atmosphere, and live music Fri nights). How else to explain an entire Mexican menu; pizza with chicken, pesto, and spinach toppings; salads that don't just rely on iceberg lettuce and which sport fat-free honey mustard dressing; and fat-free lemon cheesecake for dessert? The food is good and spicy, there's a kids' menu, and sandwiches range from po' boys to stir-fry chicken (really). Desserts like the Snicker Blitz or Candy Bar cheesecake can send you into a sugar coma.

5687 E. Commerce St. ✆ 225/635-6528. Fax 225/635-2463. www.themagnoliacafe.com. Everything under $15. MC, V. Sun–Tue 10am–4pm; Wed–Thu 10am–9pm; Fri 10am–10pm; Sat 10am–9pm.

2 Cajun Country

The official name of this area is Acadiana, and it consists of a rough triangle of Louisiana made up of 22 parishes (counties), from St. Landry Parish at the top of the triangle to the Gulf of Mexico at its base. Lafayette is Acadiana's "capital," and it's dotted with such towns as St. Martinville, New Iberia, Abbeville, and Eunice. You won't find its boundaries on any map, nor the name "Acadiana" stamped across it. But those 22 parishes are Cajun country, and its history and culture are unique in America.

MEET THE CAJUNS

The Cajun history is a sad one, but it produced a people and a culture well worth getting to know.

THE ACADIAN ODYSSEY   In the early 1600s, colonists from France began settling the southeastern coast of Canada in a region of Nova Scotia they named Acadia. They developed a peaceful agricultural society based on the values of a strong Catholic faith, deep love of family, and respect for their relatively small land holdings. The community was isolated from the mainstream of European culture for nearly 150 years. Life was defined by the company of families and friends. This pastoral existence was maintained until 1713 when Acadia became

---

Fun Fact **The Real Evangeline**

You may know Henry Wadsworth Longfellow's epic poem *Evangeline*—the story of Evangeline and Gabriel, Acadian lovers who spent their lives wandering this land searching for each other after being wrenched from their homeland. In real life, Evangeline was Emmeline Labiche, and her sweetheart was Louis Pierre Arceneaux. Their story has a different ending from the poet's—Emmeline found Louis Pierre, after years of searching, in Cajun country, in St. Martinville. The real-life tragedy was that, by then, Louis had given up hope of finding her and was pledged to another. She died of a broken heart in Louisiana, not Philadelphia.

---

the property of the British under the Treaty of Utrecht. Though the Acadians were determined to keep to their peaceful existence under the new rulers, it became clear that it would not be possible. For more than 40 years, they were harassed by the king's representatives, who tried to force them to pledge allegiance to the British crown and renounce Catholicism and embrace the king's Protestant religion. This was so abhorrent to Acadians and they were so steadfast in their refusal that, in 1755, the British governor of the region sent troops to seize their farms and deport them. Villages were burned, husbands and wives and children were separated as ships were loaded, and a 10-year odyssey began.

Some Acadians were returned to France, some went to England, many were put ashore along America's East Coast, and some wound up in the West Indies. The deportation voyages, made on poorly equipped, overcrowded ships, took a huge toll, and hundreds of lives were lost. Many of the survivors who were sent to France and England returned to America as much as 20 years later.

Louisiana, with its strong French background, was a natural destination for Acadians hoping to reestablish a permanent home, and those who were transported to the West Indies were probably the first to head there. In 1765, Bernard Andry brought a band of 231 men, women, and children to the region now known as Acadiana.

The land on which they settled differed greatly from what they had left in Nova Scotia. The swampy terrain was low-lying and boggy; interlaced with bayous and lakes; forested with live oak, willow, ash, and gum; and teeming with wildlife. Given land that mostly bounded the bayous, the Acadians built small levees (or dikes) along the banks and drained fields for small farms and pastures.

A NEW PRIDE After many decades during which Cajuns shied away from their roots (children were beaten in school for speaking French, which was considered a sign of ignorance; Cajun music was considered primitive or hokey; and so forth), the Cajun culture is experiencing a resurgence of popularity and respect as well as a new sense of community pride.

CAJUN LANGUAGE

This essay was provided by Ann Allen Savoy, who is, along with her husband, Marc, a musician in the Savoy-Doucet Cajun Band and in her own group, the Magnolia Sisters. Both groups have released CDs on the Arhoolie label. Ann is also the author of **Cajun Music Vol. 1** *(Bluebird Press, 1984), an excellent and definitive work that combines oral history with a songbook.* Evangeline Made *(Vanguard), a collection of Cajun tunes covered by artists such as Linda Ronstadt, John Fogerty, and*

Maria McKee (which Ann produced and performed on), was released in 2002 to great critical acclaim and earned a Grammy nomination for Savoy. You can see her and son Joel playing musicians in the film Divine Secrets of the Ya-Ya Sisterhood, *and she performs three songs on the soundtrack.*

The French influence in Louisiana is one of the things that sets the state apart from the rest of the United States. As soon as you get west of Baton Rouge, you can cruise down the Louisiana highways listening on your radio to French news, church services, music, and talk shows. The accent is sharp and bright with occasional English words thrown in (*"On va revenir right back"*—"We'll be right back"), so it is fun to see how much even Anglophones can follow the French story lines.

Though French is spoken by most of the older Cajuns (aged 60 and up), most middle-aged and young Louisianians don't speak the language. This is partially because the knowledge of the French language, from the 1930s on, became associated with a lack of business success or a lack of education, so a stigma became attached to it. Today, however, there is a resurgence in pride at being bilingual, particularly in larger towns and metropolitan areas. French emergence programs are cropping up here and there, and educated musicians and teachers aged 30 to 50 are learning to speak French.

CAJUN FRENCH   Where can you hear the language spoken? I recommend wandering through old grocery stores, dance halls, and feed stores, where you will hear many "natives" speaking French. This French is peppered with beautiful old words dating from Louis XIV. These words, no longer used in France, are historically intriguing. Cajun French is not a dialect of the French language, nor are there actual dialects of Cajun French from town to town in southwest Louisiana. The impression that there are various dialects could come from the fact that many words refer to particular items, and certain areas prefer particular words over others. For example, a mosquito can be called a *marougouin, moustique,* or *cousin.* One area might use only one of the words and never use the others. Remember that Cajun French is not a written language (it's only spoken), so certain words that were originally mispronounced have become part of the language. Similarly, some English words are part of the language today because, when the Acadians first came to Louisiana, there were no such things as pickup trucks, typewriters, and other modern inventions, so the English words are used.

THE CREOLE LANGUAGE   Parallel to the Cajun French language, the fascinating Creole language is still spoken by many black Louisianians. The language is a compilation of African dialects and French and is quite different from standard French. However, Cajuns and black Creoles can speak and understand both languages.

At the weekly broadcast at the Liberty Theater in Eunice, you can listen to Cajun and zydeco music and enjoy the beauty of the unique Cajun language.

CAJUN MUSIC

It's hard to decide which is more important to a Cajun: food or music. Cajuns love music so much that, even in the early days when instruments were scarce, they held dances, with *a cappella* voices providing the accompaniment. With roots probably found in medieval France, traditional Cajun music is largely an orally transmitted art form. The strains usually come in the form of a brisk two-step or a waltz. The more traditional groups still play mostly acoustic instruments—a fiddle, an accordion, a triangle, and maybe a guitar.

The best place to hear real Cajun music is on someone's back porch, the time-honored spot for gathering to eat some gumbo and listening to several generations of musicians jamming together all night long. If you don't know a Cajun and don't have access to a back-porch gathering, don't fret. Throughout Cajun country there are dance halls with something going on just about every weekend. Locals come to dance, and so should you. Don't know how to Cajun dance? Many people will be delighted to show you. Worried everyone will be watching you because you dance so badly? Observe the couples out on the dance floor. Who are you watching? That's right—the really good couples who fly in complex, almost jitterbug patterns. You aren't looking at the mediocre couples, and neither is anyone else. So don't be shy. And talk to the people around you. This is a social gathering, and Cajuns love to visit, telling stories and jokes.

Restaurants such as **Mulate's, Randol's,** and **D.I.'s** (see listings later in this chapter) offer regular live music and Cajun dancing. The regular Saturday morning jam session at the **Savoy Music Center** (p. 273) in Eunice is not to be missed—it's the closest you will get to that back-porch experience, and it is a sheer delight.

In your search for Cajun music, please don't forget zydeco, which also thrives in this region. Zydeco bands share the bill at the weekly live show at Eunice's **Liberty Theater,** and they are the house specialty at such clubs as **Slim's Y Ki-Ki** in Opelousas and **El Sido's** in Lafayette. (You can find more information on the above later in this chapter.)

PLANNING YOUR TRIP

A circular drive will allow you to take in one or two of the plantation homes en route to Baton Rouge (if you take the River Road instead of I-10) before turning west on I-10 to reach Lafayette and the land of the Cajuns. Go north of Lafayette on I-49 to reach Opelousas; Eunice is about 20 minutes west of there on Highway 190. A return to New Orleans on U.S. 90 is a trip through the history, legend, and romance of this region. There is more than a day's worth of interest in this area, so you'll probably want to plan at least an overnight stay. On I-10, the distance from New Orleans to Lafayette is 134 miles; Lafayette to New Orleans on U.S. 90 is 167 miles. Listed below (in alphabetical order) are some of the places you should not miss, but you will find scores of other Cajun country attractions on your own. Also listed are some places to stay overnight as well as some of the outstanding Cajun restaurants (rest assured, bad restaurants do not last long) in the area.

Contact the **Lafayette Parish Convention and Visitors Commission,** P.O. Box 52066, Lafayette, LA 70505 (© **800/346-1958** in the U.S., 800/543-5340 in Canada, or 337/232-3737; fax 337/232-0161; www.lafayettetravel.com). It will send you tons of detailed information to make your trip even more fun. The office is open weekdays from 8:30am to 5pm and weekends from 9am to 5pm. (See the "Lafayette" section, later in this chapter, for driving directions.)

Hands down, the best time to visit Acadiana is during festival time (p. 37). You'll have a terrific time along with native Cajuns, who celebrate with real gusto. If you miss this, however, every weekend seems to bring a smaller festival somewhere else in the area—and plenty of music at any time of the year.

TOURS

If you can't find time for an extended visit to Cajun country, a 1-day guided tour can provide an introduction to the area. **Tours by Isabelle** (© **504/391-3544;** www.toursbyisabelle.com) specializes in small tours in comfortable, air-conditioned

Cajuns Today

Growing up immersed in Cajun culture was very difficult for me. My heroes weren't football jocks or rock 'n' roll stars, but rather my old neighbors who spoke French, farmed for a living, and played the accordion or fiddle. When fiddler Dennis McGee farmed for my grandpa, it wasn't his children who were my playmates, even though they were my age—it was Dennis. I followed him in the fields while he plowed with his mule team. I wanted to hear his stories.

Needless to say, none of my classmates shared my love for what these old-timers had to offer. I guess that, on my best days, I could describe my peers' attitude toward me as indifference. I remember a beautiful girl who sat near my desk all during grade school. I would fantasize about being her boyfriend, which was of course totally impossible. She was very heavy into sports and cheerleader stuff and the mainstream, and I wasn't. Recently this same girl came into my store to purchase some Cajun CDs to send to her daughter, who was out of state and expressed a love for Cajun music. I recognized her immediately when she came in, even though 40 years had passed. We talked awhile, and when she was leaving she asked, "Where are you from?"

Even though it was difficult being Cajun in the '40s and '50s, I don't think I ever felt any anger toward the negativity expressed by the non-Cajuns or by those Cajuns who had given up their heritage. I think my feelings at this time were frustration and disappointment toward those people. To me, the choice they were making was really bad for themselves. They were turning away from this wonderful heritage in pursuit of the mainstream. They were turning their backs on a delicious bowl of gumbo in favor of a cold, tasteless American hot dog. I think my ulterior motive in 1966 in opening up a music store that specialized in Cajun music, rather than country or rock, was that I had an ax to grind. I wanted to destroy the stigma of being Cajun. I wanted to prove to the locals that heritage and success could coexist, that being Cajun and speaking French was okay. I wanted to tell outsiders how good our food was and about all these wonderful, warm, friendly, and sincere people who were called Cajuns.

The year was a turning point—Cajun music was first presented to the outside world. It happened at the Newport Folk Festival. A three-piece group of old Cajuns was up against names such as Bob Dylan and Joan Baez. The Cajuns played their first simple tune, "Grand Mamou," and before they were halfway through, an audience of 10,000 was giving them a standing ovation.

This experience did two things. First, it reinforced the passion that had kept the fire burning in the musicians' hearts. They came home with newspaper clippings and stories about the reception at Newport that surprised even the local non-Cajuns. Second, it called outsiders to come to Louisiana to search out all things Cajun. And this had a legitimizing effect on the people down here. The outsiders came down in droves, not for things they could see or hear back home but for the things the Cajuns had not allowed the Americanization process to destroy. What was once considered a stigma was now considered an asset—to be Cajun.

The Americanization process has not been completely successful down here; it has taken its toll, influencing many people who have become a caricature of Cajun. I find what is passed off as Cajun culture in major metropolitan areas rather yuppified. In the rural areas, there are a lot of snake farms hawking the Hollywood version. But in isolated rural areas, there is also a very viable culture that exists without the slickness of the modern-day mainstream. These places can be found by getting off the interstate highways and searching out the small villages through the prairie.

It is important for the tourist to know that Cajun music is localized and is never found in the forested bayou or salt marshes but in the flat prairie region. Look at the old-timers, the first people to record—they were from Crowley. Dennis McGee and Amede Ardoin were from Eunice. There were never any recordings by musicians from bayous or marshes because there were never any musicians living there. There were Cajuns living there, but the music came from the prairie. Where you find rice planted in Louisiana, you will find Cajun accordion music. The Germans brought the button accordion from their homeland, and some say they brought rice as well. My theory is this: I have an equation that prosperity equals permanence, and permanence equals roots. Having been raised on a rice farm, I know the topsoil in some places is 6 feet deep. The first settlers who came into this region could sustain themselves very easily in one spot and didn't have to move after the first spot was depleted. We also don't have big rivers. Big rivers bring in big industry and masses of people diluting the existing culture.

I don't think modern Cajuns are that different than they were in the past. Being a Cajun, a Mexican, a Native American, or any other ethnic group—it's not about one certain aspect of that culture. It's not about whether or not you play music, or eat spicy food, or speak a certain language. You can be a mute and still be an example of that culture. It isn't the person who wears costumes consisting of red bandannas, white rubber boots, and big straw hats with a plucked rubber chicken hanging from his belt. That isn't Cajun either. It's about having roots or a foundation. It's about having roots that were cultivated in good times and bad times. And because of devotion and love, those roots sink deep, deep, deep and produce a strong, strong, strong tree, which gives protection and comfort to all those who come into its embrace. It's a matter of vision, being from a certain ethnic minority. It's about how you see yourself in your environment and how you relate and function in that environment. It's about having a deep sense of the past in order to know your direction. It's about having respect and love for the things that make you who you are and prevent you from being someone else. It's not about being crowd-pleasers. It's about being natural.

—Marc Savoy

Marc Savoy supports his Cajun heritage through the craftsmanship of accordions, as a musician with the highly acclaimed Savoy-Doucet Cajun Band and the Savoy-Smith Band, and by keeping Cajun community traditions alive.

passenger vans. You'll cross the Mississippi to visit Cajun country and then take a 1½-hour narrated swamp tour. The Cajun Bayou Tour ($55) leaves New Orleans at 1pm and returns around 5:30pm. Isabelle's Grand Tour ($108) includes the Cajun Bayou Tour, a guided tour and lunch at Oak Alley Plantation, and a guided tour of Laura: A Creole Plantation.

For other Cajun country tours, see the "Organized Tours" section of chapter 8, "Sights to See & Places to Be," beginning on p. 181.

A CAJUN WEEKEND

For music lovers, a trip out of New Orleans to the source of Cajun and zydeco music is practically a must. Though it's especially tempting to go during an organized event such as Lafayette's Festival International or Breaux Bridge's Crawfish Festival, there is always plenty of music happening—so much that you can easily fill a couple of days. Here're our suggestion for a good Cajun Country weekend itinerary (all specifics can be found in more detail later in this chapter):

FRIDAY   Drive out from New Orleans (avoid rush hour, when it can take a very long time to get through Baton Rouge). Stay in Opelousas, Eunice, or Washington, pretty towns with nice B&Bs (and some basic chain hotels). That night, drive into Lafayette and hear whatever's going on at the **Grant Street Hall** or check out Opelousas's **Slim's Y Ki-Ki** or **Richard's** for the best in zydeco.

SATURDAY   Get up early and head to the **Savoy Music Center** in Eunice for the weekly jam session. Leave before noon and drive to Mamou, where **Fred's Lounge** should be jam-packed. The action at Fred's stops at 1pm, but the bar next door picks up the slack. Then head to Ville Platte and **Floyd's Record Shop** to buy some of what you've heard. Have a bite at the **Pig Stand** or back in Eunice. That night, go to Eunice's **Liberty Theater** for the live radio broadcast featuring Cajun and zydeco groups—plus plenty of Cajun folk tales and jokes. Consider dinner at **D.I.'s,** which also has live music.

SUNDAY   Spend the morning checking out picturesque Washington, strolling the wonderful gardens at **Magnolia Ridge,** or combing the many antiques shops before heading back to New Orleans.

BREAUX BRIDGE 🍴

Just off I-10 on La. 31, this little town, founded in 1859, prides itself on being the Crawfish Capital of the World. Its Crawfish Festival and Fair has drawn as many as 100,000 to the town of 4,500, and it's quite the event, with music, a unique parade, crawfish races, crawfish-eating contests, and lots more. It's held the first week in May. Some locals actually dislike the Crawfish Festival and feel that their town is at its best the rest of the year. Consider taking them up on this challenge—the town is pretty and offers some of the nicest options in the area.

ACCOMMODATIONS

Note: If the B&B listed below is full, you may be directed to the also charming Bayou Teche B&B, next door.

Maison Des Amis 🍴🍴   The winner of a national preservation award, this one-story Creole-Caribbean cabin (ca. 1860) is one the best B&Bs we've ever stayed in, for sheer comfort and style. We can't decide which we like best: the front room, with the towering half-canopy bed; the middle room with the nearly 300-year-old four-poster; or the small room with the mosquito-net-draped plantation bed (though the latter's bathroom is down the hall, which may help you make a decision). The two front rooms have private bathrooms and the biggest windows.

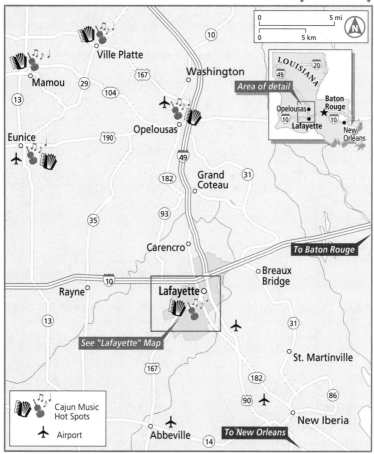

There is one communal TV with a VCR and a collection of old movies. The delightful owners are great fun and full of helpful hints (they are among those who think the Crawfish Festival is the worst time to come to town). They live above their restaurant, **Café Des Amís** (see below), where Maison guests can have breakfast. The owners now also have the **Chez Amís cottages,** which are more modern in looks and have king beds (those antique beds are small). Pets are allowed.

111 Washington, Breaux Bridge, LA 70517. 🅒 **337/507-3399.** Fax 337/332-2227. www.cafedesamis.com. 4 units, 2 with private bathrooms. $100–$125 double. Rates include full-service breakfast. AE, DISC, MC, V. **Amenities:** Restaurant, complimentary beverages; gardens; gazebo. *In room:* A/C.

DINING

Café Des Amís ★★ CAJUN   Freshly reopened after a devastating fire, this is the pride and joy of Breaux Bridge, a charming cafe that features local art and often live music in addition to meals so good at least one recent customer thought his breakfast (eggs Begnaud—eggs on a grilled biscuit topped with crawfish étouffée) worth driving up from New Orleans for. (And don't forget the *crielle de couchon*—fried dough in the shape of pigs' ears!) At dinner, try the crabmeat Napoleon or the crawfish corn bread topped with shrimp, and be sure to order the drum with andouille sausage and shrimp topped with garlic shrimp sauce (you have to order it this way, but the combination is perfect). Save room for the superb creamy white chocolate bread pudding. This restaurant is hugely popular with locals, so expect a wait for weekend breakfasts, and know that the service can be a little lacking.

140 E. Bridge St. © **337/332-5273.** Fax 337/332-2227. www.cafedesamis.com. Main courses $8.95–$22. AE, DISC, MC, V. Tue–Thu 9am–9pm; Fri–Sat 7:30am–9:30pm; Sun Zydeco Breakfast 8am–2:30pm.

Crawfish Town U.S.A. ★★ SEAFOOD/CAJUN   See if you can guess what the house specialty is here. The food is as pleasant as the heavily decorated dining room and is prepared to your taste: mild, strong, or extra hot. The staff says they serve the biggest crawfish in the world—and who are we to challenge them? The steaming platters of boiled crawfish that come out of the kitchen by the hundreds look almost like small lobsters. The crawfish étouffée and the gumbo are delicious. You shouldn't miss the bread pudding here, either. And if you just can't decide what you want, take a deep breath and go for the Seafood Festival Platter—a cup of gumbo plus jambalaya, crawfish étouffée, grilled catfish, shrimp, seafood pie, frogs' legs, crawfish, and a crawfish patty—all served with grilled potatoes, vegetables, and garlic bread.

2815 Grand Point Hwy. © **337/667-6148.** Reservations recommended. Main courses $4.95–$19. AE, DISC, MC, V. Sun–Thurs 11am–9pm; Fri–Sat 11am–10pm. From Lafayette, take I-10 to Henderson (Exit 115). Go north ½ mile and follow the signs; you can't miss it.

Mulate's Cajun Restaurant ★★ *Kids* CAJUN   This place has such a strong reputation that the owners were able to open a branch in New Orleans. Come to this one. It's gotten a bit touristy, but the food is solid (and the prices reasonable) and so is the music—Mulate's is definitely a good introduction to Cajun music and food. Stuffed crab is a specialty here. Live Cajun music is offered nightly and at noon on weekends.

325 Mills Ave. © **800/422-2586** or 337/332-4648. Fax 337/323-4013. www.mulates.com. Reservations recommended. Main courses $11–$17. AE, DC, DISC, MC, V. Daily 11am–10pm.

EUNICE ★★★

Founded in 1894 by C. C. Duson, who named the town for his wife, Eunice is a prairie town, not as picturesque as, say, Opelousas or Washington. But some of the most significant Cajun cultural happenings come out of this friendly town, including the Saturday morning jam sessions at the Savoy Music Center, the Liberty Theater's live radio broadcasts, and the exhibits and crafts demonstrations at the Prairie Acadian Cultural Center, all of which will greatly enrich your understanding of Cajun traditions and modern life. That is, if you aren't having too much fun to notice that you're also getting an education.

Liberty Theater ★★★ *Moments*   This classic 1927 theater has been lovingly restored and turned into a showcase for Cajun music. There's live music most nights, but Saturday attracts the big crowds for the "Rendezvous des Cajuns" radio show. From 6 to 8pm, Cajun historian and folklorist Barry Ancelet hosts a live program, simulcast on local radio, that features Cajun and zydeco bands. It includes anything from up-and-comers to some of the biggest names as well as folk tales and jokes. Oh, and it's all in French. Locals and tourists alike pack the seats and aisles, with dancing on the sloped floor by the stage. Don't understand what's being said? As Barry points out, turn to your neighbors—they will be happy to translate. This is the right way (actually, *the* way) to begin your Saturday night of music in Cajun country.

2nd and Park. © **337/457-7389.** www.eunice-la.com. Admission $5 adults, $3 children, free for children under 6.

Prairie Acadian Cultural Center ★★★ *Finds*   A terrific small museum, the Acadian Cultural Center is devoted to Cajun life and culture. Exhibits explain everything from the history of the Cajuns to how they worked, played, and got married. The graphics are lively and very readable and are well combined with the objects on display (most were acquired from local families who have owned them for generations). It's all quite informative and enjoyable. In other parts of the building, there might be quilting or other crafts demonstrations going on. The center has a collection of videos about Cajun life and will show any and all of them in the small theater (just ask). Anything by Les Blanc is a good choice, but you might also check out *Anything I Can Catch,* a documentary about the nearly lost art of hand-fishing (you *need* to see someone catch a giant catfish with his bare hands!).

250 West Park. © 337/262-6862. www.nps.gov/jela/PrairieAcadianCulturalCenter.htm. Free admission; donations accepted. Tues–Fri 8am–5pm; Sat 8am–6pm. Closed Christmas.

Savoy Music Center ★★★ *Moments*   On weekdays, this is a working music store with instruments, accessories, and a small but essential selection of Cajun and zydeco CDs and tapes. In the back is the workshop where musician Marc Savoy (see the "Cajuns Today" box, above) lovingly crafts his Acadian accordions—not just fine musical instruments but works of art—amid cabinets bearing his observations and aphorisms.

On most Saturday mornings, though, this nondescript Kelly-green building on the outskirts of Eunice is the spiritual center of Cajun music. Keeping alive a tradition that dates from way before electricity, Marc and his wife, Ann, host a jam session where you can hear some of the region's finest music and watch the tunes being passed down from generation to generation. Here, the older musicians are given their due respect, with octogenarians often leading the sessions while players as young as those in their preteens glean all they can—if they can keep up. Meanwhile, guests munch on hunks of boudin sausage and sip beer while listening or socializing. All comers are welcome; if they're properly respectful, they can get a member of the Savoy family or shop associate Tina Pillone to show them around. But don't come empty-handed—a pound of boudin or a six-pack of something is appropriate. And if you play guitar, fiddle, accordion, or triangle, bring one along and join in. Don't try to show off. Simply follow along with the locals, or you're sure to get a cold shoulder.

Hwy. 190 East (3 miles east of Eunice). © 337/457-9563. www.savoymusiccenter.com. Tues–Fri 9am–5pm; Sat 9am–noon.

ACCOMMODATIONS

If the following are booked, you might also try the **Best Western,** 1531 W. Laurel Ave. (© 337/457-2800), in Eunice.

Potier's Prairie Cajun Inn ★   Its bright pink exterior indicates that this tiny B&B is a bit heavy on the cute, but the location can't be beat—just a half-block from the Liberty Theater and the Acadian Cultural Center. A little kitsch can be tolerated for the sake of convenience. The tiny rooms are technically suites—itty-bitty sitting areas with separate, even smaller bedrooms and full kitchens, all decorated (again, think cutesy) by local Cajun craftsmen. A variety of snacks and breakfast foods (cereal, pastries, fruit, yogurt) are provided nightly. It also has a conference room, and each suite has a computer modem hookup. For a minimal fee, the inn provides transportation to and from the Lafayette airport.

110 W. Park, Eunice, LA 70535. © 337/457-0440. 9 units. $75 double. AE, DC, DISC, MC, V. **Amenities:** Coffee and snacks; Jacuzzi; conference room; babysitting; courtyard. *In room:* A/C, TV, dataport, kitchen.

Seale Guesthouse ⭐ A once-abandoned farmhouse has been turned into a wonderful B&B, perfect for a relaxing getaway. Eunice is only a 5-minute drive away, but the guesthouse and grounds are so inviting, sometimes it's hard to leave. Rooms are decorated with antiques, and with high ceilings, wood trim, and cozy furniture, each is more attractive and charming than the last. The large kitchen is fully stocked for guests who wish to cook. Wide verandas allow you to sit and gaze at the pretty landscaping, while animals galore (dogs, cats, always a fresh batch of kittens, various fowl, and who knows what else) gambol nearby or come over for attention. This is a hands-off guesthouse; there is no receptionist, owner Mark may not be around much (though when someone *is* around, he or she is happy to give you all kinds of good advice about local doings), and the sheets aren't changed every day. It's perfect if you want privacy, not so good if you like hotels that pick up after you.

125 Seale Lane (off Hwy. 13), Eunice, LA 70535. ✆ **337/457-3753.** Fax 337/457-3753. www.angelfire. com/la2/guesthouse. 6 units, 4 with private bathroom (1 room's bathroom is across the hall). $75 double. Rates include continental breakfast weekdays, full breakfast weekends. MC, V. **Amenities:** Wraparound porch with rockers; kitchen; wheelchair access; camper hookups. *In room:* A/C, TV, no phone.

DINING

D.I.'s Cajun Restaurant ⭐⭐ CAJUN Even when you follow the directions to D.I.'s Cajun Restaurant, you will think you are about to drive off the face off the earth, particularly if you're driving there in the dark. You'll know you're there—and that you are not alone—when you see all the cars in the gravel parking lot. Located on a back highway, D.I.'s is more or less what Mulate's was before the tourists found it: a homey family restaurant full of locals dancing to live music (except Thursdays) and stuffing themselves with crawfish and catfish. Some items are not fried, but most are—or they're stuffed or topped with a sauce—and it's all good.

Hwy. 97, Basile. ✆ **337/432-5141.** Main courses $6.75–$14. AE, DISC, MC, V. Mon–Fri 10:30am–1:30pm; Tues–Sat 5–10pm. Take Hwy. 190 to Hwy. 97; then drive 8 miles south.

Matilda's ⭐ BARBECUE For barbecue with all the fixings, this is the one sit-down place in town. It's a wood shack that some might call "quaint," but others know it's authentic. The many side dishes vary in quality, but the barbecue, while not all that spicy, is agreeable.

Hwy. 190, 611 S. St. Mary. ✆ **337/546-0329.** $3.50–$11. MC, V. Tues–Thurs 11am–7pm; Fri 11am–10pm; Sat 11:30am–8pm; Sun 11am–3pm.

SHOPPING

Lejeune's Sausage Kitchen Look for the signs or just ask, but do find your way to the Sausage Kitchen for a delicious, if perishable, souvenir. In addition to *tasso* (Cajun ham) and ponce, Lejeune's sells a variety of sausages, including a memorable garlic pork. It all freezes well, but alas, they don't ship. Open Monday through Friday from 7am to 5:30pm and Saturday from 7am to 5pm. Closed Sunday. Old Crowley Rd. 108 Tasso Circle. ✆ **337/457-8491.**

Music Machine Owner Todd Ortego claims this is the "only record store, snow cone, and pool place in the area," and he gets no dispute from us. The store features a pretty good selection of local music (on CD and cassette), and the employees should be able to help you figure out what to buy if you need guidance. Outside of Floyd's in Ville Platte (p. 287), this is probably your best local music resource. The snow cones are available only during spring and summer months. Todd is also a local DJ (you can find him on the radio playing zydeco and South Louisiana party music), and he's in the store during the week.

Finds   Boudin Joints

Boudin is Cajun sausage made of pork, usually mixed with rice, onions, and spices, and stuffed inside a chewy casing. If it's done right, it's spicy and sublime. You can get boudin (warm) at just about any grocery store or gas station, and we've spent many a day driving through Cajun country taste testing. Of course, disputes rage about who makes the best. Try for yourself—it's a cheap (just over $2 a pound), filling snack. Though boudin is easy to find, we recommend the following places.

Superette Slaughterhouse, 1044 Hwy 91 in Eunice (© 337/546-6041), is open Monday through Friday from 6am to 5pm and Saturday from 6am to noon. The name is a little unnerving to some of us urbanites, but the locals swear this is the best boudin around, and they are probably right.

Johnson's Grocery, 700 E. Maple Ave., Eunice (© 337/457-9314), has darn good boudin as well, and they ship! (Overnight, at that, so if you get a craving, you can have it filled in a matter of hours.) Hours are Monday through Friday from 6am to 6pm and Saturday from 6am to 5pm.

Poche's, 3015-A Main Hwy., Breaux Bridge (© 337/332-2108), has not only pork but also crawfish boudin plus tasso and other local tidbits—and they ship, too. Open Monday through Saturday from 5am to 8pm and Sunday from 5am to 6pm.

Ray's Grocery, 904 Shortvine (off Hwy. 190, across from Town Center), Opelousas (© 337/942-9150), has the advantage of a drive-thru window. Place your order with little interruption in your road trip. Hours are Monday through Friday from 7:30am to 6pm, Saturday from 8am to 5pm, and Sunday from 8am to 2pm.

If you are coming for a weekend of music, drop by and ask him where to go—by Thursday, he usually knows what's going on. Open daily from 10am to 7pm. 235 W. Walnut Ave. © 337/457-4846. musicmachine@geaux.org.

GRAND COTEAU

Grand Coteau seems like just a wide spot in the road, but it's worth exploring (it won't take you long). First see the beautiful, 175-year-old **Academy of the Sacred Heart,** 1821 Academy Rd. (© 337/662-5494; tours by appointment only), and its gardens. Then there are two places to eat (one where you can also shop) that are surprising in this land of Cajun cooking.

DINING

Catahoula's   CLASSIC & NOUVELLE LOUISIANA CUISINE Named for the Louisiana state dog (a hound with startling blue eyes), Catahoula's is in a 1920s general store. It's a pretty, simple place with subdued lighting that at night virtually requires candles. It serves surprisingly modern fare; this is the place to get away from local specialties, assuming you need a break from fried food and crawfish. The menu features the "best of the old and best of the new," and there is almost always something experimental. Raspberry duckling is a house specialty, as is shrimp, tasso and Gorgonzola Wellington. Try the shrimp St. Charles, a traditional New Orleans dish of shrimp sautéed in white wine with sun-dried tomatoes, served over linguine. Owner John Slaughter is also a photographer, and his photos line the walls.

234 Martin Luther King Dr. (Hwy. 93). © **888/547-BARK** or 337/662-2275. Reservations recommended. Main courses $16–$22; specials somewhat higher. AE, DISC, MC, V. Tues–Sat 5pm–until closing; Fri lunch 11am–2pm; Sun brunch 11am–2pm.

Kitchen Shop ✮ CAFE   The name is misleading, because this is actually a well-stocked, cute gift store that features kitchen, cooking, and nice food items as well as having a much larger room stuffed with local books, upscale knickknacks, jewelry (including Grandmother's Buttons [p. 263], a line made from antique buttons), and vintage-looking clothes. There is also a tiny cafe with a sweet little patio. The owner is a New York–trained pastry chef who serves quiches, delicious pastries (the specialty is Gateau Nana), and terrific café au lait. It's all packed into an 1840 building that used to be a stagecoach stop.

Corner of Cherry and King. © **337/662-3500.** Tues–Sat 10am–5pm; Sun 1pm–5pm.

LAFAYETTE ✮✮

Stop by the **Lafayette Parish Convention and Visitors Commission Center,** 1400 N.W. Evangeline Thruway (© **800/346-1958** in the U.S., 800/543-5340 in Canada, or 337/232-3808; www.lafayettetravel.com). The helpful staff will tell you everything you could possibly want to know about the region and will send you out loaded with informative materials. Turn off I-10 at Exit 103A, go south for about a mile, and you'll find the office in the center of the median. It's open weekdays from 8:30am to 5pm and weekends from 9am to 5pm. Near the intersection of Willow Street and the thruway, the attractive offices are in Cajun-style homes set on landscaped grounds that hold a pond and benches. It is a restful spot to sit and plan your Cajun country excursion.

We also highly recommend the **Festival International de Louisiane** ✮, a 6-day music and art festival that many find to be a good alternative to New Orleans's increasingly crowded Jazz Fest. Although the scope of the bands, naturally, is nothing like the big deal in New Orleans, there's an interesting lineup each year, with an emphasis on music from other French-speaking lands. The festival takes place in the center of town with streets blocked off to allow easy movement from one stage to another. In contrast to Jazz Fest, it's low-key and a manageable size. Best of all, it's free! Festival International is held at the end of April; for dates, call or write the Festival International de Louisiane, 735 Jefferson St., Lafayette, LA 70501 (© **337/232-8086;** www.festivalinternational.com).

Music can be found year-round at the **Grant Street Dance Hall,** off Cypress Street, in downtown Lafayette (© **337/237-8513;** www.grantstreetdancehall.com). This warehouse-type building features the best in local music, from Cajun to brass bands, and is where out-of-towners are most likely to play. The zydeco hot spot is **El Sido's,** 1523 N. Antoine St. (© **337/237-1959**), where combos like Nathan & the Zydeco Cha Chas hold sway. Both joints jump most any night.

SEEING THE SIGHTS

You shouldn't leave this area without exploring its bayous and swamps. Gliding through misty bayous dotted with gnarled cypress trees that drip Spanish moss, seeing native water creatures and birds in their natural habitat, and learning how Cajuns harvest their beloved crawfish is an experience not to be missed.

To arrange a voyage, contact Terry Angelle at **Angelle's Atchafalaya Basin Swamp Tours,** Whiskey River Landing, P.O. Box 111, Cecilla, LA 70521 (© **337/ 228-8567;** www.angelleswhiskeyriver.com). His tour gives you nearly 2 hours in

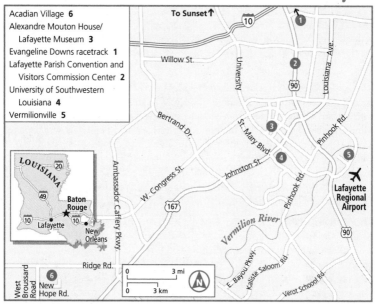

Acadian Village **6**
Alexandre Mouton House/
 Lafayette Museum **3**
Evangeline Downs racetrack **1**
Lafayette Parish Convention and
 Visitors Commission Center **2**
University of Southwestern
 Louisiana **4**
Vermilionville **5**

the third-largest swamp in the U.S. with Cajun guides who have spent their lives thereabouts and who travel the mysterious waterways as easily as you and I walk city streets. There's a glass-enclosed boat for large groups and a small, open boat for up to 14. The fares are $12 for adults, $10 for seniors, and $6 for children under 12. Departure times are 10am, 1pm, and 3pm. Angelle's features Cajun music on Sunday beginning at around 4pm. To reach Whiskey River Landing from I-10, take Exit 115 to Henderson, go through Henderson to the levee, and turn right. The landing is the fourth exit on the left. For other swamp tours, see the "Organized Tours" section in chapter 8.

If you're in Cajun country between the first week in April and Labor Day and happen to be a devotee of the sport of kings, you can enjoy an evening of horse racing at **Evangeline Downs** (© **337/896-RACE;** www.evangelinedowns.com), 3 miles north of town on I-49. Post time and racing days change periodically, so call before setting out. Don't bring the kids, though—no minors are allowed.

There's a lovely natural swamp environment in the very heart of Lafayette on the grounds of the University of Louisiana at Lafayette. Although it's small, it gives the effect of being in the wild, and during the warm months you can see alligators. Several varieties of water birds, as well as turtles, are almost always on hand, and in April, the swamp is abloom with Louisiana irises. If you want to know more about the lake and how it is used as a teaching tool, contact the **Public Relations and News Service,** University of Louisiana at Lafayette, Lafayette, LA 70504 (© **337/482-6397**). If you just want to get closer to the sort of swampland seen most often from highways, you'll like **Cypress Lake,** next to the Student Union on the ULL campus, between St. Mary Boulevard and University Avenue and Hebrard Boulevard and McKinley Street.

Acadian Village ⭐ Just south of La. 342, you'll find a reconstructed (actually, reassembled) Cajun bayou community. Houses have been moved from their original locations to this site beside a sleepy bayou, and a footpath on its banks takes you past the historic structures. The buildings hold a representative collection of Cajun furnishings.

200 Greenleaf Dr. ℭ **800/962-9133** or 337/981-2364. www.acadianvillage.org. Admission $7 adults, $6 seniors, $4 children 6–14, free for children under 6. Group rates available. Daily 10am–5pm. Closed major holidays. Take I-10 to Exit 97. Go south on La. 93 to Ridge Rd., turn right, and then turn left on West Broussard.

Alexandre Mouton House/Lafayette Museum ⋆

Louisiana's first Democratic governor, Alexandre Mouton, once lived in this antebellum town house with square columns and two galleries. Today, it is home to the Lafayette Museum. The main house was built in the early 1800s, and the cupola, attic, and second floor were added in 1849. Inside, in addition to the antiques, paintings, and historic documents, there's a colorful collection of Mardi Gras costumes that were worn by Lafayette's krewe kings and queens.

1122 Lafayette St. ℭ **337/234-2208**. Admission $3 adults, $2 seniors, $1 students. Tues–Sat 9am–4:30m; Sun 1–4pm. Closed major holidays.

Chretien Point Plantation ⋆

One of Cajun country's most intriguing plantation mansions is a short drive (about 15 miles) north of Lafayette. Allow yourself at least an hour to explore the columned home, built in 1831 on a 1776 Spanish land grant. The house is fascinating, and even more so are the tales of past owners. Its history includes links to privateer Jean Lafitte, a flamboyant gambler, his equally flamboyant widow, a ghost or two, a buried treasure, and a Civil War battle fought right out front. And if you remember the scene in *Gone With the Wind* when Scarlett O'Hara shoots a marauding Union soldier on the stairs at Tara, you'll recognize the staircase—it was copied for the movie.

The plantation also operates a **bed-and-breakfast.** The rooms are in the manor house; you get a full breakfast and a tour of the mansion plus use of the pool and tennis courts. Rooms are $125 to $225 per night.

665 Chretien Point Rd., Sunset, LA 70584. ℭ **800/880-7050** or 337/662-7050. Admission $7 adults, $6 seniors, $3 children 6–12, free for children under 4. Daily 10am–5pm and 11am–5pm April–Sept. Last tour 4pm. Closed holidays. Take I-10 west to Exit 97 and then go north about 8 miles. A little over 2 miles north of Cankton, turn left onto Parish Rd. 356 (toward Bristol) and then right on Chretien Point Rd.; the plantation is about a mile farther on the left.

Vermilionville ⋆⋆

An addition to the Lafayette scene is this reconstruction of a Cajun-Creole settlement from the 1765 to 1890 era. Vermilionville sits on the banks of the brooding Bayou Vermilion, adjacent to the airport on U.S. 90. While it may sound like a "Cajunland" theme park, it's actually quite a valid operation. Hundreds of skilled artisans labored to restore original Cajun homes and to reconstruct others that were typical of such a village. Homes of every level in society are represented, from the humblest to the most well-to-do. (It *must* be authentic; one Cajun we know refuses to go, not because he dislikes the place or finds it offensive but because "I already *live* in Vermilionville!") The costumed staff in each gives a vivid demonstration of daily life back then, and craftspeople ply their traditional crafts. In the performance center, there are plays, music, dancing, and storytelling. Vermilionville is both bigger and better than Acadian Village (see above).

300 Fisher Rd., off Surrey St. ℭ **866/99-BAYOU** or 337/233-4077. www.vermilionville.org. Admission $8 adults, $6.50 seniors, $5 students, free for children under 6. Tues–Sun 10am–4pm. Closed New Year's Eve, New Year's Day, Martin Luther King Day, Thanksgiving, Dec 24–25. Take I-10 to Exit 103A. Take Evangeline Thruway south to Surrey St. and then follow signs.

WHERE TO STAY IN & AROUND LAFAYETTE

As always, we tend toward directing you to stay at local B&Bs—mainly because they are more interesting than the alternative, which is simply a chain hotel.

However, we can't deny that prices and even the preference for what a standardized hotel has to offer can make said chain hotels even more attractive than an antique bed. Lafayette has several such options, including the **Holiday Inn Lafayette–Central,** 2032 NE Evangeline Thruway (© **800/942-4868** or 337/233-6815) and the **Lafayette Hilton & Towers,** 1521 W. Pinhook Rd. (© **800/33-CAJUN** or 337/235-6111.)

Aaah! T'Frere's Bed & Breakfast ★★★

Everything about this place cracks us up, from the name (it's so they're first in any alphabetical listing) to the evening "T'Juleps" to the owners' gorgeous son who cooked us breakfast but swore he was really a supermodel (did you hear us argue?) to the cheerful owners themselves, Pat and Maugie Pastor—the latter would be adorable even if she didn't daily preside over breakfast in red silk pajamas (she and Pat used to operate restaurants, and after years in chef's whites, she wanted as radical a change as possible). Oh, wait, did we mention the goofily named breakfasts? Daily extravaganzas, easily the best around, like the "Ooh-La-La, Mardi Gras" breakfast—eggs in white sauce on ham-topped biscuits, cheese and garlic grits, tomato grille, sweet potatoes, and chocolate muffins? Did we mention Maugie used to be a chef? And apparently still is? The rooms (and grounds) are gorgeous (Okay, the public areas are a bit Grandma-cluttered for our tastes, but maybe not for yours), though the ones in the Garconniere in the back are a bit more Country Plain than Victorian Fancy. We particularly like Mary's Room, with its priceless antique wood canopy bed and working fireplace. Look, they've been in business for years, they know how to do this right; just stay here, okay?

1905 Verot School Rd., Lafayette, LA 70508. © 800/984-9347. Fax 337/984-9347. www.tfreres.com. 8 units, all with private bathrooms. $100 double; extra person $30. Rates include full breakfast. AE, DC, DISC, MC, V. **Amenities:** Welcome drinks and Cajun canapés (*hors d'oeuvres*). *In room:* A/C, TV, dataport, coffeemaker, terry-cloth robes.

Bois des Chênes Inn ★★

Three suites at the Bois des Chênes Inn are in the carriage house, and two suites, one with an open fireplace, are in the 1820s Acadian-style plantation home known as the Charles Mouton House. Now listed on the National Register of Historical Houses, Bois des Chênes was once the center of a 3,000-acre cattle and sugar plantation. Its restoration has been a labor of love, reflected in the careful selection of antique furnishings, most of Louisiana French design. All guest rooms are tastefully furnished with antiques of different periods, and each has a small refrigerator and down pillows. The rates include a Louisiana-style breakfast, a bottle of wine, and a tour of the house. The owner, a retired geologist, conducts nature and birding trips into the Atchafalaya Swamp as well as guided fishing and hunting trips. Book as far in advance as possible.

338 N. Sterling (at Mudd Ave.), Lafayette, LA 70501. © 337/233-7816. Fax 337/233-7816. www.members.aol. com/boisdchene/bois.htm. 5 units. $100–$150 double. Rates include breakfast. Extra person $30. AE, MC, V. *In room:* A/C, TV, refrigerator.

Maison D'Andre Billeud ★★

Although it's not technically in Lafayette, it is in a small adjacent town just a few minutes down the road, so close that you can't really tell where Lafayette leaves off and the other town begins. And it's worth driving down here, if you want the classic Southern B&B experience—and by that, we mean it's full of clichés, all of which we like. Rooms in this 1903 house are done to the period, and thus you can expect huge high ceilings, half-tester beds (the one in Suite 2 is particularly impressive), pretty though no longer functional fireplaces, claw-foot tubs in big bathrooms, and a Cajun chef-owner who puts out a heck of a series of breakfasts (his crab omelets are quite the thing). The two-story "honeymoon suite" feels like a New Orleans studio and has a hodgepodge of curious items, while the Cottage room is the plainest, though still charming. The cluttered backyard even has a giant oak tree. Like we said, all the clichés, but they work for us.

203 E. Main Street, Broussard, LA 70518. ℂ 800/960-REST or 337/837-3455. www.andrehouse.com. 4 units. $95–$130. Rates include full breakfast. AE, DISC, MC, V. *In room:* AC, TV.

DINING IN & AROUND LAFAYETTE

Café Vermilionville INTERNATIONAL/CAJUN   Highly touted locally, but though it's a very pretty place to dine (it's in a beautifully restored old Acadian cypress house that dates back to 1799), we find it to be a bit disappointing. The food is extremely fussy, with layer upon layer of ingredients (as they recite specials, an entree will start out sounding lovely, but then they keep going and going describing everything that's on it, until you want to yell, "Stop!"), many of which are cream-sauce intensive. Having said that, the crawfish beignets are a perfect appetizer, and the pecan tilapia with a garlic and herb *beurre blanc* sauce comes with the sauce on the side, so the fish (crusted with pistachios and peppercorns) stays crunchy and relatively plain. Service can be inexplicably slow.

1304 W. Pinhook Rd. ℂ 337/237-0100. Fax 337/233-5599. www.cafev.com. Reservations and appropriate attire recommended. Main courses $16–$32. AE, DC, DISC, MC, V. Mon–Fri 11am–2pm; Mon–Sat 5:30–10pm. Closed major holidays.

Dean-o's ✿ *(Kids)* PIZZA   Yeah, yeah, you're supposed to be eating jambalaya and red beans and rice, to say nothing of boudin, but let's pretend you have already, or that you've got a kid who just won't touch fish or something spicy. We know, it happens, and you can't send 'em back after they are born. Anyway, to this end, Dean-o's offers up the best pizza in Lafayette, with homemade olive oil crust and several homemade sauces. Even a small pizza is big enough for two to share, and they offer a sampler—up to four of their elaborate specialty combos on one pizza, perfect for the indecisive. Stuff your kid with the T. Rex (the "ultimate meat eaters") while you try the Marie Laveau, which has bluepoint crab. But next meal, have some étouffée, *cher,* okay?

305 Bertrand (at Johnston St.). ℂ 337/233-5446. Takeout but no delivery. Main courses $5.25–$20 (for a giant specialty pizza). AE, DC, DISC, MC, V. Mon–Thurs 11am–11pm; Fri–Sat 11am–midnight; Sun 3–11pm.

Edie's ✿✿ CAJUN   This is Lafayette's favorite lunch place, and for good reason. The menu won't shock you (stuffed this, smothered that), but the deliciousness of what's on your plate might. Try to go on Sunday and Wednesdays, when the special is the pork roast with sweet potatoes. The former is perfect, melt-in-your-mouth tender, with spectacular gravy. The latter is slightly caramelized and squirted full of a gooey sauce that seems to be made of cane syrup, butter, and lots of cinnamon.

1895 W. Pinhook Rd. ℂ 337/234-2485. All main courses under $7. AE, MC, V. Sun–Fri 11am–2pm.

Prejean's ✿✿ CAJUN   From the outside, Prejean's hasn't changed at all over the years, and at first glance, it looks pretty much the way it always has. An unpretentious family restaurant, this place has live Cajun music every night. Inside, chef James Graham has turned Prejean's from a fried seafood emporium into one of Acadiana's finest restaurants, showcasing the best ingredients and styles Cajun cuisine has to offer.

Pace yourself or dance if there's room—but do whatever's necessary to sample the full range of excellent Cajun fare. Seafood is the specialty, with large menu sections devoted to fish, shrimp, oysters, crawfish, and crab dishes. One best-seller is eggplant *pirogue*—half an eggplant, hollowed out, breaded, fried, and filled with shrimp, crawfish, and crab; another is catfish Catahoula, a fresh filet stuffed with shrimp, crawfish, and crab. The extensive game menu offers exotic tastes like rack of elk and buffalo tenderloin. In the unlikely event that you have room for dessert, the chocolate Grand Marnier torte is highly recommended.

3480 I-49 North. ✆ 337/896-3247. Fax 337/896-3278. www.prejeans.com. Reservations for 8 or more. Children's menu $3.50–$8.95; main courses $15–$26. AE, DC, DISC, MC, V. Sun–Thurs 7am–10pm; Fri–Sat 7am–11pm. Take I-10 to Exit 103B and then I-49 north to Exit 2/Gloria Switch.

Randol's Restaurant and Cajun Dance Hall ✿ CAJUN   In addition to better-than-average Cajun food, Randol's offers a good-size, popular dance floor where dancers are likely to be locals enjoying their own *fais-do-do*. In fact, they eagerly volunteer when owner Frank Randol needs dancers for his traveling Cajun food and dance show. Back home, the star of the menu is seafood, all fresh from bayou or Gulf waters, and served fried, steamed, blackened, or grilled. (Given how often fried is the only option at most Cajun restaurants, the other alternatives alone make Randol's an attractive stop.) A house specialty is the seafood platter, which includes a cup of seafood gumbo, fried shrimp, fried oysters, fried catfish, stuffed crab, crawfish étouffée, French bread, and coleslaw.

2320 Kaliste Saloom Rd. ✆ 800/962-2586 or 337/981-7080. www.randols.com. Reservations accepted only for parties of 20 or more. Main courses $7.95–$18. MC, V. Sun–Thurs 5–10pm; Fri–Sat 5–11pm. Closed major holidays. From New Orleans, take I-10 west to Exit 103A. Follow Evangeline Thruway to Pinhook Rd., turn right, and follow Pinhook to Kaliste Saloom Rd. (on the right). Randol's will be on your right.

MAMOU ✿

There is one reason to come to Mamou and that's **Fred's Lounge** ✿, 420 6th St. (✆ **337/468-5411**)—and it's a darn good reason, too. At the other end of the Cajun music scale from the Savoy Music Center (p. 273), this small-town bar nonetheless offers just as essential an Acadiana Saturday-morning experience. For half a century, Fred's has been the site of Saturday daytime dances, for many years with Donald Thibodeaux & Cajun Fever playing from a "bandstand" that's really no more than a roped-off area in the middle of the floor. Couples waltz and two-step in the remaining space, and the whole thing airs from 8am to noon on radio station KVPI (1050 AM). While Savoy honors the folksy "house music" tradition, this is pure dance-hall stuff, a place for hardworking people to blow off steam and let loose. The music leans toward the country-western side of Cajun, with the band featuring steel guitar and drums along with accordion and fiddle. Everyone's welcome as long as you dive right in—though it might be a good idea to practice dancing with a drink in one hand before you give it a try here.

OPELOUSAS ✿

Opelousas, the third-oldest city in Louisiana, is the seat (and heart) of St. Landry Parish (parishes are the word for counties in Louisiana); the courthouse is there, but for the average tourist, there isn't that much to see. It's such a pretty town, though—particularly the main drag, Landry Street—that passers-through often find themselves pulling over to have a look around. Opelousas has a number of B&Bs and a couple of chain hotels, so accommodations are easy to come by.

The **Tourist Center,** 828 E. Landry St. (✆ **800/424-5442** or 337/948-6263), is open daily from 8am to 4pm. Jim Bowie lived in the building for a (really) short time as a child, and there is a small collection of ephemera devoted to him. Don't go out of your way for that, but do drop in for other tourist and lodging advice. You can also call the **St. Landry Tourist Commission** (✆ **877/948-8004;**

www.cajuntravel.com) for more info. During the spring and fall on Friday and Saturday nights, there's a live concert in the street in front of the courthouse (just off Landry St. across from the Palace Cafe). Park your car and go have a two-step. And in passing, admire the 300-year-old oak across the street from City Hall; its branches have gotten so heavy that in spots they not only touch the ground but are buried beneath the sod.

If you feel lost without proper tourist and museum-going experiences, you may drop by the **Opelousas Museum and Interpretive Center,** 315 N. Main St. (℗ **337/948-2589;** www.cityofopelousas.com; Mon–Sat 9am–5pm), or the surprisingly well-appointed **Opelousas Museum of Art,** 100 N. Union St. (℗ **800/551-9066** or 337/942-4991; www.tonychachere.com; Tues–Fri 1–5pm, Sat 9am–5pm). Cajun-cooking obsessives shouldn't miss making a pilgrimage to **Tony Chachere's Creole Foods,** 519 N. Lombard St. (℗ **337/948-4691**), where all the best Cajun spices are made and you can learn how (Mon–Fri 8am–5pm; tours on the hour).

In the fall, Opelousas features its annual long-lived and delightfully named **Yambilee Festival,** a salute to everyone's favorite Thanksgiving side dish. As for music, two of the best clubs in Cajun country are here. **Richard's,** 4 miles west of Opelousas on Hwy. 190 (no phone), is just a little shack, but it's fun. The ultimate spot for zydeco, **Slim's Y Ki-Ki** (℗ **337/942-9980**) is on Highway 81 in Opelousas. On the weekends, Slim's fills up to hot and sweaty capacity with some darn fine music. It's a must on any Cajun country weekend music tour.

ACCOMMODATIONS

Unfortunately, the two nicest B&Bs in town (one of which was perhaps the finest in the entire region) have closed. Opelousas still has a **Best Western,** 5791 I-49 Service Rd. S. (℗ **337/942-5540**), and a **Comfort Inn,** 4165 I-49 S. (℗ **337/948-9500**), but if you are looking for less generic comfort, either stay up the road in Washington (p. 287), or call the Tourist Center or Tourist Commission (listed above) to see if any new and worthy establishments have opened up.

DINING

Back in Time ⭐ SANDWICHES/SALADS   This cafe and gift store is run by Wanda Juneau, only the second owner of the building since 1921. The first, shoe repairman Mr. Grecco, may still be haunting the place; ask Wanda to tell you her ghost stories. The cafe has homemade diner-type selections: sandwiches (including muffulettas with Back in Time's own olive dressing) and salads (with not-terribly-Cajun dressings like honey-raspberry-walnut vinaigrette). The gooey desserts include Sweet Georgia Brown, a double chocolate brownie with cream cheese filling. Admire the picture from a local bar from the '20s—the man who bought the picture drank the last cup of coffee at that bar.

123 W. Landry St. ℗ **337/942-2413.** All items under $9. AE, MC, V. Mon–Fri 10am–5pm; Sat 11am–5pm (lunch 11am–2:30pm, then desserts only).

Palace Cafe ⭐ CAJUN/GREEK   Owned by the same family since 1927, the Palace Cafe is the place to sate your crawfish cravings—it serves a heck of an étouffée. If the tradition doesn't bring you into this no-frills place, the location (right on the main drag) surely will. There are daily lunch specials.

135 W. Landry St. ℗ **337/942-2142.** Main courses $5.95–$14. AE, DISC, MC, V. Mon–Sat 6am–9pm; Sun 7am–3pm.

ST. MARTINVILLE ✦

This historic town dates from 1765 when it was a military station known as the Poste des Attakapas. It is also the last home of Emmeline Labiche, Henry Wadsworth Longfellow's Evangeline (see "The Real Evangeline" box on p. 265). There was a time when it was known as la Petite Paris—many French aristocrats fled their homeland during the Revolution and settled here, bringing with them such traditions as fancy balls, lavish banquets, and other forms of high living.

SEEING THE SIGHTS

Three of St. Martinville's main attractions revolve around Longfellow's epic poem *Evangeline*.

The **Evangeline Monument,** on Main Street, is a statue to the side and slightly to the rear of St. Martin's Church. It was donated to the town in 1929 by a movie company that came here to film the epic. The star of that movie, Dolores del Rio, supposedly posed for the statue. This also reportedly marks the spot of the grave of the real-life Evangeline, Emmeline Labiche.

At Port Street and Bayou Teche is the ancient **Evangeline Oak,** where her descendants say Emmeline's boat landed at the end of her long trip from Nova Scotia. Legend has it that it was here, too, that she learned of her lover's betrothal to another. As far as a sight goes, it's just a big tree, but we like it. And it is right on the bayou, which makes for a pretty sight indeed. If you make a left at the tree, you will soon come upon a very nice memorial to the original Cajun settlers, a mural depicting their arrival after expulsion from Nova Scotia.

Also on the banks of Bayou Teche, just north of St. Martinville on La. Hwy. 31, is the **Longfellow-Evangeline State Historic Site** (✆ 888/677-2900 or 337/394-3754). The 157 acres that make up the park once belonged to Louis Pierre Arceneaux, Emmeline's real-life Gabriel. The **Olivier Plantation House** on the grounds (✆ 337/394-4284), dating from about 1765, is typical of larger Acadian homes, with bricks made by hand and baked in the sun, a cypress frame and pegs (instead of nails), and bousillage construction on the upper floor. You can also see the *cuisine* (outdoor kitchen) and *magazin* (storehouse) out back. Admission to the house is $2 for adults, free for children under 12, school groups, and seniors. It's open daily from 9am to 5pm. Tours start every hour on the hour from 9am to 4pm.

African-American Museum and Museum of the Acadian Memorial ✦
Just down the block from the Acadian Memorial (where an eternal flame commemorates the expulsion of French immigrants from Canada, the same ones who eventually made their way to Louisiana and became Cajuns) is a small but well-designed exhibit discussing the various roles of African Americans within the local Cajun communities (both as slaves and free people), while the other side of the building does the same with the story and history of the Cajun people. Both are simple but exceedingly well done. *A sweet note:* The museum has a copy of the first recorded act of the local St. Martin de Tours church, the baptism and marriage of a woman from Senegal. Recently, a local contingent took a copy of this back to a village there and presented it to the locals, symbolically returning her to her people.

123 S. New Market St. ✆ **337/394-2265**. Fax 337/394-2265. Free (but do make a donation). Daily 10am–4pm.

Finds Chef Patrick Mould's Louisiana Corn & Crab Bisque

Chef Mould is an award-winning chef, cookbook author, and television personality. (His most recent book is the very user-friendly *Recipes from a Chef.*) And you can now learn secrets de cuisine from him thanks to his highly recommended **Louisiana School of Cooking** , a terrific place to learn to make not only classic local dishes but also some of Chef Mould's own creations. It's located at 112 S. Main St., St. Martinville (© **337/394-1710**; fax 337/394-1711; www.lacooks.com); reservations are required.

Below, you'll find the recipe for the quintessential Louisiana bisque. You can use any fresh seafood, but jumbo lump crab, in my opinion, is the best.

2 tablespoons unsalted butter
1 cup chopped onion
½ cup chopped green bell pepper
½ cup chopped celery
¼ cup chopped red bell pepper
1 tablespoon minced garlic
2 cups chicken broth
½ cup dry white wine
¾ teaspoon dried thyme
½ cup blond roux (¼ cup vegetable oil and ¼ cup flour)
3½ cups heavy whipping cream
1 cup cooked corn
1 teaspoon salt
1 teaspoon hot sauce
1 pound lump crabmeat
1 tablespoon chopped parsley
1 tablespoon chopped green onion
16 crab claws, optional

Heat the butter over a low to medium heat in a 4-quart saucepot. Add onion, green bell pepper, celery, red pepper, and garlic and cook for 1 minute. Add chicken broth, white wine, and thyme. Bring to boil. In a small bowl, make blond roux by combining oil and flour and stirring until a smooth paste is formed. Whip in roux until mixture begins to thicken. Whip in cream, reduce heat to a simmer, and continue to cook until cream is blended in and beginning to thicken. Add salt, hot sauce, and corn. Simmer 5 minutes. Very carefully, in order not to break up lumps, stir in lump crabmeat, parsley, and green onions. Simmer until heated. Divide into 4 large bowls. Garnish with crab claws. Yields 4 servings.

Louisiana School of Cooking Chef Patrick Mould, veteran of several fine restaurants and a local celebrity whose visage once adorned Japanese Tabasco bottles, has opened a cooking school, with daily classes geared toward teaching you how to easily master a number of classic and Patrick-invented

Cajun dishes. Call in advance for a schedule. *Note:* Check out Chef Mould's delicious recipe for Louisiana Corn & Crab Bisque, below.

112 S. Main St. *C* **337/394-1710**. www.lacooks.com.

St. Martin de Tours Church 🂠   This is the mother church of the Acadians, 201 Evangeline Blvd. (*C* **337/394-6021**); the building was constructed in 1836 on the site of a previous church building. It is the fourth-oldest Roman Catholic church in Louisiana. Father George Murphy, an Irish priest, was the first to associate it with its patron saint, St. Martin, in the 1790s, and there's a noteworthy portrait of the saint behind the main altar. You'll also see the original box pews, an ornate baptismal font (which some say was a gift from King Louis XVI of France), and the lovely old altar. Outside is a cemetery that purportedly holds the grave of Evangeline herself. Daily 8:30am–5pm.

The **Petit Paris Museum,** 103 S. Main St. (*C* **337/394-7334**), next to the church, often has some unexpectedly interesting displays—a recent visit found a terrific St. Martinville Mardi Gras exhibit with some splendiferous costumes and the extraordinary local story that inspired the theme that year. Guided tours of the church, antebellum rectory, and museum are available; call for details.

Admission $1. Daily 9:30am–4:30pm.

ACCOMMODATIONS

Bienvenue House 🂠🂠   If you are going to stay in a small, charming town, you might as well stay in a small, charming B&B. And this one fits the bill, being housed in an 1830s building and offering nine different gourmet breakfasts as well as a welcome tray of wine and a snack. The beds aren't antiques (is that heresy?), but the owner designed each of them, and all are either canopy or four posters. The Scarlett room has two beds, perfect for parents with a child (plus a gorgeous fireplace) while the Montgomery room has its own balcony. Baths are small with claw-foot tubs (and one, unexpectedly, has hot pink accents).

421 N. Main St., St. Martinville, LA 70582. *C* **888/394-9100** or 337/394-9100. www.bienvenuehouse.com. 3 units. $85. Rates include continental breakfast. MC, V. *In room:* AC.

Old Castillo Bed & Breakfast 🂠   This rooming house—honestly, that's what it reminds us of, and indeed, it used to be a Catholic girls' school—looks promising from the outside, but once you get in, it's not nearly as interesting as local B&Bs; it's even a little (but only a little) down at the heels. But then again, the rates are cheaper than at most local B&Bs, and it's right next to the town square, though in a teeming metropolis like St. Martinville, that's not saying much. The rooms are generously sized—no. 3 is positively cavernous—if plain, but they can have food smells from the restaurant. Bathrooms (though private) are dinky, with showers only (no tubs) in the low end of the price range.

220 Evangeline Blvd., St. Martinville, LA 70582. *C* **800/621-3017** or 337/394-4010. Fax 337/394-7983. 5 units. $60–$80 double. Rates include breakfast. AE, DISC, MC, V. Free parking. *In room:* AC.

DINING

Sonny & Shirley's Thibodeaux's Cafe 🂠🂠   COUNTRY COOKING Now, if you want gourmet cuisine, go elsewhere. But if you want authentic, rib-sticking food, not to mention a meal that will barely lighten your wallet, come here. This small cafe serves up huge breakfasts and lunch specials. Less than $7 (often less than $5) will buy you a lunch plate full of such items as delicious smothered chicken or pork, rice, vegetables (out of a can, to be sure), and so forth. Nothing fancy, but pretty tasty. Chat with the friendly staff who, if they aren't busy, will give you all kinds of local info and gossip. Those who are tired of higher-profile places and want a true small-town meal will be pleased.

116 S. Main St. ℭ 337/394-6624. All items under $7. No credit cards. Daily 6:30am–3pm.

NEW IBERIA ⊛

This town dates from 1779, when a group of 300 immigrants from the Spanish province of Málaga came up Bayou Teche and settled here. It was incorporated in 1813, and its history changed drastically after the arrival of the steamboat *Plowboy* in 1836. New Iberia then became the terminal for steamboats traveling up the bayou from New Orleans, and it promptly developed the rambunctious character of a frontier town. In 1839, however, yellow fever traveled up the bayou with the steamboats and killed more than a quarter of the population. Many residents were saved, though, through the heroic nursing of a black woman called Tante Félicité, who had come here from Santo Domingo; she went tirelessly from family to family, carrying food and medicine. (She had had the fever many years before and was immune.)

During the Civil War, New Iberia was a Confederate training center and was attacked again and again. It's said that Confederate and Union soldiers alike plundered the land to such an extent that local Acadians threatened to declare war on *both* sides if any more of their chickens, cattle, and produce were appropriated. The steamboats continued coming up the bayou until 1947. (We bet you didn't know the steamboat era lasted that long anywhere in the United States.) Today, New Iberia, known as the Queen City of the Teche, continues to grow.

SEEING THE SIGHTS

Take one of Annie Miller's **Swamp and Marsh Tours** ⊛ (ℭ **504/879-3934**) for a close-up look at the bayou and its wildlife. In a comfortable boat, you'll visit a rookery of nesting egrets and herons and can say hello to the gators who come when they are called ("*Bah*-bee! *Tone*-y! *Ti*-gar!") by the friendly operators of the very personal and delightful cruises. Tours cost $15 for adults, $10 for children under 13. Be sure to call for current schedules, to find out which location (there are several) is nearest you, and to make reservations.

Note: This is also worth the drive from New Orleans. Take U.S. 90 west through Houma (about 57 miles), exit right at the tourist office on St. Charles Street, turn left at the stoplight onto Southdown/Mandalay Road, and proceed to Miller's Landing on Big Bayou Black.

Jungle Gardens ⊛ Across the street from the Tabasco factory (but not affiliated with it), these gardens cover more than 200 acres with something in bloom November through June. On a self-guided driving or walking tour, you'll see a 1,000-year-old Buddha in the Chinese Garden, sunken gardens, a bird sanctuary (with egrets and herons), and tropical plants.

La. 329, Avery Island. ℭ 337/369-6243. Admission $6 for adults, $4.25 children 6–12, free for children under 6. Daily 8am–5pm.

Shadows-on-the-Teche Plantation ⊛⊛ This beautifully preserved home was built in 1834 for David Weeks, a wealthy planter. It reflects the prevailing classical taste of the times, as seen in its Greek Revival facade. The two-story house of rose-colored brick sits amid oak trees, camellias, and azaleas. One of the most authentically restored and furnished homes in the state, it is the property of the National Trust for Historic Preservation.

317 E. Main St., New Iberia, LA 70560. ℭ **877/200-4924** or 337/369-6446. Fax 337/365-5213. www.shadow sontheteche.org. Admission $7 adults, $6.25 seniors, $4 children ages 6–11, free for children under 6. Daily

9am–4:30pm. From New Orleans (approximately 3 hr.), take U.S. 90 to La. 14 and follow La. 14 east to the inter-section with La. 182.

Tabasco Sauce Factory ⋆⋆⋆   Avery Island, south of New Iberia, sits atop a gigantic salt dome and the oldest salt-rock mine in the western hemisphere. However, it's not salt but pepper—fiery-hot peppers that grow especially well here—that's brought Avery Island its greatest fame. Tabasco brand pepper sauce, loved all over the world, is made by a close-knit family and equally close work-ers who grow the peppers and then nurse them through the fermentation process developed by Edmund McIlhenny, founder of the McIlhenny Company. Tour the Tabasco factory and visitor center, which includes an old-fashioned Tabasco Country Store. Expect to spend less than an hour.

La. 329, Avery Island. ℂ **337/365-8173.** www.tabasco.com. Free admission. Parking 50¢. Tours available daily 8am–5pm (no production Fri–Sun). From Lafayette, take Hwy. 90 to Hwy. 14, turn left to Hwy. 329, and turn right; it's about 7 miles down.

VILLE PLATTE ⋆
If you've fallen in love with Cajun music and want to take some home with you, you have a good reason to detour to the town of Ville Platte.

Floyd's Record Shop ⋆⋆   Floyd Soileau is in some ways the unofficial mayor of Acadiana and certainly one of its biggest boosters—a sort of one-man chamber of commerce. But he's meant much more to the region as one of the key entrepreneurs of bayou music. Long before Cajun and zydeco were known outside the region, he was recording and releasing the music on three labels: Swallow for Cajun, Maison de Soul for zydeco, and Jin (named after his charm-ing wife) for swamp pop, the regional offshoot of '50s and early '60s pop and soul styles. Eventually, he built a whole operation of recording, pressing (his plant was pressing vinyl well into the CD age), and selling records, by mail order and at this store. For fans of the music, this is a must-stop locale with a fine selection of Floyd's releases by such great artists as D. L. Menard (the Cajun Hank Williams) and Clifton Chenier (the King of Zydeco), as well as other releases that may be hard to find anywhere else.

434 E. Main St. ℂ **337/363-2138.** Fax 337/363-5622. www.floydsrecords.com. DISC, MC, V. Mon–Fri 8:30am–5:30pm; Sat 8:30am–5pm.

DINING
The Pig Stand ⋆⋆ PIG   As you might guess, the Pig Stand serves pig. A local institution, it even popped up in the recent Elvis Cole mystery *Voodoo River,* which erroneously described the place as having an outside window and serving boudin. In reality, it's a little dump of a local hangout (and we mean that in the best way possible) that serves divine barbecued chicken and other Southern spe-cialties for cheap prices. It's a real treat, so don't miss it. And it's just down the street from Floyd's in case you worked up an appetite buying music.

318 E. Main St. ℂ **337/363-2883.** Main courses $12 and under. MC, V. Mon–Thurs 5am–10pm; Fri–Sat 5am–11pm; Sun 5am–2pm.

WASHINGTON ⋆
This is a very small town—10 minutes will get you all the highlights—but even nonresidents will urge you to take the quick detour from Opelousas simply because it's so pretty. This is thanks in large part to an abundance of graceful old homes (more even than in other towns in the area) and trees. The many antiques stores are also a draw. At least seven of the old homes have been converted to

B&Bs; staying here is an interesting, and more attractive, experience than a night in some other towns in Cajun country.

If you plan only to drive through, it is worth getting out of the car for **Magnolia Ridge,** ½ mile north of town on Hwy. 103 (© **337/826-3027**). This 1820s house is not open to the public, but its 63 acres of gardens and paths, some winding down to the bayou, are.

There are also a couple of old **cemeteries** in Washington. All B&Bs in Washington will refer callers to others in the area if they're full on a particular night. We particularly liked **Camellia Cove,** 211 W. Hill St. (© **337/826-7362**), with double rooms (all air-conditioned but none has a TV) starting at $95, including breakfast. The nicely restored old house, including the original detached kitchen (ask to see it), has its original furniture from 1905. There are three bedrooms, two with private bathrooms—the large pink bedroom with the ornate wood bedstead is probably the best. The large front porch is perfect for sitting and rocking, and the full breakfast might feature eggs Benedict or fruit crepes, complete with fresh flowers and china. *Note:* Camellia Cove does not accept credit cards.

Appendix:
New Orleans in Depth

Throughout this book, we have talked about the mystique of New Orleans and its ineffable essence. Now it's time for some hardcore stats. The largest city in Louisiana, and one of the chief cities of the South, New Orleans is nearly 100 miles above the mouth of the Mississippi River system and stretches along a strip of land 5 to 8 miles wide between the Mississippi and Lake Pontchartrain to the north. This is a city surrounded by water—a gulf, a river, and a lake—so no wonder you, the visitor, feel moist all the time. Okay, that's the humidity. But still, one good rainfall, and the whole thing floods—it's largely under sea level, remember; in fact, the highest natural point is in City Park, a whole 35 feet above sea level!

1 History 101

IN THE BEGINNING   Two French-Canadian brothers found this spot at the turn of the 18th century. Pierre Le Moyne, Sieur d'Iberville, led an expedition from France to rediscover the mouth of the Mississippi in 1699. René Robert Cavelier, Sieur de la Salle, had claimed the region for France in 1682. (He was murdered in Texas in 1687 by his own party because his lack of navigational and leadership skills risked many of their lives.) Iberville's expedition succeeded, and he planted a cross at a dramatic bend in the river near where La Salle had stopped almost 2 decades before. On his voyage, Iberville also established a fort at Biloxi, naming it the capital of France's new and uncharted territory. His brother, 18-year-old Jean Baptiste Le Moyne, Sieur de Bienville, stayed behind in Biloxi and quickly became commanding officer of the territory. For the next 20 years, he harbored thoughts of returning up the river and establishing a new capital city at the spot where he and his brother had stopped.

In 1718, Bienville got his chance. The previous year, Louisiana had been entrusted to the Company of the West (also known as Company of the Indies

Dateline

- **1682** Sieur de la Salle stops near the present site while traveling down the Mississippi River from the Great Lakes region and plants a cross claiming the territory for Louis XIV.
- **1699** Pierre Le Moyne, Sieur d'Iberville, rediscovers and secures the mouth of the Mississippi—on Mardi Gras day, appropriately.
- **1718** The first governor of Louisiana, Iberville's brother, Jean-Baptiste Le Moyne, Sieur de Bienville, founds New Orleans.
- **1723** New Orleans replaces Biloxi as the capital of Louisiana.
- **1726** Capuchin monastery erected.
- **1752** Ursuline Convent completed.
- **1762** Louis XV secretly cedes New Orleans and all of Louisiana west of the Mississippi to Spain.
- **1768** French residents in New Orleans banish Spanish commissioner Don Antonio de Ulloa, proclaiming independence from Spain.
- **1769** The Spanish return.
- **1783** Treaty of Paris confirms Spanish possession.
- **1788, 1794** Fires destroy much of the city; new brick buildings replace wood.
- **1794** Planter Etienne de Boré granulates sugar from cane for the first time, spawning a boom in the industry.

continues

or the Mississippi Company) for development as a populated colony. The company was headed by John Law, a Scottish entrepreneur who had convinced the French monarch and many stockholders in his company that fortunes were to be had in the new land. The company authorized Bienville to find a suitable location for a settlement on the river at a spot that would also protect France's holdings in the New World from British expansion.

Bienville quickly settled on high ground at the site he had previously seen, and not only because the bend in the river would be relatively easy to defend: Although it was some 100 miles inland along the river from the Gulf of Mexico, the site was near St. John's Bayou, which provided easy water transportation directly into Lake Pontchartrain. It was convenient from a military standpoint—providing a "back door" for defense or escape should the fortunes of war turn against the French—and it gave the site great potential as a trade route because it would allow relatively easy access to the Gulf.

The new town was named New Orleans in honor of the duc d'Orléans, then the regent of France. Following the plan of a late French medieval town, a central square (the Place d'Armes) was laid out with streets forming a grid around it. A church, government office, priest's house, and official residences fronted the square, and earthen ramparts dotted with forts were built around the perimeter. A tiny wooden levee was raised against the river, which still flooded periodically and turned the streets into rivers of mud. Today, this area of original settlement is known as the Vieux Carré ("old square") and the Place d'Armes as Jackson Square.

A MELTING POT   In its first few years, New Orleans was a community of French officials, adventurers, merchants, slaves, soldiers, and convicts

- 1795 Treaty of Madrid opens port to Americans; trade thrives.
- 1800 Louisiana again becomes a French possession.
- 1803 France officially takes possession of the territory. United States then purchases it and takes possession.
- 1805 New Orleans incorporates as a city; first elections are held.
- 1812 The *New Orleans,* the first steam vessel to travel the Mississippi, arrives from Pittsburgh. Louisiana admitted as a U.S. state.
- 1815 Battle of New Orleans.
- 1831 The first (horse-drawn) railway west of the Alleghenies is completed, linking New Orleans and Milneburg.
- 1832–33 Yellow fever and cholera epidemic kills 10,000 people in 2 years.
- 1834 Medical College of Louisiana (forerunner of Tulane University) founded.
- 1837 First newspaper coverage of a Mardi Gras parade.
- 1840 Antoine Alciatore, founder of Antoine's restaurant, arrives from Marseille. New Orleans is the fourth-largest city in the United States and is second only to New York as a port.
- 1849 The Place d'Armes renamed Jackson Square.
- 1850 Booming commerce totals $200 million; cotton accounts for 45% of total trade. City becomes largest slave market in the country.
- 1852 Consolidation of municipal government; New Orleans annexes city of Lafayette.
- 1853–55 Yellow fever epidemic during the summer; 12% of the population killed in 1853 in roughly 2 months.
- 1861–62 Louisiana secedes from the Union; city captured by Adm. David Farragut. Gen. Benjamin Butler assumes command of the city and earns a reputation for harsh and unfriendly governance.
- 1865–77 Reconstruction; "carpetbaggers" swarm into the city, and tensions climax in clashes between the Crescent White League and government forces.
- 1870 Algiers and Jefferson City annexed.
- 1872 Carrollton annexed.

continues

from French prisons, all living in rude huts of cypress, moss, and clay. These were the first ingredients of New Orleans's population gumbo. The city's commerce was mainly limited to trade with native tribes and to beginning agricultural production.

To supply people and capital to the colony, John Law's company began what was essentially the first real estate scam in the New World. The territory and the city were marketed on the continent as Heaven on Earth, full of immediate and boundless opportunities for wealth and luxury. The value of real estate in the territory rose dramatically with the spreading of these lies as wealthy Europeans, aristocrats, merchants, exiles, soldiers, and a large contingent of German farmers arrived—to find only mosquitoes, a raw frontier existence, and swampy land. Ultimately, the company's scheme nearly bankrupted the French nation. It did succeed, however, in swelling the population of the territory and of New Orleans; in 1723, the city replaced Biloxi as the capital of the Louisiana territory.

In 1724, Bienville approved the *Code Noir,* which set forth the laws under which African slaves were to be treated and established Catholicism as the territory's official religion. While it codified slavery and banished Jews from Louisiana, the code did provide slaves recognition and a degree of protection under the law.

One significant natural barrier to development of the population and society in Louisiana remained: a lack of potential wives. In 1727, a small contingent of Ursuline nuns arrived in the city and set about establishing a convent. While they weren't exactly eligible, they did provide a temporary home and education to many shiploads of *les filles à la cassette.* The "cassette girls" or "casket girls"— named for the government-issue *cassettes* or casketlike trunks in which they

- **1884–85** Cotton Centennial Exposition (World's Fair) held at the present site of Audubon Park.
- **1890** Jelly Roll Morton born.
- **1890** Creole of color Homer Plessy gets arrested riding a train recently segregated by Jim Crow laws. He sues the state, efforts that culminate in the landmark U.S. Supreme Court decision *Plessy v. Ferguson.*
- **1892** First electric streetcar operates along St. Charles Avenue.
- **1897** Sidney Bechet born. Storyville established.
- **1900** Louis Armstrong born.
- **1911** Razzy Dazzy Spasm Band performs in New York, where its name is changed to Razzy Dazzy Jazz Band.
- **1917** Original Dixieland Jazz Band attains height of popularity.
- **1921** Inner-Harbor Navigational Canal built, connecting Lake Pontchartrain and the Mississippi.
- **1928** Colorful Huey P. Long elected governor of Louisiana; 4 years later, he is elected to U.S. Senate.
- **1935** Long is shot and killed.
- **1938** Tennessee Williams arrives in New Orleans; Huey P. Long Bridge built over Mississippi River.
- **1939** French Quarter Residents Association formed as an agent for preservation.
- **1956** Lake Pontchartrain Causeway, world's longest bridge, completed.
- **1960** The city's public schools integrated.
- **1973** Parades banned in the Vieux Carré, changing the character of the city's observance of Mardi Gras.
- **1975** Superdome opens.
- **1977** Ernest N. "Dutch" Morial becomes first African-American mayor.
- **1984** Louisiana World Expo draws disappointing crowds but spurs redevelopment of the riverside area between Canal and Poydras streets.
- **1988** Anne Rice moves back to New Orleans, which has enormous impact on the city.
- **1999** Harrah's opens new casino.
- **2000** The new National D-Day Museum opens along with Jazzland, a new theme park just outside the city. Mardi Gras 2000 draws record crowds.
- **2003** Jazz Fest adds an extra day to its 2-week celebration.

carried their possessions—were young women of appropriate character sent to Louisiana by the French government to be courted and married by the colonists. (If we're to believe the current residents of the city, the plan was remarkably successful: Nearly everyone in New Orleans claims descent from the casket girls or from Spanish or French nobility, which makes one wonder at the terrible infertility of the colony's earlier population of convicts and "fallen women.")

John Law's company relinquished its governance of Louisiana in 1731, and the French monarch regained direct control of the territory. In the following decades, a number of planters established estates up and down the river from New Orleans. In the city, wealthier society began to develop a courtly atmosphere on the French model. In the midst of the rough-and-tumble frontier, families competed to see who could throw the most elegant and opulent parties.

Farther afield, westward along the Gulf of Mexico, other French speakers were creating a very different kind of society in a decidedly more rural mode. During the 18th century, many French colonists, displaced by British rule from Acadia, Nova Scotia, formed an outpost on the new French territory along the coastland. Today, you'll find the Acadians' descendants living a little to the west of New Orleans, still engaged in farming and trapping, some still speaking their unique brand of French, and proudly calling themselves "Cajuns."

New Orleans experienced only modest commercial development in its first decades, in large part due to trading restrictions imposed by France: The colony could trade only with the mother country. Colonists quickly found ways around the restrictions, however, and smugglers and pirates provided alternative markets and transportation for the region's agricultural products, furs, bricks, and tar.

Despite the awkward relationship with France, New Orleanians were greatly disturbed to learn in 1764 that 2 years earlier (news traveled right slow back then) Louis XV had given their city and all of Louisiana west of the Mississippi to his cousin, Charles III of Spain, in the secret Treaty of Fontainebleau. The Spanish, in turn, took 2 more years to send a governor, Don Antonio de Ulloa, who made few friends among local residents. By 1768, a large number of French residents of New Orleans and outlying areas assembled to demand Ulloa's removal. Some proposed the formation of a Louisiana republic. Ulloa was sent packing, and for nearly 2 years, New Orleans and Louisiana were effectively independent of any foreign power. This episode ended in 1769 when Don Alexander O'Reilly (known as "Bloody O'Reilly") and 3,000 soldiers arrived in the city, dispatched by the Spanish Crown. What had been a relatively peaceful rebellion was extinguished, its leaders were executed, and Spanish rule was reimposed. With a Gallic shrug, French aristocracy mingled with Spanish nobility, intermarried, and helped to create a new "Creole" culture.

Devastating fires struck in 1788 (when more than 850 buildings were destroyed) and again in 1794 in the midst of rebuilding. From the ashes emerged a new architecture dominated by the proud Spanish style of brick-and-plaster buildings replete with arches, courtyards, balconies, and of course, attached slave quarters. Even today you'll see tile markers giving Spanish street names at every corner in the French Quarter.

The city of New Orleans was coveted by the English and the Americans—and the French, though the trade to Spain was partly motivated because the unsuccessful colony was costing them money and they could no longer afford it. The Spanish imposed the same kind of trade restrictions on the city that the French had, with even less success (these were boom years for pirates and buccaneers like the infamous Jean Lafitte and his brother Pierre). This being a period of intense imperial conflict and maneuvering, Spain did allow some American revolutionaries to trade through the city in support of the colonists' fight against Britain. France regained possession of the territory in 1800 with a surprisingly quiet transfer of ownership and held on for 3 years while Napoléon negotiated the Louisiana Purchase with the United States for the paltry (as it turned out) sum of $15 million. For Creole society, the return to French rule was unpleasant enough because France had long been facing serious financial troubles, but a sale to America was anathema. To their minds, it meant the end of a European lifestyle in the Vieux Carré.

Thus, when Americans arrived in the city, the upper classes made it known that they were welcome to settle—but across Canal Street (so named because a drainage canal was once planned along its route, although it was never constructed), away from the old city and Creole society. And so it was that New Orleans came to be two parallel cities. The American section spread outward from Canal Street along St. Charles Avenue; business and cultural institutions centered in the Central Business District, and mansions rose in what is now the Garden District, which was a separate, incorporated city until 1852. French and Creole society dominated the Quarter for the rest of the 19th century, extending toward the lake along Esplanade Avenue. Soon, however, the Americans (crass though they may have seemed) brought commercial success to the city, which quickly warmed relations—the Americans sought the vitality of downtown society, and the Creoles sought the profit of American business. They also had occasion to join forces against hurricanes, yellow fever epidemics, and floods.

FROM THE BATTLE OF NEW ORLEANS TO THE CIVIL WAR   Perhaps nothing helped to cement a sense of community more than the Battle of New Orleans, during the War of 1812. The great turning point in Creole-American relations was the cooperation of Andrew Jackson and Jean Lafitte. To save the city, Jackson set aside his disdain for the pirate, and Lafitte turned down offers to fight for the British, instead supplying the Americans with cannons and ammunition that helped swing the battle in their favor. When Jackson called for volunteers, some 5,000 citizens from both sides of Canal Street responded. Battle was joined on January 8, 1815, in a field a few miles downstream from the city, and approximately 2,000 British troops and 20 Americans were killed or wounded. The dramatic battle made a local and national hero of Jackson. Ironically, though, neither Jackson nor the British had been aware that a treaty concluding the war had been signed a full 2 weeks before on December 24, 1814.

From then until the Civil War, New Orleans was a boomtown. Colonial trade restrictions had evaporated with the Louisiana Purchase, and more importantly, the era of steam-powered river travel arrived in 1812 with the first riverboat, the aptly named *New Orleans,* delivered from a Pittsburgh shipyard. River commerce exploded, peaking in the 1840s and putting New Orleans's port on a par with New York's. Cotton and sugar made many fortunes in New Orleans and its environs; wealthy planters joined the city merchants in building luxurious town houses and attending festivals, opera, theater, banquets, parades, and spectacular balls (including "Quadroon Balls," where beautiful mulatto girls were displayed to the male gentry as possible mistresses). As always, politics and gambling were dominant pastimes of these citizens and visitors.

By the middle of the century, cotton-related business was responsible for nearly half of the total commerce in New Orleans, so it's no surprise that the city housed one of the nation's largest and most ruthless slave markets. Paradoxically, New Orleans also had one of the most extended and established populations of "free men (and women) of color" in the American South. Furthermore, racial distinctions within the city increasingly became difficult to determine; people could often trace their ancestry back to two or even three different continents. Adding to the diversity, waves of Irish and German immigrants arrived in New Orleans in this period, supplying important sources of labor to support the city's growth.

This growth—upriver and downriver from the original center and away from the river toward Lake Pontchartrain—required extensive drainage of swamps and the construction of a system of canals and levees. The only major impediments to the development of the city in these decades were occasional yellow fever epidemics, which killed thousands of residents and visitors. Despite the clearing of swampland, the mosquito-borne disease persisted until the final decades of the 19th century.

RECONSTRUCTION & BEYOND   The boom era ended rather abruptly with the Civil War and Louisiana's secession from the United States in 1861. Federal troops marched into the city in 1862 and stayed until 1877, through the bitter Reconstruction period. As was the case elsewhere in the South, this period saw violent clashes between armed white groups and the state's Reconstruction forces.

After the war, the city went about the business of rebuilding its economic life—this time without slavery. By 1880, a number of annexations had rounded out the city limits, port activity had begun to pick up, and railroads were establishing their importance to the local and national economies. Also, a new group of immigrants, Italians this time, came to put their unique mark on the city. Through it all, an undiminished enthusiasm for fun survived. Gambling again thrived in more than 80 establishments, there were almost 800 saloons, and scores of "bawdy houses" engaged in prostitution, which was illegal but uncontrolled. New Orleans was earning an international reputation for open vice, much to the chagrin of the city's polite society.

In 1897, Alderman Sidney Story thought he had figured out how to improve the city's tarnishing image. He moved all illegal (but highly profitable) activities into a restricted district along Basin Street, next door to the French Quarter. Quickly nicknamed Storyville, the district boasted fancy "sporting palaces" with elaborate decor, musical entertainment, and a wide variety of ladies of pleasure. Visitors and residents could purchase a directory (the *Blue Book*) that listed alphabetically the names, addresses, and races of more than 700 prostitutes, ranging from those in the "palaces" to the poorer inhabitants of wretched, decaying shacks (called "cribs") on the blocks behind Basin Street. Black musicians like Jelly Roll Morton played the earliest form of jazz in some of Basin Street's ornate bordellos. Although jazz predates Storyville, here it gained popularity before moving upriver and into record collections everywhere. When the secretary of the navy decreed in 1917 that armed forces should not be exposed to so much open vice, Storyville closed down and disappeared without a trace. None of the fancy sporting houses remains.

THE 20TH CENTURY   The 20th century found the city's port becoming the largest in the United States and the second busiest in the world (after Amsterdam), with goods coming in by barge and rail. Drainage problems were conquered by means of high levees, canals, pumping stations, and great spillways, which are opened to direct floodwater away from the city. Bridges have been built across the Mississippi River, including the Huey P. Long Bridge, named after Louisiana's famous politician and demagogue. New Orleans's emergence as a regional financial center, with more than 50 commercial banks, has led to the construction of soaring office buildings, mostly in the Central Business District.

As in most other American cities, the city's population has spread outward through this century, filling suburbs and nearby municipalities. Unlike other cities, however, New Orleans has been able to preserve its original town center and much of its historic architecture. Thanks to these attractions and other tourism-related improvements, it ranks near the top in U.S. tourism (conventions alone bring in more than a million visitors each year) and is one of the country's top travel destinations for foreign visitors. The 1984 World's Fair, held in New Orleans, was a highlight in this development. Although it was not very well attended, the fair permanently elevated the spirit of the city and led to the construction of a number of high-rise and luxury hotels at the river end of Canal and Poydras streets, and the renovation of a large portion of the previously derelict waterfront Warehouse District.

The Gulf, river, and lake have not changed much over the past 300 years—at least, not as much as the little island of Orleans. The city wears its changes proudly, and from the Vieux Carré out to the suburbs like Metairie and Slidell; from the Garden District to the Esplanade Ridge, it invites visitors to read its history. New Orleanians certainly live by the history of their hometown, so as you navigate through the city, try to keep the likes of Iberville and Bienville, Jackson and Lafitte, Sidney Story and Jelly Roll Morton, and Don Alexander O'Reilly and the French rebels firmly in mind.

2 Recommended Books & Recordings

BOOKS

FICTION   There are many examples of early fiction that give a good flavor of old-time New Orleans life. George Washington Cable's stories and novels are revealing and colorful; the collection to read is *Old Creole Days* (1879). Grace King answered Cable's not-always-flattering portrait of the Creoles in her short stories and in her novel *The Pleasant Ways of St. Médard* (1916). Perhaps the best writer to touch on the lives of the earliest Creoles is Kate Chopin, who lived in Louisiana for only 14 years in the late 19th century, first in New Orleans and later in Cloutierville. Many of her short stories and novels, the most famous of which is *The Awakening,* are set in the region or involve characters from here.

In the next century, William Faulkner came to New Orleans, lived on Pirates Alley, and penned *Soldier's Pay.* Several other Faulkner novels and short stories are set in New Orleans. Tennessee Williams became a devoted New Orleans fan, living in the city on and off for many years. It inspired him to write *A Streetcar Named Desire,* one of the best-known New Orleans tales. He also set *The Rose Tattoo* in the city. Frances Parkinson Keyes lived on Chartres Street for more than 25 years. Her most famous works are *Dinner at Antoine's* and *Madame Castel's Lodger,* and each has curious descriptions of life in the city at that time, along with excellent descriptions of food.

Other notable New Orleans writers include Walker Percy and Shirley Ann Grau. Percy's novels, including *The Moviegoer* and *Love in the Ruins,* are classic portrayals of the idiosyncrasies of New Orleans and its residents. Grau's most famous novel, *The Keepers of the House,* won the Pulitzer Prize in 1964. John Kennedy Toole also received a Pulitzer, but he wasn't around to know about it, having committed suicide years before. At the time of his death, none of his works had even been published. Toole's *A Confederacy of Dunces* is a timeless New Orleans tragicomedy that'll have you laughing out loud.

Among the notable modern writers is Robert Olen Butler, who won the Pulitzer in 1993 for his collection of stories, *A Good Scent from a Strange Mountain,* set primarily in New Orleans's Vietnamese community. Ellen Gilchrist is another nationally recognized contemporary fiction writer with roots in the city. *In the Land of Dreamy Dreams,* a collection of her short stories, portrays life in wealthy uptown New Orleans. Sheila Bosworth's wonderful tragicomedies perfectly sum up the city and its collection of characters—check out *Almost Innocent* or *Slow Poison,* two of our all-time favorite books. Valerie Martin's *The Great Divorce* is a retelling of *Dr. Jekyll and Mr. Hyde* set in the streets of antebellum New Orleans. Other possibilities are Nancy Levin's delightful *Lives of the Saints* and *Sportsman's Paradise,* and John Gregory Brown's critically acclaimed *Decorations in a Ruined Cemetery.* Michael Ondaatje's controversial *Coming Through Slaughter* is a fictionalized account of Buddy Bolden and the early New Orleans jazz era.

And then, of course, there is the cottage industry known as Anne Rice. Whatever you might think of her writing skills, she loves her native city and does arguably the best job of capturing its essence. (More than one person has come to New Orleans just because he or she fell in love with it from one of Rice's books.) Her *Vampire Chronicles,* set in New Orleans, are her best-known works, but the city plays a significant (and seductive) role in *The Witching Hour* and is the backdrop for a historical novel, the well-researched *Feast of All Saints,* about the free people of color in 19th-century New Orleans.

MYSTERY   Ghosts and intrigue seem to lurk around every corner in New Orleans, so it's no wonder that so many mystery novels are set here. A fantastic group of mystery writers currently lives in and writes about New Orleans. James Lee Burke's David Robicheaux detective series includes *Neon Rain, Black Cherry Blues,* and *Heaven's Prisoners* (also, a movie starring Alec Baldwin). Burke and Julie Smith, who wrote *New Orleans Mourning,* have won Edgar Awards as mystery novelists of the year. *With Extreme Prejudice,* by Frederick Barton, takes readers down both the mean streets of New Orleans and the picturesque ones of the Garden District. For a novel that captures the racial tension of the city, look for *Glass House* by Christine Wiltz.

HISTORY   Lyle Saxon's *Fabulous New Orleans* is the best and most charming place to start learning about the city's past. (Saxon was director of the writer's program under the WPA.) From there, move on to his collaboration with Robert Tallant, *Gumbo Ya-Ya.* Roark Bradford's Civil War novel, *Kingdom Coming,* contains a lot of information about voodoo. Mark Twain visited the city often in his riverboat days, and his *Life on the Mississippi* has a good number of tales about New Orleans and its riverfront life. *The WPA Guide to New Orleans* also contains some excellent social and historical background and provides a fascinating picture of the city in 1938. *Beautiful Crescent* by Joan Garvey and Mary Lou Widmer is a readable reference book on the history of New Orleans.

There are many guides to Mardi Gras including Robert Tallant's *Mardi Gras* and Myron Tassin's *Mardi Gras and Bacchus: Something Old, Something New,* both published by Pelican. The definitive account is Henri Schindler's *Mardi Gras New Orleans.* Schindler produced balls and parades for Mardi Gras for 20 years and is considered carnival's foremost historian. *Mardi Gras in New Orleans, An Illustrated History* is a concise history of the celebration from ancient times to 2001. It was produced by *Mardi Gras Guide* publisher Arthur Hardy.

LITERATURE   Many of the recent books by poet and essayist Andrei Codrescu contain pieces about his adopted city of New Orleans. Codrescu has captured the city's appeal better than anyone else in recent times—we've used quotes from him liberally throughout this text. Start with *The Muse Is Always Half-Dressed in New Orleans* (St. Martin's, 1993) and go from there.

ART, ARCHITECTURE & ANTIQUES   New Orleans's architecture is the subject of an abundance of books. *New Orleans Architecture* (Friends of the Cabildo) is a helpful and interesting series—each volume deals with a different area of the city. There is even a volume on the cemeteries.

Cemetery buffs will be delighted with Robert Florence's *New Orleans Cemeteries: Life in the Cities of the Dead* (Batture, 1997). It is the most complete look at this fascinating part of the New Orleans landscape, with photos of some of the less-traveled graveyards plus colorful human-interest stories. Florence also has a guide about St. Louis Cemetery No. 1 called *City of the Dead* (University of Louisiana, 1996). If you are interested strictly in the aesthetics of the cemeteries, try Sandra Russell Clark's *Elysium: A Gathering of the Souls* (Louisiana State University Press, 1997), a collection of haunting art photos.

FOR KIDS   Sharon Doucet has written two terrific books of Cajun folklore for children—*Why Lapin's Ears Are Long: And Other Tales from the Louisiana Bayou* (Orchard Books, 1997) and *Le Hoogie Boogie*—and the main character of Mary Alice Fontenot's series of Clovis Crawfish books (Pelican) is a crawfish struggling with everyday issues.

BOOKS ABOUT MUSIC   Scores of books discuss the music of New Orleans; the following suggestions should get you started.

We highly recommend Ann Allen Savoy's *Cajun Music Vol. 1* (Bluebird Press, 1984), a combination songbook and oral history. It features previously untranscribed Cajun music with lyrics in French (including a pronunciation guide) and English. A labor of many years, it's an invaluable resource.

John Broven's *South to Louisiana: The Music of the Cajun Bayous* (Pelican, 1987) gives an interesting introduction to the music of the Cajun people.

For a look at specific time periods, people, and places in the history of New Orleans jazz, you have a number of choices. They include William Carter's *Preservation Hall* (Norton, 1991); John Chilton's *Sidney Bechet: The Wizard of Jazz* (Oxford University Press, 1988); Gunther Schuller's *Early Jazz: Its Roots and Musical Development* (Oxford University Press, 1968); *Jazz, New Orleans* (Da Capo Press, 1983) by Samuel Charters; *New Orleans Jazz: A Revised History* by R. Collins; *Music in New Orleans* (Louisiana State University Press, 1966) by Henry Kmen; *In Search of Buddy Bolden* (Louisiana State University Press, 1978) by Donald Marquis; *New Orleans Jazz: A Family Album* (Louisiana State University Press, 1967) by Al Rose and Edmond Souchon; *New Orleans Style* by Bill Russell; and *Jazz Masters of New Orleans* by Martin Williams. Al Rose's *Storyville, New Orleans* (University of Alabama Press, 1974) is an excellent source of information about the very beginnings of jazz.

If you prefer primary sources, read Louis Armstrong's *Satchmo: My Life in New Orleans* (Da Capo Press, 1986) and Sidney Bechet's *Treat It Gentle* (Da Capo Press, 1960). Both autobiographies are captivating.

RECORDINGS

The selections listed below should give you a good start; if you want advice or recommendations on recently released recordings, drop by or call the **Louisiana Music Factory,** 210 Decatur St. (© **504/586-1094**), in New Orleans or **Floyd's Record Shop,** 434 E. Main St., Ville Platte (© **318/363-2138**). (Floyd's is about 3 hours from New Orleans, so be sure to call before heading out if you're making a special trip—see chapter 12, "Plantation Homes & Cajun Country: Side Trips from New Orleans," for more info.)

JAZZ   Most of Louis Armstrong's recordings are in print and can be found in many record stores. The same is true for Jelly Roll Morton, Wynton Marsalis, Harry Connick Jr., and Nicholas Payton—we particularly recommend his Grammy-winning *Doc Cheatham & Nicholas Payton* (Verve, 1997).

For the sound of early jazz, the following are recommended: *Streets and Scenes of New Orleans* (Good Time Jazz) by the Silver Leaf Jazz Band, *New Orleans Rhythm Kings* (Milestone), *King Oliver with Louis Armstrong* (Milestone), and the anthologies *New Orleans* (Atlantic Jazz), *Recorded in New Orleans* Volumes 1 and 2 (Good Time Jazz), and *New Orleans Jazz* (Arhoolie).

RHYTHM & BLUES   For sheer dancing delight, try the ReBirth Brass Band, *Take It to the Street* (Rounder, 1992). Don't miss Dr. John, *Gris Gris* (Atco, 1968); *Gumbo* (Atco, 1972); and *Mos Scocious: An Anthology* (Rhino, 1993). Also try the Wild Tchoupitoulas (or Mardi Gras Indians), *Wild Tchoupitoulas* (Antilles, 1976); The Meters, *Cissy Strut* (Island, 1975) and *Rejuvenation* (Reprise, 1974). You can't go wrong with hometown heroes the Neville Brothers, *Yellow Moon* (A&M, 1989) and *Treacherous: A History of the Neville Brothers, 1955–1985* (Rhino, 1986), or producer/writer Allen Toussaint, *The Complete 'Tousan' Sessions* (Bear Family Records, 1992). He's a legend for a reason. We also like Professor Longhair, *New Orleans Piano* (Atco, 1953) and *'Fess: The Professor Longhair Anthology* (Rhino, 1993). Worthwhile anthologies include *The Best of New Orleans Rhythm & Blues* Volumes 1 and 2 (Rhino, 1988), *The Mardi Gras Indians Super Sunday Showdown* (Rounder, 1992), *Mardi Gras Party* (Rounder, 1991), and *New Orleans Party Classics* (Rhino, 1992).

CAJUN & ZYDECO   One of the first Cajun musicians to be recorded was Amédé Ardoin; consider *I'm Never Comin' Back* (Arhoolie; recorded in 1930 and 1934 and released in 1995). The Balfa Brothers were the first group to gain fame outside of Cajun country—try their *J'ai Vu La Lupe, Le Renard et La Belette* (Rounder, 1977) and *The Balfa Brothers Play Traditional Cajun Music* (Swallow, 1990). Beausoleil is currently the best known and most popular Cajun band; try their *Bayou Deluxe—the Best of Beausoleil* (Rhino, 1993*), La Danse de la Vie* (Rhino, 1993), and the Grammy-winning *L'Amour La Folie* (Rhino, 1997). Beausoleil's Michael Doucet plays alongside old friends Marc and Ann Savoy in the traditional Cajun group the Savoy-Doucet Cajun Band on *Home Music with Spirits* (Arhoolie, 1992). The Hackberry Ramblers have been playing Cajun music together since the 1930s (!), and their efforts have been rewarded with the Grammy-nominated *Deep Water* (Hot Biscuits, 1997). Other great choices include Beau Jocque, *Gonna Take You Downtown* (Rounder, 1996); Buckwheat Zydeco, *100% Fortified Zydeco* (Black Top Records, 1988); Boozoo Chavis and Nathan & the Zydeco Cha-Cha's, *Zydeco Live!* (Rounder, 1989); Clifton Chenier, *Bogalusa Boogie* (Arhoolie, 1976) and *Clifton Chenier: Anthology* (Rhino, 1993); and Jo-El Sonnier, *Cajun Life* (Rounder, 1988). If you're looking for an anthology, seek out Rhino's excellent multi-volume "Alligator Stomp" series.

Ann Savoy's acclaimed tribute to Cajun music, *Evangelical Made* (Vanguard Records, 2002), features such distinguished artists as Linda Ronstadt, Nick Lowe, Rodney Crowell, and John Fogerty singing Cajun classics.

Index

See also Accommodations and Restaurant indexes, below.

ACCOMMODATIONS

RESTAURANTS

Great Trips Like Great Days Begin with a Plan

FranklinCovey and Frommer's Bring You *Frommer's Favorite Places®* Planner

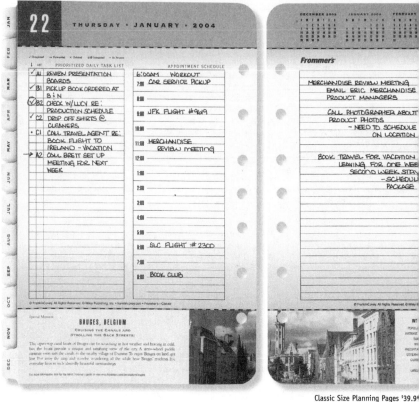

Classic Size Planning Pages $39.9

The planning experts at FranklinCovey have teamed up with the travel experts at Frommer's. The result is a full-year travel-themed planner filled with rich images and travel tips covering fifty-two of Frommer's Favorite Places.

- Each week will make you an expert about an intriguing corner of the world
- New facts and tips every day
- Beautiful, full-color photos of some of the most beautiful places on earth
- Proven planning tools from FranklinCovey for keeping track of tasks, appointments, notes, address/phone numbers, and more

Save 15%

when you purchase Frommer's Favorit Places travel-themed planner and a binder.

Order today before you next big trip.

www.franklincovey.com/frommers
Enter promo code 12252 at checkout for discount. Offer expires June 1, 2005.

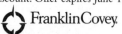

Frommer's is a trademark of Arthur Frommer.

FROMMER'S® COMPLETE TRAVEL GUIDES

FROMMER'S® DOLLAR-A-DAY GUIDES

FROMMER'S® PORTABLE GUIDES

FROMMER'S® NATIONAL PARK GUIDES

FROMMER'S® MEMORABLE WALKS

Chicago	New York	San Francisco
London	Paris	

FROMMER'S® WITH KIDS GUIDES

Chicago	Ottawa	Vancouver
Las Vegas	San Francisco	Washington, D.C.
New York City	Toronto	

SUZY GERSHMAN'S BORN TO SHOP GUIDES

Born to Shop: France	Born to Shop: Italy	Born to Shop: New York
Born to Shop: Hong Kong, Shanghai & Beijing	Born to Shop: London	Born to Shop: Paris

FROMMER'S® IRREVERENT GUIDES

Amsterdam	Los Angeles	San Francisco
Boston	Manhattan	Seattle & Portland
Chicago	New Orleans	Vancouver
Las Vegas	Paris	Walt Disney World®
London	Rome	Washington, D.C.

FROMMER'S® BEST-LOVED DRIVING TOURS

Britain	Germany	Northern Italy
California	Ireland	Scotland
Florida	Italy	Spain
France	New England	Tuscany & Umbria

HANGING OUT™ GUIDES

Hanging Out in England	Hanging Out in France	Hanging Out in Italy
Hanging Out in Europe	Hanging Out in Ireland	Hanging Out in Spain

THE UNOFFICIAL GUIDES®

Bed & Breakfasts and Country Inns in:
California
Great Lakes States
Mid-Atlantic
New England
Northwest
Rockies
Southeast
Southwest

Best RV & Tent Campgrounds in:
California & the West
Florida & the Southeast
Great Lakes States
Mid-Atlantic
Northeast
Northwest & Central Plains

Southwest & South Central Plains
U.S.A.
Beyond Disney
Branson, Missouri
California with Kids
Central Italy
Chicago
Cruises
Disneyland®
Florida with Kids
Golf Vacations in the Eastern U.S.
Great Smoky & Blue Ridge Region
Inside Disney
Hawaii
Las Vegas
London
Maui

Mexio's Best Beach Resorts
Mid-Atlantic with Kids
Mini Las Vegas
Mini-Mickey
New England & New York with Kids
New Orleans
New York City
Paris
San Francisco
Skiing & Snowboarding in the West
Southeast with Kids
Walt Disney World®
Walt Disney World® for Grown-ups
Walt Disney World® with Kids
Washington, D.C.
World's Best Diving Vacations

SPECIAL-INTEREST TITLES

Frommer's Adventure Guide to Australia & New Zealand
Frommer's Adventure Guide to Central America
Frommer's Adventure Guide to India & Pakistan
Frommer's Adventure Guide to South America
Frommer's Adventure Guide to Southeast Asia
Frommer's Adventure Guide to Southern Africa
Frommer's Britain's Best Bed & Breakfasts and Country Inns
Frommer's Caribbean Hideaways
Frommer's Exploring America by RV
Frommer's Fly Safe, Fly Smart

Frommer's France's Best Bed & Breakfasts and Country Inns
Frommer's Gay & Lesbian Europe
Frommer's Italy's Best Bed & Breakfasts and Country Inns
Frommer's Road Atlas Britain
Frommer's Road Atlas Europe
Frommer's Road Atlas France
The New York Times' Guide to Unforgettable Weekends
Places Rated Almanac
Retirement Places Rated
Rome Past & Present

Fly.
Sleep.
Save.

Now you can book your flights and
hotels together, so you can get even better deals
than if you booked them separately.

Travelocity

**Visit www.travelocity.com
or call 1-888-TRAVELOCITY**